HANDBOOK OF RESEARCH ON CORPORATE GOVERNANCE AND ENTREPRENEURSHIP

Handbook of Research on Corporate Governance and Entrepreneurship

Edited by

Jonas Gabrielsson

Professor, Halmstad University, Sweden

Edward Elgar
PUBLISHING

Cheltenham, UK • Northampton, MA, USA

Published by
Edward Elgar Publishing Limited
The Lypiatts
15 Lansdown Road
Cheltenham
Glos GL50 2JA
UK

Edward Elgar Publishing, Inc.
William Pratt House
9 Dewey Court
Northampton
Massachusetts 01060
USA

A catalogue record for this book
is available from the British Library

Library of Congress Control Number: 2016957241

This book is available electronically in the **Elgar**online
Business subject collection
DOI 10.4337/9781782545569

ISBN 978 1 78254 555 2 (cased)
ISBN 978 1 78254 556 9 (eBook)

Typeset by Servis Filmsetting Ltd, Stockport, Cheshire
Printed and bound in Great Britain by TJ International Ltd, Padstow

Contents

Figures

Contributors

Ekaterina S. Bjornali, NTNU Business School, Norwegian University of Science and Technology (NTNU), Norway.

Marita Blomkvist, School of Business, Economics and Law, University of Gothenburg, Sweden.

Stefano Bonini, Stevens Institute of Technology, USA.

Julia Brunold, School of Business, University of Skövde, Sweden.

Vincenzo Capizzi, Department of Economics and Business Studies, Università del Piemonte Orientale, Italy.

Sven-Olof Collin, School of Health and Society, Kristianstad University, Sweden.

Frédéric Delmar, Sten K. Johnson Centre for Entrepreneurship, Lund University, Sweden.

Susanne Durst, School of Business, University of Skövde, Sweden.

Asma Fattoum-Guedri, Department of Innovation and Organizational Economics, Copenhagen Business School, Denmark.

Jonas Gabrielsson, School of Business, Engineering and Science, Halmstad University, Sweden.

Morten Huse, BI Norwegian School of Business, Norway.

Eythor Ivar Jonsson, Department of Strategic Management and Globalization, Copenhagen Business School, Denmark.

Mirjam Knockaert, Department of Innovation, Entrepreneurship and Service Management, Ghent University, Belgium.

Seppo Laukkanen, Lantern Oy, Finland.

Huseyin Leblebici, Department of Business Administration, University of Illinois, USA.

Martin Lindell, Swedish School of Economics and Business Administration, Hanken, Finland.

Paola A.M. Mazzurana, Department of Economics and Statistics, University of Udine, Italy.

Teresa Nelson, Simmons College School of Management, USA.

Mari Paananen, University of Exeter Business School, UK.

Daniel Pittino, Centre for Family Enterprise and Ownership (CeFEO), Jönköping International Business School, Sweden.

Elin Smith, School of Health and Society, Kristianstad University, Sweden.

Till Talaulicar, Faculty of Economics, Law and Social Sciences, University of Erfurt, Germany.

Elien Vandenbroucke, Silverfin and Ghent University, Belgium.

Anssi Vanjoki, School of Business and Management, Lappeenranta University of Technology, Finland.

Francesca Visintin, Department of Economics and Statistics, University of Udine, Italy.

Daniel Yar Hamidi, Department of Business Administration and Textile Management, University of Borås, Sweden.

PART I

CORPORATE GOVERNANCE AND ENTREPRENEURSHIP AS A RESEARCH FIELD

1. Corporate governance and entrepreneurship: current states and future directions
Jonas Gabrielsson

INTRODUCTION

Scholarly research positioned in the intersection of corporate govern-ance and entrepreneurship has grown considerably in scale and scope during the past two decades. While mainstream research on corporate governance has been much concerned with large, publicly listed corpo-rations (Daily et al., 2003; Gabrielsson and Huse, 2004) this particular research stream has addressed issues and problems specifically related to corporate governance in entrepreneurial settings (Huse, 2000; Daily et al., 2002; Gabrielsson and Huse, 2010). The research includes a range of various entrepreneurial settings, such as start-ups (e.g., Grundei and Talaulicar, 2002; Ingley and McCaffrey, 2007), venture capital (VC)-financed ventures (e.g., Rosenstein, 1988; Gabrielsson and Huse, 2004) and fast-growing firms (e.g., Nelson and Levesque, 2007; Wirtz, 2011), as well as organized efforts to support entrepreneurship and innovation in established corporations (e.g., Zahra, 1996; Zahra et al., 2000). This volume seeks to explore and expand on the rich body of knowledge that has emerged and developed in this direction.

Both corporate governance and entrepreneurship are multidisciplinary fields of research where scholars are interested in providing actionable knowledge relevant for the phenomena studied. Research in entrepreneur-ship seeks to understand the actors, actions, resources, environmental influences and outcomes associated with the emergence of opportunities to create future goods and services and/or the emergence of new eco-nomic activities (Landström, 2010). While the most common example may include the process of starting a new business (Gartner, 1985; Davidsson, 1995) it is widely acknowledged that entrepreneurship can be found in multiple organizational contexts, including small growing firms (Davidsson, 1991; Delmar et al., 2003) and mature corporations (Covin and Miles, 1999; Garvin and Levesque, 2006) as well as public and non-profit organizations (Morris and Jones, 1999; Kearney et al., 2008).

Entrepreneurship that emerges and develops into organized forms of economic activity generates challenges with respect to the coordination and control of resources (Markman et al., 2001; Daily et al., 2002). Research in corporate governance addresses these challenges by seeking to understand how corporate power is directed in socially beneficial ways, both within and across economies (Judge et al., 2012, p. 88). While definitions of corporate governance vary, they typically include the set of systems, principles and processes by which an enterprise is directed and controlled (Thomsen and Conyon, 2012; Tihanyi et al., 2014). This encompasses a range of various institutional arrangements within firms, such as structures and forms of ownership (e.g., Pedersen and Thomsen, 2003), the board of directors (e.g., Forbes and Milliken, 1999), compensation systems for managers (e.g., Conyon, 2006), financial reporting systems (e.g., Beusenlinck and Manigart, 2007) and auditing (e.g., Cohen et al., 2010). However, it also includes a wider set of institutional arrangements surrounding the firm, such as state legislation and regulations (e.g., La Porta et al., 2000), corporate networks and managerial labor markets (e.g., Sinani et al., 2008) and competition on product markets (e.g., Giroud and Mueller, 2011), as well as pressure from the media (e.g., Bednar, 2012). In this respect, the study of corporate governance can be described as a relatively broad area of research where multiple social science disciplines collectively contribute to the scholarly understanding of the antecedents and consequences of the various institutional arrangements that conditions corporate governance in different organizational and geographical contexts.

The interest in developing scholarly knowledge in the intersection of corporate governance and entrepreneurship can in many ways be traced back to Professor Myles Mace at Harvard University, a pioneer in the study of both entrepreneurship and corporate governance. In his early observations of boards in small corporations, Mace (1948) concluded that they were seldom little more than fictional legal organs 'which included merely subservient and docile appointees of the owner-manager' (p. 87). This was also a dominant message in his book (Mace, 1971) and *Harvard Business Review* article (Mace, 1972). In the 1980s, when research on entrepreneurship and small businesses was starting to ascend as a distinct academic field of research (Landström, 2010), a number of studies continued in this direction by exploring corporate governance practices in smaller corporations (e.g., Castaldi and Wortmann, 1984; Ford, 1988; Nash, 1988; Huse, 1990). Overall, this early stream of research typically emphasized the board of directors as a potential resource in smaller firms that could serve as a valuable source of advice and counsel, offering discipline value and also acting in situations of crisis.

The body of scholarly knowledge positioned in the intersection of corporate governance and entrepreneurship has expanded considerably since the first pioneering contributions by Mace (1948, 1971) and others. The general interest in exploring and examining the corporate governance practices of small corporations has continued (e.g., Bennett and Robson, 2004; Durst and Henschel, 2014), often with a particular emphasis on the incidence, role or contribution of outside board members (e.g., Fiegener et al., 2000; Deakins et al., 2001; Cowling, 2008; Boxer et al., 2012). In addition, research on corporate governance and entrepreneurship was subsequently fuelled in the early 1990s by the growing interest in private equity markets (Sapienza et al., 1996), in particular venture capitalists and their involvement and value added in the ventures in which they invest (e.g., Rosenstein, 1988; Rosenstein et al., 1993; Fried et al., 1998). Following this, there was also a general rise in research on start-ups and fast-growing firms in the 1990s, which opened up a range of issues and challenges related to corporate governance (Daily et al., 2002). These developments were also paralleled by a growing interest in research on corporate entrepreneurship (Guth and Ginsberg, 1990; Covin and Slevin, 1991), where some scholars addressed the critical role of the corporate governance system in supporting and facilitating innovation and entrepreneurial behavior in established corporations (e.g., Zahra, 1996; Zahra et al., 2000).

Research on corporate governance and entrepreneurship has over time come to include a wide range of studies with a common interest in the set of systems, principles and processes that govern and influence the direction and performance of firms in entrepreneurial settings. However, due to the multidisciplinary character of this stream of research, with contributions from management, finance, economics, accounting and law, it can potentially be problematic to acquire a comprehensive and detailed overview of the topic. Available studies seem to be scattered across a range of different disciplines, which suggest that findings are reported in a wide range of scholarly outlets. This, in turn, risks hampering scientific progress and limiting the accumulation of research findings within the field. The situation consequently calls for a systematic effort to collect and accumulate available research evidence to support the collection and dissemination of scholarly knowledge as well as a guide for future research.

Given this, the aim of this introductory chapter is to provide an overview of the current state-of-the-art research positioned in the intersection of corporate governance and entrepreneurship. This aim will be met by means of a systematic literature review (e.g., Pittaway, Holt & Broad, 2014), where research in peer-reviewed academic journals will be identified, assessed and reported. Based on the review the chapter will then discuss the current state and possible future directions in this field of research.

The rest of the chapter is structured as follows. The next section will present details of the search methodology that has been used for identifying and analyzing research positioned in the intersection of corporate governance and entrepreneurship. This will be followed by an analysis and assessment of the current state of this stream of research with respect to main journal outlets, entrepreneurial settings, methodological approaches and empirical contexts. The chapter ends with a presentation of the chapters included in this volume with a discussion of how they explore and expand contemporary research on corporate governance and entrepreneurship.

SEARCH METHODOLOGY

The search methodology employed in this chapter has followed the general principles of a systematic literature review (e.g., Pittaway et al., 2014). This structured approach emphasizes the importance of describing the various steps undertaken in the review process. The transparent procedure in a systematic literature review has some notable advantages over traditional ad hoc reviews (Denyer and Tranfield, 2008), especially in areas that build on a highly diverse and multidisciplinary knowledge base. For example, it enhances validity, rigor and generalizability (Wang and Chugh, 2014) and also enables and opens up for reflection and integration (Pittaway et al., 2014). Following available guidelines, the systematic literature review in this chapter was structured in four action steps, as illustrated in Figure 1.1.

In the planning stage, the review objectives were defined in accordance with the overall aim of the chapter. This was followed by the development of a coding scheme to assemble and synthesize data about main journal outlets, entrepreneurial contexts, methodological approaches and empirical contexts. The coding scheme enabled systematic collection of relevant data in line with the objective of the review.

In the search stage, a number of bibliographical electronic databases were employed using the root search string 'corporate governance* AND entrepreneurship*'. ABI/INFORM Complete, Business Source Elite and Scopus were found to provide greatest coverage of full-text articles. Combinations of the following keywords were then focused in the electronic search: Corporate Governance (or) Boards of Directors (or) Ownership (and) Entrepreneurship (or) Founder (or) Venture (or) Start up (or) Small Business (or) Small Corporation (or) Small Firm. Search terms were separated when consisting of multiple words.

All multiple entries were deleted as they substantially increased the

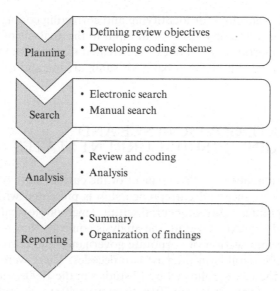

Figure 1.1   Steps in the systematic literature review

number of observed hits. The search was then limited to include only studies reported in peer-reviewed academic journals to be consistent with the review objectives. Studies that clearly lacked relevance were deleted. A narrative cross-referencing method based on a manual search of the bibliographies of all identified titles and abstracts supplemented the electronic search. The sample was then examined with respect to the review objective and aligned with the definitions expressed in the introduction. Entrepreneurship was in this examination broadly understood as the creation of future goods and services and/or the emergence of new economic activities, including the development and growth of new and small businesses and the characteristics and special problems of founders and entrepreneurs. Corporate governance was broadly understood as the set of systems, principles and processes by which an enterprise is controlled and directed. Articles that were judged as only marginally relevant for knowledge accumulation in the intersection of corporate governance and entrepreneurship were excluded. A sample of 122 articles published in international peer-reviewed academic journals remained after this screening. All identified articles were downloaded to enable full reading and analysis. A list of all articles included in the analysis is presented in Appendix 1.1.

In the analysis stage, the articles were reviewed and coded in accordance with the pre-made coding scheme. After a first round of coding a colleague was consulted for identifying and correcting coding errors. The resulting dataset was then used as an input in the analysis of the articles. In the final reporting stage, tables were created to illustrate the outcomes of the descriptive analysis as a basis for summarizing and organizing the findings.

CORPORATE GOVERNANCE AND ENTREPRENEURSHIP: CURRENT STATES

In this part an analysis and assessment of the current state of research in corporate governance and entrepreneurship is presented with respect to main journal outlets, entrepreneurial settings, methodological approaches and empirical contexts. Overall, the analysis confirms that research positioned in the intersection of corporate governance and entrepreneurship has grown considerably in the past two decades. There were five studies published in the 1980s, followed by 17 studies in the 1990s, and 60 studies in the 2000s. Between 2010 and 2016, there were 40 studies published. The 122 articles identified in the search were published in 60 different academic journals. These journals cover a wide number of academic disciplines, primarily related to business and management research. A list of all journals can be found in Appendix 1.2. A summary of the top ten journal outlets is provided in Figure 1.2.

More than half of the articles (54 percent) were published in the ten academic journals reported in Figure 1.2. Academic journals that focus on entrepreneurship and small businesses research dominate in terms of top outlets. The main scholarly outlet is *Entrepreneurship Theory and Practice*, but a significant number of contributions can also be found in journals such as *Small Business Economics, Journal of Business Venturing, Entrepreneurship and Regional Development* and *Journal of Small Business and Enterprise Development*. Three of the journals on the top ten list can be classified as field-specific outlets specifically devoted to corporate governance research: *Corporate Governance: An International Review, Journal of Management and Governance* and *International Journal of Business Governance and Ethics*. Two journals remain on the list. Of these, *Journal of Management* can be classified as a main management journal with a broad coverage of various topics, while *Long Range Planning* is a journal more specifically focused on strategic management research.

Research in the intersection of corporate governance and entrepreneurship includes a range of various entrepreneurial settings. The articles were in this respect classified with respect to the particular setting each study focused on. This procedure followed an abductive logic (e.g., Alvesson

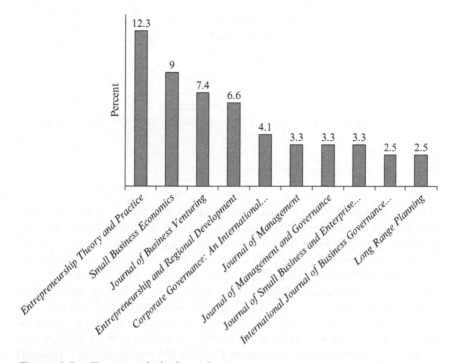

Figure 1.2   Top ten scholarly outlets

and Sköldberg, 2009), starting from preliminary conceptions based on pre-understanding and with the research purpose, framework and findings of each article then serving as inputs in the classification process. Potential new settings were identified, critically examined and potentially added as they emerged. Articles that addressed multiple settings were carefully screened and thereafter put in the category that best described their overall focus. Figure 1.3 provides a summary of the various entrepreneurial contexts studied in relation to the total number of studies.

Figure 1.3 suggests that research on corporate governance in small and medium-sized enterprises (SMEs) continues to dominate as this represents almost half of all studies (46.3 percent). A smaller but significant share of studies address corporate governance in start-ups and young firms (16.5 percent). Many of these show a particular interest in high-technology ventures. In addition, there have been notable scholarly interests in initial public offerings (IPOs) (10.7 percent) and VC-backed ventures (9.9 percent), which reflect the strong connection to issues of corporate governance in these contexts. Among the remaining studies there is a specific category of studies that focus on threshold firms (5 percent).

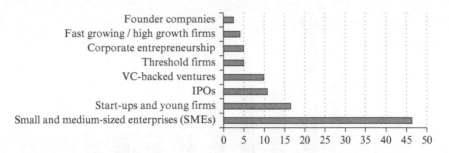

Figure 1.3   Entrepreneurial settings

Their commonality lies in that they address the evolution of corporate governance when firms grow and develop from 'entrepreneurial' to 'professional' organizations over the corporate life cycle. There is also a small but distinct stream of research on corporate governance in relation to corporate entrepreneurship (5 percent), primarily with a focus on how ownership and boards influence firms to be more or less entrepreneurial in their strategic behaviors and actions. Another small but distinct stream of research includes studies of corporate governance in fast-growing or high-growth firms (4.1 percent). Finally, a recent stream of studies also focuses on corporate governance in founder-led companies (2.1 percent) with a focus on comparing how founder versus family ownership influence firm performance.

Overall, it seems that studies in this field of research rely heavily on theories and frameworks that are used in mainstream corporate governance research (e.g., Gabrielsson and Huse, 2004; Yar Hamidi and Gabrielsson, 2014). Perhaps not surprisingly, the review shows that agency theory dominates with respect to applied theories. However, several studies use other theoretical frameworks typically found in corporate governance research, such as resource dependence theory, resource-based view of the firm, stewardship theory and institutional theory, sometimes in combination with or in contrast to agency theoretical reasoning. Other noteworthy theories applied in some of the studies are team production theory, imprinting theory and the attention-based view of the firm.

An explanation for the heavy reliance of theories and frameworks used in mainstream corporate governance research may be that many studies in the sample focus on entrepreneurial settings where the institutional arrangements that condition the structures and processes of corporate governance are relatively well defined, such as (mature) SMEs, IPOs, and even some larger publicly listed corporations, which represent a different institutional context compared to start-ups and younger

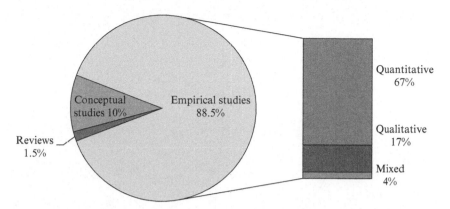

Figure 1.4   Types of methodological approach

ventures. In this respect, established theories used in mainstream corporate governance research seem to be both easy and relevant to apply in such settings.

The majority of studies are based on empirical research (88 percent). There were also a few conceptual studies (10 percent) and two reviews (e.g., Huse, 2000; Daily et al., 2002) found in the search. Of the empirical research the majority of studies employ quantitative methodological approaches (68 percent), often with data collected via questionnaires and using sophisticated statistical techniques to analyse the datasets. Much fewer but still a significant number of studies employ qualitative methodological approaches (17 percent). Interviews are the most common method of data collection among these studies. A much smaller number of studies (4 percent) use mixed methodologies in their research designs. A summary of the methodological approaches employed in research on corporate governance and entrepreneurship is presented in Figure 1.4.

A detailed review of the studies shows that most of them, about 60 percent, can be classified as 'outcome research' designed to explain effects of various corporate governance arrangements. There was also a relatively large share, about 35 percent, that can be classified as 'antecedent research' where studies focus on causes of corporate governance. Only a small share of the studies, about 5 percent, can be classified as 'characteristics research' that makes in-depth detailed examination and description to define and delimit phenomena and provide context to theory, without trying to determine cause-and-effect relationships or make predictions. Overall, this pattern is in line with the methodological approaches employed described in Figure 1.4.

The analysis was also directed towards identifying the empirical contexts

Figure 1.5   Top countries studied

studied. The large majority of the empirical studies (96 percent) present data from a single country. Only a handful of studies (e.g., Borch and Huse, 1993; Huse, 1990; Sapienza et al., 1996; Filatotchev et al., 2005; Scholes et al., 2007; Voordeckers et al., 2014; Durst and Henschel, 2014) compare and analyse data from multiple countries. With respect to countries, the United States (US) is represented in 32.4 percent of all studies. After this comes the United Kingdom (UK) (16.7 percent) and Norway (15.7 percent), followed by Sweden (11.1 percent). Overall, the findings suggest that a dominant portion of available scholarly research on corporate governance and entrepreneurship is embedded in either Anglo-American or Scandinavian models of corporate governance, each with its particular features and institutional arrangements. The top countries studied in research on corporate governance and entrepreneurship are presented in Figure 1.5.

Some final remarks can be made about the current state of research in corporate governance and entrepreneurship based on the assessment and analysis provided in this chapter. Overall, the findings suggest that research positioned in the intersection of corporate governance and entrepreneurship has become a relatively well-established area of scholarly inquiry. The search identified a large number of studies, of which 122 were assessed in the screening stage as relevant for further consideration with respect to the accumulation of scholarly knowledge within this stream of research. While the available research evidence is scattered across 60 different academic journals, about half of these studies appear in ten of them. These top ten journals are all established and well recognized by scholars within their specific fields of research. In this respect, the research field presents favorable conditions with respect to the possibility for scholars to continue to accumulate and develop scholarly knowledge on corporate governance and entrepreneurship by reading and relating to each other's work. Moreover, there seems to be ample opportunities for publishing research on corporate governance and entrepreneurship in academic journals of high quality.

The findings also suggest that research positioned in the intersection of corporate governance and entrepreneurship often focus on settings where the institutional arrangements that condition the structures and processes of corporate governance are relatively well defined, in particular SMEs, but also IPOs and larger publicly listed corporations. In this respect, studies often rely on established theories used in mainstream corporate governance research, where agency theory seems to be the dominant theoretical framework. Moreover, the findings suggest that the large majority of studies are empirical, and most of them rely on first-hand data that has been collected for the specific purpose of the research. Quantitative approaches dominate, and the data are typically analysed using rigorous statistical analyses. Most of the empirical research is conducted in the US, the UK or Scandinavia (in particular Norway and Sweden), while studies in other institutional settings are scarcer. In this respect, there seem to be ample opportunities to advance scholarly knowledge on governance and entrepreneurship by expanding efforts towards geographical and organizational settings that so far have been less studied in this stream of research.

CORPORATE GOVERNANCE AND ENTREPRENEURSHIP: FUTURE DIRECTIONS

The chapters in this volume provide a unique collection of research addressing issues of corporate governance in various entrepreneurial settings, including start-ups, owner-managed firms, fast-growing firms and IPOs, as well as how corporate governance and board leadership is associated with entrepreneurship and innovation in small and large established companies. The various chapters span a wide range of topics, methodologies and levels of analysis, all designed to contribute to the advancements of the understanding of corporate governance and entrepreneurship within and across different organizational and geographical settings.

The book is divided into four parts. Part I contains discussions about research on corporate governance and entrepreneurship as a research field. The present chapter has provided an overview of the current state-of-the-art research positioned in the intersection of the corporate governance and entrepreneurship disciplines. In Chapter 2, Jonas Gabrielsson and Morten Huse continue with a review of the historical and intellectual roots of resource dependence theory and agency theory, two dominant theories in research of boards and corporate governance, with a particular focus on how they have been applied in studies of entrepreneurial firms.

Part II focuses on corporate governance in start-ups and early-stage ventures. It starts with Chapter 3, where Eythor Jonsson examines the roles and key tasks performed by advisory boards in start-ups and growth-oriented companies from the perspective of contemporary corporate governance literature. Empirical findings from the advisory board program at Copenhagen Business School (CBS) in Denmark suggest that advisory boards play an important role for their direction and performance. However, as the underlying rationale for advisory boards is different from legal boards, the author also identifies opportunities to continue to extend and develop contemporary conceptualizations to better explain what advisory boards do and why they are valuable for entrepreneurial firms. In Chapter 4, Till Talaulicar introduces an input–mediator–outcome model implemented and developed from group theory to analyze and substantiate the effects of various structural arrangements of the organization of top management teams (TMTs) in high-tech venture firms. He discusses how installing either a command or a collegial model of TMT organization influences behavioral, cognitive and affective group processes, which in turn influence the comprehensiveness and speed of TMT decision-making. In the following chapter (Chapter 5), Ekaterina Bjornali reviews and synthesizes scholarly research on boards in high-tech start-ups as a means to accumulate and discuss state-of-the-art knowledge in the field and to identify future research directions. Overall, the chapter identifies research on boards as an extension of the top management team in high-tech start-ups as a promising, yet relatively unexplored area of scholarly inquiry. In Chapter 6, Elien Vandenbroucke and Mirjam Knockaert elaborate further on this topic by examining how TMT and outside board human capital affects innovation speed in a sample of Belgian early-stage high-tech firms. In this respect, they emphasize the need to consider the outside board as a part of the extended TMT as these are not standalone entities in an early-stage high-tech context. In Chapter 7, Stefano Bonini and Vincenzo Capizzi present a review of the main theoretical contributions and empirical results on how private equity investors influence corporate governance in young and fast-growing companies.

Part III turns attention to corporate governance in small and medium-sized enterprises (SMEs). Susanne Durst and Julia Brunhold open in

Chapter 8 with addressing how beliefs and practices of small firm owner-managers in the Rhine Valley region are reflected in their governance structures. As such, they examine what decision-makers understand by the term 'corporate governance' and which governance methods and procedures are implemented by the management of these firms. In Chapter 9, Daniel Pittino, Paola Mazzurana and Francesca Visintin examine the adoption of formal mechanisms in the governance of strategic alliances established by entrepreneurial firms in the north-east of Italy. In the study they identify that family business status plays a role in explaining interorganizational arrangements, but also that this is contingent on the size of the firm. In Chapter 10, Daniel Yar Hamidi and Jonas Gabrielsson present a study of how board chairpersons may develop innovation-promoting boards in small entrepreneurial firms in Sweden. The chapter offers insights into board development processes in such firms and identifies and describes the board leadership practices that experienced board chairpersons recommend for promoting innovation in this setting.

Part IV focuses attention on corporate governance in fast-growing firms and IPOs. In Chapter 11, Teresa Nelson and Huseyin Leblebici present and articulate an engagement theory of governance for high-growth entrepreneurial ventures. Embedded in a dynamic organizational systems view, the chapter discusses how governance relationships emerge and evolve over time during the IPO process in a negotiated organizational field of problem-solving and decision-making. In Chapter 12, Asma Fattoum-Guedri and Frédéric Delmar examine the implementation of defensive mechanism by founder-chief executive officers (CEOs) and non-founder-CEOs in French IPOs. The chapter develops a theoretical framework that explains why founder-CEOs are more likely than non-founder-CEOs to use defensive mechanisms at IPO, and the empirical results confirm the additive effects of dual class shares, pyramid control structures and voting pact agreements in shielding CEO shareholders from undesired change of control. In Chapter 13 Marita Blomkvist and Mari Paananen examine and compare differences in the quality of financial reporting between Gazelles and Non-Gazelles in Sweden. The findings imply that the quality of financial accounting is of less importance; however, corporate governance mechanisms that influence financial reporting quality have an indirect impact on the cost of debt.

Finally, Part V focuses on corporate governance and corporate entrepreneurship. Elin Smith and Sven-Olof Collin start in Chapter 14 by exploring the intertwinement between the disciplining (governance) side and the enabling (entrepreneurship) side of the firm. In the chapter they propose that such a theory needs to acknowledge the distribution of property rights and liabilities among participants of different organizational forms. Based on Swedish data they discuss how corporate entrepreneurship can be triggered by different governance mechanisms and their specific formations. In Chapter 15, Seppo Laukkanen, Martin Lindell and Anssi Vanjoki examine how corporate governance and leadership can advance entrepreneurship in a large corporation. Based on three Nokia innovation cases, they provide insights into how corporate governance and corporate entrepreneurship interact via organizational culture, strategy, administrative frameworks and sponsoring of entrepreneurial activities, as well as through critical decisions on resources.

REFERENCES

Alvesson, M. and Sköldberg, K. (2009) *Reflexive Methodology: New Vistas for Qualitative Research: Second Edition*, London: Sage Publications.
Bednar, M.K. (2012) Watchdog or lapdog? A behavioral view of the media as a corporate governance mechanism, *Academy of Management Journal*, 55, 131–150.
Bennett, R.J. and Robson, P.J.A. (2004) The role of boards of directors in small and medium-sized firms, *Journal of Small Business and Enterprise Development*, 11(1), 95–113.
Beusenlinck, C. and Manigart, S. (2007) Financial reporting quality in private equity backed companies: The impact of ownership concentration, *Small Business Economics*, 29(3), 261–274.
Borch, O.J. and Huse, M. (1993) Informal strategic networks and boards of directors, *Entrepreneurship Theory and Practice*, 18(1), 23–36.
Boxer, R., Berry, A. and Perren, L. (2012) Differing perceptions of non-executive directors' roles in UK SMEs: Governance conundrum or cultural anomaly, *Accounting Forum*, 36(1), 38–50.
Castaldi, R. and Wortman, M.S. (1984) Board of directors in small corporations: An untapped resource, *American Journal of Small Business*, 9(2), 1–11.
Cohen, J., Krishnamoorthyn, G. and Wright, A. (2010) Corporate governance in the post-Sarbanes–Oxley era: Auditors' experiences, *Contemporary Accounting Research*, 27(3), 751–786.
Conyon, M.J. (2006) Executive compensation and incentives, *Academy of Management Perspectives*, 20, 25–44.
Covin, J.G. and Miles, M.P. (1999) Corporate entrepreneurship and the pursuit of competitive advantage, *Entrepreneurship Theory and Practice*, 23(3), 47–63.
Covin, J.G. and Slevin, D.P. (1991) A conceptual model of entrepreneurship as firm behavior, *Entrepreneurship Theory and Practice*, 16(1), 7–25.
Cowling, M. (2003) Productivity and corporate governance in smaller firms, *Small Business Economics*, 20(4), 335–344.
Daily, C.M., Dalton, D.R. and Cannella, A.A. (2003) Corporate governance: Decades of dialogue and data, *Academy of Management Review*, 28(3), 371–382.
Daily, C.M., McDougall, P.P., Covin, J.G. and Dalton, D.R. (2002) Governance and strategic leadership in entrepreneurial firms, *Journal of Management*, 28(3), 387–412.
Davidsson, P. (1991) Continued entrepreneurship: Ability, need, and opportunity as determinants of small firm growth, *Journal of Business Venturing*, 6(6), 405–429.
Davidsson, P. (1995) Culture, structure and regional levels of entrepreneurship, *Entrepreneurship and Regional Development*, 7, 41–62.
Deakins, D., O'Neill, E. and Mileham, P. (2001) Chief executive officers and nonexecutive directors: Their relationships in small companies, *Environment and Planning C: Government and Policy*, 19(3), 355–372.

Delmar, F., Davidsson, P. and Gartner, W. (2003) Arriving at the high-growth firm, *Journal of Business Venturing*, 18(2), 189–216.

Denyer, D. and Tranfield, D. (2008) Producing a systematic review, in Buchanan, D. and Bryman, A. (eds), *Handbook of Organisational Research Methods*, London: Sage, pp. 671–689.

Durst, S. and Henschel, T. (2014) Governance in small firms: A country comparison of current practices, *International Journal of Entrepreneurship and Small Business*, 21(1), 16–32.

Fiegener, M.K., Brown, B.M., Dreux IV, D.R. and Dennis Jr, W.J. (2000) The adoption of outside boards by small private US firms, *Entrepreneurship and Regional Development*, 12(4), 291–310.

Filatotchev, I., Chahine, S., Wright, M. and Arberk, M. (2005) Founders' characteristics, venture capital syndication and governance in entrepreneurial IPOs, *International Entrepreneurship and Management Journal*, 1(4), 419–439.

Forbes, D.P. and Milliken, F.J. (1999) Cognition and corporate governance: Understanding boards of directors as strategic decision making groups, *Academy of Management Review*, 24, 489–505.

Fried, V.H., Bruton, G.D. and Hisrich, R.D. (1998) Strategy and the board of directors in venture capital-backed firms, *Journal of Business Venturing*, 13, 493–503.

Ford, R.H. (1988) Outside directors and the privately-owned firm: Are they necessary?, *Entrepreneurship Theory and Practice*, 13(1), 49–57.

Gabrielsson, J. and Huse, M. (2002) The venture capitalist and the board of directors in SMEs: Roles and processes, *Venture Capital*, 4(2), 125–146.

Gabrielsson, J. and Huse, M. (2004) Context, behavior, and evolution: Challenges in research on boards and governance, *International Studies of Management and Organization*, 34(3), 11–36.

Gabrielsson, J. and M. Huse (2010) Governance theory: Origins and implications for researching boards and governance in entrepreneurial firms, in Landström, H. and Lohrke, F. (eds), *The Historical Foundations of Entrepreneurship Research*, Cheltenham, UK and Northampton, MA, USA: Edward Elgar Publishing.

Gartner, W.B. (1985) A conceptual framework for describing the phenomenon of new venture creation, *Academy of Management Review*, 10, 696–706.

Garvin, D.A. and Levesque, L.C. (2006) Meeting the challenge of corporate entrepreneurship, *Harvard Business Review*, 84(10), 102–112.

Giroud, X. and Mueller, H. (2011) Corporate governance, product market competition, and equity prices, *Journal of Finance*, 66(2), 563–600.

Guth, W. and Ginsberg, A. (1990) Guest editor's introduction: Corporate entrepreneurship, *Strategic Management Journal*, Summer Special Issue, 11, 5–15.

Huse, M. (1990) Board composition in small enterprises, *Entrepreneurship and Regional Development*, 2(4), 363–373.

Huse, M. (1994) Board-management relations in small firms: The paradox of simultaneous independence and interdependence, *Small Business Economics*, 6(1), 55–72.

Huse, M. (2000) Boards in SMEs: A review and research agenda, *Entrepreneurship and Regional Development*, 12(4), 271–290.

Judge, W.Q., Weber, T. and Muller-Kahle, M. (2012) What are the correlates of interdisciplinary research impact? The case of corporate governance research, *Academy of Management Learning and Education*, 11(1), 82–98.

Kearney, C., Hisrich, R. and Roche, F. (2008) A conceptual model of public sector corporate entrepreneurship, *International Entrepreneurship and Management Journal*, 4(3), 295–313.

La Porta, R., Lopez-de-Silanes, B., Shleifer, A. and Vishny, R. (2000) Investor protection and corporate governance, *Journal of Financial Economics*, 58(1–2), 3–27.

Landström, H. (2010) *Pioneers in Entrepreneurship and Small Business Research*, New York: Springer.

Mace, M.L. (1948) *The Board of Directors in Small Corporations*, Boston, MA: Graduate School of Business Administration, Harvard University, published dissertation.

Mace, M.L. (1971) *Directors: Myth and Reality*, Boston, MA: Harvard University.

Mace, M.L. (1972) The president and the board of directors, *Harvard Business Review*, March–April, 37–49.

Markman, G.D., Balkin, D.B. and Schjoedt, L. (2001) Governing the innovation process in entrepreneurial firms, *Journal of High Technology Management Research*, 12, 273–293.

Morris, M.H. and Jones, F.F. (1999) Entrepreneurship in established organizations: The case of the public sector, *Entrepreneurship Theory and Practice*, 24, 71–91.

Nash, J.M. (1988) Boards of privately held companies: Their responsibilities and structure, *Family Business Review*, 1(3), 263–269.

Pedersen, T. and Thomsen, S. (2003) Ownership structure and value of the largest European firms: The importance of ownership identity, *Journal of Management and Governance*, 7, 27–55.

Pittaway, L., Holt, R. and Broad, J. (2014) Synthesising knowledge in entrepreneurship research: The role of systematic literature reviews, in Chell, E. and Karataş-Özkan, M. (eds), *Handbook of Research on Small Business and Entrepreneurship*, Cheltenham, UK and Northampton, MA, USA: Edward Elgar Publishing, pp. 83–105.

Rosenstein, J. (1988) The board and strategy: Venture capital and high technology, *Journal of Business Venturing*, 3(2), 159–170.

Rosenstein, J., Bruno, A.V., Bygrave, W.D. and Taylor, N.T. (1993) The CEO, venture capitalists, and the board, *Journal of Business Venturing*, 8, 99–113.

Sapienza, H.J., Manigart, S. and Vermeir, W. (1996) Venture capitalist governance and value added in four countries, *Journal of Business Venturing*, 11(6), 439–469.

Scholes, L.M., Wright, M., Westhead, P., Burrows, A. and Bruining, H. (2007) Information sharing, price negotiation and management buy-outs of private family-owned firms, *Small Business Economics*, 29(3), 329–349.

Sinani, E., Stafsudd, A., Thomsen, S., Edling, C. and Randøy, T. (2008) Corporate governance in Scandinavia: Comparing networks and formal institutions, *European Management Review*, 5(1), 27–40.

Thomsen, S. and Conyon, M. (2012) *Corporate Governance: Mechanisms and Systems*, New York: McGraw-Hill.

Tihanyi, L., Graffin, S. and George, G. (2014) From the editors: Rethinking governance in management research, *Academy of Management Journal*, 57(6), 1535–1543.

Voordeckers, W., Van Gils, A., Gabrielsson, J., Politis, D. and Huse, M. (2014) Board structures and board behaviour: A cross-country comparison of privately held SMEs in Belgium, the Netherlands and Norway, *International Journal of Business Governance and Ethics*, 9(2), 197–219.

Wang, C. and Chugh, H. (2014) Entrepreneurial learning: Past research and future challenges, *International Journal of Management Reviews*, 16(1), 24–61.

Yar Hamidi, D. and Gabrielsson, J. (2014) Developments and trends in research on board leadership: A systematic literature review, *International Journal of Business Governance and Ethics*, 9(3), 243–268.

Zahra, S.A. (1996) Governance, ownership and corporate entrepreneurship: The moderating effect of industry technological opportunities, *Academy of Management Journal*, 39(6), 1713–1735.

Zahra, S., Neubaum, D.C. and Huse, M. (2000) Entrepreneurship in medium-size companies: Exploring the effects of ownership and governance systems, *Journal of Management*, 26(5), 947–976.

APPENDIX 1.1: ARTICLES IDENTIFIED IN THE SYSTEMATIC LITERATURE REVIEW

Aaboen, L., Lindelöf, P., von Koch, C. and Löfsten, H. (2006) Corporate governance and performance of small high-tech firms in Sweden, *Technovation*, 26, 955–968.

Abor, J. and Biepke, N. (2007) Corporate governance, ownership structure and performance of SMEs in Ghana: Implications for financing opportunities, *Corporate Governance: The International Journal of Effective Board Performance*, 7(3), 288–300.

Ahn, M. (2014) Enhancing corporate governance in high-growth entrepreneurial firms, *International Journal of Innovation and Technology Management*, 11(6), 1–16.

Albu, N. and Mateescu, R.A. (2015) The relationship between entrepreneurship and corporate governance: The case of Romanian listed companies, *Amfiteatru Economic*, 17(38), 44–59.

Arthurs, J.D., Busenitz, L.W., Hoskisson, R.E. and Johnson, R. (2009) Firm-specific human capital and governance in IPO firms: Addressing agency and resource dependence concerns, *Entrepreneurship Theory and Practice*, 33(4), 845–865.

Audretsch, D.B. and Lehmann, E. (2006) Entrepreneurial access and absorption of knowledge spillovers: Strategic board and managerial composition for competitive advantage, *Journal of Small Business Management*, 44(2), 155–166.

Belghitar, Y. and Khan, J. (2013) Governance mechanisms, investment opportunity set and SMEs cash holdings, *Small Business Economics*, 40(1), 59–72.

Bennett, R.J. and Robson, P.J.A. (2004) The role of boards of directors in small and medium-sized firms, *Journal of Small Business and Enterprise Development*, 11(1), 95–113.

Berry, A. and Perren, L. (2001) The role of non-executive directors in UK SMEs, *Journal of Small Business and Enterprise Development*, 8(1), 159–173.

Beusenlinck, C. and Manigart, S. (2007) Financial reporting quality in private equity backed companies: The impact of ownership concentration, *Small Business Economics*, 29(3), 261–274.

Bishara, N.D. (2011) Governance and corruption constraints in the Middle East: Overcoming the business ethics glass ceiling, *American Business Law Journal*, 48(2), 227–283.

Bjornåli, E.S. and Aspelund, A. (2012) The role of the entrepreneurial team and the board of directors in the internationalization of academic spin-offs, *Journal of International Entrepreneurship*, 10(4), 350–377.

Bjornåli, E. and Gulbrandsen, M. (2010) Exploring board formation and evolution of board composition in academic spin-offs, *Journal of Technology Transfer*, 35(1), 92–112.

Bjornåli, E.S., Knockaert, M. and Erikson, T. (2016) The impact of top management team characteristics and board service involvement on team effectiveness in high-tech start-ups, *Long Range Planning*, doi: 10.1016/j.lrp.2015.12.014.

Block, J.H., Jaskiewicz, P. and Miller, D. (2011) Ownership versus management effects on performance in family and founder companies: A Bayesian reconciliation, *Journal of Family Business Strategy*, 2(4), 232–245.

Borch, O.J. and Huse, M. (1993) Informal strategic networks and boards of directors, *Entrepreneurship Theory and Practice*, 18(1), 23–36.

Boxer, R., Berry, A. and Perren, L. (2012) Differing perceptions of non-executive directors' roles in UK SMEs: Governance conundrum of cultural anomaly, *Accounting Forum*, 36(1), 38–50.

Boxer, R., Perren, L. and Berry, A. (2013) SME top management team and non-executive director cohesion: Precarious equilibrium through information asymmetry, *Journal of Small Business and Enterprise Development*, 20(1), 55–79.

Brunninge, O. and Nordqvist, M. (2004) Ownership structure, board composition and entrepreneurship: Evidence from family firms and venture-capital backed firms, *International Journal of Entrepreneurial Behaviour and Research*, 10(1–2), 85–105.

Brunninge, O., Nordqvist, M. and Wiklund, J. (2007) Corporate governance and strategic change in SMEs: The effects of ownership, board composition and top management teams, *Small Business Economics*, 29(3), 295–308.

Calabró, A. and Mussolino, D. (2013) How do boards of directors contribute to family SME export intensity? The moderating role of formal and informal governance mechanisms, *Journal of Management and Governance*, 17(2), 363–403.

Calabró, A., Mussolino, D. and Huse, M. (2009) The role of board of directors in the internationalization process of small and medium sized businesses, *International Journal of Globalisation and Small Business*, 3(4), 393–411.

Castaldi, R. and Wortman, M.S. (1984) Board of directors in small corporations: An untapped resource, *American Journal of Small Business*, 9(2), 1–11.

Certo, S.T., Daily, C.M. and Dalton, D.R. (2001) Signalling firm value through board structure: An investigation of initial public offerings, *Entrepreneurship Theory and Practice*, 26(2), 33–50.

Chahine, S., Filatotchev, I. and Zahra, S.A. (2011) Building perceived quality of founder-involved IPO firms: Founder's effects on board selection and stock market performance, *Entrepreneurship Theory and Practice*, 35(2), 319–335.

Chahine, S. and Saade, S. (2011) Shareholder rights and the effect of the origin of venture capital firms on the underpricing of US IPOs, *Corporate Governance: An International Review*, 19(6), 601–621.

Charas, S. and Perelli, S. (2013) Threats to board stability: Understanding SME director behavior, *Journal of Disclosure and Governance*, 10(2), 175–191.

Christy, J.A. (2013) Do board characteristics influence the shareholders' assessment of risk for small and large firm, *Abacus*, 49(2), 161–196.

Clarysse, B., Knockaert, M. and Lockett, A. (2007) Outside board members in high-tech start-ups, *Small Business Economics*, 29(3), 243–259.

Colin, B. (2001) The role of non-executive directors in high-tech SMEs, *Corporate Governance: The International Journal of Effective Board Performance*, 1(2), 34–36.

Colombo, M.G., Croce, A. and Murtinu, S. (2014) Ownership structure, horizontal agency costs and the performance of high-tech entrepreneurial firms, *Small Business Economics*, 42(2), 265–282.

Coulson-Thomas, C. (2007) SME directors and boards: The contribution of directors and boards to the growth and development of small and medium-sized enterprises (SMEs), *International Journal of Business Governance and Ethics*, 3(3), 250–261.

Cowling, M. (2003) Productivity and corporate governance in smaller firms, *Small Business Economics*, 20(4), 335–344.

Cowling, M. (2008) Small firm CEOs and outside directorships: Tenure, demonstration and synergy effects, *Manchester School*, 76(2), 160–179.

Daily, C.M. and Dalton, D.R. (1992) The relationship between governance structure and corporate performance in entrepreneurial firms, *Journal of Business Venturing*, 7(5), 375–386.

Daily, C.M. and Dalton, D.R. (1993) Board of directors leadership and structure: Control and performance implications, *Entrepreneurship Theory and Practice*, 17(3), 65–81.

Daily, C.M., McDougall, P.P., Covin, J.G. and Dalton, D.R. (2002) Governance and strategic leadership in entrepreneurial firms, *Journal of Management*, 28(3), 387–412.

Deakins, D., O'Neill, E. and Mileham, P. (2000) The role and influence of external directors in small and entrepreneurial companies: Some evidence on VC and non-VC appointed external directors, *Venture Capital*, 2, 111–127.

Deakins, D., O'Neill, E. and Mileham, P. (2000) Insiders vs. outsiders: Director relationships in small, entrepreneurial companies, *Enterprise and Innovation Management Studies*, 1(2), 175–186.

Deakins, D., O'Neill, E. and Mileham, P. (2001) Chief executive officers and nonexecutive directors: Their relationships in small companies, *Environment and Planning C: Government and Policy*, 19(3), 355–372.

Deutsch, Y. and Ross, T.W. (2003) You are known by the directors you keep: Reputable directors as signaling mechanism for young firms, *Management Science*, 49(8), 1003–1027.

Durst, S. and Henschel, T. (2014) Governance in small firms: A country comparison of current practices, *International Journal of Entrepreneurship and Small Business*, 21(1), 16–32.

Faraq, H., Mallin, C. and Ow-Kong, K. (2014) Governance, ownership, and performance of entrepreneurial IPOs in AIM companies, *Corporate Governance: An International Review*, 22(2), 100–115.

Fiegener, M.K. (2005) Determinants of board participation in the strategic decisions of small corporations, *Entrepreneurship Theory and Practice*, 29(5), 627–650.

Fiegener, M.K., Brown, B.M., Dreux IV, D.R. and Dennis Jr, W.J. (2000) The adoption of outside boards by small private US firms, *Entrepreneurship and Regional Development*, 12(4), 291–310.

Filatotchev, I., Chahine, S., Wright, M. and Arberk, M. (2005) Founders' characteristics, venture capital syndication and governance in entrepreneurial IPOs, *International Entrepreneurship and Management Journal*, 1(4), 419–439.

Finkle, T.A. (1998) The relationship between boards of directors and initial public offerings in the biotechnology industry, *Entrepreneurship Theory and Practice*, 22(3), 627–650.

Forbes, D.P., Korsgaard, M.A. and Sapienza, H.J. (2010) Financing decisions as a source of conflict in venture boards, *Journal of Business Venturing*, 25(6), 579–592.

Ford, R.H. (1988) Outside directors and the privately-owned firm: Are they necessary?, *Entrepreneurship Theory and Practice*, 13(1), 49–57.

Fortin, R. and Roth, G. (2010) Small firm governance and analyst following, *Academy of Accounting and Financial Studies Journal*, 14(2), 47–57.

Fried, V.H., Bruton, G.D. and Hisrich, R.D. (1998) Strategy and the board of directors in venture capital-backed firms, *Journal of Business Venturing*, 13, 493–503.

Gabrielsson, J. (2007a) Boards of directors and entrepreneurial posture in medium-size companies: Putting the board demography approach to a test, *International Small Business Journal*, 25(5), 511–537.

Gabrielsson, J. (2007b) Correlates of board empowerment in small companies, *Entrepreneurship Theory and Practice*, 31(5), 687–711.

Gabrielsson, J. and Huse, M. (2002) The venture capitalist and the board of directors in SMEs: Roles and processes, *Venture Capital*, 4(2), 125–146.

Gabrielsson, J. and Politis, D. (2007) The impact of board governance on firm-level entrepreneurship in small technology based firms, *ICFAI Journal of Corporate Governance*, 6(3), 43–60.

Gabrielsson, J. and Winlund, H. (2000) Boards of directors in small and medium-sized industrial firms: examining the effects of the board's working style on board task performance, *Entrepreneurship and Regional Development*, 12(4), 311–330.

Garg, S. (2013) Venture boards: Distinctive monitoring and implications for firm performance, *Academy of Management Review*, 38(1), 90–108.

Gedajlovic, E., Lubatkin, M.H. and Schulze, W.S. (2004) Crossing the threshold from founder management to professional management: A governance perspective, *Journal of Management Studies*, 41(5), 899–912.

George, G., Wiklund, J. and Zahra, S. (2005) Ownership and the internationalization of small firms, *Journal of Management*, 31(2), 210–233.

George, G., Wood, D.R. and Khan, R. (2001) Networking strategy of boards: Implications for small and medium-sized enterprises, *Entrepreneurship and Regional Development*, 13(3), 269–285.

Gill, A.S., Mand, H.S. and Mathur, N. (2012) Corporate governance and the growth of small business service firms in India, *International Research Journal of Finance and Economics*, 96, 113–123.

Gill, A.S., Biger, N., Mand, H.S. and Shah, C. (2012) Corporate governance and capital structure of small business service firms in India, *International Journal of Economics and Finance*, 4(8), 83–92.

Gnan, L., Montemerlo, D. and Huse, M. (2015) Governance systems in family SMEs: The substitution effects between family councils and corporate governance mechanisms, *Journal of Small Business Management*, 53(2), 355–381.

Grundei, J. and Talaulicar, T. (2002) Company law and corporate governance of start-ups in Germany: Legal stipulations, managerial requirements, and modification strategies, *Journal of Management and Governance*, 6(1), 1–27.

Huse, M. (1990) Board composition in small enterprises, *Entrepreneurship and Regional Development*, 2(4), 363–373.

Huse, M. (1993) Relational norms as a supplement of neo-classical understanding of directorates, *Journal of Socio-Economics*, 22(3), 219–240.

Huse, M. (1994) Board-management relations in small firms: The paradox of simultaneous independence and interdependence, *Small Business Economics*, 6(1), 55–72.

Huse, M. (1998) Researching the dynamics of board-stakeholder relations, *Long Range Planning*, 31, 218–226.

Huse, M. (2000) Boards in SMEs: A review and research agenda, *Entrepreneurship and Regional Development*, 12(4), 271–290.

Huse, M. and Zattoni, A. (2008) Trust, firm life cycle, and actual board behavior: Evidence from 'one of the lads' in the board of three small firms, *International Studies of Management and Organization*, 38(3), 71–97.

Ingley, C.B. and McCaffrey, K. (2007) Effective governance for start-up companies: Regarding the board as a strategic resource, *International Journal of Business Governance and Ethics*, 3(3), 308–329.

Jaskiewicz, P., Block, J.H., Combs, J.G. and Miller, D. (2015) The effects of founder and family ownership on hired CEOs' incentives and firm performance, *Entrepreneurship Theory and Practice*, 35(2), 319–335.

Jaskiewicz, P., Block, J.H., Miller, D. and Combs, J.G. (2014) Founder versus family owners' impact on pay dispersion among non CEO top managers: Implications for firm performance, *Journal of Management*, doi: 10.1177/0149206314558487.

Johannisson, B. and Huse, M. (2000) Recruiting outside board members in the small family business: An ideological challenge, *Entrepreneurship and Regional Development*, 12(4), 353–378.

Klein, P.G. (1999) Entrepreneurship and corporate governance, *Quarterly Journal of Austrian Economics*, 2(2), 19–42.

Knockaert, M., Bjornali, E.S. and Erikson, T. (2015) Joining forces: Top management team and board chair characteristics as antecedents of board service involvement, *Journal of Business Venturing*, 30(3), 420–435.

Knockaert, M. and Ucbasaran, D. (2013) The service role of outside boards in high tech start-ups: A resource dependency perspective, *British Journal of Management*, 24(1), 69–84.

Kroll, M., Walters, B.A. and Le, S. (2007) The impact of board composition and top management team ownership structure on post-IPO performance in young entrepreneurial firms, *Academy of Management Journal*, 50, 1198–1216.

Lappalainen, J. and Niskanen, M. (2009) Does board composition and ownership structure affect firm growth? Evidence from Finnish SMEs, *Research in Economics and Business Central and Eastern Europe*, 1(1), 66–83.

Lappalainen, J. and Niskanen, M. (2012) Financial performance of SMEs: Impact of ownership structure and board composition, *Management Research Review*, 35(11), 1088–1108.

Le, S., Kroll, M. and Walters, B.A. (2012) The influence of board composition on top management team industry- and firm-specific human capital in young IPO firms, *Journal of Managerial Issues*, 24, 412–432.

Le, S., Kroll, M. and Walters, B.A. (2013) Outside directors' experience, TMT firm-specific human capital, and firm performance in entrepreneurial IPO firms, *Journal of Business Research*, 66, 533–539.

Lynall, M.D., Golden, B.R. and Hillman A.J. (2003) Board composition from adolescence to maturity: A multitheoretic view, *Academy of Management Review*, 28(3), 416–431.

Machold, S., Huse, M., Minichilli, A. and Nordqvist, M. (2011) Board leadership and strategy involvement in small firms: A team production approach, *Corporate Governance: An International Review*, 19(4), 368–382.

Markman, G.D., Balkin, D.B. and Schjoedt, L. (2001) Governing the innovation process in entrepreneurial firms, *Journal of High Technology Management Research*, 12, 273–293.

McMahon, R.G.P. (2007) Ownership structure, business growth and financial performance amongst SMEs: From Australia's business longitudinal survey, *Journal of Small Business and Enterprise Development*, 14(3), 458–477.

Miller, D. and Le-Breton Miller, I. (2011) Governance, social identity, and entrepreneurial orientation in closely held public companies, *Entrepreneurship Theory and Practice*, 35(5), 1051–1076.

Minichilli, A. and Hansen, C. (2007) The board advisory tasks in small firms and the event of crises, *Journal of Management and Governance*, 11, 5–22.

Molokwu, V.B., Barreria, J. and Urban, B. (2013) Entrepreneurial orientation and corporate governance structures at the firm level in the South African oil and gas industry, *South African Journal of Human Resource Management*, 11(1), 1–15.

Nash, J.M. (1988) Boards of privately held companies: Their responsibilities and structure, *Family Business Review*, 1(3), 263–269.

Nelson, T. (2003) The persistence of founder influence: Management, ownership, and performance effects at initial public offering, *Strategic Management Journal*, 24(8), 707–724.

Nelson, T. and Levesque, L.L. (2007) The status of women in corporate governance in high-growth, high-potential firms, *Entrepreneurship Theory and Practice*, 31(2), 209–232.

Randoi, T. and Goel, S. (2003) Ownership structure, founder leadership, and performance in Norwegian SMEs: Implications for financing entrepreneurial opportunities, *Journal of Business Venturing*, 18(5), 619–637.

Ranft, A.L. and O'Neill, H.M. (2001) Board composition and high-flying founders: Hints of trouble to come?, *Academy of Management Executive*, 15(1), 126–138.

Ritchie, J. and Richardson, S. (2000) Smaller business governance: Exploring accountability and enterprise from the margins, *Management Accounting Research*, 11(4), 451–474.

Rosa, P. and Scott, M. (1999) The prevalence of multiple owners and directors in the SME sector: Implications for our understanding of start-up and growth, *Entrepreneurship and Regional Development*, 11(1), 21–37.

Rosenstein, J. (1988) The board and strategy: Venture capital and high technology, *Journal of Business Venturing*, 3(2), 159–170.

Rosenstein, J., Bruno, A.V., Bygrave, W.D. and Taylor, N.T. (1993) The CEO, venture capitalists, and the board, *Journal of Business Venturing*, 8, 99–113.

Sapienza, H., Korsgaard, M.A., Goutlet, P.K. and Hoogendam, J.P. (2000) Effects of agency risks and procedural justice on board processes in venture capital-backed firms, *Entrepreneurship and Regional Development*, 12(4), 331–351.

Sapienza, H.J., Manigart, S. and Vermeir, W. (1996) Venture capitalist governance and value added in four countries, *Journal of Business Venturing*, 11(6), 439–469.

Scholes, L.M., Wright, M., Westhead, P., Burrows, A. and Bruining, H. (2007) Information sharing, price negotiation and management buy-outs of private family-owned firms, *Small Business Economics*, 29(3), 329–349.

Steier, L.P. and Miller, D. (2010) Pre- and post-succession governance philosophies in entrepreneurial family firms, *Journal of Family Business Strategy*, 1(3), 145–154.

Uhlaner, L., Floren, R.H. and Geerlings, J.R. (2007a) Owner commitment and relational governance in the privately held firm: An empirical study, *Small Business Economics*, 29(3), 275–293.

Uhlaner, L., Wright, M. and Huse, M. (2007b) Private firms and corporate governance: An integrated economic and management perspective, *Small Business Economics*, 29(3), 225–241.

Vandenbroucke, E., Knockaert, M. and Ucbasaran, D. (2014) Outside board human capital and early stage high-tech firm performance, *Entrepreneurship Theory and Practice*, 40(4), 759–779.

Van den Heuvel, J., Van Gils, A. and Voordeckers, W. (2006) Board roles in small and medium-sized family businesses: Performance and importance, *Corporate Governance*, 14(5), 467–485.

Van Gils, A. (2005) Management and governance in Dutch SMEs, *European Management Journal*, 23(5), 583–589.

Voordeckers, W., Van Gils, A., Gabrielsson, J., Politis, D. and Huse, M. (2014) Board structures and board behaviour: A cross-country comparison of privately held SMEs in Belgium, the Netherlands and Norway, *International Journal of Business Governance and Ethics*, 9(2), 197–219.

Watson, R. (1991) Modelling directors' remuneration decisions in small and closely-held companies, *Journal of Business Finance and Accounting*, 18(1), 85–98.

Watson, R. (1994) An empirical analysis of financial and non-financial managers' remuneration in small and medium-sized UK enterprises, *Accounting and Business Research*, 24(94), 176–188.

Westhead, P. (1999) Factors associated with the employment of non-executive directors by unquoted companies, *Journal of Management and Governance*, 3, 81–111.

Whisler, T.L. (1988) The role of the board in the threshold firm, *Family Business Review*, 1, 309–321.

Wijbenga, F.H., Postma, T.J.B.M. and Stratling, R. (2007) The influence if the venture capitalist's governance activities on the entrepreneurial firm's control systems and performance, *Entrepreneurship Theory and Practice*, 31(2), 257–277.

Williams, D.R., Duncan, W.J. and Ginter, P.M. (2006) Structuring deals and governance after the IPO: Entrepreneurs and venture capitalists in high tech start-ups, *Business Horizons*, 49(4), 303–311.

Wirtz, P. (2011) The cognitive dimension of corporate governance in fast growing firms, *European Management Journal*, 29(6), 431–447.

Zahra, S.A. (1996) Governance, ownership and corporate entrepreneurship: The moderating effect of industry technological opportunities, *Academy of Management Journal*, 39(6), 1713–1735.

Zahra, S.A. (2014) Public and corporate governance and young global entrepreneurial firms, *Corporate Governance: An International Review*, 22(2), 77–83.

Zahra, S. and Filatotchev, I. (2004) Governance of the entrepreneurial threshold firm: A knowledge-based perspective, *Journal of Management Studies*, 41(5), 885–897.

Zahra, S.A., Filatotchev, I. and Wright, M. (2009) How do threshold firms sustain corporate entrepreneurship? The role of boards and absorptive capacity, *Journal of Business Venturing*, 24(3), 248–260.

Zahra, S., Neubaum, D.C. and Huse, M. (2000) Entrepreneurship in medium-size companies: Exploring the effects of ownership and governance systems, *Journal of Management*, 26(5), 947–976.

Zahra, S.A. Neubaum, D.O. and Naldi, L. (2007) The effects of ownership and governance on SME's international knowledge-based resources, *Small Business Economics*, 29(3), 309–327.

Zhang, J.J., Baden-Fuller, C. and Pool, J. (2011) Resolving tensions between monitoring, resourcing and strategizing: Structures and processes in high technology venture boards, *Long Range Planning*, 44(2), 95–117.

APPENDIX 1.2

Table 1A.1   Number of articles per academic journal

	No.
Abacus	1
Academy of Accounting and Financial Studies Journal	1
Academy of Management Executive	1
Academy of Management Journal	2
Academy of Management Review	2
Accounting and Business Research	1
Accounting Forum	1
American Business Law Journal	1
American Journal of Small Business	1
Amfiteatru Economic	1
British Journal of Management	1
Business Horizons	1
Corporate Governance: An International Review	5
Corporate Governance: The International Journal of Business in Society	1
Corporate Governance: The International Journal of Effective Board Performance	1
Enterprise and Innovation Management Studies	1
Entrepreneurship and Regional Development	8
Entrepreneurship Theory and Practice	14
Environment and Planning C: Government and Policy	1
European Management Journal	2
Family Business Review	2
ICFAI Journal of Corporate Governance	1
International Entrepreneurship and Management Journal	1
International Journal of Business Governance and Ethics	3
International Journal of Economics and Finance	1
International Journal of Entrepreneurial Behaviour and Research	1
International Journal of Entrepreneurship and Small Business	1
International Journal of Globalisation and Small Business	1
International Journal of Innovation and Technology Management	1
International Research Journal of Finance and Economics	1
International Small Business Journal	1
International Studies of Management and Organization	1
Journal of Business Finance and Accounting	1
Journal of Business Research	1
Journal of Business Venturing	9
Journal of Disclosure and Governance	1
Journal of Family Business Strategy	2
Journal of High Technology Management Research	1
Journal of International Entrepreneurship	1

Table 1A.1   (continued)

	No.
Journal of Management	4
Journal of Management and Governance	4
Journal of Management Studies	2
Journal of Small Business and Enterprise Development	4
Journal of Small Business Management	2
Journal of Socio-Economics	1
Journal of Technology Transfer	1
Long Range Planning	3
Management Accounting Research	1
Management Research Review	1
Management Science	1
Managerial Issues	1
Manchester School	1
Quarterly Journal of Austrian Economics	1
Research in Economics and Business Central and Eastern Europe	1
Small Business Economics	11
South African Journal of Human Resource Management	1
Strategic Management Journal	1
Technovation	1
Venture Capital: An International Journal of Entrepreneurial Finance	2
	122

2. Governance theory: origins and implications for researching boards and governance in entrepreneurial firms
*Jonas Gabrielsson and Morten Huse**

INTRODUCTION

All firms, small as well as large, new as well as old, can be described as having two complementary systems: a production system and a governance system. The production system consists of the business activities used by the firm to facilitate the transformation of input resources into the output that is offered on the market. Activities organized and carried out in most firms include procurement, operations, logistics, marketing and sales, and interaction with suppliers and customers. The overall focus is to manage the firm and its input resources to efficiently and effectively design, produce and distribute its output. The governance system, on the other hand, allocates rights and responsibilities among the various providers of input resources in and around the firm and gives some of them – generally the providers of financial resources – the power to make decisions and exercise control to influence the direction and performance of the enterprise (Huse, 2007). The overall focus is on determining how critical resources will be acquired, controlled and deployed so as to increase the wealth of the business, and how to deal with conflicts between various coalitions of resource providers who have potentially divergent goals.

The governance system in a firm includes both external and internal mechanisms that direct, administer and control the firm and its operations (O'Sullivan and Diacon, 1999; Collin, 2003). Examples of external governance mechanisms include competition on product markets, state legislation and regulations, managerial labor markets, and pressure from the media. Examples of internal governance mechanisms include the board of directors, auditing, and compensation systems for firm managers. The various external and internal mechanisms making up the governance system of the firm thus form a complex web of institutional arrangements that influence its direction and performance through particular features of incentives, supervision, best practices, 'rules of the game', links to external sources of knowledge, and internal channels to diffuse knowledge.

Entrepreneurial Firms

In this chapter we address the issue of governance in entrepreneurial firms as opposed to the large and mature corporations that most often have been studied in academic research (Gabrielsson and Huse, 2004). However, there is no accepted or consistent way of defining an entrepreneurial firm.[1] We refer in our discussion to firms that are in the early or 'entrepreneurial' stage of the organizational life cycle (Greiner, 1972; Quinn and Cameron, 1983). At this stage, firms are generally involved in building up their resource base, entering new or established markets, and searching for additional capital and allies. Entrepreneurial firms can in this respect – in an 'ideal typical' way (Weber, 1947) – be characterized as operating in one or a few product markets, with small managerial hierarchies, close relationships between owners and managers, and management of the organization in a largely personalized way. These characteristics provide a strong contrast to larger and more diversified corporations which have structurally complex organizations, distant and invisible shareholders, and multiple layers of management. The small entrepreneurial firm thus provides a fundamentally different context when it comes to issues and problems of governance.

We think that our focus on governance in entrepreneurial firms can be of interest for at least two reasons. First, entrepreneurial firms account for a relatively large share of the total amount of organized economic activity in most developed market economies. Second, these firms are considered as the most important for creating value in society, and they are often associated with positive outcomes such as job creation, innovation and economic growth (Birch, 1979; Kirchoff, 1994). Their significance, in terms of sheer numbers as well as their potential for wealth creation, makes the understanding of principles for 'good' governance highly relevant for a wide range of stakeholders in and around the entrepreneurial firm, including founders, investors and employees.

As noted above, governance refers to a broad range of mechanisms that direct, administer and control the firm and its operations. In this chapter we specifically focus on the governance provided by the 'board of directors', since this internal governance mechanism has been the most widely examined and reported in main entrepreneurship journals (e.g. Ford, 1988; Rosenstein, 1988; Daily and Dalton, 1992; Borch and Huse, 1993; Daily and Dalton, 1993; Rosenstein et al., 1993; Huse, 1994; Finkle, 1998; Fiegener et al., 2000a; 2000b; Fiegener, 2005; Gabrielsson and Winlund, 2000; Johannisson and Huse, 2000; Bennett and Robson, 2004; Gabrielsson, 2007a; 2007b; Voordeckers et al., 2007; Brunninge et al., 2007; Clarysse et al., 2007). We want to emphasize at this point that past studies do not focus solely on entrepreneurial firms (as we define these). Rather, many of them discuss boards of directors in small, often privately held firms. However, most studies include entrepreneurial firms in their samples and often address theoretical issues that are relevant to consider when studying this subset of small firms.

A widely held assumption in research on boards and governance is that the characteristics of entrepreneurial firms generally speak against active boards, as CEOs often have the authority to overrule boardroom decisions and also to directly remove board members. However, empirical studies also suggest that boards of directors in entrepreneurial firms can – and sometimes do – play an active role in shaping strategies and influencing organizational performance in this setting (e.g. George et al., 2001; Daily et al., 2002). Several theories have been employed in past research to explain the conditions under which a board of directors may take action and assert power over the direction and performance of a firm (Zahra and Pearce, 1989; Hung, 1998). Two theoretical perspectives, however, stand out when reviewing research that has addressed the issue of boards and governance in entrepreneurship research, namely 'resource dependence theory' and 'agency theory' (Huse, 2000; Gabrielsson and Huse, 2005).[2] Consequently, we focus on these two theories in the remainder of the chapter.

Aim of the Chapter

In this chapter, we aim to give an overview of the historical and intellectual roots of both resource dependence theory and agency theory with a particular focus on how they have been applied in studies of boards and governance. The underlying motivation for this endeavor is that we believe scholars interested in issues of board governance in entrepreneurial firms could benefit from such an overview for at least two reasons. First, we think that an increased understanding of the origins and history of resource dependence theory and agency theory would contribute positively to continued knowledge accumulation within the field. For example, the two theories are often seen as largely complementary perspectives that are used to justify board tasks such as resource provision and monitoring (e.g. Gabrielsson and Winlund, 2000; Voordeckers et al., 2007). There is, however, often very little reflection and discussion about the assumptions underlying each theory. Both, for example, emphasize the value in adopting outside board members[3] but the underlying reasons for this recommendation as well as the characteristics that outside board members should have to add value differ in the two theories.

Moreover, there may be some potential problems in the joint application of resource dependence theory and agency theory when researching boards and governance in entrepreneurship research. For example, resource dependence theory focuses on how the management team can control actors external to the firm so that the latter will provide or give access to critical resources. In agency theory the focus is on the very opposite – how actors external to the firm can control the management team. Thus, at first glance they seem to provide rather different implications for the design of effective board governance. An overview of the origins of resource dependence theory and agency theory and the problems each theory seeks to address may, therefore, help entrepreneurship scholars to better understand to what extent the two theories can be used together and what might be required to make them more compatible.

Second, we think that both resource dependence theory and agency theory provide interesting implications for researching behavioral aspects of boards and governance in entrepreneurial firms. Research on boards and governance has in recent years increasingly emphasized the need to more closely study behavioral processes and relational dynamics in and around the boardroom (Forbes and Milliken, 1999; Finkelstein and Mooney, 2003; Huse, 2005; Huse and Zattoni, 2008). There has, however, been an excessive bias in past entrepreneurship research towards studying only compositional aspects of boards. Actual board behavior has on the other hand been treated largely as a 'black box' (Huse, 1998) where the behavior or conduct of boards is inferred from their demographic characteristics. As a result, there has been very little attention to how boards in entrepreneurial firms actually work and how board members in this context may improve their behavior to contribute to value creation, despite the importance of such knowledge for further theory-building as well as the development of best-practice recommendations for entrepreneurial firms.

In addition to the reasons stated above, we think that an overview of the historical and intellectual roots of resource dependence theory and agency theory can be of interest for a wider audience of entrepreneurship scholars. Both theoretical perspectives have, for example, been employed in research areas within the entrepreneurship field such as franchising (Dant, 2008), family firms (Schulze et al., 2003; Lester and Cannella, 2006) and strategic alliances in small firms (Das and Teng, 2000). Although we do not specifically address the application of resource dependence theory and agency theory in these contexts, our review and discussion may be relevant for these research areas as well.

The rest of the chapter is structured as follows. The next section briefly introduces the issue of governance in entrepreneurial firms. Thereafter, we examine the historical roots of resource dependence theory followed by a similar examination of agency theory. The chapter then compares the two theories. We also address the implications for the joint application of the theories, and make suggestions for future research that seeks to better understand behavioral processes and relational dynamics in and around the boardroom in entrepreneurial firms.

GOVERNANCE IN ENTREPRENEURIAL FIRMS

Governance has traditionally not been seen as much of an issue in entre-preneurial firms, because they are characterized as relatively non-complex organizations with ownership and control consolidated in one individual (i.e. the owner-manager) where coordination is effected largely by direct supervision. This simplified view, however, has in recent years been increasingly challenged for a variety of reasons. For example, in entre-preneurial firms that start to experience growth there is eventually a need for functional managers to take on duties currently performed by the owner[4] (Greiner, 1972; Churchill and Lewis, 1983). The governance lit-erature identifies this transition as a critical step in the development from a founder-managed to a more professionally managed firm (e.g. Whisler, 1988; Daily and Dalton, 1992; Gedajlovic et al., 2004; Gabrielsson, 2007a). This transition means that job assignments become more specialized, and the increasing complexity in the organization calls for more sophisticated control systems to coordinate major elements of the growing firm. It also means that planning procedures become more formalized and that an effective compensation and reward system has to be developed. Among other things, this marks an emerging need to separate strategic and opera-tional responsibilities and to start contemplating questions about how the firm is governed rather than just managed.

Moreover, some entrepreneurial firms may already, in their early years of operations, seek additional equity from external owners (De Clercq and Manigart, 2007). Firm managers may in this respect have access to superior information regarding the resources and performance of the enterprise and can consequently take advantage of this information asym-metry for their own purposes, which in turn can cut back the returns of other investors (Markman et al., 2001). These potential problems could in turn lead to external owners demanding increased board oversight in the entrepreneurial firm. The pressure from external owners is also something which has been found both in empirical studies of the post-involvement activities of venture capitalists (Gabrielsson and Huse, 2002) and in more general studies of boards and governance in small firms (Westhead, 1999; Fiegener et al., 2000b; Gabrielsson, 2007b).

Furthermore, contemporary literature on governance tends to emphasize contractual and incentive structures in the governance process while neglecting other important tasks, such as assisting the management team in building a wider set of relationships to deal with business risks in the firm's competitive domain and extracting critical resources that are vital to firm performance (Borch and Huse, 1993; George et al., 2001). Entrepreneurial firms are in this respect often coping with liabilities of newness (Stinchcombe, 1965; Shepherd et al., 2000) and smallness (Aldrich and Auster, 1986), which create difficulties in building and maintaining stable relationships with important stakeholders and generating economies of scale. Having access to an active board of directors that can provide the firm with timely resources may, therefore, be a crucial ingredient for improving its chances of long-term survival. A governing board could identify critical strategic issues, increase the legitimacy of the firm, and provide timely access to resources that otherwise would not be accessible (Borch and Huse, 1993; Rosa and Scott, 1999; Deutsch and Ross, 2003).

The arguments above suggest that entrepreneurial firms can benefit from the support that a governing board can offer. As indicated earlier, the two theories most commonly employed for understanding principles for effective board governance in small firms are resource dependence theory and agency theory. We now continue with an overview of the history and intellectual roots of each theory.

RESOURCE DEPENDENCE THEORY

Resource dependence theory seeks to explain organizational and inter-organizational behavior in terms of the critical resources that an organization depends on. The theory posits that an organization must interact with its environment either to purchase resources or to distribute its finished products, where the key to organizational survival is the ability to acquire and maintain resources critical for its operations (Pfeffer and Salancik, 1978, p. 2). A basic premise in the theory is that organizations to a large extent are in permanent interaction with other entities in the environment where resource exchange relationships take place (e.g. Thompson, 1967), thereby creating resource dependencies. The theory predicts that the survival and success of a firm are dependent on its abilities to link the firm with its external environment. As such, the theory posits that the firm should seek to initiate and maintain control over scarce and valued resources essential to organizational survival, in order to achieve organizational effectiveness, defined as 'the ability to create acceptable outcomes and actions' (Pfeffer and Salancik, 1978, p. 7).

Organizations as Open Systems

The general thinking underlying resource dependence theory originates from open system theory, a perspective conceiving the organization as a system that is influenced by and interacts with the environment in which it operates (Katz and Kahn, 1966; Thompson, 1967). Katz and Kahn (1966, p. 16) describe the system perspective as '. . .basically concerned with problems of relationships, of structure, and of interdependence rather than with the constant attributes of objects'. Open system theory was initially developed by the biologist Ludwig von Bertanlanffy in his essay 'The theory of open systems in physics and biology' (1950). In the opening remarks of his essay he states that 'a system is closed if no material enters or leaves it; it is open if there is import and export and, therefore, change of the components' (1950, p. 23). Thus, von Bertanlanffy emphasized the idea that real systems[5] are open to their environment and interact with the environment, which results in continual change and evolution.

Before open system theory, organizations were largely seen as closed and self-contained entities which operated autonomously within relatively fixed boundaries, and studies dealt with issues such as internal operations, motivation, communication, task design, etc. (e.g. Taylor 1911; Barnard, 1938; Fayol, 1949). It should perhaps be pointed out that the idea of using a system perspective to understand organizations was not entirely novel. For example, although dealing mainly with internal operations, Chester Barnard (1938) emphasized the importance of understanding the social character of cooperation in *The Functions of the Executive*. In his book he argues that human organisms function in mutual conjunction with other organisms, with their interdependence evolving over time (p. 11). He also describes the organization as a system composed of the activities of human beings (p. 77). Hence, even if open system theory provided a fresh perspective in the study of organizations when it was introduced in the 1950s, the general idea of applying systems thinking for understanding organizations already existed. The introduction of open system theory, however, raised the idea that organizations are open to and interact in close association with what is construed to be their external environment, and the perspective introduced theoretical concepts such as input, throughput, output, system boundaries and interdependence. These concepts were then increasingly adopted and implemented by scientists across a range of different disciplines, including the study of organizations (e.g. Rhenman, 1964; Emery and Trist, 1965; Katz and Kahn, 1966).

The Organization and the External Environment

By the end of the 1960s the open system perspective was more or less mainstream thinking in organization theory. The external environment is described in this perspective as consisting of other organizations and individuals that exert economic, political and social influence on the focal organization (Katz and Kahn, 1966; Yuchtman and Seashore, 1967). Another feature of the external environment is that it provides resources that enable the organization to persist and evolve over time but also makes the organization dependent on others in order to obtain these resources (Thompson, 1967). Both these features are expected to have a critical impact on the structure and behavior of organizations. However, even if resource dependence theory conceives organizations as open systems (Pfeffer and Salancik, 1978, p. 1), it is also emphasized that the relationship between the environment and organizational structures and decisions is not perfect (Pfeffer and Salancik, 1978, p. 227). Rather, organizations are seen as 'loosely coupled' (e.g. Weick, 1976) with their environments, something which makes external relationships important but, at the same time, indeterminate. These indeterminate relationships allow potential variations in how organizations are able to manage constraints in their resource environments, by maintaining external linkages to organizations on which they depend for critical resources. These potential variations are moreover a key trigger for the analysis of resource dependence, as they point to the value of understanding how the distribution of power in and around the organization influences its behavior and design.

Two fundamental questions addressed in resource dependence theory are: who controls the organization, and how do such distributions of power and influence arise? The interest in these two questions connects resource dependence theory with early literature and research in sociology that analyze power in and around organizations. An important source for this stream of research is Philip Selznick who, in his book *TVA and the Grass Roots* (1949), uses power-based arguments to study inter-organizational relations. Organizations are described in Selznick's study as adaptive social structures affected by their environments where external groups fight for control of them, which, in turn, constrains organizational action and behaviors. An important part of his study is the analysis of co-optation as a mechanism to cope with the tensions and dilemmas caused by structural arrangements and environmental constraints. Co-optation in this context means inviting a representative of the source of constraint into the internal decision-making or advisory structure of the organization with the aim of averting threats to its stability or existence, thus trading some of the organization's autonomy for support (Selznick, 1949, p. 13).

Another important source for the development of what came to be resource dependence theory is the early work conducted by social exchange theorists such as Blau (1964) and Emerson (1962). These theorists focus on power as a function of social relations and emphasize that some form of interdependence is a necessary condition for exerting influence. Power is, moreover, not zero-sum, as two actors can have power over each other and, thus, be interdependent. The connection between social structure and the use of power is, therefore, central in this stream of research, where power is seen as the mechanics that can explain the relations of the actors in a network. There is however an important difference. Whereas social exchange theorists focus on individual actors, the attention in resource dependence theory was recast towards describing the actions of organizations.

The External Control of Organizations

There are several studies from the late 1960s until the mid-1970s that more or less explicitly build on the general idea underlying resource dependence theory, that organizational behavior is determined by external social constraints and resource interdependence (e.g. Thompson, 1967; Yuchtman and Seashore, 1967; Zald, 1970; Pfeffer, 1972a, 1972b, 1972c; Walmsley and Zald, 1973; Aldrich and Pfeffer, 1976; Pfeffer and Nowak, 1976).[6] However, the most definite reference to resource dependence theory is the book *The External Control of Organizations* by Jeffrey Pfeffer and Gerald R. Salancik, published in 1978. They develop ideas about conflicts of interest in and around organizations, and how power influences structures and patterns of behavior aimed at acquiring and maintaining necessary external resources. The result is a highly political theory that identifies and analyzes the ways in which firms become constrained by their environment and the strategies managers can employ to cope with these dependences. A basic assumption in the theory is that of political struggle, where different coalitions of actors try in a highly self-interested manner to influence each other to their own advantage, and where conflicting demands are described as largely incompatible (Pfeffer and Salancik, 1978, p. 27). In this vein, the theory posits that resource exchange and power relations in and around organizations influence the behavior and design of organizations. Moreover, organizations are seen as unable to internally generate all the resources required to maintain themselves, resulting in dependence on transactions and relations with external actors and organizations in their environment for their survival (Aldrich and Pfeffer, 1976, p. 83). This dependence on external resources constrains organizational action, and managers must effectively manage resource dependences if the organization is to survive and function. As such, organizations are involved in a constant struggle for autonomy and discretion while also being confronted with constraints and external control (Pfeffer and Salancik, 1978, p. 257).

Resource dependence theory focuses on the flow or exchange of resources between organizations (or units within the organization) and the resulting dependences and power differentials that are created. It is these dependences that provide the basis for external control over an organization. These arguments can be directly related back to the pioneering work of the social-exchange theorist Richard Emerson and his essay 'Power-dependence relations' (1962), where he developed the idea that power is the property of a social exchange relationship and not of an actor, because it 'resides implicitly in the other's dependency' (p. 32). Moreover, it is stated that 'the power of A over B is equal to and based upon the dependence of B upon A' (p. 33). Thus, in the analysis Emerson (1962) asserted that dependence and power are a function of the value that one actor places on resources controlled by another and the relative availability of alternative resources. Power is hence seen as deriving from resource connections, and those individuals, subunits or other organizations that exclusively provide the most needed resources will have the most power over or within the focal organization.

Building on these ideas, Pfeffer and Salancik (1978) apply power-dependence concepts to analyze and understand how interactions, with external actors and organizations in the environment where resource exchange relationships take place, affect and constrain an organization. A way of alleviating sources of external constraint is to strengthen the relationship with the particular sources of dependence, something that follows Selznick's (1949) insights regarding organizational co-optation. Pfeffer and Salancik (1978) thus suggest that a main task of the management is to establish 'negotiated environments' (e.g. Cyert and March, 1963, p. 119) that are favorable to the organization (Pfeffer and Salancik, 1978, p. 263). This means that the organization, instead of having to anticipate future reactions in the environment, avoids uncertainty in resource acquisition by entering and negotiating exchange relationships with other organizations. They also present a detailed analysis of specific sets of strategies and tactics that can be employed to manage these external constraints and dependences in the external environment, and they discuss the conditions under which the measures are appropriate. Strategies to manage resource dependences include mergers and acquisitions, diversification, board interlocks and co-optations, joint ventures, and direct political action (Pfeffer and Salancik, 1978, chapters 5–8).

Resource Dependence Theory and the Board of Directors

Researchers interested in issues of boards and governance have used resource dependence theory to provide a conceptual basis for how board members can assist the firm in its attempt to acquire and maintain resources critical for its operations (Zahra and Pearce, 1989; Johnson et al., 1996; Huse, 2005). As indicated above, resource dependence theory identifies the board of directors as playing a crucial role in linking the organization to its environment by co-opting representatives from important external organizations with which it is interdependent (Zald, 1969; Pfeffer, 1972c, 1973; Pfeffer and Salancik, 1978, p. 167). Board members are selected to maximize the provision of critical resources, and board members are seen as important boundary-spanners who provide timely information and convey critical resources to firm managers (Zald, 1967; Pfeffer, 1972c).

An important qualification for board members' ability to link the organization with its external environment is their personal legitimacy and reputation. Pfeffer and Salancik for example argue that 'prestigious or legitimate persons or organizations represented on the focal organization's board provide confirmation to the rest of the world of the value and worth of the organization' (1978, p. 145). The composition of the board can in this respect be seen as an important mechanism for managing resource dependencies. The emphasis on board members as boundary-spanners in resource dependence theory has moreover led to a focus on the value of having large boards composed of experienced and reputable 'outsiders' (Zahra and Pearce, 1989; Johnson et al., 1996). Through their positions and networks of relationships, these outside board members are seen as important in contributing with advice and counsel, facilitating inter-firm commitments and providing access to critical resources.

With its emphasis on mechanisms for acquiring and maintaining resources critical for business operations, resource dependence theory seems particularly applicable to the study of boards and governance in entrepreneurial firms. Entrepreneurial firms often face an uncertain environment and they may also lack both economic and political power (Pfeffer and Salancik, 1978), something which may call for the adoption of board members that can link the organization with its external environment and assist the firm in providing access to critical resources. Entrepreneurial firms may furthermore lack a sense of 'historical legitimacy' (Selznick, 1949, p. 259) and may thus benefit from using co-optation as a means to recruit representatives from important external organizations on the board, to represent the organization and become a basis for its legitimacy claims. An active board of directors can in this respect be expected to be involved in reducing dependency between the entrepreneurial firm and external contingencies and by that ultimately aid in the survival of the firm.

There are studies in the entrepreneurship field that seem to largely support the expectations derived from resource dependence theory. In a study of successful entrepreneurial firms, Daily and Dalton (1992) for example find that the number and proportion of outside board members were positively associated with higher financial performance. In another study of small corporations, Daily and Dalton (1993) report a positive association between the number and proportion of outside board members, board size and financial performance. In both cases, they interpret their findings as consistent with the resource dependence theory assumption that larger boards and more outside board members are associated with higher board involvement in service and resource provision roles, which in turn influence firm performance. There are also empirical studies presenting evidence that resource provision and networking tasks performed by board members are related to performance advantages. Borch and Huse (1993) identify the informal networks mediated by the board of directors in small firms as very important for improved environmental exchange power and in uncertainty reduction, and they find that the members of the board have to be seriously examined in order to match the firm's need for service. Consistent with the idea that interlocks are a mechanism to access scarce resources, George et al. (2001) report in a study of small and medium-sized enterprises (SMEs) that firms with a board networking strategy performed better than those firms that did not actively pursue the development of networks. Furthermore, Gabrielsson and Politis (2007) find that a higher involvement in networking activities by board members improves the competitive performance of small technology based firms by encouraging a more entrepreneurial and proactive strategic orientation. Thus, to conclude, it seems fair to argue that resource dependence theory is a viable approach for researching issues of boards and governance in entrepreneurial firms.

AGENCY THEORY

Agency theory is about the problem of divergent interests between two opportunistic and self-serving parties in a contractual relationship. An agency relationship is a contract where one or more principals hire one or more agents to perform some service, and then delegate decision-making authority to these agents (Ross, 1973; Jensen and Meckling, 1976). The theory identifies that agents are subject to moral hazard[7] when they do not bear the full economic consequences of their decisions. Moreover, delegation of decision-making authority imposes problems of information asymmetry, where the principal cannot perfectly and costlessly monitor the actions of the agent. Consequently, principals face the risk that opportunistic agents will take advantage of the situation for their own benefit by engaging in activities and behavior that harm welfare and induce unwanted costs for principals, such as free riding or shirking.

Conflict of Interests between Shareholders and Managers

Agency theory is a general theory of principal–agent relationships that has been applied to a broad range of substantive contexts. However, the specific problem that agency theory deals with in research on boards and governance is the conflict of interests between shareholders and managers.[8] The identification of this potential conflict is relatively old in the study of business enterprise and can be found in the writings of well-known economists. In *The Wealth of Nations*, Adam Smith (1776 [2000], p. 276) argued that managers could not be expected to watch over other people's money as if it were their own. For this reason, he expected that both 'carelessness and excess' would exist in these types of company. Alfred Marshall (1920, p. 212) made a similar analysis in his book *Industry and Trade*, where he suggested that salaried managers were seeking the greatest comfort and the least risk for themselves. As a result, they could not be expected to strive very energetically for improvement.

Although addressed by economists such as Smith and Marshall, among others, the potential problem of the conflict of interests between shareholders and managers was brought to a wider audience by Berle and Means (1932) in their book *The Modern Corporation and Private Property*. Their concerns were aimed at ensuring that the accumulated surplus of the organization was given to shareholders, rather than staying in the hands of the emerging powerful class of professional managers. These managers were seen as having interests that were not necessarily in line with those of the shareholders and, given the enormous freedom and power that was delegated to them, Berle and Means (1932) concluded that some kind of control mechanism had to be instituted to see that profits were properly distributed back to the rightful owners. Hence, there was a need for a system of checks and balances to align the actions and behavior of managers with the desires and preferences of shareholders.

The problem of the separation of ownership from control in the modern corporation that was raised by Berle and Means (1932) led to the subsequent development of managerial theories of the firm, in which the works of Baumol (1959), Marris (1964) and Williamson (1964) are among the most acknowledged. Managerial theories of the firm make the assumption that owners seek to maximize shareholder wealth, while managers maximize a utility function that includes remuneration, power, job security, and status. These theories moreover assume that managers have a certain level of discretion and freedom to alter the goals and objectives of the firm they are managing. It is thus suggested that managers seek to stabilize or improve their own position by maximizing, for example, revenue from sales (e.g. Baumol, 1959) or growth (e.g. Marris, 1964) at the expense of shareholders.

The Emergence of Agency Theory

Even though the problem of the separation of ownership from control has long been recognized and discussed in the economic literature, it was not until the 1970s that a common framework started to emerge for analyzing the problems associated with the separation of ownership from control. The theoretical foundations of these efforts can be traced back to the analysis of labor contracts in agrarian economies, whereby a landowner allows a tenant to use land in return for a share of the crop that is produced – something which is generally called 'sharecropping' (Otsuka et al., 1992; Casadesus-Masanell and Spulber, 2007). Dating back almost 200 years,[9] the sharecropping literature analyzes the alternative contractual arrangements that may exist between a landowner and a tenant farmer, for example the incentive effects of fixed rents compared to rent paid as a share of output produced from the rented land. According to Casadesus-Masanell and Spulber (2007), it is this origin that explains why economists primarily view agents as workers performing production tasks.

An important landmark in the development of agency theory as we know it today is Marvin Berhold who, in the essay 'A theory of linear profit-sharing incentives' (1971), develops a general model for the analysis of incentive contracts between principals and agents. In his analysis, Berhold (1971, p.461) describes the incentive function as the relationship between the monetary reward and the characteristics of the agent's performance. If the incentive function is acceptable to the agent, then an optimal incentive function (from the viewpoint of the principal) can be selected in terms of a sharing ratio and a fixed reward. The interaction between risk-sharing and performance incentives for the agent is central in his analysis of the optimal sharing ratio. Here, Berhold (1971, p.481) shows that the optimal sharing ratio decreases when the agent's risk increases, thus shifting the risk to the principal. Similarly, the optimal sharing ratio increases when the principal's risk increases, thus shifting the risk to the agent. As such, the model developed by Berhold (1971) can be considered an early version of agency theory as it emphasizes the provision of appropriate incentives so that agents act in the way principals wish.

Another important landmark for the development of agency theory is Ross's (1973) influential essay 'The economic theory of agency: the principal's problem', which reformulated agency problems and incentive contracts as embedded in agency relationships. Ross defines an agency relationship as 'when one, designated as the agent, acts for, on behalf of, or as representative for the other, designated the principal, in a particular domain of decision problems' (1973, p. 134), thus suggesting that the agency problem is generic in society. The 'principal's problem', according to Ross, is to design an incentive compensation package with fixed and performance-based pay that optimizes the expected utility of both principals and agents. As such, the problem is one of selecting an appropriate compensation system that will produce behavior by the agent consistent with the preferences of the principal.

Agency Theory and the Theory of the Firm

Both Berhold (1971) and Ross (1973) discuss the general problem of agency in relation to incentives and compensation contracting. The problem of agency was then subsequently developed and applied to the theory of the firm by Jensen and Meckling (1976) in their essay 'Theory of the firm: managerial behavior, agency costs and ownership structure'. They recognize the general nature of the agency problem, suggesting that it 'exist[s] in all organizations and in all cooperative efforts – at every level of management in firms' (Jensen and Meckling, 1976, p. 309), but they focus on the control problems that arise in firms as a result of a separation of ownership from the direct control of decision-making in the firm. Based on the ideas of Alchian and Demsetz (1972), they conceptualize the firm as a set of contracts among factors of production (owners, managers, employees, suppliers, etc.) where each factor is motivated by its self-interest.[10] Owners, in this nexus-of-contracts view of the firm, are depicted as the rightful residual claimants, because they are the only group of contracting stakeholders that bears the risk of not getting any returns on their investments. All other stakeholders (employees, suppliers, etc.) who provide factor inputs needed for production are, due to the assumption of efficient markets,[11] expected to receive an appropriate compensation for their provision of resources, which is adjusted depending on the market price for each input. Managers have a unique position in the firm as they enter into contractual relationships with other stakeholders, make strategic decisions and allocate resources.

Jensen and Meckling (1976, p. 312) state that a wholly-owned firm managed by its owner will operate decisions that maximize his or her utility. However, they go on to argue that when the owner-manager's fraction of equity falls this will encourage him or her to appropriate larger amounts of corporate resources in the form of perquisites. Thus, the separation of ownership from control induces agency problems in the entrepreneurial firm as owners will bear the costs of managerial decisions that do not maximize shareholder wealth. Opportunistic and self-serving managers can thus be expected to be involved in non-profit-maximizing activities and maximize their own pay and benefits at the expense of firm resources when they do not bear the wealth effects of their decisions. These non-profit-maximizing activities mean that the economic residual created by the firm (the owner's claim) will be reduced. These circumstances imply that owners have proper incentives to monitor the behavior and decisions of managers. To secure their best interests, agency theory thus suggests that principals should resolve potential agency problems through bonding and monitoring mechanisms.[12]

Later, Fama (1980) further developed the analysis in his essay 'Agency problems and the theory of the firm' by arguing that the two tasks usually attributed to the entrepreneur – management and risk-bearing – should be treated as naturally separate factors within the set of contracts that constitutes the firm. From this perspective, he contends that 'ownership of the firm is an irrelevant concept' (Fama, 1980, p. 290) and argues that separation of ownership[13] and control is an efficient form of economic organization as the firm is disciplined through competition from other firms. This competition forces firms to develop devices for efficiently monitoring the performance of the firm as of its individual members (in particular its managers). Moreover, he places particular emphasis on the monitoring and discipline provided by efficient markets, both within and outside the firm. As such, Fama (1980) develops the perspective on management and risk-bearing as separate factors of production where each is faced with an alternative market for its services. These markets also provide them with opportunities, where owners can take their capital elsewhere if they wish and where managers, through the managerial labor market, are motivated toward performance so that they can get promoted (internal labour market) or recruited in the future (external labor market). In sum, Fama (1980) argues that the evolution of devices for monitoring the firm is determined by market forces and that these devices have efficiency properties.

Agency Theory and the Board of Directors

In addition to the market mechanism, agency theory identifies the board of directors as a cornerstone in the governance system of a firm. In the oft-cited essay 'Separation of ownership and control', Fama and Jensen (1983) suggest that the separation of management and risk-bearing functions survives partly due to the benefits of specialization, but also because of an effective common approach to control the agency problems that arise. Here, they emphasize that the contract structures of firms separate the initiation and implementation of the decisions (i.e. decision management) from the ratification and monitoring of decisions (i.e. decision control). The latter is provided by a board of directors who are responsible for hiring, compensating, and firing the CEO and for monitoring managerial and firm performance to shield the invested stakes of shareholders from potential managerial self-interest. The board of directors, consequently, functions as an important information system that can reduce agency problems and maximize shareholder value.

The most important qualification for board members in agency theory is independence, which generally means that they should have no personal or professional relationship to the firm or firm management (Zahra and Pearce, 1989). Board members who are not independent are expected to have fewer incentives to monitor the CEO and other firm managers. An issue that could compromise the board's ability to be independent and set its own agenda is the dual leadership structure (often referred to as CEO duality), and agency theory thus recommends a separation of the CEO and board chairperson roles. Another qualification that can influence the board's ability to be independent is board members' equity compensation, as ownership aligns their own interests with those of shareholders (Jensen and Meckling, 1976). A majority of independent outside board members with an equity stake in the business is then, in turn, expected to make boards actively involved in strategic decision-making and in monitoring managerial and firm performance, thereby enabling them to take independent action and assert power (Fama and Jensen, 1983).

Agency theory is most often connected with the analysis of boards and governance in large publicly held corporations, but it can very well be applied to any firm context when the two functions of decision-making and residual risk-bearing are separated. The analytical focus of agency theory makes it applicable to use when studying effects of the separation of these two functions in the entrepreneurial firm. Agency theory would, for example, suggest that external owners exert pressure to implement independent governance structures in order to protect them from potential managerial opportunism (Jensen and Meckling, 1976). The theory would also posit that small but growing entrepreneurial firms can gain performance benefits from the external oversight an independent board can offer when the organization faces problems of asymmetric information due to increasing delegation and functional specialization (Fama and

Jensen, 1983). An active board of directors in entrepreneurial firms can, in this respect, be expected to be involved in reducing the risk of potential managerial misbehavior by instituting proper incentives (for example, performance-based pay) and by closely monitoring managerial and firm performance.

There are some studies in the entrepreneurship field that seem to support expectations derived from agency theory. For example, both Rosenstein (1988) and Gabrielsson and Huse (2002) find in their studies of firms where venture capitalists (VCs) have invested alongside management that VC-backed firms have a larger number of board seats and with outside VC-appointed board members rather than the CEO in power. Moreover, Fried et al. (1998) find that boards in VC-backed firms are more involved in both strategy formulation and evaluation compared to boards where board members do not have large ownership stakes. The findings are in line with agency theoretic expectations that outside ownership significantly changes the governance structure of small firms. This pattern is also found in more general studies of boards of directors in small firms, where influential external stakeholders, such as outside owners, often seek to avoid centralized leadership authority and the domination of the CEO in strategic decision-making by adopting outsiders on the board (e.g. Westhead, 1999; Fiegener et al., 2000b; Gabrielsson, 2007b). The adoption of independent board members seems thus to be a response to satisfy the demands from owners not directly involved in managing the company.

There are also some studies that support the idea that external monitoring by independent boards can provide proper incentives for managers to promote long-term and potentially risky strategies aimed at innovation and change. Brunninge et al. (2007), for example, find that although closely held SMEs in general exhibit less strategic change (compared to SMEs with more widespread ownership structures), they can overcome this potential weakness and achieve strategic change by adopting independent board members on the board. In a study of medium-sized corporations Gabrielsson (2007a) finds that board involvement in the ratifying and monitoring stages of strategic decision-making is positively associated with CEOs' commitment to take a more entrepreneurial strategic posture. In another study of small technology based firms Gabrielsson and Politis (2008) make a distinction between boards' involvement in strategic and financial controls,[14] and they find that boards' involvement in strategic control is positively associated with process innovation, while boards' involvement in financial control is positively associated with organizational innovation. To conclude, there consequently seems to be general support for the use of an agency theory approach when researching issues of boards and governance in entrepreneurship research.

COMPARING THE TWO THEORIES

From our review, it is evident that the two theories have similarities, complementarities, and differences. As the objective of this chapter is to give an overview of the historical and intellectual roots of resource dependence theory and agency theory with a particular focus on how they have been applied in studies of boards and governance, we want to emphasize that the characteristics and assumptions identified are not fully comprehensive, nor do we present a detailed account of all possible relevant comparative aspects. Instead, our aim has been to illustrate those similarities, complementarities and differences that may garner interest among scholars working with issues of board governance in the entrepreneurship field.

With respect to similarities, both theories have assumptions of managerial behavior guided by self-interest. Agency theory is explicit about this assumption, for example in the discussion of utility maximization in agency relationships (Jensen and Meckling, 1976, p. 308). Resource dependence theory, however, also posits that managers treat outside constituencies in a self-interested manner to suit the interests of the organization (Pfeffer and Salancik, 1978, p. 263). Thus, both theories have a self-interested position with respect to the behavior of managers. Moreover, both identify the board of directors as a cornerstone in the governance system of the firm and note especially the value of outside board members. Resource dependence theory, for example, suggests that resource-constrained firms have a considerable lack of economic and political power, which in turn creates a need to be flexible in establishing effective linkages with the external environment through outside board members (Pfeffer and Salancik, 1978). Agency theory, on the other hand, stresses the need to have a vigilant board with a majority of outside (independent) board members that can shield the invested stakes of shareholders from potential managerial self-interest (Fama and Jensen, 1983). Thus, both theories identify outside board members as key contributors in the governance process.

With respect to complementarities, each theory has a different focus. Resource dependence theory, through its attention to interorganizational relationships and power dependences between the firm and various constituencies, primarily focuses on the external environment. On the other hand, agency theory, through its attention to potential managerial self-interest, focuses on the internal environment of the firm, and, in particular, board–management relationships. The two theories are also complementary in the sense that scholars have used them to provide theoretical justifications for both a resource provisioning and monitoring role for the board (Hillman and Dalziel, 2003). Resource dependence theory emphasizes aspects of a board's resource provisioning role, encompassing tasks such as securing critical resources, providing external legitimacy, and networking. Agency theory emphasizes the board's monitoring role, which encompasses tasks such as monitoring managerial and firm performance and being involved in decision control to protect the rights of residual claimants (i.e. shareholders).

There are also some notable differences between the two theories. First, resource dependence theory acknowledges the existence of market inefficiencies and power differentials, and board members are seen as resources (or as resource providers) supporting the dominant coalition in the achievement of corporate goals. As such, the theory has no a priori definition of which stakeholder group belongs to the dominant coalition, and corporate goals and objectives are seen as the result of negotiation and political bargaining among the different coalitions of stakeholders in and around the firm. Agency theory, on the other hand, assumes that stakeholders operate in a context where markets are efficient and relatively quickly adjust to new circumstances. The contracts between all stakeholders, except shareholders, are also assumed to be made ex ante, which means that there is no room for ex post bargaining. If stakeholders do not like the terms of a contract, they can always seek a better alternative. Agency theory consequently identifies shareholders as the rightful dominant coalition, and boards are elected in their service to maximize their wealth by protecting them from opportunistic and self-serving managers.

In addition, there are differences between the two theories when it comes to their view on the rationality of decision-makers. With its close association with concepts and thinking from Cyert and March (1963), resource dependence theory more or less implicitly adopts the assumption that decision-makers in and around the firms are boundedly rational, which means that they experience limits in their ability to process information and solve complex problems (e.g. Simon, 1957). The different modes or strategies of adaptation that are delineated in resource dependence theory can, in this respect, be seen as different kinds of satisficing behavior in an environment of uncertainty. Agency theory, however, assumes that decision-makers are fully rational. This means that they are assumed to search for optimal solutions with the objective of maximizing their own benefits (Jensen and Meckling, 1976, p.307). Assuming full rationality implies that managerial discretion becomes a potential problem, as it allows greater space for managers to serve their own rather than shareholder objectives. If not constrained or in some way controlled, for example by a vigilant board of directors, increased managerial discretion may lead to agency costs which influence firm performance negatively. This can be put in contrast to resource dependence theory, which posits that managerial discretion is dictated and constrained by environmental

Table 2.1   Resource dependence theory and agency theory compared

Similarities	Complementarities	Differences
Managers are assumed to be driven largely by self-interest	Resource dependence theory is externally focused – agency theory is internally focused	Resource dependence assumes incomplete contracting setups among all stakeholders – agency theory assumes ex ante contracting between all stakeholders except between shareholders and managers
The board of directors is identified as a cornerstone in the governance system of the firm, especially outside board members	Resource dependence theory identifies a resource provision role for the board – agency theory identifies a monitoring role for the board	Resource dependence theory identifies need for boards to increase managerial discretion – agency theory identifies need for boards to constrain or control managerial discretion

conditions, which reduce the organization's ability to take independent action and pursue its objectives and goals. The boundary-spanning activities of the board of directors are, in this respect, an important means for coping in an environment of uncertainty and by that increasing managers' freedom to make decisions and choices. As such, the different views on rationality in the theories mean that they provide contradictory normative implications as to whether managerial discretion should be increased or constrained. The identified similarities, complementarities and differences are summarized in Table 2.1.

IMPLICATIONS FOR THE JOINT APPLICATION OF THE THEORIES IN ENTREPRENEURSHIP RESEARCH

Both resource dependence theory and agency theory provide rich and widely acknowledged conceptual foundations that can be used to address issues of governance in entrepreneurship research. Resource dependence theory, for example, fits well to the entrepreneurial context as new and small firms need to build and maintain favorable and stable relationships with key stakeholders to survive and prosper. Their limited influence and bargaining power may, in this respect, call for the importance of gaining access to resources, influence and legitimacy through the networks of their board members (Borch and Huse, 1993). Also, agency theory can be seen as a highly relevant perspective for understanding the risk of conflicting goals between contracting parties in entrepreneurial firms. Conflicts can in this respect arise between owners and managers, as well as between part-owners, for example in the division of the value created by the firm as well as in the struggle for power and control rights (Gabrielsson and Huse, 2005). This, in turn, calls for the need to implement governance mechanisms such as a vigilant and independent board of directors in order to reduce potential agency problems (Gedajlovic et al., 2004).

Although each theoretical perspective can be used in its own right, neither of them seems to be able to independently provide a full explanation of the complexities of governance issues in entrepreneurial firms (Daily et al., 2002). Resource dependence theory, for example, with its emphasis on the ways in which firms become constrained by their environment, has a relatively narrow focus on what goes on inside the organization. The environmental context, on the other hand, is often insufficiently examined in agency theory due to the overemphasis on the problems of agency. The joint application of both resource dependence theory and agency theory may in this respect provide a more holistic and balanced view on board governance in the entrepreneurial firm, whereby the different theories provide complementary perspectives. This combinatory approach is well in line with the growing consensus in studies of boards and governance concerning the need for theoretical pluralism (e.g. Hung, 1998; Daily et al., 2003) and where the behavior of boards can be related to the distinctive organizational characteristics and task environment of the firm (Huse, 1998; Lynall et al., 2003; Huse and Zattoni, 2008) as well as to the personal attributes of the CEO and individual board members (Hillman and Dalziel, 2003; Shen, 2003).

This joint application of resource dependence theory and agency theory in studies of boards and governance in entrepreneurial firms, however, also calls for a need to understand the basic assumptions underlying the two theories. As is evident from our overview of each theory's historical roots, they originate from different intellectual traditions and, thus, also partly rely on different assumptions. Resource dependence theory, with its roots in organizational sociology, adopts a perspective that emphasizes power differentials, market inefficiencies and political struggle to explain organizational action. Agency theory, with its roots in the financial economics discipline, on the other hand, assumes rational actors who contract for profit in efficient markets. Thus, whereas resource dependence theory acknowledges the ongoing struggle for power and influence over organizational resource-allocation decisions among different coalitions of stakeholders, the theoretical assumptions in agency theory completely overlook this possibility. Perhaps the easiest way to deal with this situation when combining the two theories is to relax at least two basic assumptions in agency theory. Relaxing these assumptions does not invalidate either the existence of agency relationships or the potential agency problems that arise from them, but it prompts consideration of some features not treated in the theory's standard version.

The first assumption to be relaxed is that of efficient markets, which means that stakeholders may not have freedom of entry into and exit from contractual relationships (Hill and Jones, 1992). Relaxing this assumption would open up the possibility for power differentials between parties in an exchange. This, in turn, rejects the idea of complete contracting ex ante for all stakeholders except between shareholders and managers (Huse et al., forthcoming). Acknowledging the existence of incomplete contracts for all stakeholders involved in resource exchange would open up the possibility for more ex post negotiation (Rajan and Zingales, 1998) while rejecting the idea that shareholders have all the bargaining power. The second assumption to be relaxed is that of fully rational economic actors.[15] The incomplete contracting between stakeholders can in this respect be explained not only by the existence of information asymmetries but also by bounded rationality. In fact, bounded rationality makes all contracts unavoidably incomplete.

The result of the two relaxations above is a slightly modified version of agency theory which – much in line with resource dependence theory thinking – acknowledges the existence of more or less temporary market inefficiencies and unequal resource dependences and power differentials between managers and stakeholders (for similar reasoning in previous studies, see Hill and Jones, 1992). These market inefficiencies create potential agency conflicts, not only between managers and shareholders, but also between managers and a wider set of stakeholders who cannot receive payments with reference to the market price as their investments have limited or no value outside the context of the firm (Blair, 1998). The board of directors is then primarily functioning as an impartial mediator that balances and interprets the sometimes conflicting interests of the value-adding stakeholders who embody the core capabilities of the firm (i.e. the dominant coalition). Moreover, incompleteness of contracts results in an increased need for ex post negotiation and bargaining among the contracting stakeholders about how to distribute the surplus (Rajan and Zingales, 1998). This creates the need for a mechanism, such as a board of directors, which can coordinate resource allocations and reduce costly and potentially value-destroying bargaining processes.[16] Furthermore, accepting that all economic actors are constrained by bounded rationality suggests that the divergence between the desires of principals and the actions of agents is not necessarily due only to agents' self-serving behavior, which is one-sidedly emphasized in standard agency theory (Jensen and Meckling, 1976), but also to the inability of agents to reliably and competently deliver what is expected (Hendry, 2002).[17] This would mean that, in addition to the risk of opportunism, there can also be agency problems related to the limited information they have, the cognitive limitations of their minds, and the finite amount of time they have to make decisions.

To conclude this section, we think the above-mentioned modifications[18] will bring the two theories closer to each other in terms of basic assumptions without violating the basic premise in agency theory that there is a need to protect the interests of principals (shareholders/stakeholders) from potential misbehavior by agents (managers) through bonding or monitoring activities. In line with resource dependence theory thinking, the changes also suggest that board members can be used to assist managers in dealing with the complexity and uncertainty of strategic decision-making by collecting and utilizing relevant and timely information, knowledge and other resources from various stakeholders in and around the firm. Moreover, we believe that the suggested changes are closer to what is already widely assumed in entrepreneurship research, for example markets in disequilibrium (Knight, 1921; Schumpeter, 1942; Kirzner, 1973), power differentials due to variations in the access to resources (Penrose, 1959; Aldrich and Auster, 1986) and decision-makers as boundedly rational economic actors (Sarasvathy, 2008).

SUGGESTIONS FOR FUTURE RESEARCH ON BOARDS AND GOVERNANCE IN ENTREPRENEURIAL FIRMS

In the introduction of this chapter we suggested that both resource dependence theory and agency theory provide implications for researching behavioral aspects of board governance in entrepreneurial firms. We have also argued in the chapter for bringing the theories closer together. In this section, we summarize a number of areas where we think further research is highly warranted to promote the accumulation of knowledge in these areas.

Researching Behavioral Aspects of Board Governance

An interest in behavioral aspects of board governance calls for closer study of how boards actually work and how board members may improve their behavior to contribute to value creation. A highly interesting area of research within a resource dependence framework is to study the motivations, intentions and behaviors of co-opted individuals on the board of directors in entrepreneurial firms. Co-opted board members, in resource dependence theory, are expected to become involved in helping the focal organization to control its environment by influencing their constituencies. Indeed, Pfeffer and Salancik suggest that, 'when an organization appoints an individual to a board, it expects the individual will come to support the organization, will concern himself with its problems, will variably present it to others, and will try to aid it' (1978, p. 167). However, there is a need to scrutinize this largely untested behavioral assumption that co-opted board members would change their loyalty so that they mainly pursue the interests of the entrepreneurial firm, instead of the organization which until recently has been their main home institution (for a more extensive critique of this assumption, see Donaldson, 1995, p. 154). It could for example be just as likely that they join the board for other reasons, for example, to monitor the focal firm to benefit their home institution.[19]

An interesting area of research from an agency theory point of view is the issue of independence in relation to board members in entrepreneurial firms. Independence is seen in agency theory as a key feature of effective boards (Fama and Jensen, 1983), and this feature has been associated with outside (or non-executive) board members. Past studies, however, have suggested a general need to distinguish between outside and independent board members (see, for example, Gabrielsson and Winlund, 2000). The adoption of outside board members and the separation of the CEO and board chairperson roles, for example, are not necessarily found to be associated with greater board involvement in shaping strategy, reviewing management policies, or contributing professional advice (Ford, 1988). Consequently, an outside board member should not, by definition, be expected to behave independently, even if he or she brings considerable competence and experience into the boardroom. Moreover, conceptualizing independence as a behavioral rather than a structural feature raises interesting questions about to what extent and under what conditions outside board members in entrepreneurial firms are acting 'independently' in the way agency theory prescribes. It also connects to recent discussions about the need to examine whether there is a trade-off between independence and the presence of firm-specific knowledge required to understand and evaluate complex firm decisions (e.g. Huse et al., 2009).

Joint Application of Resource Dependence Theory and Agency Theory

When jointly applying resource dependence and agency theory in entrepreneurial firms, there are also some areas where we think research is highly warranted. The first is how various outside board members contribute with different kinds of value-adding benefits in entrepreneurial firms. Resource dependence theory suggests that outside board members contribute added value by bringing different linkages and resources to a board. Agency theory suggests that outside board members contribute added value by introducing checks and balances to correct potential harmful managerial behavior and protect the assets of the firm. Past research, however, has primarily relied on relatively rough distinctions between inside and outside board members (Gabrielsson, 2007b), whereas a more fine-grained analysis of different categories of outside (and perhaps also inside) board members could provide a much more detailed understanding of what kind of value-added contributions a given type of board member is likely to bring to the board (Hillman et al., 2000).

Another interesting area of research when jointly applying resource dependence and agency theory is the extent to which the entrepreneurial firm is able to effectively implement and use the value-added contributions provided by outside board members. Such attempts may need to distinguish between 'potential' contributions and 'realized' contributions. Potential contributions would here refer to the set of potential benefits that the entrepreneurial firm can receive from its outside board members. The realized contributions, on the other hand, would refer to the successful implementation and incorporation of such resource contributions into the venture's operations with the hope of improving its performance. This conceptual distinction suggests that entrepreneurial firms can vary significantly in their ability to effectively implement and utilize the value-adding contributions that outside board members can bring. Making such a distinction would also allow researchers to abandon viewing the value-adding benefits from outside board members as a simple transferring process, and instead turn more attention towards the study of why some attempts to contribute resources fail while others thrive.

A third area of research when jointly applying resource dependence and agency theory is to study how board members' involvement in monitoring versus resource provision tasks evolves and changes as the entrepreneurial firm develops and moves through the organizational life cycle (e.g. Lynall et al., 2003; Bonn and Pettigrew, 2009). This may also include studies of how boards in entrepreneurial firms balance (or fail to balance) the speed and flexibility in decision-making that often are seen as critical features for competitiveness in small firms (e.g. O'Gorman, 2000) against the need to formalize rules, reporting procedures and job descriptions as the firm grows. Such endeavors would not only contribute to our scholarly knowledge of how processes of board governance emerge and develop over time, but would also go beyond the fundamentally static conceptions of boards of directors that often dominate research on corporate governance (Gabrielsson and Huse, 2004).

CONCLUSIONS

Studies of boards and governance have a long history in business research. Although these studies traditionally have focused on large firms (Gabrielsson and Huse, 2004) this interest has also spilled over to include firms that are in the entrepreneurial stages of the organizational life cycle. In this chapter we have provided an overview of the historical and intellectual roots of resource dependence theory and agency theory with a particular focus on how they have been applied in studies of boards and governance. Despite the frequent use of these theories by scholars addressing issues of governance in entrepreneurial firms, they also tend to be used in a largely metaphorical sense to justify the need for board members to perform resource provision and monitoring tasks. Thus, our underlying motivation for the review has been that a better understanding of the origins and thinking behind the theories should contribute positively to knowledge accumulation within the field.

In short, our review suggests that both resource dependence theory and agency theory provide powerful conceptual foundations that can be used to address issues of board governance in entrepreneurship research. Based on this, we also discuss some similarities, complementarities, and differences between the two theories that may have implications when combining arguments from resource dependence theory and agency theory. With regard to similarities and complementarities, there seems to be enough common ground for their joint application in studies of boards and governance. With regard to differences, however, we identify a need to relax some of the assumptions in agency theory to bring the two theories closer together. This, we hope, will stimulate further research on how board members, through their performance of resource provision and monitoring tasks, can contribute to the creation of wealth, value and satisfaction for the range of stakeholders in and around the entrepreneurial firm.

ACKNOWLEDGMENTS

We are indebted to Franz Lohrke and Hans Landström, the editors of this book, for their valuable comments on earlier drafts of this chapter. We are also grateful for the comments given by Diamanto Politis in the course of developing this work.

NOTES

*   Gabrielsson, J. and Huse, M. (2010) Governance theory: Origins and implications for researching boards and governance in entrepreneurial firms, in Landström, H. and Lohrke, F.T. (eds) *Historical Foundations of Entrepreneurship Research*, Cheltenham: Edward Elgar Publishing.

1.   'Entrepreneurial' can refer to such different firm characteristics as being young (Daily et al., 2002), innovative (Covin and Slevin, 1988), fast-growing (Daily and Dalton, 1993) or owner-controlled (Carland et al., 1984).

2.   The dominance of resource dependence theory and agency theory is the case also in studies of boards of directors in general. For an overview, see for example Gabrielsson and Huse (2004).

3.   Outside directors have in entrepreneurship research often been defined as directors who are not executive managers or relatives of the CEO (whether employed by the firm or not) (Fiegener et al., 2000b; Gabrielsson, 2007b).

4.   Research on small firm growth indicates that managerial appointments are usually made when a firm reaches a size between 10 to 20 employees (Storey, 1994, p. 10).

5.   von Bertanlanffy discussed living organisms as open systems in his article, hence the term 'real systems'.

6.   Please note that the terminology varies. Yuchtman and Seashore (1967) refer to the systems-resource approach, Zald (1970) and Walmsley and Zald (1973) refer to the political economy model, and Thompson (1967) refers to the power-dependency model.

7.   Moral hazard means that people act less carefully when they are protected from some (or all) risk than when they are fully exposed to risk. The moral hazard problem originates from the analysis of insurance market contracts where an individual may influence the probability of the insured event to his advantage (e.g. Spence and Zeckhauser, 1971).

8.   A distinction is sometimes made between two different types or versions of agency theory in the literature: the 'positivist' approach and the 'principal–agent' approach. The positivist approach is most often used in corporate governance research. It is more empirical, largely verbal and concentrates on the problem of separation of ownership from control (e.g. Fama and Jensen, 1983). The 'principal–agent' approach is used to analyse all principal/agent relationships. It is more normative, much more mathematical and concentrates on the design of specific ex ante contract specifications (e.g. Holmström, 1979). In this chapter we are referring to the positivist approach in our discussion. However, even if there are some differences in focus and style between the two approaches, we want to emphasize that the background and analytical core is pretty much the same.

9.   Early contributors to the economic analysis of labor contracts in sharecropping include for example both Smith (1776) and Marshall (1890).

10.   Antecedents of this perspective can be found in Coase (1937) and Coase (1960).

11.   Agency theory assumes that markets are in or near an efficient equilibrium (e.g. Fama, 1980; Jensen, 1983).

12.   Bonding mechanisms – such as compensation packages – reward agents when they

achieve the goals of the principals and penalize them when they violate the interests of principals. Monitoring mechanisms – such as a vigilant board of directors – observe the behavior and performance of the agents.

13. Ownership of capital (risk bearing) should here not be confused with ownership of the firm.

14. The distinction is based on Hoskisson and Hitt (1988) and Baysinger and Hoskisson (1990). Financial controls are clear and unambiguous and based on objective decision areas such as the organizational budget, equity, liquidity and finance. Strategic controls recognize the more long-term dimensions of business enterprise and are based on strategically relevant decision criteria that are more subjective, for example decisions related to external market and user needs and new products.

15. This relaxed assumption is not very controversial as it appears in Eisenhardt's (1989) widely cited article.

16. These resource allocations may of course not lead to a fair return on investments as unequal resource dependencies may make ex post surplus and ex ante investments sharing unrelated.

17. Accepting bounded rationality also suggests that principals cannot always express exactly what they want, but this is another problem not dealt with here. See for example Hendry (2005).

18. These modifications also open the way for the application of new theoretical approaches, such as team production theory, in studies of boards and governance in entrepreneurial firms (Huse et al., 2008).

19. We want to point out that this possibility is far from ignored in resource dependence theory. On the contrary, it was discussed by Selznick (1949) and also in later work by Palmer (1983) and Mizruchi and Stearns (1988). However, we are not aware of any attempts that examine the loyalty of co-opted board members in the entrepreneurship literature.

REFERENCES

Alchian, A.A. and H. Demsetz (1972), 'Production, information costs, and economic organization', *American Economic Review*, **62**, 777–95.

Aldrich, H.E. and E. Auster (1986), 'Even dwarfs started small: liabilities of age and size and their strategic implications', *Research in Organizational Behavior*, **8**, 165–98.

Aldrich, H.E. and J. Pfeffer (1976), 'Environments of organizations', *Annual Review of Sociology*, **2**, 79–105.

Barnard, C.I. (1938), *The Functions of the Executive*, Cambridge, MA: Harvard University Press.

Baumol, W.J. (1959), *Business Behavior, Value and Growth*, New York: Macmillan.

Baysinger, B.D. and R.E. Hoskisson (1990), 'The composition of boards of directors and strategic control: effects on corporate strategy', *Academy of Management Review*, **15**, 72–80.

Bennett, R.J. and P.J.A. Robson (2004), 'The role of boards of directors in small and medium-sized firms', *Journal of Small Business and Enterprise Development*, **11**(1), 95–113.

Berhold, M. (1971), 'A theory of linear profit-sharing incentives', *Quarterly Journal of Economics*, **85**(3), 460–82.

Berle, A.A. and G.C. Means (1932), *The Modern Corporation and Private Property*, New York: Macmillan.

Bertanlanffly, L. von (1950), 'The theory of open systems in physics and biology', *Science*, **3**, 23–29.

Birch, D.L. (1979), *The Job Generating Process*, Cambridge, MA: MIT Press.

Blair, M.M. (1998), 'For whom should corporations be run? An economic rationale for stakeholder management', *Long Range Planning*, **31**(2), 195–200.

Blau, P.M. (1964), *Exchange and Power in Social Life*, New York: John Wiley and Sons.
Bonn, I. and A. Pettigrew (2009), 'Towards a dynamic theory of boards: an organisational life cycle approach', *Journal of Management and Organization*, **15**(1), 2–16.
Borch, O.J. and M. Huse (1993), 'Informal strategic networks and the board of directors', *Entrepreneurship Theory and Practice*, **18**(1), 23–37.
Brunninge, O., M. Nordqvist and J. Wiklund (2007), 'Corporate governance and strategic change in SMEs: the effects of ownership, board composition and top management teams', *Small Business Economics*, **29**(3), 295–308.
Carland, J.W., F. Hoy, W.R. Boulton and J.C. Carland (1984), 'Differentiating entrepreneurs from small business owners: a conceptualization', *Academy of Management Review*, **9**(3), 354–59.
Casadesus-Masanell, R. and D.F. Spulber (2007), 'Agency revisited', Northwestern University Working Paper, Boston, MA: Northwestern University.
Churchill, N.C. and V.L. Lewis (1983), 'The five stages of small business growth', *Harvard Business Review*, **61**(3), 30–50.
Clarysse, B., M. Knockaert and A. Lockett (2007), 'Outside board members in high tech start-ups', *Small Business Economics*, **29**(3), 243–59.
Coase, R.H. (1937), 'The nature of the firm', *Economica*, **4**(16), 386–405.
Coase, R.H. (1960), 'The problem of social cost', *Journal of Law and Economics*, **3**, 1–44.
Collin, S.-O. (2003), 'The mastering of the corporation: an integrated model of corporate governance', unpublished manuscript, Department of Business Studies, Kristianstad University College, Sweden.
Covin, J.G. and D.P. Slevin (1988), 'The influence of organization structure on the utility of an entrepreneurial top management style', *Journal of Management Studies*, **25**(3), 217–35.
Cyert, R.M. and J.G. March (1963), *A Behavioral Theory of the Firm*, Englewood Cliffs, NJ: Prentice Hall.
Daily, C.M. and D.R. Dalton (1992), 'The relationship between governance structure and corporate performance in entrepreneurial firms', *Journal of Business Venturing*, **7**, 375–86.
Daily, C.M. and D.R. Dalton (1993), 'Board of directors leadership and structure: control and performance implications', *Entrepreneurship Theory and Practice*, **17**(3), 65–81.
Daily, C.M., D.R. Dalton and A.A. Cannella (2003), 'Corporate governance: decades of dialogue and data', *Academy of Management Review*, **28**, 371–82.
Daily, C.M., P.P. McDougall, J.G. Covin and D.R. Dalton (2002), 'Governance and strategic leadership in entrepreneurial firms', *Journal of Management*, **28**(3), 387–412.
Dant, R.P. (2008), 'A futuristic research agenda for the field of franchising', *Journal of Small Business Management*, **46**, 91–98.
Das, T.K. and B.-S. Teng (2000), 'Instabilities of strategic alliances: an internal tensions perspective', *Organization Science*, **11**(1), 77–101.
De Clercq, D. and S. Manigart (2007), 'The venture capital post investment phase: opening up the black box of involvement', in H. Landström (ed.), *Handbook of Research on Venture Capital*, Cheltenham, UK and Northampton, MA, USA: Edward Elgar, pp. 193–218.
Deutsch, Y. and T.W. Ross (2003), 'You are known by the directors you keep: reputable directors as a signaling mechanism for young firms', *Management Science*, **49**(8), 1003–17.
Donaldson, L. (1995), *American Anti-Management Theories of Organization*, Cambridge, MA: Cambridge University Press.
Eisenhardt, K.M. (1989), 'Agency theory: an assessment and review', *Academy of Management Review*, **14**, 57–74.
Emerson, R.M. (1962), 'Power-dependence relations', *American Sociological Review*, **27**, 31–40.
Emery, F.E. and E.L. Trist (1965), 'The causal texture of organizational environments', *Human Relations*, **18**(1), 21–32.
Fama, E.F. (1980), 'Agency problems and the theory of the firm', *Journal of Political Economy*, **88**(2), 288–307.
Fama, E.F. and M.C. Jensen (1983), 'Separation of ownership and control', *Journal of Law and Economics*, **26**, 301–25.

Fayol, H. (1949), *General and Industrial Management*, Pitman: London.

Fiegener, M.K. (2005), 'Determinants of board participation in the strategic decisions of small corporations', *Entrepreneurship Theory and Practice*, **29**(5), 627–50.

Fiegener, M.K., B.M. Brown, D.R. Dreux and W.J. Dennis Jr (2000a), 'CEO stakes and board composition in small private firms', *Entrepreneurship Theory and Practice*, **24**(4), 5–24.

Fiegener, M.K., B.M. Brown, D.R. Dreux and W.J. Dennis Jr (2000b), 'The adoption of outside boards by small private US firms', *Entrepreneurship and Regional Development*, **12**(4), 291–310.

Finkelstein, S. and A.C. Mooney (2003), 'Not the usual suspects: how to use board process to make boards better', *Academy of Management Executive*, **17**(2), 101–13.

Finkle, T.A. (1998), 'The relationship between boards of directors and initial public offering in the biotechnology industry', *Entrepreneurship Theory and Practice*, **22**(3), 5–29.

Forbes, D.P. and F.J. Milliken (1999), 'Cognition and corporate governance: understanding boards of directors as strategic decision making groups', *Academy of Management Review*, **24**(3), 489–505.

Ford, R.H. (1988), 'Outside directors and the privately-owned firm: are they necessary?', *Entrepreneurship Theory and Practice*, **13**(1), 49–57.

Fried, V.H., G.D. Bruton and R.D. Hisrich (1998), 'Strategy and the board of directors in venture capital-backed firms', *Journal of Business Venturing*, **13**, 493–503.

Gabrielsson, J. (2007a), 'Boards of directors and entrepreneurial posture in medium-size companies: putting the board demography approach to a test', *International Small Business Journal*, **25**(5), 511–37.

Gabrielsson, J. (2007b), 'Correlates of board empowerment in small companies', *Entrepreneurship Theory and Practice*, **31**(5), 687–711.

Gabrielsson, J. and M. Huse (2002), 'The venture capitalist and the board of directors in SMEs: roles and processes', *Venture Capital*, **4**(2), 125–46.

Gabrielsson, J. and M. Huse (2004), 'Context, behavior and evolution – challenges in research on boards and governance', *International Studies in Management and Organization*, **34**(2), 11–36.

Gabrielsson, J. and M. Huse (2005), 'Outside directors in SME boards: a call for theoretical reflections', *Corporate Board: Roles, Duties and Composition*, **1**(1), 28–37.

Gabrielsson, J. and D. Politis (2007), 'The impact of ownership and board governance on firm-level entrepreneurship in small technology-based firms', *Icfai Journal of Corporate Governance*, **6**(3), 43–60.

Gabrielsson, J. and D. Politis (2008), 'Board control and innovation: an empirical study of small technology-based firms', in M. Huse. (ed.), *The Value Creating Board: Corporate Governance and Organizational Behaviour*, London: Routledge, pp. 505–19.

Gabrielsson, J. and H. Winlund (2000), 'Boards of directors in small and medium-sized industrial firms: examining the effects of the board's working style on board task performance', *Entrepreneurship and Regional Development*, **12**(4), 311–30.

Gedajlovic, E., M.H. Lubatkin and W.S. Schulze (2004), 'Crossing the threshold from founder management to professional management: a governance perspective', *Journal of Management Studies*, **41**(5), 899–912.

George, G., D.R. Wood and R. Khan (2001), 'Networking strategy of boards: implications for small and medium-sized enterprises', *Entrepreneurship and Regional Development*, **13**(3), 269–85.

Greiner, L.E. (1972), 'Evolution and revolution as organizations grow', *Harvard Business Review*, **50**(4), 37–46.

Hendry, J. (2002), 'The principals' other problems: honest incompetence and management contracts', *Academy of Management Review*, **27**, 98–113.

Hendry, J. (2005), 'Beyond self-interest: agency theory and the board in a satisficing world', *British Journal of Management*, **16** (special issue), 55–64.

Hill, C.W. and T.M. Jones (1992), 'Stakeholder-agency theory', *Journal of Management Studies*, **29**(2), 132–54.

Hillman, A.J. and T. Dalziel (2003), 'Boards of directors and firm performance: integrating agency and resource dependence perspectives', *Academy of Management Review*, **28**(3), 383–96.

Hillman, A.J., A.A. Cannella and R.L. Paetzold (2000), 'The resource dependence role of corporate directors: strategic adaptation of board composition in response to environmental change', *Journal of Management Studies*, **37**(2), 235–55.

Holmström, B. (1979), 'Moral hazard and observability', *Bell Journal of Economics*, **10**, 74–91.

Hoskisson, R.E. and M.A. Hitt (1988), 'Strategic control systems and relative R&D investment in large multiproduct firms', *Strategic Management Journal*, **9**, 605–21.

Hung, H. (1998), 'A typology of the theories of the roles of governing boards', *Corporate Governance: An International Review*, **6**, 101–11.

Huse, M. (1994), 'Board–management relations in small firms: the paradox of simultaneous independence and interdependence', *Small Business Economics*, **6**(1), 55–73.

Huse, M. (1998), 'Researching the dynamics of board–stakeholder relations', *Long Range Planning*, **31**, 218–26.

Huse, M. (2000), 'Boards in SMEs: a review and research agenda', *Entrepreneurship and Regional Development*, **12**(4), 271–90.

Huse, M. (2005), 'Accountability and creating accountability: a framework for exploring behavioural perspectives of corporate governance', *British Journal of Management*, **16** (special issue), 65–80.

Huse, M. (2007), *Boards, Governance and Value Creation*, Cambridge: Cambridge University Press.

Huse, M. and A. Zattoni (2008), 'Trust, firm life cycle, and actual board behavior: evidence from "one of the lads" in the board of three small firms', *International Studies of Management and Organization*, **38**(3), 71–97.

Huse, M., J. Gabrielsson and A. Minichilli (2009), 'Knowledge and accountability: outside directors' contribution in the corporate value chain', in P.-Y. Pierre-Yves Gomez and R. Moore (eds), *Board Members and Management Consultants: Redefining the Boundaries of Consulting and Corporate Governance*, Information Age Publishing, pp. 137–53.

Huse, M., R. Hoskisson, J. Gabrielsson and R. White (2008), 'Governance in small and medium-sized entrepreneurial firms: the case for team production theory', paper presented at the 28th Annual International Conference of the Strategic Management Society, Cologne, Germany.

Huse, M., R. Hoskisson, A. Zattoni and R. Vigano (forthcoming), 'New perspectives on board research: changing the research agenda', paper to appear in *Journal of Management and Governance*, DOI: 10.1007/s10997-009-9122-9.

Jensen, M.C. (1983), 'Organization theory and methodology', *Accounting Review*, **50**, 319–39.

Jensen, M.C. and W.H. Meckling (1976), 'Theory of the firm: managerial behavior, agency costs and ownership structure', *Journal of Financial Economics*, **2**, 305–60.

Johannisson, B. and M. Huse (2000), 'Recruiting outside board members in the small family business: an ideological challenge', *Entrepreneurship and Regional Development*, **12**(4), 353–78.

Johnson, J.L., C.M. Daily and A.E. Ellstrand (1996), 'Boards of directors: a review and research agenda', *Journal of Management*, **22**(3), 409–38.

Katz, D. and R.L. Kahn (1966), *The Social Psychology of Organizations*, New York: Wiley.

Kirchoff, B. (1994), *Entrepreneurship and Dynamic Capitalism*, London: Praeger.

Kirzner, I.M. (1973), *Competition and Entrepreneurship*, Chicago, IL: University of Chicago Press.

Knight, F.H. (1921), *Risk, Uncertainty and Profit*, Chicago: University of Chicago Press.

Lester, R.H. and A.A. Cannella (2006), 'Interorganizational familiness: how family firms use interlocking directorates to build community-level social capital', *Entrepreneurship Theory and Practice*, **30**(6), 755–75.

Lynall, M.D., B.R. Goldenand and A.J. Hillman (2003), 'Board composition from adolescence to maturity: a multi-theoretical view', *Academy of Management Review*, **28**, 416–31.

Markman, G.D., D.B. Balkin and L. Schjoedt (2001), 'Governing the innovation process in entrepreneurial firms', *Journal of High Technology Management Research*, **12**, 273–93.

Marris, R. (1964), *Economic Theory and 'Managerial' Capitalism*, New York: Free Press.

Marshall, A. (1890), *Principles of Economics: An Introductory Volume*, London: Macmillan and Co.

Marshall, A. (1920), *Industry and Trade: A Study of Industrial Technique and Business Organization; and of Their Influence on the Conditions of Various Classes and Nations*, 3rd edition, London: Publisher's green cloth.

Mizruchi, M.S. and L.B. Stearns (1988), 'A longitudinal study of the formation of interlocking directorates', *Administrative Science Quarterly*, **33**, 194–210.

O'Gorman, C. (2000), 'Strategy and the small firm', in S. Carter and D. Jones-Evans (eds), *Enterprise and Small Business: Principles, Practice and Policy*, Harlow: Financial Times, pp. 283–99.

O'Sullivan, N. and S. Diacon (1999), 'Internal and external governance mechanisms: evidence from the UK insurance industry', *Corporate Governance: An International Review*, **7**(4), 363–73.

Otsuka, K., H. Chuma, and Y. Hayami (1992), 'Land and labor contracts in agrarian economies: theories and facts', *Journal of Economic Literature*, **30**(4), 1965–2019.

Palmer, D. (1983), 'Broken ties: interlocking directorates and intercorporate coordination', *Administrative Science Quarterly*, **28**, 40–55.

Penrose, E. (1959), *The Theory of the Growth of the Firm*, Oxford: Oxford University Press.

Pfeffer, J. (1972a), 'Interorganizational influence and managerial attitudes', *Academy of Management Journal*, **15**, 317–30.

Pfeffer, J. (1972b), 'Merger as a response to organizational interdependence', *Administrative Science Quarterly*, **17**, 382–94.

Pfeffer, J. (1972c), 'Size and composition of corporate boards of directors: the organization and its environment', *Administrative Science Quarterly*, **17**, 218–28.

Pfeffer, J. (1973), 'Size, composition and function of hospital boards of directorates', *Administrative Science Quarterly*, **18**(3), 349–64.

Pfeffer, J. and P. Nowak (1976), 'Joint ventures and interorganizational interdependence', *Administrative Science Quarterly*, **21**(3), 398–418.

Pfeffer, J. and G. Salancik (1978), *The External Control of Organizations: A Resource Dependence Perspective*, New York: Harper and Row.

Quinn, R.E. and K. Cameron (1983), 'Organizational life cycles and shifting criteria of effectiveness: some preliminary evidence', *Management Science*, **29**, 33–51.

Rajan, R.G. and L. Zingales (1998), 'Power in a theory of the firm', *Quarterly Journal of Economics*, **113**, 387–432.

Rhenman, E. (1964), *Företaget som ett styrt system*, Stockholm: Nordstedts.

Rosa, P. and M. Scott (1999), 'The prevalence of multiple owners and directors in the SME sector: implications for our understanding of start-up and growth', *Entrepreneurship and Regional Development*, **11**(1), 21–37.

Rosenstein, J. (1988), 'The board and strategy: venture capital and high technology', *Journal of Business Venturing*, **3**, 159–70.

Rosenstein, J., A.V. Bruno, W.D. Bygrave and N.T. Taylor (1993), 'The CEO, venture capitalists, and the board', *Journal of Business Venturing*, **8**, 99–113.

Ross, S. (1973), 'The economic theory of agency: the principal's problem', *American Economic Review*, **63**(2), 134–39.

Sarasvathy, S.D. (2008), *Effectuation: Elements of Entrepreneurial Expertise*, Cheltenham, UK and Northampton, MA, USA: Edward Elgar.

Schulze, W.S., M.H. Lubatkin and R.N. Dino (2003), 'Exploring the agency consequences of ownership dispersion among the directors of private family firms', *Academy of Management Journal*, **46**(2), 179–94.

Schumpeter, J.A. (1942), *Capitalism, Socialism, and Democracy*, New York: Harper and Row.

Selznick, P. (1949), *TVA and the Grass Roots: A Study in the Sociology of Formal Organization*, New York: Harper and Row.

Shen, W. (2003), 'The dynamics of the CEO–board relationships: an evolutionary perspective', *Academy of Management Review*, **28**, 466–76.

Shepherd, D.A., E.J. Douglas and M. Shanley (2000), 'New venture survival: ignorance, external shocks, and risk reduction strategies', *Journal of Business Venturing*, **15**(5–6), 393–410.

Simon, H.A. (1957), *Models of Man: Social and Rational*, New York: John Wiley and Sons.

Smith, A. (1776 [2000]), *An Inquiry into the Nature and Causes of the Wealth of Nations*, New York: Random House International.

Spence, M. and R. Zeckhauser (1971), 'Insurance, information, and individual action', *American Economic Review*, **61**(2), 380–87.

Stinchcombe, A.L. (1965), 'Social structure and organizations', in J. March (ed.), *Handbook of Organizations*, Chicago: Rand McNally, pp. 142–93.

Storey, D.J. (1994), *Understanding the Small Business Sector*, London: Routledge.

Taylor, F.W. (1911), *The Principles of Scientific Management*, New York: Harper and Brothers Publishers.

Thompson, J.D. (1967), *Organizations in Action*, New York: McGraw-Hill.

Voordeckers, W., A. Van Gils and J. Van den Heuvel (2007), 'Board composition in small and medium-sized family firms', *Journal of Small Business Management*, **45**(1), 137–56.

Walmsley, G. and M. Zald (1973), *The Political Economy of Public Organizations*, Lexington, MA: Lexington Books.

Weber, M. (1947), *The Theory of Social and Economic Organization*, New York: The Free Press.

Weick, K.E. (1976), 'Educational organizations as loosely coupled systems', *Administrative Science Quarterly*, **21**, 1–19.

Westhead, P. (1999), 'Factors associated with the employment of non-executive directors by unquoted companies', *Journal of Management and Governance*, **3**, 81–111.

Whisler, T.L. (1998), 'The role of the board in the threshold firm', *Family Business Review*, **1**, 309–21.

Williamson, O.E. (1964), *The Economics of Discretionary Behavior: Managerial Objectives in a Theory of the Firm*, Englewood Cliffs, NJ: Prentice-Hall.

Yuchtman, E. and S.E. Seashore (1967), 'A system resource approach to organizational effectiveness', *American Sociological Review*, **32**, 891–903.

Zahra, S.A. and J.A. Pearce (1989), 'Boards of directors and corporate financial performance: a review and integrative model', *Journal of Management*, **15**, 291–334.

Zald, M.N. (1967), 'Urban differentiation, characteristics of boards of directors, and organizational effectiveness', *American Journal of Sociology*, **73**, 261–72.

Zald, M.N. (1969), 'The power and functions of boards of directors: a theoretical synthesis', *American Journal of Sociology*, **75**, 97–111.

Zald, M.N. (1970), 'Political economy: a framework for analysis', in M.N. Zald (ed.), *Power in Organizations*, Nashville: Vanderbilt University Press, pp. 221–61.

PART II

CORPORATE GOVERNANCE IN START-UPS AND EARLY-STAGE VENTURES

3. Advisory boards in entrepreneurial companies
Eythor Ivar Jonsson

INTRODUCTION

What role do advisory boards play for the direction and performance of entrepreneurial companies? It is an interesting question that relates to a broader, and central, question of corporate governance, for example whether legal boards of directors contribute to firm performance (Nicholson and Kiel, 2007). Extensive research in corporate governance (e.g. Zahra and Pearce, 1989; Pettigrew, 1992; Johnson et al., 1996; Bhagat and Black, 1999) has failed to identify a link between the board of directors and corporate performance (Nicholson and Kiel, 2007; Huse et al., 2010). Advisory boards and legal boards are not the same, but it has not been established how they are similar or differ in terms of roles and tasks (Zahra et al., 2011).

Companies can be described as evolving through progressive stages such as start-up, early growth, later growth and maturity (Churchill and Lewis, 1983; Kazanjian and Drazin, 1989; Hite and Hesterly, 2001). The transition from start-up to early growth calls for resources and decision capabilities that improve growth potential and performance (Parker, 2011; Koen et al., 2011). One of the approaches is to use external advisors who have relevant experience and capabilities to help the company to develop (Morkel and Posner, 2002). There is however limited empirical research available which examines the importance and role of this relationship with advisory boards in entrepreneurial settings (Zahra et al., 2011).

The aim of this chapter is to examine the roles and key tasks performed by advisory boards in start-ups and growth-oriented companies from the perspective of contemporary corporate governance literature. The focus on advisory boards complements existing corporate governance literature by shedding light on an often used, but seldom studied, entity in the governance structure of companies (Morkel and Posner, 2002). The empirical data have been gathered via a quasi-experimental case study approach during a period of more than ten years and involving approximately 100 start-ups and early-growth companies participating in the advisory board programme at Copenhagen Business School in Denmark. The perspectives of entrepreneurs and advisors during the advisory board process are used to extract the roles and key tasks of advisory boards.

The chapter proceeds as follows. The next section presents an overview of corporate governance theories addressing the role of boards of directors. Thereafter follows a desription of the methodology. The next section focuses on the results and discussions. The final section summarizes the main conclusions.

CORPORATE GOVERNANCE THEORIES ADDRESSING BOARD ROLES

It can be argued that three theoretical paradigms dominate corporate governance research and the roles and key tasks performed by boards (Nicholson and Kiel, 2007). The three theoretical paradigms are agency theory (Jensen and Meckling, 1976; Fama and Jensen, 1983; Eisenhardt, 1989), stewardship theory (Donaldson, 1990; Donaldson and Davis, 1991, 1994) and resource dependency theory (Zald, 1969; Pfeffer, 1972, 1973; Pfeffer and Salancik, 1978). These theories will be discussed below, and are summarized in Table 3.1.

Agency Theory

Agency theory is usually described as part of organizational economics (Barney and Ouchi, 1986; Donaldson and Preston, 1995) or new institutional economics (Eggertsson, 1990). As originated in the study by Berle and Means (1932 [1968]), the use of new institutional economics in relation to corporate governance has primarily focused on the relationship

Table 3.1   Three different theoretical perspectives

	Agency theory	Stewardship theory	Resource dependency
Role of board	Control/monitor	Strategy/directing	Linking/service
Theory rational	Monitor agents	Stewardship of assets	Co-optative resources
Theory origin	Economics/finance	Org. theory, psychology, sociology	Org. theory, sociology
Behaviour	Self-serving	Collective-serving	Network-serving
Management	Control orientation	Involvement orientation	External orientation

between shareholders and managers of large public companies (Ulhøi, 2007). There are serious doubts as to whether the theory is applicable in other settings, or even whether it was ever intended for any other settings (Ulhøi, 2007; Lubatkin, 2007). As observed by Gabrielsson and Huse (2004), agency theory is the most common approach in empirical research within the corporate governance field. It has been considered the dominant theoretical perspective in corporate governance (Shleifer and Vishny, 1997; Dalton et al., 2003). Furthermore, it is often used synonymously with governance theory (Lubatkin, 2007).

Agency theory is concerned with the problems arising when one party (the principal) contracts with another (the agent) to make decisions on behalf of the principals (Fama and Jensen, 1983). Three factors play a key role in this problem and capture the nature of the principal–agent relationship: (1) information asymmetry between principals and agents; (2) bounded rationality by both principals and agents; and (3) potential goal conflict (Gomez-Mejia and Wiseman, 2007). The separation of ownership and control gives rise to conflicts of interest between shareholders and managers, their agents, because of the opportunism of managers (Lubatkin, 2007).

Williamson (1975, 1984, 1992) and Fama and Jensen (1983) argue that the role of the board of directors, and more generally of the corporate governance system, is to harmonize agency conflicts. The board is principally an instrument by which managers control other managers (Williamson, 1984). It is an instrument of control with the primary role of monitoring management activities in order to minimize agency costs, and thereby protecting shareholder interests (Stiles and Taylor, 2001). It can therefore be argued that agency theory is at least partially, if not completely, about control (Mace, 1971; Boyd, 1990; Zahra and Pearce, 1992) and power (Finkelstein and Hambrick, 1996; Pettigrew and McNulty, 1998). The contractual relationship of the principal and the agent is related to potential moral hazard and adverse selection problems (Gomez-Mejia and Wiseman, 2007). Moral hazard arises when agents shirk their responsibilities, as they believe their behaviour is unobservable (Arrow, 1962). Adverse selection arises when one party has information that the other party in the contract cannot obtain without some cost (Akerlof, 1970). Moral hazard and adverse selection create the need for a governance mechanism (Gomes-Mejia and Wiseman, 2007). As information asymmetries increase, it becomes harder for the principal to know whether the agent is fulfilling his contract (Balkin et al., 2000).

The main assumptions of agency theory are still being debated, as recent publications demonstrate (Lubatkin, 2007; Ulhøi, 2007; Gomez-Mejia and Wiseman, 2007; Zahra, 2007). It is argued that some researchers emphasize the opportunism of managers too heavily, as the main premise is not distrust (Ulhøi, 2007), but rather insurance or protective measures. In other words, 'it is better to be safe than sorry'. There is, however, little debate on whether 'monitoring' and 'control' are the main theoretical areas for board role research.

Stewardship Theory

Stewardship theory takes a different view from new institutional economics of the relationship between management and the board of directors. It can be described as a counter theory to agency theory. Managers are considered to be good stewards of corporate assets, rather than opportunistic and self-interested actors as within agency theory (Donaldson, 1990). The theory originates from organizational psychology and sociology, claiming that executives are generally trustworthy (Herzberg et al., 1959; Argyris, 1964; Donaldson and Davis, 1991; Muth and Donaldson, 1998). Davis et al. (1997) compare the two theories and point out that the limits and boundaries of the two theories rest in their definition of behaviour, or the model of man. While both theories concentrate on the relationship between the board (or shareholders) and management, they view that relationship in totally different ways. According to agency theory, managers are self-serving individualists focused on the short term; while stewardship theory focuses on managers who serve the collective and are long-term orientated (Davis et al., 1997).

Stewardship theory and agency theory are described in terms of Theory of X and Theory Y (Gay, 2001), originating from McGregor (1960). From the Y perspective, from which stewardship theory draws its insight, individuals need development and achievement (Davis et al., 1997). Furthermore, shareholder interests and executive interest are often naturally aligned (Davis et al., 1997; Lane et al., 1998; Daily et al., 2003) and reputations and careers are naturally interwoven (Baysinger and Hoskisson, 1990). In this sense monitoring is less important as a function for the board (Donaldson and Davis, 1994), although some researchers argue for the need to review strategies formulated and implemented by management (Andrews, 1980). The role of the board within this theory is defined by its activity and involvement in guiding management to achieve the corporate mission and objectives (Hung, 1998). Directors and executives seek to become a team for governing the company, thereby creating value for shareholders (Zahra and Pearce, 1991; Sundaramurthy and Lewis, 2003; Davis et al., 1997). This may be considered an argument for combining the roles of the chief executive and the chairman (Stiles and Taylor, 2001).

Resource dependency theory

The main claim of resource dependency theory is that the board serves as a 'co-optive' mechanism to link the company to the external environment, to secure resources and protect against adversity (Stiles and Taylor, 2001). The board is a linking instrument between the organization and the external environment (Hung, 1998; Kiel and Nicholson, 2003). The board focuses on resource exchange between companies and the external environment, essential for survival and effective performance (Pfeffer and Salancik, 1978; Pearce and Zahra, 1992). However, as the theory stems from interest in distribution of power in the firm (Zahra and Pearce, 1989) and the market, it uses interlocking directorates to facilitate and obtain valuable resources (Zeitlin, 1974; Pfeffer and Salancik, 1978). In companies where executives lack experience, non-executive directors provide skill and knowledge about the external environment (Pfeffer and Salancik, 1978; Castaldi and Wortmann, 1984; Borch and Huse, 1993; Carpenter and Westphal, 2001).

Resource dependency theory focuses on the importance of human and social capital (Kiel and Nicholson, 2004). Human capital consists of experience, expertise and reputation; while social capital consists of networks, status and goodwill (Nahapiet and Ghoshal, 1998; Hillman and Dalziel, 2003). Social capital, described as a network of individuals, is used to leverage information, influence and solidarity, as well as talent and external information (Adler and Knoeber, 2002; Rosenstein et al., 1993; Davis, 1991; Haunschild, 1993).

Carpenter and Westphal (2001) suggest that networks of directors through appointments to other boards are important in determining whether boards have the appropriate strategic knowledge and perspective to monitor and advise management. Socio-cognitive perspective indicates that experience on other boards can either enhance or diminish directors' ability to contribute to strategy by focusing their attention on relevant strategic issues. The theory suggests that individuals cope with complex decision-making tasks by relying upon the schemata or 'knowledge structures' they have developed about their environment (Kiesler and Sproull, 1982; Walsh, 1995). In the absence of more complete information, or given uncertainty regarding the relevance of different pieces of information, individuals tend to follow a top-down or theory-driven approach to decision-making, rather than a bottom-up or data-driven approach based on current information (Abelson and Black, 1986; Nisbett and Ross, 1980; Ocasio, 1997). This is important given the extreme information complexity facing directors evaluating strategic decisions (Lorsch and MacIver, 1989). This perspective is based on the assumption that the knowledge structures individuals use to cope with information processing demands are developed from experience in similar roles (Dearborn and Simon, 1958; Walsh, 1995). Useem (1982) notes that executives use their board appointments as a way to scan the environment for timely and pertinent information. Directors treat experience on other boards as a vehicle for learning (Useem, 1982) and to observe consequences of management decisions (Haunschild, 1993). Information acquired from fellow directors may be particularly influential, because it often comes from a trusted source (Davis, 1991; Useem, 1982; Weick, 1995).

Board Roles

There is ambiguity in the literature as to what roles boards perform and how these roles are defined (Heuvel et al., 2006). Many different labels for roles seem to be overlapping, and researchers interpret these roles differently. The first study of roles can be traced back to Mace (1948). However, there are not many studies on the role of boards. Gabrielsson and Huse (2005) found 127 empirical articles on boards and governance in six leading academic journals from 1990 to 2002, only 27 with primary data. Heuvel et al. (2006) note that around 30 articles discussed board roles and tasks from 1980 to 2004. It is not surprising there has been a constant call for research focused on board roles and tasks (Zahra and Pearce, 1989; Stiles and Taylor, 2001; Leblanc and Gillies, 2005).

The most common approach is to aggregate board roles based on various tasks that boards are expected to perform (Zahra and Pearce, 1989; Nicholson and Kiel, 2004; Huse, 2005; Kula, 2005; Heuvel et al., 2006). The starting point for discussion is often the literature review by Zahra and Pearce (1989). The control, strategy and service roles are often considered representative of the key activities that boards need to address (Nicholson and Kiel, 2004; Huse, 2005). However, there is some debate in the literature about what these roles constitute in terms of tasks.

There is least debate about what constitutes the control role (Heuvel et al., 2006). According to agency theorists, effective boards independently monitor strategic challenges facing the firm, and evaluate management performance in addressing them (Beatty and Zajac, 1994; Fama and Jensen, 1983). Directors may overturn poor decisions and replace 'underperforming' managers as a result of such monitoring (Brudney, 1982). The board, therefore, controls management by monitoring its decisions and actions. The definition of the control role is much the same in the integrated model, where directors monitor managers as fiduciaries of stockholders (Zahra and Pearce, 1989).

The strategy role has attracted most debate. Sometimes it is described as part of the control role, such as in Zahra and Pearce (1989). However, sometimes it is part of the service role or defined as a separate role on its own. For example, in the review of Johnson et al. (1996), which is an update on Zahra and Pearce's (1989) work, the strategy role is omitted, and the service role, control role and resource dependence role are used instead. Johnson et al. (1996) define the service role as directors advising the chief executive officer (CEO) and top managers on administrative and other managerial issues, as well as more actively initiating and formulating strategy. The strategy role described by Zahra and Pearce (1989) is therefore partially included in the revised definition of the service role. The resource dependence role, facilitating the acquisition of resources critical to the firm's success, is found in the description of resource dependence theory (Johnson et al., 1996; Gabrielsson and Huse, 2010).

Researchers typically emphasize the importance of the strategic role (Zahra, 1990; Demb and Neubauer, 1992; Stiles and Taylor, 2001), where boards may provide ongoing advice to top managers on possible strategic changes, or the implementation of existing strategies (Demb and Neubauer, 1992; Lorsch and MacIver, 1989). Nicholson and Kiel (2004b) add a separate strategy role for three reasons: (1) increasing performance pressures applied by institutional investors (Black, 1992); (2) board perception of the importance of the strategizing role (Tricker, 1984); and (3) recent legal precedent placing corporate goal-setting and strategic direction within the board's charter (Kesner and Johnson, 1990). Nicholson and Kiel (2004) use four roles in their study: monitoring and controlling; strategizing; providing advice and counsel; and providing access to resources. However, many authors have noted the persistent challenge of allowing directors to make a meaningful contribution to company strategy, even though they have the power to do so (Demb and Neubauer, 1992; Lorsch and MacIver, 1989; Westphal, 1999; Westphal and Zajac, 1997). Others have noted that the strategic role is only relevant in cases of crisis (Mace, 1971; Stiles and Taylor, 2001).

For the analysis the list of tasks compiled from Heuvel et al. (2006) who based their list on five recent literature reviews and research (e.g. Zahra and Pearce, 1992; Finkelstein and Hambrick, 1996; Johnson et al., 1996; Hillman et al., 2000; Hillman and Dalziel, 2003). They identify 11 tasks (Heuvel et al., 2006). As has been noted, however, the limitations of the strategy role in this list were evident (Jonsson, 2013), and it was therefore decided to follow Ingley et al. (2015) who added items derived from Zahra and Pearce's (1990) study and Rindova's (1999) discussion to make a more complete list of tasks which would represent the three

Table 3.2   Board tasks and roles

Control/monitoring tasks	Service tasks	Strategy tasks
Supervising company accounts and budgets	Building company's reputation	Scanning company's environment
Overseeing the firm's performance	Networking and maintaining relations	Discussing strategic alternatives
Evaluating executive performance	Gathering external information	Taking decisions on long-term strategy
Ratifying strategic decisions	Accessing critical resources	Implementing strategic decisions
Setting executives' compensation	Advising company's executives	Evaluating strategy outcomes
Appointing board members		
Hiring and dismissing senior executives		

Source: Adapted from Ingley et al. (2015).

different roles. The final scale, which included 17 board tasks, is found in Table 3.2.

Advisory Boards

Advisory boards can be unique and influential contributors in different contexts (Zahra et al., 2011). Some boards are informal forums where members exchange ideas (Vermeulen, 2003), while others tend to be more formal in their composition and operations (Zahra et al., 2011). Typically, an advisory board is a group of professionals brought together to help the client to pursue and accomplish its mission (Akers and Giacomino, 2004; Reiter, 2003). Given the limited research on advisory boards and theoretical discussions, researchers have tried to link the academic discussion to the corporate governance literature (Zahra et al., 2011) with the aim of describing advisory boards within different theoretical traditions.

Although advisory boards for start-ups have been common in practice, they are not widely discussed in corporate governance literature. Advisory boards seem to have potential to add value by coaching and supporting the CEO (Morkel and Posner, 2002). There thus seems to be a need for empirical studies of advisory boards, which may help to explain and describe what advisory boards can do to contribute to their own effectiveness, and ultimately influence the direction and performance of the organization (Zahra et al., 2011; Morkel and Posner, 2002).

METHODOLOGY

The data analysed in this chapter are based on the advisory board programme at Copenhagen Business School (CBS) in Denmark. The advisory board programme was set up as a research project with the aim of understanding what makes advisory boards effective in start-ups and early-growth companies. Between 2005 and 2014 more than 100 start-ups have participated in the programme.

Quasi-Experimental Approach

The research approach is quasi-experimental as the cases of the advisory boards are all part of the same programme and not a random choice of advisory boards. It is an observation of variables of the system rather than manipulation of one or few variables, as would happen in more controlled experiments. The quasi-experimental approach was developed for research in social science and has also been recognized in other fields of research, such as medical informatics, software engineering, environmental research and economics (Shadish et al., 2002; Sjøberg et al., 2005).

The research approach in this chapter is based on more than 100 cases, which minimized the selection bias influence on internal validity (Shadish et al., 2002). The general advice of Cook and Campbell (1979) for analysing quasi-experiments was followed: (1) plan the design carefully, so as to have available as much information that is required for the analysis as possible; (2) use multiple and open-minded analyses; and (3) use an explicit appraisal of the validity of the findings and the plausibility of alternative explanations.

Cases

Companies approved for the advisory board programme were approached with the assistance of key stakeholders of the Danish entrepreneurial ecosystem. Venture capitalist funds, accelerators, incubators, mentor networks, competitions, media and start-up databases were used to make introductions and inquiries about the advisory board programme. The programme was presented as an advisory programme for start-ups and early-growth companies.

The companies portray a diverse scope of industries, although many of them have an information technology (IT) focus with an emphasis on the global market. Being start-ups and early-growth companies, many of them had existed for only a few years. The youngest companies were about one year old, while there also were a few more established companies with a longer history of about 20 years. On average the companies had existed for about four years.

The entrepreneurs were in all ages, the youngest being 22 years old, while the oldest was over 60. The age of the entrepreneurs was on average about 35. The typical profile of the entrepreneur was a university graduate from either an engineering or a business discipline, often with some previous experience in start-ups or working in industry.

Directors of the Advisory Boards

The directors of the advisory boards were in nearly all cases full-time MBA students at Copenhagen Business School. More than 90 per cent of the MBA participants tend to come from outside of Denmark and they typically had more than seven years of working experience from diverse industries and organizational functions. Each advisory board therefore on average had at least three different nationalities, with some cases having up to five different nationalities. Roughly 40 per cent of the directors were female, while 60 per cent were male.

Purpose and Process

The advisory board programme had a clear purpose: to create value for the company. This was communicated to the entrepreneurs and the directors. The objective of the board was to figure out how they could help the company and create value. The process of the board was designed around three advisory board meetings, based on a three-step model: analyse, explore and recommend. It was emphasized that the first meeting should be about information gathering about the entrepreneur, the company, the industry and the key problem issues that the board could focus on. The task of the board was to define by the end of the first meeting how the advisory board should be used to create value for the company. The second meeting emphasis was about exploring options and possibilities regarding the focus of the board, which was defined in the first meeting. The third and last meeting focused on presenting and discussing the recommendations of the board and reflecting on the process. The three meetings were held within an eight-month period. The first meetings were held in November or December, the second meetings in February, and the last meetings in February–April.

Data Collection

Several data gathering approaches were used to document the work of the advisory boards. Before every meeting, a detailed agenda was provided by the advisors with key topics and times for each topic. Minutes of each meeting were provided by the advisors with information about who attended the meeting, discussions about previous minutes, updates from the company, key issues and decisions. At the end of the programme the advisory board wrote a short report about the recommendations it had for the company. Furthermore each director made their own reflections about the company and the entrepreneur, about the team and about the process and output.

The researcher attended all the meetings and made notes on the discussions and the contribution of the board. In the final meeting the researcher furthermore organized a round of reflections from the entrepreneur and the directors about the process and purpose. This means that for each board there were agendas and minutes for three meetings, reports with recommendations, three to four reports of reflections from the directors, transcripts of key issues during the meetings, as well as a summary of reflections from the last meeting.

Analysis

The aim of the study is to examine the roles and key tasks performed by advisory boards. Therefore the unit of analysis selected was the board rather than individual directors (Beverland, 2000; Nicholson and Kiel, 2007). Each case was analysed separately, where the coding focused on determining the tasks of the board and the value creation of the board. The tasks that were noted and the perception of value creation that was expressed by entrepreneurs and directors were then compared to the tasks identified in the corporate governance literature. The aim was to look for gross matches or mismatches and 'in which even an "eyeballing" technique is sufficiently convincing to draw a conclusion' (Yin, 1994, p. 110). The importance of specific tasks was furthermore classified as high, medium or low for this process (Nicholson and Kiel, 2007).

RESULTS AND DISCUSSION

Monitoring Role

The monitoring role had seven tasks that could be associated with it from the literature (Table 3.3). Six out of the seven tasks could not be found in the data for the advisory boards. The seventh task, regarding ratifying strategic decisions, could be found in some cases where the advisory board was looking at past and current strategic decisions with critical

Table 3.3   The importance of monitoring tasks

Monitoring tasks	Importance
Supervising company accounts and budgets	Low
Overseeing the firm's performance	Low
Evaluating executive performance	Low
Ratifying strategic decisions	Medium
Setting executives' compensation	Low
Appointing board members	Low
Hiring and dismissing senior executives	Low
Monitoring role	*Low*

eyes, approving or disapproving those decisions. The monitoring role as a bundle of monitoring tasks is therefore approximately non-existing in the case of the advisory boards.

Agency theory is the underlying theory emphasizing the monitoring role and tasks. As a theory focused on monitoring, it can be regarded as not a relevant theory for explaining the advisory boards. That is what might being expected, as agency theory has primarily focused on the relationship between shareholders and managers of large public companies (Ulhøi, 2007). Advisory boards were not focused on the relationship between shareholders and managers and therefore had limited motivation to monitor management. The context of start-ups might furthermore decrease the importance of agency theory as it focuses on larger organizations and the issues of new and small organizations are thought to be different. More likely is that agency theory simply has little relevance in these different settings (Ulhøi, 2007; Lubatkin, 2007) as it does not focus on principal–agent issues (Fama and Jensen, 1983).

Service Role

The service role had five tasks derived from the literature (Table 3.4). Two out of the five tasks could not be found in the data for the advisory boards: building company's reputation, and networking and maintaining relations. The reason for the lack of importance could be related to the time span of the advisory boards, which was 6–8 months, short term rather than long term. Building reputation and maintaining relationships are, however, activities that are long-term issues. On the other hand they could be the tasks of the CEO rather than the advisory board. One task was estimated to have medium importance: accessing critical resources. Some of the boards did have issues regarding accessing venture capital

Table 3.4 The importance of service tasks

Service tasks	Importance
Building company's reputation	Low
Networking and maintaining relations	Low
Gathering external information	High
Accessing critical resources	Medium
Advising company's executives	High
Service role	*Medium*

and employees. It was not, however, of high importance. The last two tasks – gathering external information and advising the company's executives – were graded as highly important. As the boards were defined as advisory boards, this was also their main task. The importance of gathering information was highly important because the advisers somewhat represented external information in terms of their knowledge and experience. However, to be able to solve the issues that the board was focusing on, gathering external information was vital. The evidence of the service role as a bundle of service tasks is therefore mixed, as half of the tasks are highly important while the other half are not.

Resource dependency theory is associated with the service tasks and role. As a theory it can be regarded as relevant for explaining advisory boards. The argument for advisory boards is in line with resource dependency theory because executives lack experience, and non-executive directors provide skill and knowledge about the external environment (Pfeffer and Salancik, 1978; Castaldi and Wortmann, 1984; Borch and Huse, 1993; Carpenter and Westphal, 2001). It is further supported by the importance of human and social capital (Kiel and Nicholson, 2004) in providing insight and advice for the company. Furthermore social capital is used to leverage information, influence and solidarity, as well as talent and external information (Adler and Knoeber, 2002; Rosenstein et al., 1993; Davis, 1991; Haunschild, 1993).

Strategy Role

The strategy role had five tasks that could be associated with it from the literature (Table 3.5). Three out of five tasks were regarded as being of medium importance: taking decisions on long-term strategy, implementing strategic decisions and evaluating strategy outcomes. It can be argued that the advisory board gives advice but do not take decisions; that is the task of the CEO. In some cases, however, joint decisions

Table 3.5   The importance of strategy tasks

Strategy tasks	Importance
Scanning company's environment	High
Discussing strategic alternatives	High
Taking decisions on long-term strategy	Medium
Implementing strategic decisions	Medium
Evaluating strategy outcomes	Medium
Strategy role	*Medium to high*

were taken. Although implementation cannot be regarded as a task of advisors, some of the boards did implement short-term strategies in an effort to help the CEO. This was not, however, the general rule. The advisory board also in some cases evaluated strategy outcomes of previously implemented strategies in an effort to understand what had worked, or not, previously. The boards were however in most cases forward-thinking and did not spend much time on evaluating previous decisions. Two of the strategy tasks were of high importance. Scanning the company's environment was essential for the board to understand the company and the competitive landscape. Discussing strategic alternatives was probably the key task of the advisory board, which during the second meeting discussed strategic options, and during the last meeting suggested one or more options. The strategy role as a bundle of strategy tasks is therefore very important in the case of the advisory boards.

Stewardship theory is associated with the strategy tasks and role. As a theory it can be regarded as highly relevant for explaining advisory boards. Advisory boards are more likely to regard managers as good stewards of corporate assets, rather than opportunistic and self-interested actors as within agency theory (Donaldson, 1990). Advisers have limited reason to build the relationship with management on other than they are trustworthy (Herzberg et al., 1959; Argyris, 1964; Donaldson and Davis, 1991; Muth and Donaldson, 1998), serve the collective and are long-term orientated (Davis et al., 1997). It might further be argued that they are more likely to adapt to the theory perspective where individuals need development and achievement (Davis et al., 1997) rather than being perplexed by self-interest and shirking. Shareholder interests and executive interests are expected to be naturally aligned (Davis et al., 1997; Lane et al., 1998; Daily et al., 2003), as reputations and careers are naturally interwoven (Baysinger and Hoskisson, 1990). It can also be argued that advisory boards are defined by their activity and involvement in guiding

Table 3.6   The importance of advisory tasks

Advisory tasks	Importance
Gathering external information	High
Advising company's executives	High
Scanning company's environment	High
Discussing strategic alternatives	High
Ratifying strategic decisions	Medium
Accessing critical resources	Medium
Taking decisions on long-term strategy	Medium
Implementing strategic decisions	Medium
Evaluating strategy outcomes	Medium
Advisory roles	*High*

management to achieve the corporate mission and objectives, just like the role of board under stewardship implies (Hung, 1998). Directors of the advisory board and executives seek to become a team for creating value for shareholders (Zahra and Pearce, 1991; Sundaramurthy and Lewis, 2003; Davis et al., 1997).

Advisory Role

Based on the corporate governance literature and the tasks identified, the advisory role of the advisory board can be described as a bundle of nine tasks (Table 3.6). Four of them are most important: advising company executives, gathering external information, scanning the company environment and discussing strategic alternatives. As the purpose of an advisory board is advising executives it does not come as a surprise that this has high importance. Access to external information has high importance which is somewhat in line with stewardship theory, although stewardship theory emphasizes insiders while advisory boards are generally built of external advisors. Exploring strategic alternatives and discussing strategy in general have the most importance for advisory boards in the context of start-ups.

Stewardship theory, and to some extent resource dependency theory, are helpful to explain what the advisory boards do and why. The data seem to suggest that the importance of advisory boards might be much broader than has been suggested before, and somewhat different from what traditional corporate governance theories imply in terms of the roles which they suggest boards should have.

CONCLUSIONS

In this chapter the aim has been to provide empirical data about advisory boards and to explore them from the perspective of the corporate governance literature with the goal of explaining better what the role and tasks of an advisory board are. Three roles – the monitoring role, service role and strategy role – were defined, based on three different theories: agency theory, resource dependency theory and stewardship theory. The roles were then conceptualized as bundles of tasks (Heuvel et al., 2006).

Overall the findings suggest that advisory boards play an important role for the direction and performance of start-ups and early-growth companies by performing certain board tasks. The findings also indicate that the importance of the three roles is different: the monitoring role is practically non-existent, the service role is only partly important, and the strategy role is highly important. From a theoretical perspective the findings suggest that agency theory has a very limited explanatory power in the context of advisory boards. Research dependency theory is relevant in this context, but has limited explanatory power in terms of the roles performed by advisory boards. Stewardship theory, which advocates the strategy role, is instead the most relevant in this context.

There is, however, a contradiction in using stewardship theory in the context of advisory boards, as it emphasizes the importance of insiders rather than outsiders. This defeats the objective of the advisory board, which is to gather external advisors and offer information and direction to help the fledging organization forward. Given that the underlying rationale for an advisory board is somewhat different from that of a legal board, this opens opportunities to continue to extend and develop contemporary conceptualizations to better explain what advisory boards do and why they are valuable.

This chapter has addressed the role of advisory boards in start-ups and early-growth firms. However, while the findings offer valuable insights, further research is needed to explore advisory boards in other settings. Such research efforts could offer typologies of advisory boards, explaining factors that make them different, and contribute to our theoretical and practical understanding of the advisory role of boards in corporate governance.

REFERENCES

Abelson, R.P. and Black, J.B. (1986). Introduction. In R.P. Abelson and J.B. Black (eds), *Knowledge Structures*. Hillsdale, NJ: Erlbaum.

Adler, P.S. and Knoeber, C.R. (2002). Social Capital: Prospects for a New Concept. *Academy of Management Review*, 27: 17–40.

Akerlof, G. (1970). The Market for 'Lemons': Quality Uncertainty and the Market Mechanism. *Quarterly Journal of Economics*, 84: 488–500.

Akers, M. and Giacomino, D. (2004). Boards of Advisors in Small Businesses: An Empirical Profile of their Composition and Use. *Journal of Business and Economics Research*, 2(6): 27–35.

Andrews, K.R. (1980). Directors' Responsibility for Corporate Strategy. *Harvard Business Review*, 58: 30–42.

Aram, J.D. and Cowan, S.S. (1983). *Information for Corporate Directors: The Role of the Board in the Management Process*. New York: National Association of Accountants.

Argyris, C. (1964). *Integrating the Individual and the Corporation*. New York: Wiley & Sons.

Arrow, K.J. (1962). Economic Welfare and the Allocations of Resources for Invention. In *The Rate and Direction of Inventive Activity*. Princeton, NJ: Princeton University Press.

Balkin, D.B., Markman, G. and Gomez-Mejia, L.R. (2000). Is CEO Pay in High-Technology Firms Related to Innovation?. *Academy of Management Journal*, 43: 1118–1130.

Barney, J.B. and Ouchi, W. (eds) (1986). *Organizational Economics*. San Francisco, CA: Jossey-Bass.

Baysinger, B.D. and Hoskisson, R.E. (1990). Diversification Strategy and R&D Intensity in Multiproduct Firms. *Academy of Management Journal*, 32: 310–332.

Beatty, R.P. and Zajac, E.J. (1994). Top Management Incentives, Monitoring and Risk Bearing: A Study of Executive Compensation, Ownership and Board Structure in Initial Public Offerings. *Administrative Science Quarterly*, 39: 313–336.

Berle, A.A. and Means, G.G. (1932 [1968]). *The Modern Corporation and Private Property*. New York: Macmillan.

Beverland, M. (2000). Uncertainty and Opportunity as Determinants of Strategic Alliances: Evidence from Four Case Studies. *Australasian Marketing Journal*, 8: 19–31.

Bhagat, S. and Black, B.S. (1999). The Uncertain Relationship between Board Composition and Firm Performance. *Business Lawyer*, 54, 921–963.

Black, B.S. (1992). Agents Watching Agents: The Promise of Institutional Investor Voice. *UCLA Law Review*, 39(4): 811–893.

Borch, O.J. and Huse, M. (1993). Informal Strategic Networks and Boards of Directors. *Entrepreneurship Theory and Practice*, 18(1): 23–36.

Boyd, B. (1990). Corporate Linkages and Organisational Environment: A Test of the Resource Dependence Model. *Strategic Management Journal*, 11: 419–430.

Brudney, V. (1982). The Independent Director – Heavenly City or Potemkin Village?. *Harvard Law Review*, 95: 597–659.

Campbell, J.C. Stanley (1963). *Experimental and Quasi-Experimental Designs for Research*. Boston, MA: Houghton Mifflin Company.

Carpenter, M.A. and Westphal, J.D. (2001). The Strategic Context of External Network Ties: Examining the Impact of Director Appointments on Board Involvement in Strategic Decision-Making. *Academy of Management Journal*, 44: 639–660.

Castaldi, R. and Wortman, M.S. (1984). Board of Directors in Small Corporations: An Untapped Resource. *American Journal of Small Business*, 9(2): 1–11.

Churchill, N.C. and Lewis, V.L. (1983). The Five Stages of Small Business Growth. *Harvard Business Review*, 61(3): 30–50.

Cook, T.D. and Campbell, D.T. (1979). *Quasi-Experimentation: Design and Analysis Issues for Field Settings*. Boston, MA: Houghton Mifflin Co.

Daily, C.M. and Dalton, D.R. (2003). Dollars and Sense: The Path to Board Independence. *Journal of Business Strategy*, May/June: 41–43.

Dalton, D.R., Daily, C.M., Certo, S.T. and Roengpitya, R. (2003). Meta-analysis of Financial Performance and Equity: Fusion or Confusion?. *Academy of Management Journal*, 19: 13–26.

Dalton, D.R., Hitt, M.A., Certo, S.T. and Dalton, C.M. (2007). The fundamental agency problem and its mitigation: Independence, equity, and the market for corporate control.

In A. Brief and J. Walsh (eds), *Academy of Management Annals*, 3: 1–64. London, UK: Routledge.

Davis, J.H., Schoorman, F.D. and Donaldson, L. (1997). Toward a Stewardship Theory of Management. *Academy of Management Review*, 22(1): 20–47.

Dearborn, D. and Simon, H. (1958). Selective Perception: A Not on the Departmental Identifications of Executives. *Sociometry*, 21: 140–144.

Demb, A. and Neubauer, F.F. (1992). *The Corporate Board*. New York: Oxford University Press.

Donaldson, L. (1990). The Ethereal Hand: Organizational Economics and Management Theory. *Academy of Management Review*, 15: 369–381.

Donaldson, L. and Davis, J.H. (1991). Stewardship Theory or Agency Theory: CEO Governance and Shareholder Returns. *Australian Journal of Management*, 16(1): 49–64.

Donaldson, L. and Davis, J.H. (1994). Boards and Company Performance: Research Challenges the Conventional Wisdom. *Corporate Governance: An International Review*, 2: 151–160.

Donaldson, T. and Preston, L.E. (1995). The Stakeholder Theory of the Corporation: Concepts, Evidence, and Implications. *Academy of Management Review*, 20(1): 65–91.

Eggertsson, T. (1990). *Economic Behavior and Institutions*. Cambridge: Cambridge University Press.

Eisenhardt, K.L. (1989). Agency Theory: A Review and Assessment. *Academy of Management Review*, 14(1): 57–74.

Fama, E.F. and Jensen, M. (1983). Separation of Ownership and Control. *Journal of Law and Economics*, 26: 301–325.

Finkelstein, S. and D'Aveni, R.A. (1994). CEO Duality as a Double Edged Sword: How boards of Directors Balance Entrenchment Avoidance and Unity of Command. *Academy of Management Journal*, 37(3): 1079–1108.

Finkelstein, S. and Hambrick, D. (1996). *Strategic Leadership: Top Executives and Their Effects on Organisations*. St Paul, MN: West.

Gabrielsson, J. and Huse, M. (2004). Context, Behaviour, and Evolution. *International Studies of Management and Organizations*, 34(2): 11–36.

Gay, K. (2001). An Empirical Study of the Impact of the Cadbury Nexus on the Work of Non-Executive Directors of FTSE 350 Companies. Doctoral thesis. Henley Management College/Brunel University.

Gomez-Mejia, L.R. and Wiseman, R.M. (2007). Does Agency Theory have Universal Relevance? A Reply to Lubatkin, Lane, Collin, and Very. *Journal of Organisational Behaviour*, 28: 81–88.

Haunschild, P.R. (1993). Interorganisational Imitation: The Impact of Interlocks on Corporate Acquisition Activity. *Administrative Science Quarterly*, 38: 564–592.

Herman, E. (1981). *Corporate Control, Corporate Power*. New York: Cambridge University Press.

Herzberg, F., Mausner, B. and Snyderman, B. (1959). *The Motivation to Work*. New York: Wiley.

Heuvel, J.V.D., Gils, A.V. and Voordeckers, W. (2006). Board Roles in Small and Medium-Sized Family Businesses: Performance and Importance. *Corporate Governance: An International Review*, 5: 467–485.

Hillman, A.J., Cannella, A.A. and Paetzold, R. (2000). The Resource Dependence Role of Corporate Directors: Strategic Adaptation of Board Composition in Response to Environmental Change. *Journal of Management Studies*, 37: 235–256.

Hillman, A., and Dalziel, T. (2003). Boards of Directors and Firm Performance: Integrating Agency and Resource Dependence Perspectives. *Academy of Management Review*, 28(3): 383–396.

Hite, J. and Hesterly, S. (2001). The Evolution of Firm Networks: From Emergence to Early Growth of the Firm Source. *Strategic Management Journal*, 22(3): 275–286.

Hung H. (1998). A Typology of the Theories of the Roles of Governing Boards. *Corporate Governance: An International Review*, 6(2): 101–111.

Huse, M. (2005). Accountability and Creating Accountability: A Framework for Exploring Behavioural Perspectives of Corporate Governance. *British Journal of Management*, 16: 65–79.

Huse, M., Hoskisson, R.E., Zattoni, A. and Vigano, R. (2010). New Perspectives on Board Research: Changing the Research Agenda. *Journal of Management and Governance*, published online November 2009.

Jensen, M.C. and Meckling, W.H. (1976). Theory of the Firm, Managerial Behaviour, Agency Costs and Ownership Structure. *Journal of Financial Economics*, October: 305–360.

Johnson, J.L., Dayly, C.M. and Ellstrand, A.E. (1996). Boards of Directors: A Review and Research Agenda. *Journal of Management*, 22: 409–438.

Karoui, L., Khlif, W. and Ingley, C. (2005). Board Governance and Proximity in Private SMEs: Beyond Homogeny. Unpublished.

Kazanjian, R.K. and Drazin, R. (1989). An Empirical Test of a Stage of Growth Progression Model. *Management Science*, 35, 1489–1503.

Kesner, I.F. and Johnson, R.B. (1990). An Investigation of the Relationship between Board Composition and Stockholder Suits. *Strategic Management Journal*, 11(4): 327–336.

Kiel, G.C. and Nicholson, G.J. (2003). Board Composition and Corporate Performance: How the Australian Experience Informs Contrasting Theories of Corporate Governance. *Corporate Governance: An International Review*, 11(3): 189–205.

Kiesler, S. and Sproull, L. (1982). Managerial Response to Changing Environments: Perspectives on Problem Sensing from Social Cognition. *Administrative Science Quarterly*, 27: 548–570.

Koen, P.A., Bertels, H.M. and Elsum, I.R. (2011). The Three Faces of Business Model Innovation: Challenges for Established Firms. *Research-Technology Management*, 54(3): 52–59.

Kula, J. (2005). The Impact of the Role, Structure and Process of Boards on Firm Performance: Evidence from Turkey. *Corporate Governance: An International Review*, 2: 264–276.

Lane, P.J., Cannella, A.A. and Lubatkin, M.H. (1998). Agency Problems as Antecedents to Unrelated Mergers and Diversification: Amihud and Lev Reconsidered. *Strategic Management Journal*, 19: 555–578.

Leblanc, R. and Gillies, J. (2005). *Inside the Boardroom: How Boards Really Work and the Coming Revolution in Corporate Governance*. Toronto: John Wiley & Sons.

Lorsch, J.W. and MacIver, E. (1989). *Pawns or Potentates: The Reality of America's Corporate Boards*. Boston, MA: Harvard University Press.

Lubatkin, M. (2007). One More Time: What is a Realistic Theory of Corporate Governance?. *Journal of Organisational Behaviour*, 28: 59–67.

Mace, M.L. (1948). The Board of Directors in Small Corporations. Unpublished PhD dissertation, Graduate School of Business Administration, Harvard University.

Mace, M.L. (1971). *Directors: Myth and Reality*. Boston, MA: Harvard University Press.

Molz, R. (1985). The Role of the Board of Directors: Typologies of Interaction. *Journal of Business Strategy*, 5(4): 86–93.

Morkel, H. and Posner, A. (2002). The Effectiveness of Corporate Advisory Boards. *Corporate Governance*, 2(3): 4–12.

Nadler, D. (2004). Building Better Boards. *Harvard Business Review*, May: 102–112.

Nahapiet, J. and Ghoshal, S. (1998). Social Capital, Intellectual Capital, and the Organisational Advantage. *Academy of Management Review*, 23: 242–440.

Nicholson, J.G. and Kiel, G.C. (2007). Can Directors Impact Performance? A Case-Based Test of Three Theories of Corporate Governance. *Corporate Governance: An International Review*, 15(4): 585–605.

Nisbett, R. and Ross, L. (1980). *Human Inference: Strategies and Shortcomings of Social Judgment*. Englewood Cliffs, NJ: Prentice-Hall.

Ocasio, W. (1997). Toward an Attention-Based View of the Firm. *Strategic Management Journal*, 18: 187–206.

Parker, S. (2011). *Recession, Business Cycles and Entrepreneurship*. Cheltenham, UK and Northampton, MA, USA: Edward Elgar Publishing.

Pearce, J.A. and Zahra, S.A. (1992). Board Composition from a Strategic Management Perspective. *Journal of Management Studies*, 29(4): 411–438.

Pettigrew, A.M. (1992). On Studying Managerial Elites. *Strategic Management Journal*, 13(Special Issue: Winter): 163–182.

Pettigrew, A.M. and McNulty, T. (1995). Power and Influence In and Around the Boardroom. *Human Relations*, 48(8): 845–873.

Pfeffer, J. (1972). Size and Composition of Corporate Boards of Directors: The Organization and Its Environment. *Administrative Science Quarterly*, 17: 218–228.

Pfeffer, J. (1973). Size, Composition and Function of Hospital Boards of Directors: A Study of Organization–Environment Linkage. *Administrative Science Quarterly*, 18: 349–364.

Pfeffer, J. and Salancik, G.R. (1978). *The External Control of Organizations: A Resource Dependence Perspective*. New York: Harper & Row.

Reiter, B.J. (2003). The Role and Value of an Effective Advisory Board. *Ivey Business Journal*, September/October: 1–10. Retrieved from http://www.iveybusinessjournal.com/view_ article.asp? intArticle_ID440.

Rindova, V. (1999). What Corporate Boards Have To Do with Strategy: A Cognitive Perspective. *Journal of Management Studies*, 36: 953–975.

Rosenstein, J., Bruno, A.V., Bygrave, W.D. and Taylor, N.T. (1993). The CEO, Venture Capitalists, and the Board. *Journal of Business Venturing*, 8: 99–113.

Shadish, W.R, Cook, T.D. and Campbell, D.T. (2002). *Experimental and Quasi-Experimental Designs for Generalized Causal Inference*. Boston, MA: Houghton, Mifflin.

Shleifer, A. and Vishny, R.W. (1997). A Survey of Corporate Governance. *Journal of Finance*, 52: 737–384.

Sjøberg, D.I., Hannay, J.E., Hansen, O., Kampenes, V.B., Karahasanovic, A., Liborg, N.-K. and Rekdal, A.C. (2005). A Survey of Controlled Experiments in Software Engineering. *IEEE Transactions on Software Engineering*, 31(9): 733–753.

Stiles, P. and Taylor, B. (2001). *Boards at Work – How Directors View their Roles and Responsibilities*. Oxford: Oxford University Press.

Sundaramurthy, C. and Lewis, M. (2003). Control and Collaboration: Paradoxes of Governance. *Academy of Management Review*, 28: 397–415.

Tricker, R.I. (1984). *The Evolution of the Company – How the Idea has Changed. Corporate Governance: Practices, Procedures and Powers in British Companies and their Boards of Directors*. Aldershot: Gower, 25–41: 282–285.

Ulhøi, J.P. (2007). Revisiting the Principal–Agent Theory of Agency: Comments on the Firm-Level and Cross-National Embeddedness Theses. *Journal of Organizational Behaviour*, 28: 75–80.

Useem, M. (1982). Classwide Rationality in the Politics of Managers and Directors of Large Corporations in the United States and Great Britain. *Administrative Science Quarterly*, 27: 199–226.

Vance, S.C. (1983). *Corporate Leadership: Boards, Directors and Strategy*. New York: McGraw-Hill.

Vermeulen, B. (2003). Advisory Boards and Advisors. Retrieved from http://www.corp21. com/080524/download/AdvisoryBoards 030720.pdf.

Walsh, J. (1995). Managerial and Organisational Cognition: Notes from a Trip Down Memory Lane. *Organization Science*, 6: 280–321.

Weick, K. (1995). What Theory is Not, Theorizing Is. *Administrative Science Quarterly*, 40(3): 385–390.

Westphal, J.D. (1999). Collaboration in the Boardroom: Behavioural and Performance Consequences of CEO–Board Social Ties. *Academy of Management Journal*, 42(1): 7–24.

Westphal, J.D. and Zajac, E.J. (1997). Defections from the Inner Circle: Social Exchange, Reciprocity and the Diffusion of Board Independence in US Corporations. *Administrative Science Quarterly*, 42: 161–183.

Williamson, O. (1975). *Markets and Hierarchies*. New York.

Williamson, O.E. (1984). Corporate Governance. *Yale Law Journal*, 93: 1197–1230.
Williamson, O.E. (1985). *The Economic Institutions of Capitalism*. New York: Free Press.
Wood, M.M. (1983). From the Boardroom: What Role for College Trustees?. *Harvard Business Review*, 61(3): 52–62.
Yin, R.K. (1989). *Case Study Research: Design and Methods*, 1st edn. Thousand Oaks, CA: Sage.
Zahra, S.A. (2007). An Embeddedness Framing of Governance and Opportunism: Towards a Cross-Nationally Accommodating Theory of Agency – Critique and Extension. *Journal of Organisational Behaviour*, 28: 69–73.
Zahra, S.A. and Pearce, J.A. (1989). Boards of Directors and Corporate Financial Performance: A Review and Integrative Model. *Journal of Management*, 15(2): 291–334.
Zahra, S.A. and Pearce, J.A. (1991). The Relative Power of CEOs and Boards of Directors; Associations with Corporate Performance. *Strategic Management Journal*, 12: 135–153.
Zahra, S.A., Newey, L. and Shaver, J.M. (2011). Academic Advisory Boards' Contributions to Education and Learning: Lessons From Entrepreneurship Centers. *Academy of Management Learning and Education*, 10(1): 113–129.
Zald, M.N. (1969). The Power and Functions of Boards of Directors: A Theoretical Synthesis. *American Journal of Sociology*, 74: 97–111.
Zeitlin, M. (1974). Corporate Ownership and Control: The Large Corporation and the Capitalist Class. *American Journal of Sociology*, 79: 1073–1119.

4. Top management team organization of high-tech venture firms: structural arrangements and their potential consequences
Till Talaulicar

INTRODUCTION

How to organize the top management team (TMT) is a core issue in the design of the organization and governance structure of newly founded high-tech venture firms or start-ups (these terms are used interchangeably in the present chapter). The TMT denotes the small group of people at the apex of the organizational hierarchy (Finkelstein et al., 2009, p. 3) who have the responsibility and the authority to make major business decisions and eventually to run the firm.

There has been a long academic debate about whether or not management matters. According to the deterministic view which was most prominently taken by population ecology (Hannan and Freeman, 1977) and also utilized to study organizational founding rates (Hannan and Freeman, 1987; Aldrich, 1990; Lomi, 1995), management does not really have an impact on the fate of the firm, which is rather largely specified by the corporate environment which contains important resources and favors and selects those organization forms that best fit with the conditions of their environment. Evolutionary mechanisms on the level of firm populations are accordingly much too complex and uncertain to be influenced by (groups of) individuals (like TMTs) who can only randomly or accidentally create organizational variations (Hannan and Freeman, 1977). In contrast, the strategic choice perspective claims that managers do matter because they make strategic decisions about the goals, the strategy and the structure of the firm that may have a huge impact on the success and survival of the firm (Child, 1972). While evolutionary mechanisms may influence firm viability and some environmental conditions are clearly beyond managerial discretion, there is nonetheless wide agreement that management at least also matters. Firm performance therefore depends on TMTs and the decisions they make (Norburn and Birley, 1988; Carpenter, 2002; Judge et al., 2015).

Conceding the importance of TMTs, there is a vast literature on TMTs, their composition and their potential impact on various forms of organizational outcomes. Corresponding research has, *inter alia*, addressed associations between TMT variables such as TMT size (Haleblian and Finkelstein, 1993), TMT tenure (Finkelstein and Hambrick, 1990), TMT functional background and expertise (Michel and Hambrick, 1992), TMT education (Wiersema and Bantel, 1992), TMT industry experience (Kor, 2003), TMT international experience (Athanassiou and Nigh, 2002), TMT advice networks (Athanassiou and Nigh, 1999) and TMT social networks (Collins and Clark, 2003), on the one hand, and corporate financial performance (Cannella et al., 2008), social performance (Wong et al., 2011), diversification (Krishnan et al., 1997), growth (Kor, 2003), internationalization (Athanassiou and Nigh, 2002), innovativeness (Bantel and Jackson, 1989), ambidextrous orientation (Lubatkin et al., 2006), propensity to strategic change (Wiersema and Bantel, 1992) and illegal activity (Daboub et al., 1995), on the other. Regarding TMT composition, prior research has also particularly analyzed the various effects associated with different forms of TMT heterogeneity, or TMT diversity, based on demographic characteristics of individual TMT members (Hambrick et al., 1996; Carpenter, 2002; Naranjo-Gil et al., 2008) and more recently particularly their gender (Dwyer et al., 2003; Krishnan and Park, 2005; Welbourne et al., 2007).

Evidently, this stream of research shares the view that TMTs and their composition are essential determinants of firm performance. Surprisingly, however, this research has largely ignored how the competencies and responsibilities within the group of people at the apex of the company are formally organized; that is, differentiated or structured. Hence, an organization design perspective on how to – intentionally and formally – organize the TMT is still missing. In extant research, structure refers solely to demographics of TMT members (e.g., Keck, 1997; Priem et al., 1999; Carpenter, 2002) and does not capture the formal division of labor within the top executive group. While some research has addressed chief executive oficer (CEO) dominance (Haleblian and Finkelstein, 1993) and power within the TMT (Finkelstein, 1992), this research mainly reflects informal relations within the TMT and does not intend to provide insights on how the TMT should be formally organized to better achieve organizational goals. Design aspects are tackled within the rich literature on TMT compensation (Carpenter and Sanders, 2002). Again, however, this research ignores the formal structure within the TMT and how it can, or should, be organized.

Organization design issues always emerge when competencies and responsibilities, as well as capacities and resources, are to be delivered – or could be differentiated – between more than one organizational member (Galbraith, 1974; Tushman and Nadler, 1978; Burton et al., 2011). TMTs include at least two individuals. Therefore, the question arises of how to organize the TMT, or how to design its structure. The formal structure of an organization is basically concerned with the division of labor within the firm and can be described and designed by means of various dimensions such as centralization (Huber et al., 1990), configuration (Ketchen et al., 1993), coordination (Van de Ven et al., 1976), formalization (Hall et al., 1967) and specialization (Carter and Keon, 1989). More recent research has indicated that these dimensions can also be applied to the team structure of lower-level working groups, such as self-managed production teams or research and development (R&D) teams, and turn out to be powerful predictors of team learning and performance (Bunderson and Boumgarden, 2010; Bresman and Zellmer-Bruhn, 2013). However, these structural dimensions have not yet been analyzed for the structural organization within the high-level and high-status TMT. This is an important omission, because TMT structure can also be expected to influence TMT processes and outcomes. However, these effects may vary because relationships among team constructs have been shown to differ in different types of teams (Barrick et al., 2007; Bell et al., 2011; de Wit et al., 2012) and the TMT is a unique type of team with some peculiarities, due to its high level and status, that other types of teams do not share.

In order to start to fill this research gap, I will analyze one very crucial aspect of the vertical division of labor, namely the hierarchical differentiation between the TMT members. More specifically, and following prior research (see Werder, 1987), I will distinguish collegial models, where all TMT members share collective responsibilities for TMT decisions that are jointly made on equal terms; and command models, where a subgroup of the TMT has the right to issue directives to the remaining TMT members and to make overall decisions without considering the expertise or concerns of the remaining and consequently subordinate TMT members.

Structural determinants of firm performance and organizational outcomes have frequently been criticized due to their black box modeling (Lawrence, 1997; Pelled et al., 1999; Kilduff et al., 2000). That is, corresponding empirical research may have established an association between structural characteristics and organizational outcomes. However, the underlying mechanisms and processes on why this association occurs, including its direction of causality and potential issues of endogeneity, remain unclear. In this regard, prior TMT research has shown the fruitfulness of analyzing specific TMT processes. Important TMT processes indicated in extant studies include affective and cognitive conflict (Amason and Sapienza, 1997), behavioral integration (Lubatkin et al., 2006), debate (Simons, 1995), social cohesion (Michel and Hambrick, 1992), social integration (Smith et al., 1994), strategic consensus (Knight et al., 1999) and intragroup trust (Simons and Peterson, 2000).

Against this background, I will introduce an integrative comprehensive framework borrowed and developed from group theory to analyze and substantiate the effects of various structural arrangements of TMT organization in more depth. Group theory is applicable as TMTs are a specific type of group. I will come up with an input–mediator–outcome model to capture the various determinants of firm performance and their interrelatedness. More specifically, I will elaborate on behavioral, cognitive and affective group processes and how installing either a command or a collegial model of TMT organization influences them. This process perspective allows to better predict the expected effects of TMT organization on significant task related outcomes, namely comprehensiveness and speed of TMT decision-making.

The remainder is organized as follows. In the next section I will introduce and discuss peculiarities of high-tech venture firms that explain the vital importance of the TMT and its organization in this type of company. Subsequently, I will provide a more precise definition of the TMT and explain the structural alternatives of the command and the collegial model of TMT organization in more detail. In the following section, I develop a comprehensive input–mediator–outcome model of TMT effectiveness. Based on this model, I provide an in-depth analysis of the strengths and weaknesses of the alternative models of TMT organization and how they are related to major TMT mediators and eventually to outcomes of TMT decision-making. The final section concludes.

PECULIARITIES OF HIGH-TECH VENTURE FIRMS

High-tech venture firms are newly founded companies that operate in technology-based industries such as biotech, microelectronics, software or the internet (Talaulicar et al., 2005; Clarysse et al., 2007; Colombo and Piva, 2012). These entrepreneurial firms share a number of peculiarities that make it particularly promising to study the potential consequences of various forms of TMT organization within this type of company.

Since they are newly founded companies, high-tech venture firms are initially of small size (Grundei and Talaulicar, 2002; Clarysse et al., 2007; Colombo and Rossi-Lamastra, 2013). Due to their small size and newness, one may expect an even stronger influence, or more direct effects (Daily and Dalton, 1992; Hmieleski and Ensley, 2007; Klotz et al., 2014), of the TMT and its organization when compared to larger and more established firms that may be much more inertial (see Hannan and Freeman, 1984). Furthermore, the TMT and its organization may be essential to add or signal legitimacy to the business as perceived by important constituencies (Cohen and Dean, 2005) because these newly founded firms may still lack reputation in the marketplace (Hannan and Freeman, 1984; Romanelli, 1989; Fried and Hisrich, 1995) and suffer from a liability of newness (Stinchcombe, 1965; Singh et al., 1986; Castrogiovanni, 1996).

At the same time, high-tech ventures operate in high-velocity environments (Eisenhardt, 1989) and face tremendous growth opportunities (Feeser and Willard, 1990; Himmelberg and Petersen, 1994; Nunes et al., 2012). Their size may therefore increase rapidly in these quickly evolving high-tech industries. Leading a high-technology, fast-growing company in a very competitive environment first and foremost requires substantial resources (Hambrick and Crozier, 1985). Technologies and growth create demand for substantial financial and human resources (Chandler and Hanks, 1998). These firms are therefore often not founded by one person but rather by a group of persons (Roure and Maidique, 1986; Watson et al., 1995; Almus and Nerlinger, 1999). The founders generally know each other well; sometimes friendship ties exist between them (Roure and Maidique, 1986; Eisenhardt and Schoonhoven, 1990; Schoonhoven et al., 1990; Baron et al., 1999; Baron and Markman, 2000). Moreover, venture firms tend to have significant external and professional equity investors (Freear and Wetzel, 1990; Garg, 2013; Lim et al., 2013) whose attraction also depends on the TMT (see Higgins and Gulati, 2003), its reputation and network ties (Shane and Cable, 2002).

As high-tech ventures are started in high-velocity environments and sometimes lack founders with general management experience (Forbes and Milliken, 1999; Lechner and Dowling, 1999), they have a substantial need for information and expertise in order to make sound management decisions (Young et al., 1999). However, in these high-velocity environments, not only the quality but also the pace of decision-making is crucial (Judge and Miller, 1991). Thus, governance structures in general and TMT organization in particular must allow for efficient decision-making, that is, decisions which are comprehensively prepared for and at the same time conducted in a timely manner (Eisenhardt, 1989; Grundei and Talaulicar, 2002; Talaulicar et al., 2005).

ALTERNATIVES OF TMT ORGANIZATION

Definition of the Top Management Team

There is a wide variety of alternative definitions of who constitutes the top management team of a company (Finkelstein et al., 2009). Similar concepts include the inner circle of executives (Finkelstein, 1992; Raes et al., 2011; Colbert et al., 2014), the dominant coalition (Cyert and March, 1963; Child, 1972; Pearce, 1995), the upper echelons (Hambrick and Mason, 1984; Carpenter et al., 2004; Hambrick, 2007) or the top management group (Wagner et al., 1984; Murray, 1989; Siegel and Hambrick, 2005). Teams are commonly a specific type of groups that share more intense interaction among members and are hence characterized by a higher degree of 'teamness' (Katzenbach and Smith, 1993); although this conceptual distinction between teams and groups may be elusive and the notion of teamness may not always apply to each TMT in practice (Katzenbach, 1997).

Common definitions of the TMT include all executives who report directly to the CEO (Sutcliffe, 1994; Boeker, 1997; Dietz et al., 2004), who are identified by the CEO to belong to the TMT (Bantel and Jackson, 1989), who are at the vice-president level or higher (Michel and Hambrick, 1992), who belong to the two highest levels of the organizational hierarchy (Wiersema and Bantel, 1992), who are inside directors of the board within a one-tier board structure, as in the US (Haleblian and Finkelstein, 1993), who are members of the management board within a two-tier board structure, as in Germany (Talaulicar et al., 2005), and/or who are the five highest-paid managers within the firm (Carpenter et al., 2001). In sum, TMTs consist of high-status and highly paid executives with major responsibilities for their firm and its multiple constituencies (Barrick et al., 2007).

Some of these definitions, however, appear to be less eligible for the purpose of the present chapter as they predetermine structural arrangements of decision authorities that may be related to specific job titles and descriptions, such as CEO, chief finance officer (CFO) or treasurer. Some definitions rest on specific governance systems that are not universally available and hence only applicable either in one-tier board systems where the board may consist of inside and outside directors, or in two-tier board systems with their strict separation between a management and a supervisory board. Reference to remuneration may also raise concerns as there are some industries, most notably in the financial sector, where the highest-paid members of the organization are not involved in strategic decision-making but provide specific expertise for investment banking, mergers and acquisitions (M&A) or research and development (R&D).

Moreover, it remains elusive how to specify the number of top-paid executives who may accordingly constitute the TMT. In contrast, I seek for a definition that can be widely applied and does not predetermine the structural organization of decision authorities and responsibilities, because these have to remain to be specified by the design of a structural model of TMT organization.

In this chapter, the top management team includes those executives who are highly involved in forming and executing major strategic decisions that affect the overall performance and viability of the firm. This definition may admittedly require some more operationalization to be utilized in an empirical study, but is sufficiently precise and parsimonious for the purpose of the present chapter. In particular, this definition leaves open how authorities and responsibilities of strategic decision-making are structured and differentiated within the group. Accordingly, the TMT may have a 'clearly defined leader' (Barrick et al., 2007, p. 544) such as a CEO who is allowed to issue instructions to the remainder of the team. Alternatively, this definition is also compatible with the view that the TMT is 'the inner circle of executives who collectively formulate, articulate, and execute the strategic and tactical moves of the organization' (Raes et al., 2011, p. 102).

Dimensions of Organizational Structures

The organizational structure basically determines the division of labor within the firm and the corresponding tasks, competencies and roles as well as relations and interdependencies that arise from this division of labor. Consequently, the organizational structure of the TMT refers to the division of labor among the members of the TMT (Werder, 1987). As indicated above, this division of labor can be described and designed by means of various dimensions such as centralization (Huber et al., 1990), configuration (Ketchen et al., 1993), coordination (Van de Ven et al., 1976), formalization (Hall et al., 1967) and specialization (Carter and Keon, 1989). Bunderson and Boumgarden (2010), as well as Bresman and Zellmer-Bruhn (2013), have analyzed selected terms of team structure for lower-level working groups. Their measure of team structure integrates the dimensions of hierarchy (which refers to the vertical division of labor and, more specifically, the differentiation into supervisors and subordinates), specialization (horizontal division of labor) and formalization (explicit articulation of the division of labor and related procedures, priorities and regulations). Based on an empirical study of 40 self-managed manufacturing teams of a Fortune 100 high-tech firm (Bunderson and Boumgarden, 2010) and 62 self-managed teams operating in 13 pharmaceutical R&D units (Bresman and Zellmer-Bruhn, 2013), this research suggests that higher degrees of team structure tend to be associated with favorable team processes and outcomes such as, in particular, team learning. At the same time, however, this research also suggests that the corresponding relations may depend on the task environment and the overall structure of the organization and are therefore not to be generalized to different types of teams. This particularly holds true for TMTs because their tasks differ fundamentally from those of lower-level working groups (Cohen and Bailey, 1997; Barrick et al., 2007; de Wit et al., 2012).

TMTs in high-tech ventures need to make efficient decisions, that is, their decisions have to be based on sound problem analysis (decision comprehensiveness) and made in a timely manner (decision speed). TMT organization should therefore be designed primarily to facilitate the efficiency of forming and executing these strategic decisions (see Huber and McDaniel, 1986). To commence the inquiry of potential effects of various forms of TMT organization, I will in the present chapter refer to the vertical division of labor within the TMT. Basically, this design dimension is concerned with the vertical differentiation and the hierarchical relation between TMT members. I constrain my initial analysis to the dichotomous design alternatives: (1) whether there is a vertical differentiation into superior and subordinate TMT members (constituting a command model of TMT organization); or (2) whether any hierarchical differentiation is absent among TMT members (constituting a collegial model of TMT organization). More fine-grained analyses are conceivable as this vertical division of labor could be more or less pronounced and even establish various levels of hierarchical differentiation among TMT members, but are dispensable in an initial study because they mainly increase complexity without adding substantial insights. Moreover, this concept of hierarchy is related to, but needs to be distinguished from, the construct of centralization. The design alternatives to establish either a command model or a collegial model of TMT organization stem only from the organizational design decision on whether or not to differentiate between (superior and subordinate) TMT members and, consequently, whether or not to establish hierarchical levels between the members of the TMT. The organizational design dimension of centralization, in contrast, refers to the relations between vertically differentiated levels of the hierarchy and basically determines the degree to which competencies are delegated from the superior to the subordinate level of the organizational hierarchy. Vertical differentiation therefore constitutes the structural precondition to design the degree of centralization between (vertically differentiated) levels of the organizational hierarchy.

Basic Organizational Arrangements

Command model of TMT organization
In the command model of TMT organization, there is a vertical differentiation between members of the TMT. Consequently, some TMT members are superior to other members of the team and hence authorized to issue instructions to the subordinate members. I therefore refer to this form as the command model of TMT organization. TMT decisions are accordingly not made on equal terms. Rather, the superior team members could also make decisions on their own without consulting with the remaining TMT members who may provide input and information to better prepare the decisions made on the superior level. The command model may be attractive for start-ups whose managing founders intend to recruit outside executives and to appoint them to the TMT without compromising their own discretion and control about the overall courses of action of their company.

Irrespective of their exclusion from the overall strategic decision-making of the firm, subordinate TMT members may nonetheless have important responsibilities and, for instance, authority to lead major corporate units and divisions. However, these competencies do not follow from the vertical differentiation of the TMT but primarily depend on how many competencies are delegated to the second level of the organizational hierarchy (that is, the degree of decentralization) and how the firm is organized on this second level of the organizational hierarchy (that is, the horizontal division of labor).

One specific sub-form of the command model of TMT organization is the CEO model (Talaulicar et al., 2005). In this case, only one member of the TMT has a superior position – that is, the CEO – and is allowed to issue instructions to the remaining team members. Consequently, one single individual (the CEO) is eventually allowed to make major business decisions on his or her own without consulting or considering the input and the expertise that all the remaining TMT members may have with regard to the matters of the decision-making.

The command model, particularly in the form of its subtype of the CEO model, is very common in the United States (US). In the US, the CEO frequently also holds the position of the chairperson of the board of directors, which is referred to as CEO duality (Rechner and Dalton, 1991; Dalton and Dalton, 2011; Krause et al., 2014). In other governance regimes, for instance in the German stock corporation, legal stipulations prohibit the installation of a form of TMT organization that is associated with vertical differentiations between the members of the management board (Grundei and Talaulicar, 2002). Hence, at least formally, command models of TMT organization are incompatible with the regulations of the German Stock Corporation Act.

Collegial model of TMT organization

Absence of a vertical differentiation among TMT members constitutes a collegial model of TMT organization. The term 'collegial' is used as all TMT members have equal rights to be involved in decision-making of the TMT, and are on a par with each other because there are no supervisors or subordinates within the TMT. Decisions of the TMT accordingly have to be made collectively by all TMT members. In this regard, various forms of the collegial model can be distinguished, as there may be different requirements that need to be met in order to reach a collective decision (that is, unanimity versus various forms of majority voting rules). Moreover, the collegial model is compatible with installing a chairperson of the TMT who may have a second vote in the event of a tie. However, such a chairperson may be authorized only to dissolve an equality of votes but is not enabled to enforce decisions against the majority of the TMT members.

The collegial model may appear to be peculiar, or at least rarely utilized, from a US perspective where a powerful CEO who frequently is also the chair of the board of directors (CEO duality) is common. However, the collegial model is quite widespread in other governance environments. Depending on the legal form of the firm, it is even mandatory in some countries. In the German stock corporation, for instance, the collegial model has to be applied whenever more than one person is appointed to the management board. For high-tech start-ups, the collegial model may be an attractive option if managing founders who have a high-tech background and lack general management experience intend to strengthen the management expertise within the TMT by hiring outside executives, and to signal to external constituencies that the professional management knowledge and skills of these outside executives has equal weight when TMT decisions are formed and executed.

EVALUATION OF STRENGTHS AND WEAKNESSES

Group Theoretical Framework

In order to substantiate the potential consequences of various models of TMT organization, I refer to group theory and develop an elaborated input–mediator–outcome model of TMT, or group, effectiveness. Research on the effectiveness of teams has a long tradition in small-group research (for reviews, see Bettenhausen, 1991; Cohen and Bailey, 1997;

Mathieu et al., 2008). The factors that influence team effectiveness are modelled in an input–mediator–outcome (IMO) framework (Ilgen et al., 2005; Mathieu et al., 2008; Klotz et al., 2014). Inputs are antecedent factors which form the basis for teamwork. Mediators capture interactions between group members transforming inputs to outcomes and can be differentiated in group interaction processes and emergent states. Processes include group members' actions to accomplish a task or a series of simultaneously evolving tasks. Emergent states capture cognitive, motivational or affective states that are dynamic and dependent on the inputs, processes and outcomes in the past. Outcomes are the results of team activities and indicate task performance. Some authors refer to an IMOI (rather than IMO) model (e.g., Ilgen et al., 2005) to emphasize the dynamic nature of teamwork, as past task performance constitutes an input to a new, subsequent task episode (symbolized by the final 'I' of IMOI).

There is an increasing awareness that corporate governance, board and TMT research can largely benefit from procedural perspectives grounded in group effectiveness theory. Finkelstein and Mooney (2003) and Pettigrew (1992) notice that not only the 'usual suspects' – as the structural characteristics of board composition are often called – have to be analyzed, but also the intervening processes leading to task performance (see also McNulty and Pettigrew, 1999; Roberts et al., 2005; Huse et al., 2011). This call for more process studies also stems from the observation that the predominant studies on the usual suspects have yielded inconsistent findings on the relation between structural characteristics and outcomes (Zahra and Pearce, 1989; Daily and Schwenk, 1996; Johnson et al., 1996). In order to open the black box between structural characteristics and performance (Lawrence, 1997; Pelled et al., 1999; Kilduff et al., 2000), an integrative theoretically driven framework, based on the process-related findings of the group effectiveness research, needs to be developed. While the need for such studies is widely acknowledged, there is still only scarce corresponding research available (Minichilli et al., 2009).

Extant research suggests that group mediators can be behavioral, cognitive and affective, as they refer to behavioral aspects of interaction among TMT members, their thinking or their feelings (see Kozlowski and Klein, 2000; Marks et al., 2001; DeChurch and Mesmer-Magnus, 2010b; Klotz et al., 2014). In order to ensure both sufficient comprehensiveness and efficient parsimony of the model, I include two behavioral, two cognitive and two affective mediators that have been shown to be influential for group effectiveness and can be expected to be related to the design of the organizational arrangement for the TMT in general and also in high-tech ventures. The behavioral mediators are open communication and participation; the cognitive mediators are shared mental models and task conflict; and the affective mediators are relationship conflict and cohesion. In the following, I will briefly define and explain each mediator and propose how the mediator will be related to the command model and the collegial model of TMT organization.

Process Consequences

Behavioral mediators

I refer to open communication and participation as essential behavioral mediators. Open communication is defined as the frank discussion of task-related differences and the advocacy, by different TMT members, of competing solutions to the tasks of the TMT (Simons et al., 1999). The communication and sharing of information among group members is essential for group effectiveness (Campion et al., 1996; Mesmer-Magnus and DeChurch, 2009; Li Lu and McLeod, 2012), particularly in complex task environments (Jia et al., 2014) such as the ones high-tech ventures face, as it allows for utilizing and creating knowledge among TMT members (Smith et al., 2005) and orchestrating how TMT tasks are to be done and performed (Barrick et al., 2007).

Vertical differentiation among the TMT members may, on the one hand, function as an incentive system (Halevy et al., 2011) and motivate subordinate members to put forward insights for problem solutions in order to boost their own career chances by pleasing their superiors. On the other hand, and more importantly, hierarchy may inhibit open communication, as subordinate TMT members may withhold either information that is not in line with the perspectives of their superiors, or ideas the value of which may only be reaped by these superiors. Tost et al. (2013) have moreover shown that formal power of superiors, as provided by the command model, reduces open communication within the team because superiors spend more time talking and the subordinate members consequently have fewer chances to express their opinions and hold them back more frequently. All else being equal, I therefore propose:

Proposition 1: The command model (in contrast to the collegial model) of TMT organization tends to be associated with lower levels of open communication among the TMT members.

To benefit from a TMT member's knowledge and skills, they have to have the chance to contribute to, or to participate in, decision-making preparation. Therefore, the second mediator is participation, that is, the degree to which the TMT members, in practice, take part in preparing and making decisions on equal terms (see Knoop, 1991). Participation tends to enhance the intrinsic motivation of team members (see Kirkman and Rosen, 1999), and to be particularly important for the performance of interdependent and complex tasks (Yammarino and Naughton, 1992) that are characteristic of start-ups in high-technology industries.

Carmeli et al. (2009) have shown that participatory decision-making is also positively related to decision-making effectiveness and firm performance in TMTs. Installing a command model, by definition, does not preclude that all TMT members participate in preparing for and substantiating TMT decisions. The degree of participation, however, depends on the willingness of the superior TMT members to request, and to consider, the inputs, ideas and insights of their subordinates. Consequently, subordinate TMT members can be expected to be less inclined to participate actively in preparing for decisions that are eventually made by the superior TMT members, because the command model provides subordinate TMT members with less discretion and a lesser sense of responsibility in decision-making (see Cao et al., 2010). This leads to:

Proposition 2: The command model (in contrast to the collegial model) of TMT organization tends to be associated with lower levels of TMT member participation.

Cognitive mediators
With regard to cognitive mediators, I analyze the relations to shared mental models and task conflict. Shared mental models measure the degree to which TMT members have knowledge structures or knowledge representations in common (Kozlowski and Ilgen, 2006). Related constructs have also been studied in entrepreneurial settings to reveal how they are associated with venture success (Ensley and Pearce, 2001).

On the one hand, shared mental models allow for efficient decision-making as they enable TMT members to acquire, organize and exchange information more easily in order to develop and evaluate potential courses of action. Consequently, they have been shown to be positively related to team performance (Edwards et al., 2006; DeChurch and Mesmer-Magnus, 2010a; Turner et al., 2014). On the other hand, a too-high degree of similarity and overlap of shared mental models could also become detrimental to firm performance (see Smith et al., 2006) as this may inhibit exploration of innovative problem solutions which TMTs may particularly be supposed to come up with (see Bantel and Jackson, 1989), especially in high-tech industries.

The development of shared mental models tends to be facilitated when team members have backgrounds, experiences, task challenges and environmental conditions in common. In this regard, each organizational differentiation also tends to differentiate competencies as well as the challenges and conditions that team members pay attention to. Hence I expect that TMT mental models tend to be shared to a lower degree when the TMT is organized as a command model (rather than as a collegial model):

Proposition 3: The command model (in contrast to the collegial model) of TMT organization tends to be associated with lower levels of shared mental models among TMT members.

Task conflict occurs when TMT members perceive disagreements on viewpoints and opinions pertaining to their task (Jehn and Mannix, 2001). For non-routine tasks which characterize the task environment of a TMT in general, and particularly in a high-tech start-up setting, task conflict tends to facilitate task performance (see Jehn, 1995; Kozlowski and Ilgen, 2006; Mathieu et al., 2008). This relation has been shown to be more positive in TMTs than in non-top management teams (de Wit et al., 2012).

Vertical differentiation, on the one hand, may facilitate task conflict because TMT members view task-related problems from different perspectives and may therefore have, or at least perceive, competing rather than converging task-related opinions. On the other hand, task conflict requires that TMT members become aware of disagreements about task-related viewpoints and opinions. This appears to be less likely when the command model has been chosen, which tends to result in lower levels of open communication and less participation of TMT members. In sum, therefore, task conflict can be expected to be less pronounced when a command model (rather than a collegial model) of TMT organization has been installed:

Proposition 4: The command model (in contrast to the collegial model) of TMT organization tends to be associated with lower levels of task conflict among TMT members.

Affective mediators

Relationship conflict and cohesion are incorporated in the TMT effectiveness model as essential affective mediators. Relationship conflict is tantamount to the awareness of interpersonal incompatibilities among TMT members, and includes emotional components such as feeling tension and friction (Jehn and Mannix, 2001). Meta-analyses have revealed stable negative associations between relationship conflict and group outcomes (De Dreu and Weingart, 2003; de Wit et al., 2012). This relationship has also been shown in venture teams (Ensley and Pearce, 2001; Higashide and Birley, 2002; de Jong et al., 2013).

On the one hand, vertical differentiation creates some dissimilarities among TMT members and may therefore foster relationship conflict. On the other hand, hierarchy establishes some formal distance between vertically differentiated members, which may make the arousal of affective conflicts less likely. Subordinates furthermore anticipate that conflict may be detrimental to their career chances, such as getting promoted (Halevy et al., 2011). More unambiguously, prior TMT research has demonstrated that relationship conflicts can particularly be triggered by task conflicts (Simons and Peterson, 2000; Ensley et al., 2002; Mooney et al., 2007). Therefore, one may expect the degree of affective conflict to be less pronounced in a command (rather than a collegial) model of TMT organization:

Proposition 5: The command model (in contrast to the collegial model) of TMT organization tends to be associated with lower levels of relationship conflict among TMT members.

Cohesion is defined as the degree to which TMT members are attracted to each other and motivated to stay in the group (see Forbes and Milliken, 1999). In general, meta-analyses indicate that cohesion tends to be moderately positive for team task performance (Evans and Dion, 1991; Gully et al., 1995; Chiocchio and Essiembre, 2009), whereas this effect may vary by context (Mullen and Copper, 1994; Beal et al., 2003; Chiocchio and Essiembre, 2009) and remains theoretically somewhat unclear (Casey-Campbell and Martens, 2009). However, conceptual considerations also suggest that cohesion could become too much of a good thing. On the one hand, a TMT needs a certain minimum level of interpersonal attraction and joint commitment to function at all. Moreover, cohesion may promote motivation and engagement of TMT members. On the other hand, too much mutual attraction may advance groupthink (Janis, 1972) or overconfidence (Clark and Maggitti, 2012) of the TMT, which tends to be detrimental to group task performance.

According to similarity theory (Bowers et al., 2000), more homogeneous TMTs tend to experience more mutual attraction and hence greater cohesion (see Wiersema and Bantel, 1992; Smith et al., 1994; Webber and Donahue, 2001). Regarding the TMT as a whole, vertical differentiation therefore tends to decrease cohesion because the hierarchical separation creates dissimilarities in status and competencies. Although there is also strong evidence that cohesion tends to be negatively affected by interpersonal conflicts within the TMT (Ensley and Pearce, 2001; Ensley et al., 2002), cohesion may mitigate the negative effects of affective conflicts and promote the positive effects of cognitive conflict (see Ensley and

Pearce, 2001). In sum, one may expect that cohesion tends to be lower in command models of TMT organization (when compared to collegial models of TMT organization):

Proposition 6: The command model (in contrast to the collegial model) of TMT organization tends to be associated with lower levels of cohesion within the TMT.

Outcome Consequences

Upper echelons theory suggests that overall firm performance tends to be a reflection of the TMT and its structural characteristics (Hambrick and Mason, 1984; Carpenter et al., 2004; Hambrick, 2007). The effect between TMT characteristics and firm performance tends to be even more direct in entrepreneurial venture firms which are of smaller size and younger compared to mature and more inertial firms (Daily and Dalton, 1992; Hmieleski and Ensley, 2007; Klotz et al., 2014). However, these direct effects leave open the question of which underlying mechanisms associate specific TMT characteristics with higher or lower firm performance. In addition, the caveat remains that overall firm performance is a rather complex construct that is influenced by a multitude of potential, partly lagged and interrelated determinants, which highly complicate explanations and predictions of performance variation (March and Sutton, 1997). To complete the conceptual analysis, I therefore refer to TMT performance measures that are more closely related to TMT task work and teamwork, but nonetheless of vital importance to the success and survival of high-tech ventures. As introduced above, these are the comprehensiveness and speed of TMT decision-making, which can be expected to depend on the mediators discussed in the prior subsection.

Decision comprehensiveness refers to the degree to which the choice of a strategic course of action is based on a thorough problem analysis. The behavioral mediators of open communication and participation as well as cognitive conflict tend to contribute to decision comprehensiveness, because TMT members articulate various perspectives and competing solutions in relation to the complex tasks of the TMT (Simons et al., 1999), that are considered in decision preparation more impartially (Talaulicar et al., 2005) and rest on different viewpoints and opinions pertaining to these tasks (Jehn and Mannix, 2001). Consequently, these mediators can be expected to be beneficial to decision comprehensiveness because the synthesis from this broader knowledge base and the contesting perspectives tends to enhance the quality of forming and executing strategic decision-making (Amason, 1996; Talaulicar et al., 2005; Olson et al., 2007).

In contrast, affective conflict can be expected to be detrimental to a thorough and impartial preparation for strategic decision-making because TMT members are distracted from an unbiased problem solution and may compromise valuable arguments in favor of promoting personal disputes. Regarding (cognitive) shared mental models and (affective) cohesion within the TMT, one may expect an inverse U-shaped relationship with decision quality. Some degree of shared mental models and cohesion allows both better information exchange and mutual search for feasible problem solutions. Too much of these two mediators, though, may lead to a rather narrow search of problem solutions, inhibit creative ideas and entrench the TMT, which consequently disregards or discounts arguments that appear not to fit with shared knowledge structures or to imperil group coherence. One may therefore expect that installing a command (rather than a collegial) model of TMT organization tends to be associated with lower levels of decision comprehensiveness:

Proposition 7: The command model (in contrast to the collegial model) of TMT organization tends to be associated with lower levels of TMT decision comprehensiveness.

Decision speed refers to how fast strategic choices are made. One may expect that the behavioral mediators of open communication and participation as well as (cognitive and affective) conflict tend to decelerate the pace of decision-making. Open communication of multiple viewpoints and opinions enlarges the information base to be considered and processed for decision-making. Higher degrees of participation furthermore imply that all TMT members take part in evaluating how to assess and utilize this broader information base. Task and relationship conflict tend to result in disputes, and make it more difficult, and consequently time-consuming, to reach consensus.

In contrast, shared mental models and cohesion within the TMT may tend to smooth speedy decision-making because joint knowledge structures and mutual attraction, mainly based on similarities, tend to make reaching consensus easier (Priem, 1990; Iaquinto and Fredrickson, 1997; Knight et al., 1999; Kellermanns et al., 2005) and accordingly also faster (Clark and Maggitti, 2012). In sum, one may expect that strategic decisions tend to be made faster in the command model (rather than in the collegial model) of TMT organization:

Proposition 8: The command model (in contrast to the collegial model) of TMT organization tends to be associated with faster TMT decision-making.

DISCUSSION AND CONCLUSION

The above analyses reveal how the vertical differentiation between members of the TMT and the corresponding model of TMT organization may be related to specific TMT outcomes – that is, comprehensiveness and speed of strategic decision-making – that are deemed of vital importance to the success and survival of high-tech ventures. The input–mediator–outcome (IMO) model of team effectiveness also illuminates the underlying group processes that transform TMT inputs into outcomes, and therefore explains why certain outcomes of TMT performance are to be expected. Table 4.1 displays these major relations.

Three limitations are worth noting as they also provide promising avenues for future research to build on and refine the present analysis. First, a more in-depth examination of the mediator consequences of the command and the collegial model may take into consideration more advanced approaches from group theory such as the faultline concept (Lau and Murnighan, 1998, 2005; Thatcher and Patel, 2012) and various types of subgroups (Carton and Cummins, 2012) that may be beneficial to explain and predict whether the proposed relations may be expected to be more or less pronounced, depending on the specific composition and practice of the TMT and its vertical differentiation. More specifically, the type and degree of vertical differentiation may be related to the strength of faultlines, which has already been indicated to also depend on structural

Table 4.1   Mediator and outcome consequences of alternative models of TMT organization

Group variables	Model of TMT organization	
	Command model	Collegial model
Behavioral mediators		
Open communication	Lower	Higher
Member participation	Lower	Higher
Cognitive mediators		
Shared mental models	Lower	Higher
Task conflict	Lower	Higher
Affective mediators		
Relationship conflict	Lower	Higher
Cohesion	Lower	Higher
Outcome consequences		
Decision comprehensiveness	Lower	Higher
Decision speed	Faster	Slower

factors (Lim et al., 2013), and the extent of subgroup formation. Second, the above analysis rests on only one, albeit very crucial, dimension of TMT organization structure. Further research may take into account additional dimensions of TMT organization, to which reference has been made above. Considering additional design dimensions and their interrelatedness will help to provide more comprehensive insights on the options for TMT organization design, as well as their pros and cons. Last but not least, the analysis has incorporated extant research, whenever possible with specific reference to TMTs in high-tech venture firms, in order to better substantiate the associations under study. This, of course, does not make an empirical validation dispensable. In this regard, the developed propositions could be employed as testable hypotheses, and corresponding empirical studies could utilize established measures that are available for most of the above constructs.

The analyses suggest that the command model (in contrast to a collegial model) of TMT organization tends to inhibit: (1) the behavioral mediators of open communication and participation; (2) the cognitive mediators of shared mental models and task conflict; and (3) the affective mediators of relationship conflict and cohesion. The underlying group effectiveness model therefore provides insights as to why the command model of TMT organization tends to be associated with lower levels of decision comprehensiveness, which at the same time can be accomplished faster than in a collegial model of TMT organization. All else being equal, the collegial model of TMT organization, in contrast, allows for a more thorough, but less timely preparation of strategic decisions to be made by the TMT. In sum, both models have strengths and weaknesses. Prioritizing them will depend on contingencies and the strategy of the firm, which influence whether the quality or the pace of strategic decision-making are deemed to be more essential.

REFERENCES

Aldrich, H.E. (1990), Using an Ecological Perspective to Study Organizational Founding Rates. *Entrepreneurship Theory and Practice*, **14** (3), 7–24.

Almus, M. and Nerlinger, E.A. (1999), Growth of New Technology-Based Firms: Which Factors Matter?. *Small Business Economics*, **13**, 141–154.

Amason, A.C. (1996), Distinguishing the Effects of Functional and Dysfunctional Conflict on Strategic Decision Making: Resolving a Paradox for Top Management Teams. *Academy of Management Journal*, **39**, 123–146.

Amason, A.C. and Sapienza, H.J. (1997), The Effects of Top Management Team Size and Interaction Norms on Cognitive and Affective Conflict. *Journal of Management*, **23**, 495–516.

Athanassiou, N. and Nigh, D. (1999), The Impact of US Company Internationalization on Top Management Team Advice Networks: A Tacit Knowledge Perspective. *Strategic Management Journal*, **20**, 83–92.

Athanassiou, N. and Nigh, D. (2002), The Impact of the Top Management Team's International Business Experience on the Firm's Internationalization: Social Networks at Work. *Management International Review*, **42**, 157–181.

Bantel, K.A. and Jackson, S.E. (1989), Top Management and Innovations in Banking: Does the Composition of the Top Team Make a Difference?. *Strategic Management Journal*, **10**, 107–124.

Baron, J.N., Burton, M.D. and Hannan, M.T. (1999), Engineering Bureaucracy: The Genesis of Formal Policies, Positions, and Structures in High-Technology Firms. *Journal of Law, Economics, and Organization*, **15**, 1–41.

Baron, R.A. and Markman, G.D. (2000), Beyond Social Capital: How Social Skills Can Enhance Entrepreneurs' Success. *Academy of Management Executive*, **14** (1), 106–116.

Barrick, M.R., Bradley, B.H., Brown, K., Amy, L. and Colbert, A.E. (2007), The Moderating Role of Top Management Team Interdependence: Implications for Real Teams and Working Groups. *Academy of Management Journal*, **50**, 544–557.

Beal, D.J., Cohen, R.R., Burke, M.J. and McLendon, C.L. (2003), Cohesion and Performance in Groups: A Meta-Analytic Clarification of Construct Relations. *Journal of Applied Psychology*, **88**, 989–1004.

Bell, S.T., Villado, A.J., Lukasik, M.A., Belau, L. and Briggs, A.L. (2011), Getting Specific about Demographic Diversity Variable and Team Performance Relationships: A Meta-Analysis. *Journal of Management*, **37**, 709–743.

Bettenhausen, K.L. (1991), Five Years of Groups Research: What We Have Learned and What Needs to Be Addressed. *Journal of Management*, **17**, 345–381.

Boeker, W. (1997), Strategic Change: The Influence of Managerial Characteristics and Organizational Growth. *Academy of Management Journal*, **40**, 152–170.

Bowers, C.A., Pharmer, J.A. and Salas, E. (2000), When Member Homogeneity is Needed in Work Teams: A Meta-Analysis. *Small Group Research*, **31**, 305–327.

Bresman, H. and Zellmer-Bruhn, M. (2013), The Structural Context of Team Learning: Effects of Organizational and Team Structure on Internal and External Learning. *Organization Science*, **24**, 1120–1139.

Bunderson, J.S. and Boumgarden, P. (2010), Structure and Learning in Self-managed Teams: Why 'Bureaucratic' Teams Can Be Better Learners. *Organization Science*, **21**, 609–624.

Burton, R.M., Obel, B. and DeSanctis, G. (2011), *Organizational Design: A Step-by-Step Approach*, 2nd edition, Cambridge, UK and New York, USA: Cambridge University Press.

Campion, M.A., Papper, E.M. and Medsker, G.J. (1996), Relations between Work Team Characteristics and Effectiveness: A Replication and Extension. *Personnel Psychology*, **49**, 429–452.

Cannella Jr, A.A., Park, J.H. and Lee, H.U. (2008), Top Management Team Functional Background Diversity and Firm Performance: Examining the Roles of Team Member Colocation and Environmental Uncertainty. *Academy of Management Journal*, **51**, 768–784.

Cao, Q., Simsek, Z. and Zhang, H. (2010), Modelling the Joint Impact of the CEO and the TMT on Organizational Ambidexterity. *Journal of Management Studies*, **47**, 1272–1296.

Carmeli, A., Sheaffer, Z. and Halevi, M.Y. (2009), Does Participatory Decision-making in Top Management Teams Enhance Decision Effectiveness and Firm Performance?. *Personnel Review*, **38**, 696–714.

Carpenter, M.A. (2002), The Implications of Strategy and Social Context for the Relationship between Top Management Team Heterogeneity and Firm Performance. *Strategic Management Journal*, **23**, 275–284.

Carpenter, M.A., Geletkanycz, M.A. and Sanders, W.G. (2004), Upper Echelons Research Revisited: Antecedents, Elements, and Consequences of Top Management Team Composition. *Journal of Management*, **30**, 749–778.

Carpenter, M.A. and Sanders, W.G. (2002), Top Management Team Compensation: The

Missing Link between CEO Pay and Firm Performance? *Strategic Management Journal*, **23**, 367–375.

Carpenter, M.A., Sanders, W.G. and Gregersen, H.B. (2001), Bundling Human Capital with Organizational Context: The Impact of International Assignment Experience on Multinational Firm Performance and CEO Pay. *Academy of Management Journal*, **44**, 493–511.

Carter, N.M. and Keon, T.L. (1989), Specialization as a Multidimensional Construct. *Journal of Management Studies*, **26**, 11–28.

Carton, A.M. and Cummings, J.N. (2012), A Theory of Subgroups in Work Teams. *Academy of Management Review*, **37**, 441–470.

Casey-Campbell, M. and Martens, M.L. (2009), Sticking It All Together: A Critical Assessment of the Group Cohesion–Performance Literature. *International Journal of Management Reviews*, **11**, 223–246.

Castrogiovanni, G.J. (1996), Pre-startup Planning and the Survival of New Small Businesses: Theoretical Linkages. *Journal of Management*, **22**, 801–822.

Chandler, G.N. and Hanks, S.H. (1998), An Examination of the Substitutability of Founders Human and Financial Capital in Emerging Business Ventures. *Journal of Business Venturing*, **13**, 353–369.

Child, J. (1972), Organizational Structure, Environment, and Performance: The Role of Strategic Choice. *Sociology*, **6**, 1–22.

Chiocchio, F. and Essiembre, H. (2009), Cohesion and Performance: A Meta-Analytic Review of Disparities Between Project Teams, Production Teams, and Service Teams. *Small Group Research*, **40**, 382–420.

Clark, K.D. and Maggitti, P.G. (2012), TMT Potency and Strategic Decision-Making in High Technology Firms. *Journal of Management Studies*, **49**, 1168–1193.

Clarysse, B., Knockaert, M. and Lockett, A. (2007), Outside Board Members in High Tech Start-ups. *Small Business Economics*, **29**, 243–259.

Cohen, B.D. and Dean, T.J. (2005), Information Asymmetry and Investor Valuation of IPOs: Top Management Team Legitimacy as a Capital Market Signal. *Strategic Management Journal*, **26**, 683–690.

Cohen, S.G. and Bailey, D.E. (1997), What Makes Teams Work: Group Effectiveness Research from the Shop Floor to the Executive Suite. *Journal of Management*, **23**, 239–290.

Colbert, A.E., Barrick, M.R. and Bradley, B.H. (2014), Personality and Leadership Composition in Top Management Teams: Implications for Organizational Effectiveness. *Personnel Psychology*, **67**, 351–387.

Collins, C.J. and Clark, K.D. (2003), Strategic Human Resource Practices, Top Management Team Social Networks, and Firm Performance: The Role of Human Resource Practices in Creating Organizational Competitive Advantage. *Academy of Management Journal*, **46**, 740–751.

Colombo, M.G. and Piva, E. (2012), Firms' Genetic Characteristics and Competence-Enlarging Strategies: A Comparison Between Academic and Non-Academic High-Tech Start-Ups. *Research Policy*, **41**, 79–92.

Colombo, M.G. and Rossi-Lamastra, C. (2013), The Organizational Design of High-Tech Start-Ups: State of the Art and Directions for Future Research. In Grandori, Anna (ed.), *Handbook of Economic Organization: Integrating Economic and Organization Theory*, Cheltenham, UK and Northampton, MA, USA: Edward Elgar Publishing, pp. 400–415.

Cyert, R.M. and March, J.G. (1963), *A Behavioral Theory of the Firm*, Englewood Cliffs, NJ: Prentice-Hall.

Daboub, A.J., Rasheed, A.M.A., Priem, R.L. and Gray, D.A. (1995), Top Management Team Characteristics and Corporate Illegal Activity. *Academy of Management Review*, **20**, 138–170.

Daily, C.M. and Dalton, D.R. (1992), The Relationship between Governance Structure and Corporate Performance in Entrepreneurial Firms. *Journal of Business Venturing*, **7**, 375–386.

Daily, C.M. and Schwenk, C. (1996), Chief Executive Officers, Top Management Teams, and Boards of Directors: Congruent or Countervailing Forces?. *Journal of Management*, **22**, 185–208.

Dalton, D.R. and Dalton, C.M. (2011), Integration of Micro and Macro Studies in Governance Research: CEO Duality, Board Composition, and Financial Performance. *Journal of Management*, **37**, 404–411.

De Dreu, C.K.W. and Weingart, L.R. (2003), Task versus Relationship Conflict, Team Performance, and Team Member Satisfaction. *Journal of Applied Psychology*, **88**, 741–749.

De Jong, A., Song, M. and Song, L.Z. (2013), How Lead Founder Personality Affects New Venture Performance: The Mediating Role of Team Conflict. *Journal of Management*, **39**, 1825–1854.

De Wit, F.R.C., Greer, L.L. and Jehn, K.A. (2012), The Paradox of Intragroup Conflict: A Meta-Analysis. *Journal of Applied Psychology*, **97**, 360–390.

DeChurch, L.A. and Mesmer-Magnus, J.R. (2010a), Measuring Shared Team Mental Models: A Meta-Analysis. *Group Dynamics: Theory, Research, and Practice*, **14**, 1–14.

DeChurch, L.A. and Mesmer-Magnus, J.R. (2010b), The Cognitive Underpinnings of Effective Teamwork: A Meta-Analysis. *Journal of Applied Psychology*, **95**, 32–53.

Dietz, J., Pugh, S.D. and Wiley, J.W. (2004), Service Climate Effects on Customer Attitudes: An Examination of Boundary Conditions. *Academy of Management Journal*, **47**, 81–92.

Dwyer, S., Richard, O.C. and Chadwick, K. (2003), Gender Diversity in Management and Firm Performance: The Influence of Growth Orientation and Organizational Culture. *Journal of Business Research*, **56**, 1009–1019.

Edwards, B.D., Day, E.A., Arthur Jr, W. and Bell, S.T. (2006), Relationships among Team Ability Composition, Team Mental Models, and Team Performance. *Journal of Applied Psychology*, **91**, 727–736.

Eisenhardt, K.M. (1989), Making Fast Strategic Decisions in High-Velocity Environments. *Academy of Management Journal*, **32**, 543–576.

Eisenhardt, K.M. and Schoonhoven, C.B. (1990), Organizational Growth: Linking Founding Team, Strategy, Environment, and Growth among US Semiconductor Ventures, 1978–1988. *Administrative Science Quarterly*, **35**, 504–529.

Ensley, M.D. and Pearce, C.L. (2001), Shared Cognition in Top Management Teams: Implications for New Venture Performance. *Journal of Organizational Behavior*, **22**, 145–160.

Ensley, M.D., Pearson, A.W. and Amason, A.C. (2002), Understanding the Dynamics of New Venture Top Management Teams: Cohesion, Conflict, and New Venture Performance. *Journal of Business Venturing*, **17**, 365–386.

Evans, C.R. and Dion, K.L. (1991), Group Cohesion and Performance: A Meta-Analysis. *Small Group Research*, **22**, 175–186.

Feeser, H.R. and Willard, G.E. (1990), Founding Strategy and Performance: A Comparison of High and Low Growth High Tech Firms. *Strategic Management Journal*, **11**, 87–98.

Finkelstein, S. (1992), Power in Top Management Teams: Dimensions, Measurement, and Validation. *Academy of Management Journal*, **35**, 505–538.

Finkelstein, S. and Hambrick, D.C. (1990), Top-Management-Team Tenure and Organizational Outcomes: The Moderating Role of Managerial Discretion. *Administrative Science Quarterly*, **35**, 484–503.

Finkelstein, S., Hambrick, D.C. and Cannella Jr, A.A. (2009), *Strategic Leadership. Theory and Research on Executives, Top Management Teams, and Boards*, Oxford, UK and New York, USA: Oxford University Press.

Finkelstein, S. and Mooney, A.C. (2003), Not the Usual Suspects: How to Use Board Process to Make Boards Better. *Academy of Management Executive*, **17**, 101–113.

Forbes, D.P. and Milliken, F.J. (1999), Cognition and Corporate Governance: Understanding Boards of Directors as Strategic Decision-Making Groups. *Academy of Management Review*, **24**, 489–505.

Freear, J. and Wetzel Jr, W.E. (1990), Who Bankrolls High-tech Entrepreneurs?. *Journal of Business Venturing*, **5**, 77–89.

Fried, V.H. and Hisrich, R.D. (1995), The Venture Capitalist: A Relationship Investor. *California Management Review*, **37** (2), 101–113.

Galbraith, J.R. (1974), Organization Design: An Information Processing View. *Interfaces*, **4** (5), 28–36.

Garg, S. (2013), Venture Boards: Distinctive Monitoring and Implications for Firm Performance. *Academy of Management Review*, **38**, 90–108.

Grundei, J. and Talaulicar, T. (2002), Company Law and Corporate Governance of Start-ups in Germany: Legal Stipulations, Managerial Requirements, and Modification Strategies. *Journal of Management and Governance*, **6**, 1–27.

Gully, S.M., Devine, D.J. and Whitney, D.J. (1995), A Meta-Analysis of Cohesion and Performance: Effects of Level of Analysis and Task Interdependence. *Small Group Research*, **26**, 497–521.

Haleblian, J. and Finkelstein, S. (1993), Top Management Team Size, CEO Dominance, and Firm Performance: The Moderating Roles of Environmental Turbulence and Discretion. *Academy of Management Journal*, **36**, 844–863.

Halevy, N., Chou, E.Y. and Galinsky, A.D. (2011), A Functional Model of Hierarchy: Why, How, and When Vertical Differentiation Enhances Group Performance. *Organizational Psychology Review*, **1**, 32–52.

Hall, R.H., Haas, J.E. and Johnson, N.J. (1967), Organizational Size, Complexity, and Formalization. *American Sociological Review*, **32**, 903–912.

Hambrick, D.C. (2007), Upper Echelons Theory: An Update. *Academy of Management Review*, **32**, 334–343.

Hambrick, D.C., Cho, T.S. and Chen, M.J. (1996), The Influence of Top Management Team Heterogeneity on Firms' Competitive Moves. *Administrative Science Quarterly*, **41**, 659–684.

Hambrick, D.C. and Crozier, L.M. (1985), Stumblers and Stars in the Management of Rapid Growth. *Journal of Business Venturing*, **1**, 31–45.

Hambrick, D.C. and Mason, P.A. (1984), Upper Echelons: The Organization as a Reflection of Its Top Managers. *Academy of Management Review*, **9**, 193–206.

Hannan, M.T. and Freeman, J. (1977), The Population Ecology of Organizations. *American Journal of Sociology*, **82**, 929–964.

Hannan, M.T. and Freeman, J. (1984), Structural Inertia and Organizational Change. *American Sociological Review*, **49**, 149–164.

Hannan, M.T. and Freeman, J. (1987), The Ecology of Organizational Founding: American Labor Unions, 1836–1985. *American Journal of Sociology*, **92**, 910–943.

Higashide, H. and Birley, S. (2002), The Consequences of Conflict between the Venture Capitalist and the Entrepreneurial Team in the United Kingdom from the Perspective of the Venture Capitalist. *Journal of Business Venturing*, **17**, 59–81.

Higgins, M.C. and Gulati, R. (2003), Getting Off to a Good Start: The Effects of Upper Echelon Affiliations on Underwriter Prestige. *Organization Science*, **14**, 244–263.

Himmelberg, C.P. and Petersen, B.C. (1994), R&D and Internal Finance: A Panel Study of Small Firms in High-Tech Industries. *Review of Economics and Statistics*, **76**, 38–51.

Hmieleski, K.M. and Ensley, M.D. (2007), A Contextual Examination of New Venture Performance: Entrepreneur Leadership Behavior, Top Management Team Heterogeneity, and Environmental Dynamism. *Journal of Organizational Behavior*, **28**, 865–889.

Huber, G.P. and McDaniel, R.R. (1986), The Decision Making Paradigm of Organizational Design. *Management Science*, **32**, 572–589.

Huber, G.P., Miller, C.C. and Glick, W.H. (1990), Developing More Encompassing Theories About Organizations: The Centralization–Effectiveness Relationship as an Example. *Organization Science*, **1**, 11–40.

Huse, M., Hoskisson, R., Zattoni, A. and Vigano, R. (2011), New Perspectives on Board Research: Changing the Research Agenda. *Journal of Management and Governance*, **15**, 5–18.

Iaquinto, A.L. and Fredrickson, J.W. (1997), Top Management Team Agreement about the Strategic Decision Process: A Test of Some of Its Determinants and Consequences. *Strategic Management Journal*, **18**, 63–75.

Ilgen, D.R., Hollenbeck, J.R., Johnson, M. and Jundt, D. (2005), Teams in Organizations: From Input–Process–Output Models to IMOI Models. *Annual Review of Psychology*, **56**, 517–543.

Janis, I.L. (1972), *Victims of Groupthink. A Psychological Study of Foreign-Policy Decisions and Fiascoes*, Boston, MA: Houghton Mifflin.

Jehn, K.A. (1995), A Multimethod Examination of the Benefits and Detriments of Intragroup Conflict. *Administrative Science Quarterly*, **40**, 256–282.

Jehn, K.A. and Mannix, E.A. (2001), The Dynamic Nature of Conflict: A Longitudinal Study of Intragroup Conflict and Group Performance. *Academy of Management Journal*, **44**, 238–251.

Jia, L., Shaw, J.D., Tsui, A.S. and Park, T.Y. (2014), A Social-Structural Perspective on Employee–Organization Relationships and Team Creativity. *Academy of Management Journal*, **57**, 869–891.

Johnson, J.L., Daily, C.M. and Ellstrand, A.E. (1996), Boards of Directors: A Review and Research Agenda. *Journal of Management*, **22**, 409–438.

Judge, W.Q., Hu, H., Gabrielsson, J., Talaulicar, T., Witt, M.A., et al. (2015), Configurations of Capacity for Change in Entrepreneurial Threshold Firms: Imprinting and Strategic Choice Perspectives. *Journal of Management Studies*, **52**, 506–530.

Judge, W.Q. and Miller, A. (1991), Antecedents and Outcomes of Decision Speed in Different Environmental Contexts. *Academy of Management Journal*, **34**, 449–463.

Katzenbach, J.R. (1997), The Myth of the Top Management Team. *Harvard Business Review*, **75** (6), 82–91.

Katzenbach, J.R. and Smith, D.K. (1993), The Discipline of Teams. *Harvard Business Review*, **71** (2), 111–120.

Keck, S.L. (1997), Top Management Team Structure: Differential Effects by Environmental Context. *Organization Science*, **8**, 143–156.

Kellermanns, F.W., Walter, J., Lechner, C. and Floyd, S.W. (2005), The Lack of Consensus About Strategic Consensus: Advancing Theory and Research. *Journal of Management*, **31**, 719–737.

Ketchen Jr, D.J., Thomas, J.B. and Snow, C.C. (1993), Organizational Configurations and Performance: A Comparison of Theoretical Approaches. *Academy of Management Journal*, **36**, 1278–1313.

Kilduff, M., Angelmar, R. and Mehra, A. (2000), Top Management-Team Diversity and Firm Performance: Examining the Role of Cognitions. *Organization Science*, **11**, 21–34.

Kirkman, B.L. and Rosen, B. (1999), Beyond Self-Management: Antecedents and Consequences of Team Empowerment. *Academy of Management Journal*, **42**, 58–74.

Klotz, A.C., Hmieleski, K.M., Bradley, B.H. and Busenitz, L.W. (2014), New Venture Teams. A Review of the Literature and Roadmap for Future Research. *Journal of Management*, **40**, 226–255.

Knight, D., Pearce, C.L., Smith, K.G., Olian, J.D., Sims, H.P., Smith, K.A. and Flood, P. (1999), Top Management Team Diversity, Group Process, and Strategic Consensus. *Strategic Management Journal*, **20**, 445–465.

Knoop, R. (1991), Achievement of Work Values and Participative Decision Making. *Psychological Reports*, **58**, 775–781.

Kor, Y.Y. (2003), Experience-Based Top Management Team Competence and Sustained Growth. *Organization Science*, **14**, 707–719.

Kozlowski, S.W.J. and Ilgen, D.R. (2006), Enhancing the Effectiveness of Work Groups and Teams. *Psychological Science in the Public Interest*, **7**, 77–124.

Kozlowski, S.W.J. and Klein, K.J. (2000), A Multilevel Approach to Theory and Research in Organizations: Contextual, Temporal, and Emergent Processes. In Klein, K.J. and Kozlowski, S.W.J. (eds), *Multilevel Theory, Research, and Methods in Organizations: Foundations, Extensions, and New Directions*, San Francisco, CA: Jossey-Bass, pp. 3–90.

Krause, R., Semadeni, M. and Cannella Jr, A.A. (2014), CEO Duality: A Review and Research Agenda. *Journal of Management*, **40**, 256–286.

Krishnan, H.A., Miller, A. and Judge, W.Q. (1997), Diversification and Top Management

Team Complementarity: Is Performance Improved by Merging Similar or Dissimilar Teams?. *Strategic Management Journal*, **18**, 361–374.

Krishnan, H.A. and Park, D. (2005), A Few Good Women – On Top Management Teams. *Journal of Business Research*, **58**, 1712–1720.

Lau, D.C. and Murnighan, J.K. (1998), Demographic Diversity and Faultlines: The Compositional Dynamics of Organizational Groups. *Academy of Management Review*, **23**, 325–340.

Lau, D.C. and Murnighan, J.K. (2005), Interaction with Groups and Subgroups: The Effects of Demographic Faultlines. *Academy of Management Journal*, **48**, 645–659.

Lawrence, B.S. (1997), The Black Box of Organizational Demography. *Organization Science*, **8**, 1–22.

Lechner, C. and Dowling, M. (1999), The Evolution of Industrial Districts and Regional Networks: The Case of the Biotechnology Region Munich/Martinsried. *Journal of Management and Governance*, **3**, 309–338.

Li Lu, Y.C.Y. and McLeod, P.L. (2012), Twenty-Five Years of Hidden Profiles in Group Decision Making: A Meta-Analysis. *Personality and Social Psychology Review*, **16**, 54–75.

Lim, J-A.Y-K., Busenitz, L.W. and Chidambaram, L. (2013), New Venture Teams and the Quality of Business Opportunities Identified: Faultlines Between Subgroups of Founders and Investors. *Entrepreneurship Theory and Practice*, **37**, 47–67.

Lomi, A. (1995), The Population Ecology of Organizational Founding: Location Dependence and Unobserved Heterogeneity. *Administrative Science Quarterly*, **40**, 111–144.

Lubatkin, M.H., Simsek, Z., Ling, Y. and Veiga, J.F. (2006), Ambidexterity and Performance in Small-to Medium-Sized Firms: The Pivotal Role of Top Management Team Behavioral Integration. *Journal of Management*, **32**, 646–672.

March, J.G. and Sutton, R.I. (1997), Organizational Performance as a Dependent Variable. *Organization Science*, **8**, 698–706.

Marks, M.A., Mathieu, J.E. and Zaccaro, S.J. (2001), A Temporally Based Framework and Taxonomy of Team Processes. *Academy of Management Review*, **26**, 356–376.

Mathieu, J., Maynard, M.T., Rapp, T. and Gilson, L. (2008), Team Effectiveness 1997–2007: A Review of Recent Advancements and a Glimpse Into the Future. *Journal of Management*, **34**, 410–476.

McNulty, T. and Pettigrew, A. (1999), Strategists on the Board. *Organization Studies*, **20**, 47–74.

Mesmer-Magnus, J.R. and DeChurch, L.A. (2009), Information Sharing and Team Performance: A Meta-Analysis. *Journal of Applied Psychology*, **94**, 535–546.

Michel, J.G. and Hambrick, D.C. (1992), Diversification Posture and Top Management Characteristics. *Academy of Management Journal*, **35**, 9–37.

Minichilli, A., Zattoni, A. and Zona, F. (2009), Making Boards Effective: An Empirical Examination of Board Task Performance. *British Journal of Management*, **20**, 55–74.

Mooney, A.C., Holahan, P.J. and Amason, A.C. (2007), Don't Take It Personally: Exploring Cognitive Conflict as a Mediator of Affective Conflict. *Journal of Management Studies*, **44**, 733–758.

Mullen, B. and Copper, C. (1994), The Relation between Group Cohesiveness and Performance: An Integration. *Psychological Bulletin*, **115**, 210–227.

Murray, A.I. (1989), Top Management Group Heterogeneity and Firm Performance. *Strategic Management Journal*, **10**, 125–141.

Naranjo-Gil, D., Hartmann, F. and Maas, V.S. (2008), Top Management Team Heterogeneity, Strategic Change and Operational Performance. *British Journal of Management*, **19**, 222–234.

Norburn, D. and Birley, S. (1988), The Top Management Team and Corporate Performance. *Strategic Management Journal*, **9**, 225–237.

Nunes, P.M., Serrasqueiro, Z. and Leitão, J. (2012), Is There a Linear Relationship between R&D Intensity and Growth? Empirical Evidence of Non-high-tech vs. High-tech SMEs. *Research Policy*, **41**, 36–53.

Olson, B.J., Parayitam, S. and Bao, Y. (2007), Strategic Decision Making: The Effects of

Cognitive Diversity, Conflict, and Trust on Decision Outcomes. *Journal of Management*, **33**, 196–222.

Pearce, J.A., II (1995), A Structural Analysis of Dominant Coalitions in Small Banks. *Journal of Management*, **21**, 1075–1095.

Pelled, L.H., Eisenhardt, K.M. and Xin, K.R. (1999), Exploring the Black Box: An Analysis of Work Group Diversity, Conflict, and Performance. *Administrative Science Quarterly*, **44**, 1–28.

Pettigrew, A.M. (1992), On Studying Managerial Elites. *Strategic Management Journal*, **13**, 163–182.

Priem, R.L. (1990), Top Management Team Group Factors, Consensus, and Firm Performance. *Strategic Management Journal*, **11**, 469–478.

Priem, R.L., Lyon, D.W. and Dess, G.G. (1999), Inherent Limitations of Demographic Proxies in Top Management Team Heterogeneity Research. *Journal of Management*, **25**, 935–953.

Raes, A.M.L., Heijltjes, M.G., Glunk, U. and Roe, R.A. (2011), The Interface of Top Management Team and Middle Managers: A Process Model. *Academy of Management Review*, **36**, 102–126.

Rechner, P.L. and Dalton, D.R. (1991), CEO Duality and Organizational Performance: A Longitudinal Analysis. *Strategic Management Journal*, **12**, 155–160.

Roberts, J., McNulty, T. and Stiles, P. (2005), Beyond Agency Conceptions of the Work of the Non-Executive Director: Creating Accountability in the Boardroom. *British Journal of Management*, **16**, 5–26.

Romanelli, E. (1989), Environments and Strategies of Organization Start-up: Effects on Early Survival. *Administrative Science Quarterly*, **34**, 369–387.

Roure, J.B. and Maidique, M.A. (1986), Linking Prefunding Factors and High-Technology Venture Success: An Explorative Study. *Journal of Business Venturing*, **1**, 295–306.

Schoonhoven, C.B., Eisenhardt, K.M. and Lyman, K. (1990), Speeding Products to Market: Waiting Time to First Product Introduction in New Firms. *Administrative Science Quarterly*, **35**, 177–207.

Shane, S. and Cable, D. (2002), Network Ties, Reputation, and the Financing of New Ventures. *Management Science*, **48**, 364–381.

Siegel, P.A. and Hambrick, D.C. (2005), Pay Disparities Within Top Management Groups: Evidence of Harmful Effects on Performance of High-Technology Firms. *Organization Science*, **16**, 259–274.

Simons, T. (1995), Top Management Team Consensus, Heterogeneity, and Debate as Contingent Predictors of Company Performance: The Complementarity of Group Structure and Process. *Academy of Management Journal*, **38**, 62–66.

Simons, T.L., Pelled, L.H. and Smith, K.A. (1999), Making Use of Difference: Diversity, Debate, and Decision Comprehensiveness in Top Management Teams. *Academy of Management Journal*, **42**, 662–673.

Simons, T.L. and Peterson, R.S. (2000), Task Conflict and Relationship Conflict in Top Management Teams: The Pivotal Role of Intragroup Trust. *Journal of Applied Psychology*, **85**, 102–111.

Singh, J.V., Tucker, D.J. and House, R.J. (1986), Organizational Legitimacy and the Liability of Newness. *Administrative Science Quarterly*, **31**, 171–193.

Smith, A., Houghton, S.M., Hood, J.N. and Ryman, J.A. (2006), Power Relationships among Top Managers: Does Top Management Team Power Distribution Matter for Organizational Performance?. *Journal of Business Research*, **59**, 622–629.

Smith, K.G., Collins, C.J. and Clark, K.D. (2005), Existing Knowledge, Knowledge Creation Capability, and the Rate of New Product Introduction in High-Technology Firms. *Academy of Management Journal*, **48**, 346–357.

Smith, K.G., Smith, K.A., Olian, J.D., Sims Jr, H.P., O'Bannon, D.P. and Scully, J.A. (1994), Top Management Team Demography and Process: The Role of Social Integration and Communication. *Administrative Science Quarterly*, **39**, 412–438.

Stinchcombe, A.L. (1965), Social Structure and Organizations. In James G. March (ed.), *Handbook of Organizations*, Chicago, IL: Rand McNally, pp. 142–193.

Sutcliffe, K.M. (1994), What Executives Notice: Accurate Perceptions in Top Management Teams. *Academy of Management Journal*, **37**, 1360–1376.

Talaulicar, T., Grundei, J. and Werder, A. (2005), Strategic Decision Making in Start-ups: The Effect of Top Management Team Organization and Processes on Speed and Comprehensiveness. *Journal of Business Venturing*, **20**, 519–541.

Thatcher, S.M.B. and Patel, P.C. (2012), Group Faultlines: A Review, Integration, and Guide to Future Research. *Journal of Management*, **38**, 969–1009.

Tost, L.P., Gino, F. and Larrick, R.P. (2013), When Power Makes Others Speechless: The Negative Impact of Leader Power on Team Performance: In *Academy of Management Journal*, **56**, 1465–1486.

Turner, J.R., Chen, Q. and Danks, S. (2014), Team Shared Cognitive Constructs: A Meta-Analysis Exploring the Effects of Shared Cognitive Constructs on Team Performance. *Performance Improvement Quarterly*, **27**, 83–117.

Tushman, M.L. and Nadler, D.A. (1978), Information Processing as an Integrating Concept in Organizational Design. *Academy of Management Review*, **3**, 613–624.

Van de Ven, A.H., Delbecq, A.L. and Koenig Jr, R. (1976), Determinants of Coordination Modes within Organizations. *American Sociological Review*, **41**, 322–338.

Wagner, W.G., Pfeffer, J. and O'Reilly, C.A., III (1984), Organizational Demography and Turnover in Top-Management Groups. *Administrative Science Quarterly*, **29**, 74–92.

Watson, W.E., Ponthieu, L.D. and Critelli, J.W. (1995), Team Interpersonal Process Effectiveness in Venture Partnerships and Its Connection to Perceived Success. *Journal of Business Venturing*, **10**, 393–411.

Webber, S.S. and Donahue, L.M. (2001), Impact of Highly and Less Job-Related Diversity on Work Group Cohesion and Performance: A Meta-Analysis. *Journal of Management*, **27**, 141–162.

Welbourne, T.M., Cycyota, C.S. and Ferrante, C.J. (2007), Wall Street Reaction to Women in IPOs: An Examination of Gender Diversity in Top Management Teams. *Group and Organization Management*, **32**, 524–547.

Werder, A. (1987), Organisation der Unternehmungsleitung und Haftung des Top-Managements. *Der Betrieb*, **40**, 2265–2273.

Wiersema, M.F. and Bantel, K.A. (1992), Top Management Team Demography and Corporate Strategic Change. *Academy of Management Journal*, **35**, 91–121.

Wong, E.M., Ormiston, M.E. and Tetlock, P.E. (2011), The Effects of Top Management Team Integrative Complexity and Decentralized Decision Making on Corporate Social Performance. *Academy of Management Journal*, **54**, 1207–1228.

Yammarino, F.J. and Naughton, T.J. (1992), Individualized and Group-Based Views of Participation in Decision Making. *Group and Organization Management*, **17**, 398–413.

Young, M., Wyman, S.M. and Brenner, C.T. (1999), Assessment of Small Business Perception of Needed Information and Assistance. *Journal of Business and Entrepreneurship*, **11** (1), 99–105.

Zahra, S.A. and Pearce, J.A. II (1989), Boards of Directors and Corporate Financial Performance: A Review and Integrative Model. *Journal of Management*, **15**, 291–334.

5. Research on the board of directors in high-tech start-ups: an assessment and suggestions for future research
Ekaterina S. Bjornali

INTRODUCTION

While entrepreneurship research has undergone drastic changes over the past 40 years, scholars have increasingly recognized that the formation of new high-technology-based firms is a collective action by the founding teams and other people involved (Wright and Vanaelst, 2009). High-tech start-ups are defined as early-stage firms that are one to ten years old, operate in multiple high-tech sectors, and have significant equity investment from multiple professional investors (Burgel and Murray, 2000; Burgel et al., 2004; Garg, 2013). Early-stage high-tech firms are considered to be a significant source of economic growth and innovation (Kortum and Lerner, 2000). High-tech start-ups are also firms in transition as they go through a number of stages of activity and need to develop resources and capabilities in order to bring their innovative products or services to market under highly uncertain and changing conditions.

Today, the development and growth of research-based high-tech firms is much emphasized by policy-makers as a way to support innovation and job creation (Steffensen et al., 2000; Wright et al., 2004). The composition and functioning of the entrepreneurial team are often identified as critical determinants of the survival and success of these firms (Cooper and Daily, 1997; Birley and Stockley, 2000; Ensley and Hmieleski, 2005; Clarysse and Moray, 2004; Vanaelst et al., 2006). However, there is often a limited amount of recognition that the entrepreneurial team in these firms often includes both the top management team (TMT) and board members. This is surprising, since the board of directors in high-tech start-ups appears to be more actively involved in the company's strategic decisions compared to large established companies (Gabrielsson and Huse, 2002). Further, the service role of the outside board seems to be crucial for early-stage high-tech firms in terms of acquiring additional resources through new board members that the TMT lacks (Bjørnåli and Gulbrandsen, 2010; Knockaert and Ucbasaran, 2013). Zhang et al. (2011) even suggest that the outside board members can be seen as an extension of the full-time internal TMT, and all together play a vital role as 'collective entrepreneurs' in the early venturing process.

While the boundaries between the TMT and the board are blurred in the early stages of start-up development, they are nevertheless embedded in institutional and financial structures that over time divide and separate these two leadership entities (Vanaelst et al., 2006). Hence, understanding the development and growth of high-tech start-ups requires a joint understanding of how the TMT and board members shape and influence a firm's direction. Unfortunately, scholarly knowledge about these issues is limited in several respects since studies of TMTs and boards are often carried out within different research traditions, with TMT scholars being in one camp and corporate governance scholars in another. Moreover, existing studies in both traditions are scattered across various research streams and reported in different scholarly outlets, and this fragmentation hampers knowledge accumulation.

Previous studies have extensively examined the characteristics of the founders and TMTs (Eisenhardt and Schoonhoven, 1990; Smith et al., 1994; Chandler et al., 2005; Beckman et al., 2007; Foo, 2010), while several literature reviews have extensively covered the issues related to TMTs in new high-tech firms (e.g. Cooper and Daily, 1997; Birley and Stockley, 2000; Klotz et al., 2014). Yet, these studies have neglected an important extension of the entrepreneurial TMT: the board of directors. One exception is the studies that investigate how TMT characteristics affect relationships with venture capital (VC) investors who are often board members (e.g. Busenitz et al., 1997; Franke et al., 2006, 2008). Thus, there is a need to make an effort to collect, review and synthesize the current body of scholarly knowledge about boards in high-tech start-ups to start unifying these streams of research. This can be used to inform policy and practice about the state of the art in this field of research, as well as helping to identify areas in which there is a need for further scholarly inquiry.

Consequently, the aim of this chapter is to review and synthesize scholarly research on boards in high-tech start-ups as a means of accumulating and discussing current knowledge in the field, and to identify areas in which further scholarly inquiry is highly warranted. In particular, I attempt to conduct a comprehensive review of the literature that deals with boards in high-tech start-ups. The assessment and synthesis should make this research topic more accessible to scholars and practitioners, thus contributing to its diffusion.

The chapter is structured in several sections. This introduction is followed by a theoretical discussion, ending in a framework as the basis for a sorting logic. Additionally, the unique features of high-tech start-up board are also presented here. Next, I describe the search methodology, and present the descriptive overview of the field and findings of the thematic analysis along three dimensions: group inputs, processes and outcomes. Lastly, I propose future research directions and present the conclusions, implications and limitations of this review.

THEORETICAL FRAMEWORK

In this section I attempt to build an overarching framework to encompass the different elements that comprise the board studies included in this literature review. The development of such a framework is a worthwhile attempt because it is quite difficult to advance the field without an agreed-upon categorization scheme (Christensen et al., 2002). The framework may serve as a useful tool, which makes the existing body of knowledge more accessible and easier to understand for novice researchers; this in turn should enhance the diffusion of the research topic and its impact. Below, I first elaborate on the unique features of boards in high-tech start-ups, and then describe how and why the chosen framework is suitable for structuring the reviewed board studies.

Distinctive Characteristics of Boards in High-Tech Start-Ups

High-tech start-ups are early-stage entrepreneurial firms in transition that evolve into more stable organizations and often aim at reaching an initial public offering (IPO) (Filatotchev et al., 2006a). As such, these firms attempt to overcome various thresholds, for example gathering human resources, and achieving entrepreneurial milestones such as attracting external funding (Vohora et al., 2004; Clarysse and Moray, 2004; Vanaelst et al., 2006). As shown by Vanaelst et al. (2006), during legal incorporation the founding team is divided into two major leadership groups: the top management team and the board of directors. In newly established firms, these groups most often overlap, as the original founder becomes a formal member of both the TMT and the board, while an external financier will typically require a seat on the board. As the firm develops further, founders may seek outside equity investments from professional investors, such as venture capitalist (VC) firms and corporate venture capital (CVC) firms (Clarysse et al., 2007; Katila et al., 2008). They usually contribute financial capital and their commercial knowledge in return for stock ownership. An increasing stake for external owners represents a reduction in TMT ownership, which implies that some founders have to leave the board. Therefore, as the firm develops, both the TMT and the board will most likely undergo changes.

Indeed, prior studies of high-tech start-ups have shown that TMTs are dynamic and experience turnover during a company's life cycle (Boeker and Karichalil, 2002; Chandler et al., 2005). Following Marks et al. (2001), along with team member exits and entries, transition processes also include activities that teammates undertake between performances, episodes to reflect on past accomplishments and to prepare for future actions, for example mission analysis, goal specification and strategic planning. In high-tech start-ups, boards are also quite dynamic, and in addition to board membership changes, they experience higher levels of internal dynamics than public corporations (Garg, 2013). For instance, board members may have more diverse and conflicting interests among themselves and with the start-up firm, although while all are interested in the firm, they may be interested for different reasons. A founding TMT may have a strong psychological attachment to and passion for the firm, whereas investors are primarily focused on growth that leads to an eventual liquidity exit through an IPO or acquisition. External board members are typically senior executives from relevant industries who are selected for their expertise (Lerner, 1995; Bjørnåli and Gulbrandsen, 2010). Their reasons to serve on the board may vary. They may be interested in enhancing their status and reputation, and in having more director appointments.

The misalignment of interests between the founding TMT members, investors and other external board members is expected to give rise to interpersonal processes such as conflict, while the common strategic interest in the firm will initiate action processes such as planning and goal setting. Interpersonal processes are activities that involve the management of interpersonal relationships, for example conflict management, motivating and confidence building, all of which affect management (Marks et al., 2001). Activities during performance episodes that facilitate goal achievement, for example, monitoring progress and group coordination, are referred to as action processes (Marks et al., 2001). As a result of both divergent and common strategic interests being present in high-tech start-ups, boards may experience higher levels of dynamics in terms of conflict or goal-setting processes compared to large corporations (Garg, 2013). To sum up, similarly to the new-venture team, the board undergoes internal and external processes that may influence the firm's performance.

Overall, the ongoing processes occurring within and between the TMT and the board, coupled with the board service role in terms of providing access to external resources, make the board in a high-tech start-up a crucial component of the venture's management that affects firm development.[1] As such, the key dimensions considered in the framework below, and originally developed for TMTs, will be also highly relevant for boards in early-stage high-tech firms.

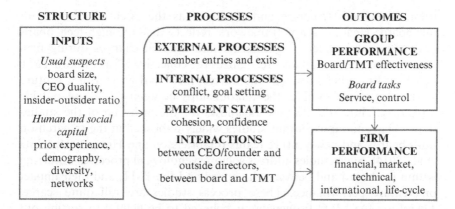

Figure 5.1   Input–processes–outcome (I-P-O) framework for boards and TMTs in high-tech start-ups

An Input–Processes–Outcome Framework

An input–processes–outcome framework has been suggested by several TMT and board scholars (see Figure 5.1; Forbes and Milliken, 1999; Vykarnam and Handelberg, 2005; Mathieu et al., 2008), which seems to include all specific aspects of a high-tech start-up board or TMT. This framework is rooted in the field of organizational behaviour, and seeks to understand group performance and other group-level outcomes as the consequence of the inputs and processes that determine them (Klotz et al., 2014). As such, it includes two key dimensions: group structure and processes. Board members' inputs, for example human and social capital, constitute group structure; while board processes include the processes both across and within the group boundaries, that is, external and internal processes. External processes refer to transition processes (for example, member addition or departure), whereas internal processes refer to interpersonal processes (for example, conflict) or action processes (for example, planning, goal setting), as described above. Some conditions may arise within a board which can be categorized as neither structure nor process. Instead, these are referred to as emergent states; for example, cohesion, confidence (Mathieu et al., 2008; Klotz et al., 2014). Finally, there may be interactions between external board members and internal TMT members; for instance, the relationship between chief executive officer (CEO) and outside directors has been previously studied. The overarching input–processes–outcome (I-P-O) framework for considering the board and TMT in high-tech start-ups is displayed in Figure 5.1.

This input–processes–outcome framework has a number of advantages.

First, it includes structure and processes as the essential elements of the board. Hence, such a framework reflects that the high-tech board is dynamic and undergoing external and internal changes during firm development. Second, it also recognizes the collective effort of both TMT and board members, towards the development and growth of a venture (formed by, for example, the relationships between CEO and outside directors). Third, the framework allows for the inclusion of the studies that go beyond input–output studies widely published in the research on both boards and new-venture teams (Gabrielsson and Huse, 2004; Klotz et al., 2014). Such studies address socio-psychological processes occurring within the board and between the board and the TMT, and their impact on venture performance. These process studies are still quite scarce. Therefore, the I-P-O framework is believed to be helpful in sorting out interesting avenues for future research on the board and interaction processes in early-stage high-tech firms.

SEARCH METHODOLOGY

The search of the literature and the subsequent review were carried out following the procedures developed for conducting systematic literature reviews (Tranfield et al., 2003; Gough et al., 2012). Specifically, inspired by other reviews using similar procedures (Hamidi and Gabrielsson, 2014), this review was conducted in four steps: planning, search, analysis and reporting.

First, the objectives that would help to achieve the overall aim of the review were identified, and a coding scheme was developed: to assemble and synthesize data on the authors' and publications' names, the articles' year and focus, theories, methodologies, empirical contexts, variables, methodology and key findings.

Second, I started with an extended search in electronic databases such as ISI Web of Knowledge, Wiley and Francis & Taylor. I searched for combinations of the following terms with the word 'board(s)' or 'director(s)': start-up (start*), entrepreneurial (entrepr*), venture, high* and technology (tech*), within the major management and entrepreneurship journals, considered also in the review by Klotz et al. (2014). A full list of journals and other publication channels is provided in Appendix 5.1.

The articles had to address the topic pertaining to the board in a high-tech start-up, which is defined as an early-stage firm between one to ten years old operating in a high-tech sector and having no single external shareholder holding a majority stake (Burgel and Murray, 2000; Burgel et al., 2004; Garg, 2013). However, the first search produced few results.

The second search was thus expanded to other journals that were identified by reviewing the references in the articles found initially, for example *Small Business Economics*. Simultaneously, the definition of a high-tech start-up was broadened to include university and academic spin-offs or spin-outs, venture capital-backed firms and IPO firms. The abstracts and often the body text of the articles were examined to assure that the sample of the firms fell into a category of early-stage high-tech firms. For example, such firms could be described as threshold firms (Zahra et al., 2009), young entrepreneurial IPO firms (Kroll et al., 2007) or *de novo* organizations operating (Beckman et al., 2014). In a few cases the studies on small and medium-sized enterprises (SMEs) were chosen because they either contained a sample resembling the characteristics of high-tech start-ups (Cowling, 2003; Brunninge et al., 2007; Zahra et al., 2007) or provided valuable insights into board issues (Borch and Huse, 1993; George et al., 2001; Audretsch and Lehmann, 2006, 2014). A manual search within each journal was made to assure that no important article had been omitted.

Additionally, the CVs of the researchers who seemed to specialize in the topic of the board in high-tech start-ups have been reviewed. This way, four book chapters and two conference papers were found and included in this review. Such inclusion was justified because these additional publications were found in widely recognized international publication channels, that is, books published by Edward Elgar Publishing and Routledge, and the *Academy of Management Proceedings*. The search yielded 38 empirical and conceptual articles. Finally, review articles of corporate governance in SMEs and entrepreneurial firms were selected to provide a backdrop against which the studies of high-tech boards were analysed. Hence, the final search yielded a total of 44 articles, which form the basis of the literature review. See Appendix 5.2 for a list of the articles.

In the third step, I read and analysed these articles, and created a detailed database in which I coded the following data: (1) author name(s), journal name and year; (2) article's focus; (3) theory; (4) empirical context, including industry, number of firms and the country; (5) dependent variable(s); (6) independent dependent variable(s); (7) methodology, main design and data used; and (8) key findings. The risk of subjective bias is minimized as these data are quite objective. These data form a basis for a descriptive overview of the field.

The simplest and most widely used form of research synthesis is a narrative review that attempts to identify what has been written on a given subject or topic (Tranfield et al., 2003, p. 208). An alternative approach to synthesis is meta-analysis, which enables the pooling of data from individual studies to allow for an increase in statistical power and a more precise estimate of effect size (Glass, 1976). Board/TMT studies of entrepreneurial firms rarely measure a phenomenon in the same way (Daily et al., 2002). Such a lack of consistency across variables, in addition to a lack of reliance on the same performance indicators and independent variables, makes a meta-analysis difficult to implement. Therefore, a thematic analysis of the articles was carried out using narrative method.

The final step in the systematic literature review is descriptive and thematic reporting. Below, I start with providing a descriptive overview of the research on boards in high-tech start-ups. Then, the results of the thematic analysis are presented, following the structure of the input–processes–output framework.

RESEARCH ON BOARDS IN HIGH-TECH START-UPS: A DESCRIPTIVE OVERVIEW

In this section, I report on the descriptive characteristics of the research on the board in high-tech start-ups. An interesting pattern that emerged during the coding and analysis is that the board studies appear to be twofold: one stream addresses board issues only, while another stream considers both board and TMT (or founder/CEO) characteristics explicitly. In the latter joint board/TMT research stream, the board is often considered as an extended team. Therefore, the results below report on both of these streams.

Publication Channels

The studies on board and joint board/TMT studies are scattered across various outlets. The *Journal of Business Venturing* and *Small Business Economics* have published the most articles on the topic (six); the former – three articles in the 1990s and three very recently, between 2003 and 2007. These journals are followed by the *Academy of Management Review*, *Entrepreneurship Theory and Practice* and the *Entrepreneurship and Regional Development Journal*, which have published three articles each. Otherwise, the articles are distributed across different academic journals and other publication channels where the search was made. See Appendix 5.1 for a full list of journals and other publication channels.

Year

Early-stage high-tech board studies have been published in both the early and the late 1990s, and almost every other year from 2000 onwards (see

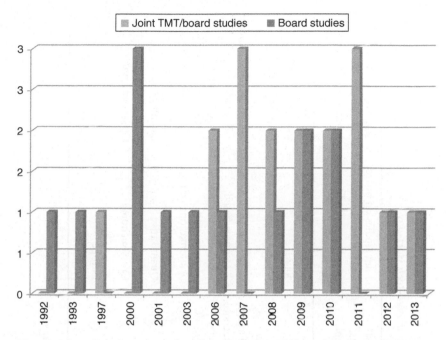

Figure 5.2   Development of studies on high-tech board and board/TMT

Figure 5.2). Joint board/TMT studies seem to represent an emergent research stream that appeared in the publications after 2003. Following recent calls for collectively studying the TMT and board (Nielsen, 2009; Zhang et al., 2011), the number of joint board/TMT articles will most likely increase in the coming years.

Country

In both research streams, 30 per cent of the data come from the United States (US). In the rest of the studies, the data are mainly collected in Europe. Joint board/TMT studies exploit data from the United Kingdom (UK), Norway and Belgium, and two studies use data from Sweden and Germany. Board studies use data from Norway, the UK, Scotland, Sweden and Belgium. One board study is from Australia, and another examines new ventures at IPO in China. Other descriptive characteristics of the studies are summarized in Table 5.1 and described below:

Table 5.1 Descriptive characteristics of the articles on boards in high-tech start-ups

	Studies on board characteristics as antecedents of firm performance	Studies on board characteristics as dependent variables	Joint studies on board/TMT characteristics as antecedents of firm performance	Joint studies on board/TMT characteristics as dependent variables
Number of studies*	9 (24%)	11 (29%)	8 (21%)	10 (26%)
Era	2000–	2000–	2006–	2006–
Dominant study characteristic	Empirical (8), conceptual (1)	Empirical (8), conceptual (3)	Empirical (8)	Empirical (10)
Theoretical frameworks	Eclectic frameworks that were previously applied to large publicly listed corporations	Combination of agency, resource dependence, network, general governance and VC perspectives	Combination of resource-based, resource dependence, agency and internationalization views	Combination of resource dependence, agency, upper-echelon, IPO and general governance perspectives
Methodological approach	Quantitative	Qualitative and quantitative	Quantitative	Quantitative
Study design	Cross-sectional and longitudinal	Cross-sectional	Cross-sectional	Cross-sectional
Empirical context	US	Europe	Europe	Europe
Data sources	Secondary	Primary	Primary	Primary

Note: * Total of 38 studies, since review articles are excluded from this overview.

120

Board Characteristics as Antecedents of Firm Performance

Similarly to the input–output studies on TMT, board researchers have attempted to identify the essential ingredients for building effective boards. These studies are quantitative and draw on frameworks that were applied to large publicly listed corporations, linking the 'usual suspects' (for example, CEO duality, insider–outsider ratio) and board demographic characteristics, including human and social capital (for example, size and prior experience), to firm performance. Most of the studies are empirical using quantitative either cross-sectional or longitudinal data (equally), but most often from secondary sources (databases). The dominant empirical context is the US.

Board Characteristics as Dependent Variables

Studies that treat board composition and processes as dependent variables are both quantitative and qualitative, using mainly cross-sectional primary data. Five studies use general board literature, and cite previous empirical results. The rest of the studies explicitly develop a theoretical framework, drawing upon multiple theoretical perspectives. Agency theory and a resource dependence view are the most frequently used theories combined with social networks. For deeper insights into the origins of resource dependence and agency theories and their implications for governance research on entrepreneurial firms, see Gabrielsson and Huse (2009).

Board/TMT Characteristics as Antecedents of Firm Performance

The majority of the TMT/board studies are quantitative, using cross-sectional primary data from Europe. All studies draw upon multiple theories, including resource-based theory, resource dependence view, agency theory and absorptive capacity. They also draw on internationalization and upper-echelon theories and input–output studies of TMT/boards in large public companies.

Board/TMT Characteristics as Dependent Variables

Fewer studies in this category use general board/TMT literature only, and more studies draw on theories in combination with the board/TMT literature. The examples are resource dependence view, agency theory, conflict theory, social networks, power theory and procedural justice. The empirical context studied is Europe. Most of the studies are quantitative and use cross-sectional primary data. This is comprehensible, because one needs to ask board/TMT members directly in order to collect data about internal board/TMT processes (for example, effectiveness, social integration) and emergent states (for example, cohesion). Two quantitative studies use longitudinal data, and two studies are qualitative. No conceptual studies were registered.

THEMATIC ANALYSIS

Below, I report on the results of the thematic analysis that are structured according to the I-P-O framework presented above (see Figure 5.1).

Inputs (Structure)

'Usual suspects'
Board size   Boards help firms to establish links with the external environment in order to secure resources, and a large board will handle this task better than a small board (Pfeffer and Salancik, 1978). The greater the need for external linkages, the larger the board should be. While the ideal board size is believed to be seven to eight members Jensen (1993), the board tends to be small in threshold (VC-backed) firms, with significant activity and influence shared among all its members (e.g. Sapienza et al., 2000). Larger boards which are actively engaged in networking activities may facilitate new team member additions in entrepreneurial firms that often experience a recruitment of new TMT members as a challenge (Bjørnåli and Erikson, 2010; Leung et al., 2006).

Venture capital investors   Studies on boards in high-tech start-ups have indicated that venture capitalists are often a key stakeholder group (Rosenstein, 1988; Fried et al., 1998). Beyond financial help, venture capitalists may provide managerial competence and perform other value-added activities, all of which can be a great help for young start-ups (Deakins et al., 2000a; Gabrielsson and Huse, 2002). Recent research shows that venture capitalists serve as catalysts to new-venture internationalization through the provision of knowledge and reputation resources (Fernhaber and McDougall-Covin, 2009), invest in more risky entrepreneurial IPO firms (Filatotchev et al., 2006b), and are a positive contextual factor which in tandem with the founder director matters for the firm's IPO performance (Wang and Song, 2016).

Board human and social capital
High-tech start-up board studies highlight that the main benefits of having outside directors on the board are human capital, for example specialized commercial or marketing expertise (Rosenstein, 1988; Clarysse et al., 2007; Bjørnåli and Gulbrandsen, 2010), and social capital, for example board networking activity (Borch and Huse, 1993; Deakins et al., 2000a; Bjørnåli and Erikson, 2010).

Board complements TMT's resources   Previous governance studies theorize which competencies board members should have to be effective, thus contributing to the firm's success (Forbes and Milliken, 1999; Huse, 2007). For example, board members in high-tech firms should preferably have the functional area knowledge and skills (finance, marketing, and so on), not to mention firm-specific knowledge and skills (Kotz, 1998; Forbes and Milliken, 1999).

Bjørnåli and Gulbrandsen (2010) have tested these assumptions on a selection of academic spin-offs based in the US and Norway that represent an important subset of high-tech start-ups. The addition of key board members was positively associated with the firm's performance. Furthermore, these key members contributed with additional resources that TMT members did not possess. In the initial stages of a venture's life cycle, the board members were investors and industry representatives helping to secure financing and with strategic positioning. In later rounds, professional executives and external members with market-specific knowledge were added to the board. Moreover, Clarysse et al. (2007) show that whether board human capital complements or substitutes for the founding team depends on the human capital of the team and on the company's origin (academic or independent start-up). Kor and Misangyi (2008) show that the lower the levels of industry experience in the TMT, the higher the levels of industry experience among outside directors.

Board/TMT demographic and task-related diversity   Bjørnåli et al. (2010) have tested which finance, TMT and board features contribute to firm performance in terms of obtaining VC capital. TMT size and TMT members' functional and industry background diversity were positively associated with the academic spin-off's ability to attract VC funding, although the authors did not find support for board diversity features. However, prior seed funding and industry financing were the predominant predictors of subsequent VC financing, with the results indicating that the board members' contribution and ability to use their human and social capital may be more important than their background per se.

To sum up, the research on board inputs (structure) in high-tech start-ups resembles to some degree 'input–output' governance studies done on large listed corporations. This research produces significant insights into which structural characteristics of the board as a whole, as well as characteristics of specific board members such as venture capital investors and other types of outside director, contribute to a superior firm performance. Most of the studies are quantitative studies based on empirical results produced from one country, either the US or from Europe. Hence, testing whether the results hold in different contexts (for example, in different multiple countries or even continents) may be one future research path. More research is also needed on uncovering how the structural characteristics unfold over time, for example with a firm's life cycle, and how they interact with the processes occurring within the board and TMT (which are the subject of the next subsection).

Processes

There is little research on board processes in high-tech start-ups. This is most likely highly correlated with the status of the research on new-venture teams, in which some research exists on some transition and inter-personal processes (for example, membership changes, conflict), while no prior work has specifically addressed action processes (for example, planning, goal setting) (Klotz et al., 2014). Furthermore, while some TMT research has examined the emergent states such as collective cognition (for example, comprehensiveness, strategic cognition and polychronicity) and TMT cohesion, no board studies of emergent states in high-tech start-ups were identified in this literature review. As such, the research on mediating processes in the high-tech boards represents a fruitful future research avenue, and entails a unique opportunity to investigate both the TMT and the board simultaneously, thereby considerably improving our understanding of how TMT and board members jointly shape and influence a firm's direction.

External (transition) processes
TMT research demonstrates that in high-tech firms, both greater CEO and VC ownership and increasing VC representation on the board are likely to lead to more TMT changes in terms of replacing TMT members, rather than adding new members (Boeker and Wiltbank, 2005; Hellman and Puri, 2002; Fiet et al., 1997). Very few high-tech board studies have yet investigated transition processes on the board.

Board member additions   As shown in a qualitative study by Bjørnåli and Gulbrandsen (2010), the process of board formation is primarily driven by the social networks of the founders. Subsequent changes in the board are driven by the social networks of the board chair, and the addition of key board members is associated with the progress of a venture developing from one stage to another.

Internal (interpersonal and action) processes and emergent states

As previously mentioned, very few studies were found in this subcategory. Forbes et al. (2010) show that venture boards experience more relationship conflict when they make financial decisions that involve a devaluation of the venture. This effect is moderated by whether the CEO is a founder or not.

Research conducted on the board as a group in high-tech start-ups is virtually non-existent. According to Huse (2007), it is not common to consider the board as a team, as one reason for this is that the board meets infrequently. However, a board consists of people who have a psychological dependence on each other, so board members will therefore have to relate to group rather than individual norms (Huse, 2007). Forbes and Milliken (1999) integrate the demographic literature on boards with the literature on group dynamics, and discuss criteria that may distinguish effective boards from ineffective ones. For boards to become more effective – that is, to meet the task expectations – researchers are advised to focus on socio-psychological processes, and in particular on those related to group participation and interaction, the exchange of information and critical decisions (for example, cohesiveness, openness). Nonetheless, there is still a need to open the 'black box' between board composition and firm performance to better understand how the processes within the board impact on firm development (Daily et al., 2003; Gabrielsson and Huse, 2004).

Interactions between the TMT and the board

On the level of individuals, the relationships between outside directors and the CEO/leading entrepreneur were examined (Deakins et al., 2000a, 2000b). On a group level, Bjørnåli et al. (2011) find that the relationship between TMT diversity and TMT effectiveness is mediated by an involvement of the board in the firm's strategic decisions. Furthermore, Knockaert et al. (2015) find that, first, the service involvement by the board diminishes as TMT size increases, especially in cases of limited board chair industry experience; and second, the positive relationship between TMT diversity and board service involvement is stronger when CEO duality is present, that is, when the CEO is also board chair.

More research is needed to generate insights into interaction processes in early-stage high-tech firms. For example, whether and how trust or behavioural integration between TMT and board members influence how effectively a board performs its role. Does the absence of trust or behavioural integration lead to the board being involved in a monitoring rather than a service role?

Group-Level Outcomes

Board role and tasks
Governance scholars argue that having board members who are able to contribute to the development of the firm's resources may considerably increase the venture's growth and chances of survival (Filatotchev et al., 2006a; Huse, 2007). The studies on VC investors have been able to empirically demonstrate the value added that is delivered to entrepreneurs. However, more empirical research in this area is needed to expand our knowledge about the contributions made by other types of outside directors, and collectively by the board to the firm's development.

Board service role   Due to liabilities of smallness and newness, the various service tasks of the board in early-stage high-tech firms will be more highly valued than in large companies (Huse, 2007; Knockaert and Ucbasaran, 2011). The boards are shown to have an active involvement by, for example, offering legitimacy in the business community or helping with networking, rather than merely performing monitoring and control (e.g. Deakins et al., 2000a, 2000b; Huse, 2007). The board service role will be perceived differently depending on the resource base of the high-tech start-up. For instance, in the founding TMTs where research and development (R&D) experience and technological resources are lacking, boards will be seen as crucial for building technological resources by providing the legitimacy the venture needs to develop technological partnerships (Knockaert and Ucbasaran, 2011).

Further, Knockaert et al. (2015) show that TMT diversity and CEO duality are important antecedents of board involvement in the service role in high-tech start-ups. While the former positively affects the board service involvement, the latter has an opposite effect. Moreover, interesting interactions have been observed by the authors: the industry experience of the chairperson positively moderates the relationship between TMT size and board service involvement, whereas CEO duality reinforces the relationship between TMT diversity and board service involvement.

Board monitoring role   Garg (2013) focuses on distinctive features of the board monitoring function in new ventures and implications for firm performance. The author theoretically highlights a potential principal problem that could emerge as the separation of ownership and control is reduced, and develops propositions about which board inputs and venture attributes may potentially be associated with increased venture board monitoring.

Other tasks of outside directors include counselling and advisory (Daily and Dalton, 1992), the impact on strategic planning processes, as well as an involvement in recruitment, training and staff development (Deakins et al., 2000a). More recent studies provide evidence regarding the extent to which, for example, board networking and advising actually contribute to assembling the necessary resources that would move the firm forward (Bjørnåli and Erikson, 2010; Bjørnåli and Gulbrandsen, 2010).

Zhang et al. (2011) have qualitatively explored the tensions between board monitoring, resourcing and strategizing tasks in UK high-tech start-ups. The authors conclude that early venture boards do not monitor managements in the traditional sense, nor are they detached from their firm's operations as these boards are quite active in resource gathering and strategizing activities aimed at securing their venture's growth. As such, the results of whether a board in high-tech start-ups provides more of a service role or is more involved in monitoring remain contradictory. Future researchers could resolve these contradictions by, for example, examining in which stages of firm development or in what strategic contexts cither the service or monitoring board role prevails.

Board and TMT effectiveness

Zahra et al. (2009) argue that effective boards can substitute for poor absorptive capacity and vice versa, thereby influencing the intensity of corporate entrepreneurship activities. Bjørnåli et al. (2011) show that TMT diversity has an indirect impact on TMT effectiveness through the board's involvement in strategy. This means that higher levels of TMT diversity are positively related to higher levels of board involvement in the firm's strategy, in turn generating higher levels of TMT effectiveness in high-tech start-ups.

More studies could be done in this interesting area of future research. Examples of possible research questions are: how do the interactions between TMT and board members affect board/TMT effectiveness? What processes are most detrimental or conducive to board/TMT effectiveness? Are effective teams also more cohesive and better networked, and thereby capable of attracting effective boards?

Firm-Level Outcomes

In joint board/TMT studies, firm performance has been measured as a firm's internationalization (Bjørnåli and Aspelund, 2012), a firm's attraction of VC funding (Bjørnåli et al., 2010), IPO performance (holding period returns) (Kroll et al., 2007) and corporate entrepreneurship activities (Zahra et al., 2009). In high-tech board studies, firm performance is measured financially (return on assets, ROA; return on equity, ROE) (George et al., 2001) and in a less traditional manner, namely as a dependence on a key entrepreneur (Arthurs et al., 2009), a diverse alliance portfolio emergence (Beckman et al., 2014), and as a market versus technical performance (Vandenbroucke et al., 2014). One study attempts to link board tasks (for example, group-level outcomes) to firm innovation (Gabrielsson and Politis, 2009). This variation in the measure of firm performance makes it difficult to compare studies and conduct a meta-analysis, which also reflects the complexity of the phenomenon of new-venture growth (Chandler and Hanks, 1993; Davidsson et al., 2007).

IPO performance
The percentage of original TMT board members and their ownership participation is demonstrated to be positively associated with post-IPO performance in a study by Kroll et al. (2007). A few more studies link TMT and board outputs to IPO-related firm outcomes (e.g. Filatotchev, 2006; Chahine et al., 2009; Chancharat et al., 2012; Wang and Song, 2016). Even so, there may be a long path prior to the initial public offering. Early-stage high-tech firms need to pass several thresholds before they reach an IPO (Rasmussen, 2011; Rasmussen et al., 2011). Qualitative and longitudinal studies of whether and how the initial formation processes imprint on future paths directions are welcome in this research area.

A firm's life cycle
Lynall et al. (2003) theorize about that board composition and firm performance are a reflection of both the firm's life cycle stage and the relative power of the CEO and external financiers at the time of founding. Filatotchev et al. (2006a) have attempted to link the corporate governance parameters to strategic thresholds in the firm's life cycle. The authors show that a successful transition over a threshold is accompanied by a rebalancing in the structure and roles of corporate governance compared with each previous stage in the cycle. Bjørnåli and Gulbrandsen (2010) have attempted to link board member additions to the firm's development stages, proof of viability and maturity. Combining a life cycle perspective with process theories from small group research most likely has considerable potential for creating valuable insights into how and when board/TMT socio-psychological processes come into play and become critical for a firm's development. Key variables used in the studies on boards including joint board/TMT studies in high-tech start-ups are summarized in Table 5.2.

Table 5.2 Variable characteristics in the articles on boards in high-tech start-ups

	Studies on board characteristics as antecedents of firm performance	Studies on board characteristics as dependent variables	Joint studies on board/TMT characteristics as antecedents of firm performance	Joint studies on board/TMT characteristics as dependent variables
Inputs used	Board members' and founder's demographic characteristics, network positions, turnover, usual suspects (e.g. CEO duality, board size, independence, tenure)	Board size and composition, board members' backgrounds, CEO founder status	Board/TMT size, heterogeneity, demographic characteristics, including experience, board tenure, share ownership	Board/TMT size, heterogeneity, demographic characteristics, including experience, share ownership, the ratio of outside directors, presence of VC, prestige
Process variables used	Board financial decision control and strategic control roles; networking strategy	Board members' social networks, resource provision and monitoring roles, power	Board service and strategic roles, board effectiveness, absorptive capacity	Board networking and strategic roles, board behaviour, TMT cohesion
Group outcome is measured as		The relationship between entrepreneur and external board members, board monitoring role, value added contribution by outside directors, board conflict, board formation and evolution	Levels of corporate entrepreneurship	Board/TMT membership changes, human capital on the board/TMT, TMT effectiveness, board control and service roles
Firm performance is measured as	ROA, ROE, survival, innovation, forming alliance portfolio, firm's dependence on a key entrepreneur, number of patents, IPO premium	Firm development, including life cycle, firm's corporate governance functions	Internationalization, including international sales, acquisition of VC funding, holding period returns, strategic change, productivity	Holding period returns

FUTURE RESEARCH DIRECTIONS

For scholars interested in pursuing research on the group level in the context of high-tech start-up firms, I suggest that four main future research areas would be the most promising to address. First, researchers are encouraged to continue opening the 'black box'. The conclusion of this literature review echoes other calls (e.g. Gabrielsson and Huse, 2004; Daily et al., 2003; Huse et al., 2011) that we still know relatively little about the actual behaviour of the board. Future research is needed to examine decision-making processes, relationships and cognitions among board directors, and how this would affect board effectiveness and a firm's development. Insights into the processes would add significantly to our knowledge of effective boards and governance. To be able to open up the 'black box' of actual board behaviour, van Ees et al. (2009) have argued for the need for new directions and alternative theorizing in research on boards and governance. In general, van Ees et al. (2009) propose a behavioural theory of boards and corporate governance with a focus on problems of coordination, exploration and knowledge creation rather than on the problems of conflict of interest, exploitation and the distribution of value.

In the context of high-tech start-ups, as the results indicate, it is highly important to enhance our understanding of the interactions between the board and TMT behaviour and their joint influence on the early-stage high-tech firm performance. Hence, our understanding of the impact of joint board/TMT inputs on high-tech start-ups would be extended by augmenting archival data sources with the direct measurement of behavioural group characteristics and by applying alternative theories. One such alternative is the team production theory of the firm, which may help to explain governance phenomena and board behaviour (Blair and Stout, 1999; Kaufman and Englander, 2005). In the contemporary team production perspective, firms are conceptualized as a nexus of team-specific assets, with an investment by shareholders, board members, managers, employees and other stakeholders, all of whom hope to profit from team production (Blair and Stout, 1999; Gabrielsson et al., 2007; Kaufman and Englander, 2005). In and of itself, the board can be viewed as a team that co-produces values (Forbes and Milliken, 1999). Following the logic of team production theory, boards are viewed as cooperative teams that contribute to firms' value creation through their strategy involvement (Machold et al., 2011). Related to team production is the issue of effective and accountable board leadership, which is about ensuring that the knowledge and skills of the board members are used to create value (Finkelstein and Mooney, 2003; Huse et al., 2011; Hamidi and Gabrielsson, 2014).

Second, for early-stage high-tech firms, in which the board operates as an extension of the top management team, a fruitful future research approach to opening up the 'black box' would be by developing input–processes outcome models of board/TMT functioning. Some work has been done on transition processes (for example, board/TMT member additions and departures) and interpersonal processes (for example, conflict) in the reviewed board studies. Prior work has not yet addressed many of the other types of processes, for example action processes and emergent states. In general, more future work could be done in this area that would address transition, interpersonal and action processes occurring in the board and between the TMT and board members. Similarly to calls within new-venture team research (Klotz et al., 2014), future research could seek to achieve a more balanced understanding of how each of these types of group processes (within-board and TMT and jointly) influences high-tech start-up performance. For instance, while the link between cohesion and new-venture team performance has been extensively explored (Ensley et al., 2002; Foo et al., 2006), we know little about cohesion among board members, its antecedents and its consequences for an interaction between the TMT and the board, and the subsequent high-tech firm performance. With regard to emergent states, one could gain inspiration and borrow constructs from small-group studies, upper-echelon research and new-venture team research. Some examples are self-efficacy, which refers to the beliefs in one's capabilities to mobilize the motivation, cognitive resources and courses of action needed to meet given situational demands (Bandura, 1986); and team potency: a shared general belief that the group will be effective (Lester et al., 2002). Emergent states embrace both cognitive-based and affective-based constructs (Barsade and Gibson, 2007). While focusing on cognitive constructs would mean examining thinking and decision-making processes on the board, focusing on affective constructs would imply investigating the feelings and moods of the board members.

Third, TMT studies have shown that the initial entrepreneurial team composition has an imprinting effect on the subsequent TMT composition and high-tech firm performance (Beckman and Burton, 2008). In other words, founding TMTs directly shape the initial structure, systems and processes of their firms. This influence has long-term imprinting effects that continue to impact upon the strategy of firms, often long after most TMT members have moved on and been replaced. Investigating whether the initial board composition has some imprinting effects on the subsequent board composition and firm performance is an interesting future research path for entrepreneurship and governance scholars interested in a high-tech context. An increased understanding of the initial imprinting effects of both TMTs and boards in early-stage high-tech firms may further help strategy researchers to achieve a fuller understanding of how firms evolve, and what factors influence their ability to develop and maintain competitive advantages in their industries.

Lastly, Finkelstein and Hambrick (1996) specifically include the board of directors in their book on strategic leadership and executive effects, defining the construct of a 'Supra TMT' composed of both top executives and board members. Future studies could test this construct in a high-tech start-up context: for instance, when and how the boundaries of a Supra TMT change. Furthermore, as research on positive organizational behaviour increases (Luthans et al., 2007), it has been suggested that new-venture teams would seem to be a natural unit of examination with respect to groups that are truly agentic (that is, actively able to shape their own fortunes; see Bandura, 2001; Klotz et al., 2014). While positive organizational behaviour researchers could examine how both the TMT and the board members can flourish under challenging conditions that typically exist in high-tech start-ups, entrepreneurship scholars could examine how the TMT and board members jointly actually shape their environment in order to flourish.

In addition to applying alternative theories, there is also an opportunity to apply alternative methods and conduct studies in other institutional contexts. Most published studies to date are from the US and developed European countries, and few studies are conducted across countries. Hence, the scholars should be careful when interpreting past results and take into account cultural specifics, for example with the US, or with TMT culture, board culture and internal processes in the UK. In terms of research methods, most high-tech joint board/TMT and quite a few board studies rely on survey designs. Thus, future research may benefit from using inductive qualitative methods that enable the generation of new insights into processes and emergent states, both within and between the board and TMT in early-stage high-tech firms. Longitudinal quantitative studies could be a useful addition to existing cross-sectional quantitative and conceptual studies. In the former case, such studies may strengthen the generalizability and validity of prior findings if conducted in other countries (for example, outside North America and Europe). In the latter case, such studies would test the theoretically derived propositions, and contribute to the further development of the field.

CONCLUSIONS

This literature review chapter has sought to review and synthesize scholarly research on boards in high-tech start-ups as a means to accumulate and discuss state-of-the-art knowledge in the field, and to identify future research directions. The board in early-stage high-tech firms is a promising, yet unexplored, research stream and high-tech start-ups represent an interesting dynamic context for studying the board as an important extension of the top management team. The studies that explicitly consider both board and TMT characteristics, and their joint influence on firm performance, constitute an emerging research stream. However, more joint board/TMT studies, both empirical and conceptual, are needed and welcomed in order to improve our understanding of how TMT and board members shape and influence a firm's direction.

Overall, there is much about boards and TMTs in high-tech start-ups that has not been systematically studied, which presents numerous opportunities for future research. In this review, I have attempted to identify key promising research areas. For researchers wishing to contribute to high-tech start-up studies on the group level, there are many opportunities to address the existing gaps related to board/TMT inputs and processes and their relationships to firm performance. For instance, there is a need to respond to recent calls of the TMT and board researchers to treat both groups as dynamic entities and to use theories other than those traditionally applied to the TMT and the board in large organizations such as upper-echelon and agency theory. The resource-based view, team production theory, stage-based and small-group behaviour approaches can fruitfully be applied in this context, whereas the main future research questions remaining to be answered are how the TMT and the board can jointly contribute to sustained firm development, and how the TMT and the board can be important resources that add value to a high-tech start-up.

This chapter is not without limitations. First, since there are still only a few board and joint board/TMT studies in high-tech start-ups, I have attempted to provide some key directions for future research that could develop this area. Therefore, the relationships between some variables have received a greater amount of attention depending on whether or not they have been addressed by previous research. Future researchers may attempt to identify and focus on the relationships between certain variables, which have been extensively studied in other contexts or disciplines (for example, corporate governance, upper-echelon studies), and theorize about, or even test the applicability of, these relationships in a high-tech start-up context. Second, new-venture teams have been quite extensively studied and reviewed (Cooper and Daily, 1986; Birley and Stockley, 2000; Wright and Vanaelst, 2009; Klotz et al., 2014). Arguing that the outside board members in early-stage high-tech firms function as an extension of the TMT, I focused on board and joint board/TMT studies in this review, and I attempted to relate the results to what is known about new-venture teams.

ACKNOWLEDGMENTS

The author gratefully acknowledges the helpful suggestions of the anonymous reviewers and participants of the XI Norefjell Research Workshop on Board Governance 'Learning from Practice', the 2014 Academy of Management Annual Meeting, and the 2014 European Academy of Management conference, and would like to thank the colleagues at NTNU and the editor of this book for the comments on earlier drafts of this chapter.

NOTE

1. For broader overview of corporate governance mechanisms in entrepreneurial firms and explanations of how and why they may differ from those mechanisms in large and publicly traded corporations, see Audretsch and Lehmann (2014) and Audretsch and Lehmann (2011).

REFERENCES

Note: References listed here are those cited in the text which do not appear in the Appendix 5.2 list. For instance, if a reference is cited in the text, but does not appear in this reference list, please, check Appendix 5.2 list.

Audretsch, D.B. and Lehmann, E.E. (2014), 'Corporate governance and entrepreneurial firms', *Foundations and Trends in Entrepreneurship*, **10** (1–2), 1–160.
Bandura, A. (1986), *Social Foundations of Thought and Action: A Social Cognitive Theory*, Englewood Cliffs, NJ: Prentice Hall.
Bandura, A. (2001), 'Social cognitive theory: An agentic perspective', *Annual Review of Psychology*, **52**, 1–26.
Barsade, S.G. and Gibson, D.E. (2007), 'Why does affect matter in organizations?', *Academy of Management Perspectives*, **21** (1), 36–59.
Beckman, C.M. and Burton, M.D. (2008), 'Founding the future: Path dependence in the evolution of top management teams from founding to IPO', *Organization Science*, **19**, 3–24.
Beckman, C.M., Burton, M.D. and O'Reilly, C. (2007), 'Early teams: The impact of team demography on VC financing and going public', *Journal of Business Venturing*, **22** (2), 147–173.
Birley, S. and Stockley, S. (2000), 'Entrepreneurial teams and venture growth', in Landström, H. and Sexton, D.L. (eds), *The Blackwell Book of Entrepreneurship*, Oxford: Blackwell, pp. 287–307.
Blair, M. and Stout, L.A. (1999), 'A team production theory of corporate law', *Virginia Law Review*, **85**, 247–328.

Boeker, W. and Karichalil, R. (2002), 'Entrepreneurial transitions: Factors influencing founder departure', *Academy of Management Journal*, **45** (4), 818–826.
Boeker, W. and Wiltbank, R. (2005), 'New venture evolution and managerial capabilities', *Organization Science*, **16** (2), 123–133.
Burgel, O. and Murray, G.C. (2000), 'The international market entry choices of start-up companies in high-technology industries', *Journal of International Marketing*, **8** (2), 33–62.
Burgel, O., Fier, A. and Licht, G. (2004), *Internationalisation of Young High-Tech Firms: An Empirical Analysis in Germany and the United Kingdom*, Heidelberg: Physica-Verlag.
Chandler, G. and Hanks, S.H. (1993), 'Measuring the performance of emerging businesses: A validation study', *Journal of Business Venturing*, **8**, 381–408.
Chandler, G.N., Honig, B. and Wiklund, J. (2005), 'Antecedents, moderators, and performance consequences of membership change in new venture teams', *Journal of Business Venturing*, **20** (5), 705–725.
Christensen, C.M., Carlile, P. and Sundahl, D. (2002), 'The process of theory-building', Working paper, Harvard Business School, Boston, MA.
Clarysse, B. and Moray, N. (2004), 'A process study of entrepreneurial team formation: The case of a research-based spin-off', *Journal of Business Venturing*, **19** (1), 55–79.
Cooper, A.C. and Daily, C.M. (1997), 'Entrepreneurial teams', in Sexton, D. and Smilor, R. (eds), *Entrepreneurship 2000*, Chicago, IL: Upstart Publishing, pp. 127–149.
Daily, C., Dalton, D. and Cannella, A. (2003), 'Corporate governance: Decades of dialogue and data', *Academy of Management Review*, **28** (3), 371–382.
Dalton, D.R., Daily, C.M., Ellstrand, A.E. and Johnson, J.J. (1998), 'Meta-analytical reviews of board composition, leadership structure, and financial performance', *Strategic Management Journal*, **19** (3), 269–290.
Davidsson, P., Steffens, P. and Fitzsimmons, J. (2007), 'Performance assessment in entrepreneurship research: is there a pro-growth bias?', available at http://eprints.qut.edu.au/archive/00012040.
Eisenhardt, K.M. and Schoonhoven, C.B. (1990), 'Organizational growth: Linking founding team, strategy, environment, and growth among US semiconductor ventures 1978–1988', *Administrative Science Quarterly*, **35** (3), 504–529.
Ensley, M.D. and Hmieleski, K.M. (2005), 'A comparative study of new venture top management team composition, dynamics and performance between university-based and independent start-ups', *Research Policy*, **34** (7), 1091–1105.
Ensley M.D., Pearson, A.W. and Amason, A.C. (2002), 'Understanding the dynamics of new venture top management teams: Cohesion, conflict, and new venture performance', *Journal of Business Venturing*, **17** (4), 365–386.
Fernhaber, S.A. and McDougall-Covin, P.P. (2009), 'Venture capitalists as catalysts to new venture internationalization: The impact of their knowledge and reputation resources', *Entrepreneurship Theory and Practice*, **33** (1), 1042–2587.
Finkelstein, S. and Hambrick, D.C. (1996), *Strategic Leadership: Top Executives and their Effects on Organizations*, St Paul, MN: West Publishing.
Finkelstein, S. and Mooney, A.C. (2003), 'Not the usual suspects: How to use board process to make boards better', *Academy of Management Executive*, **17** (2), 101–113.
Foo, M.D. (2010), 'Member experience, use of external assistance and evaluation of business ideas', *Journal of Small Business Management*, **48** (1), 32–43.
Foo, M.D., Sin, H.P. and Yiong, L.P. (2006), 'Effects of team inputs and intrateam processes on perceptions of team viability and member satisfaction in nascent ventures', *Strategic Management Journal*, **27**, 389–399.
Franke, N., Gruber, M., Harhoff, D. and Henkel, J. (2006), 'What you are is what you like – similarity biases in venture capitalists' evaluations of startup teams', *Journal of Business Venturing*, **21**, 802–826.
Franke, N., Gruber, M., Harhoff, D. and Henkel, J. (2008), 'Venture capitalists' evaluations of startup teams: Trade-offs, knock-out criteria, and the impact of VC experience', *Entrepreneurship Theory and Practice*, **32**, 459–483.
Fried, V.H., Bruton, G.D. and Hisrich, R.D. (1998), 'Strategy and the board of directors in

venture capital-backed firms: Venture capital and high technology', *Journal of Business Venturing*, **13** (6), 493–503.

Gabrielsson, J. and Huse, M. (2004), 'Context, behavior, and evolution: Challenges in research on boards and governance', *International Studies of Management and Organization*, **34** (2), 11–36.

Gabrielsson, J., Huse, M. and Minichilli, A. (2007), 'Understanding the leadership role of the board chairperson through a team production approach', *International Journal of Leadership Studies*, **3** (1), 21–39.

Glass, G.V. (1976), 'Primary, secondary, and meta-analysis of research', *Educational Researcher*, **5** (2), 3–8.

Gough, D., Oliver, S. and Thomas, J. (2012), *An Introduction to Systematic Reviews*, London: SAGE Publications.

Hambrick, D.C. and Abrahamson, E. (1995), 'Assessing managerial discretion across industries – a multimethod approach', *Academy of Management Journal*, **38** (5), 1427–1441.

Hamidi, D.Y. and Gabrielsson, J. (2014), 'Developments and trends in research on board leadership: A systematic literature review', *International Journal of Business Governance and Ethics*, **9** (3), 243–268.

Hellmann, T. and Puri, M. (2002), 'Venture capital and the professionalization of start-up firms: Empirical evidence', *Journal of Finance*, **57** (1), 169–197.

Huse, M. (2007), *Boards, Governance and Value Creation: The Human Side of Corporate Governance*, Cambridge: Cambridge University Press.

Huse, M., Hoskisson, R., Zattoni, A. and Vigano, R. (2011), 'New perspectives on board research: Changing the research agenda', *Journal of Management Governance*, **15** (5), 5–28.

Jensen, M.C. (1993), 'The modern industrial revolution, exit, and the failure of internal control systems', *Journal of Finance*, **48** (3), 831–880.

Katila, R., Rosenberger, J.D. and Eisenhardt, K.M. (2008), 'Swimming with sharks: Technology ventures, defense mechanisms and corporate relationships', *Administrative Science Quarterly*, **53**, 295–332.

Kaufman, A. and Englander, E. (2005), 'A team production model of corporate governance', *Academy of Management Executive*, **19** (3), 9–22.

Klotz, A.C., Hmieleski, K.M., Bradley, B.H. and Busenitz, L.W. (2014), 'New venture teams: A review of the literature and roadmap for future research', *Journal of Management*, **40** (1), 226–255.

Kotz, R. (1998), 'Technology company boards: A new model', *Directors and Boards*, **22** (3), 26–28.

Kuhn, T.S. (1962), *The Structure of Scientific Revolutions*, Chicago, IL: University of Chicago Press.

Lerner, J. (1995), 'Venture capitalists and the oversight of private firms', *Journal of Finance*, **50**, 301–318.

Lester, S.W., Meglino, B.M. and Korsgaard, M.A. (2002), 'The antecedents and consequences of group potency: A longitudinal investigation of newly formed groups', *Academy of Management Journal*, **45**, 352–368.

Leung, A., Zhang, J., Wong, P.K. and Foo, M.D. (2006), 'The use of networks in human resource acquisition for entrepreneurial firms: Multiple "fit" considerations', *Journal of Business Venturing*, **21** (5), 664–686.

Luthans, F., Youssef, C.M. and Avolio, B.J. (2007), *Psychological Capital: Developing Human Competitive Advantage*, New York: Oxford University Press.

Machold, S., Huse, M., Minichilli, A. and Nordqvist, M. (2011), 'Board leadership and strategy involvement in small firms: A team production approach', *Corporate Governance: An International Review*, **19** (4), 1467–8683.

Marks, M.A., Mathieu, J.E. and Zaccaro, S.J. (2001), 'A temporally based framework and taxonomy of team processes', *Academy of Management Review*, **26**, 356–376.

Mathieu, J.E., Maynard, M.T., Rapp, T. and Gilson, L. (2008), 'Team effectiveness 1997–2007: A review of recent advancements and a glimpse into the future', *Journal of Management*, **34**, 410–476.

Nielsen, S. (2010), 'Top management team diversity: A review of theories and methodologies', *International Journal of Management Reviews*, **12**, 301–316.

Pfeffer, J. and Salancik, G. (1978), *The External Control of Organizations: A Resource Dependence Perspective*, New York: Harper & Row.

Rasmussen, E. (2011), 'Understanding academic entrepreneurship: Exploring the emergence of university spin-off ventures using process theories', *International Small Business Journal*, **29**, 448–471.

Rasmussen, E., Mosey, S. and Wright, M. (2011), 'The evolution of entrepreneurial competencies: A longitudinal study of university spin-off venture emergence', *Journal of Management Studies*, **48**, 1314–1345.

Rosenstein, J. (1988), 'The board and strategy: Venture capital and high technology', *Journal of Business Venturing*, **3** (2), 159–170.

Rosenstein, J., Bruno, A.V., Bygrave, W.D. and Taylor, N.T. (1993), 'The CEO, venture capitalists, and the board', *Journal of Business Venturing*, **8** (2), 99–113.

Smith, K., Smith, K., Olian, J., Sims, H., O'Bannon, D. and Scully, J. (1994), 'Top management team demography and process: The role of social integration and communication', *Administrative Science Quarterly*, **39**, 412–438.

Steffensen, M., Rogers, E.M. and Speakman, K. (2000), 'Spin-offs from research centers at a research university', *Journal of Business Venturing*, **15** (1), 93–111.

Tranfield, D.R., Denyer, D. and Smart, P. (2003), 'Towards a methodology for developing evidence informed management knowledge by means of systematic review', *British Journal of Management*, **14** (3), 207–222.

Van Ees, H., Gabrielsson, J. and Huse, M. (2009), 'Toward a behavioral theory of boards and corporate governance', *Corporate Governance: An International Review*, **17** (3), 307–319.

Vanaelst, I., Clarysse, B., Wright, M., Lockett, A., Moray, N. and S'Jegers, R. (2006), 'Entrepreneurial team development in academic spinouts: An examination of team heterogeneity', *Entrepreneurship Theory and Practice*, **30** (2), 249–271.

Vohora, A., Wright, M. and Lockett, A. (2004), 'Critical junctures in the development of university high-tech spinout companies', *Research Policy*, **33** (1), 147–175.

Vykarnam, S. and Handelberg, J. (2005), 'Four themes of the impact of management teams on organizational performance: Implications for future research of entrepreneurial teams', *International Small Business Journal*, **23** (3), 236–256.

Wright, M. and Vanaelst, I. (eds) (2009), *Entrepreneurial Teams and New Business Creation*, The International Library of Entrepreneurship, An Elgar Reference Collection, Cheltenham, UK and Northampton, MA, USA: Edward Elgar Publishing.

Wright, M., Vohora, A. and Lockett, A. (2004), 'The formation of high-tech university spinouts: The role of joint ventures and venture capital investors', *Journal of Technology Transfer*, **29** (3–4), 287–310.

APPENDIX 5.1: LIST OF JOURNALS AND OTHER PUBLICATION CHANNELS

Name of journal	No. of articles
Academy of Management Journal	2
Academy of Management Review	3
Administrative Science Quarterly	0
British Journal of Management	2
Corporate Governance: An International Review	1
Enterprise and Innovation Management Studies	1
Entrepreneurship and Regional Development	3
Entrepreneurship Theory and Practice	3
International Journal of Managerial Finance	1
International Journal of Management Reviews	0
Journal of Business Research	1
Journal of Business Venturing	6
Journal of International Entrepreneurship	1
Journal of Management	2
Journal of Organizational Behavior	0
Journal of Small Business Management	1
Journal of Technology Transfer	1
Long Range Planning	1
Management Science	0
Research Policy	0
Small Business Economics	6
Strategic Entrepreneurship Journal	0
Strategic Management Journal	1
Venture Capital: An International Journal of Entrepreneurial Finance	2
Other publication channels	
Academy of Management Proceedings	2
Book chapters: Routledge	1
Book chapters: Edward Elgar Publishing	3
Total no. of articles	44

APPENDIX 5.2: STUDIES ON BOARDS IN EARLY STAGE HIGH-TECH FIRMS

1 *   iv   Arthurs, J.D., Busenitz, L.W., Hoskisson, R.E. and Johnson, R.A. (2009), 'Firm-specific human capital and governance in IPO firms: Addressing agency and resource dependence concerns', *Entrepreneurship Theory and Practice*, **33** (4), 845–865.

2 ** iv   Audretsch, D.B. and Lehmann, E. (2006), 'Entrepreneurial access and absorption of knowledge spillovers: Strategic board and managerial composition for competitive advantage', *Journal of Small Business Management*, **44** (2), 155–166.

3 *   iv   Beckman, C.M., Schoonhoven, C.B., Rottner, R.M. and Kim, S-J. (2014), 'Relational pluralism in de novo organizations: Board of directors as bridges or barriers to diverse alliance portfolios?', *Academy of Management Journal*, **57**, 460–483.

4 ** iv   Bjørnåli, E.S. and Aspelund, A. (2012), 'The role of the entrepreneurial team and the board of directors in the internationalization of academic spin-offs', *Journal of International Entrepreneurship*, **10** (4), 350–377.

5 ** dv   Bjørnåli, E. and Erikson, T. (2010), 'Board features associated with new team member addition in academic spin-offs', in Brush, C., Kolvereid, L., Widding, L.Ø. and Sørheim, R. (eds), *The Life Cycle of New Ventures: A Cross National Investigation*, Cheltenham, UK and Northampton, MA, USA: Edward Elgar Publishing, pp. 157–171.

6 ** dv   Bjørnåli, E., Erikson, T. and Knockaert, M. (2011), 'The impact of top management team characteristics and board strategic involvement on team effectiveness in high-tech start-ups', Academy of Management, Annual Meeting Proceedings.

7 *   dv   Bjørnåli, E.S. and Gulbrandsen, M. (2010), 'Exploring board formation and evolution of board composition in academic spin-offs', *Journal of Technology Transfer*, **35** (1), 92–112.

8 ** iv   Bjørnåli, E.S., Sørheim, R. and Erikson, T. (2010), 'Design characteristics associated with venture capital acquisitions in academic spin-offs', in Brush, C., Kolvereid, L., Widding, Ø. and Sørheim, R. (eds), *The Life Cycle of New Ventures: A Cross National Investigation*, Cheltenham, UK and Northampton, MA, USA: Edward Elgar Publishing, pp. 157–171.

9 *   dv   Borch, O.J. and Huse, M. (1993), 'Informal strategic networks and the board of directors', *Entrepreneurship Theory and Practice*, **18** (1), 23–26.

10 ** iv   Brunninge, O., Nordqvist, M. and Wiklund, J. (2007), 'Corporate governance and strategic change in SMEs: The effects of ownership, board composition and top management teams', *Small Business Economics*, **29**, 295–308.

11 ** dv   Chahine, S., Filatotchev, I. and Zahra, S.A. (2009), 'Building
                perceived quality of founder-involved IPO firms: Founders'
                effects on board selection and stock market performance',
                Entrepreneurship Theory and Practice, 1042–2587.
12 *   iv   Chancharat, N., Krishnamurti, C. and Tian, G. (2012), 'Board
                structure and survival of new economy IPO firms', *Corporate
                Governance: An International Review*, **20** (2), 144–163.
13 ** dv   Clarysse, B., Knockaert, M. and Lockett, A. (2007), 'Outside board
                composition in high tech start-ups', *Small Business Economics*, **29**
                (3), 243–260.
14 ** iv   Cowling, M. (2003), 'Productivity and corporate governance in
                smaller firms', *Small Business Economics*, **20**, 335–344.
15 *   iv   Daily, C.M. and Dalton, D.R. (1992), 'The relationship between
                governance structure and corporate performance in
                entrepreneurial firms', *Journal of Business Venturing*, **7**, 375–386.
16 R   Daily, C.M., McDougall, P.P., Covin, J. and Dalton, D.R. (2002),
                'Governance and strategic leadership in entrepreneurial firms',
                Journal of Management, **28** (3), 387–412.
17 *   dv   Deakins, D., O'Neill, E. and Mileham, P. (2000a), 'The role and
                influence of external directors in small, entrepreneurial
                companies: Some evidence on VC and non-VC appointed
                external directors', *Venture Capital*, **2** (2), 111–127.
18 *   dv   Deakins, D., O'Neill, E. and Mileham, P. (2000b), 'Insiders
                vs outsiders: Director relationships in small, entrepreneurial
                companies', *Enterprise and Innovation Management Studies*, **1** (2),
                175–186.
19 *   dv   Fiet, J.O., Busenitz, L.W., Moesel, D.D. and Barney, J.B. (1997),
                'Complementary theoretical perspectives on the dismissal of new
                venture team members', *Journal of Business Venturing*, **12** (5),
                347–366.
20 ** dv   Filatotchev, I. (2006), 'Effects of executive characteristics and
                venture capital involvement on board composition and share
                ownership in IPO firms', *British Journal of Management*, **17**, 75–92.
21 *   dv   Filatotchev, I., Toms, S. and Wright, M. (2006a), 'The firm's
                strategic dynamics and corporate governance life-cycle',
                International Journal of Managerial Finance, **2** (4), 256–279.
22 *   dv   Filatotchev, I., Wright, M. and Arberk, M. (2006b), 'Venture
                capitalists, syndication and governance in initial public offerings',
                Small Business Economics, **26**, 337–350.
23 *   dv   Forbes, D.P., Korsgaard, M.A. and Sapienza, H.J. (2010),
                'Financing decisions as a source of conflict in venture boards',
                Journal of Business Venturing, **25** (6), 579–592.
24 *   iv   Forbes, D.P. and Milliken, F.J. (1999), 'Cognition and corporate
                governance: Understanding boards of directors as strategic
                decision-making groups', *Academy of Management Review*, **24**
                (3), 489–505.

25 R   Gabrielsson, J. and Huse, M. (2002), 'The venture capitalist and the board of directors in SMEs: Roles and processes', *Venture Capital*, **4** (2), 125–146.

26 R   Gabrielsson, J. and Huse, M. (2009), 'Governance theory: Origins and implications for researching boards and governance in entrepreneurial firms', in Landström, H. and Lohrke, F. (eds), *Historical Foundations of Entrepreneurship Research*, Cheltenham, UK and Northampton, MA, USA: Edward Elgar Publishing, pp. 229–252.

27 * iv Gabrielsson, J. and Politis, D. (2009), Board control and innovation: An empirical study of small technology-based firms', in Huse, M. (ed.), *The Value Creating Board: Corporate Governance and Organizational Behavior*, London: Routledge.

28 * dv Garg, S. (2013), 'Venture boards: Distinctive monitoring and implications for firm performance', *Academy of Management Review*, **38** (1), 90–108.

29 * iv George, G., Robley Wood Jr, D. and Khan, R. (2001), 'Networking strategy of boards: Implications for small and medium-sized enterprises', *Entrepreneurship and Regional Development*, **13** (3), 269–285.

30 R   Huse, M. (2000), 'Boards of directors in SMEs: A review and research agenda', *Entrepreneurship and Regional Development*, **12** (4), 271–290.

31 ** dv Knockaert, M., Bjornali, E.S. and Erikson, T. (2015), 'Joining forces: Top management team and board chair characteristics as antecedents of board service involvement', *Journal of Business Venturing*, **3** (30), 420–435.

32 ** dv Knockaert, M. and Ucbasaran, D. (2011), 'The service role of outside boards in high tech start-ups: A resource dependency perspective', *British Journal of Management*, **24** (1), 1467–8551.

33 ** dv Kor, Y.Y. and Misangyi, V.F. (2008), 'Outside directors' industry-specific experience and firms' liability of newness', *Strategic Management Journal*, **29** (12), 1345–1355.

34 ** iv Kroll, M., Walters, B.A. and Le, S.A. (2007), 'The impact of board composition and top management team ownership structure on post-IPO performance in young entrepreneurial firms', *Academy of Management Journal*, **50** (5), 1198–1216.

35 ** dv Le, S.A., Kroll, M. and Walters, B.A. (2013), 'Outside directors' experience, TMT firm-specific human capital, and firm performance in entrepreneurial IPO firms', *Journal of Business Research*, **66**, 533–539.

36 * dv Lynall, M.D., Golden, B.R. and Hillman, A.J. (2003), 'Board composition from adolescence to maturity: A multitheoretic view', *Academy of Management Review*, **28** (3), 416–431.

37 *   dv Rosenstein, J., Bruno, A.V., Bygrave, W.D. and Taylor, N.T.
                (1993), 'The CEO, venture capitalists, and the board', *Journal of
                Business Venturing*, **8** (2), 99–113.
38 *   dv Sapienza, H.J., Korsgaard, M.A., Goulet, P.K. and Hoogendam,
                J.P. (2000), 'Effects of agency risks and procedural justice
                on board processes in venture capital-backed firms',
                Entrepreneurship and Regional Development, **12** (4), 331–351.
39 R   Uhlaner, L., Wright, M. and Huse, M. (2007), 'Private firms and
                corporate governance: An integrated economic and management
                perspective', *Small Business Economics*, **29** (3), 225–241.
40 *   iv Vandenbroucke, E., Knockaert, M. and Ucbasaran, D. (2014),
                'Outside board human capital and early stage high tech firm
                performance', *Entrepreneurship Theory and Practice*, **40** (4),
                759–779.
41 *   iv Wang, T. and Song, M. (2016), 'Are founder directors detrimental
                to new ventures at initial public offering?', *Journal of
                Management*, **42** (3), 644–670.
42 ** iv Zahra, S.A., Filatotchev, I. and Wright, M. (2009), 'How do
                threshold firms sustain corporate entrepreneurship? The role of
                boards and absorptive capacity', *Journal of Business Venturing*,
                24, 248–260.
43 ** iv Zahra, S.A., Neubaum, D.O. and Naldi, L. (2007), 'The effects of
                ownership and governance on SMEs' international knowledge-
                based resources', *Small Business Economics*, **29**, 309–327.
44 ** dv Zhang, H.J., Baden-Fuller, C. and Pool, J.K. (2011), 'Resolving
                the tensions between monitoring, resourcing and strategizing:
                Structures and processes in high technology venture boards',
                Long Range Planning, **44**, 95–117.

Note: * iv, * dv = the studies on board inputs and processes as antecedents of high-tech start-up performance and as dependent variables; **iv, **dv = the joint studies on board/TMT inputs and processes as antecedents of high-tech start-up performance and as dependent variables; R = review article.

6. Corporate governance in early-stage high-tech ventures: the impact of top management team and outside board human capital on innovation speed
Elien Vandenbroucke and Mirjam Knockaert

INTRODUCTION

Early-stage high-tech firms have the potential to contribute significantly to individual wealth and regional transformation (Venkataraman, 2004). At the same time, however, these firms are faced with a number of challenges. First, early-stage high-tech firms are confronted with the liability of newness as they lack resources and legitimacy compared to established organizations (Stinchcombe, 1965; Kor and Misangyi, 2008). As such, they may struggle to develop relationships with potential business partners (Stinchombe, 1965) and have difficulties in developing and acquiring necessary knowledge (Schoonhoven et al., 1990; Choi and Shepherd, 2005). Next, these firms encounter the liability of smallness, which arises as they are unable to buffer themselves from market contractions due to insufficient resources and capabilities (Aldrich and Auster, 1986; Fackler et al., 2013). Additionally, early-stage high-tech firms are often highly innovative and operate in new and rapidly changing markets (Ittner and Larcker, 1997). As time is a scarce resource and demand for speed in the workplace is increasing (Holder, 1992), speeding up innovation becomes more important. Generally, a higher speed at which products are brought to market creates a sustainable competitive advantage (Kessler and Chakrabarti, 1996), confers strategic opportunities (Eisenhardt and Martin, 2000) and is tied to new wealth creation (Markman et al., 2005). This speed is even more important for early-stage high-tech firms as they operate in dynamic environments (Zahra and Bogner, 1999) which causes them to bring products faster to market than their counterparts in more stable settings (Kessler and Chakrabarti, 1996). Indeed, time is crucial for these firms (Lynn et al., 1999) and the pace at which they move from technological development to marketable product will be essential for survival (Knockaert et al., 2011). Consequently, in order for early-stage high-tech firms to survive and flourish, they need to develop sufficient innovation speed, defined as the time elapsed between initial development and ultimate market introduction (Kessler and Chakrabarti, 1996). Accordingly, Schoonhoven et al. (1990) indicate that shipping a first product for revenues is a major milestone for an early-stage high-tech firm.

While Schoonhoven et al. (1990) and Leonard and Sensiper (1998) highlight a number of internal and external factors which are likely to affect innovation speed, they emphasize the importance of top management team (TMT) human capital in generating sufficient innovation speed. Nevertheless, the TMT in early-stage high-tech ventures often remains fragile in terms of its human resource and knowledge base. Specifically, these TMTs are often largely homogeneous in terms of education, industry experience and functional expertise (Franklin et al., 2001), as team members typically have superior technical skills, but are less competent in the area of business development (Klofsten and Jones-Evans, 1996), and tend to select team members from their own network (Ensley and Hmieleski, 2005). Following these human capital deficiencies in the TMT (Clarysse et al., 2007; Bjornali and Gulbrandsen, 2010), research has pointed to the need to study the extended TMT. While the limited (and frequently studied) TMT is defined as the group of top managers involved in strategic decision-making, as identified by the chief executive officer (CEO) (Amason, 1996), the extended TMT consists of this TMT together with outside board members and advisors (Vanaelst et al., 2006). Such outside board members and advisors could complement the TMT in the striving for innovation speed. Indeed, while outside boards may engage in a control or service role (Zahra and Pearce, 1989; Fiegener, 2005), researchers highlighted the importance of board engagement in the service role for early-stage high-tech firms (Lynall et al., 2003; Knockaert and Ucbasaran, 2013). Through this role, the outside board provides access to resources (Deutsch and Ross, 2003; Hillman and Dalziel, 2003) and increases the firm's legitimacy through its relational and reputational capital (Certo et al., 2001). Zhang et al. (2011) even suggest that boards and TMTs in entrepreneurial new ventures can be seen as 'collective entrepreneurs', and Vanaelst et al. (2006) consider the outside board as part of the extended TMT in an early-stage environment. Subsequently, in this chapter, we focus on the nature of the extended TMT human capital in early-stage high-tech firms and how it relates to innovation speed. Particularly, we consider the role of the outside board as a complement for the (limited) TMT and study the relationship between this TMT human capital and innovation speed, while also taking into account the impact of outside board human capital on innovation speed. Figure 6.1 presents the terminology used in this chapter.

In pursuing our research objectives, we build upon a unique, hand-

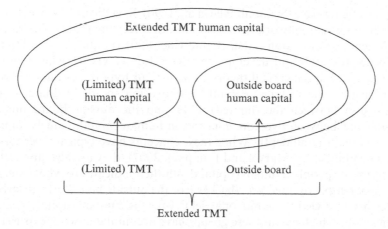

Figure 6.1   Terminology used in the chapter

collected dataset containing longitudinal data on 80 Belgian early-stage high-tech firms. In what follows, we first elaborate on our conceptual framework, followed by a description of our methodology. Subsequently, we present our results, and finally, we discuss the implications and limitations of the research presented in this chapter.

CONCEPTUAL FRAMEWORK

The entrepreneurship literature offers abundant evidence of the central role of the (limited) TMT for firm performance. Specifically, numerous studies provide support for TMT human capital as a key factor in explaining organizational performance (e.g. Bruderl et al., 1992; Delmar and Shane, 2002; Hitt et al., 2001), and recent studies have indicated that the same positive relationship holds for technology-based new firms (Colombo and Grilli, 2010; Shrader and Siegel, 2007). Human capital has been presented as the most universally valuable and imperfectly imitable resource (Crook et al., 2011; Grant, 1996; Kogut and Zander, 1992), consisting of achieved attributes, work experience and habits which are linked to firm competitiveness (Becker, 1975; Crook et al., 2011; Parnes, 1984). Human capital theory posits that individuals with greater human capital achieve higher performance in executing relevant tasks (Dimov and Shepherd, 2005). By consequence, given the resource gaps in the TMT, outside boards can be expected to contribute to the human capital in early-stage high-tech firms. Indeed, (extended) teams with more human capital are better able to implement new technologies more effectively (Link and Siegel, 2007), and thus at a faster pace (Schoonhoven et al., 1990). Specifically, Wincent et al. (2010) show that network board capital can affect the type of (radical or incremental) innovation pursued, and Chen (2013) indicates that boards influence research and development (R&D) decisions. In what follows, we build on human capital theory to derive our hypotheses linking TMT and outside board human capital to innovation speed. In doing so, we distinguish between the (limited) TMT and the outside board human capital and between two core concepts in human capital, namely human capital breadth and depth. While these concepts have typically been used for individuals (e.g. Marvel and Lumpkin, 2007), they are also applicable to groups of people. Human capital depth then indicates to what extent a group of people (in this case: the TMT or the outside board) has absorbed specialist knowledge within one field, whereas human capital breadth indicates to which extent these groups have accumulated work experience in different areas of work, or have a more generalist profile (Gabrielsson and Politis, 2012).

Human Capital Depth: Marketing and Sales Experience as a Prerequisite for Innovation Speed

TMTs in early-stage high-tech firms often consist of people with predominantly technical human capital (Ensley and Hmieleski, 2005). At the same time, many authors have commented on the importance of incorporating sufficient marketing and sales human capital into the TMT. For instance, Knockaert et al. (2011) found that incorporating people with a commercial mindset and experience is important in reaching adequate post-founding speed to first product in the case of academic spin-off firms. Schoonhoven et al. (1990) contend that TMTs including experts in marketing will be advantaged in speeding products to market. Indeed, attractive products in the marketplace have product features desired by customers, therefore requiring a good understanding of customer needs (Schoonhoven et al., 1990). In addition, Marvel (2013) shows that prior knowledge of ways to serve markets, acquired through sales and marketing experience, provides access to information about how a technology can be developed or packaged as a product that satisfies customer needs. Consequently, it will be important to add marketing and sales experience to the (often) technical TMT in early-stage high-tech firms as both technical and market experience are required to bring a product to the market (Burkart, 1994; Flynn, 1993).

Indeed, people who have gained larger levels of human capital depth in a particular domain can be expected to better absorb and combine concepts within that particular field. Therefore, following human capital theory and insights from the determinants of innovation speed, we argue that firms incorporating TMTs with higher levels of marketing and sales experience will generate higher levels of innovation speed and will exhibit shorter waiting times until the first product is shipped. As such, we claim that marketing and sales experience within the TMT is beneficial to the firm's innovation speed.

Additionally, firms lacking marketing and sales experience may try to complement the highly technical nature of the TMT by attracting this type of human capital through external advisors, such as outside board members. Subsequently, the availability of marketing and sales experience, and particularly the depth of such experience, is also of great value within the outside board, which complements the TMT (Nielsen, 2010). Following the extensive dedication of outside board members in these firms to the service role (Knockaert and Ucbasaran, 2013), we state that higher levels of marketing and sales experience within the outside board will positively affect innovation speed. We offer the following hypotheses:

H1a: TMT marketing and sales experience will positively affect innovation speed.

H1b: Outside board marketing and sales experience will positively affect innovation speed.

Human Capital Breadth: Functional Diversity as a Prerequisite for Innovation Speed

While marketing and sales experience in either the TMT or outside board will be crucial for new venture success, it is likely that also other types of human capital will be valuable in speeding products to market. Specifically, teams comprising members with different backgrounds are likely to have more diverse perspectives at their disposal which leads to improved decision-making and therefore to innovative new product introductions (Bantel and Jackson, 1989; Shrader and Siegel, 2007). First, high-technology ventures often require extensive new knowledge creation and technological synthesis which calls for high levels of technical expertise (Eisenhardt and Schoonhoven, 1990) necessary to compete in rapidly changing markets (Jarillo, 1989) and to enhance firm performance (McGee and Dowling, 1994). Indeed, Knockaert et al. (2011) show that the availability of specific technical knowledge within the TMT is likely to speed up the development process and subsequently decreases time to first product. Second, expertise in manufacturing is expected to reduce the time to first product (Schoonhoven et al., 1990). Wheelwright (1988) showed that new ventures with timely product innovations acknowledged the importance of manufacturing experience at an early stage in the product development phase. Third, Bruderl and Preisendorfer (2000) demonstrated that founders' management experience predicted whether a start-up would become a fast-growing business. Therefore, management experience is also crucial in order to speed up the innovation rate and to improve early-stage venture performance (Stuart and Abetti, 1990). Finally, financial experience has been found to be key for early-stage high-tech firms (Oakey, 1984) as obtaining financial resources might be important in order to achieve firm survival and growth (Cooper et al., 1994). As a result, the complexity related to bringing products to market may require a mix of human capital types. Indeed, the greater the human capital breadth within a group of people, the greater the number of puzzle pieces they can draw from, which will be required to successfully bring a product to market (Casson, 1995; Marvel and Lumpkin, 2007). We subsequently argue that human capital breadth, or the diversity in the TMT's human capital relating to different functional domains, will lead to a decrease in the time to commercialize new products and will therefore positively affect innovation speed. This is in line with previous research stating that teams need to be cross-functional and require diverse roles in order to successfully bring a product to market (Ancona and Caldwell, 1990). At the same time, while sufficiently high levels of human capital breadth within the TMT may be optimal for early-stage high-tech firms, these firms often lack significant (financial) resources (Henderson, 1999) and therefore often consist of team members with a homogeneous (technological) profile. In such circumstances, the required diversity may still be obtained by composing a diverse outside board, which may complement the lack of human capital breadth in early-stage high-tech TMTs. Through their interventions within and outside of the board room, board members can help firms to successfully commercialize products. Therefore, we offer the following hypotheses:

H2a: TMT functional diversity will positively affect innovation speed.

H2b: Outside board functional diversity will positively affect innovation speed.

METHODOLOGY

Sample and Data Collection

Our longitudinal dataset, constructed in 2011–13, contains early-stage high-tech firms located in Belgium. Belgium is a federal state in the

European Union (EU) with three culturally different regions: Flanders, Wallonia and the capital city of Brussels. It is an export-driven economy and has relatively large levels of R&D intensity (2 percent of gross domestic product), targeting an increase towards 3 percent by 2020. As regards innovation, Belgium is seen as an 'innovation follower', with an innovation performance above the European average (EC, 2011). Belgian companies have a predominantly controlled ownership structure and the country has a significant presence of small (listed) companies (Allen & Overy, 2012). As regards corporate governance, there is a general code, the Belgian 2009 code, just as the 'code Lippens' for listed companies and the 'code Buysse' for non-listed companies. As in the other member states of the EU, these codes are a compromise between the national corporate governance traditions and practices and European directives and recommendations. The Belgian 2009 code contains an extensive set of ethical and qualitative rules of conduct for directors. Belgium is a forerunner in a number of aspects, for instance in the field of legal provisions related to director remuneration (Allen & Overy, 2012).

The new ventures selected in Belgium had not existed for more than ten years and as such were founded between 2001 and 2011 (Burgel and Murray, 2000). Further, we selected new ventures from multiple high-tech sectors, as classified by Burgel et al. (2004). They used the high-tech industries of Butchart (1987), complemented by a number of high-tech service sectors.

We identified all early-stage high-tech firms in Belgium meeting these requirements by using the official public database Bel-First, containing general, financial, team and board-related information on each Belgian company. Applying our selection criteria to this database resulted in a sample of 179 firms. Given that the focus of this chapter's study is on both the TMT and the outside board, those firms without at least one outside board member were eliminated from our sample. An outside board member cannot be part of the top management team, or an associate or families, or relative of a TMT member of the firm or its subsidiaries, nor a member of the immediate past top management group (Pearce and Zahra, 1991). Applying this assumption reduced our sample to 129 early-stage high-tech firms of which 80 firms were willing to cooperate.

The longitudinal data were collected during face-to-face interviews with the firms' CEOs after sending a letter to introduce our study and calling them a week later to make an appointment. While doing face-to-face interviews was time-consuming, this procedure was essential to gain often confidential information and to acquire a high response rate. Specifically, the primary data contain longitudinal information on the TMT and outside board human capital, the new venture's performance, and a number of firm-related variables such as venture ownership. Even though interviewing the CEO is relevant as they typically possess the most comprehensive knowledge on the organization (Carter et al., 1994), we deemed it necessary to collect information from multiple sources. Through the interviews with the CEOs, we obtained the contact information of all TMT and outside board members. Consequently, they received a request to complete an online survey which allowed us to verify the information provided by the CEO. Out of the 239 TMT members in our dataset, 83 replied to our survey (35 percent), as well as 75 of the 315 outside board members (24 percent), which allowed us to validate the data provided by the CEO. Additionally, we verified the received responses with information gathered from other secondary sources such as Bel-First (providing validation for board membership and a number of control variables, for instance firm age) and LinkedIn (a professional social network website), to ensure data reliability.

Measures

In what follows, we elaborate on the measures used.

Dependent variable

Innovation speed is defined following Schoonhoven et al. (1990), arguing that shipping a first product for revenues is a major milestone for new high-tech organizations. They indicate that the speed at which such an organization sells its product is important to accelerate financial independence; to gain visibility, legitimacy and early market share; and to increase the likelihood of survival. As such, we created a dummy variable, *product launched*, which takes a value of 1 in the year when the first product is shipped for revenues. Given the panel nature of our data, this variable provides an indication of how long it took for the firm to sell its first product.

Independent variables

TMT marketing and sales experience is the total number of years the TMT is experienced in marketing or sales. On average, the TMT has 5.02 years of marketing and sales experience. Likewise, *outside board marketing and sales experience* is the total number of years of experience the outside board has in marketing or sales, which is 6.23 years on average.

TMT diversity is calculated using Teachman's (1980) diversity measure:

$$H = -\sum_{i=1}^{N} P_i(\ln P_i).$$

Pfeffer and O'Reilly (1987) have shown that this formula can be used to index the heterogeneity in a system (H), where P_i is the probability that the system will be found in state i, if there are N possible states in which the system can be. In our case, P represents the proportion of the TMT's years of working experiences assigned to management, marketing/sales/promotion, accounting/controlling/financing, engineering/R&D, production or personnel (Canter et al., 2010).

TMT diversity ranges from 0 (indicating a very homogeneous TMT in terms of working experiences) to 1.68 (specifying a very diverse TMT). In line with TMT diversity, *outside board diversity* is also calculated by Teachman's (1980) diversity measure: $H = -\sum_{i=1}^{N} P_i (\ln P_i)$, with P representing the proportion of the outside board's years of working experiences assigned to management, marketing/sales/promotion, accounting/controlling/financing, engineering/R&D, production or personnel (Canter et al., 2010). The average outside board diversity index is 1.11.

Control variables
Several other factors may affect the hypothesized relationships. Hence, we control for firm characteristics (firm age, firm independence, firm industry and VC ownership), TMT characteristics (TMT tenure and TMT R&D experience) and outside board characteristics (outside board tenure, outside board R&D experience, frequency of board meetings and CEO duality).

Firm characteristics   We control for *firm age* by taking the natural log of the number of years the new venture has existed to ensure that none of the identified effects are the result of age-related processes. In particular, since older firms may be more likely to have developed products, it becomes important to control for firm age. The sampled high-tech start-ups are on average 4.52 years old. *Firm independence* is a dummy variable equaling 1 if the firm is an independent start-up and 0 otherwise. An independent start-up emerges from the ideas and knowledge of one or more independent entrepreneurs (Shrader and Simon, 1997), while dependent start-ups include corporate and academic spin-offs. This control variable is necessary as the presence of a related corporation, university or public institute can have an influence on the speed of technological development (Perez and Sanchez, 2003). Sixty-nine percent of our sample are independent early-stage high-tech firms. *Firm industry* is controlled for by introducing two dummies: ICT industry, and health and life sciences industry. These variables equal 1 if the firm belongs to this industry category, and 0 otherwise. We control for the technological domain as institutional theory suggests that organizational practices may be related to industry-specific norms (Eisenhardt, 1988). Fifty-two percent of the firms in our sample belong to the ICT industry and 20 percent operate in the health and life sciences industry. *VC ownership* is a dummy variable (0/1) indicating whether the company has raised venture capital or not. Thirty-nine percent of the firms in our sample are VC-backed, which is high but not surprising, as this type of financing is often seen as one of the most appropriate ways of funding early-stage high-tech firms (Gompers and Lerner, 2001). We control for VC ownership, as VC-backed early-stage high-tech firms have been found to outperform non-VC-backed firms (Baum and Silverman, 2004).

TMT characteristics   *TMT tenure* is important to create a shared understanding of the company's needs (Tihanyi et al., 2000), leading to an increased speed at which first products are developed and reach the market (Schoonhoven et al., 1990). TMT tenure is measured as the number of years TMT members belonged to the TMT. The average TMT has a tenure of 10.41 years. *TMT R&D experience* is controlled for, as many high-tech TMTs are composed of members with technical expertise (Mosey and Wright, 2007), necessary to speed up projects (Gomory, 1989). Therefore, we also control for TMT R&D experience, calculated as the total number of years the TMT is skilled in engineering or R&D, which is 17.36 years on average.

Outside board characteristics   *Outside board tenure*: developing new products is a result of learning by doing (Delmar and Shane, 2002), and as outside board members will interact more frequently if they have served longer on the board, we control for outside board tenure. Indeed, the longer the outside board members serve on the board, the more they develop an understanding of the company's needs (Kor and Sundaramurthy, 2009) and the better they are able to absorb relevant knowledge on the firm's functioning and to effectively exchange information (Rutherford and Buchholtz, 2007), which in turn may lead to new ideas for product development (Tsai, 2001). Outside board tenure is measured as the total number of years the outside board members have served on the board. The average outside board has 12.44 years of tenure. *Outside board R&D experience* measures the total number of years of experience the outside board has in engineering or R&D, which is 13.59 years on average. Outside board R&D experience can complement the TMT R&D experience as new ventures need to quickly gain technical capabilities to compete in rapidly changing markets (Jarillo, 1989). The *frequency of board meetings* is controlled for, following Vafeas (1999). The more frequently board meetings are held, the better

Table 6.1   Means, standard deviations and correlations

Variable	Mean	s.d.	1	2	3	4	5	6	7	8	9	10	11	12	13	14	15
Firm age (ln)	1.29	0.71															
Firm independence	0.69	0.46	0.06														
ICT industry	0.52	0.50	−0.05	0.13*													
Health & life sciences industry	0.20	0.40	−0.04	−0.32*	−0.52*												
VC ownership	0.39	0.49	0.14*	−0.17*	−0.09*	0.36*											
TMT tenure	10.41	9.38	0.62*	−0.06	0.09*	0.12*	0.30*										
TMT R&D experience	17.36	16.17	0.03	−0.21*	−0.14*	0.46*	0.25*	0.31*									
Outside board tenure	12.44	12.67	0.56*	−0.19*	−0.17*	0.15*	0.23*	0.60*	0.28*								
Outside board R&D experience	13.59	14.51	0.13*	−0.40*	−0.14*	0.29*	0.39*	0.22*	0.29*	0.49*							
Frequency of board meetings	6.32	3.18	0.00	0.01	−0.04	0.06	−0.08	−0.10	−0.09*	−0.17*	−0.12*						
CEO duality	0.41	0.49	−0.00	0.25*	0.22*	−0.12*	−0.13*	−0.14*	−0.14*	−0.06	−0.16*	0.00					
TMT marketing and sales experience	5.02	7.78	0.13*	−0.07	−0.04	0.03	0.27*	0.40*	0.13*	0.16*	0.12*	−0.11*	−0.12*				
Outside board marketing and sales experience	6.23	7.37	0.10*	0.14*	0.01	−0.11*	0.04	0.09*	0.00	0.16*	0.04	0.04	−0.03	0.07			
TMT diversity	0.94	0.49	0.08	−0.17*	−0.09*	0.19*	0.33*	0.39*	0.15*	0.21*	0.16*	−0.27*	−0.09*	0.42*	0.02		
Outside board diversity	1.11	0.49	0.27*	−0.06	−0.07	0.15*	0.25*	0.24*	0.21*	0.40*	0.32*	−0.11*	−0.02	0.07	0.29*	0.20*	
Time to first product launched	0.66	0.47	0.31*	0.18*	0.29*	−0.57*	−0.20*	0.14*	−0.25*	0.13*	−0.09*	−0.14*	0.19*	0.09*	0.16*	0.06	0.22*

Notes:
N = 440
* p < 0.05
Variables 2, 3, 4, 6, 7, 16 and 18 are binary and their correlations should be interpreted with care.

153

the board members are informed about the firm's situation (Demb and Neubauer, 1992), which is necessary to provide tailored support in order to enhance innovation speed. We measure the number of board meetings organized on a yearly basis. The firms in our sample on average hold 6.32 meetings a year. Gabrielsson (2007) explains that early-stage high-tech firms may benefit from *CEO duality*, as it creates a centralized representative, resulting in clarity and flexibility in a dynamic high-tech environment. CEO duality equals 1 if the CEO of the company is also the board chair, 0 otherwise. Forty-one percent of the firms in our sample reported CEO duality. Table 6.1 provides the descriptive statistics for all variables used.

Analytical Techniques

For every early-stage high-tech firm in our sample, we created observations for each year of the firm's existence, starting from the founding year. As these ventures were established between 2001 and 2011, we have a maximum of 11 observations for each venture. The later the venture was founded, the fewer the number of observations available. For instance, an early-stage high-tech firm founded in 2005 is represented by seven observations. Thus, the length of the time series of each early-stage high-tech firm will be different based upon its founding year. Our dataset consists of 562 firm-year observations.

As causal inference is facilitated by the temporal precedence of the independent variables to the dependent variables, we lead the dependent variables by one year (Finkel, 1995; Katila and Ahuja, 2002). As such, we assume that TMT and outside board human capital depth and breadth will only have an impact on innovation speed in the following year, thereby limiting potential endogeneity issues (Brav, 2009). As our dependent variable is dichotomous, we used a Cox proportional hazard model to assess which TMT and outside board variables affect innovation speed. Cox proportional hazard models are frequently used for event history analysis. In our analyses, the event takes into account the occurrence of a product introduction while estimating the effect of other variables. The cases are however right censored, as some firms may not have a product by the end of the observation period. The dependent variable then becomes the waiting time before the event takes place, thus the time it takes to ship a first product for revenues. Therefore, the hazard ratios are reported in Table 6.2. A hazard ratio greater than 1 implies that the variable reduces the waiting time until the event, while a hazard ratio lower than 1 points to an increase in the waiting time.

Table 6.2   Results of the Cox proportional hazard model

	Innovation speed	
	Base model	Full model
Control variables		
Firm age (ln)	–	–
	(–)	(–)
Firm independence	1.05	0.80
	(0.30)	(0.22)
ICT industry	1.09	1.14
	(0.23)	(0.21)
Health & life sciences industry	0.08**	0.11**
	(0.07)	(0.08)
VC ownership	0.59*	0.46**
	(0.16)	(0.13)
TMT tenure	1.02	0.98
	(0.04)	(0.04)
TMT R&D experience	1.00	0.99
	(0.01)	(0.01)
Outside board tenure	1.02	0.99
	(0.03)	(0.03)
Outside board R&D experience	1.02	1.01
	(0.01)	(0.01)
Frequency of board meetings	0.97	0.99
	(0.03)	(0.03)
CEO duality	1.39	1.32
	(0.26)	(0.24)
Independent variables		
TMT marketing and sales experience		1.03*
		(0.01)
Outside board marketing and sales experience		1.02*
		(0.01)
TMT diversity		1.32
		(0.28)
Outside board diversity		2.17***
		(0.48)
No. of observations	254	254
No. of groups	80	80
Chi²	38.85***	82.91***

Notes:
*** $p < 0.001$, ** $p < 0.01$, * $p < 0.05$.
Hazard ratios of the Cox proportional hazard models are displayed.

RESULTS

Table 6.2 shows the results. The base model includes only the control variables and provides a number of interesting insights. First, firms in the health and life sciences industry tend to have longer waiting times to first product, which is in line with the literature as companies in this sector typically have a longer product development phase (Rothaermel and Deeds, 2004). Further, also VC-backed early-stage high-tech firms are likely to have a longer waiting time to first product compared to non-VC-backed ones.

Adding the independent variables to the base model led to significant improvements, as can be seen in the full model. We first assess the impact of specific marketing and sales experience on innovation speed. The impact of TMT marketing and sales experience on innovation speed is significantly positive, just as the impact of outside board marketing and sales experience on innovation speed. As such, we find support for H1a and H1b. Second, we evaluate the impact of diversity on innovation speed. We find that higher levels of TMT and outside board diversity positively affect innovation speed, while the results are statistically significant only for outside board diversity. Consequently, we do not find support for H2a and find support for H2b.

Post Hoc Analysis and Robustness Checks

We conducted post hoc analyses to assess the robustness of our results and to provide more fine-grained insights into the impact of TMT and outside board human capital on innovation speed. First, it has been suggested that functional diversity may be beneficial only up to a certain point, after which further diversity has a marginally negative effect (Johnson et al., 2013). As such, we tested for the existence of curvilinearity. Our analysis however does not provide support for such curvilinear effect. It is unclear whether this is due to the relatively limited age of firms in our sample or whether this is due to the non-existence of such relationship. Further research into this issue may be warranted.

Finally, if TMT and outside board members can be considered part of the extended TMT (Vanaelst et al., 2006), it can be expected that marketing and sales experience and diversity of this extended TMT will positively affect innovation speed. In order to test for this assertion, we removed the TMT and outside board human capital variables from the analysis, and included the extended TMT human capital. Our results show that the extended TMT marketing and sales experience as well as the extended TMT functional diversity positively affect innovation speed. This emphasizes that it is useful to consider human capital characteristics in a broader way than merely the TMT human capital, and that TMTs may beneficially source complementary human capital from external sources.

DISCUSSION AND IMPLICATIONS

This chapter aimed at understanding how the extended TMT human capital affects innovation speed in early-stage high-tech firms. Both the TMT and the outside board are part of the extended TMT as these are not standalone entities in an early-stage high-tech context (Nielsen, 2010). We build on human capital theory in order to assess the impact of TMT and outside board human capital on innovation speed, measured as the time it takes to ship a first product for revenues (Schoonhoven et al., 1990). We hypothesized that innovation speed will benefit from higher levels of both marketing and sales experience and diversity in the TMT as well as in the outside board.

In general, following our post hoc analyses, we find that both the extended TMT marketing and sales experience and extended TMT diversity positively affect innovation speed. Thus, it is essential for the often technical TMT to complement its human capital by adding the necessary skills and experience to either the TMT or the outside board. This is an interesting finding as TMTs in early-stage high-tech firms often try to complement the founding team by new team members, but in doing so frequently select team members from their own network (Ensley and Hmieleski, 2005). However, even when such selection of new team members results in human capital gaps, these can be neutralized by adding complementary profiles to the outside board. Our main analyses, differentiating between the (limited) TMT and the outside board, provide more insights into which human capital is beneficial at which level. Specifically, we find that it is beneficial to have sufficient levels of marketing and sales experience available within the TMT or the outside board. Further, innovation speed can then be strengthened by composing the outside board in a diverse way, comprising many different profiles. As such, our findings are in line with Knockaert et al.'s (2011) assertion that the (limited) TMT requires both technical and commercial human capital. It further shows that diversity is advantageous to innovation speed, but especially at the level of the outside board. More diverse outside boards bring the heterogeneous human capital needed to introduce a product into the market (Schoonhoven et al., 1990) and are likely to have more diverse perspectives leading to improved decision-making and innovative product introductions (Shrader and Siegel, 2007).

Our research has implications for academic research and practice. First, the study presented in this chapter makes a number of contributions to the corporate governance and entrepreneurship literatures. Specifically, by studying the relationship between extended TMT human capital and innovation speed in early-stage high-tech ventures, we focus on an under-studied type of firm. A focus on these ventures is warranted, given the particular difficulties they are faced with and their expected large contribution to economic development. Furthermore, traditional corporate governance studies have typically taken an agency perspective, hereby largely focusing on the composition and functioning of boards in large firms. Given the importance of the service role which outside board members in early-stage high-tech firms fulfill, we introduce a human capital perspective which is more relevant in this context. Additionally, this chapter complements the entrepreneurship literature, which has largely focused on studying the relationship between TMT characteristics and firm performance, but has so far focused on the limited TMT, without integrating outside board members bringing valuable input to the TMT. As such, we offer a potential explanation for previous research finding contradictory results on the relationship between TMT composition and firm performance, and respond to a call by Machold et al. (2011) who recommend studying TMTs and outside boards together.

Second, this chapter has some implications for practice. It can provide further indications to entrepreneurial founders on how entrepreneurial teams should ideally be composed. Specifically, it shows the need to integrate marketing and sales experience within the TMT. However, while other types of experience such as manufacturing and financial human capital may be beneficial, this type of human capital can be sourced externally, for instance by composing the outside board in a diverse way. These insights might further be interesting to policy-makers who have recently, especially in Europe, established schemes and policy measures stimulating new ventures to attract outside board members (Conyon et al., 2001).

LIMITATIONS AND DIRECTIONS FOR FUTURE RESEARCH

While our study is one of the first to shed light on how the extended TMT human capital can affect early-stage high-tech innovation speed, it has a number of limitations which lead to further research directions. First, this chapter focuses on a sample of companies located in one specific country, namely Belgium. Although this enabled us to select all early-stage high-tech firms belonging to our sample and to collect highly valuable data through face-to-face interviews, it may be more difficult to generalize our results to other (non-European) regions, where regulations and traditions related to board composition may be different from the Belgian situation. Therefore, future studies could analyze the extent to which our findings hold in other contexts. Second, this chapter concentrates on innovation speed as an important performance indicator for early-stage high-tech firms. While innovation speed is a key performance measure for these firms, future research could investigate the impact of extended TMT human capital on other performance indicators, such as patent activity or multiple product introductions (Hagedoorn and Cloodt, 2003; Vandenbroucke et al., 2016). Finally, while we found outside board human capital to contribute significantly to innovation speed, our findings provide little insight into the mechanisms and processes through which outside board members employ this human capital. Future research could use observational or qualitative designs to study under which conditions (for example, formality and openness of board meetings, chair leadership style, trust in the boardroom) and through which mechanisms (for example, CEO duality) the TMT can optimally benefit from the outside board's human capital. Finally, other types of diversity (for example, demographical diversity, diversity in terms of the interest groups outside board members represent) and other types of outside board capital (for example, outside board social capital), and their impact on innovation speed could be investigated.

REFERENCES

Aldrich, H.E. and Auster, E.R. (1986), 'Even dwarfs started small: liabilities of age and size and their strategic implications', *Research in Organizational Behavior*, **8**, 165–198.

Allen & Overy (2012), *Corporate Governance Comparative Study*, Brussels.

Amason, A.C. (1996), 'Distinguishing the effects of functional and dysfunctional conflict on strategic decision making: resolving a paradox for top management teams', *Academy of Management Journal*, **39** (1), 123–148.

Ancona, D.G. and Caldwell, D.F. (1990), 'Improving the performance of new product teams', *Research Technology Management*, **33** (2), 25–29.

Bantel, K.A. and Jackson, S.E. (1989), 'Top management and innovations in banking – does the composition of the top team make a difference?', *Strategic Management Journal*, **10**, 107–124.

Baum, J.A.C. and Silverman, B.S. (2004), 'Picking winners or building them? Alliance, intellectual, and human capital as selection criteria in venture financing and performance of biotechnology startups', *Journal of Business Venturing*, **19** (3), 411–436.

Becker, G.S. (1975), *Human Capital: A Theoretical and Empirical Analysis, with Special Reference to Education*, 2nd edn, New York: National Bureau of Economic Research / Columbia University Press.

Bjornali, E.S. and Gulbrandsen, M. (2010), 'Exploring board formation and evolution of board composition in academic spin-offs', *Journal of Technology Transfer*, **35** (1), 92–112.

Brav, O. (2009), 'Access to capital, capital structure, and the funding of the firm', *Journal of Finance*, **64** (1), 263–308.

Bruderl, J. and Preisendorfer, P. (2000), 'Fast-growing businesses: empirical evidence from a German study', *International Journal of Sociology*, **30** (3), 45–70.

Bruderl, J., Preisendorfer, P. and Ziegler, R. (1992), 'Survival chances of newly founded business organizations', *American Sociological Review*, **57** (2), 227–242.

Burgel, O., Fier, A. and Licht, G. (2004), *Internationalisation of Young High-Tech Firms: An Empirical Analysis in Germany and the United Kingdom*, Heidelberg: Physica-Verlag.

Burgel, O. and Murray, G.C. (2000), 'The international market entry choices of start-up companies in high-technology industries', *Journal of International Marketing*, **8** (2), 33–62.

Burkart, E.E. (1994), 'Reducing R&D cycle time', *Research Technology Management*, **37**, (3), 27–31.

Butchart, R.L. (1987), 'A new UK definition of the high technology industries', *Economic Trends 400*, 82–88.

Canter, U., Goethner, M. and Stuetzer, M. (2010), 'Disentangling the effects of new venture team functional heterogeneity on new venture performance', Working paper no. 2010-029, Jena Economic Research Papers.

Carter, N.M., Stearns, T.M., Reynolds, P.D. and Miller, B.A. (1994), 'New venture strategies: theory development with an empirical base', *Strategic Management Journal*, **15**, 21–41.

Casson, M. (1995), *Entrepreneurship and Business Culture*, Aldershot, UK and Brookfield, VT, USA: Edward Elgar Publishing.

Certo, S.T., Daily, C.M. and Dalton, D.R. (2001), 'Signaling firm value through board structure: an investigation of initial public offerings', *Entrepreneurship Theory and Practice*, **26** (2), 33–50.

Chen, H-L. (2013), 'CEO tenure and R&D investment: the moderating effect of board capital', *Journal of Applied Behavioral Science*, **49** (4), 437–459.

Choi, Y.R. and Shepherd, D.A. (2005), 'Stakeholder perceptions of age and other dimensions of newness', *Journal of Management*, **31**(4), 573–596.

Clarysse, B., Knockaert, M. and Lockett, A. (2007), 'Outside board members in high tech start-ups', *Small Business Economics*, **29** (3), 243–259.

Colombo, M.G. and Grilli, L. (2010), 'On growth drivers of high-tech start-ups: exploring the role of founders' human capital and venture capital', *Journal of Business Venturing*, **25** (6), 610–626.

Conyon, M., Peck, S. and Read, L. (2001), 'Performance pay and corporate structure in UK firms', *European Management Journal*, **19** (1), 73–82.

Cooper, A.C., Gimeno-Gascon, F.J. and Woo, C.Y. (1994), 'Initial human and financial capital as predictors of new venture performance', *Journal of Business Venturing*, **9**, 371–395

Crook, T.R., Todd, S.Y., Combs, J.G., Woehr, D.J. and Ketchen, D.J. (2011), 'Does human capital matter? A meta-analysis of the relationship between human capital and firm performance', *Journal of Applied Psychology*, **96**, 443–456.

Delmar, F. and Shane, S. (2002), 'Legitimating first: organizing activities and the survival of new ventures', *Journal of Business Venturing*, **19** (3), 385–410.

Demb, A. and Neubauer, F.F. (1992), *The Corporate Board*, Oxford: Oxford University Press.

Deutsch, Y. and Ross, T.W. (2003), 'You are known by the directors you keep: reputable directors as a signaling mechanism for young firms', *Management Science*, **49** (8), 1003–1017.

Dimov, D.P. and Shepherd, D.A. (2005), 'Human capital theory and venture capital firms: exploring "home runs" and "strike outs"', *Journal of Business Venturing*, **20** (1), 1–21.

EC (2011), *Innovation Union Competetiveness Report*, European Union.

Eisenhardt, K. (1988), 'Agency- and institutional-theory explanations: the case of retail sales compensation', *Academy of Management Journal*, **31**, 488–511.

Eisenhardt, K. and Martin, L. (2000), 'Dynamic capabilities: what are they?', *Strategic Management Journal*, **21** (10–11), 1105–1121.

Eisenhardt, K. and Schoonhoven, C.B. (1990), 'Organizational growth – linking founding team, strategy, environment, and growth among United States semiconductor ventures', *Administrative Science Quarterly*, **35** (3), 504–529.

Ensley, M. and Hmieleski, K. (2005), 'A comparative study of new venture top management team composition, dynamics and performance between university-based and independent start-ups', *Research Policy*, **34**, 1091–1105.

Fackler, D., Schnabel, C. and Wagner, J. (2013), 'Establishment exits in Germany: the role of size and age', *Small Business Economics*, **41** (3), 683–700.

Fiegener, M.K. (2005), 'Determinants of board participation in the strategic decisions of small corporations', *Entrepreneurship Theory and Practice*, **29** (5), 627–650.

Finkel, S.E. (1995), *Causal Analysis with Panel Data*, Thousand Oaks, CA: Sage Publications.

Flynn, B.B. (1993), 'The role of quality management and organizational infrastructure in fast cycle/time-driven innovation', Center of Innovation Management Studies, Lehigh University, Bethlehem, PA.

Franklin, S., Wright, M. and Lockett, A. (2001), 'Academic and surrogate entrepreneurs in university spin-out companies', *Journal of Technology Transfer*, **26** (1–2), 127–141.

Gabrielsson, J. (2007), 'Correlates of board empowerment in small companies', *Entrepreneurship, Theory and Practice*, **31** (5), 687–711.

Gabrielsson, J. and Politis, D. (2012), 'Work experience and the generation of new business ideas among entrepreneurs: an integrated learning framework', *International Journal of Entrepreneurial Behaviour and Research*, **18** (1), 48–74.

Gomory, R.E. (1989), 'From the ladder of science to the product development cycle', *Harvard Business Review*, **67** (6), 99–105.

Gompers, P. and Lerner, J. (2001), 'The venture capital revolution', *Journal of Economic Perspectives*, **15** (2), 145–168.

Grant, R.M. (1996), 'Toward a knowledge-based theory of the firm', *Strategic Management Journal*, **17**, 109–122.

Hagedoorn, J. and Cloodt, M. (2003), 'Measuring innovative performance: is there an advantage in using multiple indicators?', *Research Policy*, **32** (8), 1365–1379.

Henderson, A.D. (1999), 'Firm strategy and age dependence: a contingent view of the liabilities of newness, adolescence, and obsolescene', *Administrative Science Quarterly*, **44** (2), 281–314.

Hillman, A.J. and Dalziel, T. (2003), 'Boards of directors and firm performance: integrating agency and resource dependence perspectives', *Academy of Management Review*, **28** (3), 383–396.

Hitt, M.A., Bierman, L. and Shimizu, K. (2001), 'Direct and moderating effects of human capital on strategy and performance in professional service firms: a resource-based perspective', *Academy of Management Journal*, **44** (1), 13–28.

Holder, R.J. (1992), 'Time in the new workplace', *Journal for Quality and Participation*, **15** (6), 30–38.

Ittner, C. and Larcker, D. (1997), 'Product development cycle time and organizational performance', *Journal of Marketing Research*, **34**, 13–23.

Jarillo, J.C. (1989), 'Entrepreneurship and growth: the strategic use of external resources', *Journal of Business Venturing*, **4** (2), 133–147.

Johnson, S.G., Schnatterly, K. and Hill, A.D. (2013), 'Board composition beyond independence: social capital, human capital, and demographics', *Journal of Management*, **39** (1), 232–262.

Katila, R. and Ahuja, G. (2002), 'Something old, something new: a longitudinal study of search behavior and new product introduction', *Academy of Management Journal*, **45** (6), 1183–1194.

Kessler, E.H. and Chakrabarti, A.K. (1996), 'Innovation speed: a conceptual model of context, antecedents, and outcomes', *Academy of Management Review*, **21** (4), 1143–1191.

Klofsten, M. and Jones-Evans, D. (1996), 'Stimulation of technology-based small firms – a case study of university–industry cooperation', *Technovation*, **16** (4), 187–193.

Knockaert, M. and Ucbasaran, D. (2013), 'The service role of outside boards in high-tech start-ups: a resource dependency perspective', *British Journal of Management*, **24**, 69–84.

Knockaert, M., Ucbasaran, D., Wright, M. and Clarysse, B. (2011), 'The relationship between knowledge transfer, top management team composition, and performance: the case of science-based entrepreneurial firms', *Entrepreneurship Theory and Practice*, **35** (4), 777–803.

Kogut, B. and Zander, U. (1992), 'Knowledge of the firm, combinative capabilities, and the replication of technology', *Organization Science*, **3** (3), 383–397.

Kor, Y.Y. and Misangyi, V. (2008), 'Outside directors' industry-specific experience and firms' liability of newness', *Strategic Management Journal*, **29** (12), 1345–1355.

Kor, Y.Y. and Sundaramurthy, C. (2009), 'Experience-based human capital and social capital of outside directors', *Journal of Management*, **35** (4), 981–1006.

Leonard, D. and Sensiper, S. (1998), 'The role of tacit knowledge in group innovation', *California Management Review*, **40**, 112–132.

Link, A.N. and Siegel, D.S. (2007), *Innovation, Entrepreneurship, and Technological Change*, Oxford: Oxford University Press.

Lynall, M.D., Golden, B.R. and Hillman, A.J. (2003), 'Board composition from adolescence to maturity: a multitheoretic view', *Academy of Management Review*, **28** (3), 416–431.

Lynn, G.S., Skov, R.B. and Abel, K.D. (1999), 'Practices that support team learning and their impact on speed to market and new product success', *Journal of Product Innovation Management*, **16** (5), 439–454.

Machold, S., Huse, M., Minichilli, A. and Nordqvist, M. (2011), 'Board leadership and strategy involvement in small firms: a team production approach', *Corporate Governance – An International Review*, **19** (4), 368–383.

Markman, G.D., Gianiodis, P.T., Phan, P.H. and Balkin, D.B. (2005), 'Innovation speed: transferring university technology to market', *Research Policy*, **34**, 1058–1075.

Marvel, M.R. (2013), 'Human capital and search-based discovery: a study of high-tech entrepreneurship', *Entrepreneurship, Theory and Practice*, **37** (2), 403–419.

Marvel, M. and Lumpkin, G.T. (2007), 'Technology entrepreneurs' human capital and its effects on innovation radicalness', *Entrepreneurship Theory and Practice*, **31** (6), 807–828.

McGee, J.E. and Dowling, M.J. (1994), 'Using R&D cooperative arrangements to leverage managerial experience: a study of technology-intensive new ventures', *Journal of Business Venturing*, **9** (1), 33–48.

Mosey, S. and Wright, M. (2007), 'From human capital to social capital: a longitudinal study of technology-based academic entrepreneurs', *Entrepreneurship Theory and Practice*, **31** (6), 909–935.

Nielsen, S. (2010), 'Top management team internationalization and firm performance', *Management International Review*, **50** (2), 185–206.

Oakey, R. (1984), *High Technology Small Firms*, New York: St Martin's Press.

Parnes, H.S. (1984), *People Power*, Beverly Hills, CA: Sage Publications.

Pearce, J.A. and Zahra, S.A. (1991), 'The relative power of CEOs and board of directors – associations with corporate performance', *Strategic Management Journal*, **12** (2), 135–153.

Perez, P.M. and Sanchez, M.A. (2003), 'The development of university spin-offs: early dynamics of technology transfer and networking', *Technovation*, **23**, 823–831.

Pfeffer, J. and O'Reilly, C.A. (1987), 'Hospital demography and turnover among nurses', *Industrial Relations*, **26**, 158–173.

Rothaermel, F.T. and Deeds, D.L. (2004), 'Exploration and exploitation alliances in biotechnology: a system of new product development', *Strategic Management Journal*, **25**, 201–221.

Rutherford, M.A. and Buchholz, A.K. (2007), 'Investigating the relationship between board characteristics and board information', *Corporate Governance: An International Review*, **15** (4), 576–584.

Schoonhoven, C.B., Eisenhardt, K.M. and Lyman, K. (1990), 'Speeding products to market: waiting time to first product introduction in new firms', *Administrative Science Quarterly*, **35** (1), 177–207.

Shrader, R. and Siegel, D.S. (2007), 'Assessing the relationship between human capital and firm performance: evidence from technology-based new ventures', *Entrepreneurship Theory and Practice*, **31** (6), 893–908.

Shrader, R. and Simon, M. (1997), 'Corporate versus independent new ventures: resource, strategy, and performance differences', *Journal of Business Venturing*, **12** (1), 47–66.

Stinchcombe, A.L. (1965), 'Social structure and organization', in J.G. March (ed.), *Handbook of Organizations*, Chicago, IL: Rand McNally, pp. 142–193.

Stuart, R.W. and Abetti, P.A. (1990), 'Impact of entrepreneurial and management experience on early performance', *Journal of Business Venturing*, **5**, 151–162.

Teachman, J.D. (1980), 'Analysis of population diversity – measures of qualitative variation', *Sociological Methods and Research*, **8** (3), 341–362.

Tihanyi, L., Ellstrand, A.E., Daily, C.M. and Dalton, D.R. (2000), 'Composition of the top management team and firm international diversification', *Journal of Management*, **26** (6), 1157–1177.

Tsai, W.P. (2001), 'Knowledge transfer in intraorganizational networks: effects of network position and absorptive capacity on business unit innovation and performance', *Academy of Management Journal*, **44** (5), 996–1004.

Vafeas, N. (1999), 'Board meeting frequency and firm performance', *Journal of Financial Economics*, **53**, 113–142.

Vanaelst, I., Clarysse, B., Wright, M., Lockett, A., Moray, N. and S'Jegers, R. (2006), 'Entrepreneurial team development in academic spinouts: an examination of team heterogeneity', *Entrepreneurship Theory and Practice*, **30** (2), 249–271.

Vandenbroucke, E., Knockaert, M. and Ucbasaran, D. (2016), 'Outside board human capital and early stage high-tech firm performance', *Entrepreneurship Theory and Practice*, **40** (4), 759–779.

Venkataraman, S. (2004), 'Regional transformation through technological entrepreneurship', *Journal of Business Venturing*, **19**, 153–167.

Wheelwright, S.C. (1988), 'Product development and manufacturing start-up', in M. Tushman and W. Moore (eds), *Readings in the Management of Innovation*, 2nd edn, Cambridge, MA: Ballinger, pp. 444–453.

Wincent, J., Anokhin, S. and Örtqvist, D. (2010), 'Does network board capital matter? A study of innovative performance in strategic SME networks', *Journal of Business Research*, **63** (3), 265–275.

Zahra, S.A. and Bogner, W.C. (1999), 'Technology strategy and software new ventures' performance: exploring the moderating effect of the competitive environment', *Journal of Business Venturing*, **15**, 135–173.

Zahra, S. and Pearce, J. (1989), 'Boards of directors and corporate financial performance: a review and integrative model', *Journal of Management*, **15**, 291–334.

Zhang, H.J., Baden-Fuller, C. and Pool, J.K. (2011), 'Resolving the tensions between monitoring, resourcing and strategizing: structures and processes in high technology venture boards', *Long Range Planning*, **44**, 95–117.

7. The effects of private equity investors on the governance of companies
Stefano Bonini and Vincenzo Capizzi

INTRODUCTION

Companies that receive external equity typically experience a separation of ownership and control, where owners who are not involved in the company (principals) have to rely on the management team (agents) for achieving expected goals and target levels. Theoretical literature argues that when ownership and control are separated, principals develop governance structures to reduce agency costs and align agents' incentives (Berle and Means, 1932; Jensen and Meckling, 1976; Grossman and Hart, 1986; Zingales, 1995). Likewise, optimal financial structure design by financial intermediaries can effectively help to mitigate agency problems by identifying self-enforcing equilibria (Diamond, 1984; Fama and Jensen, 1985; Stiglitz, 1985; Bhattacharya and Thakor, 1993; Barry, 1994).

In general terms, governance and financial devices can be thought of as either internal control mechanisms (such as the board) or external control mechanisms (such as the market for corporate control). An increasingly important external control mechanism affecting the governance of young and fast-growing companies worldwide is the emergence of institutional and private equity investors, as equity owners. Institutional investors have the potential to influence management's activities directly through their ownership, and indirectly by trading their shares (Gillan and Starks, 2003). In this respect private equity investors are differentiated from institutional ones in the longer-term view and in the significantly more hands-on approach that they pursue when investing in a portfolio company. As a result, companies backed by private equity investors represent a fruitful environment to investigate the use and efficiency of a multitude of control mechanisms.

The surge over the last 30 years in investment activity by private equity investors at large has given rise to an increased specialization of this class of investors conditional on the risk return profiles associated with different investment and firm life cycle stages. For instance, business angels supporting the archetypical 'paper company' start-up face a risk exposure that in terms of both magnitude and characteristics is significantly different from that incurred by a private equity investor acquiring control of a mature company. Yet, investors in this market share common traits such as a value maximization approach, risk–return informed decisions, and a deep knowledge of governance mechanisms. As such their influence on portfolio company governance mechanisms is largely similar in terms of depth and breadth. In this chapter we aim at presenting an up-to-date review of the main theoretical contributions and empirical results in this active and growing field of research.

PRIVATE EQUITY INVESTORS: STAGE FOCUS AND INVOLVEMENT IN CORPORATE GOVERNANCE

A broad definition of private equity is the provision of capital by financial investors to high-growth, private companies (see the National Venture Capital Association, NVCA, and European Venture Capital Association, EVCA, guidelines). A more accurate definition identifies investors as either venture capital or, strictly speaking, private equity investors according to the stage of development of the target firm. In particular, formal venture capital (VC) is the provision of capital to young ventures in need of resources to start up, develop or expand a business by a professional investor. Formal venture capital, as part of the larger private equity model, is characterized by the separation of fund provisioning (largely restricted to the so-called 'limited partners') and the management of capital, normally mandated to a group of professional investors organized as a management company. However, as Bygrave et al. (2003) show, the overwhelming majority of capital provided by non-family members to young, high-growth companies is provided by so-called 'informal venture capital' sources, mainly through investors known as 'business angels'. Crucially, business angels provide funding out of their own endowments rather than through external fundraising. A question still hotly debated in the literature is whether business angels (BAs) and venture capitalists are to be looked at as complements or substitutes. The general consensus seem to point at business angels, both as individuals and as organized groups of individuals (known as business angels groups), as precursors of proper venture capital investors, in that they target essentially only newborn firms in the seed phase of development and they adopt very similar valuation models, monitoring structures and exit strategies. However a few recent contributions (most notably Hellmann et al., 2015) provide preliminary evidence of increased competition between these two classes of early-stage investors, making them 'dynamic complements'. We reckon that this is an area of fruitful research that, through the availability of more granular data on the financing sequencing of start-ups, will help to answer this pressing question.

Differently from formal or informal VC, strictly defined private equity is referred to as a later-stage type of organized investment that usually provides capital to support the buyout, further expansion or turnaround of an established company (EVCA, 2006). As such, PE investors target fast-growing companies that have unexploited potential that investors can unleash through the so-called 'operational re-engineering' and/or appropriate financial structuring.

A crucial characteristic of all these three forms of professional investors is the finite life of their holding periods: the main purpose of the investment is in fact to maximize the return on capital and sell the company to a later-stage investor or a private entity, or to the market through the listing of shares. This feature generates an endogenous incentive to exert strict control on the portfolio company through a variety of mechanisms, among which corporate governance control mechanisms are of the utmost importance. In fact, while sound governance may not necessarily lead to strong performance, there is an implicit understanding among the vast majority of investors that poorly governed companies are more prone to failure. Hence, there is a strong element of self-interest for private equity managers to ensure that their funds are invested only in well-governed companies or in companies that are willing and able to improve their governance, and to avoid investing in poorly governed companies that demonstrate no inclination to improve their governance.

Despite these common objectives, the different stages of development of the target firms and the different risk–return profiles of the investment generate significantly different approaches in the implementation of control and monitoring procedures and, ultimately, in shaping the corporate governance of portfolio companies. In the following we present evidence on the impact of business angels, venture capitalists and later-stage private equity investors on the governance of portfolio companies.

INFORMAL VENTURE CAPITAL AND CORPORATE GOVERNANCE

The market for informal venture capital includes various typologies of investors, among which the most important are business angels, who are private investors providing finance to small and newly established companies with their own private savings by underwriting equity capital

(Sørheim and Landström, 2001). Differently from formal venture capitalist, it is often noted (e.g. Shane, 2008) that BAs' objective function is two-sided: on one hand they share with formal VC a value-maximization goal. On the other, though, there seems to be a significant component driving BA investment decisions provided by non-monetary benefits associated with prestige, visibility and involvement in successful ventures. As several authors note (Haines et al., 2003; Morrisette, 2007; Ibrahim, 2008; Hsu et al., 2014), there seem to be a strong component of personal reward motivating business angels, such as playing an entrepreneurial role, mentoring highly talented and creative people, discovering new technologies, and interacting with other angels and players. In this respect, the contribution they provide to financed firms is at least as much related to knowledge, advice, mentoring and personal networks as to capital injection (Harrison and Mason, 1992; Landström, 1993; Politis, 2008).

From a research perspective BAs and venture capitalists have intuitive similarities and interesting differences. Crucially, both venture capitalists and BAs share a common approach to capital provision through direct equity underwriting which allows for the extension to BAs of much of the empirical evidence on the process and structure of venture capital investing. However, business angels differ deeply from formal venture capitalists in several respects. Firstly and probably most importantly, business angels invest their own capital and not funds committed by third parties through a closed-end fund vehicle (Freear et al., 1992; Coveney and Moore, 1998). This characteristic generates a higher risk exposure on the investor side and, arguably, a greater involvement in the investment selection and monitoring process. Secondly, business angels' available funds are generally rather limited when compared to the average size of assets under management by venture capital firms. This generates an almost mechanical focus on smaller and younger companies with a steep growth potential. This evidence largely holds true despite a trend observed in recent years among business angels of syndicating investment to finance larger and more 'developed' projects (Harrison and Mason, 2000; Sohl and Hill, 2007). Thirdly, they have no or limited diversification strategies, nor do they commit themselves simultaneously to multiple investments, having as a major risk management technique the small proportion of invested capital over their total personal assets, which by construction should limit the impact of a negative performance on their net worth (Freear et al., 1992; Harrison and Mason, 1996; Van Osnabrugge, 2000; Johnson and Sohl, 2012; Capizzi, 2015). These differences suggest the existence of a complementarity, rather than a competition, between BAs and venture capitalists. According to data compiled by the United States (US) Angel Capital Association and reported in Table 7.1, there

Table 7.1   VC and BA investment activity

	Angel Investors	Venture Capital
Invested capital	$24.8 bn	$29.6 bn
Number of investors	298 000	548
Total deals	71 000	4050
Seed	32 000	120
Early stage	29 000	1375
Expansion	9200	2550

Note: This table provides summary statistics on the investment activity in start-up companies. Figures are for the fiscal year 2013 obtained by the National Venture Capital Association and the Angel Capital Association.

Source: Table compiled by the authors on US ACA data.

is striking evidence of similar capital contributions by angels and formal VC investors. However, business angels invest in about 16 times more companies than are financed by formal VC, and disproportionately in the seed and early-stage phase.

Given this evidence, it is not surprising that since the 1990s informal venture capitalists have tried to increase the quality of their operations by gathering in semi-formal associations or groups of angels, usually on a territorial or industrial basis, sharing presentation pitches from potential entrepreneurs, due diligence over the potential investment opportunities, transaction costs and investment deals to be implemented by syndicates of group members (Mason, 2006; Sohl, 2007; Paul and Whittam, 2010; Kerr et al., 2014a). These associations, called business angel networks (BANs), angel investment organizations (AIOs) or angel groups, have grown to regional levels (for example, Tech Coast Angels in southern California or CommonAngels in Massachusetts), national levels (for example, ACA in the US, BBAA in the United Kingdom, IBAN in Italy) and super-national levels (for example, EBAN in Europe).

This evidence notwithstanding, research on business angels and their impact on portfolio companies is still limited by significant data availability issues and is therefore mainly qualitative and largely incomplete. Yet, preliminary results seem suggestive of a different set of objectives and techniques than those observed in VC contracts (Landström, 2007). Venture capitalists typically address the problem of opportunistic behavior of entrepreneurs – arising from uncertainty, information asymmetries and agency costs faced by the outside equity investors – by:

1. Pooling the risks coming from many investments through a portfolio diversification approach.
2. Sharing the risks with other investors through a syndication approach.
3. Designing investment contracts aimed at aligning inside and outside investors' incentives. Such an alignment is obtained through a deal-specific combination of five different mechanisms:
   a. Staged financing, a funding mechanism conditioning the follow-on investments to some pre-specified performance milestones to be reached over a given time period.
   b. Dual class shares, aimed at providing a priority status to outside equity investors in case of payout policies and in case of a company sale, bankruptcy or liquidation.
   c. Board seats, allowing the VCs to exert control over the company.
   d. Negative covenants (or veto rights), which are specific contractual clauses aimed at preventing the target companies from implementing predetermined actions, operations or investments which could increase the equity risk for already existing outside investors.
   e. Exit rights, including, but not limited to, redemption rights, 'tag and drag along' rights, demand registration rights, conversion rights.

Whether any of these techniques is actually adopted by business angels remains an opaque issue. Wong et al. (2009), in their seminal study, provide evidence on business angels' contract design, looking at a sample of 215 angel investment rounds in 143 companies from across the United States during the period 1994–2001. Their results show that angels are not given the traditional control rights that venture capitalists typically use. Rather, one of the primary mechanisms to control agency costs is the alignment of the entrepreneur's interests with those of the firm through the large ownership positions. Additionally, angels make smaller investments and increase syndication when investing in the riskier ventures. Wong et al. (2009) provide a tentative answer to the puzzling question as to why angels provide capital in highly uncertain operations without much formal protection from expropriation. In particular, Wong et al. (2009) argue that a proximity effect plays a role: angels tend to invest in ventures located very closely to their home base. Therefore they can engage in direct monitoring and indirect network monitoring in a spirit similar to Sorenson and Stuart (2001). This effect is reinforced by business angels who generally invest in ventures operating in businesses which the investor is extremely familiar with due to prior or current experience.

BAs invest in the very first stages of the firm life where the issues of uncertainty, information asymmetries and agency costs are the highest. Yet, Ibrahim's (2008) evidence provides additional support to Wong et al.'s (2009) results showing that their typical investment contracts very seldom show the adoption of the standard VC control and governance provisions. As Ibrahim puts it, '[BA contracts] are surprisingly non aggressive and striking in their informality', with a puzzling lack of contractual protection.

Ibrahim proposes three major arguments to explain these observed differences. First, angel investors anticipate that as the company grows and increases the unit size of its operating investments, it will become eligible for a follow-up financing round by a formal venture capital fund. In such a case, a formal VC investor, as illustrated above, would inevitably require appropriate control and governance tools that would make a prior contract design by a business angel either too binding (thereby potentially unraveling the deal) or simply of limited use and therefore a loss-making investment, as suggested also by Gompers and Lerner (2006) in the VC context. This implies that 'the start-up's need for further funding from venture capitalists sets de facto limits on the terms of the angel investment contract' (Ibrahim, 2008).

Second, Ibrahim (2008) suggests that some informal substitutes for contractual monitoring are available to business angels. In particular, aligned with Wong et al.'s (2009) networking conjecture, Ibrahim (2008) shows that angel investors tend to join start-ups either operating in industries they know because of their past personal experience, or controlled by entrepreneurs they are familiar with. Finally, as previously noted by Wong et al. (2009), BAs invest in start-ups geographically close to the BA's location, thus building trust, and offering mentoring and leverage on the BA network.

Elaborating on the network argument, Ibrahim (2008) also introduces the evolving trend in angel financing toward structured or semi-structured angel investment organizations (AIOs). These networks provide angels with a valuable set of opportunities at reduced costs, including a constant stream of deal flow, joint valuation, due diligence and legal advisory services, training courses, interaction with other investors and the chance to participate in larger deals through the syndication mechanism. However, the more investors organize as semi-formal venture capital investment companies, the less AIO angels can leverage on informal substitutes for monitoring. As a consequence, the progressive institutionalization and formalization of angel investing may lead to an increase in the use of structured contractual mechanisms to minimize information asymmetries and agency costs.

In a recent contribution on this topic, Kerr et al. (2014a) investigate whether and how entrepreneurial financiers affect the success and growth of new ventures. Despite not providing specific evidence on the effects on governance practices of target companies, Kerr et al. (2014a) show that angel groups exhibit much more structured investment selection processes and that the level of favorable review of the investment proposal, initial presentation and due diligence at the group rather than individual level is strongly predictive of investment success. Kerr et al. (2014a) additionally show that receiving financing from a group, as opposed to a single angel investor, is associated with improved likelihood of survival for four or more years, higher levels of employment and more visibility in the market. However, Kerr et al. (2014a) also show that with regard to the role of angel funding in facilitating access to future formal venture capital financing, the evidence is mixed: on one hand, strongly positive prospects are significantly more likely to receive follow-on financing rounds. On the other hand, however, the evidence quickly decreases for less positively evaluated projects that still received angel group financing.

Chua and Wu (2012) provide explicit, valuable evidence of the effects of post-investment involvement (PII) of BAs in invested companies. Their research design looks at both the characteristics of PII and the effects on performance. Chua and Wu's (2012) empirical analysis builds on a new survey-based dataset provided by the Kauffmann Foundation of 539 BAs, affiliated to 86 BANs in North America that recorded 1137 exits from their angel investments. The results show that PII has a significant positive effect on the returns (internal rate of return, IRR) earned by angels on their venture investments. However, such returns seem to be more significantly associated to mentoring and value-adding activities, rather than 'standard' monitoring activities such as serving on the board, designing the strategy and providing additional financing rounds (similarly to Kerr et al., 2014b). These results are aligned with those documented by Capizzi (2015) on one of the first panel data large samples of angel investments.

VENTURE CAPITAL AND CORPORATE GOVERNANCE

Venture capital deals are primarily characterized by asymmetric information between entrepreneurs and financiers and almost exclusive capital infusion by outsiders. In such a context, Gorman and Sahlman (1989) and Sahlman (1990) first suggested that the value of VC lies not only in providing capital but also in superior selectivity by consistently picking high-growth firms, and most importantly in the provision of supplementary services such as entrepreneurial advice, hiring executives and shaping strategy, resulting in a valuable professionalization of portfolio companies. Following these seminal contributions, a large number of studies have investigated the mechanisms adopted by VCs to mitigate principal–agent conflicts, identifying three broad classes of control mechanisms:

intense pre-investment screening, the development of accurate financing contracts, and continuous post-investment monitoring and advice. Admati and Pfleiderer (1994), Lerner (1994) and Hochberg et al. (2004) shed light on pre-investment screening and syndication. Sahlman (1990), Berglof (1994), Gompers (1995) and Bergmann and Hege (1998) provide extensive evidence on the increasing level of complexity in the design of VC financing contracts through the introduction of staging, monitoring, governance and exit rules. Cumming (2005) supports this evidence by showing that agency problems can be explicitly addressed by appropriate security design and that the degree of contractual sophistication changes over time due to learning effects. A stream of research has given specific attention to the valuable activities performed by venture capitalists beyond their financing function. In particular, value-added tasks of venture capitalists include helping firms to shape strategies, and providing technical and commercial advice (Bygrave and Timmons, 1992; Hellmann, 1998; Hellmann and Puri, 2002; Baker and Gompers, 2003; Cornelli and Yosha, 2003). These contributions paved the way to answering a second set of questions, that is, the extent of VC influence on the governance of firms, the channels through which these effects are transmitted to portfolio companies, and the ultimate effects on corporate performance.

The Extent of VC Influence on the Governance of Firms

Fama and Jensen (1983) and Williamson (1983) first conjectured that the composition of the board should be shaped by the need for oversight. Lerner (1995) tests this intuition in the VC industry by looking at board representation of portfolio companies. Assuming that venture capitalists are significant providers of managerial oversight, their representation on boards should be larger when there is a greater need for oversight. His findings show that venture capitalists are more likely to join or be added to the boards of private companies in periods when the chief executive officer (CEO) of the company changes. Baker and Gompers (1999) focus on board composition at initial public offerings (IPOs). They argue that the optimal choice for board structure is made at the time of the IPO, since existing shareholders bear the cost of suboptimal governance. Using data from 1116 IPO prospectuses, they describe board size and composition for a set of firms with a median age of less than six years and a median equity capitalization of $42 million. According to their analysis, the number of insiders is 27 percent smaller in VC-backed firms, and the number of instrumental directors is 20 percent smaller. Kroszner and Strahan (2001), using banks' board representation, obtain similar results. Hellmann and Puri (2002) provide additional insights on a set of governance actions in a hand-collected survey sample of 149 start-ups in Silicon Valley. The authors show that venture capitalists are influential not only at the top of the organization, in terms of replacing the original founders with an outside CEO as in Lerner (1995), but also in developments further down the organization. Differently from previous studies, Kaplan and Stromberg (2000, 2003, 2004) document direct evidence on venture capitalist actions and monitoring. Analyzing investment decisions on portfolio companies at the time of the initial investment, they find that while in 14 percent of the investments the venture capitalists play an active role in advising the management, they trade off this activity with the costs of devoting excessive attention to a single venture.

Hochberg (2004) compares governance in VC-backed and non-VC-backed IPO firms using a unique database assembled by supplementing data from four publicly available databases with additional information gathered from two hand-collected datasets. Results show that VC backing reduces the level of earnings management in the firm (as proxied for by discretionary accruals); furthermore, VC-backed firms are more likely to follow 'conservative' rather than 'aggressive'[1] accounting practices than non-VC-backed firms. Additionally, VC-backed firms experience higher abnormal returns than non-VC-backed firms upon the announcement of the adoption of a shareholder rights agreement, and have more independent board structures at the time of the IPO. In a similar set-up, Suchard (2009) explores the effect of VC backing on the size and composition of the board of directors of investees at the time of the IPO, showing that venture capitalists are influential in determining the number of board members and in appointing independent directors with substantial industry-related skills. Cumming (2008) addresses the issue of the governance of VC-backed companies conditional on the legal and economic framework. The results, although focused on a broad set of corporate variables relating to governance style by VC investors, offer a first hint at the existence of profound differences in the governance choices by VC investors conditional on their geographical origins.

The Transmission Channels of the VC Influence on the Governance of Firms

These contributions confirm the intuition that venture capitalists do affect the governance of their portfolio companies by intense monitoring, providing advice, shaping strategies and accelerating companies' growth. The existence of causal links calls for understanding the transmission channels through which venture capitalists exert their influence on the governance of their firms.

Several contributions have identified the investment size as a relevant factor in the selection and management process of VC-backed companies. Kanniainen and Keuschnigg (2003, 2004) and Bernile et al. (2007) show that since the size of a VC management company cannot be easily scaled to the number of ventures in its portfolio, the screening, monitoring and advice activity of that management company is upper bounded. As a consequence, VC investors will optimize their available time and effort by carefully selecting the size of the portfolio (number of investments) to achieve optimal passive diversification, and the stake in each venture, in order to optimally allocate their monitoring (scarce) resources. The latter decision can be also interpreted as a diversification effect as venture capitalists will devote more resources to projects where they have larger interests, and accept more risks on projects where they have smaller stakes (Jääskeläinen et al., 2006). Bernile et al. (2007) test this empirical prediction on a survey-based sample of 42 VC-backed companies. Their results confirm the theoretical model, showing that VC investors jointly optimize the size of the portfolio and the relative weight of each invest-ment. Cumming (2006) addresses the portfolio size issue, showing that additional factors such as industry, stage, syndication and geographical region contribute to the portfolio size selection.

Bonini et al. (2012) provide a specific set of tests on the correlation between the amount of VC funding in a company and the venture capital-ist's influence on the governance practices. In particular, their main tests aim at identifying a causal relationship between the VC investment size and the effect on governance practices at the top of the company and across the whole organization. Looking at data from a novel hand-collected, questionnaire-based survey sample of 164 VC-backed companies in the US and Europe, they gather information on top-management and organ-ization-wide variables that they then relate to investment size and a set of control variables. All variables are operationalized as Likert-type items with values ranging from 1 to 4, where 1 indicates no VC influence, and 4 indicates high VC influence, with the exception of *CEO-replaced* which is a dichotomous item. Variables are modeled as follows:

- Top-management items: *CEO-replaced, CEO hiring (CEO), Executive compensation (EXE), Board decisions (BODD), Board appointments (BODA).*
- Organization-wide variables: *HR practices (HR), Employee incentives (INCENT), Strategy direction (STR), Investment planning (INV).*

Table 7.2 reports results for a set of univariate and multivariate OLS regressions.

Table 7.2 Linear regressions of VC influence on governance practices

	CEO	CEO	HR	HR	EXE	EXE	INCENT	INCENT	BODD	BODD	STR	STR	BODA	BODA	INV	INV
Intercept	1.92***	1.73***	1.72***	1.90***	2.73***	2.59***	2.08***	2.05***	3.08***	3.03***	3.01***	2.36***	2.83***	2.72***	2.85***	2.89***
	(0.27)	(0.49)	(0.17)	(0.36)	(0.18)	(0.28)	(0.19)	(0.33)	(0.20)	(0.32)	(0.18)	(0.29)	(0.18)	(0.30)	(0.18)	(0.34)
VC%	1.10**	1.23**	0.37	0.4	0.72***	0.72**	0.53**	0.58*	0.66**	0.56*	0.01	0.06	0.85***	0.77***	0.29	0.26
	(0.36)	(0.39)	(0.23)	(0.23)	(0.23)	(0.23)	(0.25)	(0.27)	(0.25)	(0.23)	(0.24)	(0.23)	(0.23)	(0.22)	(0.25)	(0.26)
#ofVCs		-0.01		0.04*		0.02		0.01		0.03		0.04+		0.02		0.01
		(0.04)		(0.02)		(0.02)		(0.02)		(0.02)		(0.02)		(0.02)		(0.02)
LnAGE		0.13		0.12		-0.01		0.00		-0.14		-0.09		-0.11		-0.04
		(0.16)		(0.11)		(0.09)		(0.11)		(0.10)		(0.10)		(0.09)		(0.12)
Ln#EE		0.06		-0.08		0.01		-0.03		0.01		0.15**		0.00		-0.04
		(0.09)		(0.07)		(0.06)		(0.06)		(0.06)		(0.05)		(0.06)		(0.06)
Computer		-0.03		-0.16		0.12		-0.12		0.22		-0.19		0.31*		0.18
		(0.25)		(0.15)		(0.17)		(0.17)		(0.15)		(0.15)		(0.14)		(0.17)
Medical		-0.11		-0.14		0.12		0.03		0.19		0.13		0.24+		0.21
		(0.25)		(0.18)		(0.14)		(0.17)		(0.16)		(0.16)		(0.14)		(0.17)
Expansion		-0.17		-0.34*		0.05		0.14		0.18		0.03		0.16		-0.07
		(0.26)		(0.18)		(0.17)		(0.18)		(0.17)		(0.18)		(0.17)		(0.18)
Later Stage		-0.87*		-0.59+		-0.41		-0.36		-0.01		-0.56*		0.02		-0.06
		(0.43)		(0.31)		(0.35)		(0.30)		(0.24)		(0.26)		(0.31)		(0.28)
Europe		-0.10		0.22+		-0.08		0.03		-0.03		0.33*		0.04		0.18
		(0.22)		(0.13)		(0.14)		(0.14)		(0.14)		(0.13)		(0.13)		(0.14)
F	9.44	1.68	2.66	2.31	9.66	1.52	4.05	1.37	7.01	2.09	0.00	3.41	13.71	2.46	1.35	0.83
R²	0.05	0.08	0.01	0.10	0.05	0.09	0.02	0.07	0.05	0.11	0.00	0.14	0.09	0.14	0.01	0.04
N	164	164	164	164	164	164	164	164	164	164	164	164	164	164	164	164

Note: This table presents results for univariate and multivariate OLS regressions. The dependent variables are VC influence on *CEO* hiring, *HR* practices, Executive compensation, Employee incentives, Board decisions, Board appointments, Strategy, and Investment, which are likert-type variables ranging from 1 to 4, 1 representing no influence and 4 indicating high influence. The independent variables are the proportion of VC funding received by sample companies; # VCs which is the number of different VC investors funding sample companies; LnAge which is a natural logarithm of the company age; Ln # Employees which is a natural logarithm of the number of company employees; industry controls are performed through the Computer and Medical dummy variables with "Other industries" as a baseline; Stage controls are performed through the Expansion and Later stage dummy variables with "Start-up" stage as the baseline; region control is performed in Panel A through the "Europe" dummy variable with "US" as the baseline. Robust standard errors are reported in parentheses. Significance at the 0.1%, 1%, 5% and 10% level is denoted by ***, **, *, and + respectively.

Source: Based on Bonini et al. (2012).

The percentage of VC funding is statistically significant in explaining the variance in venture capitalists' influence in some governance structures: as the percentage of funding increases, venture capitalists' influence on CEO hiring, executive compensation, employees' incentives, board decisions and board appointments grows accordingly. As shown by Gompers (1995), VC investors frequently require seats on the board of directors of portfolio companies as a monitoring covenant, since this allows better access to information and ongoing oversight on managerial decision-making. Confirming this preliminary evidence, results show that the proportion of funding and influence on board decisions and appointments is highly significant ($\beta = 0.662$, $p < 0.01$ and $\beta = 0.852$, $p < 0.001$).

VC is a well-known case of a principal–agent problem where the venture capitalist as a principal is exposed to large moral hazard issues not only by the entrepreneurs but also by a larger workforce which can be critical to the success of the venture. In such a case incentive alignment mechanisms such as profit sharing and pay-per-performance plan can be useful in reducing risk. The *EXE* and *INCENT* models confirm this intuition, showing increasing effects the larger the investment by the venture capitalist.

Given the categorical nature of the survey response variables, Bonini et al. (2012) perform appropriate ordinal logistic tests to overcome the problems highlighted by Menard (1995) in adopting linear approaches in a non-linear context. Results reported in Table 7.3 are aligned with those obtained in ordinary least squares (OLS) specifications.

As expected, significance increases both for the overall model and for the single estimated parameters. Figure 7.1 provides a graphical interpretation of the O-logit results plotting the predicted probabilities for the extreme response categories (1 = 'No or low influence' and 4 = 'High influence') for the four most significant dependent variables, namely: *CEO hiring (CEO)*, *Executive compensation (EXE)*, *Board of Directors decisions (BODD)* and *Board of Directors appointment (BODA)*.

The dashed lines graph the predicted probabilities for the response category 1 for each variable while the solid lines graph the predicted probabilities for the response category 4. Estimations are computed for changes in the VC ownership stake keeping all other variables constant at their mean values. Due to the non-linear nature of categorical models the interpretation of this graph is not straightforward: each line represents the predicted probabilities of observing a high or low influence of the amount of VC invested on the selected independent variable. For instance, when the VC stake is at its mean value of 70.35 percent looking at the effect on board of directors appointment, the model predicts a probability of recording a high influence slightly below 60 percent compared with a probability for a

Table 7.3   Ordinal Logistic Regressions of VC influence on governance practices

| | Panel A – Full sample | | | | | | | |
	CEO	HR	EXE	INCENT	BODD	STR	BODA	INV
VC%	1.76**	1.07+	1.82**	1.23*	1.63**	0.08	2.05***	0.67
	(0.61)	(0.59)	(0.56)	(0.60)	(0.61)	(0.61)	(0.59)	(0.55)
#ofVCs	-0.01	0.11*	0.07	0.01	0.11	0.10*	0.04	0.02
	(0.06)	(0.05)	(0.06)	(0.06)	(0.06)	(0.05)	(0.06)	(0.06)
LnAGE	0.24	0.26	0.12	-0.01	-0.35	-0.33	-0.29	-0.11
	(0.23)	(0.27)	(0.22)	(0.24)	(0.32)	(0.26)	(0.26)	(0.26)
Ln#EE	0.05	-0.27	-0.04	-0.05	0.02	0.37*	-0.06	-0.1
	(0.12)	(0.16)	(0.13)	(0.12)	(0.16)	(0.15)	(0.15)	(0.14)
Computer	0.07	-0.29	0.47	-0.19	0.72	-0.51	0.93*	0.4
	(0.37)	(0.35)	(0.40)	(0.37)	(0.47)	(0.38)	(0.41)	(0.37)
Medical	-0.1	-0.42	0.24	0.13	0.58	0.3	0.55	0.39
	(0.36)	(0.42)	(0.35)	(0.38)	(0.46)	(0.39)	(0.40)	(0.39)
Expansion	-0.22	-0.71+	0.15	0.42	0.59	-0.03	0.53	-0.07
	(0.42)	(0.43)	(0.38)	(0.39)	(0.50)	(0.44)	(0.46)	(0.39)
Later stage	-1.25+	-1.38+	-0.68	-0.61	-0.33	-1.46*	0.28	-0.09
	(0.69)	(0.80)	(0.86)	(0.68)	(0.67)	(0.63)	(0.78)	(0.59)
Europe	-0.2	0.46	-0.12	0.09	-0.2	0.84*	0.11	0.34
	(0.33)	(0.31)	(0.33)	(0.30)	(0.39)	(0.33)	(0.35)	(0.30)

Table 7.3 (continued)

				Panel A – Full sample				
	CEO	HR	EXE	INCENT	BODD	STR	BODA	INV
No influence	0.48	−0.77	−1.31	−0.86	−2.19	−2.14	−2.32	−2.46
Low influence	1.05	1.38	−0.11	0.98	−0.64	0.13	−0.38	−0.86
Moderate influence	1.71	3.25	2.01	3.16	0.72	2.29	1.44	1.00
χ^2	12.82	20.95	12.76	10.52	22.54	26.17	19.43	7.73
Pseudo-R^2	0.03	0.05	0.04	0.03	0.07	0.06	0.07	0.02
N	164	164	164	164	164	164	164	164

Note: This table presents results for a set of Ordinal logistic regressions. The dependent variables are Likert-type variables ranging from 1 (no influence) to 4 (high influence) capturing the VC influence on: *CEO* hiring, *HR* practices, Executive compensation, Employee incentives, Board decisions, Board appointments, Strategy, and Investment. Parameters estimated are presented at the mean values of the independent variables. The independent variables are the proportion of VC funding received by sample companies; # VCs which is the number of different VC investors funding sample companies; LnAge which is a natural logarithm of the company age; Ln # Employees which is a natural logarithm of the number of company employees; industry controls are performed through the Computer and Medical dummy variables with "Other industries" as a baseline; Stage controls are performed through the Expansion and Later stage dummy variables with "Start-up" stage as the baseline; region control is performed in Panel A through the "Europe" dummy variable with "US" as the baseline. Cut points are reported for the No influence (response 1), Low influence (response 2) and Moderate influence (Response 3) categories of the dependent variable. Robust standard errors are reported in parentheses. Significance at the 0.1 %, 1%, 5% and 10% level is denoted by ***, **, * and + respectively.

Source: Based on Bonini et al. (2012).

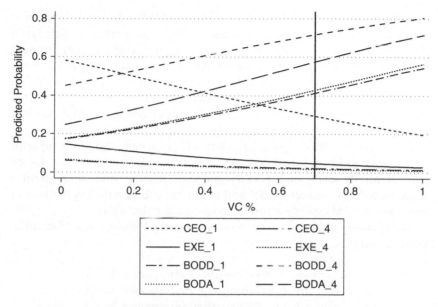

Note: This figure plots predicted probabilities for the four dependent variables significant at the 1% level or more from the full-sample ordinal logistic regression reported in Table 7.3. The four variables are: influence on CEO hiring (*CEO*), influence on Executive compensation (*EXE*), influence on Board of directors decisions (*BODD*) and influence on Board of directrors appointment (*BODA*). The dashed lines plot the predicted probabilities for the 'No or low influence' outcome (i.e. response category = 1), while the solid lines report the predicted probabilities associated with the 'High influence' outcome (i.e. response category = 4). Predicted probabilities are computed setting all other variables at their mean values. The vertical line reports the mean level of VC contribution.

Source: Based on Bonini et al. (2012).

Figure 7.1 Full sample predicted probabilities

low influence of less than 5 percent. Probabilities are increasing in the VC amount for the high category and decreasing for the low one.

VC Influence on Governance and Financial Performance of Portfolio Firms

The previous results clearly illustrate the existence of strong influence by VC investors on the design of governance mechanisms within firms. A connected question is whether more elaborated governance structures also lead to superior financial performance. Farag et al. (2014) tackle this issue by looking at VC-backed firms listing on the United Kingdom (UK) Alternative Investment Market (AIM). Given the extensive set of possible governance variables, Farag et al. (2014) develop an ad hoc comprehensive corporate governance (CG) measure: the CGAIM50 Index. This index is obtained by aggregating 50 governance items. Each item is modeled as a dummy variable taking the value of 1 if the item is found as being present in the observed firm and 0 otherwise. All items are then equally weighted to avoid any potential scoring and scaling biases to yield a final score that ranges between 0 and 1. A company with a sophisticated and articulated governance structure would exhibit a CG index close to 1 as opposed to a weakly governed firm that would rank not far from 0.

Farag et al. (2014) conjecture that VC ownership leads to superior governance which in turn leads to superior financial performance. Given the potentially severe endogeneity and simultaneity issues they adopt a three-stage least squares model and an alternative generalized method of moments (GMM) specification to cross-validate the results.

The first step in their approach is to design the following set of simultaneous equations:

$$Governance = f(Ownership, Performance, \Xi, \varepsilon_1)$$
$$Ownership = f(Governance, Performance, \Xi, \varepsilon_2)$$
$$Performance = f(Ownership, Governance, \Xi, \varepsilon_3)$$

where Ξ is a vector of control variables.

To empirically establish the dynamic relationship between corporate governance, VC ownership structure and financial performance of AIM companies, Farag et al. (2014) run a three-stage least squares (3SLS) model to estimate the previous equations jointly within a system of simultaneous equations in which they are treated as endogenous variables. The essential advantage of the 3SLS estimation technique is that it allows not only for simultaneity among corporate governance, VC ownership and financial performance, but also for correlations among the error components. As a robustness check the authors estimate also simpler 2SLS and OLS models. Results of this exercise are reported in Table 7.4.

Panel A shows that there is a positive and significant relationship between governance characteristics and both the percentage of VC ownership and financial performance. Panel B reveals a positive and significant relationship between governance characteristics and financial performance; however there is no significant relationship between VC ownership and financial performance. This result supports the conjecture that causality flows from VC ownership to governance and that better governance translates into superior financial performance. Finally, the results reported in panel C show that there is no direct relationship between VC ownership and both financial performance and corporate governance. Their findings can be interpreted as follows: companies with

Table 7.4 *Simultaneous equation systems*

	Panel A: Governance equation			Panel B: Performance equation			Panel C: VC Ownership equation		
	3SLS	2SLS	OLS	3SLS	2SLS	OLS	3SLS	2SLS	OLS
Lagged CG index	0.937*** (0.46)	0.937*** (0.46)	0.876*** (0.16)						
CG index				0.891** (0.386)	0.995** (0.368)	0.565* (0.294)	0.501 (0.427)	0.501 (0.436)	0.157 (0.772)
Lagged VC own							0.602** (0.205)	0.571** (0.217)	0.501** (0.198)
VC own	0.031** (0.011)	0.022* (0.010)	0.032** (0.012)	0.248 (0.205)	0.251 (0.212)	0.250 (0.231)			
Lagged ROA				0.008*** (0.002)	0.009** (0.003)	0.002* (0.001)			
ROA	0.034** (0.011)	0.026* (0.011)	0.001† (0.001)				0.678 (0.521)	0.674 (0.524)	0.679 (0.521)
Lnmcap	0.017*** (0.005)	0.014** (0.005)	0.007*** (0.002)	0.391** (0.140)	0.299* (0.141)	0.268* (0.139)	0.108 (0.107)	0.112 (0.109)	0.097 (0.077)
Debt/TA	−0.029 (0.023)	−0.022 (0.025)	−0.005 (0.010)	−1.065 (0.812)	−1.062 (0.819)	−1.039 (0.819)	−0.016 (0.530)	−0.014 (0.534)	−0.029 (0.452)
R&D/sales	0.004*** (0.001)	0.002* (0.001)	0.001 (0.001)	−0.005*** (0.001)	−0.002* (0.001)	−0.001 (0.001)	0.013*** (0.003)	0.011* (0.005)	0.127*** (0.003)
No. risk factors	0.011* (0.005)	0.014* (0.006)	0.005* (0.002)	0.238† (0.137)	0.239† (0.139)	0.228† (0.139)	0.012 (0.100)	0.012 (0.101)	0.018 (0.077)

Table 7.4 (continued)

	Panel A: Governance equation			Panel B: Performance equation			Panel C: VC Ownership equation		
	3SLS	2SLS	OLS	3SLS	2SLS	OLS	3SLS	2SLS	OLS
VC reputation	0.003**	0.002*	0.001	0.009**	0.008***	0.006	0.231***	0.245***	0.239***
	(0.001)	(0.01)	(0.001)	(0.003)	(0.002)	(0.004)	(0.018)	(0.011)	(0.014)
Age	0.001	0.002	0.002	0.004	0.005	0.002	−0.037	−0.038	−0.036
	(0.001)	(0.003)	(0.004)	(0.044)	(0.045)	(0.045)	(0.025)	(0.027)	(0.025)
Foreign	−0.022†	−0.023†	−0.016*	0.105	0.108	0.073	0.301	0.301	0.287
	(0.012)	(0.013)	(0.007)	(0.588)	(0.593)	(0.591)	(0.325)	(0.328)	(0.326)
CEO/founder	0.014	0.016	0.007	0.827†	0.778†	0.682	−0.281	−0.281	−0.261
	(0.011)	(0.013)	(0.005)	(0.443)	(0.466)	(0.545)	(0.256)	(0.258)	(0.245)
Lockup period	−0.001	−0.001	−0.001	−0.001	−0.002	−0.001	0.002*	0.003	0.005
	(0.001)	(0.01)	(0.003)	(0.003)	(0.003)	(0.003)	(0.001)	(0.002)	(0.012)
Constant	0.228*	0.236*	0.045†	8.351***	8.302***	8.289***	0.609	0.686	0.664
	(0.104)	(0.105)	(0.025)	(2.180)	(2.254)	(2.251)	(2.464)	(2.482)	(1.249)
Ind. dummy	Yes	Yes	Yes	Yes	Yes	Yes	Yes	Yes	Yes
Time dummy	Yes	Yes	Yes	Yes	Yes	Yes	Yes	Yes	Yes
Firm dummy	Yes	Yes	Yes	Yes	Yes	Yes	Yes	Yes	Yes

	(0.000)	(0.031)	(0.003)	(0.000)	(0.031)	(0.003)	(0.000)
System Chi sq. (p-value)	0.651	0.185	0.418	0.651	0.185	0.418	0.651
System weighted R sq.	0.418	0.185	0.418	0.185	0.418	0.185	

Hausman Specification Tests	
OLS vs 3SLS	(0.000)
p-value	
OLS vs 2SLS	(0.009)
p-value	
2SLS vs 3SLS	(0.239)
p-value	

183

Note: This table reports the result of a three-stage least squares (3SLS) model to empirically establish the dynamic relationship between corporate governance, VC ownership structure and financial performance of AIM companies. Variables are defined as follows. CG index: CGAIM50 index; VC Own: percentage of total number of shares outstanding owned by VCs. *ROA*: return on assets; Tobin's Q: (Book value of assets + market value of common stock) − (book value of common stock + deferred taxes)/the book value of assets. Lnmcap: natural logarithm of market cap as a proxy for company size; Debt/TA: long-term debt/total assets as a proxy for leverage; *R&D*/sales: research & development/total sales as a proxy for growth; No. risk factors: total number of risk factors (e.g., technology, competition, legal aspects, and exchange rate changes). We assign the value of one for each risk factor if it is mentioned in the *IPO* prospectus/annual reports and zero otherwise; VC reputation: total market value of all companies taken public by the VC firm for a given calendar year and normalize it by the aggregate market value of all VC-backed companies that went public in the same calendar year; Age: company age measured by the difference between founding year and IPO year (AIM admission year); Foreign: dummy variable takes the value of 1 if the company is foreign and 0 otherwise; CEO/Founder: dummy variable takes the value of 1 if the *CEO* is the founder of the company and 0 otherwise. Lockup: the length of the lockup period in days. Clustered standard errors in parentheses. ***, **, * and † indicates significance at the .1, 1, 5 and 10 percent levels respectively.

Source: Based on Farag et al. (2014).

better financial performance are keen to develop their governance mechanism and characteristics through employing high-profile and experienced directors, in particular non-executive directors. Similarly, companies with better corporate governance characteristics have better-quality management and this is reflected in the decision-making process and thus the overall financial performance of the firm.

PRIVATE EQUITY AND CORPORATE GOVERNANCE

Many academics and practitioners have argued that the success of private equity-backed buyouts stems in part from a more effective corporate governance structure implemented after a company is acquired. Most obviously, ownership changes from a dispersed base of public shareholders, none of which may have adequate incentives to participate fully in governance, to a small number (often one) of buyout funds whose own success and remuneration depends on the returns provided by their investments and which are thus highly motivated to maximize value.

Several studies have examined governance features of companies with private equity (PE) or specifically buyout fund sponsorship to determine the extent to which governance structures indeed differ between these companies and companies without a professional investor sponsorship. The features that are typical of private company governance, such as small, engaged boards and high pay–performance sensitivity, can be adopted by public as well as private companies but they may appear redundant for the case of concentrated private ownership that characterizes PE deals. Accordingly, private equity sponsors – given their own performance-based compensation and retained equity stakes – may implement less of these features in their portfolio companies. A rival conjecture though might be that given that exits are mainly expected through IPOs, PE-backed firms may align to best practices related to board independence and dilution from equity compensation plans to attract investors who, as minority shareholders, attach significant value to governance mechanisms. The relevance of these questions in terms of economic and welfare effects has spurred a number of studies investigating the effects of PE sponsors on several governance structures.

Private Equity and CEO and Management Turnover

According to agency theory, companies with a high level of undistributed free cash and a low level of leverage suffer from severe agency problems, among which are CEOs enjoying private benefits and engaging in 'empire building' activities. Jensen (1989) argues that private equity buyouts are a form of governance mechanism that addresses the inefficiencies observed in companies that have incurred agency costs beyond an equilibrium point. In particular, PE firms investing in companies characterized by significant agency costs are more likely to remove incumbent CEOs. In such a case, the CEO replacement, firm restructuring and eventual firm sale – in short, the PE intervention – generates value for the economy as a whole, and in particular for minority shareholders.

Many studies (among others, Baker and Wruck, 1989; Lehn and Poulsen, 1989; Leslie and Oyer, 2009), have addressed the intervention channels of PE sponsors at the operating level, through the implementation of so-called operational re-engineering strategies; and at the incentive mechanism level, through the design and enforcement of pay-per-performance compensation schemes at multiple organization levels. Surprisingly, though, few studies have specifically looked into the differential degree of CEO turnover in PE-backed companies.

Gong and Wu (2011) filled the gap by looking at a US sample of 126 PE-sponsored leveraged buyouts (LBOs)[2] that occurred between 1998 and 2006. A methodological issue affecting the size of the sample is that when gathering buyout data, all MBOs have to be excluded, in that MBOs are almost always initiated by the former management led by the pre-buyout CEO, thus determining a sharp decline in available data points. Gong and Wu's (2011) results indicate an unconditional CEO replacement probability of 51 percent, which strikingly exceeds by a factor of five the market average replacement rate of 11 percent documented by Parrino (1997) and Farrell and Whidbee (2003). Moving to a standard logistic regression approach they include in the analysis a set of important agency cost controls.

Results reported in Table 7.5 show that some sources of agency costs appear to have a meaningful and large effect on the likelihood of observing a CEO replacement. In particular, leverage is strongly negatively related to CEO turnover, providing a confirmation of Jensen's (1986) hypothesis: debt acts as a disciplining mechanisms for CEOs. Since leverage is by and large determined by managerial discretion, a new owner will most likely face a conflict with the incumbent CEO who chose a suboptimal capital structure and this will generate an almost mechanical pressure for CEO replacement. In a similar spirit we can interpret the positive coefficient of the free cash flow. Very interestingly the strongly significant, very large and negative coefficient for return on assets (ROA), a measure of the efficiency in asset exploitation, indicates that the company was underperforming its peers, most likely due to agency costs. A comforting

Table 7.5   Logistic regression for CEO replacement

| | Simultaneous equation systems | | | | | | | | |
| | Panel A: Governance equation | | | Panel B: Performance equation | | | Panel C: VC Ownership equation | | |
	3SLS	2SLS	OLS	3SLS	2SLS	OLS	3SLS	2SLS	OLS
Lagged CG index	0.937*** (0.046)	0.937*** (0.046)	0.876*** (0.016)						
CG index				0.891** (0.386)	0.995** (0.368)	0.565* (0.294)	0.501 (0.427)	0.501 (0.436)	0.157 (0.772)
Lagged VC Own							0.602** (0.205)	0.571** (0.217)	0.501** (0.198)
VC Own	0.031** (0.011)	0.022* (0.010)	0.032** (0.012)	0.248 (0.205)	0.251 (0.212)	0.250 (0.231)			
Lagged ROA				0.008*** (0.002)	0.009** (0.003)	0.002* (0.001)			
ROA	0.034** (0.011)	0.026* (0.011)	0.001† (0.001)	0.391** (0.140)	0.299* (0.141)	0.268* (0.139)	0.678 (0.521)	0.674 (0.524)	0.679 (0.521)
Lnmcap	0.017*** (0.005)	0.014** (0.005)	0.007*** (0.002)				0.108 (0.107)	0.112 (0.109)	0.097 (0.077)
Debt/TA	−0.029 (0.023)	−0.022 (0.025)	−0.005 (0.010)	−1.065 (0.812)	−1.062 (0.819)	−1.039 (0.819)	−0.016 (0.530)	−0.014 (0.534)	−0.029 (0.452)
R&D/sales	0.004*** (0.001)	0.002* (0.001)	0.001 (0.001)	−0.005*** (0.001)	−0.002* (0.001)	−0.001 (0.001)	0.013*** (0.003)	0.011* (0.005)	0.127*** (0.003)
No. risk factors	0.011* (0.005)	0.014* (0.006)	0.005** (0.002)	0.238† (0.137)	0.239† (0.139)	0.228† (0.139)	0.012 (0.100)	0.012 (0.101)	0.018 (0.077)
VC reputation	0.003** (0.001)	0.002* (0.01)	0.001 (0.001)	0.009** (0.003)	0.008*** (0.002)	0.006 (0.004)	0.231*** (0.018)	0.245*** (0.011)	0.239*** (0.014)
Age	0.001 (0.001)	0.002 (0.003)	0.002 (0.004)	0.004 (0.044)	0.005 (0.045)	0.002 (0.045)	−0.037 (0.025)	−0.038 (0.027)	−0.036 (0.025)

186

	(1)	(2)	(3)	(4)	(5)	(6)	(7)	(8)	(9)
Foreign	−0.022†	−0.023†	−0.016*	0.105	0.108	0.073	0.301	0.301	0.287
	(0.012)	(0.013)	(0.007)	(0.588)	(0.593)	(0.591)	(0.325)	(0.328)	(0.326)
CEO/founder	0.014	0.016	0.007	0.827†	0.778†	0.682	−0.281	−0.281	−0.261
	(0.011)	(0.013)	(0.005)	(0.443)	(0.466)	(0.545)	(0.256)	(0.258)	(0.245)
Lock up period	−0.001	−0.001	−0.001	−0.001	−0.002	−0.001	0.002*	0.003	0.005
	(0.001)	(0.01)	(0.003)	(0.003)	(0.003)	(0.003)	(0.001)	(0.002)	(0.012)
Constant	0.228*	0.236*	0.045†	8.351***	8.302***	8.289***	0.690	0.686	0.664
	(0.104)	(0.105)	(0.025)	(2.180)	(2.254)	(2.251)	(2.464)	(2.482)	(1.249)
Ind. dummy	Yes	Yes	Yes	Yes	Yes	Yes	Yes	Yes	Yes
Time dummy	Yes	Yes	Yes	Yes	Yes	Yes	Yes	Yes	Yes
Firm dummy	Yes	Yes	Yes	Yes	Yes	Yes	Yes	Yes	Yes
System Chi sq. (p-value)	(0.000)	(0.003)	(0.031)	(0.000)	(0.003)	(0.031)	(0.000)	(0.003)	(0.031)
System weighted R sq.	0.651	0.418	0.185	0.651	0.418	0.185	0.651	0.418	0.185

Hausman Specification Tests

OLS vs 3SLS p-value	(0.000)
OLS vs 2SLS p-value	(0.009)
2SLS vs 3SLS p-value	(0.239)

Note: This table exhibits results for our logistic regressions. Variable definitions are provided in Table 7.2. All monetary variables are adjusted for inflation to the 1990 dollar. Significance levels are denoted by: †p < .1, *p < .05, **p <0.01, ***p < .001 (one-tailed test for variables with predicted signs, two-tailed test otherwise). Huber–White's heteroscedasticity consistent standard errors are used to calculate the z-statistics (reported in parentheses).

Source: Based on Gong and Wu (2011).

result from a welfare perspective is the very weak effect of the experience or quality of the PE sponsor on the replacement likelihood. The sign of the parameter is positive but most often insignificant, meaning that one can expect the average PE fund to recognize inefficiencies and, following an investment, address them through appropriate actions.

Supporting these results, Cornelli and Karakas (2014) show that following CEO replacement the turnaround of CEOs in PE-backed firms is essentially null, which again compares with an unconditional expected replacement rate of 11 percent for the market. This result suggests that by actively intervening in companies characterized by an abnormal level of agency costs, private equity investors alleviate board myopia and generate value for all stakeholders.

Private Equity and Boards

The role of boards in public companies is to provide management supervision in the presence of fragmented shareholders and in particular of small, minority investors who express a need for protection. However, firms acquired by private equity firms lack this characteristic, as the rationale often given for the success of private equity is exactly that it concentrates the ownership in the hands of a few shareholders, allowing direct, more efficient control. In such respect the intervention of a PE investor may significantly alter the composition and powers of the board of a company. In particular, because PE investors could provide advice and monitoring without a board, one could argue that boards may be considerably diminished in terms of both size and powers. A counter-argument though is that, as Lerner (1995) showed for VC firms, investors tend to exert their influence by taking board seats. Following this analogy, one could expect boards to be vastly dominated by PE members empowered with superior, direct monitoring and that independent directors would essentially be absent. These arguments suggest that there is a clear rationale for expecting board composition and powers to be significantly different in PE-backed firms.

In a seminal study Gertner and Kaplan (1996) explored this question by comparing board characteristics of 59 companies target of a reverse-LBO with a sample of industry and size matched peers. The authors found that the reverse-LBO companies' boards were smaller, owned more equity and met less frequently. At the director level, boards were younger, directors had served for shorter time periods, were less likely to be women and were at least as likely to serve on other boards. This preliminary evidence has been complemented by Cao (2008) who examined post-IPO ownership by buyout sponsors and insiders and governance characteristics in a sample of reverse-LBO companies between 1981 and 2006. Cao shows that buyout sponsors' ownership drops from 60 percent equity ownership to 40 percent immediately following the IPO. However, the residual stake diminishes only slowly over time to an average of 24 percent three years after the IPO. Importantly, however, Cao finds that buyout sponsors continue to be active investors after the IPO, in that they retain significant control of board and board committees. In particular, Cao's results indicate that buyout sponsors retain control over compensation and nominating committees disproportionately to their ownership stakes.

Cornelli and Karakas (2014) address this compelling research question by looking at a sample of 142 public-to-private transactions in the UK between 1998 and 2003. Out of this initial sample, 88 deals are pure PE-sponsored transactions and are compared with other transactions where there was no involvement of a PE firm. Their analysis yields a number of results. First, the presence of a PE sponsor is not significantly related with a change in board size: both sponsored and unsponsored public-to-private transactions experience a drop in board size by about two units from an unconditional mean of 6.5. However, experience matters in that PE-backed deals where the PE sponsor has considerable experience (this variable also partially captures reputation) experience a much bigger shrinkage in board size. In a way, experienced PE seems to be taking a more direct, hands-on approach, and almost exclusive management of the company. Supporting this view, Cornelli and Karakas (2014) show that independent directors practically disappear from boards after the company has been taken private.

Private Equity and Takeover Defenses

An issue of hot debate is the perception by non-PE investors that post-IPO PE firms tend to maintain disproportionate control rights through a plethora of mechanisms to the disadvantage of investors at large. When a portfolio company completes an IPO, the buyout fund sponsor usually does not dispose of its entire investment in the offering; instead, it retains an equity stake, which diminishes over time. For example, sponsors of a 'vote no' campaign against directors at Safeway in 2004 objected to the presence on Safeway's board of four directors affiliated with buyout sponsor KKR, which owned only 9 percent of Safeway's shares, as well as the existence of related-party transactions involving KKR. An open question is therefore whether PE-backed firms exhibit stronger and more articulated anti-takeover practices and whether these add or destroy value.

Klausner (2003), building on survey data from the Investor Responsibility

Research Center (IRRC), unveiled the striking effect of PE investors in introducing and maintaining anti-takeover provisions in newly listed PE-backed companies. Klausner (2003) first notices the booming share of PE-backed firms in the IPO market that went from a few percentage points in the early 1980s to about 40 percent by the end of the century. In the same time frame IRRC data reported in Bebchuck (2003) show a spectacular increase in the presence of anti-takeover provisions at the time of the IPO. For instance, classified boards went from being present in 36.2 percent of the newly listed firms in the period 1988–92 to more than 82 percent in 1999. Similarly, provisions limiting the right to call for special meeting skyrocketed from 12.4 percent to 84.8 percent of the cases.

Barret et al. (2009) in a follow-up IRRC-sponsored study show that, despite harsh criticism by shareholders and advocates of corporate governance practices, this phenomenon has continued. In their study, Barret et al. (2009) show that IPO companies backed by buyout funds had significantly stronger takeover defenses than companies brought public by non-private-equity sponsors. Additionally, companies backed by buyout funds were more likely than others to have classified boards, 'poison pills', and restrictions on director removal by shareholders.

A recent report (WilmerHale, 2014) on IPO data between 2007 and 2012 compiled by WilmerHale, a large law data provider, provides an effective overview of this phenomenon. As reported in Table 7.6, PE (and VC) funds introduce strong anti-takeover provisions in their portfolio company charters, with classified boards, supermajority and exclusive forum defense mechanisms showing the largest difference with non-PE-sponsored firms.

The prevailing view seems to be that anti-takeover provisions reduce shareholder value, and are meant only to entrench existing firm management, allowing them to maintain control and extract private benefits of control. This entrenchment hypothesis has been partially supported by Daines and Klausner (2001). In an important paper, Field and Karpoff (2002), in contrast to this view, did not find evidence of poorer performance conditional on the presence of takeover defenses. Chemmanur and Jiao (2005) addressed this empirical puzzle by proposing a model in which, in the presence of asymmetric information, takeover defenses allow managers to engage in riskier but value-creating long-term projects that could not be pursued if the company could easily be target to a proxy contest. Chemmanur and Jiao's (2005) model goes further in showing that their results hold conditional on managers' quality: when managers exhibit high quality the expected effect on performance is positive and large. Conversely, if managers are of low quality, anti-takeover provisions destroy value because they generate inefficient investment decisions.

Table 7.6   Anti-takeover provision in IPO companies

	All IPO companies (%)	VC-backed (%)	PE-backed (%)	Other IPO companies (%)
Classified board	72	83	72	48
Supermajority voting requirements to approve mergers or change corporate charter and bylaws	62	72	65	37
Prohibition of stockholders' right to act by written consent	83	91	84	64
Limitation of stockholders' right to call special meetings	89	94	94	73
Advance notice provisions	93	96	95	86
Section 203 of the Delaware corporation statute	79	95	51	76
Blank check preferred stock	94	96	98	84
Multi-class capital structure	7	7	4	10
Exclusive forum provisions	27	22	44	14
Stockholders' rights plan	2	4	1	2

Note: This table reports the fraction of IPO companies exhibiting an anti-takeover provision at the time of the IPO. Data are compiled from SEC filings from 2007 to 2012 for US issuers.

Source: Based on WilmerHale (2014).

Consequently, the model predicts that highly reputable managers are more likely to put defense mechanisms into place so that they can pursue longer-term, value-creating strategies. Since a building block of PE firms is that they provide not only capital but also valuable managerial skills, the evidence that PE firms exhibit stronger defense mechanisms seems to confirm Chemmanur and Jiao's (2005) model. This hypothesis implies that firms with strong protection provisions and high-quality managers should exhibit superior performance. In a follow-up study, Chemmanur et al. (2011) answer this question by looking at a large sample of IPOs from 1993 to 2000. They define management quality through eight different dimensions: managerial team size; education; professional certification; prior experience; prior experience in a law or accounting firm; CEO dominance; length of tenure; and tenure heterogeneity across team members. However, given that each measure may have unique limitations as a measure of the underlying unobservable construct, they develop an aggregate, principal components quality score that captures the overall management quality and is increasing in it.

Their comprehensive results robustly show that the abnormal holding period returns of IPO firms with stronger anti-takeover protection are significantly larger than those of IPO firms with weaker anti-takeover protection. The differences in mean abnormal holding period returns are statistically significant at conventional levels and hold across a number of robustness tests. In particular, despite IPOs' performance being generally lower than the benchmark as already pointed out by Ritter (1991), Loughran and Ritter (1995), Brav and Gompers (1997) and Teoh et al. (1998), firms with high-quality managers and strong anti-takeover provisions significantly mitigate such an endogenous downward bias and align more to the benchmark. In a recent paper Karpoff et al. (2015) further extend this evidence, providing alternative interpretations of the transmission channel that allows anti-takeover provisions to generate value. In particular, they argue and show that firm stability in the absence of an external risk of takeover allows the generation of valuable relationships with the economic environment (the bonding hypothesis) that ultimately translate into superior performance.

CONCLUSIONS

Private equity investors have risen to be one of the most notable forces shaping corporate governance practices in young and fast-growing companies as well as in established market players. The significantly increasing volume of investment has given rise to multiple classes of investors specialized in different stages of the life of a company. As such, the market is now populated by business angels, venture capitalists and later-stage private equity investors. This specialization has also contributed to shape different practices, including the extent and design of corporate governance practice in portfolio companies. Surprisingly, the literature on this topic is fairly recent and relatively preliminary, and several questions are still unanswered. First, despite business angels being an investor class comparable to formal venture capital in terms of invested capital, little is known about the performance of their investments, the characteristics of the investment decision process and the governance of portfolio companies. Second, there is a wide gap in our understanding of the links between informal and formal venture capital. Since informal venture capital appears to be an obvious precursor (or pre-screening device) for formal venture capitalists, it would be natural to observe significant connections between angel investors and proper venture capital funds, and considerably higher rates of success in securing follow-up investments by business angel-sponsored firms. None of these expected links is robustly observed. Confirming this apparent puzzle and understanding its drivers are crucial in advancing our knowledge of the development of entrepreneurial activity. Third, there is still ambiguous evidence on the effects of anti-takeover and protection mechanisms in PE-backed deals. While there is a clear, general consensus on limiting these practices, there is also a striking and puzzling evidence of the widespread adoption of such provisions in firms controlled by private equity investors. Whether this is beneficial or detrimental to firms, stakeholders and the market at large is largely an open question. We envision these to be fruitful areas for future research.

NOTES

1. The definition of 'aggressive' versus 'conservative' accounting practices is the one adopted by Hochberg (2004) and Teoh et al. (1998), who consider accounting policies as 'aggressive' when characterized by higher discretionary accruals, as opposed to lower discretionary accruals for 'conservative' policies.
2. A leveraged buy-out (LBO) is a type of acquisition by a financial investor that relics significantly on external debt financing. A special class of LBO is the management buy-out (MBO), an LBO initiated by the existing management team that seeks support of a financial sponsor to buy out the company from its existing shareholders.

REFERENCES

Admati, A. and Pfleiderer, P. (1994), 'Robust financial contracting and the role for venture capitalists', *Journal of Finance*, **49** (2), 371–402.

Barret, A., Gladman, K., Hodgson, P., Lamb, M., Marshall, R. and Young, B. (2009), *What Is the Impact of Private Equity Buyout Fund Ownership on IPO Companies' Corporate Governance?*, Portland, ME: IRRC Institute / The Corporate Library.

Baker, M. and Gompers, P.A. (1999), 'Executive ownership and control in newly public firms: The role of venture capitalists', Harvard University Working Paper.

Baker, M. and Gompers, P.A. (2003), 'The determinants of board structure at Initial Public Offering', *Journal of Law and Economics*, **46** (2), 569–598.

Baker, G.P. and Wruck, K.H. (1989), 'Organizational changes and value creation in leveraged buyouts: The case of O.M. Scott & Sons Company', *Journal of Financial Economics*, **25** (2), 163–190.

Barry, C. (1994), 'New directions in venture capital research', *Journal of Financial Management*, **23** (3), 15.

Bebchuk, L.A. (2003), 'Why firms adopt antitakeover arrangements', *University of Pennsylvania Law Review*, **152**, 713–753.

Berglöf, E. (1994), 'A control theory of venture capital finance', *Journal of Law, Economics and Organization*, **10** (2), 247–267.

Bergmann, D. and Hege, U. (1998), 'Dynamic venture capital financing, learning, and moral hazard', *Journal of Banking and Finance*, **22** (6–8), 703–735.

Berle, A.A. and Means, G.C. (1932), *The Modern Corporation and Private Property*, New York: Macmillan.

Bernile, G., Cumming, D. and Lyandres, E. (2007), 'The structure of private equity fund portfolios: Theory and international evidence', *Journal of Corporate Finance*, **4**, 564–590.

Bhattacharya, S. and Thakor, A. (1993), 'Contemporary banking theory', *Journal of Financial Intermediation*, **3** (1), 2–50.

Bonini, S., Alkan, S. and Salvi, A. (2012), 'The effects of venture capitalists on the governance of firms', *Corporate Governance: An International Review*, **20** (1), 21–45.

Brav, A. and Gompers, P.A. (1997), 'Myth or reality? The long-run underperformance of initial public offerings: Evidence from venture and nonventure capital-backed companies', *Journal of Finance*, **52** (5), 1791–1821.

Bygrave, W.D., Hay, M., Ng, E. and Reynolds, P. (2003), 'Executive forum: A study of informal investing in 29 nations composing the Global Entrepreneurship Monitor', *Venture Capital: An International Journal of Entrepreneurial Finance*, **5** (2), 101–116.

Bygrave, W. and Timmons, J. (1992), *Venture Capital at the Crossroads*, Boston, MA: Harvard Business School Press.

Cao, J. (2008), 'What role does private equity play when leveraged buyouts go public?', Unpublished PhD dissertation, Boston College.

Capizzi, V. (2015), 'The returns of business angel investments and their major determinants', *Venture Capital*, **17** (4), 271–298.

Chemmanur, T. and Jiao, Y. (2005), 'Seasoned equity issues with "soft" information: Theory and empirical evidence', SSRN Working Paper Series, SSRN.com/abstract#674102.

Chemmanur, T.J., Paeglis, I. and Simonyan, K. (2011), 'Management quality and antitakeover provisions', *Journal of Law and Economics*, **54** (3), 651–692.

Chua, J.H. and Wu, Z. (2012), 'Value added by angel investors through post-investment involvement: Empirical evidence and ownership implications', *Handbook of Entrepreneurial Finance*, New York: Oxford University Press.

Cornelli, F. and Karakaş, O. (2014), 'CEO turnover in LBOs: The role of boards', Working Paper, London Business School.

Cornelli, F. and Yosha, O. (2003), 'Stage financing and the role of convertible securities', *Review of Economic Studies*, **70** (1), 1–32.

Coveney, P. and Moore, K. (1998), *Business Angels: Securing Start-Up Finance*, Chichester: Wiley.

Cumming, D. (2005), 'Global venture capital transactions', *Venture Capital*, **7** (2), 185–201.

Cumming, D.J. (2006), 'The determinants of venture capital portfolio size: Empirical evidence', *Journal of Business*, **79**, 1083–1126.

Cumming, D.J. (2008), 'Contracts and exits in venture capital finance', *Review of Financial Studies*, **21** (5), 1947–1982.

Daines, R. and Klausner, M. (2001), 'Do IPO charters maximize firm value? Antitakeover protection in IPOs', *Journal of Law, Economics, and Organization*, **17** (1) 83–120.

Diamond, D.W. (1984), 'Financial intermediation and delegated monitoring', *Review of Economic Studies*, **51** (3), 393–414.

EVCA (2006), 'Private equity fund structures in Europe', European Venture Capital Association.

Fama, E.F. and Jensen, M.C. (1983), 'Separation of ownership and control', *Journal of Law and Economics*, **26** (2), 301–325.

Fama, E.C. and Jensen, M.C. (1985), 'Organizational forms and investment decisions', *Journal of Financial Economics*, **14**, 101–119.

Farag, H., Mallin, C. and Ow-Yong, K. (2014), 'Governance, ownership structure, and performance of entrepreneurial IPOs in AIM companies', *Corporate Governance: An International Review*, **22** (2), 100–115.

Farrell, K.A. and Whidbee, D.A. (2003), 'The impact of firm performance expectations on CEO turnover and replacement decisions', *Journal of Accounting and Economics*, **36** (1), 165–196.

Field, L.C. and Karpoff, J.M. (2002), 'Takeover defenses of IPO firms', *Journal of Finance*, **57** (5), 1857–1889.

Freear, J., Sohl, J.E. and Wetzel Jr, W.E. (1992), 'The investment attitudes, behavior and characteristics of high net worth individuals', *Frontiers of Entrepreneurship Research*, 374–387.

Gertner, R.H. and Kaplan, S.N. (1996), 'The value-maximizing board', University of Chicago.

Gillan, S.L. and Starks, L.T. (2003), 'Corporate governance, corporate ownership, and the role of institutional investors: A global perspective', *Journal of Applied Finance*, **13** (2), 1–19.

Gompers, P. (1995), 'Optimal investment, monitoring, and the staging of venture capital', *Journal of Finance*, **50** (5), 1461–1489.

Gompers, P. and Lerner, J. (2006), *The Venture Capital Cycle*, Cambridge, MA: MIT Press.

Gong, J.J. and Wu, S.Y. (2011), 'CEO turnover in private equity sponsored leveraged buyouts', *Corporate Governance: An International Review*, **19** (3), 195–209.

Gorman, M. and Sahlman, W.A. (1989), 'What do venture capitalists do?', *Journal of Business Venturing*, **4** (4), 231–248.

Grossman, S. and Hart, O. (1986), 'The costs and benefits of ownership: A theory of vertical and lateral integration', *Journal of Political Economy*, **94**, 691–719.

Haines Jr, G.H., Madill, J.J. and Riding A.L. (2003), 'Informal investment in Canada: Financing small business growth', *Journal of Small Business & Entrepreneurship*, **16** (3–4), 13–40.

Harrison, R.T. and Mason, C.M. (1992), 'International perspectives on the supply of informal venture capital', *Journal of Business Venturing*, **7** (6), 459–475.

Harrison, R.T. and Mason, C.M. (1996), '*Informal Venture Capital: Evaluating the Impact of Business Introduction Services*', Hemel Hempstead, UK: Prentice Hall.

Harrison, R.T. and Mason, C.M. (2000), 'Venture capital market complementarities: The link between business angels and venture capital funds in the United Kingdom', *Venture Capital: An International Journal of Entrepreneurial Finance*, **2** (3), 223–242.

Hellmann, T. (1998), 'The allocation of control rights in venture capital contracts', *Rand Journal of Economics*, **29** (1), 57–76.

Hellmann, T. and Puri, M. (2002), 'Venture capital and the professionalization of start-up firms: Empirical evidence', *Journal of Finance*, **57** (1), 169–197.

Hellmann, T., Schure, P. and Vo, D. (2015), 'Angels and venture capitalists: Complements or substitutes?', Said Business School, Working Paper No. 2015-2.

Hochberg, Y. (2004), 'Venture capital and corporate governance in the newly public firm', Stanford University, Mimeo.

Hochberg, Y., Ljungqvist, A. and Lu, Y. (2004), 'Who you know matters: Venture capital networks and investment performance', Cornell University working paper.

Hsu, D.K., Haynie, J.M., Simmons, S.A. and McKelvie, A. (2014), 'What matters, matters differently: A conjoint analysis of the decision policies of angel and venture capital investors', *Venture Capital*, **16** (1), 1–25.

Ibrahim, D.M. (2008), 'The (not so) puzzling behavior of angel investors', *Vanderbilt Law Review*, **61** (5), 1405–1452.

Jääskeläinen, M., Maula, M. and Seppä, T. (2006), 'Allocation of attention to portfolio companies and the performance of venture capital firms', *Entrepreneurship Theory and Practice*, **30** (2),185–206.

Jensen, M.C. (1986), 'Agency costs of free cash flow, corporate finance, and takeovers', *American Economic Review*, **76** (2), 323–329.

Jensen, M.C. (1989), 'Active investors, LBOs, and the privatization of bankruptcy', *Journal of Applied Corporate Finance*, **2** (1), 35–44.

Jensen, M.C. and Meckling, W.H. (1976), 'Theory of the firm: Managerial behavior, agency costs and ownership structure', *Journal of Financial Economics*, **3** (4), 305–360.

Johnson, W.C. and Sohl, J. (2012), 'Angels and venture capitalists in the initial public offering market', *Venture Capital: An International Journal of Entrepreneurial Finance*, **14** (1), 27–42.

Kanniainen, V. and Keuschnigg, C. (2003), 'The optimal portfolio of start-up firms in venture capital finance', *Journal of Corporate Finance*, **9** (5), 521–534.

Kanniainen, V. and Keuschnigg, C. (2004), 'Start-up investment with scarce venture capital support', *Journal of Banking and Finance*, **28** (8), 1935–1959.

Kaplan, S. and Stromberg, P. (2000), 'How do venture capitalists choose and manage their investments', University of Chicago working paper.

Kaplan, S. and Stromberg, P. (2003), 'Financial contracting theory meets the real world: Evidence from venture capital contracts', *Review of Economic Studies*, **70** (2), 281–315.

Kaplan, S. and Stromberg, P. (2004), 'Characteristics, contracts, and actions: Evidence from venture capitalist analyses', *Journal of Finance*, **59** (5), 2177–2210.

Karpoff, J.M., Johnson, W.C. and Yi, S. (2015), 'The bonding hypothesis of takeover defenses: Evidence from IPO firms', *Journal of Financial Economics*, **117** (2), 307–332.

Kerr, W.R., Lerner, J. and Schoar, A. (2014a), 'The consequences of entrepreneurial finance: Evidence from angel financings', *Review of Financial Studies*, **27** (1), 1–19.

Kerr, W.R., Lerner, J. and Schoar, A. (2014b), 'The consequences of entrepreneurial finance: A regression discontinuity', *Review of Financial Studies*, **27** (1), 20–55.

Klausner, M. (2003), 'Institutional shareholders, private equity, and anti-takeover protection at the IPO stage', *University of Pennsylvania Law Review*, **152**.

Kroszner, R.S. and Strahan, P.E. (2001), 'Bankers on boards: Monitoring, conflicts of interest, and lender liability', *Journal of Financial Economics*, **62** (3), 415–52.

Landström, H. (1993), 'Informal risk capital in Sweden and some international comparisons', *Journal of Business Venturing*, **8** (6), 525–540.

Landström, H. (2007), *Handbook of Research on Venture Capital*, Cheltenham, UK and Northampton, MA, USA: Edward Elgar Publishing.

Lehn, K. and Poulsen, A. (1989), 'Free cash flow and stockholder gains in going private transactions', *Journal of Finance*, **44**, 771–788.

Lerner, J. (1994), 'The syndication of venture capital investments', *Financial Management*, **23**, 16–27.

Lerner, J. (1995), 'Venture capitalists and the oversight of private firms', *Journal of Finance*, **50**, 301–318.

Leslie, P. and Oyer, P. (2009), 'Managerial incentives and value creation: Evidence from private equity', Working Paper, Stanford University.

Loughran, T. and Ritter, J.R. (1995), 'The new issue puzzle', *Journal of Finance*, **50**, 23–51.

Mason, C.M. (2006), 'Informal sources of venture finance', in Parker, S.C. (ed.), *The Life Cycle of Entrepreneurial Ventures*, New York: Springer, pp. 259–299.

Menard, S. (1995), 'Applied logistic regression analysis', Sage University Papers Series on Quantitative Applications in the Social Sciences, No. 106, Thousand Oaks, CA: Sage.

Morrisette, S.G. (2007), 'A profile of angel investors', *Journal of Private Equity*, **10** (3), 52–66.

Parrino, R. (1997), 'CEO turnover and outside succession: A cross sectional analysis', *Journal of Financial Economics*, **46**, 165–197.

Paul, S. and Whittam, G. (2010), 'Business angel syndicates: An exploratory study of gatekeepers', *Venture Capital: An International Journal of Entrepreneurial Finance*, **12** (3), 241–256.

Politis, D. (2008), 'Business angels and value added: What do we know and where do we go?', *Venture Capital: An International Journal of Entrepreneurial Finance*, **10** (2), 127–147.

Ritter, J.R. (1991), 'The long-run performance of initial public offerings', *Journal of Finance*, **46**, 3–27.

Sahlman, W.A. (1990), 'The structure and governance of venture capital organizations', *Journal of Financial Economics*, **27**, 473–524.

Shane, S. (2008), 'The importance of angel investing in financing the growth of entrepreneurial ventures', SBA Office of Advocacy Working Paper, No. 331, Washington, DC.

Sohl, J.E. and Hill, L. (2007), 'Women business angels: Insights from angel groups', *Venture Capital: An International Journal of Entrepreneurial Finance*, **9** (3), 207–222.

Sorenson, O. and Stuart, T.E. (2001), 'Syndication networks and the spatial distribution of venture capital investments', *American Journal of Sociology*, **106** (6), 1546–1588.

Sørheim, R. and Landström, H. (2001), 'Informal investors – a categorization with policy implications', *Entrepreneurship and Regional Development*, **13** (4), 351–370.

Stiglitz, J.E. (1985), 'Credit markets and the control of capital', *Journal of Money, Credit and Banking*, **17**, 133–152.

Suchard, J.A. (2009), 'The impact of venture capital backing on the corporate governance of Australian initial public offerings', *Journal of Banking and Finance*, **33**, 765–774.

Teoh, S.H., Welch, I. and Wong, T. (1998), 'Earnings management and the long-run performance of initial public offerings', *Journal of Finance*, **53**, 1935–1974.

Van Osnabrugge, M. (2000), 'A comparison of business angel and venture capitalist investment procedures: An agency theory-based analysis', *Venture Capital: An International Journal of Entrepreneurial Finance*, **2** (2), 91–109.

Williamson, O.E. (1983), 'Organization form, residual claimants, and corporate control', *Journal of Law and Economics*, **26**, 351–366.

WilmerHale (2014), '2013 M&A Report', Boston, MA: WilmerHale Associates.

Wong, A., Bhatia, M. and Freeman, Z. (2009), 'Angel finance: The other venture capital', *Strategic Change*, **18** (7–8), 221–230.

Zingales, L. (1995), 'What determines the value of corporate votes?', *Quarterly Journal of Economics*, **110**, 1047–1073.

PART III

CORPORATE GOVERNANCE IN SMES

8. Corporate governance practices in smaller privately held businesses: insights from the Rhine Valley region
Susanne Durst and Julia Brunold

INTRODUCTION

Corporate governance represents an area of immense research interest (Cadbury, 1992; Shleifer and Vishny, 1997; Johnson and Greening, 1999). However, when we consider governance in small firms, then the opposite is true: there is a lack of research (Audretsch and Lehmann, 2011; Gill et al., 2012; Lappalainen and Niskanen, 2012). The lack of interest in governance of small firms is surprising given the importance of this category of firms to most economies. Small firms are important drivers of economic growth, employment, technological development and structural change (OECD, 2002); consequently an understanding of how (corporate) governance is practiced is a key issue in the development and support of this entrepreneurial segment of the economy.

Additionally, the study of corporate governance is mainly dominated by quantitative research methods (McNulty et al., 2013; Zattoni et al., 2013). As a result, our understanding of the topic is rather unilateral and focused on confirming the well-known, which therefore prevents us from taking advantage of alternative approaches and insights (Bansal, 2013). Indeed, the continued dominance of agency theory and its assumption of rational economic agents could have hampered the application of other research methodologies (Bansal, 2013). Moreover, and noteworthy in this regard, many journals predominantly publish quantitative research. In prestigious journals such as the *Academy of Management Journal*, only a small number of qualitative papers are published, which suggests that potential contributors to these journals would be better off developing papers that are grounded in deductive research, even though there have been calls from several editors for an increased number of qualitative papers (e.g. Bansal, 2013; Zattoni et al., 2013). Finally, extant research has been carried out in the United States (US) and United Kingdom (UK) contexts (Huse, 2005) and lacks cross-cultural studies (Gispert et al., 2005; Voordeckers et al., 2014). Findings presented have implied that they are generalizable, which may not be the case (Uhlaner et al., 2007b). As far as the study of corporate governance in smaller firms is concerned, the focus thus far has been on conceptual papers (e.g. Uhlaner et al., 2007b).

Against the background of the discussion above it is not surprising that the few empirical studies that have been conducted have mostly used a positivist or deductive methodology, where quantitative methods have been used to test for significant relationships between the types of variables (for example, the characteristics of the board of directors) that have been associated with the study of corporate governance in listed firms. Applying this framework to the study of small or family-owned firms is problematic, particularly as there is an implicit assumption of a separation of ownership from control within the firms being studied (Brunninge et al., 2007; Zahra et al., 2007; Voordeckers et al., 2007). Moreover, our understanding of actual corporate governance practices is rather limited (Voordeckers et al., 2014).

As a response to these knowledge gaps, our chapter examines how corporate governance is practiced in smaller firms in the Rhine Valley region, more precisely in parts of both Austria and the Principality of Liechtenstein. The aim of this chapter is to address a number of issues that will help us to develop our understanding of how governance is being implemented in smaller firms. Firstly, what exactly do the decision-makers in small firms understand by the term 'corporate governance'? And secondly, which governance methods and procedures are implemented by the management of these firms? In sum, the chapter's intention is to provide insights into how beliefs and practices of small firm owner-managers are reflected in their governance structures. In order to do so, we take a bottom-up approach, meaning that the issue of corporate governance is approached from a practitioner's perspective rather than a prescriptive one. This perspective can help to build a stronger bridge between theory and practice (Taylor, 2006).

In this chapter, a smaller firm is defined as any business that is an independent company in which an overlap between ownership and management exists and with no more than 250 employees. This firm can be run by an individual or a team of individuals (which do not have to be relatives).

The chapter is organized as follows. In the next section, the literature related to the research purpose is briefly presented, followed by a description of the methodology adopted. The results are then presented, followed by a discussion, and the conclusions of the chapter are laid out in the final section.

THEORETICAL BACKGROUND

Smaller Firms

The type of firm that represents the focus of our chapter cannot be understood without reference to the owner-manager, who is normally the central decision-maker within the firm (Bridge and O'Neill, 2013). In addition, this individual is often the longest-tenured member of the firm, which in turn makes it possible to develop a specific knowledge about the firm (He, 2008). Therefore, in such an environment increased attention must be given to this person. In the situation of complete ownership concentration, one can expect that the owner-manager will undertake certain actions concerning the organizational structure and selection of environment that help them to reach their goals. This standing will also influence the firm's response to new ideas and information (Child, 1972). Even though this type of owner-manager disposes of more or less unlimited power, the decisions made and, particularly, the likelihood of their success will be influenced by the remaining organization members' willingness to back them. Consequently, internal negotiations play a critical role (Child, 1997). As owner-managers of those firms are less constrained by shareholders compared with larger listed companies, they are in a position to take advantage of a wider range of alternatives regarding decision-making (Child, 1997).

Corporate Governance

As far as definitions of corporate governance are concerned, there is a variety of definitions available. For example, the Cadbury Report (1992) defines corporate governance as:

> The systems by which companies are directed and controlled, boards of directors are responsible for the governance of their companies. The shareholders' role in governance is to appoint the directors and auditors and to satisfy themselves that an appropriate governance structure is in place in the organization. The responsibilities of the board include setting the company's strategic aims, providing leadership to put them into effect, supervising the management of the business and reporting to shareholders on their stewardship. The board's actions are subject to laws, regulations and the shareholders' general meeting. (Cadbury, 1992, Para. 2.5)

Shleifer and Vishny (1997) argue that corporate governance 'deals with the ways in which suppliers of finance to corporations assure themselves of getting a return on their investment' (p. 737). Aguilera and Jackson (2003) view corporate governance as 'the relationships among stakeholders in the process of decision making and control over firm resources' (p. 450). Mallin (2010) stresses that corporate governance also comprises the mechanisms that help firms to attain their corporate objectives; thereby monitoring performance is viewed as a key element in achieving these goals. For Carney (2005), arguing from a family business perspective, 'systems of corporate governance embody distinct incentives, authority structures, and norms of accountability that generate specific organizational propensities' (p. 249). And according to Papesch (2010), arguing from the same perspective, corporate governance structures include the balancing of management and control with different stakeholders' interests, as well as the processes and structures facilitating a firm's long-term survivability.

In the small firm context where formal structures and processes are rare (Miller, 1983), and owner-managers 'often rely on informal social controls rather than on contractual governance' (Uhlaner et al., 2007a, p. 276), the term 'relational governance' might be more appropriate. According to Mustakallio et al. (2002, p. 206), relational governance 'is based on the creation and usage of social capital embedded in social relationships among the owner-family members and management'. Even though the authors are addressing family firms, the existence of close (social) relationships can be expected in small firms as well (O'Donnell, 2013). According to Zaheer and Venkatraman (1995), these social relationships are characterized by trust, cooperation and stability. The existence of trust in particular is viewed as the main condition for relational governance (Granovetter, 1985). In situations of trust, it is further argued that it may act as compensation for high levels of control (Zaheer and Venkatraman, 1995). In the context of small firms, we expect that long-term relationships in particular – that is, long-term employments – foster the existence of trust in employer and employee relations as well as among employees (Blomqvist, 1997). Over time, the parties involved can develop, test, observe and confirm the existence of trust as well as other preconditions of close relationships (Poppo and Zenger, 2002). Consequently, the existence of informal governance structures may be more likely than that of formal governance structures (Uhlaner et al., 2007a).

Therefore, in this chapter the term 'relational governance' is used, which involves the structures, processes and relationships with relevant stakeholders that support owner-managers in measures concerning corporate governance and organizational development. This definition makes clear that our understanding of good corporate governance is not limited to a monitoring function, but also fulfills an enterprising function in order to prepare firms for present and future business challenges. Consequently, corporate governance systems are viewed as a fundamental basis for organizational development and thus the firms' long-term success.

Additionally, the definition puts a strong emphasis on relationships with different stakeholders, taking into account the smaller firms' dependency on those groups (for example, employees). By taking a broader view of corporate governance, this chapter joins recent research activities that are interested in understanding additional roles of corporate governance beyond that of control (Uhlaner et al., 2007b; Wirtz, 2011).

Corporate Governance in Small Firms

Having in mind what has been outlined so far, it is surprising to see that the few studies conducted in the area put an emphasis on corporate governance variables that have been developed for large and listed companies (e.g. Brunninge et al., 2007), apparently assuming that what works in those firms will work in small firms as well. This appears inappropriate, as those firms are typically based on separation of ownership and management and control (Wesel, 2010). A transfer to smaller privately held firms would assume that this separation is the only suitable organizational form, thus ignoring alternative corporate ownership structures as found around the world (La Porta et al., 1999). Moreover, by implementing approaches originally developed for larger firms, the danger is that smaller firms are losing their distinct characteristics and at the end their capability to act.

When looking at the research topics that have received the most attention, an emphasis on the study of boards, in particular, can be established (e.g. Huse, 1990; Voordeckers et al., 2007; Minichilli and Hansen, 2007; Neville, 2011; Calabrò and Mussolino, 2013). This finding is questionable, as many smaller firms do not have one (Van Gils, 2005). Indeed, the underlying assumptions of these boards may better apply to the structures found in large and listed companies (Velayutham, 2013). The worst, however, is that this situation limits our openness regarding alternatives that might be better suited to the nature of smaller firms, which brings us back to the introduction of this chapter. One noteworthy exception is the study by Voordeckers et al. (2014) which examined formal board structures and actual board behavior in privately held small and medium-sized enterprises (SMEs) in Belgium, the Netherlands and Norway. The study demonstrated the decoupling of formal board structures and actual board behavior. Furthermore, the findings imply that actual governance practices and behavior in small firms are in fact very similar.

Generally, when researching smaller firms, it is claimed that the issue of heterogeneity is taken into account (Curran and Blackburn, 2001), which makes the idea of one single governance system nearly impossible. Moreover, based on contingency theory, some authors argue that certain corporate governance systems work in different situations (Giovannini,

2010). Huse (2005), for example, argues that there is no best corporate governance system as contexts (for example, national, geographical and cultural differences; industry and industrial environment; ownership dispersion; firm size; life-cycle variations; and chief executive officer tenure, attributes and background) and actors are the relevant variables influencing the actual design. Consequently, suitable governance systems would take into consideration the specific attributes and requirements of smaller firms (Mustakallio et al., 2002). This would call for governance systems that are not too rigid, but flexible enough to support a small firm's moves in the business environment. Additionally, these systems take into account the different needs depending on the firm's life cycle (Lynall et al., 2003; Uhlaner et al., 2007b). This notion is shared by Lubatkin et al. (2007) who highlight the dynamism of the governance system as a result of knowledge sharing and learning. The authors further underline that corporate governance is influenced by the owners' and/or executives' viewpoints. In the same vein, Filatotchev and Bishop (2002) conclude that 'corporate governance factors may be affected by strategic actions and outcomes and the choice of the various governance options could be associated with changes in organizational strategy and firm performance' (p. 953).

In sum, the extant body of knowledge regarding corporate governance in small firms can be assessed as rather fragmented, and exhibits an emphasis on quantitative research approaches intended to test governance variables that have been developed for large listed companies. Thereby, the study of boards dominates. Our understanding of how corporate governance is actually understood and practiced in small firms is ill-developed. This situation calls for intense exploratory (qualitative) research approaches that can contribute to insights and developments at both theoretical and empirical levels.

METHOD

Given the aim of our chapter, an exploratory (qualitative) research approach was chosen. A qualitative approach allowed us to get closer to the participants and their thinking; in order to scrutinize the entire research problem in depth. These insights would not be possible using a quantitative approach (Maykut and Morehouse, 1994; Miles and Huberman, 1994).

The companies selected for our chapter were small firms from Austria (more precisely, from the Vorarlberg province) and the Principality of Liechtenstein. This region, known as the Rhine Valley, is characterized by an 'Alemannic' mentality. Inhabitants of this region are seen as hard-working and ambitious. The translation of 'working' is *schaffa*, which means 'to create'. People have a high sense of goal-orientation and individual responsibility: they want to do their work on their own, taking control over outcomes, and to avoid solely relying on others. Besides, the Rhine Valley as a region has been shaped predominantly by privately held businesses (Pleininger, 2012). The sample of firms chosen for the chapter included firms from a number of different sectors. Both countries have a high preponderance of small firms and are comparable in their business practices due to the mentality they share.

As far as the corporate governance system is concerned, the Principality of Liechtenstein and Austria represent similar systems. In 2012, the then acting government in Liechtenstein enacted a Public Corporate Governance Code to be applied for the first time in the 2013 financial year. The Liechtenstein corporate governance model is derived from the continental European two-tier model of a supervisory board and a separate management or executive committee of executive directors. In the Principality of Liechtenstein – similarly to Switzerland – however, a flexible constitution of the organizational structure is admitted. Consequently, a board of directors can fulfill both a supervisory function and a management function (one-tier system) whereas the management function may be delegated by the board (Marxer, 2009). In Austria the Austrian Code of Corporate Governance was presented to the public on 1 October 2002 and follows the continental European two-tier model (without the flexible constitution as found in Liechtenstein). The Austrian Code addresses primarily Austrian exchange-listed companies including exchange-listed European companies (*societas Europaea*) registered in Austria. Private firms are recommended to follow this code.

Because of the fact that we were not able to rely on a database, we had to take advantage of contacts of the Institute for Entrepreneurship (University of Liechtenstein) as well as personal contacts. This, in turn, suggested that a lot of time was required in order to gain access to suitable research subjects.

The interviews were mainly conducted with executive staff (that is, managing directors, owner-managers) of the firms. Twenty-five individuals were involved. We collected data through semi-structured interviews. This type of interview is appropriate when the planned study comprises an exploratory element (Saunders et al., 2009). Although this type of interview is flexible regarding the order of questions – providing the opportunity to explore aspects in greater depth – the discussion is centered upon the research topic which is introduced by the interviewer (Mayring, 1990).

The interview process was supported by an interview guide consisting of four parts. Open-ended questions were used to underline the chapter's exploratory character. The interview guide was tested on a managing director from Liechtenstein. This course of action led to some amendments to the wording of the questions. The final interview guide focused on the following points: general facts about the business and the managing director; the understanding of corporate governance and its application in the firm; and the measures used to support organizational development. The interviews were conducted between September 2011 and October 2012, took place in the interviewees' work environment, and lasted up to 90 minutes. They were tape-recorded and then transcribed. Note-taking during and after the interviews was used as a means to record thoughts and seemingly important aspects related to the phenomena under investigation.

To analyze the data we applied the data display and analysis approach as proposed by Miles and Huberman (1994). The authors divide the analysis process into three sub-processes. First, the data are reduced, meaning they are summarized. For this process, we reworked the field notes from each interview together with the tape recordings. Afterward, interview summaries were produced which included the most important aspects discovered. Second, data display is conducted by organizing the data into charts, diagrams or other visual forms. In our chapter, this meant that the most important data from each interviewee were displayed in an Excel matrix under different broad themes. The themes developed represented an outcome of searching for themes which appeared to be of importance for the understanding of the phenomenon under investigation (Fereday and Muir-Cochrane, 2006), for example, ownership structure, understanding of corporate governance, process of decision-making, employee involvement. After all of the interviewees' data were displayed under these themes, an overview of the most relevant collected data was made. This helped us to compare the data, find similarities or differences, and draw conclusions. The overall data analysis process involved both of us, which allowed for multiple perspectives for each interview and for cross-case analysis (Eisenhardt, 1989). The characteristics of the interviewees and the interviewees' firms are summarized in Table 8.1.

Table 8.1 clarifies that a fairly balanced mix of micro, small and medium-sized enterprises, and a range of company ages, were represented. A balance regarding the industry and the industry's characteristics was also apparent. Additionally, the table suggests that staff are very loyal to the company they work for, and that experienced employee teams can be expected.

Table 8.1 Demographic characteristics of the participants

Interviewee	Industry	Industry characteristic	Position	Company's age	Number of employees	Staff turnover rate
1	Spice	Stable	Managing director (MD)	39	13	low
2	Trade (software and computer accessory)	Rather dynamic	MD	15	23	low
3	Printing	Dynamic	MD	85	50	low
4	Mechatronics	Rather stable	MD	61	12	low
5	Corrosion prevention	Dynamic	Managing partner	153	40	low
6	Software (medical)	Rather dull	Founder and MD	8	15	low
7	Main contract work	Conservative	MD	38	37	low
8	Printed media	Dynamic	Owner-manager	26	40	low
9	Printing machines	Dynamic	MD	0.75	21	low
10	Engineering (drive technology)	Stable	International sales manager	62	220	low
11	Retailing (PC games)	Dynamic	Founder and MD	5	8	low
12	Creation of synthetics	Stable	Owner-manager	47	10	low
13	Timber trade	Stable	MD	59	8	low
14	Logistics	Dynamic	Owner-manager	43	45	low
15	CNC manufacturing	Dynamic	MD	35	50	low
16	Hotel and tourism	Dynamic	Owner-manager	160	35	low
17	Software (logistics)	Dynamic	Founder and MD	20	96	low
18	Optician	Dynamic	Owner-manager	37	14	moderate
19	Furniture	Dynamic	Assistant to management	34	34	low
20	Butcher	Dynamic	Owner-manager	39	50	low
21	Retail and print	Stable	MD	58	180	low
22	Supplier for mechanical engineering	Dynamic	MD	36	150	low
23	Air transport	Dynamic	MD	38	50	low
24	Fruit and snack trade	Dynamic	Owner-manager	3	10	moderate
25	Coffee roasters	Stable	Owner-manager	3	3	very low

FINDINGS

In this section, the chapter's findings are presented. We include quotes from the informants where appropriate.

Understanding of Corporate Governance

One issue of concern for this chapter was the extent to which managing directors in small firms understand the term 'corporate governance'. Each interviewee was asked what they understood by the term 'corporate governance'. Six respondents had not heard of the term before, whereas the remaining respondents associated the term with a code of behavior, responsible management, controlling, ethics, cooperation and a set of values. In particular, the handling of employees was stressed, which underlines the strong employee orientation often found in smaller firms (Hine and Ryan, 1999). The findings reveal that the interviewees have a relatively broad perception of the term, yet they also show that the term is not associated with having a board or other more formal structures. The statements recorded also illustrated that the term, according to the interviewees, is less associated with control but more with ways of working together with different stakeholders. The following presents some statements on this issue:

> For me, Corporate Governance is a code of behavior. How the company itself, how managers and employees deal with customers . . . How they behave related to the external and to the internal environment. (Interviewee 5)

> Business ethics, firm ethics, employee ethics, environment ethics . . . actually it has a lot to do with questions on how to behave properly when doing business. (Interviewee 21)

> I personally find that it is kind of a catalog of values the company feels responsible for and this catalog comprises questions concerning the following topics: How do we deal with employees? How do we deal with customers? How do we deal with suppliers? So it is kind of a trial to give all actions kind of an ethic corridor. (Interviewee 1)

Governance Structure

Information on the companies regarding ownership and governance are presented in Table 8.2.

Table 8.2 shows that 12 firms are characterized by complete ownership concentration (that is, 100 percent). Ownership in the remaining firms is distributed over two and three individuals, respectively. In firm

Table 8.2 Ownership and governance

Company	Owner-managed	Ownership structure	TMT	Board
1	Yes	100% family	No	Yes
2	Yes	Founders 45% each; former employer 10%	Yes	No
3	Yes	100% father	No	Yes
4	Yes	50% MD, 25% brother & 25% sister	No	No
5	Yes	50% managing partner & 50% brother	No	No
6	Yes	100%	No	No
7	Yes	50% MD, 25% partner & 25% the partner's son	Yes	Yes
8	Yes	100%	No	No
9	No	100%	Yes	No
10	Yes	100%	Yes	No
11	Yes	100% MD	Yes	No
12	Yes	100% owner-manager	Yes	Yes
13	No	75% sister & 25% sister's husband	Yes	No
14	Yes	100% owner-manager	Yes	No
15	Yes	50% MD & 50% his wife	Yes	No
16	Yes	100% owner-manager	Yes	No
17	Yes	50% MD & 50% his wife	Yes	No
18	Yes	50% owner-manager & 50% his wife	Yes	No
19	Yes	Three owners (father, daughter, son)	Yes	Yes
20	Yes	Two owners (brothers)	Yes	No
21	No	100% MD	No	Yes
22	No	Four owners (comprising 3 families)	Yes	Yes
23	No	Two owners (sisters)	No	No
24	Yes	Two owners	Yes	No
25	Yes	100% owner-manager	No	No

22, ownership is distributed among four shareholders. These findings confirm the high concentration of ownership typically found in smaller firms (Neville, 2011). Many of the firms involved are managed by a top management team (2, 7, 9, 10, 11, 12, 15, 17, 20, 22 and 24) or something similar (13, 14, 16, 18 and 19). The latter refers to management teams that are not officially communicated, but are formed informally. Regardless of the type of management team, they commonly consist of persons performing different responsibilities (for example, technical tasks versus business tasks). A board is established in eight companies (1, 3, 7, 12, 15, 19, 21 and 24). The number of board members is in the range of 2–6. Almost all cases reported that the board was established because of legal obligation, so a passive (inactive) approach dominates. Interviewee 15, for example, emphasized that their board takes a very informal role. It consists of six people – four family members and two external persons – and serves as a way of involving the closest people in business issues, which happens bi-yearly at the maximum. Interviewee 19 stated that at the moment the board has an inactive role, which mainly means that she and her father use it as an opportunity to spend some pleasant time together. In the future, however, this situation should change according to the interviewee, and the board's task will be to give her father an opportunity to control her business activities and if necessary to intervene. All board members have links to the firms, which is in line with previous research (Pearce and Zahra, 1992). Additionally, the boards appear to be less open to outsiders, which might reflect the region's mentality. This observation is comparable to Corbetta and Montemerlo's (1999) findings from Italy. None of the firms surveyed reported the establishment of an advisory board or council or other more formal governance constructs.

Internal and External Collaboration and Exchange

As shown in Table 8.1, the firms are primarily characterized by low turnover rates, so teams of experienced organization members are rather likely. This, in turn, could have led to a close working atmosphere and smooth operations. The findings indicate that firms in which this scenario occurs are characterized by teams showing cohesion and a strong bond to the firm. Interviewee 24 stated:

> We are a great team. Our employees identify to 100% with the company, almost too much. Sometimes I get a call from my employees on Sundays because they have an idea. That's real nice.

And Interviewee 15 reported:

> The cohesion in our company is strong; people feel they belong to us. We regularly organize events with employees . . . I am very proud of the prizes that our apprentices win in competitions.

Several interviewees emphasized team-based activities that are organized regularly (for example, Interviewees 2, 6, 10, 15, 16, 17, 23 and 24). When it comes to assigning responsibilities to employees, not surprisingly, trust plays an important role. Indeed, the 'autocrats' of important functions such as accounting or sales are often close collaborators, friends or family members (Interviewees 2, 3, 5, 12, 13, 15, 17 and 24).

Concerning collaboration with external actors, some respondents turn to their informal network (that is, long-time companions) with whom they have built very specific trust relationships when discussing strategic issues (17 and 24). Interviewee 17 stated that the person in question provides 'emotional support' (Bruderl and Preisendorfer, 1998) in the case of important decisions:

> I have an old friend, who was an entrepreneur as well. Since a few years, we sit together every once a while and discuss the issues that are on the table. He supports me a lot with his experiences, and sometimes I just need his approval for difficult decisions. (Interviewee 17)

Many respondents mentioned the use of networks as a means for exchange, advice and/or gathering new information (O'Donnell, 2013):

> There is also another friend, he is over 65 years old and our business idea is the result of him. He takes over a 'support' role I would say. We contact him when it comes to different questions . . . These are mostly important issues, for example about strategy, where I like to hear his opinion. (Interviewee 24)

The findings indicate that these external contacts are also used to provide an independent outside view or to obtain a different perspective on business issues. As one would expect, different network partners fulfill different roles. Existing customers, 'friendly' firms and main suppliers represent the primary external contacts. The chapter's findings are in line with prior research regarding the significance of networking in smaller firms (Gilmore et al., 2001).

Decision-Making

When it comes to decision-making the interviewees primarily involve close confidants from within the firm, which is a logical consequence of earlier statements. These confidants seem to enjoy the interviewees' confidence and trust. These groups of people, called 'cadre' in firms 2, 3 and 8, are relatively fixed, even though new individuals are added on certain occasions. This occurs, for example, if expert knowledge is needed (4 and 10). The meetings take place regularly and resemble 'kitchen cabinets' (Frisch, 2011).

In terms of operative business issues, the firms primarily follow a decentralized decision-making approach, whereas with strategic issues a centralized approach is pursued. As illustrated in the previous subsection, the firms surveyed stand out by showing a strong employee involvement. This is also reflected in the decision-making process. Several respondents highlighted team decisions as the main approach to decision-making (5, 6, 10, 11, 12, 13, 15 and 17). On that matter, Interviewee 11 stated:

> In our company the whole team has its coffee break together, current topics are discussed and decided jointly. The opinions of the other employees are always listened to when it's a matter of, for example, the purchase of a new machine.

And Interviewee 17 reported:

> Employees are always involved. I always gather my employees together first. Okay, you can only do this up to a point. I have the final say if we cannot agree. Usually, though I always try to reach a consensus with the departmental heads beforehand, to establish how they would like to see it.

By having involved their employees, the interviewees' decision-making process is supported in that they obtain a broader picture of the issues. Additionally, it helps to promote mutual understanding of and agreement on forthcoming business activities. Consequently, it can reinforce a sense of community. This atmosphere may also result in faster decision-making.

The findings provide evidence that employees represent the first point of information when critical decisions regarding company development are pending. Only when the employees are not able to provide answers to this issue do the managing directors turn to other individuals of their (extended) network (O'Donnell, 2013). The managing directors (as indicated by Interviewee 17, and not surprisingly) are the ones who make the final decisions. Beforehand, however, the findings indicate that each organization member has an equal position.

Given the number of network partners to which the interviewees have access, some interviewees (3, 4, 5, 6, 12, 13, 14, 18 and 24) involve befriended external individuals (for example, from 'friendly' companies, from the same industry, from the guild, suppliers and customers) in the decision-making process as a means of having access to outside perspectives or opinions. Here too the existence of trust is underlined. Interviewee 13 said that 'trust replaces written contracts, even though trust can be abused too'.

As expected in a small firm environment, decision-making tends to follow an informal approach, and the interviewees did not mention the application of tools that could support the process. Regular but informal rituals, such as a discussion during the coffee break involving all organization members, appear to dominate.

Concerning the generation of new ideas in order to further develop the firm, several interviewees reported that ideas are generated at every level of the firm (10, 11, 12, 15, 16, 17, 23 and 24), which is a further illustration of the strong involvement of staff. The organization members seem to feel somewhat responsible for the firm's continuous development and thus its long-term success.

DISCUSSION

The findings underline that when it comes to corporate governance the respondents take advantage of simple structures, which are primarily people-focussed. Indeed, the structures found can be assigned to informal and relational governance systems (Mustakallio et al., 2002). The development of these structures might have been internally favored by low staff turnover. Low staff turnover also contributes to a stronger identification of the organization members with their firm, and an increased willingness of engaging in firm issues. This situation, in conjunction with the existence of well-integrated teams that are characterized by trust, compensates for more formal (contractual) governance approaches (Mustakallio et al., 2002). The findings suggest that the practice of corporate governance in the firms surveyed is not so much about control as it is understood in the frequently cited definitions of corporate governance provided by the Cadbury Report (1992) or Shleifer and Vishny (1997), but more about ways of working together with different stakeholders. As a result, the findings seem to be more in line with corporate governance definitions as provided by Aguilera and Jackson (2003) and Papesch (2010). On the other hand, the existence of frequent exchanges makes informal control possible (Jones et al., 1997). Consequently, in such environments, there is no need for strong and costly governance mechanisms as a means of accomplishing a control function (Bowey and Easton, 2007).

Regarding the people approach to corporate governance, the findings highlight the particular role ordinary employees play in terms of the firm's further development and corporate governance. Interactions with employees are very close, and the statements clarify that the managing directors continuously involve their staff in the strategic decision-making process, thereby reducing to some extent the burden of being the sole decision-maker within the firm (Deakins et al., 2000). The managing directors make use of their employees and their knowledge to solve problems, to discuss new product ideas and so on, which underlines the contribution of networking to company development (O'Donnell, 2013) and the general role of employees in SME business operations (Cowling, 2003). This finding also supports Rajan and Zingales's (2000) argumentation that valuable resources (human capital in particular) are found everywhere in the company and not only among top management. So one may conclude that the managing directors have realized that in order to survive and compete in a knowledge-driven business environment they have to include their employees in business decisions at all levels of the firm (Muthusamy et al., 2011). Consequently, the findings presented in this chapter suggest that small firms provide a setting where the ideas of co-determination (that is, employee participation in corporate governance) are highly applicable (Muthusamy et al., 2011). The findings also clarify that in privately held firms an emphasis is placed on other stakeholders compared with the prioritizations in large listed firms (Blair, 1998).

Given the interdependence between managing directors and employees in small firms concerning the achievement of desired objectives (Pfeffer and Salancik, 1978), the increasing importance of human capital, and the situation that a growing number of industries and firms are exposed to skills shortages (Interviewee 4, for example, reported increasing difficulties in recruiting staff), the position of employees has changed over time. This is, *inter alia*, reflected in the firms by the influence – that is, a greater say – that the employees have in directing business decisions. Indeed, the findings seem to confirm Blair's (1998) theoretical reasoning that in situations in which different types of assets (that is, knowledge assets, and financial and tangible assets) are dependent on each other, neither asset has much value without the other. Therefore, even if complete ownership concentration or high ownership concentration is present, it does not allow the managing directors to alter the organizational context at their own discretion. Consequently, one could argue that to a certain extent the employees assume the role of active board members as suggested in the literature (McNulty and Pettigrew, 1999; Mustakallio et al., 2002; Lynall et al., 2003).

Concerning (external) networks, the findings illustrate that the managing directors make great use of external formal and informal contacts. These contacts are used not only for information but also for advice (O'Donnell, 2013). Besides, the networks are characterized by spatial proximity: that is, the majority of contacts are located in the region. This circumstance apparently fosters economic efficiency of the actors involved, as a face-to-face exchange can easily and quickly be managed (Huggins and Johnston, 2010). It is also an indicator of the specific region under investigation, where firms apparently prefer to network with local and regional actors.

In general, networks comprising members with suitable competencies and know-how regarding the firm and the industry can help overcome a lack of resources and at the same time enable the firm to better address organizational development (Barringer, 1997). Well-functioning networks can also mean a source of competitive advantage in smaller firms (O'Donnell, 2013). Transferred to the study of corporate governance, the findings can be referred to as 'governance by network' (Jones et al., 1997), which not only contributes to present business challenges and problems, but can also systematically be used for activities addressing the firm's future well-being. In such an environment, network activities take a

strategic role in assuming those tasks that in the existent corporate governance literature are normally associated with boards. In the present chapter,
network activities primarily function as a means of broadening the resource
basis. However, as the networks also comprise employees (that is, internal
networks), one can argue that these persons take on a control role as well,
as they provide feedback or express disapproval should the managing
directors act differently to what had originally been planned or decided.
Consequently, both perspectives on boards (control and resource provider)
are covered to a certain extent (Corbetta and Salvato, 2004).

Additionally, the findings demonstrate the position that 'kitchen cabinets' have in the firms surveyed, so confirming Frisch's (2011) line of
argumentation. These cabinets are used in particular to address company
development, whereby their composition tends to vary depending on the
issue at hand. By involving a variety of organization members in terms of
their functional background, that is, their functional-specific knowledge,
the managing directors increase the likelihood of coming up with alternative solutions as well as a higher number of different ideas (Sundaramurthy
and Lewis, 2003). In many of the firms studied, the 'kitchen cabinet' is an
informal but a very powerful approach that is applied spontaneously once
a specific incident arises, acting as a facilitator for decisions, new ideas,
improvements, suggestions, and so on. Given the evidence provided, these
'kitchen cabinets' also take on some tasks associated with more formal and
institutionalized boards (Mustakallio et al., 2002; Deakins et al., 2000).

CONCLUSION

This chapter has examined the practice of governance in smaller firms in
the Rhine Valley region – that is, parts of both Austria and the Principality
of Liechtenstein – from a practitioner's perspective. Therefore, this
chapter has responded to calls for more qualitative research in order to
further develop our understanding of corporate governance (Bansal,
2013; Zattoni et al., 2013). Additionally, this chapter has addressed the
lack of cross-country research on corporate governance (Gispert et al.,
2005; Voordeckers et al., 2014). It has also addressed the situation that
the study of corporate governance continues to be dominated by an
emphasis on large and listed companies (Lynall et al., 2003; Bansal, 2013).
Given the fact that smaller firms represent the backbone of most economies, our understanding of the topic would benefit from more research.
Consequently, the present chapter's intention was to make a small contribution to this gap.

The findings illustrate a governance approach that mainly follows a relational one. The firms involved put an emphasis on informal and relational governance systems involving internal and external stakeholders. In this context, trust and well-integrated teams can be emphasized: trust forms an essential prerequisite for collaboration with internal and external stakeholders; the existence of well-integrated and long-term teams helps to jointly address present and future business challenges. Both trust and long-term teams also seem to compensate for more formal (contractual) approaches (Mustakallio et al., 2002). Employee involvement is regarded as critical for company development, and in combination with low staff turnover contributes to a stronger identification with the firm.

The mix of companies involved – that is, older firms versus younger firms, variety of industries, and family firms versus non-family firms – also showed no striking differences with regard to the governance approach chosen, which is interesting in terms of existing research suggesting distinctions as a consequence of evolution over time (e.g. Filatotchev and Wright, 2005).

From an academic point of view, our chapter draws particular attention to the relational governance approach as more appropriate when discussing governance from a small firm perspective. Therefore, we position our chapter in recent research activities regarding alternative governance approaches for studying small firm governance (e.g. Uhlaner et al., 2007a; Mustakallio et al., 2002). Our research expands this discussion by bringing in the role of employees in corporate governance. So far, the role of non-executive employees has been neglected in the study of corporate governance in privately held firms and/or family businesses, which may be explained by a rather traditional top-down perspective when relationships between owner-managers and employees are discussed (Bridge and O'Neill, 2013). In many smaller firms, however, this kind of hierarchical thinking is not present, and would also be rather dangerous in terms of the firm's development. This is also reflected in the governance mechanisms applied in the firms surveyed. Indeed, the findings suggest that the firms take a very modern approach to corporate governance, one that is based on co-determination (Muthusamy et al., 2011).

The role that trust plays also contributes to recent developments intended to include it in the study of corporate governance (e.g. Eddleston et al., 2010; Calabrò and Mussolino, 2013). The findings also indicate that greater attention needs to be paid to the role of networking in small firm governance. The findings make us believe that more research should turn to the internal and external networks and their role concerning governance issues in smaller firms.

From a practical point of view, our chapter's findings may help managing directors of smaller firms to better understand and exploit the benefits of relational governance mechanisms in their efforts to cope with the firm's development. The findings may also be used by business consultants, helping them to expand their service offer regarding corporate governance. Policy-makers too can benefit from the chapter's findings, as the latter provides the basis for narrowing the gap between prescriptive thinking and actual business practice. Additionally, and maybe more importantly, a better understanding of the actual governance practices in small firms can contribute to the development of corporate governance codes and best practice recommendations that are not adopted from large corporate settings but embedded in corporate governance practices as understood and carried out in small firms.

We are aware that the presented chapter has several limitations. First, the results were gained from a relatively small number of small firms; thus, the reliability of our findings is limited. Future studies should focus on a larger number of firms. Another limitation is related to the fact that only executive personnel were included in the interviews, meaning that only a limited view of the topic was provided. Future research could also include other perspectives, for example that of the firm's key employees, to obtain a more balanced understanding of governance practices in small firms. Finally, the emphasis on this particular geographic region may have introduced another limitation, rendering the findings at least partly unsuitable for application in other countries. The findings by Voordeckers et al. (2014) that actual governance practices and behavior in SMEs are often very similar, however, provide support that the present chapter's findings about relational governance practices in small firms are applicable across countries. Overall, the chapter's findings have contributed to an expansion of our understanding of governance practices in small firms in different parts of the world (Calabrò and Mussolino, 2013).

ACKNOWLEDGEMENTS

Susanne Durst and Julia Brunold gratefully acknowledge support from the University of Liechtenstein Science Foundation in the context of a research project on corporate governance in SMEs.

REFERENCES

Aguilera, R.V. and Jackson, G. (2003), 'The cross-national diversity of corporate governance: Dimensions and determinants', *Academy of Management Review*, **28** (3), 447–465.
Audretsch, D.B. and Lehmann, E.E. (2011), 'Introduction', in Audretsch, D.B. and Lehmann,

E.E. (eds), *Corporate Governance in Small and Medium-Sized Firms*, Cheltenham, UK and Northampton, MA, USA: Edward Elgar Publishing, pp. xiii–xxvii.

Bansal, P. (2013), 'Commentary. Inducing frame-breaking insights through qualitative research', *Corporate Governance: An International Review*, **21** (2), 127–130.

Barringer, B.R. (1997), 'The effects of relational channel exchange on the small firm: A conceptual framework', *Journal of Small Business Management*, **35** (2), 65–79.

Blair, M.M. (1998), 'For whom should corporations be run? An economic rationale for stakeholder management', *Long Range Planning*, **31** (2), 195–200.

Blomqvist, K. (1997), 'The many faces of trust', *Scandinavian Journal of Managemet*, **13** (3), 271–286.

Bowey, J.L. and Easton, G. (2007), 'Entrepreneurial social capital unplugged', *International Small Business Journal*, **25** (3), 273–306.

Bridge, S. and O'Neill, K. (2013), *Understanding Enterprise. Entrepreneurship and Small Business*, 4th edn, Basingstoke: Palgrave Macmillan.

Bruderl, J. and Preisendorfer, P. (1998), 'Network support and the success of newly founded businesses', *Small Business Economics*, **10** (3), 213–225.

Brunninge, O., Nordqvist, M. and Wiklund, J. (2007), 'Corporate governance and strategic change in SMEs: The effects of ownership, board composition and top management teams', *Small Business Economics*, **29**, 295–308.

Cadbury, A. (1992), *The Report of the Committee on the Financial Aspects of Corporate Governance*, London: Gee & Co.

Calabrò, A. and Mussolino, D. (2013), 'How do boards of directors contribute to family SME export intensity? The role of formal and informal governance mechanisms', *Journal of Management and Governance*, **17**, 363–403.

Carney, M. (2005), 'Corporate governance and competitive advantage in family-controlled firms', *Entrepreneurship Theory and Practice*, **29** (3), 249–265.

Child, J. (1972), 'Organizational structure, environment and performance: The role of strategic choice', *Sociology*, **6**, 1–22.

Child, J. (1997), 'Strategic choice in the analysis of action, structure, organizations and environment: Retrospect and prospect', *Organization Studies*, **18** (1), 43–76.

Corbetta, G. and Montemerlo, D. (1999), 'Ownership, governance, and management issues in small and medium-size family businesses: A comparison of Italy and the United States', *Family Business Review*, **12** (4), 361–374.

Corbetta, G. and Salvato, C.A. (2004), 'The boards of directors in family firms: One size fits all?', *Family Business Review*, **17** (2), 119–134.

Cowling, M. (2003), 'Productivity and corporate governance in smaller firms', *Small Business Economics*, **20** (4), 335–344.

Curran, J. and Blackburn, R.A. (2001), *Researching the Small Enterprise*, London: Sage.

Deakins, D., O'Neill, E. and Mileham, P. (2000), 'The role and influence of external directors in small entrepreneurial companies: Some evidence on VC and non-VC appointed external directors', *Venture Capital*, **2** (2), 111–127.

Eddleston, K.A., Chrisman, J.J., Steier, L.P. and Chua, J.H. (2010), 'Governance and trust in family firms: An introduction', *Entrepreneurship Theory and Practice*, **34** (6), 1043–1056.

Eisenhardt, K.M. (1989), 'Building theories from case study research', *Academy of Management Review*, **14** (4), 532–550.

Fereday, J. and Muir-Cochrane, E. (2006), 'Demonstrating rigor using thematic analysis: A hybrid approach of inductive and deductive coding and theme development', *International Journal of Qualitative Methods*, **5** (1), 1–11.

Filatotchev, I. and Bishop, K. (2002), 'Board composition, share ownership, and "underpricing" of UK IPO firms', *Strategic Management Journal*, **23**, 941–955.

Filatotchev, I. and Wright, M. (2005), 'The corporate governance life cycle', in Filatotchev, I. and Wright, M. (eds), *The Life Cycle of Corporate Governance*, Cheltenham, UK and Northampton, MA, USA: Edward Elgar Publishing, pp. 1–19.

Frisch, B. (2011), 'Who really makes the big decisions in your company?', *Harvard Business Review*, **89** (12) 104–111.

Gill, A., Biger, N., Mand, H.S. and Shah, C. (2012), 'Corporate governance and capital structure of small business service firms in India', *International Journal of Economics and Finance*, **4** (8), 83–92.

Gilmore, A., Carson, D. and Grant, K. (2001), 'SME marketing in practice', *Marketing Intelligence and Planning*, **19** (1), 6–11.

Giovannini, R. (2010), 'Corporate governance, family ownership and performance', *Journal of Management Governance*, **14** (2), 145–166.

Gispert, C., de Jong, A., Kabir, R. and Renneboog, L. (2005), 'The impact of corporate governance on firm performance and growth potential: An analysis of three different European governance regimes', in Filatotchev, I. and Wright, M. (eds), *The Life Cycle of Corporate Governance*, Cheltenham, UK and Northampton, MA, USA: Edward Elgar Publishing, pp. 233–252.

Granovetter, M. (1985), 'Economic action and social structure: The problem of embeddedness', *American Journal of Sociology*, **91** (3), 481–510.

He, L. (2008), 'Do founders matter? A study of executive compensation, governance structure and firm performance', *Journal of Business Venturing*, **23**, 257–279.

Hine, D. and Ryan, N. (1999), 'Small service firms – creating value through innovation', *Managing Service Quality*, **9** (6), 411–422.

Huggins, R. and Johnston, A. (2010), 'Knowledge flow and inter-firm networks: The influence of network resources, spatial proximity and firm size', *Entrepreneurship and Regional Development*, **22** (5), 457–484.

Huse, M. (1990), 'Board composition in small enterprises', *Entrepreneurship and Regional Development*, **2**, 363–373.

Huse, M. (2005), 'Accountability and creating accountability: A framework for exploring behavioural perspectives of corporate governance', *British Journal of Management*, **16**, S65–S79.

Johnson, R.A. and Greening, D.W. (1999), 'The effects of corporate governance and institutional ownership types on corporate social performance', *Academy of Management Journal*, **42** (5), 564–576.

Jones, C., Hesterly, W.S. and Borgatti, S.P. (1997), 'A general theory of network governance: Exchange conditions and social mechanisms', *Academy of Management Review*, **22** (4), 911–945.

La Porta, R., Lopez-de-Silanes, F. and Shleifer, A. (1999), 'Corporate ownership around the world', *Journal of Finance*, **54** (2), 471–517.

Lappalainen, J. and Niskanen, M. (2012), 'Financial performance of SMEs: Impact of ownership structure and board composition', *Management Research Review*, **35** (11), 1088–1108.

Lubatkin, M., Lane, P.J., Collin, S. and Very, P. (2007), 'An embeddedness framing of governance and opportunism: Towards a cross-nationally accommodating theory of agency', *Journal of Organizational Behaviour*, **28**, 43–58.

Lynall, M.D., Golden, B.R. and Hillman, A.J. (2003), 'Board composition from adolescence to maturity: A multitheoretic view', *Academy of Management Review*, **28** (3), 416–431.

Mallin, C.A. (2010), *Corporate Governance*, 3rd edn, Oxford: Oxford University Press.

Marxer, P. (2009), *Liechtensteinisches Wirtschaftsrecht*, Vaduz: Liechtenstein Verlag.

Maykut, P. and Morehouse, R. (1994), *Beginning Qualitative Research. A Philosophic and Practical Guide*, London: Falmer Press.

Mayring, P. (1990), *Einführung in die qualitative Sozialforschung*, Munich: Psychologie Verlags Union.

McNulty, T. and Pettigrew, A. (1999), 'Strategists on the board', *Organization Studies*, **20** (1), 47–74.

McNulty, T., Zattoni, A. and Douglas, T. (2013), 'Developing corporate governance research through qualitative methods: A review of previous studies', *Corporate Governance: An International Review*, **21** (2), 183–198.

Miles, M.B. and Huberman, A.M. (1994), *An Expanded Sourcebook. Qualitative Data Analysis*, 2nd edn, Thousand Oaks, CA: Sage.

Miller, D. (1983), 'The correlates of entrepreneurship in three types of firms', *Management Science*, **29** (7), 770–791.

Minichilli, A. and Hansen, C. (2007), 'The board advisory tasks in small firms and the event of crises', *Journal of Management and Governance*, **11** (1), 5–22.

Mustakallio, M., Autio, E. and Zahra, S.A. (2002), 'Relational and contractual governance in family firms: Effects on strategic decision making', *Family Business Review*, **15** (3), 205–222.

Muthusamy, S., Bobinski, P.A. and Jawahr, D. (2011), 'Toward a strategic role for employees in corporate governance', *Strategic Change*, **20**, 127–138.

Neville, M. (2011), 'The role of boards in small and medium-sized firms', *Corporate Governance*, **11** (5), 527–540.

O'Donnell, A. (2013), 'The contribution of networking to small firm marketing', *Journal of Small Business Management*, doi: 10.1111/jsbm.12038.

OECD (2002), *Small and Medium Enterprise Outlook*, OECD: Paris.

Papesch, M. (2010), *Corporate Governance in Familienunternehmen. Eine Analyse zur Sicherung der Unternehmensnachfolge*, Wiesbaden: Gabler.

Pearce, J.A. and Zahra, S.A. (1992), 'Board composition from a strategic contingency perspective', *Journal of Management Studies*, **29** (4), 411–438.

Pfeffer, J. and Salancik, G.R. (1978), *The External Control of Organizations: A Resource Dependence Perspective*, New York: Harper & Row.

Poppo, L. and Zenger, T. (2002), 'Do formal contracts and relational governance function as substitutes or complements?', *Strategic Management Journal*, **23**, 707–725.

Pleininger, H. (2012), 'Wachstumschancen sind da, aber der Platz wird eng', available at http://wirtschaftsblatt.at/home/nachrichten/oesterreich/vorarlberg/1317772/Wachstum-schancen-sind-da-aber-der-Platz-wird-eng (accessed 5 December 2013).

Rajan, R.G. and Zingales, L. (2000), 'The governance of the new enterprise', in Vives, X. (ed.), *Corporate Governance: Theoretical and Empirical Perspectives*, Cambridge: Cambridge University Press, pp. 201–227.

Saunders, M., Lewis, P. and Thornhill, A. (2009), *Research Methods for Business Students*, 5th edn, Harlow: Pearson Education.

Shleifer, A. and Vishny, R.W. (1997), 'A survey of corporate governance', *Journal of Finance*, **42** (2), 737–783.

Sundaramurthy, C. and Lewis, M. (2003), 'Control and collaboration: Paradoxes of governance', *Academy of Management Review*, **28** (3), 397–415.

Taylor, S. (2006), 'Acquaintance, meritocracy and critical realism: Researching recruitment and selection processes in smaller and growth organizations', *Human Resource Management Review*, **16**, 478–489.

Uhlaner, L.M., Floren, R.H. and Geerlings, J.R. (2007a), 'Owner commitment and relational governance in the privately-held firm: An empirical study', *Small Business Economics*, **29**, 275–293.

Uhlaner, L., Wright, M. and Huse, M. (2007b), 'Private firms and corporate governance: An integrated economic and management perspective', *Small Business Economics*, **29**, 225–241.

Van Gils, A. (2005), 'Management and governance in Dutch SMEs', *European Management Journal*, **23** (5), 583–589.

Velayutham, S. (2013), 'Governance without boards: The Quakers', *Corporate Governance*, **13** (3), 223–235.

Voordeckers, W., Van Gils, A., Gabrielsson, J., Politis, D. and Huse, M. (2014), 'Board structures and board behaviour: A cross-country comparison of privately held SMEs in Belgium, the Netherlands and Norway', *International Journal of Business Governance and Ethics*, **9** (2), 197–219.

Voordeckers, W., Van Gils, A. and Van den Heuvel, J. (2007), 'Board composition in small and medium-sized family firms', *Journal of Small Business Management*, **45** (1), 137–156.

Wesel, M.A. (2010), *Corporate Governance im Mittelstand*, Berlin: Erich Schmidt Verlag.

Wirtz, P. (2011), 'The cognitive dimension of corporate governance in fast growing entrepreneurial firms', *European Management Journal*, **29**, 431–447.

Zaheer, A. and Venkatraman, N. (1995), 'Relational governance as an interorganizational strategy: An empirical test of the role of trust in economic exchange', *Strategic Management Journal*, **16**, 373–392.

Zahra, S.A., Neubaum, D.O. and Naldi, L. (2007), 'The effects of ownership and governance on SMEs international knowledge-based resources', *Small Business Economics*, **29**, 309–327.

Zattoni, A., Douglas, T. and Judge, W. (2013), 'Developing corporate governance theory through qualitative research', *Corporate Governance: An International Review*, **21** (2), 119–122.

9. Alliance governance in entrepreneurial firms: the influence of family control and organizational size
Daniel Pittino, Francesca Visintin and Paola A.M. Mazzurana

INTRODUCTION

Strategic alliances can be defined as long-term agreements between two or more organizations, aimed at the joint pursuit of strategic goals. The creation of alliances is a viable choice for large, medium-sized and small enterprises (Roijakkers and Hagedoorn, 2007; Street and Cameron, 2007; Hoskisson et al., 2011).

Small and medium-sized enterprises (SMEs) are in the vast majority of the cases entrepreneurial firms, characterized by flexibility and personality in the management of the organization (Gabrielsson and Huse, 2010), and these features lead to both advantages and shortcomings. Thus, the use of alliances among SMEs might support the pursuit of entrepreneurial goals, either by leveraging on the unique features of these organizations or by overcoming their structural limitations. In particular, among SMEs, alliances have been proven to speed up the new product development processes (Deeds and Hill, 1996; Hyder and Abraha, 2004; Haeussler et al., 2012; Ma et al., 2012), to foster corporate entrepreneurship (Teng, 2007), to support projects of international venturing (Dodd et al., 2002; Guillen, 2000; Milanov and Fernhaber, 2014) and, in general, to enhance innovation capabilities (Thorgren et al., 2009; Wincent et al., 2010).

Quite often the implementation of the above-mentioned strategies requires the adoption of formal mechanisms in the governance of the alliance (Dyer and Singh, 1998; Thorgren et al., 2009). Alliance governance refers to the effective combination of structures and systems ensuring the control and coordination of activities and the allocation of resources, rights, duties and rewards among partners (Nickerson and Zenger, 2004; Gulati et al., 2005; De Man and Roijakkers, 2009). The literature on inter-organizational relationships identifies two main modes of alliance governance: formal governance mechanisms and relational governance mechanisms. According to the theory of organizational control (Ouchi,

1979; Eisenhardt, 1985), formal and relational mechanisms ensure, respectively, formal and social (informal) control over partners' activities and behaviors.

Empirical evidence on alliances in SMEs emphasizes the importance of social control mechanisms; however research also points out that formal arrangements are crucial in establishing effective control in cases of high uncertainty, ambiguity and risk of expropriation (Williamson, 1985; Poppo and Zenger, 2002). Thus, given the relevance of formal governance mechanisms for the alliance performance in entrepreneurial firms, in this chapter we draw from organizational control theory to identify and discuss some determinants that may affect the adoption of formal arrangements in the governance structure of alliances.

In particular, since family control is widespread among SMEs (Brunnige et al., 2007), we primarily evaluate the effect of family business status on the adoption of formal inter-organizational control mechanisms. Family business status is potentially relevant for the decisions on alliance governance since family firms are usually portrayed as organizations that prefer social and relational governance arrangements to formal ones (e.g., Carney, 2005; Mustakallio et al., 2002).

Assuming a contingent point of view, we subsequently assess to what extent organizational size affects the importance of family control in alliance governance choices. The contingent perspective suggests that the firms' behaviors and structures (Donaldson, 2001) can be predicted according to a number of situational factors. Among them, size is an organizational characteristic that has been often investigated and related to an increase in the organizational complexity (Pondy, 1969), or to a change in organizational structures and procedures, as the life cycle stage models suggest (see, e.g., Greiner, 1972; Churchill and Lewis, 1985). In the alliance governance literature, alliance characteristics are often identified as contingencies affecting the choice of the governance structures (Lee and Cavusgil, 2006; Mellewigt et al., 2007), however these studies do not specifically investigate organizational size as a contingency. Our argument is that the increase in organizational size creates higher complexity, therefore reduces the 'discretion' in the entrepreneurial choices and tends to nullify the effect of family control in the alliance governance decisions.

Our research thus contributes to the literature on governance choices in entrepreneurial firms by evaluating the effect of family control on the adoption of formal arrangements in the governance of inter-organizational relationship. Our study also adds to the literature on organizational control by analyzing, in a contingent perspective, two relevant determinants of formal inter-organizational control mechanisms. The analysis is carried out on a sample of 253 SMEs involved in strategic alliances and operating in the Italian region of Friuli-Venezia Giulia.

The chapter is organized as follows. It first describes the theoretical background, focusing on the importance of formal control mechanisms in the alliance governance choices of SMEs; the next section presents the hypotheses of our research, focusing on the family business status and its interplay with organizational size as determinants of the adoption of formal mechanisms. The chapter then describes the sample and method of our study, and presents the results, which are then discussed, highlighting also the main theoretical and managerial implications of our findings. The final section concludes.

THEORETICAL BACKGROUND: FORMAL ALLIANCE GOVERNANCE AND ITS IMPORTANCE FOR SMES

In this chapter we adopt a theoretical perspective based on the organizational control framework (Ouchi, 1979; Eisenhardt, 1985). Organizational control deals with the rules and monitoring processes that affect the way activities are carried out. Leifer and Mills define control as 'a regulative process by which the elements of a system are made more predictable through the establishment of standards in the pursuit of some desired objective or state' (Leifer and Mills, 1996, p. 117). Organizational control can be exerted through formal or social (informal) mechanisms (Smith et al., 1995). Formal control mechanisms focus on the monitoring of inputs and actions and on the measurement of outcomes (Ouchi, 1979; Eisenhardt, 1985).

In Ouchi's (1979) view, formal control is typical of markets and bureaucracies: market prices provide information, and work as mechanisms for solving the problem of goal incongruity; while in bureaucracies behaviors are aligned through organizational mechanisms providing norms and rules, and specifying procedures and standards (Ouchi, 1979). On the other hand, social control is essentially based on mechanisms inducing self-regulation (Ouchi, 1979), and it is appropriate when both the task programmability and the output measurability are low. Examples of social control modes are close interactions, informal and participatory decision-making processes and shared values and beliefs.

The literature on alliance governance points out that formal governance arrangements rely on contractual or organizational mechanisms (for example: joint planning, shared programs, rules, standard operating procedures, detailed contractual prescriptions and dispute resolution procedures, performance control systems, goals setting, incentive systems and reward structures) (Dekker, 2004), whereas relational governance mechanisms are based on informal and social control modes that facilitate coordination and ensure the alignment of interest between partners, mainly through mutual trust and a common frame of reference in terms of values and beliefs (Das and Teng, 2001; Dekker, 2004). Examples of arrangements promoting relational governance are teams, task forces, committees, meetings, transfer of managers or personnel, mechanisms for shared decision-making and partner development activities (Dekker, 2004).

Previous studies on alliance governance among SMEs emphasize the prevalence of social control mechanisms in such settings; however, the pursuit of particular strategic goals through inter-organizational partnerships often requires the adoption of formal arrangements. As Lee and Cavusgil (2006) suggest, formal mechanisms may serve as a basis in the initial stages of the relationship. This phase is characterized by high levels of uncertainty and ambiguity, due to the lack of previous interactions. Thus, formal arrangements help to avoid misunderstandings between partners, and support the process of sense-making of the relationship (Vlaar et al., 2006; Thorgren et al., 2009). These dimensions are crucial, for example, in alliances with foreign partners (O'Dwyer and O'Flynn, 2005; Blomqvist et al., 2008), when different cultures and values could make it difficult to establish trustful relationships (Steemsma et al., 2000).

Power asymmetry is another situation where formal mechanisms are particularly recommended. Power asymmetry is typical when SMEs establish alliances with larger counterparts. In such cases, the use of formalized arrangements may limit the potential of opportunism, for example by controlling the type and amount of information shared so that they do not exceed the intended goals, or as a safeguard in the case of conflicts (Lee and Cavusgil, 2006; Blomqvist et al., 2008). Formal governance can also prevent opportunistic behaviors, hold-up problems and risks of knowledge expropriation in situations where partners' actions cannot be specified *ex ante*, and it is crucial to allocate property rights on the outcomes of the alliance, as in the case of joint research and development (R&D) projects (Hoetker and Mellewigt, 2009; Dickson et al., 2006).

Thus, the relative importance of formal and social control modes in the design of alliance governance mechanisms depends on various alliance attributes: the type and level of risk faced by the partners (Das and Teng, 1998; De Man and Roijakkers, 2009), the asset type (property-based and knowledge-based assets), the attributes of the knowledge involved (tacit versus explicit) (Contractor and Ra, 2002) and the environmental dynamism (Lee and Cavusgil, 2006). In addition to the determinants mentioned, which refer to the alliance features in terms of resources and activities involved in the relationship, other dimensions at the organizational level might be important for the choice of the governance mechanisms. In particular, we argue that in entrepreneurial firms family control and organizational size play a crucial role.

HYPOTHESES DEVELOPMENT

Family Firms and Alliance Governance

It is surprising to observe that very few contributions combine the analysis of family firms' characteristics and the study of alliances, as if the 'familiness' that appears to impact on almost all aspects of the governance of a company, and on the subsequent performance results, had no influence on inter-firm relationships and, in particular, on strategic alliances. Indeed, the vast majority of contributions that in the past decade or so have dealt with the use of strategic alliances in family business have as a major concern of analysis the process of internationalization. Alliance formation in these studies is included among the various phases of the internationalization process, particularly useful as a means of resource gathering. For example, Dyer and Mortesen (2005) show how alliances with partners in developed countries can play a significant role in the competitive advantage of family businesses active in underdeveloped economies. Fernandez and Nieto (2005) highlight the importance of inter-firm agreements for family SMEs as providers of the necessary resources for the undertaking of internationalization processes. Very few other contributions focus on other business concerns. Zahra (2005) includes strategic alliances among the instances of entrepreneurial risk-taking behavior of family firms, while Miller and Le Breton-Miller (2006) suggest that highly competitive publicly traded family firms invest in networks and alliances as means for the support to the future generations (see also Naphiet and Goshal, 1998; Bubolz, 2001).

Few studies focus on the type of alliances that family firms undertake (e.g., Pittino et al., 2013), and in particular no study considers the distinction between formal and informal agreements. This is a significant empirical and theoretical shortcoming as, on the one side, as explained above, alliances are a significant part of the competitive strategies of small and medium-sized enterprises, and on the other, as mentioned above, processes of strategic change of any kind (product innovation, internationalization, and so on) may require a level of formalization that is usually not typical of the governance style of family firms.

Carney (2005) suggests that in comparison with other forms of governance (managerial and alliance), family firms are freer in choosing different arrangements without a specific, predictable criteria. According to the author, such freedom stems from the personal and particular style of corporate governance. The owner-manager style of decision-making is personal in that family members 'operate under fewer internal constraints as they may exempt themselves from the internal bureaucratic constraints that limit managerial authority in other modes of governance. For example, owner-managers of family firms may be unwilling to abide by formalized human resources management practices that inhibit their ownership prerogatives' (p. 255). In addition, 'family control rights permit the family to intervene in the affairs to substitute other [instead of rational-calculative], "particularistic" criteria of their choosing'.

One could extend the argument to the governance of strategic alliances. As much as for the human resource management practices, the owner-manager will try to rely on informal forms of governance so as to extend their personal and particular prerogatives to the relationships with the external partners. It is likely that such partners will be chosen on the basis of their propensity towards such informal systems of coordination, with similar value systems, possibly among other family firms (e.g., Pittino and Visintin, 2011).

As a matter of fact, the very few studies that refer to strategic alliances in family firms postulate a preference towards informal types of agreements, often not even of the contractual type. For example, Habbershon and Blank (2005) underline the role played by the family owner-manager in building strong personal and informal links with important customers; likewise Miller and Le Breton-Miller (2005), in describing the long-term success of great family firms, explain that such success is leveraged on the stability of relationships with customers, mostly of the relational type. In sum, previous theory and research suggest the following hypothesis:

Hypothesis 1: Family control negatively influences the adoption of formal mechanisms in alliance governance.

The Moderating Role of Organizational Size

We argue, however, that such somewhat taken-for-granted peculiar characteristics of family firms are not equally distributed across firms of different sizes. In other words, we put forward a contingent view of the governance of strategic alliances in family firms. The 'organizational contingencies' literature (see, e.g., Blau, 1970) posits that a number of contingencies, including size, affect the degree of organizational complexity, which in turn require higher levels of codification and formalization of organizational procedures, including control processes (Pondy, 1969; Hall et al., 1967). The same may hold true for the governance and control of strategic alliances. As the firm grows, the owner-manager, whose cognitive resources are constrained, is progressively forced to delegate his decision-making power to other members of the organization, giving up the personal and particular style of decision-making. The entrepreneurial attention (Gifford, 1992), the limited resource allocated to direct supervision and coordination activities, is progressively less sufficient as the company grows in size. The delegation process in the initial growth phases may occur through a value-based alignment of interests, and this is especially true for family-controlled firms. However, above a certain degree of complexity, organizational coordination requires a formalized system of procedures, programming and control. The same holds true for the inter-organizational coordination in the case of strategic alliance management. We can therefore propose the following:

Hypothesis 2: The adoption of formalized forms of governance of strategic alliances in family-controlled SMEs is contingent on organizational size.

Theory and research on SMEs generally distinguish between micro, small and medium-sized firms as they pose differences in their structural and operational complexity (Ghobadian and O'Regan, 2006; Gabrielsson, 2007). By considering different size classes we can further develop the argument summarized in our Hypothesis 2. First, in micro companies, we do not expect differences between the corporate governance style of a family owner-manager and of an individual entrepreneur. In these companies, the decisions of the entrepreneurs are usually not constrained by rigid bureaucratic structures and we can expect that the management of strategic alliances are strongly influenced by the personal style of the entrepreneur. In very small companies, the direct supervision by the entrepreneur and their direct involvement in day-to-day operations is an effective common feature (Hall et al., 1967; Moreno and Casillas, 2008; Wolf and Pett, 2000). In addition, in these companies, boundary-spanning activity is so strategic that is usually carried out exclusively by the owner-entrepreneur.

As the firm grows, direct supervision of inter-firm relationships becomes progressively more difficult. Family firms, however, may continue to effectively rely on informal mechanisms more frequently than non-family firms, as value-based systems of coordination that are extensively used by these companies might still play a significant role in the governance of the alliance, particularly through processes of delegation to other members of the family (Pittino and Visintin, 2011). Our argument is therefore that as the firm grows out of the entrepreneurial size, non-family firms will rely more extensively on formal mechanisms for the governance of the alliance.

Above a certain size and level of complexity, however, the entrepreneurial attention, even when supported by other familial resources through a family coalition, becomes insufficient and the direct management of the strategic alliance ought to be complemented by formal mechanisms, procedures, control systems and inter-organizational coordination bodies. In sum, our arguments extend the previous hypothesis (Hypothesis 2) as follows:

Hypothesis 2a: In micro enterprises, there is no significant difference between family and non-family firms in the adoption of formal alliance governance mechanisms.

Hypothesis 2b: In small enterprises, family firms have a significantly lower degree of adoption of formal alliance governance mechanisms.

Hypothesis 2c: In medium-sized enterprises, the difference in the adoption of formal alliance governance mechanisms between family and non-family firms is lower compared to small firms.

METHOD

The hypotheses were tested on a dataset of 253 small to medium-sized companies involved in strategic alliances. The dataset is based on a survey carried out on a representative sample of firms based in the Italian region Friuli-Venezia Giulia, located in the north-east of Italy.

Sample

The dataset was collected within a research project financed by the local Chamber of Commerce (Chamber of Commerce of the Udine Province) and aimed at exploring the cooperation attitude and strategies of small to medium-sized enterprises. Data were collected in the period October–December 2010 through phone interviews carried out by professional interviewers working for a social research company. Information was gathered through a structured questionnaire that was built by the authors of this chapter, who also provided training and instructions to the interviewers.

The initial sample was made up of 1192 firms. Following a preliminary e-mail contact, 508 companies agreed to participate in the survey (42.62

percent response rate). The final sample is representative of the population of enterprises operating in Friuli-Venezia Giulia, in terms of size and industry. For the aims of our analysis, we selected the enterprises which had set up alliances in the previous ten years. For the purpose of this research, we define as 'strategic alliance' any long-term collaborative agreement between two or more companies, aimed at the pursuit of a common goal, either through concerted action or through performance of complementary functions (respectively, confederate collectives and conjoint collectives, according to the definition by Astley and Fombrun, 1983).

The final dataset is made up of 253 companies involved in strategic alliances. The questionnaire had three sections: the first section was devoted to the collection of general data about the firm and its ownership and management structure; the second section was about the strategic posture of the company and product–market combinations; the third section was focused on the establishment of inter-firm alliances. In particular, we were interested in collecting information about the features of alliances in terms of:

- aims and goals of alliances (for example, conjoint R&D activities, marketing, distribution and commercial, co-production);
- partners involved (for example, business of the same industry, university and research centers);
- problems faced with partners;
- financial and human resources employed;
- organizational forms (for example, informal, contractual, equity-based agreements);
- coordination mechanisms and governance modes (for example, employees' exchange, planning and budgeting systems, standard operating procedures).

In line with previous work, we invited respondents to focus on their most important alliances (Hoetker and Mellewigt, 2009). The respondents were company-level key informants: chief executive officers (CEOs), entrepreneurs, executives or employees in charge of the management of inter-organizational relationships.

The companies involved operate mainly in the manufacturing industry (43.1 percent), building and construction (18.9 percent) and commerce (26.1 percent). The remaining companies belong to agriculture, transport, hospitality (mainly accommodation and restaurants), and information and communication industries. Family firms represent 55.9 percent of the companies of the sample. The companies on average have 35.8 employees

Table 9.1   Characteristics of the sample

Industries	N	%
Agriculture	2	0.79
Manufacturing	109	43.08
Building and construction	48	18.97
Commerce	66	26.09
Transport	9	3.56
Hospitality	2	0.79
Information and communication services	3	1.19
Real estate	4	1.58
Professional and business services	9	3.56
Other services	1	0.40
	Mean	SD
Year of establishment	1984	18
Number of employees	35.80	54.84
Sales (000 euros)	7169	11 775

and €7.16 million of average turnover. Detailed descriptive information is reported in Table 9.1.

Our sample includes only contractual (non-equity) alliances (Das and Teng, 1996). In 34 percent of cases alliances have a predominant exploration goal, aimed at creating a new valuable pool of resources through processes of searching and learning (for example, joint R&D and technology development projects). The remaining agreements focus mainly on exploitation goals, involving a set of resources, assets or capabilities already under the control of the partner companies (for example, technology licensing, marketing, distribution) (Levinthal and March, 1993; Koza and Lewin, 1998; Rothaermel and Deeds, 2004).

Variables

Dependent variables
We adopted a multivariate dependent measure, made up by five variables, accounting for the degree of formalization of the alliance governance. Each variable refers to a distinctive governance mechanism and is drawn from previous literature on strategic alliances (Faems et al., 2008; Hoetker and Mellewigt, 2009; Lee and Cavusgil, 2006; Murray and Kotabe, 2005; Nielsen, 2010; Poppo and Zenger, 2002): (1) complexity of bilateral contracts (Poppo and Zenger, 2002; Lee and Cavusgil, 2006), which refers to the degree to which the parties create a complex contract to deal with

future contingencies; (2) adoption of performance control mechanisms (Faems et al., 2008; Murray and Kotabe, 2005), which accounts for the presence of program milestones, target dates and performance standards; (3) organizational roles aimed at monitoring and coordinating partners' behavior, which refers to the existence of managers in charge of the inter-organizational relationship (e.g., Grandori and Soda, 2005); (4) formal budgeting and business planning, which measures the extent to which financial targets are set formally (Hoetker and Mellewigt, 2009); and (5) information systems and procedures, which captures the relevance of systems that support information and communication flows between partners (Grandori and Soda, 2005). The importance of each dimension was assessed on a seven-point Likert scale, ranging from 1 (low importance) to 7 (high importance).

Independent variable
Our independent variable is the family-controlled business status of the company. Family-controlled business status is a dichotomous variable assuming value 1, according to the definition by Westhead and Cowling (1998), if a family controls the company through the majority of voting shares and the family is represented in the entrepreneurial and management team, 0 otherwise.

Moderating variable
The moderating variable is the size of the organization, measured by the number of employees. The number of employees has been widely used as a proxy of the structural complexity of an organization (e.g., Pugh et al., 1968; Blau, 1970). For the purposes of the research, we divided the sample into three size groups, according to the conventional distinction (European Commission, 2003) between micro (less than ten employees), small (between ten and 50 employees) and medium-sized enterprises (more than 50 and less than 250 employees). The distribution of family and non-family companies in the three size groups is presented in Table 9.2.

Control variables
In addition to the variables featured in the hypotheses, the following control variables were considered. Size of the partner company: the size of the partner may influence the decision on governance mechanisms, since a larger partner might explicitly dictate a more formalized design and management of the agreement (e.g., O'Dwyer and O'Flynn, 2005; Yang et al., 2014). As for the organizational size variable, the size of partner company is measured by the number of employees.

Industry's technological intensity: technological intensity of the

Table 9.2   Distribution of the SMEs of the sample according to organizational size and family firm status

Organizational size (no. employees)	Non-family firms	(N)	Family-controlled firms	(N)	Total	(N)
Less than 10 employees (micro)	51.2	(39)	48.8	(41)	100	80
10 to 50 employees (small)	50.5	(55)	49.5	(54)	100	109
50 to 250 employees (medium)	59.4	(38)	40.6	(26)	100	64
Total						253

industry may affect the type of knowledge involved in the alliance and therefore influence the choice of governance mechanisms (e.g., Contractor et al., 2011; Contractor and Ra, 2002). Technological intensity is measured on a scale ranging from 1 to 3, according to the OECD (2013) definitions of R&D intensity in manufacturing and knowledge intensity in services.

Alliance goal: the goal of the alliance influences the type of knowledge involved (Nielsen, 2010), thus affecting the governance mode. In particular, we distinguished between alliances aimed at resource exploration and alliances aimed at resource exploitation (Koza and Lewin, 1998; Rothaermel and Deeds, 2004; Lavie et al., 2011) using a dichotomous variable that assumes value 1 if the alliance has an exploration goal and 0 in the case of exploitation goal.

Alliance experience: previous alliance experience may lead the companies to systematically prefer certain governance arrangements over others (e.g., Lee et al., 2010). We measured alliance experience by the number of alliances initiated by the company in the previous ten years. Descriptive statistics and correlations among variables are provided in Table 9.3.

Data Analysis Technique

The hypotheses were tested through multivariate analysis of variance (MANOVA) aimed at identifying the influence of family-controlled firms status and size on the adoption of the different alliance governance mechanisms. We chose not to construct a 'summated' index of formalization since we are interested in evaluating to what extent the different governance mechanisms are simultaneously adopted as mutual complements. To provide a more comprehensive picture, we also present the univariate

Table 9.3 *Means, standard deviations and correlations*

	Mean	SD	1	2	3	4	5	6	7	8	9	10	11
1 Size	33.12	50.06	1.00										
2 Family-controlled firm	0.32	0.48	0.02	1.00									
3 Contractual complexity	4.98	2.25	0.14	-0.28	1.00								
4 Performance control	4.62	2.52	0.08	-0.15	0.12	1.00							
5 Monitoring and integration roles	2.43	2.56	0.13	-0.01	0.06	0.09	1.00						
6 Formal planning and budgeting	3.57	2.58	0.27	0.01	0.03	0.13	0.28	1.00					
7 Shared information systems	2.41	2.55	0.10	0.00	0.08	0.11	0.31	0.37	1.00				
8 Technological intensity	1.32	2.07	-0.08	0.13	-0.38	-0.03	-0.11	-0.08	-0.11	1.00			
9 Alliance experience	2.07	1.44	0.01	0.00	-0.11	-0.29	0.03	-0.13	-0.15	0.18	1.00		
10 Partner's company size	36.50	18.40	-0.20	-0.05	0.06	-0.16	-0.18	-0.23	-0.08	0.09	-0.05	1.00	
11 Alliance goal	3.02	2.43	0.00	0.03	0.04	-0.06	-0.05	-0.03	0.06	-0.02	-0.07	-0.08	1.00

analysis of variance between family-controlled and non-family firms at different sizes according to the single mechanisms.

First we perform a multivariate analysis of variance on the entire sample, estimating the main effects of size and family/non-family firm status on the governance mechanisms; we also introduce in the MANOVA an interaction effect, namely family-controlled firm interacted with size, to assess whether the family control effect on formalized governance is moderated by organizational size. Finally, we consider separately the effect of family-controlled/non-family firm status within each size group of firms (micro, small and medium). All models also include the control variables.

RESULTS

Multivariate analysis of variance was used first to test the influence of the family-controlled firm variable in the entire sample. Results reported in Table 9.4 confirm that being a family-controlled firm indeed has an impact (positive or negative) on the use of formal governance mechanisms; at the same time, firm size is significantly related to the formalization of alliance governance. Both values of Wilk's Lambda are significant at p-level < 0.01. Introducing the interaction effect (family-controlled firm * size) we also observe that the effect of family-controlled firm status depends significantly on the size of the firm ($p = 0.03$). Thus we obtain initial and partial support to Hypothesis 1 and Hypothesis 2 is thus

Table 9.4   *MANOVA analysis for the effects of independent variable and interaction effect on formal governance (entire sample)*

Effect	Wilk's Lambda	F-value	Sig.
Intercept	0.67	23.14	0.00
Size	0.93	3.76	0.00
Family-controlled firm	0.91	4.83	0.00
Family-controlled firm * Size	0.95	2.43	0.03
Technological intensity	0.86	7.81	0.00
Alliance experience	0.87	7.29	0.00
Partner's company size	0.93	3.95	0.00
Alliance goal	0.98	1.18	0.32

Note: Design: intercept + family-controlled firm + organizational size + family-controlled firm * organizational size + technological intensity + Alliance experience + Partner's size + Alliance goal.

*Table 9.5   Univariate analysis of variance of the effect of family-
controlled firm status on the single mechanisms of formal
governance (entire sample)*

	FCFs	NFFs	F-value	Sig.
Contractual complexity	4.14	5.45	12.097	0.00
Performance control	4.14	4.90	4.881	0.01
Monitoring and integration roles	2.48	2.05	0.924	0.09
Formal planning and budgeting	3.43	3.59	8.977	0.54
Shared information systems	2.34	2.52	6.865	0.52

Note: FCFs: family-controlled firms. NFFs: non-family firms.

supported. The control variables, with the exception of the alliance goals, are also significant in discriminating between high and low formalization in alliance governance.

The univariate analysis of the single mechanisms reveals that over the entire sample the significant differences between family-controlled and non-family firms emerge in the contractual complexity and in the use of performance assessment systems (Table 9.5). In the establishment of monitoring functions the differences between the two types of firm is weakly significant, while there are not significant differences in the adoption of planning and budgeting systems, and shared information systems. This gives full support to the predictions of Hypothesis 1 on the effect that family-controlled business status has on the adoption of formal procedures, even if it reveals that the preferences are not the same among different types of formal mechanism.

The significance of the interaction term in Table 9.5 motivates the breakdown of the sample in three size groups; we then observe the multivariate and univariate effect of family firm status in each size group (Tables 9.6 and 9.7). In firms with less than ten employees, as predicted by Hypothesis 2a, there is no significant difference between family and non-family firms in the formalization of governance (p = 0.28). The univariate analysis reported in Table 9.7 shows that there is no difference between family-controlled and non-family enterprises, with the exception of the weakly significant lower level of complexity in the formal contracts (p = 0.09).

In the small firms group, as expected and according to Hypothesis 2b, significant differences emerge between family-controlled and non-family SMEs in the degree of formalization of alliance governance, with respect to all the mechanisms. Differences at p-level < 0.01 are observed particu-

Table 9.6   *MANOVA analysis for the effects of independent variables on formal governance adoption; comparison of the effects for each sub-sample*

Effect	Less than 10 employees (micro)			10 to 50 employees (small)			50 to 250 employees (medium)		
	Wilk's Lambda	F	Sig.	Wilk's Lambda	F	Sig.	Wilk's Lambda	F	Sig.
Intercept	0.68	13.53	0.00	0.65	5.81	0.00	0.26	16.65	0.00
Family-controlled firm	0.96	1.27	0.28	0.64	6.08	0.00	0.84	1.11	0.37
Technological intensity	0.75	9.64	0.00	0.68	4.91	0.00	0.60	3.84	0.01
Alliance experience	0.95	1.26	0.20	0.78	0.64	0.00	0.73	2.18	0.08
Partner's company size	0.81	6.87	0.00	0.83	2.13	0.07	0.69	2.57	0.05
Alliance goal	0.92	1.23	0.30	0.94	1.89	0.09	0.47	3.17	0.06

Note: Design: intercept + family-controlled firm + technological intensity + Alliance experience + Partner's size + Alliance goal.

larly in the complexity of formal contracts and in the use of performance assessment systems. Non-family firms are also more likely to establish formal roles to manage the relationship and to rely on financial plans and information systems.

In the group of medium-sized enterprises (50 to 250 employees) the gap between family and non-family SMEs narrows again. As results in Table 9.6 show, no significant differences emerge (p-value = 0.37 for the family firm variable), and Hypothesis 2c is thus supported. Univariate comparison highlights that contractual complexity is the only mechanism that is significantly more important for non-family firms (Table 9.7). The significance of control variables holds across the three size groups.

DISCUSSION

The results of the empirical analysis provide rather robust support to our theoretical predictions. On average, family-controlled SMEs make less use of formal alliance governance mechanisms compared to non-family ones; the robustness of the results is enhanced since family control proves to be a

Table 9.7 *Univariate analysis of variance of the effect of family-controlled firm status on the single components of formal governance; comparison of the differences between family (FF) and non-family firms (NFF) in each sub-sample*

	Less than 10 employees (micro)				10 to 50 employees (small)				50 to 250 employees (medium)			
	FCFs	NFFs	F	Sig.	FCFs	NFFs	F	Sig.	FCFs	NFFs	F	Sig.
Contractual complexity	3.69	4.96	3.01	0.09	4.28	5.61	12.39	0.00	5.45	6.00	3.35	0.07
Performance control	3.69	4.87	2.45	0.12	3.79	4.57	4.39	0.00	4.31	4.85	1.16	0.29
Monitoring and integration roles	2.31	2.38	0.00	0.92	3.14	4.04	3.88	0.08	3.76	4.14	0.29	0.59
Formal planning and budgeting	2.12	2.87	0.84	0.36	2.65	3.11	2.67	0.10	2.91	3.22	0.20	0.65
Shared information systems	2.38	2.21	0.04	0.82	3.26	3.83	2.74	0.10	3.82	4.41	1.75	0.19

significant discriminant controlling also for technological intensity, previous alliance experience, goals and even partner's size.

This confirms the preference of family-controlled enterprises for informal governance mechanisms and also supports the idea that family SMEs prefer to establish inter-organizational relationships based on shared values, trust and family control, extending outside the boundaries of the organization the personalistic management style adopted in the internal processes (Carney, 2005; Gedajlovic and Carney, 2010; Lester and Cannella, 2006).

Our results however indicate that the family control influence on the (less frequent) adoption of formal governance arrangements is particularly important in firms with a number of employees ranging from ten to 50, whereas in micro firms (less than ten employees) and in larger ones (between 50 and 250 employees) the differences are not significant. This seems to suggest that family influence on formal alliance governance mechanisms is more likely to occur: (1) when it is appropriate to use coordination and control mechanisms alternative to direct supervision and personal involvement of the leader-entrepreneur; and (2) when structural constraints are flexible enough to allow a discretional choice of mechanisms by the dominant coalition.

In micro firms we do not observe differences between family and non-family enterprises because in both situations direct supervision of the agreement's progress and the leader's personal commitment are the most appropriate and convenient governance mechanisms for the inter-organizational partnership; formal governance systems would be redundant and costly, given the intensity and binding power of trust and personal involvement.

In medium-sized organizations (companies with 50 to 250 employees), again, we do not observe any significant difference because organizational size imposes structural constraints on the choices of the dominant coalition, pushing towards the adoption of formal governance practices in internal and external relationships. In organizations of intermediate size (small firms with ten to 50 employees) the previous conditions (1) and (2) are both verified: the leader's personal commitment needs to be supplemented by other mechanisms, and the family influence is free enough from structural constraints to choose whether to continue in the use of informal mechanisms or to switch to professional ones.

From the theoretical point of view, our results can also be interpreted as different ways through which entrepreneurial companies deal with the issue of control and governance, when organizational growth tends to saturate entrepreneurs' attention and cognitive capacities. Non-family firms tend to switch more quickly to formal mechanisms compared to family

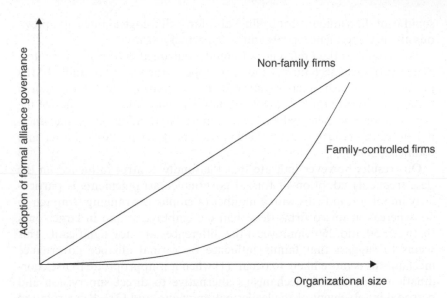

*Figure 9.1   A possible representation of the effect of organizational size
on the adoption of formal alliance governance mechanisms in
family versus non-family firms*

firms. The evolution of family-controlled firms thus seems to follow a different path, compared to non-family firms. As the life cycle stage models show, the growth of firms is characterized by an increase in complexity, which leads to an increase in the use of formal structures and systems (Churchill and Lewis, 1985). As Greiner (1972) suggests, formal control mechanisms are adopted to overcome the 'crisis of control' and respond to the greater need of coordination imposed by an increasingly articulated organizational structure. However, whereas entrepreneurial non-family firms seem to follow a linear path and to reach the crossover point rapidly, family-controlled firms reach that point later. The familiness has thus an impact on the timing in the adoption of formal control mechanisms, and seems to delay the emergence of a crisis of control. Figure 9.1 provides a possible, intuitive, graphical representation of the phenomenon.

This argument might have relevant managerial implications: as previously highlighted, alliances are an important strategy to ensure growth and competitive success for entrepreneurial firms. Since formal governance mechanisms are often strictly required to ensure proper management of the alliances, family-controlled firms expose themselves to higher risks of alliance failure, due to their absolute preference towards informal arrangements; this failure risk is more likely to occur during a critical growth stage, namely the transition between the status of micro firm and the status of medium-sized firm. Thus, family firms' managers should be aware of this threat, and carefully consider the need to adopt formal arrangements in the management of partnerships as a part of the organizational growth process, even if this choice might be in contradiction with the established organizational culture and management style.

CONCLUSIONS

In this chapter we have presented an empirical study investigating the adoption of formal mechanisms in the governance of strategic alliances established by entrepreneurial firms. Formal governance mechanisms are crucial for the success of those alliances characterized by high uncertainty, ambiguity and risk of expropriation. Drawing from organizational control theory, we evaluated the role of family business status as a determinant of alliance governance choices; then we assumed a contingency perspective to assess the effect of organizational size in moderating the consequences of family influence over the inter-organizational arrangements. The empirical findings indicate that the impact of family control on the adoption of formal alliance governance is more likely to occur when organizational structure does not impose too many restrictions on the entrepreneurial discretionary choices. Thus, in this research organizational size appears to be an important variable that may reduce the impact of the family component on the business decisions. This finding could inspire further studies on family business and, more generally, entrepreneurial firms' governance fields, in order to assess the role of structural contingencies in the design of governance arrangements by such firms.

REFERENCES

Astley, W.G. and Fombrun, C.J. (1983), 'Collective strategy: Social ecology of organizational environments', *Academy of Management Review*, **8** (4), 576–587.

Blau, P.M. (1970), 'A formal theory of differentiation in organisations', *American Sociological Review*, **35**, 201–218.

Blomqvist, K., Hurmelinna-Laukkanen, P., Nummela, N. and Saarenketo, S. (2008), 'The role of trust and contracts in the internationalization of technology-intensive Born Globals', *Journal of Engineering and Technology Management*, **25** (1), 123–135.

Brunninge, O., Nordqvist, M. and Wiklund, J. (2007), 'Corporate governance and strategic change in SMEs: The effects of ownership, board composition and top management teams', *Small Business Economics*, **29** (3), 295–308.

Bubolz, M. (2001), 'Family as a source, user and builder of social capital', *Journal of Socio-Economics*, **30**, 129–131.

Carney, M. (2005), 'Corporate governance and competitive advantage in family-controlled firms', *Entrepreneurship Theory and Practice*, **29**, 249–66.

Churchill, N.C. and Lewis, V.L. (1985), 'Profitability of small business lending', *Journal of Bank Research*, **16** (2), 63–71.

Contractor, F.J. and Ra, W. (2002), 'How knowledge attributes influence alliance governance choices: a theory development note', *Journal of International Management*, **8** (1), 11–27.

Contractor, F.J., Woodley, J.A. and Piepenbrink, A. (2011), 'How tight an embrace? Choosing the optimal degree of partner interaction in alliances based on risk, technology characteristics, and agreement provisions', *Global Strategy Journal*, **1** (1–2), 67–85.

Das, T.K. and Teng, B.S. (1996), 'Risk types and inter-firm alliance structures', *Journal of Management Studies*, **33** (6), 827–843.

Das, T.K. and Teng, B.S. (1998), 'Between trust and control: Developing confidence in partner cooperation in alliances', *Academy of Management Review*, **23** (3), 491–512.

Das, T.K. and Teng, B.S. (2001), 'Trust, control, and risk in strategic alliances: An integrated framework', *Organization Studies*, **22** (2), 251–283.

De Man, A.P. and Roijakkers, N. (2009), 'Alliance governance: Balancing control and trust in dealing with risk', *Long Range Planning*, **42**, 75–95.

Deeds, D.L. and Hill, C.W. (1996), 'Strategic alliances and the rate of new product development: An empirical study of entrepreneurial biotechnology firms', *Journal of Business Venturing*, **11** (1), 41–55.

Dekker, H.C. (2004), 'Control of inter-organizational relationships: Evidence on appropriation concerns and coordination requirements', *Accounting, Organizations and Society*, **29** (1), 27–49.

Dickson, P.H., Weaver, K.M. and Hoy, F. (2006), 'Opportunism in the R&D alliances of SMES: The roles of the institutional environment and SME size', *Journal of Business Venturing*, **21** (4), 487–513.

Dodd, S.D., Jack, S. and Anderson, A.R. (2002), 'Scottish entrepreneurial networks in the international context', *International Small Business Journal*, **20** (2), 213–219.

Donaldson, L. (2001), *The Contingency Theory of Organizations*, Thousand Oaks, CA: Sage.

Dyer, J. and Singh, H. (1998), 'The relational view: Cooperative strategy and sources of inter-organizational competitive advantage', *Academy of Management Review*, **23** (4), 660–679.

Dyer, W. and Mortensen, P.S. (2005), 'Entrepreurship and family business in an hostile environment: The case of Lithuania', *Family Business Review*, **18** (3), 247–258.

Eisenhardt, K.M. (1985), 'Control: Organizational and economic approaches', *Management Science*, **31** (2), 134–149.

Faems, D., Janssens, M., Madhok, A. and Van Looy, B. (2008), 'Toward an integrative perspective on alliance governance: Connecting contract design, trust dynamics, and contract application', *Academy of Management Journal*, **51** (6), 1053–1078.

Fernandez, Z. and Nieto, M.J. (2005), 'Internationalization strategy of small and medium sized family business: Some influential factors', *Family Business Review*, **18** (1), 77–89.

Gabrielsson, J. (2007), 'Boards of directors and entrepreneurial posture in medium-size companies: Putting the board demography approach to a test', *International Small Business Journal*, **25** (5), 511–537.

Gabrielsson, J. and Huse, M. (2010), 'Governance theory: Origins and implications for researching boards and governance in entrepreneurial firms', in H. Landström and F. Lohrke (eds), *Historical Foundations of Entrepreneurial Research*, Cheltenham, UK and Northampton, MA, USA: Edward Elgar Publishing, pp. 229–255.

Gedajlovic, E. and Carney, M. (2010), 'Markets, hierarchies and families: Toward a transaction cost theory of the family firm', *Entrepreneurship Theory and Practice*, **34** (6), 1145–1171.

Ghobadian, A. and O'Regan, N. (2006), 'The impact of ownership on small firm behaviour and performance', *International Small Business Journal*, **24** (6), 555–586.

Gifford, S. (1992), 'Allocation of entrepreneurial attention', *Journal of Economic Behavior and Organisation*, **19**, 265–284.

Grandori, A. and Soda, G. (2005), 'Inter-firm networks: Antecedents, mechanisms and forms', *Organization Studies*, **16** (2), 183–214.

Greiner, L.E. (1972), 'Evolution and revolution as organizations grow', *Harvard Business Review*, July–August, 37–46.

Guillen, M.F. (2000), 'Business groups in emerging economies: A resource-based view', *Academy of Management Journal*, **43** (3), 362–380.

Gulati, R., Lawrence, P.R. and Puranam, P. (2005), 'Adaptation in vertical relationships: Beyond incentive conflict', *Strategic Management Journal*, **26** (5), 415–440.

Habbershon, T.G. and Blank, A.M. (2005), 'Innovation in dominant regional family firms: A model for assessing the familiness factor', unpublished paper, Babson College, Institute for Family Enterprising.

Haeussler, C., Holger, P. and Zahra, S.A. (2012), 'Strategic alliances and product development in high technology new firms: The moderating effect of technological capabilities', *Journal of Business Venturing*, **27** (2), 217–233.

Hall, R.H., Haas, J.E. and Norman, N.J. (1967), 'Organisational size, complexity and formalisation', *American Sociological Review*, **32** (6), 903–912.

Hoetker, G. and Mellewigt, T. (2009), 'Choice and performance of governance mechanisms: Matching alliance governance to asset type', *Strategic Management Journal*, **30** (10), 1025–1044.

Hoskisson, R.E., Covin, J., Volberda, H.W. and Johnson, R.A. (2011), 'Revitalizing entrepreneurship: The search for new research opportunities', *Journal of Management Studies*, **48** (6), 1141–1168.

Hyder, A.S. and Abraha, D. (2004), 'Product and skills development in small and medium-sized high-tech firms through international strategic alliances', *Singapore Management Review*, **26** (2), 1–24.

Koza, M.P. and Lewin, A.Y. (1998), 'The co-evolution of strategic alliances', *Organization Science*, **9** (3), 255–264.

Lavie, D., Kang, J. and Rosenkopf, L. (2011), 'Balance within and across domains: The performance implications of exploration and exploitation in alliances', *Organization Science*, **22** (6), 1517–1538.

Lee, J., Hoetker, G. and Qualls, W. (2010), 'Alliance experience and accommodation in the choice of alliance governance structure', available at SSRN 1691094.

Lee, Y. and Cavusgil, S.T. (2006), 'Enhancing alliance performance: The effects of contractual-based versus relational-based governance', *Journal of Business Research*, **59** (8), 896–905.

Leifer, R. and Mills, P.K. (1996), 'An information processing approach for deciding upon control strategies and reducing control loss in emerging organizations', *Journal of Management*, **22** (1), 113–137.

Lester, R.H. and Cannella, A.A. (2006), 'Interorganizational familiness: How family firms use interlocking directorates to build community-level social capital', *Entrepreneurship Theory and Practice*, **30** (6), 755–775.

Levinthal, D.A. and March, J.G. (1993), 'The myopia of learning', *Strategic Management Journal*, **14** (S2), 95–112.

Ma, C., Yang, Z., Yao, Z., Fisher, G. and Fang, E.E. (2012), 'The effect of strategic alliance resource accumulation and process characteristics on new product success: Exploration of international high-tech strategic alliances in China', *Industrial Marketing Management*, **41** (3), 469–480.

Mellewigt, T., Madhok, A. and Weibel, A. (2007), 'Trust and formal contracts in interorganizational relationships – substitutes and complements', *Managerial and Decision Economics*, **28** (8), 833–847.

Milanov, H. and Fernhaber, S.A. (2014), 'When do domestic alliances help ventures abroad? Direct and moderating effects from a learning perspective', *Journal of Business Venturing*, **29** (3), 377–391.

Miller, D. and Le Breton-Miller, I. (2005), *Managing for the Long Run*, Boston, MA: Harvard Business School Press.

Miller, D. and Le Breton-Miller, I. (2006), 'Family governance and firm performance: Agency, stewardship, and capabilities', *Family Business Review*, **19** (1), 73–87.
Moreno, A.M. and Casillas, L.C. (2008), 'Entrepreneurial orientation and growth of SMEs: A causal model', *Entrepreneurship Theory and Practice*, **32** (3), 507–528.
Murray, J.Y. and Kotabe, M. (2005), 'Performance implications of strategic fit between alliance attributes and alliance forms', *Journal of Business Research*, **58** (11), 1525–1533.
Mustakallio, M., Autio, E. and Zahra, S.A. (2002), 'Relational and contractual governance in family firms: Effects on strategic decisions making', *Family Business Review*, **15** (3), 205–222.
Naphiet, J. and Ghoshal, S. (1998), 'Social capital, intellectual capital, and organizational advantage', *Academy of Management Review*, **23** (2), 242–266.
Nickerson, J.A. and Zenger, T.R. (2004), 'A knowledge-based theory of the firm: The problem-solving perspective', *Organization Science*, **15** (6), 617–632.
Nielsen, B.B. (2010), 'Strategic fit, contractual, and procedural governance in alliances', *Journal of Business Research*, **63** (7), 682–689.
O'Dwyer, M. and O'Flynn, E. (2005), 'MNC–SME strategic alliances: A model framing knowledge value as the primary predictor of governance modal choice', *Journal of International Management*, **11** (3), 397–416.
Organisation for Economic Co-operation and Development (OECD) (2013), *OECD Science, Technology and Industry Scoreboard 2013: Innovation and Performance in the Global Economy*, Organisation for Economic Co-operation and Development.
Ouchi, W.G. (1979), 'A conceptual framework for the design of organizational control mechanisms', *Management Science*, **25** (9), 833–848.
Pittino, D. and Visintin, F. (2011), 'The propensity toward inter-organizational cooperation in small-and medium-sized family businesses', *Journal of Family Business Strategy*, **2** (2), 57–68.
Pittino, D., Visintin, F., Bau, M. and Mazzurana, P. (2013), 'Collaborative technology strategies and innovation in family firms', *International Journal of Entrepreneurship and Innovation Management*, **17** (1–3), 8–27.
Pondy, L.R. (1969), 'Effects of size, complexity, and ownership on administrative intensity', *Administrative Science Quarterly*, **14** (1), 47–60.
Poppo, L. and Zenger, T. (2002), 'Do formal contracts and relational governance function as substitutes or complements?', *Strategic Management Journal*, **23** (8), 707–725.
Pugh, D.S., Hickson, D.J., Hinings, C.R. and Turner, C. (1968), 'Dimensions of organization structure', *Administrative Science Quarterly*, **13** (1), 65–105.
Roijakkers, N. and Hagedoorn, J. (2007), 'Strategic and organizational understanding of inter firm partnerships and networks', in H. Hanusch and A. Pyka (eds), *Elgar Companion to Neo-Schumpeterian Economics*, Cheltenham, UK and Northampton, MA, USA: Edward Elgar Publishing, pp. 201–210.
Rothaermel, F.T. and Deeds, D.L. (2004), 'Exploration and exploitation alliances in biotechnology: A system of new product development', *Strategic Management Journal*, **25** (3), 201–221.
Smith, K.G., Carroll, S.J. and Ashford, S.J. (1995), 'Intra-and interorganizational cooperation: Toward a research agenda', *Academy of Management Journal*, **38** (1), 7–23.
Steensma, H.K., Marino, L., Weaver, K.M. and Dickson, P.H. (2000), 'The influence of national culture on the formation of technology alliances by entrepreneurial firms', *Academy of Management Journal*, **43** (5), 951–973.
Street, C. and Cameron, A.F. (2007), 'External relationships and the small business: A review of small business alliance and network research', *Journal of Small Business Management*, **45** (2), 239–266.
Teng, B.S. (2007), 'Corporate entrepreneurship activities through strategic alliances: A resource-based approach toward competitive advantage', *Journal of Management Studies*, **44** (1), 119–142.
Thorgren, S., Wincent, J. and Örtqvist, D. (2009), 'Designing interorganizational networks

for innovation: An empirical examination of network configuration, formation and governance', *Journal of Engineering and Technology Management*, **26** (3), 148–166.

Vlaar, P.W., Van den Bosch, F.A. and Volberda, H.W. (2006), 'Coping with problems of understanding in interorganizational relationships: Using formalization as a means to make sense', *Organization Studies*, **27** (11), 1617–1638.

Westhead, P. and Cowling, M. (1998), 'Family firm research: The need for a methodological rethink', *Entrepreneurship Theory and Practice*, **23**, 31–56.

Williamson, O.E. (1985), *The Economic Institutions of Capitalism: Firms, Markets, Relational Contracting*, New York: Free Press.

Wincent, J., Anokhin, S. and Örtqvist, D. (2010), 'Does network board capital matter? A study of innovative performance in strategic SME networks', *Journal of Business Research*, **63** (3), 265–275.

Wolf, J.A. and Pett, T.L. (2000), 'Internationalisation of small firms: An examination of export competitive patterns, firm size and export performance', *Journal of Small Business Management*, **38** (2), 34–47.

Yang, H., Zheng, Y. and Zhao, X. (2014), 'Exploration or exploitation? Small firms' alliance strategies with large firms', *Strategic Management Journal*, **35** (1), 146–157.

Zahra, S.A. (2005), 'Entrepreneurial risk taking in family firms', *Family Business Review*, **18** (1), 23–40.

10. Corporate governance and innovation in small entrepreneurial firms: the board chairperson's role

Daniel Yar Hamidi and Jonas Gabrielsson

INTRODUCTION

The board of directors is an untapped resource in many small firms (Castaldi and Wortman, 1984; Huse, 2000). Research shows that active boards may contribute ideas and new perspectives on how to develop small firms and their operations (Borch and Huse, 1993; George et al., 2001; Gabrielsson and Politis, 2007). This research stream finds that active boards can help small firms to discover and exploit market opportunities and can facilitate new product development (Borch et al., 1999; Zahra et al., 2000; Gabrielsson, 2007a). Given these findings, the small firm may well benefit from actively using its board of directors in ways that promote its innovation, leading to increased competitiveness.

Empirical studies suggest that the chairperson may play a key role for leading and developing the board of directors in small firms (Gabrielsson et al., 2007; Huse and Zattoni, 2008; Machold et al., 2011). However, most research that has addressed questions related to the chairperson has been heavily influenced by theoretical and methodological approaches that treat the inner workings of boards as a black box (Gabrielsson and Huse, 2004; Huse and Gabrielsson, 2012). This research relies primarily on agency theory in its conception of the firm (Fama and Jensen, 1983) where the question has been whether or not the chief executive officer (CEO) should be removed from the chairperson position (Daily and Dalton, 1993; Daily et al., 2003). On the other hand, the few studies that have been conducted on chairpersons and their leadership behaviours have so far been largely descriptive (Leblanc, 2005; Huse and Gabrielsson, 2012). Thus, there is a lack of theory on the leadership role of board chairpersons and how they can promote innovations via the board of directors in small entrepreneurial firms.

Against this backdrop, the overall objective of the chapter is to build a framework that addresses how board chairpersons can develop innovation-promoting boards in small entrepreneurial firms. We use Miller and Friesen's (1982) definition of the entrepreneurial firm as a firm that seeks innovation and accepts the related changes and risks (see also Miller, 1983). Moreover, we use the conceptualization of innovation as the generation and/or adoption (or use) of new ideas or behaviours in organizations (Damanpour, 1991; Gopalaskrishnan and Damanpour, 1997).

In this chapter we contribute to theory and research on corporate governance in entrepreneurial contexts in several ways. The first contribution is our proposal of a conceptual framework for how board chairpersons may create and sustain innovation-promoting boards of directors in small entrepreneurial firms. We develop this framework using a qualitative interview methodology in which we examine how board leadership can support and nurture innovation. With this examination, we respond to the research call to open up the board of directors' 'black box' (Huse, 2005; Huse and Zattoni, 2008).

The chapter's second contribution is its comparison of innovation-promoting practices by the boards of small entrepreneurial firms with other practices by such boards. This comparison reveals no fundamental difference between such practices; rather, innovation-promoting practices are an extension and continuation of other board activities.

The chapter's third contribution is the finding that the dynamics of board behaviour in small entrepreneurial firms can be seen as relatively complex social systems (Huse, 1998; Sonnenfeld, 2002) largely embedded in processes of interdependency and causal asymmetry. This finding calls for theoretical frameworks and methodological approaches that emphasize and acknowledge such complexity in their logic and design.

The rest of the chapter is structured as follows. In the next section we review the contemporary research literature on innovation and corporate governance. We then describe our qualitative interview methodology. Thereafter we present our findings and a discussion on how these findings contribute to the research on board leadership. The chapter concludes with a summary of our main findings and with comments on the implications of our research for theory and practice.

LITERATURE REVIEW

Innovation and Corporate Governance

Intense competition and technological development in many industries exert pressure on small firms to respond and adapt to rapid changes in their environments (Mazzarol and Reboud, 2009). These changes create constant pressure to develop new products and more efficient production processes. Innovations – the very lifeblood of firms – are essential for sustained competitiveness and long-term survival. An explicit commitment to innovation is increasingly prioritized in small firms as a way to come up with novel solutions to customer problems and for the creation of future revenue streams (Messeghem, 2003; Wiklund and Shepherd, 2005; Lechner and Gudmundsson, 2014).

Our focus in this chapter is the generation or adoption of innovations at the level of the firm (Burns and Stalker, 1961 [1994]; Thompson, 1965) rather than the process by which innovations are communicated among members of a social system (e.g., Rogers, 2003). We also focus on firm innovations that can (at minimum) result in a new product, service, process, market, organizational structure or administrative system (Zahra, 1991; Gopalakrishnan and Damanpour, 1997).

Research suggests that a firm's corporate governance structure has a profound influence on its innovative capacity (Zahra, 1996; Zahra et al., 2000; Gabrielsson, 2007a). Hambrick et al. (2008, p. 381) define corporate governance as 'the formal structures, informal structures, and processes that exist in oversight roles and responsibilities in the corporate context'. These oversight roles and responsibilities include the development and implementation of organizational routines and reward systems that encourage attitudes and behaviour consistent with the firm's mission and goals.

Corporate Governance in Small Firms

Much of the research on corporate governance is concerned with large, publicly owned corporations in which there is a clear separation between ownership and management (Gabrielsson and Huse, 2004). This research emphasizes the necessity for independent corporate governance structures that give managers the incentive to act in the interest of the owners rather than in their own self-interest (Zahra et al., 2000; Gabrielsson, 2007a). In small firms, however, there is often a close relationship between owners and managers; in some cases, the owner and manager are the same person. In this situation, independent corporate governance structures are less critical (Jensen and Meckling, 1976).

Small firms, in relation to larger firms, generally have fewer resources and competencies (Mazzarol and Reboud, 2009), less experience, and less economic and political power (Pfeffer and Salancik, 1978). Thus small firms must be more flexible in their use of their resources and competencies that are essential for their long-term viability and health (Mazzarol and Reboud, 2009). For competitive advantage, small firms require supportive governance functions (Warren, 2003) that can expand their competencies and experience when developing, reviewing and revising long-term plans (Brunninge et al., 2007; Gabrielsson and Politis, 2007;

Minichilli and Hansen, 2007), and that can establish effective linkages with strategically important stakeholders (Borch and Huse, 1993; Huse and Zattoni, 2008).

The Board of Directors and the Role of the Chairperson

The board of directors is a key component of good corporate governance (Huse, 2000), especially in small entrepreneurial firms engaged in innovation (Zahra et al., 2000; Gabrielsson, 2007a). Board members in small firms are typically charged with supervising the overall development of the organization (Bennett and Robson, 2004), managing relationships with key stakeholders (Borch and Huse, 1993; Huse, 1998; George et al., 2001) and acting as the CEO's partner in setting strategic directions (Fiegener, 2005; Knockaert et al., 2015). Effective board members are thus a powerful strategic resource for the creation of competitive advantage. They often contribute important business networks, specialized know-how and experience to the firm's strategic decision-making processes (Gabrielsson et al., 2007; Machold et al., 2011).

Empirical research, however, finds that developing the boards of directors in a small firm is a particularly challenging task. Surveys of board members at small firms (e.g. Ward and Handy, 1988; Fiegener et al., 2000; Gabrielsson, 2007b) indicate that the boards of such firms typically consist of the owner-manager and their family members. If a firm has additional board members, these people are often the firm's attorney and/or friends and business associates of the CEO (Corbetta and Tomaselli, 1996; Johannisson and Huse, 2000). A patriarchal power structure may exist when board members are linked to the firm by family ties or friendship (Ward and Handy, 1988). These board members may also be influenced by 'group think' (Brouthers et al., 1998). As a result, the small firm's board of directors may lack the power and integrity needed in their governance support function.

Small firms seeking to empower their board of directors often recruit an external board member as the board chairperson (Huse and Zattoni, 2008). The chairperson, who has the same voting rights as any other board member (Baxt, 2009), has additional responsibilities. These responsibilities typically include scheduling board meetings, overseeing board processes, and developing a board culture that encourages participation and supports decision-making (Furr and Furr, 2005; Kakabadse et al., 2006). In addition, the chairperson is expected to run board meetings in a way that permits discussion aimed at ensuring that strategic and policy decisions are consistent with company goals, owner directives and bylaws (Parker, 1990; Leblanc, 2005).

However, with no formal authority over other board members, the board chairperson must rely on their personal experience and leadership qualities to turn a group of people with diverse personalities and backgrounds into an interacting and collective team (Gabrielsson et al., 2007). Therefore, the board chairperson must take an active role as a boardroom leader to unlock the potential on the team (Parker, 1990; Cascio, 2004). Small entrepreneurial firms especially require competent and forceful board chairpersons who can facilitate board leadership and drive the organization forward (Huse and Zattoni, 2008).

The selection of an effective board chairperson requires an understanding of behavioural dynamics in and around the boardroom, and this is an understanding not often addressed in the general theories and models on board leadership (Huse and Gabrielsson, 2012). Much of the research on board leadership is grounded in agency theory (Fama and Jensen, 1983), in which the emphasis is on the independence of the board from the firm's managers, in particular the CEO. This research has often focused on when the same individual holds both the CEO and the board chairperson positions (Daily and Dalton, 1993; Gabrielsson and Huse, 2004).

While this research stream has provided valuable insights into the drivers of board effectiveness at large, publicly held corporations (Krause et al., 2014), the findings have less relevance for the analysis of boards of directors and their chairpersons in small entrepreneurial firms (Huse, 2000). In addition, no theory or model has been developed that addresses how the board chairperson may promote innovation and an entrepreneurial culture (Huse and Gabrielsson, 2012).

METHODOLOGY

Because board of directors' meetings are inaccessible research settings (McNulty and Pettigrew, 1999; Huse, 2000), most research on boards relies on data from various published reports about and by large, publicly held companies (e.g., Gabrielsson and Huse, 2004). As an alternative data collection methodology for this research, we mainly used qualitative interviews with board chairpersons in Sweden. This approach (see Silverman, 2001; Rubin and Rubin, 2012) is useful for building theories in new or emerging areas where development is needed at both theoretical and empirical levels (Eisenhardt, 1989). We also used a number of other sources to verify and crosscheck data from the interviews. These sources included annual reports, press releases and newspaper articles.

Data Collection

We first designed a preliminary interview questionnaire that we could use with small entrepreneurial firms engaged in innovation. The questionnaire consisted of questions about the generation and/or adoption of innovations (Rogers, 2003; see also Damanpour, 1991) and how this work related to the board chairperson's efforts to lead and influence board members (Huse, 2005; Huse and Gabrielsson, 2012). We tested this preliminary questionnaire in a pilot test with an experienced board chairperson. Based on this input, we revised and finalized our interview questionnaire.

Sample

We used purposeful sampling (e.g., Patton, 2002) to identify respondents who could provide relevant data. This procedure is appropriate for our qualitative interview methodology and our goal of generalizing our findings (Yin, 2003). We had three criteria for the selection of our sample. First, each firm would have a history of growth that was driven by the generation or adoption of innovations. Second, each firm's board chairperson would have extensive managerial and board of director experience. Third, each firm's board chairperson would be an outsider without controlling ownership in the firm.

We determined our sample size following the principle of theoretical saturation (e.g., Glaser and Strauss, 1967). Thus, we ceased interviewing respondents when our data no longer added new insights to our research. Our final sample consisted of six respondents with considerable experience as board members and as board chairpersons at entrepreneurial firms. Some of these companies were fully owned family businesses, while others were partially owned by investment companies. All respondents had been externally recruited as board chairpersons and had no other employment or assignments at the firms. Either the investment companies or the owner-manager chose the chairpersons. Table 10.1 describes the six respondents.

We used our interview questionnaire for all interviews. Because we did not intend to test any formal hypotheses, we used open-ended questions that could lead to inductive theories (Kvale, 1983; Eisenhardt, 1989). Thus our questions were flexible yet sufficiently structured that the present and past work experiences of the board chairpersons were always in focus.

We also used a chart in the interviews that was constructed on the basis of theories about the generation and adoption of innovations (Rogers, 2003; Damanpour and Wischnevsky, 2006). Using this chart, we invited the respondents to describe their involvement with business innovation.

The interviews lasted about one hour. We tape-recorded and transcribed

Table 10.1 *Description of the respondents*

	Alex	Burt	Chandler	Douglas	Ephraim	Figaro
Age	68	52	57	70	58	72
Educational background	Law	Engineering	Engineering	Engineering	Business/ economics	Engineering
Main industries	Banking, production, professional services	Textile, chemical production, service	Production plants, metal, services, finance	Metal, production plants, professional services	Construction, production plants	Software, production plants, professional services
Total no. of board engagements	13	8	17	7	21	9
Total no. of board engagements as chairperson	5	4	6	2	4	5

all interviews. In addition, we conducted a number of follow-up telephone interviews where clarification of responses was required.

Method of analysis

We analysed our interview data using a systematic process of theory building (Eisenhardt, 1989; Yin, 2013). We verified some factual data in the interview responses by comparisons with other sources. In our analysis, we identified observations and patterns that could lead to general conclusions.

We began our data analysis at the same time that we collected data. This analytical method is a recommended strategy in qualitative research (Glaser and Strauss, 1965; Eisenhardt, 1989). Therefore, we analysed our first interview with the intent of identifying the building blocks of a framework that explains how the board chairperson may support innovation in small entrepreneurial firms. Concurrently, we thought about how this initial framework might relate to existing theory. As we analysed all the interview data, we conducted within-case analyses and cross-case analyses. Our goal was to determine whether the framework applied only to areas of interest in the first interview, or to all interviews (Miles and Huberman, 1994). In short, we analysed each chairperson's responses individually as well as jointly with the other chairpersons' responses. We continued this iterative process until all the interviews were analysed and compared.

ANALYSIS AND DISCUSSION

The Role of the Board Chairperson

Our analysis suggests that the chairpersons have a very pragmatic understanding of their role as leaders of the board of directors. Their mandate, which is to a large extent based on trust (Huse, 1998), is typically to act as moderators and facilitators. Chairperson Ephraim stated:

> Usually it [the leadership] is very unpretentious. There is no leadership [in a formal sense]. I do not see it [my chairpersonship] as [formally] leading others. I see my role more as a catalyst or maybe somehow, someone who moderates the meetings to make them as effective as possible.

Several chairpersons emphasized trust and confidence as central features of the relationship between the chairperson, the other board members, the CEO and the owners. A trusting relationship gives the chairperson the authority to conduct board meetings. Chairperson Chandler stated:

> Yes, chairpersonship in this kind of company is very much about high trust between the chairperson and the owners. By building trust in the board and by allowing other board members to take the lead in discussions in which they are most knowledgeable, the chairperson may convince the owners to take some action. This may include investing in risky innovation processes.

The owners set the course for the firm that provides the overall frame for the responsibilities and activities of the board chairperson. The chairperson must understand and follow the mandate to develop the firm's innovation work. Otherwise the board, lacking commitment, will only pay lip service to innovation. Chairperson Douglas stated:

> You must be animated by the idea of renewing the firm. Probably not all directors are inspired by it [promoting innovation] and understand its consequences. I can very well imagine that many see themselves as the chairperson who should monitor and control instead of taking a proactive position.

The Framework for Innovation Promotion by Boards of Directors

We identified the building blocks of a framework that explains how a board chairperson may support innovation in small entrepreneurial firms. These building blocks are: (1) structures; (2) processes; (3) culture; and (4) cognition. The first three building blocks are essential for innovation-promoting boards although they are not directly associated with the support of innovation. The fourth building block, cognition, is directly associated with the support of innovation.

In interpreting, systemizing and structuring our data, we were inspired by Herzberg's (1966) two-factor theory of motivators and hygiene factors. This theory proposes that some factors in the workplace create job satisfaction, while other factors create job dissatisfaction. The theory concludes that satisfiers and dissatisfiers are not on a continuum whereby the increase in one factor causes another factor to decrease. Rather, the theory, which proposes an asymmetric structure of causal effects, requires an understanding of all factors if desired results are to be achieved.

We identified similar signs of an asymmetric structure in the analysis of our data. We identified three building blocks, categorized as enablers, which create the basis of effective board work. Enablers are the board leadership practices related to structures, processes and culture that support the development of a well-functioning board of directors. In addition, we identified a fourth building block, categorized as energizers, that directly contributes to innovation. Energizers include the board leadership practices that influence the cognitive dimensions of the board's work. Figure 10.1 depicts the building blocks of the framework for inno-

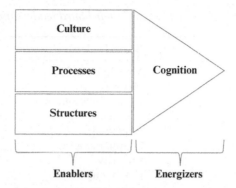

Figure 10.1   Building blocks for the development of innovation-promoting boards

vation promotion by boards of directors, divided between enablers and energizers.

Our analysis reveals that, for a firm's board to perform its tasks properly, well-functioning boardroom structures and processes as well as an appropriate boardroom culture must exist. However, to promote innovation, board members must also actively and openly exchange knowledge and experience and engage in constructive cognitive work in the support of the firm's development activities. The board chairperson's most important responsibility is to show leadership by implementing the leadership practices associated with the four building blocks. See Table 10.2.

Enablers: Board Leadership Practices that Support Well-Functioning Boards

Many board leadership practices support the development of well-functioning boards rather than promote innovation. Based on previous research on the boards of directors at small firms (e.g., Huse, 1998; Gabrielsson and Winlund, 2000), we associate these support practices with three of the framework's building blocks: structures, processes and culture.

Structures
Structures refer to the board leadership practices that structure and organize the board's work (Huse, 1998; Gabrielsson and Winlund, 2000). In the analysis we specifically identified board leadership that influences the presence and quality of meeting agendas, protocols and instructions and policies for the board's work. The findings emphasize the need to

Table 10.2   The building blocks and their board leadership practices

Building blocks	Board leadership practices
Structures	Meeting agendas
	Protocols
	Instructions and policies
Processes	Coaching
	Follow-ups
	Summarizing
Culture	Integrity
	Generosity
	Cohesiveness
Cognition	Knowledge sharing
	Cognitive conflict
	Strategy development

implement proper meeting agendas that bring up relevant development aspects at board meetings. This provides direction and focus to board meetings and provides a platform for constructive debate. The meeting agendas should include clear and pertinent instructions that provide direction and focus for the board's activities. They should also include reports about key performance indicators that are in line with the current and future development of the firm. Chairperson Douglas stated: 'I do not believe it is enough with quarterly economic reports. We need to set other parameters and include suitable key performance indicators. I think, for example, that one must be able to follow product renewal.' Chairperson Douglas also stated: 'At the board meetings we had these questions [development projects] on our agenda quarterly, and we had a follow up on several projects running in parallel.'

The findings also emphasize the importance of protocols. Law often regulates the existence of protocols from board meetings. However, when decisions are filed in protocols these decisions should be clearly formulated. The board chairperson has an important task in overseeing board protocols to ensure that they clearly describe decisions in a permanent record for use in reviews of firm activities and the assignment of responsibility. Chairperson Ephraim stated:

> When a decision is filed in a protocol, it is the chairperson's task to ensure that it is what the board agreed on and to follow up on its execution. Sometimes there may be a delay [in execution], but then a discussion by the board is required. The board's decision should be respected and followed. It is what external chairpersons in this kind of company should do.

Furthermore, the findings suggest that the chairperson has an important task in coordinating instructions and policies that describe the topics for discussion in the meetings, the communications to the CEO and owners, and the follow-up plans for current and future projects. These instructions and policies should include information of how current projects and activities in the firm will be followed up. Often there are some instructions and policies in place, but they need to be continuously reviewed and (if necessary) updated as the firm is developing. Chairperson Ephraim stated: 'I just expect it [reporting instructions and information flow] to work well. However, it actually doesn't work sometimes. And that is something that must be taken care of immediately.'

Processes

Processes refer to the board leadership practices associated with the working processes in and around the boardroom (Huse, 1998; Gabrielsson and Winlund, 2000). In the analysis we specifically identified board leadership related to coaching (the CEO), summarizing board discussions, as well as following up the execution and implementation of board decisions.

The findings suggest that coaching the CEO is a very important part of the work of the chairperson in small entrepreneurial firms. The CEO must deal with both everyday activities and crisis events, by supporting the coordination of the firm's operations and goals. The chairperson, who is removed from the daily activities, can provide a long-term and wider perspective on the firm's strategic decisions. Chairperson Figaro stated:

> For the chairperson, it is a question of pushing the CEO in the right direction by making him understand what must be done. As the firm is growing, with more and more employees, it is important that the CEO trusts the organization instead of demanding total control. The CEO must delegate responsibility to others.

In providing such coaching, the chairperson is most effective if they suggest options, rather than direct advice, for example by offering decision-making frameworks to the CEO. Chairperson Chandler stated: 'I believe that it [helping the firm to innovate] requires a very specific process of educating the entrepreneur and getting him to dare create resources [for innovation]!'

The findings also emphasize the chairperson's role in summarizing the board's discussions. The chairperson encourages all members to freely state their opinion before a decision is made. The chairperson then summarizes the board's discussions so that all board members' opinions and viewpoints are explicitly aired. Chairperson Burt stated: 'much [of a chairperson's role] is about keeping the discussions open and ongoing, following the meeting agendas, and making sure everyone on the board can express their opinions . . . It is the chairperson's role to reduce discussions to a summary and make a decision.'

Furthermore, the chairperson has an important task in overseeing follow-ups on various activities to determine whether decisions were implemented properly. Follow-ups may include the use of such instruments as growth targets and key performance indicators aimed at measuring the achievement of strategic goals. Chairperson Chandler stated: 'It is of utmost importance to have some relevant criteria for follow-ups. For example, we support product renewal by tracking sales statistics on newly developed products instead of total sales of some firms.'

Culture
Culture refers to the board leadership practices associated with a system of shared board member assumptions, values and beliefs (Huse, 2005). In the analysis we specifically identified board leadership practices that influence and encourage integrity, generosity and cohesiveness in the boardroom.

The chairpersons emphasize the importance of creating a high level of integrity among all board members. Honesty and fairness at the board level sets the right tone from the top and establishes a culture for the entire firm. It is also something that promotes an open culture and allows board members to act according to the values, beliefs and principles they hold. Chairperson Chandler stated: 'There are two very important things to look for in a board member – extensive experience . . . and great integrity.'

The findings also emphasize the chairperson's role in encouraging generosity in the boardroom. A board member exhibits a generous spirit insofar as they share opinions and experience with other board members. This generosity is also evident in a willingness to listen to others. Chairperson Chandler stated:

> He [a director on one of my boards] had an absolutely fantastic manner at the board meetings. He could listen [to others]. When he had stated his own ideas, he shared his perspective very generously with other directors. He was not afraid to lose face in the discussions or risk criticism. He just shares his ideas very generously.

Furthermore, the analysis emphasizes the need for the board chairperson to create cohesion among board members by stressing the spirit of teamwork. The board members ultimately need to act and speak as a unit, especially when facing tough or challenging situations. Chairperson Douglas stated:

> If the owners demand some kind of renewal [in the firm], defined by their conditions, then you need someone taking the lead on the board. This requires both an understanding of what it means [to lead] and what will be required [of others] in working together in the boardroom as well as in relation to management.

Energizers: Board Leadership Practices that Drive Innovation

Board leadership practices that drive, rather than support, innovation are associated with the building block of cognition (see Rindova, 1999). These practices are critical to implement in small entrepreneurial firms as they directly relate to the promotion of innovation.

Cognition

The building block entitled cognition relates to the cognitive aspects of the board's work (Forbes and Milliken, 1999; Rindova, 1999). In the analysis we specifically identified board leadership practices that influence knowledge sharing and cognitive conflicts in the boardroom, and the active use of this input into strategy development.

The analysis identifies the chairperson's task of facilitating knowledge sharing as an exclusive and critical contribution that they offer when developing innovation-promoting boards. The chairperson shares their knowledge with the other board members and with the CEO. This knowledge includes ideas, perspectives, evaluations, and so on, all of which are valuable in the discussion on strategic decision-making. Chairperson Chandler stated:

> A board can have the world's top consultants as board members, but if they do not share their ideas, knowledge, experiences, networks and assessments, nothing will happen! This passivity deceives the board into believing that management's proposals are right for the firm. Sometimes, when management's proposal are the best suggestions, then great! But there are rarely any ideas so well developed that you cannot tweak or change things a bit to make them better.

The chairperson, however, is also comfortable with admitting when they lack the knowledge to evaluate a particular issue. Chairperson Ephraim stated:

> Take Company A. I was with them from the time when we grew from a turnover of ninety million [Swedish crowns] to about two hundred and six million. There was strong growth for more than three years. I had an early discussion with the owners about the situation in which there was a set of new problems

that I really had no experience with. I explained that I have been with other companies that have had these problems, but I was not the chairperson. I told the company that they should look around for someone who can comple-ment my role . . . When I left, we parted as friends, about six months after this discussion.

Another contribution made by board chairpersons in the effort to develop innovation-promoting boards was the deliberate creation of respectful cognitive conflicts among board members (see Forbes and Milliken, 1999). Such conflicts are useful in challenging taken-for-granted assumptions and so-called common wisdom. When the chairperson is out-spoken and frank, other board members are encouraged to express their opinions. Chairperson Ephraim stated: '"Why do you do that?" Doing this [asking why] will raise many ideas. You should ask yourself: "Why do I do this?: And, of course, as often is the case, the answer may be that it has always been done this way!' Chairperson Burt stated:

> That's the problem [why the firm does not grow]. They [owner-managers] are happy and satisfied with what they have . . . maybe they want to develop new products, but these are always very much like those of competitors because they have no new ideas. Managers and owner entrepreneurs are not successful at finding new patterns. They do not know how or where to look for renewal for their firms.

Furthermore, the findings suggest that board chairpersons who aim to promote innovation have an important task in assimilating and channel-ling the new insights and perspectives into the strategic decision-making process. The chairperson guides the firm's strategic development by engag-ing board members in framing and defining problems (e.g., Lindenberg, 2003; Rindova, 1999). This practice requires that the chairperson estab-lish a trusting work relationship with the CEO as they set firm strategy. Without such cooperation, the board's knowledge, skills and expertise are left unused, with little impact on strategic outcomes (Forbes and Milliken, 1999). Chairperson Figaro stated: 'Basically, it is about guiding the CEO in his work, so that some parts are cut off while other parts are expand-ing. This process must be fully integrated in the strategy [of the firm] and continually followed up.'

CONCLUSION AND IMPLICATIONS

The chapter proposes a conceptual framework for how board chairper-sons may develop innovation-promoting boards in small entrepreneurial firms. Our interest in this topic stems from our observations that the chairperson, by their leadership practices, can play a key role at small firms (Gabrielsson et al., 2007; Machold et al., 2011). Previous research has largely treated the board of directors as a black box (Gabrielsson and Huse, 2004; Huse and Gabrielsson, 2012). The implication is that the board of directors is isolated from the firm. Our purpose in this chapter, using data from qualitative interviews with board chairpersons in small entrepreneurial firms, is to open up that black box and show how the board chairperson's leadership practices may influence the direction and performance of such firms.

The findings reported in the chapter provide empirical and theoretical insights into how chairpersons may develop the organizational capacity to support and nurture innovations in entrepreneurial firms by developing the work of the board of directors. Our framework consists of four building blocks: structures, processes, culture and cognition. Enablers refer to the first three building blocks; energizers refer to the fourth building block. Each building block has a set of board leadership practices that board chairpersons can use to support innovation-promoting boards.

We acknowledge that our analysis is based on contemporary interviews with six board chairpersons of firms located in Sweden. Given this research setting, we recognize the potential limitations for broader generalizations of the findings across temporal and spatial contexts. We thus welcome further studies on this topic that can support or develop our conceptual framework.

However, despite this limitation, we think our conceptual framework can be useful for chairpersons in small entrepreneurial firms. The framework identifies and describes the board leadership practices that experienced board chairpersons recommend for promoting innovation at such firms. The board chairperson may assist such development by organizing, overseeing and encouraging the activities of the entire board in a collective endeavour.

This chapter also offers insights into processes of board development in small entrepreneurial firms. Boards may organize their work in different ways. We find that board leadership practices aimed at developing well-functioning boards are not fundamentally different from board leadership practices aimed at developing innovation-promoting boards. Innovation-promoting board work can in this respect be conceptualized as an extension and continuation of ordinary (effective) board work. This process is illustrated in Figure 10.2.

Overall, our findings suggest that the relationship between various board leadership practices and the development of innovation-promoting boards in small entrepreneurial firms is, to a large extent, embedded in complex systemic processes. In this respect we find that some factors

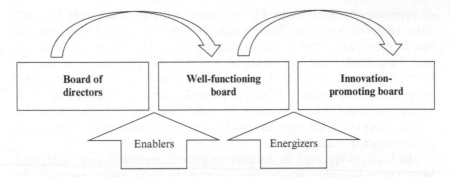

Figure 10.2   Process model for the development of innovation-promoting boards

(enablers) create building blocks for well-functioning boards while other factors (energizers) create building blocks for innovation-promoting boards. Both sets of factors are thus necessary, but not sufficient, building blocks for innovation-promoting boards. While some research assumes independence between predictors and asymmetry in causal connections (see Fiss, 2011), these assumptions may be too restrictive when researching the dynamics of board behaviour in small entrepreneurial firms (see Huse, 1998). The potential interdependencies observed in our data may call for alternative approaches in future empirical studies. One such approach is a configurational examination of causal relationships (e.g. Flynn and Chan, 1992; Judge et al., 2015; see also Fiss, 2011). We think such alternative approaches may advance our understanding of how chairpersons promote innovation in small entrepreneurial firms.

REFERENCES

Baxt, B. (2009), *Duties and Responsibilities of Directors and Officers*, Sydney: Australian Institute of Company Directors.

Bennett, R.J. and Robson, P.J.A. (2004), 'The role of boards of directors in small and medium-sized firms', *Journal of Small Business and Enterprise Development*, **11** (1), 95–113.

Borch, O.J. and Huse, M. (1993), 'Informal strategic networks and the board of directors', *Entrepreneurship Theory and Practice*, **18**, 23–36.

Borch, O.J., Huse, M. and Senneseth, K. (1999), 'Resource configuration, competitive strategies, and corporate entrepreneurship: An empirical examination of small firms', *Entrepreneurship Theory and Practice*, **24**, 49–70.

Brouthers, K.D., Andriessen, F. and Nicoales, I. (1998), 'Driving blind: Strategic decision-making at small companies', *Long Range Planning*, **31** (1), 130–38.

Brunninge, O., Nordqvist, J. and Wiklund, J. (2007), 'Corporate governance and strategic change in SMEs: The effects of ownership, board composition and top management teams', *Small Business Economics*, **29** (3), 295–308.

Burns, T.E. and Stalker, G.M. (1961 [1994]), *The Management of Innovation*, Oxford: Oxford University Press.

Cascio, W.F. (2004), 'Board governance: A social systems perspective', *Academy of Management Executive*, **18**, 97–100.

Castaldi, R. and Wortman, M.S. (1984), 'Board of directors at small companies: An untapped resource', *American Journal of Small Business*, **9** (2), 1–11.

Corbetta, G. and Tomaselli, S. (1996), 'Boards of directors in Italian family businesses', *Family Business Review*, **9** (4), 403–21.

Daily, C.M. and Dalton, D.R. (1993), 'Board of directors leadership and structure: Control and performance implications', *Entrepreneurship Theory and Practice*, **17**, 65–81.

Daily, C.M., Dalton, D.R. and Cannella Jr, A.A. (2003), 'Corporate governance: Decades of dialogue and data', *Academy of Management Review*, **28**, 371–82.

Damanpour, F. (1991), 'Organizational innovation: A meta-analysis of effects of determinants and moderators', *Academy of Management Journal*, **34**, 555–90.

Damanpour, F. and Wischnevsky, D.J. (2006), 'Research on innovation in organizations: Distinguishing innovation-generating from innovation-adopting organizations', *Journal of Engineering and Technology Management*, **23**, 269–91.

Eisenhardt, K.M. (1989), 'Building theories from case study research', *Academy of Management Review*, **14**, 532–50.

Fama, E.F. and Jensen, M.C. (1983), 'Separation of ownership and control', *Journal of Law and Economics*, **26**, 301–26.

Fiegener, M.K. (2005), 'Determinants of board participation in the strategic decisions of small corporations', *Entrepreneurship Theory and Practice*, **29** (5), 627–50.

Fiegener, M.K, Brown, B.M., Dreux, D.R. and Dennis W.J. (2000), 'The adoption of outside boards by small private US firms', *Entrepreneurship and Regional Development*, **12**, 291–309

Fiss, P. (2011), 'Building better causal theories: A fuzzy set approach to typologies in organization research', *Academy of Management Journal*, **54**, 393–413.

Flynn, J.E. and Chan, P.S. (1992), 'Configurations of board of director composition and structure, strategic attributes and business performance', *Journal of Applied Business Research*, **8** (3), 24–37.

Forbes, D.P. and Milliken, F.J. (1999), 'Cognition and corporate governance: Understanding boards of directors as strategic decision-making groups,' *Academy of Management Review*, **24** (3), 489–505.

Furr, R.M. and Furr, L.J. (2005), 'Is your chairman a leader?', *Corporate Board*, **26**, 11–15.

Gabrielsson, J. (2007a), 'Boards of directors and entrepreneurial posture in medium-size companies: Putting the board demography approach to a test', *International Small Business Journal*, **25** (6), 511–37.

Gabrielsson, J. (2007b), Correlates of board empowerment at small companies', *Entrepreneurship Theory and Practice*, **31**, 687–711.

Gabrielsson, J. and Huse, M. (2004), 'Context, behavior, and evolution', *International Studies of Management and Organization*, **34**, 11–36.

Gabrielsson, J., Huse, M. and Minichilli, A. (2007), 'Understanding the leadership role of the board chairperson through a team production approach', *International Journal of Leadership Studies*, **3** (1), 21–39.

Gabrielsson, J. and Politis, D. (2007), 'The impact of ownership and board governance on firm-level entrepreneurship at small technology based firms', *ICFAI Journal of Corporate Governance*, **6**, 43–60.

Gabrielsson, J. and Winlund, H. (2000), 'Boards of directors in small and medium-sized industrial firms: Examining the effects of the Board's working style on board task performance', *Entrepreneurship and Regional Development*, **12**, 311–30.

George, G., Wood, D.R. and Khan, R. (2001), 'Networking strategy of boards: Implications for small and medium-sized enterprises', *Entrepreneurship and Regional Development*, **13** (3), 269–85.

Glaser, B.G. and Strauss, A.L. (1965), 'Discovery of substantive theory: A basic strategy underlying qualitative research', *American Behavioral Scientist (pre-1986)*, **8** (6), 5–12.

Glaser, B.G. and Strauss, A.L. (1967), *The Discovery of Grounded Theory: Strategies of Qualitative Research*, London: Wiedenfeld & Nicholson.

Gopalakrishnan, S. and Damanpour, F. (1997), 'A review of innovation research in economics, sociology and technology management', *Omega*, **25**, 15–28.

Hambrick, D.C., Werder, A. and Zajac, E.J. (2008), 'New directions in corporate governance research', *Organization Science*, **19** (3), 381–85.

Herzberg, F. (1966), *Work and the Nature of Man*, Cleveland, OH: World Publishing.

Huse, M. (1998), 'Researching the dynamics of board–stakeholder relations', *Long Range Planning*, **31**, 218–26.

Huse, M. (2000), 'Boards of directors in SMEs: A review and research agenda', *Entrepreneurship and Regional Development*, **12**, 271–90.

Huse, M. (2005), 'Accountability and creating accountability: A framework for exploring behavioural perspectives of corporate governance', *British Journal of Management*, **16**, 65–79.

Huse, M. and Gabrielsson, J. (2012), 'Board leadership and value creation: An extended team production approach', in T. Clarke and D. Branson (eds), *The SAGE Handbook of Corporate Governance*, London: SAGE, pp. 233–53.

Huse, M. and Zattoni, A. (2008), 'Trust, firm life cycle, and actual board behavior: Evidence from "one of the lads" in the board of three small firms', *International Studies of Management and Organization*, **38** (3), 71–97.

Jensen, M.C. and Meckling, W.H. (1976), 'Theory of the firm: Managerial behavior, agency costs and ownership structure', *Journal of Financial Economics*, **3**, 305–60.

Johannison, B. and Huse, M. (2000), 'Recruiting outside board members in the small family business: An ideological challenge', *Entrepreneurship and Regional Development*, **12**, 353–78.

Judge, W.Q., Hu, H.W., Gabrielsson, J., Talaulicar, T., Witt, M.A., et al. (2015), 'Configurations of capacity for change in entrepreneurial threshold firms: Imprinting and strategic choice perspectives', *Journal of Management Studies*, **52** (4), 506–30.

Kakabadse, A., Kakabadse, N.K. and Barratt, R. (2006), 'Chairman and chief executive officer (CEO): That sacred and secret relationship', *Journal of Management Development*, **25**, 134–50.

Knockaert, M., Bjørnåli, E.S. and Erikson, T. (2015), 'Joining forces: Top management team and board chair characteristics as antecedents of board service involvement', *Journal of Business Venturing*, **30** (3), 420–35.

Krause, R., Semanedi, M. and Canella Jr, A.A. (2014), 'CEO duality: A review and research agenda', *Journal of Management*, **40** (1), 252–82.

Kvale, S. (1983), 'The qualitative research interview: A phenomenological and a hermeneutical mode of understanding', *Journal of Phenomenological Psychology*, **14**, 171–96.

Leblanc, R. (2005), 'Assessing board leadership', *Corporate Governance: An International Review*, **13** (5), 654–66.

Lechner, C. and Gudmundsson, S.V. (2014), 'Entrepreneurial orientation, firm strategy and small firm performance', *International Small Business Journal*, **32** (1), 36–60.

Lindenberg, S. (2003), 'The cognitive side of governance', in V. Buskens, W. Raub and C. Snijders, C. (eds), *The Governance of Relations in Markets and Organizations*, Amsterdam: JAI, pp. 47–76.

Machold, S., Huse, M., Minichilli, A. and Nordqvist, M. (2011), 'Board leadership and strategy involvement at small firms: A team production approach', *Corporate Governance: An International Review*, **19** (4), 368–83.

Mazzarol, T. and Reboud, S. (2009), *The Strategy of Small Firms: Strategic Management and Innovation in the Small Firm*, Cheltenham, UK and Northampton, MA, USA: Edward Elgar Publishing.

McNulty, T. and Pettigrew, A. (1999), 'Strategists on the board', *Organization Studies*, **20**, 47–74.

Messeghem, K. (2003), 'Strategic entrepreneurship and managerial activities in SMEs', *International Small Business Journal*, **21** (2), 197–212.

Miles, M.B. and Huberman, A.M. (1994), *Qualitative Data Analysis: An Expanded Sourcebook*, London: SAGE Publications.

Miller, D. (1983), 'The correlates of entrepreneurship in three types of firms', *Management Science*, **29** (7), 770–91.

Miller, D. and Friesen, P.H. (1982), 'Innovation in conservative and entrepreneurial firms: Two models of strategic momentum', *Strategic Management Journal*, **3**, 1–25.

Minichilli, A. and Hansen, C. (2007), 'The board advisory tasks in small firms and the event of crisis', *Journal of Management and Governance*, **11** (1), 5–22.

Parker, H. (1990), 'The company chairman: His roles and responsibilities', *Long Range Planning*, **23**, 35–43.

Patton, M. (2002), *Qualitative Evaluation and Research Methods*, Newbury Park, CA: Sage.

Pfeffer, J. and Salancik, G. (1978), *The External Control of Organizations*, New York: Harper & Row Publishers.

Rindova, V. (1999), 'What do corporate boards have to do with strategy: A cognitive perspective', *Journal of Management Studies*, **36**, 953–77.

Rogers, E.M. (2003), *Diffusion of Innovations*, New York: Free Press.

Rubin, H. and Rubin, L.S. (2012), *Qualitative Interviewing: The Art of Hearing Data*, 3rd edn, Thousand Oaks, CA: Sage.

Silverman, D. (2001), *Interpreting Qualitative Data: Methods for Analysing Talk, Text and Interaction*, 2nd edn, London: Sage.

Sonnenfeld, J.A. (2002), 'What makes great boards great', *Harvard Business Review*, **80**, 106–113.

Thompson, V.A. (1965), 'Bureaucracy and innovation', *Administrative Science Quarterly*, **10** (1), 1–20.

Ward, J.L. and Handy, J.L. (1988), 'A survey of boards practices', *Family Business Review*, **1** (3), 289–308.

Warren, R. (2003), 'Corporate governance for competitive advantage in SMEs', in Jones, O. and Tilley, F. (eds), *Competitive Advantage in SMEs: Organising for Innovation and Change*, Chichester: Wiley & Sons, pp. 54–70.

Wiklund, J. and Shepherd, D.A. (2005), 'Entrepreneurial orientation and small business performance: A configurational approach', *Journal of Business Venturing*, **20** (1), 71–91.

Yin, R.K. (2013), *Case Study Research: Design and Methods*, 5th edn, Thousand Oaks, CA: SAGE Publications.

Zahra, S.A. (1991), 'Predictors and financial outcomes of corporate entrepreneurship: An exploratory study', *Journal of Business Venturing*, **6** (4), 259–85.

Zahra, S.A. (1996), 'Governance, ownership, and corporate entrepreneurship: The moderating impact of industry technological opportunities', *Academy of Management Journal*, **39**, 1713–35.

Zahra, S.A., Neubaum, D.O. and Huse, M. (2000), 'Entrepreneurship in medium-size companies: Exploring the effects of ownership and governance systems', *Journal of Management*, **26**, 947–76.

PART IV

CORPORATE GOVERNANCE IN FAST-GROWING FIRMS AND IPOS

11. An engagement theory of governance: the dynamics of governance structures in high-growth, high-potential firms

Teresa Nelson and Huseyin Leblebici

INTRODUCTION

Two characteristics distinguish this chapter from the bulk of management literature on governance. First, we are interested in a dynamic organizational systems view: we would like to know how governance relationships emerge and evolve over time. Perhaps, we hypothesize, this occurs in some path-dependent fashion, likely complex in nature. Here we focus on entrepreneurial high-growth, high-potential firms[1] because it gives the opportunity to consider high-stakes governance situations. These firms have less historical baggage, more influential management members and teams, and smaller groups of owners and stakeholders. High-growth industry settings present dynamic conditions that deliver more change, more often. In addition, these firms are also most responsible for most real firm growth and growth in employment in the United States, so there are policy and practice implications of merit (Kauffman Foundation, 2011).

Second, we want to look beyond the valuable, though limited, theoretical and empirical findings of the principal–agent and ownership–control paradigms to examine governance in the context of the firm as it moves over time. We do this from a conceptual orientation that respects the interrelated, interdependent, emergent quality of organizational governance in practice. We integrate thinking on the multidisciplinary field of complexity studies and related points of view to enrich our examination. We also consider current theoretical work on path dependence, as well as other theory bases in organizational studies, to understand how these bodies of ideas may exist complementarily.

Moving from these bases, we propose a new conceptual framework, the 'Engagement Theory of Governance', which includes managers, key employees, owner groups, and other individuals and groups participating in a negotiated organizational field of problem-solving and decision-making. From this perspective, governance can be viewed as the outcome of mutual promises made, at least in part, to facilitate the survival and prosperity of the firm. We believe that these multi-party, ongoing relationships find expression in an array of governance and strategic arrangements and decisions that are interesting and valuable to understand.

The contributions of the chapter include, first, discussion of the ideas of governance and the ways the topic can be approached, particularly for entrepreneurial firms. We have shared our research process, as well as our progress and thoughts on future work. Second, we present and discuss an Engagement Theory of Governance. Through this model, we begin to articulate a multi-party concept of strategic leadership that can be considered in relation to firm problem-solving, decision-making and performance outcomes. We conceptualize the model as dynamic, changing over time as participants enter and exit, take action and continue action. We also consider which partners are present and which are not, and when, as key identifiers of the relationship mix.

Third, as a supplement, we reflect on the complexity of the governance system by sharing elements of our ongoing research process investing the growth and development of a set of firms accomplishing and moving beyond initial public offerings (IPOs) over a 20-year period (1991–2011) in the United States in relationship to the founder role. This placement of theory in practice serves to illustrate the principles presented rather than to stand as a comprehensive empirical treatment of the phenomena discussed. Our goal is to explicate the richness of the governance system as a contrast to more common reductionist approaches that consider two or three governance variables in a linear fashion *sans* time and context interplays. We begin by presenting three narratives to show key elements of governance roles and events of high-growth firms as companies strategically and voluntarily transform the firm from private to public status. As the future direction of the firm is actualized, various parties are engaged in varied ways.

Next, we discuss our findings from the broader case study project as well as steps we have taken to move the research forward. We conclude the chapter by proposing further research directions. We make the case for continued exploration of the governance systems of entrepreneurial firms using dynamic models. We suggest that the continued application of corporate governance models that have been built to describe large, ongoing corporations are not appropriate, for a variety of reasons, to build understanding of the rich and precious conditions and opportunities of growth firms as they emerge.

Our study has limitations. First, it is United States (US)-centric in its application, though we hope not in its relevance. Second, while highlighting the complexity of governance systems in high-growth firms, we have greatly simplified parts of the discussion due to issues of complexity. Our primary purpose is to present an alternative view while considering alternate empirical tools to the norm. Third, we examine this phenomenon primarily with strategic management and organizational theory views. This is our expertise; other approaches would be equally valid. On the plus side, much of existing governance research from a management perspective has been in these disciplines. We see this as the continuation of a wider, interdisciplinary project with multiple theoretical homes including, for example, path dependence, complexity, institutional theory, strategic management and chaos theory.

CONCEPTUAL GROUNDING: GOVERNANCE

From a historical, strategic perspective, the field of corporate[2] governance research has focused on the involvement and relative power and influence of key stakeholders in relation to the structure, strategy and performance of the firm. Questions of interest include: how do the preferences of owners, managers, board members, funders and other influential players interact, and what is the impact of this on the organization? How is leadership expressed through governance? Who plays what roles to what outcome? Who controls resources and decision-making? And how does influence translate into particular goals, activities and outcomes of the enterprise? These are some of the questions of interest to academics, business people and government because of the influence exercised at this node of business activity.

Since the early 1980s agency theory has been a dominant paradigm used by strategists and other organizational scientists to understand these questions, and most particularly the role of incentives and controls in aligning the interests of critical firm participants who hold diverse goals. The current model perhaps begins with Berle and Means (1932), and owes substantial credit to Fama (1980) and Jensen and Meckling (1976), as well as to many others who have explored its application to date. As Gerald Davis says:[3]

> Berle and Means's view of an economy dominated by a handful of ever-larger corporations run by an unaccountable managerial class inspired scholarship from sociologists (who were convinced they were right) to financial economists (who wanted to prove them wrong) to lawyers (who contemplated the rights and obligations implied by this system). (Davis, 2011, p. 1121)

To simplify greatly, within the agency theory framework, the organization is collectively owned through shares by the dispersed shareholders, and alignment toward their interests of personal wealth creation through firm profitability is the purpose of governance and the company. The system of governance directs and controls the organization (Cadbury, 1992), and there is a special focus on managers, whose self-interest is expected to pull value from the owners without appropriate alignment, oversight and regulation.

Frequently invoked as an alternate governance framework to agency theory, stakeholder theory (for example, as in Donaldson and Preston, 1995) posits a different philosophical position with regard to the purpose and role of the firm. Stakeholder theory values the 'stake' that various role-holders, groups, individuals and entities (for example, nature, society) have in the firm as a result of its social (including economic) activities. Therefore, the governance structure is envisioned to include these parties as significant players, while it acknowledges self-interest as well as other motivations of governance parties, including top management team members. These relationships and the varied goals involved are envisioned to be moderated, often by top managers as organizational representatives (e.g., Davis et al., 1997). This membership inclusion of the governance system to organizations not part of the firm's legal structure, as well as a more socially responsible firm core, has found robust application of late for topics such as corporate social responsibility and environmental protection.

In terms of entrepreneurial firms, we see a contribution of these meta-theories in positing governance as the interaction of role-based entities that, more or less, are legislated, incentivized and made responsible for the outcomes that emerge from governance action. We believe for entrepreneurial firms that a certain kind of intra-firm competitiveness for benefits, as expressed in agency theory, is applicable: benefits, at least in the short term, are limited. We also see stakeholder theories offering the idea of collaboration for a wider, more complex purpose as useful. We do however see gaps in both models in terms of: (1) representation of the complexity of the interactions; (2) the reality of how relationships are played out over time; (3) the embedded power of human and institutional relations as a prerequisite for forward movement; (4) the need for more and different governance roles; (5) the role of variety, uncertainty and unpredictability in firm outcomes; and (6) an awareness of the interactive, networked nature of governance over time.

For example, entrepreneurial firms present different ownership constructions than large, public firms. The identity of participants, their relative power, their entrance and exit, and the ramifications of governance growth in terms of firm growth are different in kind. Also, the role of the top management team, particularly company founders, is difficult to place in a principal–agent framework. This is true not only because founders often start the firm as 100 percent owners, but because the nature of new ventures often entails intense commitment of founders (and employees and capital providers, and so on) beyond financial commitment (Arthurs and Busenitz, 2003). At the same time, the process of capital acquisition for new, high-potential firms usually entails a pattern of sale of portions of the company to access growth resources. Often these new owners participate in the development of the firm in different ways than corporate shareholders might in their own milieu. Finally, roles cannot be completely and distinctly classified: that is, individuals or organizations, for example, can hold one or more roles, or not, from organization to organization or from one organization T_1 to T_2.

Our proposition is that another view of governance is needed, particularly for entrepreneurial firms. In this chapter we present, model and consider an 'engagement theory of governance' to unearth the complexity of arrangements that bring together key entrepreneurial players including venture capitalists, founders, bootstrap investors and new venture employees including key professional employee innovators, over time, in the context of an organization. We want to consider how organizations launch, grow and change. While much of existing governance research investigates two or three discrete variables of governance, we want to propose governance as a system – a complex system – that can be considered more robustly using ideas drawn from the interdisciplinary field of complexity studies and integrating elements of path dependence and other organizational points of view. We take up these issues next.

CONCEPTUAL GROUNDING: COMPLEXITY THEORY AND ITS MANAGEMENT NEIGHBORS

> How can interdependent yet self-interested organisms come together on solving problems that affect the survival of the whole? (Mitchell, 2009, p. xii)

An intellectual movement to consider complex adaptive systems emerged near the end of the last century, drawing on advances in physics, metaphysics, cybernetics, system theory and other bases (for an orientation, we suggest Mitchell, 2009; Lineweaver et al., 2013, particularly Part 4, 'Philosophical perspectives'; Page, 2010, and other editions in the Primers in Complex Systems series, Princeton Press[4]). A strong impetus for this new effort came from the natural sciences, particularly physics, yet the paradigm proponents have been committed to an interdisciplinary focus from the start and the study of human systems through the social sciences are integral to the movement. Phenomena such as technology development (the internet), disease and weather patterns, the dynamics of political and economic systems, and the emergence of artificial intelligence – all these and more caused scholars to realize that interdisciplinary study was necessary to see and come to understand the patterns of complex systems themselves, in contrast and as a supplement to building knowledge of complexity within a single system.

Key elements in complexity theory are interacting agents, predictability and unpredictability, emergent patterns, dynamics, self-organization, information, adaptation, chaos, feedback loops, systems and networks. Hierarchy and its partner, control, are largely absent; links between agents are key and evolution (learning) happens. Synergies are present and therefore linearity is not expected. As is often stated in introductions to complexity theory, the whole is more than the sum of its parts. Small differences in initial conditions can cause very high levels of unpredictability over time (that is, chaos), or not. Therefore the type of phenomena of interest directs an empirical approach: mathematical reasoning is common, linear models of complex systems are bemoaned. Variables are many and averages are thought to be not illuminative, even misleading. Reductionism is challenged (Mitchell, 2009).

The Santa Fe Institute (SFI), the complexity theory think-tank established in 1984, has provided a central hub for researchers throughout the world to explore complex systems in a networked fashion (www.santafe.edu). Describing the core of interest of complexity theory, SFI complexity theory scholars in the domain suggest:[5]

> 'Complex systems have many interacting, active components and the interactions between components have non-trivial or nonlinear interactions. . .this leads to unpredictable behavior. All of the components are either learning or modifying their behavior in some way while the system is behaving. . .this leads to complex dynamics.' (Stephanie Forrest).

> 'Complex systems . . . don't yield to compact forms of representation or description . . . when it comes to properties of the brain or . . . human systems . . . there are no beautiful, elegant solutions . . . Why is that? . . . (these systems) encode long histories . . . complex systems extract from its environment information in order to use it to behave adaptively . . .' (David Krakauer).

> 'Complex systems tend to be things that are different from simpler, physical systems. Parts are not the same (heterogeneous), many are open-ended (firms, people) – they can keep on evolving. (These are) hardest to study in terms of making predictions: they also typically have chains of causations mechanisms that make things happen that are circular – both positive and negative – these are more difficult to study than linear systems' (Luis Bettencourt).

> 'Complex systems have a lot of interacting parts . . . something about the way those parts behave when they interact is qualitatively different than when you look at them individually' (Doyne Farmer).

> '(Complex systems) in addition to being diverse and interconnected . . . are also interdependent . . . the actions of one agent in the system influences or has implications for another agent . . . (and) agents adapt and respond to the environment in which they are in . . . it's not just a case of them following simple rules . . . they adapt . . . adaptation is really a higher order rule . . . you could say they are rule based, but they are meta-rule based. They allow for behavior that can respond to information they are getting locally and globally' (Scott Page).

In contrast to an agency theory approach, a complex systems theory paradigm is interested in dynamics, as opposed to causality; non-linearity in contrast to predictability; and patterned novelty (sense making) versus rule enactment. In terms of governance systems of entrepreneurial companies, this provides a variety of attractive features that allow us to think about and model interactions and outcomes over time.

Integration of the concept of complexity is not foreign to management. On the contrary, a review of organization theory and strategic management writings shows that 'complexity' is often discussed as an external variable that impacts the system under study, more than an inherent part of the system and its elemental interaction. Alternately, conditions of the company, the team and the individual are often defined as 'complex'; this can mean that many parts are present, or that uncertainty is present, or some other condition. What complexity is and how it impacts the system can be seen to vary by degree across cases (for example, the difference between the cement industry versus hypercompetitive technology sectors) but perhaps not within the case so much (for example, within hypercompetitive environments). Very often, high levels of complexity are assumed as a constant force.

Looking from another perspective, complexity as a concept is explored in management scholarship to the extent that research draws on fundamental ideas common to the complex systems domain: for example, network theory (e.g., Parkhe et al., 2006; Kadushin, 2011; Borgatti and Halgin, 2011), social construction (e.g., Berger and Luckman, 1967; Elder-Vass, 2013), path dependence (e.g., Sydow et al., 2009; Marquis and Tilcsik, 2013), adaptation and adaptability (e.g., Staber and Sydow, 2002; Boisot and Child, 1999), dynamism, the learning organization (Argyris, 1999; Senge, 2006; Easterby-Smith and Lyles, 2011) and, generally, longitudinal approaches which investigate dynamic processes. Complex systems theory looks at emergent behavior, particularly as it relates to information flow, so from this perspective the ideas of complexity theory are found in organizational studies. As per Giddens (1984) and Weick (1969), organizations are interpretive, adaptive systems that create and then re-create. Members make sense by reducing complexity and absorbing it. Here is a bridge.

EMPIRICAL APPROACHES

The power of the complex systems view for governance in entrepreneurial firms is also that it aligns with the realities of governing a young, growth, high-potential firm where stability is not standard. Theoretically we are ready to explore then but empirically, complexity theory poses serious challenges. As noted by Zia et al. (2012):

> Although different types of algorithms and Turing-complete machines that underlie agent based models have opened up new vistas of scientific discovery to simulate decision-making by heterogeneous agents in artificial societies . . . there are significant limits of the algorithmic approach for simulating creative decision making by intelligent agents in rapidly shifting environments and social dynamics.

Put simply, human systems are especially difficult to model and predict.[6]

Boschetti et al. (2011) provide some intellectual structure to move forward. In 'Can we learn how complex systems work?', the authors discuss the human, organizational and cognitive dimensions of complex problems that serve as barriers in applying complexity theory. Complexities that are dynamical (the mathematical and statistical behavior of the system) and organizational (the network system interactions of information flow) are understood and processed under conditions of cognitive (amount of information under uncertainty) and interrelational (environmental tie-ins creating phases and tipping points) complexities. Distinguishing these varieties of complexity, relating the problem itself with the process of working on the problem, is useful as a conceptual frame and, we propose, part of an empirical approach for organizational scientists. We can address our difficulty as researchers in part by getting our minds around the complex situation of governance structures as well as the complexity we have in modeling and understanding that system. Further, a goal of prediction of outcome with few degrees of freedom must be set aside, although patterns of behavior stay in focus and outcomes can often and clearly be understood as bounded.

We suggest researchers must hold the idea of the system as a whole, the idea of system elements, the flows within the system, and a temporal dimension within in the mind approximately in considering governance systems. While we are cognitively challenged in this endeavor, we can use framing techniques to help. For example, the focus of our research design and interpretation of findings can stay global while empirical investigation goes local.

EMERGENCE, PATH DEPENDENCE AND IMPRINTING

Emergence, path dependence and imprinting are temporal issues of special significance when considering entrepreneurial firms and their governance systems. From gestation to start-up through growth, companies evolve and employ the governance system to bridge the environment to access resources, determine strategy and build the firm (Nelson, 2003). Notably, population ecology (see Hannah and Freeman, 1993) and more recently

Padgett and Powell (2012) (and many scholars between) have examined this dynamic process in terms of a patterned historical trail across firms and industries. While a full exploration of these ideas is not possible here, we call them out and distinguish them for future research attention.

Entrepreneurial firms emerge from existing networks; they innovate relations. 'Nodes and ties in social networks are not reified dots and lines; they are the congealed residues of history – in particular, the history of iterated production rules and communication protocols in interaction (Padgett and Powell, 2012, p. 3). A start-up's success is dependent on the creation and extension of networks: owners, customers, employees and top management team members. The governance system is a leadership function in the creation of those networks and the building of links to access resources for the company and its actors. The rules of the roles of the governance system create the networks that then provide the yeast for continued innovation. 'In the short run, actors create relations; in the long run, relations create actors' (Padgett and Powell, 2012, p. 2).

Emergence begets development or extinction. Development, here assuming no particular level of success beyond survival, involves implementation of structures, routines, expectations, meaning, and so on by founders. Founders use the history record of their own experiences and networks to begin the creation of the new organization's history. Development is not random or completely new, but patterned and historically informed.

There are a variety of theoretical lens that adopt a 'history matters' focus, including imprinting and path dependence. Imprinting, as per Marquis and Tilcsik (2013, p. 199), is 'a process whereby, during a brief period of susceptibility, a focal entity develops characteristics that reflect prominent features of the environment, and these characteristics continue to persist despite significant environmental changes in subsequent periods'. The idea of imprinting could be used in governance research to understand how initial conditions for groups or cohorts of firms are influenced by conditions at time T_0.

Path dependence is a pattern of emergence whereby 'past conditions influence present outcomes' (Marquis and Tilcsik, 2013, p. 193). Beyond agreement that history has a non-random impact, recent scholarship on path dependence presents different views on definition and domain. Sydow et al. (2009) and Dobusch and Schussler (2011) link path dependence to a lock-in consequence. Sydow et al. (2009) propose a framework that differentiates three developmental phases: '1) singular historical events, 2) which may, under certain conditions transform themselves into self-reinforcing dynamics 3) that possibly end up in an organizational lock-in'. Dobusch and Schüßler (2011, p. 620) add: 'what matters is that the path dependence construct pays attention to which dynamics lead to which kinds of outcomes, whereas other constructs focus more on early events (e.g. imprinting) or final outcomes (e.g. structural inertia)'.

Vergne and Durand (2010) suggest that initial conditions, trigger events and sustaining mechanisms are path-dependent phenomena. Feedback mechanisms define a path-dependent process, though whether path dependence includes negative as well as positive feedback loops is under debate (Vergne and Durand, 2011; Sydow et al., 2009; Vergne and Durand, 2010). Dobusch and Schüßler (2011) suggest that, 'if the object to be explained – a rigidified action pattern – is clearly defined and (if) the causal mechanisms – network effects or increasingly shared cognitions – are carefully spelled out at the different relevant analysis levels, path dependence can indeed be widely applied as an explanatory concept'. Sydow et al. (2009) propose coordination effects, complementarity effects, learning effects and adaptive expectations as path-dependent mechanisms visible in rules resources, practices and strategies.

We relate this work to the empirical work of Beckman and Burton (2008) and to other scholarship of the Stanford (University) Project in Emerging Companies (Baron et al., 1996; Baron and Hannan, 1999; Hannan et al., 1996; Burton et al., 2002) on Silicon Valley start-ups. Beckman and Burton (2008) empirically tested whether initial functional structures of new ventures predicted a deepening of those structures over time, among other questions on emergent practices. Beckman and Burton (2008): 'the pattern of results suggest that the range of prior experience held by the founding team is an important correlate of VC [venture capital] financing, and firms that start with both experience and structure reach this milestone faster than other firms.' This body of work from Stanford University, while not directly focused on governance, provides in our opinion the strongest model to date of empirical study for path dependence and emergence of entrepreneurial firms under conditions of complexity.

Pentland et al. (2012) take a somewhat different approach in path dependence theory development. With the intent of explaining the micro-foundation of routines, they link micro-level actions to macro-level phenomena. They take action as their focus, rather than agents. '*Action* refers to steps in a process of accomplishing an organizational task such as paying an invoice (Pentland et al., 2010) . . . There can be no action without actors, but in the theory we present here, actions are the starting point for the inquiry' (Pentland et al. 2012, p. 1484). In contrast to the work of Sydow et al. (2009), Pentland et al. (2012) do not restrict their path-dependent process to a lock-in finale, rather stating that lock-in must be possible but not inevitable.

Following Schulz (2008), Pentland et al. (2012) propose that path dependence is manifest in two ways: within performances, and between performances:

Within each performance or iteration of a pattern of action, each action is dependent on the prior actions. Thus, as each action is taken, it is more or less likely that other specific actions will follow. Path dependence within a performance makes the pattern *recognizable*. As a pattern of action develops in response to a stimulus, it becomes more likely that a similar pattern will occur in response to a similar stimulus. (Pentland et al., 2012, p. 1487)

For their empirical approach, the authors use a simulation via a transition matrix comprised of conditional probabilities as an investigative tool:

Theoretically, this transition matrix incorporates both the interpretations of history as causal force and as observable outcome. Each conditional probability can be seen as the likelihood or 'disposition' of the sociomaterial ensemble to take a subsequent action . . . each conditional probability also expresses the actual and potential performances (or ostensive aspects) that could be generated by the routine. (Pentland and Feldman, 2008)

When there is no history, all actions are equally likely (Pentland et al., 2012).

A SPOTLIGHT ON ROLES

As we worked to develop this research, it became apparent to us that our construction relied on the idea of roles held by individuals and groups in the governance system. Much of governance research depends on an articulation of roles conceptually and empirically, yet we found the concept and its application underdeveloped. We speculate at least two causes. First, roles are a ubiquitous construction with meaning assumed. Second, some roles, particularly in governance, have been explicitly defined and practiced in the context of law, and this serves as a default system of articulation for researchers. For example, a limited number of roles are completely segmented through law: shareholder, director and chief executive officer (CEO), for example.[7] Other important roles such as lead investor or scientific advisory board member are then often in the shadows. In terms of the former, this leaves us talking across ourselves. For the latter, a rather impoverished understanding of roles from a social and organizational perspective is before us. Together, these suggest a renewed spotlight on roles, especially for governance theory building in entrepreneurship where the parties are important and richly played.

Conceptually, roles can be traced back to the articulation of the division of labor (Marx, 1977; Durkheim, 1893; Taylor, 1911); linguistically, 'roles' arrived via the theater. Roles give definition for how work is to be done (Katz and Kahn, 1978) and 'roles (are explained) by presuming that persons are members of social positions and hold expectations for their own behaviors and those of other persons' (Biddle, 1986, p. 67). Therefore, roles are defined by context, by others, and through self-identification.

Role holders change roles and/or may play roles sequentially, in an overlapping fashion, or simultaneously. Roles have functional, symbolic, structural, interactionist and cognitive dimensions (Biddle, 1986; Stryker and Statham, 1985). They also have a temporal dimension: some end instantaneously (for example, shares are sold), others have negotiated end dates (for example, the voluntary departure of a CEO), and still others are perpetuated (for example, founder). Roles are enforced at and across multiple levels.

Attention to roles makes governance a multi-level theory extending to the individual, the group, horizontally across organizations, and interorganizationally from organization to institutional domains. For example, the venture capitalist holds a role through self-identification and it is expressed on a company board in concert with others, within venture capital networks, and through normative structures, for example in law and regulation (from securities law to tax law, and so on). We are also interested in roles from a social perspective because they are potentially additive and perhaps synergistic. A CEO may be a shareholder and a founder. A venture capitalist may be a shareholder and a director, or not. This complexity has not been addressed, yet it is likely influential, particularly for young and growing firms.

This variety of approaches to the definition of roles is simply illustrated by comparing legal roles of CEO, shareholder and director, for example, with Mintzberg's (2007) classic articulation of leadership roles: (1) interpersonal roles: figurehead, liaison and leader; (2) information roles: monitor, disseminator and spokesperson; and (3) decision roles: entrepreneur, disturbance handler, resource allocator and negotiator, which are also relevant for governance players. Adding an additional level of complexity, roles can be seen from an institutional perspective as professions (for example, venture capitalist, CEO, lawyer, and so on), which for Scott (2008, p. 219) are the 'preeminent institutional agents of our time'. From this theoretical overview, we move to present an engagement theory of governance that intends to actualize these issues of theory in regard to the governance structures of entrepreneurial firms.

AN ENGAGEMENT THEORY OF GOVERNANCE

As an expression of mutual promises made by governance parties, this model encompasses managers, owners, employees and other groups (roles) of key stakeholders as they provide critical resources for firm growth and survival over time. We see governance parties as interdependent, because they need each other to achieve the benefits of the firm. Negotiation and decision-making within the governance system are taken as the common modes of action. We propose that it is important to consider what role is not represented at a given time within the system, as well as what role is represented; the path not taken, as well as the one taken. This brings an options sensibility into play. It also allows us to distinguish the network which links the firm through actors to the 'environment'. For example, we can see a venture capitalist at one degree of separation from the CEO, and that this is a different governance situation than a venture capitalist at three degrees of separation.

We use the concept of engagement in governance to include the following nuances. Engagement as:

- Betrothal, a future pledge (for example, we have engaged the employees in a new stock ownership program).
- A hostile meeting of opposing forces, a conflict (for example, large block stockholders engaged top brass at the annual meeting).
- A meeting arranged in advance, a scheduled engagement (for example, in 2015 we are engaged to present our research findings to our corporate partner).
- An emotional sign-up, participation of members (for example, the team was extraordinarily engaged in the new product development project).
- Things fitting together, as with gears (for example, top management team members across functions were engaged in putting together the IPO prospectus).

Moving away from the ideas of stewardship theory (Hernandez, 2012; Davis et al., 1997; Haskins et al., 1998), we envision promises to not necessarily be cooperative (that is, 'We will defend our rights as shareholders'). Goals across the group may be shared or fragmented, but we assume there is enough in common to move forward. We also allow for varying degrees of engagement from different parties not based solely on financial investment. This still assumes that all roles can be important and essential or non-essential to firm survival and success. Founders may maintain high levels of commitment even when their financial ownership levels fall; venture capitalists may be intensely involved in the firm, but only for a while. In the other case, founders are essential as firm creation does not happen without them, and outside investors are important as a rule, but not essential as firms do grow on internal reinvestment and founder(s) investment alone. Different than agency theory, this concept of governance provides room for a range of 'ownership' concepts including financial, psychological, legal and moral.

A key aspect for this theoretical development is awareness of the development of conditions over time. A promise is made at Time T but fulfilled, or not, in Time T+1; that is the nature of a promise. Therefore to explore this proposal around governance we examine longitudinal governance arrangements of key stakeholders as they are tied to strategic operational and performance outcomes.

In summary, change is present in the following ways:

- The firm persists, or not.
- Pattern of growth of the company; at its simplest: steady state, smaller, larger.
- Definition of firm success.
- Identity of the governance parties engaged, and not engaged, through roles.
- Relative power of the governance parties.
- Level of engagement by governance party.
- Kind of engagement by governance party.
- Relations of the governance parties.
- Goals of the governance parties, in addition to firm success.
- The role network extending from the firm through actors.
- And each of the items above varies over time.

This accounts for the system as a whole, the idea of system elements, the flows within the system, and a temporal dimension as discussed in the theoretical sections above. See Figures 11.1 and 11.2.

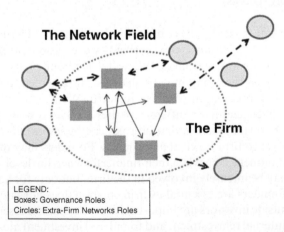

The Network Field

The Firm

LEGEND:
Boxes: Governance Roles
Circles: Extra-Firm Networks Roles

Figure 11.1   Engagement theory of governance negotiated field, static view, model 1

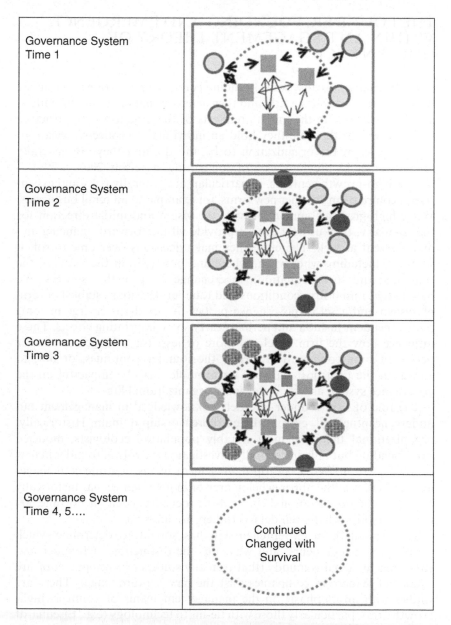

Figure 11.2   Engagement theory of governance negotiated field, continuing view, model 2

THE FOUNDER, FOUNDING AND EMERGENCE WITHIN AN ENGAGEMENT THEORY OF GOVERNANCE

Every firm exists because some founding person or group of persons made the decision to establish a firm and then acted on that decision. 'Founders, as firm creators, are the initial architects of the organization's structure and strategy; in this role they hold an individual or collective vision of what they want the organization to be and do, and they are generally unconstrained by previous ways of doing things' (Nelson, 2003, p. 709).

New high-growth ventures, in particular, are generally risky and expensive in comparison to other new firms, for example small retail businesses. While high-growth founders provide the vision and initial direction for the company, they usually cannot provide all the forward financing and management as well. Therefore they make decisions over time to solicit partners, including who, when, where and how (within the limits of the economic and social equation), in exchange for growth resources. We believe that initial firm conditions and founder decisions establish a form of system and a set of governance parties that perhaps emerge in some path-dependent fashion and perhaps carry some imprinting effects. These influence how the firm develops, more or less, for a longer or shorter period of time comparatively. How the founder continues, or not, to engage in the firm post-start-up, for example, may be impactful on the governance system as well as the wider organizational life.

The role of firm founder is widely acknowledged in management but underconceptualized, even in the entrepreneurship domain. Historically, organizational theorists, most notably population ecologists, modeled firm founding but only incidentally investigated the role of founder in new venture creation. Work on top management teams in strategic management, whether in the upper echelon area or in governance, has historically examined the organizational elite but the focus has been on Fortune 500 type companies where founders as leaders are unusual.

Traits research in entrepreneurship has sought to determine which people are entrepreneurs, and why, but the distinction of founder and entrepreneur remains muddy (that is, many studies of 'entrepreneurs' are studies of leaders in companies past the new venture stage). There are studies with an emphasis on the management teams of younger, high-growth firms, particularly those with tie-ins to technology (e.g., Eisenhardt and Schoonhoven, 1990 as an early model) where founders may be, but are not always, recognized as organizational players. Founders have also been credited as valuable information sources on organizational start-up (Hannan et al., 1996) and as directors of human resource and strategy patterns of the firm (Baron et al., 2001). Some of these studies use the founder role as a variable of study, but the term is not defined when it is.

A more recent, small body of research on founders over the last two decades has come primarily through scholarship on high-technology venture development and through the study of new venture finance (usually also high technology) in the field of finance. A brief review of this work is included here; we find it lends some support for a range of theoretical ideas discussed in this chapter even though none is conceptualized using a systems or complexity framework.

Comparing founder and non-founder CEOs, for example, Souder et al. (2013) find higher levels of market aggression in the firms of founder CEOs, as well as high levels of motivation, power and knowledge for founder CEOs. Also comparing founder CEOs and non-founder CEOs, Wasserman investigates (2004) succession from founder CEO and identifies how the patterns are significantly different than those of non-founder CEO succession:

> The critical differences between later-stage succession and Founder-CEO succession include the higher level of attachment between Founder-CEOs and the firms they create, the much larger equity holdings of Founder-CEOs (which give them much more control of the firm), the fact that many Founder-CEOs remain in the firm (even though it is being run by their successors), and the fact that nearly all early-stage succession events involve outside successors (in contrast to later-stage succession research, which has focused on the insider-outsider distinction). (2003, p. 149)

To contribute to the temporal dimension of governance and firm development, Wasserman identifies the key events of product development and the raising of each round of financing from outside investors as times when founder presence in the firm tends to shift.

Other studies investigate the history of founders and their teams pre-start-up including Fern et al. (2012) who report that founder's past experience directs their firm's strategy choices; the wider the diversity of experience of the founder and the founder team, the more options are found in the firm's strategy development over time. Gruber et al. (2012) also examine the founder's pre-entry market stance showing that the extent and nature of the firm's pre-entry opportunity set has a significant effect on the likelihood that the firm will later diversify. Constraints on the choice sets of the founder(s) can be seen in the growth trajectories of the firms over time.

Finance research lends support to the role of founder as it finds support for founder reputation expediting the venture's quick access to public, but not private financing. Further, venture capital (VC) financing obtained early on is related to delays in market financing for founders holding extensive public reputations (Mahto and Khanin, 2013). Gao and Jain (2012) find that the presence of founder-CEOs reduces the likelihood of post-IPO change of control but enhances target IPO firm wealth by increasing acquisition premiums. Controlling for the effect of performance on founder-CEO status, Fahlenbrach (2009) identifies a positive causal effect of founder-CEOs on firm performance that is 'quantitatively larger than the effect estimated through standard OLS [ordinary least squares] regressions' (Fahlenbrach, 2009, p. 439). The author reports:

> Founder-CEO firms differ systematically from successor-CEO firms with respect to firm valuation, investment behavior, and stock market performance. Founder-CEO firms invest more in research and development, have higher capital expenditures, and make more focused mergers and acquisitions. An equal-weighted investment strategy that had invested in founder-CEO firms from 1993 to 2002 would have earned a benchmark-adjusted return of 8.3% annually. The excess return is robust; after controlling for a wide variety of firm characteristics, CEO characteristics, and industry affiliation, the abnormal return is still 4.4% annually. (Fahlenbrach, 2009)

Supporting this finding in another setting, Nelson (2003) found that the stock market rewarded founder-CEOs with a stock price premium at IPO.

Fauchart and Gruber (2011) identify three archetypes of founders and they find evidence that archetype type is related to firm strategy over time. The authors propose that imprinting of the firm occurs in relation to the founders' distinct self-concepts. Arvanitis and Stucki (2012) find a greater than 40 percent increase in the likelihood of innovative activities in a firm based on founder characteristics including university education (at best a combination of technical and commercial education), prior experience in research and development (R&D), and strong motivation to realize own innovative ideas. Especially interesting in relation to the idea of simultaneous, multiple roles, Li and Srinivansan (2011) report that when non-CEO founders serve on the board of directors of the firm they launched, the board provides more high-powered incentives in the form of pay and retention policies than the average US board. Compared with non-founder firms, founder-director firms show stock returns around mergers and acquisitions (M&A) announcements.

Taken together, this research suggests that, in general, there appears to be a role termed 'founder' which is recognizable in relation to a variety of firm functions. Further, the founder role can be distinguished before, during and after firm founding, including network effects to firm external and firm internal partners. Evidence suggests that founders have an impact on firm design, operations and performance and that relative qualities of founders (for example, education) have varied effects.

DEFINING THE ROLE OF THE FOUNDER, FOR INSTANCE[8]

To define a founder one can begin by defining the organization which is founded. This process is conceptualized by Hannan and Freeman (1989) as one that involves a series of steps: initiation, resource mobilization, legal establishment, social organization and operational start-up undertaken by an individual or group of individuals. Founders then actualize some or all of the steps of organizational founding. They play a distinct role in organizations, that is, they 'engage in a set of expected behavior patterns that are attributed to occupying a given position in a social unit' (Robbins, 2000, p.90). Clearly, some threshold level of activity, in terms of the amount and/or the kind of activity, distinguishes the founder(s) from others who participate in the new venture process. Single or multiple founders per organization are possible. The steps of organizational founding will involve tasks that are tangible and intangible, practical and symbolic. Completing the founding steps will take time as some are sequential, and some require the founders to interact with outside individuals and organizations. Finally, there is a beginning and an end to the founding process. Once the organization is operational, founding is complete.

From this discussion, it is possible to formulate a set of connotations for the founder construct: (1) founders organize and take initiative in the organizational founding process; (2) founders are likely to work on important organizing tasks; (3) the initiation step is particularly important because it is likely to establish ownership of the process, define its scale and scope, and imprint an organizational pattern; (4) founders' efforts are likely to persist over time and contribute to completion of the founding event; (5) an organization may have one or more founders; and (6) for a founder to be declared, a company must become operational.

Note that the founder role itself does not confer structural authority or financial return. Further, being a founder does not necessarily or logically associate with any other particular role post-founding. However, given the founder's responsibility (sole or joint) as initial organizational architect, the roles assumed are likely to be in the upper echelon of the organization, for example, as owner, management executive, board member, or head of an operational unit that exploits the founder's expertise (for example, scientist in a biotechnology company or chief architect in an architectural firm).

All founders will exit, whether early or late in the life of the firm, unless the organization fails first. Multiple founders may leave together, or some may leave earlier than others. We know from anecdotal stories (e.g., Arkebauer, 1991) and case study research (e.g., Mintzberg and Waters,

1982) that founders depart from management leadership positions willingly and unwillingly. They may die, or be fired or displaced into subordinate positions by owners displeased with their performance. In other cases they may relinquish management and/or equity stakes voluntarily. When the population of post-start-up firms is considered, some will have active founders and others will not. For the latter group, a great variety of configurations of founders in the firm may exist: there will be differing numbers of original and remaining founders, founders will fill different roles, and they will make varying contributions to the firm's continuation and success.

Specific mechanisms for founder influence post-start-up may be additive and/or interactive. Founders in the working organization could carry the following influences (Nelson, 2010):

> Founder as focal point: When founders are visible in the organization they may serve as a focal point for other decision-makers because of their knowledge, experience, and organizational stature (Pfeffer & Salancik, 1978). This influence may lead founders to play an extraordinary role in defining the mission, structure, and behavior of the firm for other members of the top management team (Kunze, 1990; Vesper, 1996).
>
> Founder imprinting: The founder sets the initial structure, strategy, and culture of the organization through early decisions, including many that occur pre-start-up. As Baron, Hannan, and Burton (2001) state, 'Once formulated and articulated, a founder's organizational blueprint likely 'locks in' the adoption of particular structures, as well as certain premises that guide decision-making.'
>
> Founder psychological commitment: The idea of psychological commitment rests in the assumption that some firms deliver not only profits, but also personal psychological benefits to their managers, as supported by Smith and Miner 1983), Lafuente and Salas (1989), Donaldson (1994), and England (1967, 1975). Gimeno, Folta, Cooper & Woo (1997) demonstrate that the probability of firm shut-down negatively correlates to 'psychic income from entrepreneurship' derived by managers of new ventures. Fama and Jensen (1983) discuss how the extraordinary commitment of some individuals in the governance system of the firm may reduce their drain on organizational resources – an 'anti'-agency cost, if you will. The work of Dutton, Dukerich, and Harquail (1994) on members' identification with organizational image supports this logic.
>
> Founder ownership control: Founders often are start-up owners. Extraordinary power accrues to owners who hold large absolute or relative stakes. While 50% ownership represents legal control, lesser percentages may deliver significant influence over firm affairs (Monks & Minow, 1995).
>
> Founder structural authority: The CEO and other top managers within the organizational structure hold authority and responsibility for high-level decision making. The structure bridging owners and managers, i.e., the board of directors, holds additional positions of individual and joint command, especially the officers of the board (Mace, 1971; Pound, 1995).
>
> Founder tenure: Active founders, ipso facto, will be the longest tenured members of the organization. Tenure results in firm and industry level experi-

ence that builds valuable knowledge and practice for the firm (Penrose, 1959). Tenure allows for the development of information sources, relationships, and problem-solving routines (Katz, 1982). The joint tenure of managers may lead to an increased strength in the group's dominant logic, or collective mindset. Dominant logic guides managerial choices and is considered 'sticky'; it is embodied to a disproportionately large degree in the minds of the longest-tenured managers (Prahalad & Bettis, 1986).

These mechanisms of founder influence are exercised in relation to organizational stakeholders brought into the network of firm activity by the founders and others pre- or post-start-up. One way to conceptualize the founder's relationship with the organization and other stakeholders over time is to consider the founder as 100 percent owner-manager of the firm at some point in the founding process. Jensen and Meckling (1976) use the example of the 100 percent owner-manager to establish the governance starting point, where the goals of managers and owners are 100 percent aligned. This position must change if the firm is to grow. Founders need additional resources (for example, capital, human, technological) to accomplish organizational goals, and economic organization delivers an efficient structure within which to do so (Alchian and Demsetz, 1972). As Pfeffer and Salancik (1978, p. 24) write, 'organizations are not so much concrete social entities as a process of organizing support sufficient to continue existence'.

Sometime in an organization's early life, founders engage social agents, be they investors, employees or suppliers; some are governance parties. Within the framework of the organization, these parties exchange inducements and contributions to enhance firm survival, and perhaps prosperity. Starting with the 100 percent owner-manager, one can think about the supra-categories of ownership and management as domains where important exchanges take place; for example, a founder exchanges x percent of ownership for capital to fund operations. Founders hire additional workers and relinquish to them certain authority and decision-making power. To incorporate with the state, officers meeting certain requirements must be appointed. To go public, a board of certain numbers, with certain experience, fulfilling certain responsibilities, must be in place.

Within this logic, founders balance the value of their immediate, personal control of the organization with its survival and growth needs, taking into account the immediate benefits they derive from the exchange. Within some parameters, founders likely express their preferences on this balance, and the organization is affected as a result. For example, founders may decide against venture capital funding or public stock ownership so as to retain more ownership and management authority, and/or to explore other options. This may result in the firm growing at a slower pace, and perhaps survival chances will be influenced.

At some point founders may lose control of the ownership structure (that is, who can own company stock and how much). This outcome could be a decisive or a cumulative event. Control in this sense, though ultimately tied to the legal idea of what person or coalition holds greater than 50 percent ownership, can clearly occur under other configurations as well. For example, when ownership is diffused to a great extent, even a 20 percent owner can be highly influential. By the time a firm has thousands of stockholders, the distinction of owner and investor is relevant. Even before this, some 'hands-off' investors simply buy and sell among offerings that fit their portfolio, while other investors are committed to specific firms and they will participate in their management through exercise of ownership rights. Beyond the absolute degree of ownership control held by individual and collective investors, the rate of diffusion of ownership over the life of the firm may also be relevant to its strategic direction and performance.

USING DATA

Fundamental assumptions that are engrained in each algorithm about the behavioral rules, intelligence, creative decision-making, learning, treatment of uncertainty and so forth, constrain the modeling of emergence, self-organization and adaptation in complex systems. No matter which decision theory is used to describe decision rules and strategy spaces of agents in complex systems, assignment of decision rules and strategy spaces for agents poses significant challenges. Zia et al. (2012):

> Maybe there is no algorithm that allows you to leapfrog across time. So you may have to do a laborious process of moving through the history.
> (Cris Moore)[9]

Proposing a complex system base for governance research demands that great care be taken in the specification of an empirical approach to the investigation of data. Earlier we presented the idea that researchers must hold the idea of the system as a whole, the idea of system elements, the flows within the system, and a temporal dimension within the mind approximately. This still allows us to initiate local investigation which contributes to global understanding. What is critical is that the context of the system starts and ends the process and, we believe, that temporal and system effects be considered primary, with flows next, and system elements last, as the latter is where research attention has already focused for the most part. In this section we review some ideas that may be useful as research designs are prepared, and we present some preliminary findings of our own current research.

The Event and Temporal Dimensions

What is a proper thread to illuminate the workings of a high-growth, high-potential firm governance system in emergence, given our cognitive limitations to know at once a complete vision of a governance system? Here is a list of potential variables that can be tied to events and studied over time across a governance system.

- The presence or absence of roles.
- The outcomes of firm strategy.
- The existence and use of new information.
- The networks in the firm and across the firm.
- The allocation of resources.
- The rules that divide action.
- The decisions that influence firm emergence and growth.

With these ideas in mind we found it useful to distinguish the temporal dimension regarding emergence and enacted history for firms identified as high growth and high potential from an event action point of view. First, we note the importance of determining whether things happen for firms, and how this is different from how things happen for firms over time. These questions exist within the context of how long a firm continues to exist post-founding. This issue of existence and non-existence is not as bifurcated a case as it may seem (for example, firms may be 'walking dead'), although at some points in time we can say with confidence that there is a firm, and at others that there is not.

In Table 11.1, we indicate our understanding of events that tend to happen to firms across a group of similar firms: always, often or rarely. We also note our opinions on how these events happen: only once, occasionally or repeatedly. More categories could be better in terms of outlining temporal patterns, yet we found where there was question among categories showed us variability that was worth a discussion. Also, it could be valuable to create a category of 'never happens' or 'usually happens' for the insight this provides; perhaps in contrast, for example, to very large, multinational firms. Building this kind of thought structure helped us to identify the types of patterns within the governance structure that we could select for deeper investigation. It provides evidence for the difference between entrepreneurial high-growth firms and other types of firms.

Table 11.1   Temporal dimension of events of high-growth, high-potential firms

	Does it happen?			How often does it happen?		
	Always happens	Often happens	Rarely happens	Happens only once	Happens occasionally	Happens repeatedly
Strategy						
Founder/s found the firm	x			x		
Firm puts some form of legal structure in place	x				x	
Firm diversifies into multiple industries		x			x	x
Firm adopts an industry strategy		x	x		?	?
Firm vertically integrates			x		x	
Firm adopts a business unit strategy		x	x			x
Firm structures internal operations	x					x
Firm hires employees	x					x
Firm innovates products/services	x				x	x
Firm exists for a very short period of time (e.g., months)		x				
Firm exists for a very long period of time (e.g., 20+ years)			x			
Firm is acquired		x		x		
Firm acquires other firms		x			x	x
Firm acquires other firms and is acquired		x				
Firm merges with equal			x	x		

Table 11.1   (continued)

	Does it happen?			How often does it happen?		
	Always happens	Often happens	Rarely happens	Happens only once	Happens occasionally	Happens repeatedly
Bankruptcy legally declared			x	x		
Chapter 11 legally declared			x		x	
Finance						
Funders other than founder emerge	x					x
Firm decides to reinvest profits in company			x		x	
Income produced		x			x	x
Profit produced			x		x	
Bank debt acquired	X	x			x	x
Initial public offering			x	x		
Follow-on stock offered on public market		x			x	
Operations, RandD						
Products sold		x				
Customers acquired		x				
Employees hired	x				x	
Founder replaced as CEO		x		x		
Firm invents something very new			x	x	x	
Firm evolutionizes an existing product/ service		x			x	x

The technique could also be used to explore cross-cultural and/or cross-national differences in high-growth firms.

Finally, regarding the temporal dimension, we note that the first time something happens is potentially different in kind from the second time, or third time, or last time. For example, the first product sold is very important for the high-growth firm as it symbolizes that a phase of R&D has been completed and that a network to customers has been established. This event would be more momentous than the 2345th product sold, most likely. This logic is true for many 'firsts' which are hallmarks of the entrepreneurial phase. In fact, things so numbered may in fact be completely different events, no more related to each other than to other events, but they are commonly grouped and so we have a norm at work. For example, an IPO may be substantially different in a number of dimensions than a secondary stock offering, though both share a process of moving stock onto public markets.

We have confined ourselves in the table to governance decisions and actions that we categorize (lightly) with common organizational structure areas (for example, strategy, finance, operations) to help us to be more aware of a range of firm events. We have not attempted to be comprehensive, but to share the concept as a thinking tool. We note our own bias for strategy and finance events, as this is what we have studied for many years. As a result, one proposal we have for future research is to conduct a Delphi study of scholars of high-growth firms to identify key events over time, including common and rare events, to be used to understand emergence and the governance system at work. The Delphi study is a qualitative research technique that allows investigation of complex problems without clear data sources through rounds of interrogation of a group of experts, with the goal of consensus while preserving the contribution of all voices (Charlton, 2004). Examples of research using Delphi techniques in entrepreneurship, while rare, include Evans and Volery (2001) and Pardo-del-Val (2010).

As many researchers propose, we found that preparing short case studies, in our case on the population of firms, was useful in identifying variables and outliers of interest while promoting our understanding of human network flows and roles, as well as types of information flows. Statistics can be useful, too, to identify trends across firms and to better understand relationships among variables across firms. Solutions for empirically investigating complex systems of governance are beyond the scope of this chapter. However, we will next provide a look at a few investigations we have conducted to begin an ongoing research agenda.

The 1991 US Initial Public Offering Cohort Seven Years and Younger

For a number of years we have been following the strategic events and governance parties as relates to the group of firms aged 1–7 which make up the cohort of IPO firms in the US in 1991. Our foundational question of interest has been: how do governance systems structure firm existence and growth over time and under conditions of complexity? Sources of data have been varied including official filings to the Securities and Exchange Commission, telephone surveys of company executives, company websites, competitor filings and websites, supplier filings and websites, employee interviews, and media news sources, including those that are business focused.

We include here brief case histories of three of the 57 IPO cohort companies of 1991 to illustrate the process and the variety of governance roles and events occurring variously across firms, across time. We chose these firms to conveniently represent a variety of industry and governance styles to illustrate variety in governance relationships.

Sam & Libby Inc.
Sam and Libby Edelman founded the company in October 1987 with the intent to manufacture leather goods; more specifically, women and girl's footwear, children's footwear, handbags and private label-related apparel. The four-year-old company went public in 1991 with 120 employees. Mr and Mrs Edelman held 80 percent of the ownership at IPO. The remaining 20 percent was held by three private, unaffiliated investors.

The company's ongoing strategy was to design and market products under the Sam & Libby brand name with the goal of providing high-fashion content at affordable prices. Advertising was a key investment and costs were contained through offshore manufacturing outsourcing in Brazil, Taiwan and China. In 1994 and 1995 the company closed its subsidiary operations in Hong Kong and Brazil. By 1996 the company had 39 employees.

From founding through 1996, Sam Edelman served as Chair, President and CEO of the company. Louise Edelman, a co-founder and consistent board member, served as Sr. VP-Image from founding through the second quarter of 1992, when she assumed the title of Executive VP-Corporate Development. In 1996 there were six members of the board of directors including Mr and Mrs Edelman and Kenneth Sitomer, the COO and CFO who had served in an executive position with the company since 1993. Together these six individuals owned 59 percent of the common shares of stock in the company.

The years 1994–96 saw falling sales and growing liabilities for Sam &

Libby, Inc. Net income statements recorded a loss of $3–16 million each for the years 1993–95. Effective in 1996, the company's common stock was removed from trading on the Nasdaq National Market for failure to meet certain listing requirements. There were 1096 shareholders of record. No one, other than the members of the board of directors, owned more than 5 percent of the company. There were no institutional or corporate owners.

In late 1996 the company was renamed Utopia Marketing. Also in that year the company entered into an agreement with Maxwell Shoe Company to sell all worldwide rights to the company's trademarks, trade names and intellectual property rights. The Sam & Libby brand shoe remains for sale in 2005; until 2004 under the ownership of Maxwell Shoe, and then through Maxwell Shoe's acquirer, Jones Apparel. On 3 November 2000, Utopia Marketing, Inc. filed an assignment for the benefit of its creditors, entering receivership and bankruptcy proceedings.

Applied Extrusion Technology (AET)
When AET went public in 1991 it was a leading developer and manufacturer of highly specialized plastic films used primarily in consumer product labeling, flexible packaging and health care applications in North America. By 1999 the company's labels were used on soft drink containers for Coca-Cola and Pepsi-Cola and its packaged film was used for food products by Frito-Lay, Nabisco, Kellogg's and Hershey Foods.

The company was founded by Amin Khoury in 1986. Mr Khoury jointly held the roles of Chairman and CEO until 1993. Then he served as Board Chair through 2004. In 2002–04 he again served as CEO. In 2004 he retired from both roles. In 1990 Khoury owned 13.7 percent of the company stock, and corporate owners, including one venture capital firm, held 17 percent. Net income was approximately $16 million pre-IPO in 1990. The company then operated with a net loss from 1991 (~$4 million) to 2004 ($47 million). In 1996, 15 percent of common stock was held by three mutual and pension funds. Representatives of these investors did not serve on the board. In 1997 there were 12 members of the board. By 2004 there were only six, four of whom had served in that capacity since 1986. All were unaffiliated with any corporate investor. Five corporations owned less than 10 percent each of the company at that time; Mr Khoury maintained ownership of about 5.5 percent of stock.

In 1994, the firm acquired the OPP films business of Hercules, Inc. and established a production facility in Varennes, Canada. In 1999 the assets of AEP Borden were acquired. Then in 2001, AET purchased the assets of QPF LLC, an OPP films business of Hood Companies. In 2004 the company filed a Chapter 11 plan of reorganization. Significant debt obligations and adverse industry economic conditions, particularly the unforeseen escalations in costs of petroleum and associated products such as propylene and polypropylene resin, the company's primary raw material, were credited with the move.

In its filing document the company proposed that noteholders receive 100 percent of the common equity of the private company with new senior notes to be issued. The solicitation of votes for the prepackaged Chapter 11 plan was held in November with 95 percent of the dollar amount of 'large' beneficial holders, counting only those claims that actually voted, voting in favor of the plan. 'Small' note holders holding less than $500 000 in principal amount voted to reject the plan. The plan was accepted by the Bankruptcy Court. As a privately held company. Mr Khoury, the founder, retired and was replaced as CEO and Chairman.

AET holds 50 active patents and approximately 15 trademarks and applications and since 2010 has invested more than $20 million in research and development. In 2012, AET was acquired by Taghleef Industries, headquartered in Dubai. $143 million in financing to Taghleef Industries for the acquisition of AET was provided by GE Capital. In addition to the production facility in Canada, the company operates a distribution center in Terre Haute, Indiana (moved from Indianapolis in 2005).

Anergen

Anergen was founded in 1988 by Dr Somesh Sharma and Dr Brian Clark. At the company's inception neither man served as a company manager, but respectively as Vice-President of Research and Vice-President of Scientific Development. Pre-IPO the four company board positions were held by two venture capital firms, by the CEO, and by an outside investor. There was no Chairman of the Board position designated. The first CEO held 3.6 percent of ownership which he cashed out at IPO; three venture capital companies held more than 58 percent of shares and the two founders held 3.7 percent each. These were held through IPO, though the percentages were reduced through dilution.

The intent of the company was to conduct R&D, 'on its own behalf and on behalf of its corporate partners (SEC S-1 filing)'. Its intended products were pharmaceutical applications in biotechnology, to include autoimmune treatments to combat multiple sclerosis and rheumatoid arthritis. Through 1996 the company did not have any products available for sale, nor did it expect to have any products commercially available for at least several years, if at all. Anergen maintained a Scientific Advisory Board made up of researchers from Stanford University and Vanderbilt Medical Center. As of year-end 1996 the company had 65 full-time employees and the founders had exited their executive and ownership positions.

Anergen developed strategic partnerships with Novo Nordisk and with

Organon. In exchange for certain marketing rights, the partner companies funded research and development and they agreed to pay royalties on product sales, if any. At the time of the agreement with Novo Nordisk, that company made an $8 million equity investment in Anergen. This agreement was extended through 1998. In 1996, Anergen entered into a collaborative agreement with Organon under which Organon, in exchange for certain marketing rights, supported research and development on a separate project to incorporate a proprietary peptide discovered by Organon. Under the arrangement, the company received a one-time license fee of $2 million with agreements for milestone payments and royalties on sales, if any. In addition, Anergen maintained collaborations with academic and clinical researchers to perform certain research, development and clinical trial activities.

As of 1997 about 19 million shares of the company's common stock were issued and outstanding and held of record by approximately 357 shareholders and were beneficially owned by more than 400 shareholders. The company officers, directors and principal shareholders, namely Warburg, Pincus Ventures, International Biotechnology Trust and Novo Nordisk, collectively beneficially owned approximately 50 percent of the company's outstanding common stock. Under a 1995 common stock purchase agreement with Warburg and IBT, the company was obligated to include in the slate of nominees recommended by the company's board of directors and management, at each election of directors, two candidates selected by Warburg, one candidate selected by IBT, and one candidate mutually agreed to by IBT and Warburg. Additionally, while not obligated to do so, since 1993, the company included a representative of Novo Nordisk in its slate of nominees for the Board of Directors.

In September 1998 the company announced that it did not have enough cash to make it to the end of the year. In October it announced its inability to secure financing, so the company was restructured. In early 1999, Anergen became a wholly owned subsidiary of Corixa Corporation.

Moving forward with the project
What we discovered through this open-ended discovery process is that many statements concerning high-growth entrepreneurial firms and IPO presented in textbooks and as summary introductions to the field in research articles and reports were either presenting findings on select sets and/or presenting average findings that obscured the complexity and actual situation of the governance systems of high-growth, high-potential firms. This was especially true, we saw, as high-tech was frequently assumed to be a synonym for high growth, and as constituting the bulk of firms going public, but this was not the case, at least for the samples we

Table 11.2   *Strategic outcome of firms going public (seven years and under) over time*

	At IPO 1991	1991–95	1996–2000	2001–05	2006–10
Firm exists and continues in identity as public firm, or with name change only	57 (100%)	49 (86%)	30 (53%)	25 (44%)	9 (16%)
Firm identity extinguished via:					
Fail: Bankruptcy			3		4
Fail: Liquidate without bankruptcy			2		1
Fail: Acquired			1		3
Acquired as healthy (2 went private)		8	13	4	8
Merger of equals				1	
Exit in prior period			8	27	32
TOTAL	57	57	57	57	57
Went public a second time from private status				1	1
Went private			2	2	1

examined. In our survey of 1991, 1995 and 1999 IPO firms in the US, for example, in contrast to the 'common knowledge', founders were present in about 60 percent of firms as CEO, not having been replaced by 'professional management'; high-tech industry participants comprised about half of firms, not the majority; and venture capitalists of various kinds were present in about 80 percent of cases, thus one-fifth of all IPO firms got there without venture funding. Therefore, some of these empirical issues and interpretation issues had to do with research design, some were definitional, some were temporal, and some were based on statistical analysis choices.

In Tables 11.2 and 11.3 we show some of our data collection for the cohort of firms seven years and younger (N = 57) which went public in 1991 in the US to provide contrast to common assumptions and the actual data for some growth ventures through our research. For simplicity, we have aggregated the data into time phases. There are no databases where information of this sort is easily available and it must be painstakingly pieced together from a variety of sources.

For us, the founder role with the system over time was a priority for

Table 11.3   Founder in the firm for firms going public (seven years and under) over time

	1991–95 (firms in existence)	1996–2000 (firms in existence)	2001–05 (firms in existence)	2006–10 (firms in existence)
Founder active in top management team*	45 (79%)	22 (39%)	12 (21%)	3 (5%)
Founder CEO	33 (58%)	18 (32%)	6 (10%)	1 (0.02)

Note: * Defined here as CEO, top management team member, Chair of Board or board member.

investigation. This was for a number of reasons including the fact that: (1) the founder was an emergence role always present; (2) the role is not legally defined but socially constructed; (3) we had discovered much variety in the number of founders and the roles they played; and (4) the founder had been conceptually developed as a key driver in the establishment of the governance system. So we began with simple questions that were difficult to answer: when were founders present, and when were they not? What roles did founders hold in addition to founder? How did founder roles change over time? To answer these questions we determined that we had to step back and establish the historical paths of the firms themselves: had they survived during the study period? And because of our interest in growth: what major strategic decisions had been taken in regard to the growth of the company?

Our recommendations at this stage concerning research on the governance systems of entrepreneurial firms can be summarized in three points. Firstly, we doubt the continued value of exploring governance through the delineation of three or five variables of interest: a system approach is warranted. Early governance research helped to focus on key governance parties and their relationship to key organizational outcomes through linear regressions, but the value derived from such work has likely been accumulated. Secondly, as difficult as it is, we need to explore complex system research techniques that take more variety, more complexity, more interaction and more change into account. Thirdly, we need to allow old research to be assigned as historical. Studies of governance structures from the 1970s may be informative, but too often they are used as the basis of argument and hypothesis development despite the fact that the contexts of then and now are dramatically different. Taking just one example, the field of equity provision has been deeply reordered with the arrival of public funding via the internet, and as a result of the ascendancy of angel invest-ing and syndication across equity types as common financing methods. Change in approach and perspective is needed.

CONCLUSION

The goal of this chapter has been to articulate the conceptual roots and the design of an engagement theory of governance for high-growth entre-preneurial ventures. We have presented a dynamic organizational systems view that lies within a paradigm of complexity theory from a social sci-ences perspective. This means that we are interested in interacting agents, predictability and unpredictability, emergent patterns, dynamics, adapta-tion, systems and networks. Such phenomena cannot be studied with a reductionist approach; still, local study can be used to accomplish global understanding. Differences in the complexity of the problem, and the complexity facing the researcher in understanding the problem, should be distinguished and acknowledged.

We acknowledge the conceptual bases in strategic management and organizational theory that are aligned and even embedded in this para-digm, including especially network theory, path dependency, imprinting, role theory, organizational emergence, organizational learning, social construction, and population ecology and institutional theory. We also acknowledge the relevance of certain aspects of agency and stakeholder theory to the building of a robust model for high-growth firms, though each of these theories is found to be incomplete and in some ways inac-curate for the high-growth firm setting.

We would like to know how governance relationships emerge and evolve over time, and how what has occurred in the past relates to the past, the present and the future. We see the elements of the governance system to be mostly individuals, but sometimes also groups and organizations, who assume governance roles. We hypothesize that it is important which roles are filled, and which are not, at any point in time.

We see governance to be made up of actions of negotiation and decision processes as parties make promises, at least in part, to facilitate the sur-vival and prosperity of the firm. We believe the governance process over time can be examined through events (that is, performances), and that there are event and non-event periods that relate to each other over time. Sometimes, but not always, we believe that decisions made within the gov-ernance system lead to a restriction in the range of options available to the firm, even including a lock-in of options.

This research also serves to highlight firms at a particularly important point in their organizational life: the IPO. Substantial excitement over new issues has been generated due to the phenomenal initial secondary market success of particular offerings. Understanding more about the transition of private to public status over time helps us to understand the IPO process and its value: who is participating, what these firms look like structurally, and what happens to them in the years following their public debut:

> Historical path dependency does not imply that there are no transformational principles at the base of endless open-ended generation. Scientific prediction in open-ended, creative systems such as life is not the specification of a fixed-point equilibrium. It is the description of processual mechanisms of genesis and selection in sufficient detail to be capable, in the rich interactive context of the study system, of specifying a limited number of possible histories. This is the biology, not the physics, view of science. (Padgett and Powell, 2012, p. 2)

NOTES

1. The descriptor 'high-growth' marks an organization that has achieved some strong increase in measured performance, often sales. Such firms may be of any size: for example, a small business that doubles sales in a year has experienced high growth. In this research, however, we are interested in the set of firms that have firm and market conditions that hold the possibility for the firm to become large and influential. This is an interest in a mid- to long-term trajectory and it may be tied to year-over-year sales increases or not (for example, capital-intensive conditions as found in biotechnology, for instance, will not exhibit profits for years, if at all). These 'high-growth, high-potential' firms will be called simply 'high-growth' in this chapter to enhance readability.
2. Use of the word 'corporate' here as a descriptor of governance is somewhat of a misnomer in the context of our research, as we focus not on the traditional corporation, but rather on young firms that may or may not meet the legal corporation descriptor. However, 'corporate governance' is the term widely used in these discussions and we respond to this semantic legacy for three reasons. First, we want to acknowledge the theoretical tradition and its contributions in this area. Second, in reference to the wealth of literature in other fields, in particular public administration, political science, international relations and sociology, which are also developing governance research around organizations, networks and governments. Third, we are interested in for-profit governance arrangements which are closer to a corporate outlook than to, say, a non-profit one.
3. Davies, G. (2011). 'The twilight of the Berle and Means corporation', *Seattle University Law Review*, 34, 1121–1138.
4. http://press.princeton.edu/catalogs/series/pics.html.
5. This series of quotes is taken from a video lecture prepared and delivered by Melanie Mitchell, accessed 1.5.2014 at: http://www.complexityexplorer.org/online-courses/3.
6. 'The phenomena of preference reversal, irrational decision making, incomplete knowledge of what agents want and so forth demonstrate that there will always be a statistical probability that the algorithms that are trying to represent decision making by adaptive agents in complex systems will contain some error' (ibid., p. 91).
7. For a good overview of the legal approach from a US perspective, see 'Report of the Task Force of the ABA Section of Business Law Corporate Governance Committee on Delineation of Governance Roles and Responsibilities' (2009), accessed 01.1.2014 at: http://apps.americanbar.org/buslaw/committees/CL260000pub/materials/20090801/delineation-final.pdf.

8. This section is elaborated from earlier work by Nelson, including Nelson (2010, 2003, 1998).
9. This quote is taken from a video lecture prepared and delivered by Melanie Mitchell, accessed 1.5.2014 at: http://www.complexityexplorer.org/online-courses/3.

REFERENCES

Alchian, A.A. and Demsetz, H. (1972), 'Production, information costs, and economic organizations', *American Economic Review*, **62**, 777–795.

Argyris, C. (1999), *On Organizational Learning*, Oxford, UK: Wiley-Blackwell.

Arkebauer, J.B. (1991), *Cashing Out: The Entrepreneur's Guide to Going Public*, New York: Harper Business.

Arthurs, J.D. and Busenitz, L.W. (2003), 'The boundaries and limitations of agency theory and stewardship theory in the venture capitalist/entrepreneur relationship', *Entrepreneurship Theory and Practice*, **28** (2), 145–162.

Arvanitis, S. and Stucki, T. (2012), 'What determines the innovation capability of firm founders?', *Industrial and Corporate Change*, **21** (4), 1049–1084.

Baron, J.N., Burton, M.D. and Hannan, M.T. (1996), 'The road taken: Origins and evolution of employment systems in emerging companies', *Industrial and Corporate Change*, **5**, 239–275.

Baron, J. and Hannan, M. (1999), 'Building the iron cage: Determinants of managerial intensity in the early years of organizations', *American Sociological Review*, **64**, 527–548.

Baron, J., Hannan, M. and Burton, M.D. (2001), 'Labor pains: organizational change and employee turnover in young, high-tech firms', *American Journal of Sociology*, **106**, 960–1012.

Beckman, C.M. and Burton, M.D. (2008), 'Founding the future: Path dependence in the evolution of top management teams from founding to IPO', *Organization Science*, **19** (1), 3–24.

Berger, P. and Luckman, T. (1967), *The Social Construction of Reality*, Anchor.

Berle Jr, A. and Means, G. (1932), *The Modern Corporation and Private Property*, New York: Macmillan.

Biddle, B. (1986), 'Recent development in role theory', *Annual Review of Sociology*, **12**, 67–92.

Boisot, M. and Child, J. (1999), 'Organizations as adaptive systems in complex environments', *Organization Science*, **10** (3), 328–345.

Borgatti, S. and Halgin, D. (2011), 'On network theory', *Organization Science*, **22** (5), 1168–1181.

Boschetti, F., Hardy, P.Y., Grigg, N. and Horwitz, P. (2011), 'Can we learn how complex systems work?', *Emergence: Complexity and Organization*, **13** (4), 47–62.

Burton, M., Sorensen, J. and Beckman, C. (2002), 'Coming from good stock: Career histories and new venture formation', in Lounsbury, M. and Ventresca, M. (eds), *Research in the Sociology of Organizations*, **19**, 229–262.

Cadbury, A. (1992), 'The Cadbury Report, the Committee on the Financial Aspects of Corporate Governance', accessed 1 January 2014 at http://www.jbs.cam.ac.uk/cadbury/report/index.html.

Charlton, J. (2004), 'Delphi technique', in Lewis-Beck, M.S., Bryman, A. and Liao, T.F. (eds), *The Sage Encyclopedia of Social Science Research Methods*, Thousand Oaks, CA: Sage Publications, pp. 245–246.

Davis, G. (2011), 'The twilight of the Berle and Means corporation', *Seattle University Law Review*, **34**, 1121–1138.

Davis, J., Schoorman, F. and Donaldson, L. (1997), 'Toward a stewardship theory of management', *Academy of Management Review*, **22** (1), 20–47.

Dobusch, L. and Schüßler, E. (2013), 'Theorizing path dependence: A review of positive feedback mechanisms in technology markets, regional clusters, and organizations', *Industrial and Corporate Change*, **22** (3), 617–647.

Donaldson, G. (1994), *Corporate Restructuring*, Boston, MA: Harvard University Press.

Donaldson, T. and Preston, L. (1995), 'The stakeholder theory of the corporation: Concepts, evidence and implications', *Academy of Management Review*, **21** (1), 65–91.

Durkheim, E. (1893), *De la Division du Travail Social*, Presses Universitaires de France.

Dutton, J., Dukerich, J. and Harquail, C. (1994), 'Organizational images and member identification', *Administrative Science Quarterly*, **39**, 239–260.

Easterby-Smith, M. and Lyles, M. (2011), *Handbook of Organizational Learning and Knowledge Management*, 2nd edn, Chichester, UK: Wiley.

Eisenhardt, K.M. and Schoonhoven, C.B. (1990), 'Organizational growth: Linking founding team, strategy, environment, and growth among US semiconductor ventures, 1978–1988', *Administrative Science Quarterly*, **35**, 504–529.

Elder-Vass, D. (2013), *The Reality of Social Construction*, UK: Cambridge University Press.

England, G.W. (1967), 'Personal value systems of American managers', *Academy of Management Journal*, **10**, 53–68.

England, G.W. (1975), *The Manager and His Values*, Cambridge, MA: Ballinger.

Evans, D. and Volery, T. (2001), 'Online business development services for entrepreneurs', *Entrepreneurship and Regional Development*, **13**(4), 333–350.

Fahlenbrach, R. (2009), 'Founder-CEOs, investment decisions, and stock market performance', *Journal of Financial and Quantitative Analysis*, **33** (2), 439–466.

Fama, E. (1980), 'Agency problems and the theory of the firm', *Journal of Political Economy*, **88** (2), 288–307.

Fama, E. and Jensen, M. (1983), 'Organizational forms and investment decisions', *Journal of Financial Economics*, **14**, 101–119.

Fauchart, E. and Gruber, M. (2011), 'Darwinians, communitarians, and missionaries: The role of founder identity in entrepreneurship', *Academy of Management Journal*, **54** (5), 935–957.

Fern, M., Cardinal, L. and O'Neill, H. (2012), 'The genesis of strategy in new ventures: Escaping the constraints of founder and team knowledge', *Strategic Management Journal*, **33** (4), 427–447.

Gao, N. and Jain, B. (2012), 'Founder management and the market for corporate control for IPO firms: The moderating effect of the power structure of the firm', *Journal of Business Venturing*, **27** (1), 112–126.

Giddens, A. (1984), *The Constitution of Society: Outline of the Theory of Structuration*, Cambridge: Polity Press.

Gimeno, J., Folta, T., Cooper, A. and Woo, C. (1997), 'Survival of the fittest: Entrepreneurial human capital and the persistence of underperforming firms', *Administrative Science Quarterly*, **42**, 750–783.

Gruber, M., MacMillan, I. and Thompson, J. (2013), 'Escaping the prior knowledge corridor: What shares the number and variety of market opportunities identified before market entry of technology start-ups', *Organization Science*, **24** (1), 280–300.

Hannan, M., Burton, M.D. and Baron, J. (1996), 'Inertia and change in the early years: Employment relations in young, high technology firms', *Industrial and Corporate Change*, **5**, 503–536.

Hannan, M. and Freeman, J. (1989), *Organizational Ecology*, Cambridge, MA: Harvard University Press.

Haskins, M.E., Liedtka, J. and Rosenblum, J. (1998), 'Beyond teams: Toward an ethic of collaboration', *Organizational Dynamics*, **26** (4), 34–50.

Hernandez, M. (2012), 'Toward an understanding of the psychology of stewardship', *Academy of Management Review*, **37** (2), 172–193.

Jensen, M. and Meckling, W. (1976), 'Theory of the firm: Managerial behavior, agency costs and ownership structure', *Journal of Financial Economics*, **3**, 305–360.

Kadushin, C. (2011), *Understanding Social Networks: Theories, Concepts, and Findings*, New York: Oxford University Press.

Katz, R. (1982), 'The effects of group longevity on project communication and performance', *Administrative Science Quarterly*, **27**, 81–104.

Katz, D. and Kahn, R. (1978), *The Social Psychology of Organizations*, 2nd edn, Chichester, UK: Wiley.

Kauffman Foundation (2011), 'Where Will the Jobs Come From?', accessed 1 October 2014 at http://www.kauffman.org/what-we-do/research/firm-formation-and-growth-series/where-will-the-jobs-come-from.

Kunze, R.J. (1990), *Nothing Ventured*, New York: Harper.

Lafuente, A. and Salas, V. (1989), 'Types of entrepreneurial firms: The case of new Spanish firms', *Strategic Management Journal*, **10**, 17–30.

Li, F. and Srinivasan, S. (2011), 'Corporate governance when founders are directors', *Journal of Financial Economics*, **102** (2), 454–469.

Lineweaver, C., Davies, P. and Ruse, M. (eds) (2013), *Complexity and the Arrow of Time*, Cambridge: Cambridge University Press.

Mace, M. (1971), *Directors: Myth and Reality*, Cambridge, MA: Harvard Business School Press.

Mahto, R. and Khanin, D. (2013), 'Speed of venture financing for emerging technology-based entrepreneurial firms as a function of founder reputation', *Creativity and Innovation Management*, **22** (1), 84–95.

Marquis, C. and Tilcsik, A. (2013), 'Imprinting: Toward a multilevel theory', *Academy of Management Annals*, **7** (1), 193.

Marx, K. (1977), *Capital: A Critique of Political Economy*, Vol. 1, New York: Vintage Books.

Mintzberg, H. (1973), 'Strategy-making in three modes', *Regents of the University of California*, **16** (2), 44–53.

Mintzberg, H. and Waters, J. (1982), 'Tracking strategy in an entrepreneurial firm', *Academy of Management Journal*, **25**, 465–499.

Mitchell, M. (2012), *Complexity: A Guided Tour*, Oxford, UK: Oxford University Press.

Monks, R. and Minow, N. (1995), *Corporate Governance*, Cambridge, MA: Blackwell.

Nelson, T. (1998), *Evidence of Entrepreneurial Resources: Firm Founder Effects on the Performance, Governance and Product Level of the Firm at Initial Public Offering*, Champaign-Urbana, IL: University of Illinois.

Nelson, T. (2003), 'The persistence of founder influence: Management, ownership, and performance effects at initial public offering', *Strategic Management Journal*, **24** (8), 707–724.

Nelson, T. (2010), 'Firm founders', in Bournois, F., Duval-Hamel, J., Roussillon, S. and Scaringella, J-L. (eds), *Handbook of Top Management Teams*, London: Palgrave.

Padgett, J. and Powell, W. (2012), *The Emergence of Organizations and Markets*, Princeton University Press.

Page, S. (2010), *Diversity and Complexity*, Primers in Complex Systems, Princeton University Press.

Pardo-del-Val, M. (2010), 'Services supporting female entrepreneurs', *Service Industries Journal*, **30** (9), 1479–1498.

Parkhe, A., Wasserman, S. and Ralston, D.A. (2006), 'New Frontiers in network theory development', *Academy of Management Review*, **31** (3), 560–568.

Penrose, E.E. (1959), *The Theory of the Growth of the Firm*, New York: Oxford University Press.

Pentland, B. and Feldman, M. (2008), 'Designing routines: On the folly of designing artifacts, while hoping for patterns of action', *Information and Organization*, **18**, 235–250.

Pentland, B., Feldman, M., Becker, M. and Peng, L. (2012), 'Dynamics of organizational routines: A generative model', *Journal of Management Studies*, **49** (8), 1484.

Pentland, B., Hærem, T. and Hillison, D. (2010), 'Comparing organizational routines as recurrent patterns of action', *Organization Studies*, **31** (7), 917.

Pfeffer, J. and Salancik, G. (1978), *The External Control of Organizations*, New York: Harper & Row.

Pound, J. (1995), 'The promise of the governed corporation', *Harvard Business Review*, **73** (2), 89–98.

Prahalad, C.K. and Bettis, R. (1986), 'The dominant logic: A new linkage between diversity and performance', *Strategic Management Journal*, 7, 485–501.

Robbins, S.P. (2000), *The Essentials of Organizational Behavior*, Upper Saddle River, NJ: Prentice Hall.

Schulz, M. (2008), 'Staying on track: A voyage to the internal mechanisms of routine reproduction', in Becker, M.C. (ed.), *Handbook of Organizational Routines*, Cheltenham, UK and Northampton, MA, USA: Edward Elgar Publishing, pp. 228–255.

Scott, W.R. (2008), 'Lords of the dance: Professionals as institutional agents', *Organization Studies*, **29** (2), 219.

Senge, P. (2006), *The Fifth Discipline: The Art and Practice of the Learning Organization*, New York: Doubleday.

Smith, N.R. and Miner, J.R. (1983), 'Type of entrepreneur, type of firm, and managerial motivation: Implications for organizational life cycle theory', *Strategic Management Journal*, **4**, 325–340.

Souder, D., Simsek, Z. and Johnson, S. (2012), 'The differing effects of agent and founder CEOs on the firm's market expansion', *Strategic Management Journal*, **33** (1), 23–41.

Staber, U. and Sydow, J. (2002), 'Organization adaptive capacity: A structuration perspective', *Journal of Management Inquiry*, **11** (4), 408–424.

Stryker, S. and Statham, A. (1985), 'Symbolic interaction and role theory', in Lindzey, G. and Aronson, E. (eds), *The Handbook of Social Psychology*, New York: Random House, pp. 311–378.

Sydow, J., Schreyogg, G. and Koch, J. (2009), 'Organizational path dependence: Opening the black box', *Academy of Management Review*, **34** (4), 689–709.

Taylor, F. (1911), *The Principles of Scientific Management*, New York, USA and London, UK: Harper & Brothers.

Vergne, J-P. and Durand, R. (2010), 'The missing link between the theory and empirics of path dependence: Conceptual clarification, testability issue, and methodological implications', *Journal of Management Studies*, **47** (4), 736–759.

Vergne, J-P. and Durand, R. (2011), 'The path of most persistence: An evolutionary perspective on path dependence and dynamic capabilities', *Organization Studies*, **32** (3), 365–382.

Vesper, K.H. (1996), *New Venture Experience*, Seattle, WA: Vector Books.

Wasserman, N. (2003), 'Founder-CEO succession and the paradox of entrepreneurial success', *Organization Science*, **14** (2), 149–172.

Weick, K. (1969), *The Social Psychology of Organizing*, Addison-Wesley Publishers.

Zia, A., Kauffman, S. and Niiranen, S. (2012), 'Complexity and philosophy: The prospects and limits of algorithms in simulating creative decision making', *Emergence: Complexity and Organization*, **14** (3), 89–109.

12. Founder status and defensive mechanisms at IPO: evidence from French firms
Asma Fattoum-Guedri and Frédéric Delmar

INTRODUCTION

This chapter reports the results from a longer ongoing research effort on founder-chief executive officer (CEO) behavior at initial public offering (IPO) and the consequences of their behavior on short-term and long-term company valuation (Fattoum and Delmar, 2011, 2013). The empirical context is France.

An IPO confronts founder-CEOs with a demanding trade-off between the often incompatible goals of obtaining additional resources needed to sustain growth and maintaining control of the company. On the one hand, an IPO permits founder-CEOs to raise money from a larger pool of investors and to cut company cost of capital (Brau and Fawcett, 2006; Modigliani and Miller, 1963). In addition, an IPO offers opportunities for portfolio diversification to founder-CEOs who wish to sell a small share of their holdings in the company after it has become successful (Bruton et al., 2009; Dalziel et al., 2011; Daily et al., 2003; Daily et al., 2005). Such portfolio diversification opportunities are especially attractive when founder-CEOs can take advantage of bull markets and favorable time windows to seize the highest possible offering prices for their investment (Brau and Fawcett, 2006; Lowry and Schwert, 2002). Moreover, as an IPO exposes the company to scrutiny of the market for corporate control, it may increase visibility, prestige and reputation of successful founder-CEOs (He, 2008).

On the other hand, IPOs bring several important challenges, which if not properly dealt with, may lead to destabilizing and perilous consequences for founder-CEOs. For instance, beyond the considerable financial cost and complexity of the IPO process in itself, an IPO may jeopardize the extent of founder-CEOs' control of the company (Arthurs et al., 2008; Dalziel et al., 2011). In fact, at IPO ownership structure goes through important changes in terms of concentration and identity of main shareholders. Explicitly, ownership structure becomes more diluted and founder-CEOs no longer have the discretion to freely select new shareholders. This situation simplifies transfer of company control to new shareholders, who can easily start significant modifications at the top management team level. These possible consequences are not a threat for founder-CEOs who are actually using an IPO as an exit strategy and a means to transfer ownership and management of the company, but they are a substantial threat for those who desire to keep full control of the company post-IPO and who are undertaking an IPO only to access financial resources needed for future investments.

This situation raises two important theoretical and empirical research questions. First, what kinds of mechanisms do founder-CEOs use to lower the threat of losing company control at IPO? Second, are companies with founder-CEOs more likely to use defensive mechanisms than companies led by non founder-CEOs at the IPO? This chapter addresses these two research questions in the context of the French IPO market for the 1992–2010 period.

In particular, this research effort investigates the practice of defensive mechanisms disconnecting cash flow rights from voting rights. The most popular of these defensive mechanisms include dual-class shares, pyramid control structures and voting pact agreements (Almeida and Wolfenzon, 2006; Bennedsen and Wolfenzon, 2000; Bhaumik and Gregoriou, 2010; Cronqvist and Nilsson, 2003; Villalonga and Amit, 2009; Volpin, 2002). By preserving controlling shareholders' voting rights at high levels despite diluted cash-flow rights, defensive mechanisms simplify control over company governance and reduce undesired takeover events (Bebchuk et al., 2000; Roosenboom and Schramade, 2006; Smart and Zutter, 2003).

Moreover, based upon previous studies on founders' emotional biases, we suggest that founder-CEOs are more inclined than non-founder CEOs to put in place defensive mechanisms at IPO such as dual-class shares, pyramid control structure and voting pact agreements. Indeed, a rich body of research suggests that founder-CEOs experience deeper feelings of psychological ownership, identification, attachment and commitment towards their companies than non founder-CEOs (Arthurs and Busenitz, 2003; Gao and Jain, 2011; He, 2008; Souder et al., 2012; Wasserman, 2006). This, in turn, escalates founder-CEOs' perception of possessiveness, propensity to resist change, and feeling that they are the sole individuals legitimate to own and run the company. We suggest that such biases will ultimately increase founder-CEOs' determination to put defensive mechanisms in place (Arthurs et al., 2007; Ikävalko et al., 2010; Wasserman, 2008).

The chapter proceeds as follows. First, after having presented the French corporate governance context, we illustrate how dual-class shares, pyramid control structure and voting pact agreements allow controlling shareholders to exercise their control over and above their equity stake. Then, we develop a theoretical framework that explains why founder-CEOs are more likely than non-founder-CEOs to implement several defensive mechanisms at IPO. Next, we describe the extent of defensive mechanisms implementation in the population of all 467 IPOs undertaken in the French capital market from January 1992 to December 2010. Finally, we conclude by discussing theoretical and empirical contributions.

THEORETICAL FRAMEWORK

The French Corporate Governance Context

The use of disconnecting mechanisms varies substantially across countries. Such mechanisms are seldom used in the United States and the United Kingdom, but they are widespread in France, Sweden and Italy (Zingales, 1994; La Porta et al., 1998). The propensity to adopt disconnecting mechanisms is linked to the protection awarded to minority shareholders (Bruton et al., 2010; La Porta et al., 1998; Nenova, 2003). The limited protection bestowed to minority shareholders as well as the resulting popular use of disconnecting mechanisms in French civil law countries makes France an interesting context to study the impact of those mechanisms on both company and founder-CEO welfare.

The protection of investors is important because it will influence the possibility for a company to raise capital and the cost of doing so. Capital is needed to compete, innovate, diversify and grow. If such protection is weak, investors might be reluctant to invest unless they become controlling shareholders. Strong regulations clearly define transactions, disclosure and possibility for shareholder participation in important decisions of the company, and set clear standards for accountability for company insiders such as CEOs (World Bank, 2013; OECD, 2004). If protection is weak, investors are likely to refrain from investing or to ask for a premium to do so. Weak protection will decrease the access to capital and increase its cost.

As discussed in the World Bank's (2013) 'Doing Business' report, the protection of investors in France is below that of the United States and the United Kingdom, as well as the members of 'OECD high income'. The Protecting Investor index is one of the World Bank's (2013) 'Doing Business' indicators. It is composed of three measures of investor protection: extent of disclosure, extent of director liability and ease of shareholder suits. The index ranges from 0 to 10, with higher values indicating more disclosure, greater liability of directors, and more power

Table 12.1   World Bank protecting investor index by country

Economy	Extent of disclosure index	Extent of director liability index	Ease of shareholder suits index	Protecting investor index (mean)
OECD high income	7	5	7	6.3
Argentina	7	2	6	5.0
Australia	8	2	7	5.7
Brazil	5	8	3	5.3
Canada	8	9	9	8.7
Denmark	7	5	7	6.3
France	10	1	5	5.3
Germany	5	5	5	5.0
India	7	4	8	6.3
Indonesia	10	5	3	6.0
Italy	7	4	7	6.0
Netherlands	4	4	6	4.7
Singapore	10	9	9	9.3
South Africa	8	8	8	8.0
Sweden	8	4	7	6.3
Switzerland	0	5	4	3.0
United Kingdom	10	7	7	8.0
United States	7	9	9	8.3

Source: World Bank (2013), 'Doing Business 2013', available at http://www.doingbusiness.org.

for shareholders to question decisions. As shown in Table 12.1, which presents the Protecting Investor index by country, France scores an average value of 5.3. This can be compared to a value of 6.3 for the OECD high income average, a value of 8 for the United Kingdom and a value of 8.3 for the United States. Some important differences are to be noted. First, France scores high on extent of disclosure with a value of 10, compared to the Organisation for Economic Co-operation and Development (OECD) value of 6, and the United States of 7. Second, France scores very low to liability of directors with a value of 1 compared to 5 for the OECD, 7 for the United Kingdom (UK) and 9 for the United States (US). Third, shareholders' ability to sue officers and directors for misconduct in France is restricted (score of 5) compared to the United Kingdom (score of 7) and the United States (score of 9). There have been few changes during the last six years.

In short, French investors have superior access to information, but little possibility to influence major decisions or to monitor self-serving behavior of agents such as CEOs. This means that on average they will ask for a premium if investing. The size of the premium is going to increase if they believe there is a risk of self-serving behavior or extraction of personal benefits by executive directors such as the CEO. The use of mechanisms separating cash flow from voting rights diminishes even more the already limited influence by investors. Hence, firms using such mechanism should not be favorably traded by investors. In connection with our discussions of defensive mechanisms below, we also discuss the French context specifically for each mechanism.

Mechanisms Separating Cash-Flow Rights From Voting Rights

To disconnect cash-flow rights from voting rights, controlling shareholders can rely on several mechanisms such as dual-class shares, pyramid structures, voting pact agreements, cross-shareholdings, voting rights ceilings and ownership ceilings (Almeida and Wolfenzon, 2006; Bennedsen and Wolfenzon, 2000; Bhaumik and Gregoriou, 2010; Cronqvist and Nilsson, 2003; Villalonga and Amit, 2009; Volpin, 2002). Although these defensive mechanisms rely on different techniques and processes, they produce similar results. They provide controlling shareholders with voting power that is greater than their capital at risk. Among this large array of mechanisms available for controlling shareholders to disconnect cash-flow rights from voting rights, the most widely used worldwide are dual-class shares, pyramid structures and voting pact agreements (Claessens et al., 2002; ISS et al., 2007; La Porta et al., 1999).

Dual-class shares
Issuing distinct classes of shares, which are endowed with different voting rights, allows controlling shareholders to significantly leverage their voting power. For example, a company may issue a first class of shares that is owned predominantly by controlling shareholders and which grants ten voting rights per share. In parallel, the company can issue at IPO a second class of shares, with single or no voting rights, intended primarily for new shareholders. To compensate for reduced voting rights, this second class of shares may provide in some cases special cash-flow rights such as preferential (that is, higher or guaranteed) dividends. Dual-class shares can be highly effective in disconnecting cash-flow rights from voting rights. For instance, dual-class shares allow Mark Zuckerberg to preserve control of Facebook with less than 10 percent of cash flow rights (Davidoff, 2013). Similarly, the double voting rule put in place at Louis Vuitton Moet Hennessy (LVMH) allows the Arnault family to control 62 percent of voting rights with a direct ownership of only 46 percent.

Empirical evidence consistently shows that issuing dual-class shares has been a popular defensive mechanism all over the world for the last 30 years. In the United States, 7 percent of all IPOs undertaken between 1990 and 1994 adopted dual-class shares. They represent about 11 percent of the aggregate market capitalization of IPO companies (Smart and Zutter, 2003). From 1994 to 1998, the propensity of dual-class shares in IPOs increased significantly to reach almost 12 percent of all IPOs, accounting for about 31 percent of IPO market capitalization (Smart and Zutter, 2003). Gompers et al. (2010) report that about 6 percent of the 7000 companies included in the Compustat database issued dual-class shares, representing about 8 percent of the market capitalization of all companies. Similarly, using a sample of Fortune 500 companies listed in the US stock markets during 1994–2000 period, Villalonga and Amit (2009) report that about 12 percent of these companies had two or more common share classes.

Outside the US, dual-class shares are even more common. For example, Cronqvist and Nilsson (2003) report descriptive statistics based on a panel sample of 309 listed Swedish companies during the 1991–97 period, where about 76 percent of companies have dual-class shares. The vast majority of those companies have superior voting shares that provide ten votes per share. Similarly, in their study of large corporations' ownership structures in 27 countries, La Porta et al. (1999) found dual-class shares to explain the significant gap between cash-flow rights and voting rights observed in Denmark, Norway, Finland, Italy, Mexico, the Netherlands and Switzerland. In contrast, La Porta et al.'s (1999) data show the use of dual-class shares to be rare in the UK, Ireland, Australia, Japan, New Zealand, South Korea and Israel.

In France, two distinct instruments have been applied to deviate from the one share, one vote rule. The first instrument permitted by French law consists in the delivery of Investment Certificates. Investment Certificates provide their holders with cash-flow rights but no voting rights. Investment Certificates were introduced in 1983 by French national banks and state-owned companies to raise capital from stock markets without losing corporate control (Nenova, 2007). However, their use has been very rare since 1989 because the laws regulating Investment Certificates have been repeatedly changed and are severely constraining to shareholders (Nenova, 2007).

The second instrument applied in France to depart from the one share, one vote rule consists in endowing double voting rights upon common shares, which are held by the same shareholder for a specific period of time (Nenova, 2007; Roosenboom and Schramade, 2006). The period of time needed to grant double voting rights to ordinary shares held by a shareholder is specified in the provisions of a company's statutes. The period generally varies between two and five years. Any time a shareholder sells shares carrying double voting rights to a different shareholder, the transferred shares inevitably lose their double voting advantage and become ordinary one-vote shares for the whole period needed to acquire double voting benefits again. Hence, what sets the French context apart from other settings is that double voting stocks are not a special category of stocks: they are ordinary shares gaining temporary double voting rights if they are held by the same shareholder for a specific period of time. Moreover, double voting rights are not transferable to other shareholders after a sale transaction, as they do not represent a special category of stocks.

Dual-class shares are common among the population of 467 companies that have undertaken an IPO in France between 1992 and 2010. Indeed, 343 out of 467 companies (73 percent) implemented the double voting rule at IPO. Among these 343 companies, the typical period of time needed to grant double voting rights to ordinary shares held by a shareholder was equal to two years. More precisely, the required period was equal to: (1) two years in 54 percent of cases; (2) three years in 10 percent of cases; and (3) four years in 36 percent of cases.

Pyramid control structures
Pyramid control structures permit deviation from the proportionality between cash flow rights and voting rights through implementation of a multitude of control chains and sequences of holding companies (Claessens et al., 2002; Faccio and Lang, 2002; Johnson, 2000). For example, in a two-tier pyramid structure a controlling shareholder having 51 percent of the voting rights in a holding company, which in turn controls 51 percent of voting rights in the company going public, can gain complete control of an IPO company although they own only 26 percent (51 percent x 51 percent) of the ultimate cash flow stake (Almeida and Wolfenzon, 2006; Bebchuk et al., 2000). The larger the number of holding companies involved in the control chain, the greater the gap between cash-flow rights and voting rights. For instance, the ultimate cash-flow stake needed for full control in a three-tier pyramid control structure is 13.2 percent (51 percent × 51 percent × 51 percent). Hence, pyramid structures can be very effective in leveraging voting power. As an example, Marco Tronchetti Provera has been able to control 18 percent of Telecom Italia voting rights through a pyramid structure involving five holding companies, although he owned only 0,7 percent of cash-flow rights (Smith et al., 2013).

Intermediary holding companies used in a pyramid control structure can be either public or private (Villalonga and Amit, 2009). However, minority shareholders of those intermediary holding companies are never allowed to hold more than 50 percent of voting rights at each level of the pyramid (Morck and Yeung, 2003). Formal control of 50 percent of voting rights throughout the chain is only allowed to the focal shareholder.

The use of pyramid control structures throughout the world is more widespread than dual-class shares, but distribution across the world is uneven (Almeida and Wolfenzon, 2006; Bhaumik and Gregoriou, 2010; La Porta et al., 1999). Specifically, in their analysis of company ownership structures in 27 countries, La Porta et al. (1999) found that 31 percent of companies are controlled through pyramids in countries with weak shareholder protection. This quantity falls to 18 percent in countries with strong shareholder protection. The use of pyramid control structures as defensive mechanisms is especially widespread in Asian countries. For example, based on 1996 data relating to 2980 companies from eight Asian countries, Claessens et al. (2000) reported that pyramid control structures were used in 38.7 percent of companies. Notably, pyramid control structures are very popular in Indonesia (66 percent of companies), Singapore (55 percent of companies) and Taiwan (49 percent of companies).

Equally, pyramid control structures are very common in some European countries such as Austria, Belgium, France, Germany, Spain and Sweden (Bebchuk et al., 2000; La Porta et al., 1999). In France, among the population of all 467 companies that undertook an IPO between 1992 and 2010, 155 companies (33 percent) implemented pyramid control structures. In contrast, such structures are uncommon in the US, UK, Finland and Denmark, where regulation is more obliging (Bhaumik and Gregoriou, 2010; ISS et al., 2007).

Voting pact agreements
Formal voting pact agreements binding founder-CEOs and other blockholders, such as family members, employees and venture capital institutions, are also helpful in preserving a high level of control in the hands of founder-CEOs (Bennedsen and Wolfenzon, 2000; Cronqvist and Nilsson, 2003; Villalonga and Amit, 2006). These formal agreements specify pre-emptive rights and expected transactional behavior of shareholders who are members of the pact. They may also define specific conditions that govern pooling of voting rights held by pact members in relation to important strategic and corporate governance issues. Implementing pact agreements allows founder-CEOs to better control transactional and voting behavior of important blockholders that are members of the pact. Therefore, pact agreements substantially reduce risks of loss of control of the firm (Bennedsen and Wolfenzon, 2000; Gianfrate, 2007; Roosenboom and Schramade, 2006; Volpin, 2002).

In France, as in most European countries and the United States, voting pact agreements are publicly disclosed in newspapers, prospectuses and annual reports (Gianfrate, 2007). Contracting shareholders are also legally required to register pact agreements and all subsequent amendments with the financial markets authorities, for example with the AMF, the security and exchange authority in France; and with the Security and Exchange Commission (SEC), Form 13-D, in the United States. They last generally between three and five years and can be renewed.

Whereas shareholder pact agreements are legally permitted in all European Union member states, their actual use is common only in Italy, Belgium and France. More specifically, the ISS et al. (2007) study shows that shareholder pact agreements are implemented in 40 percent of Italian firms, 25 percent of Belgian firms and 15 percent of French firms. In the remaining 13 European Union member states under study, the proportion of firms that reported the presence of shareholder pact agreements was lower than 5 percent (ISS et al., 2007). In the population of 467 companies that have undertaken an IPO in France between 1992 and 2011, 78 companies (17 percent) have disclosed explicit pact agreements involving mainly CEOs, insider directors, venture capitalists and industrial companies.

An illustrative example
A simple example, represented graphically in Figure 12.1, might illustrate the different mechanisms put in place by incumbent controlling shareholders to prevent loss of corporate control post-IPO. Rigiflex International, today known as Prismaflex International, is a leading manufacturer of advertising displays and a digital printing services provider. The company was created by four founders: Pierre-Henry Bassouls, Nathalie Bassouls, Jean-Philippe Delmotte and Eric Bihr. It is located in Haute Rivoire (about 90 kilometers south-west of the French city of Lyon). In March 1999, Rigiflex International went public. The four founders instigated three layers of defensive mechanisms to create a gap between cash-flow rights and voting rights.

First, several years before IPO the four founders voted provisions to grant double voting rights to all ordinary shares held by the same shareholder for more than four years. The creation of the double voting rule allowed the four founders, just before the IPO and through their holding company JPN Fixations, to control 65.2 percent of voting rights resulting from an ownership stake of 53.6 percent. On the first day of IPO, the double voting rule granted the founders, via their holding company, almost 50 percent of the voting rights. This corresponded to a direct ownership stake of only 37.3 percent.

Second, the four founders established a two-tier pyramid structure to

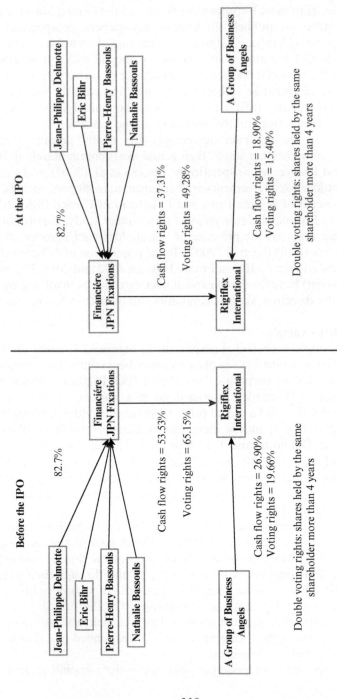

Figure 12.1   Different defensive mechanisms put in place by Rigiflex International founders before and at IPO

control Rigiflex International. Their ownership was achieved through the holding company JPN Fixations in which they own 82.7 percent of cash-flow rights. Consequently, on the first day of IPO they were able to control almost 50 percent of voting rights in Rigiflex International with an ultimate cash-flow stake of only 31 percent (equal to 82.7% x 37.31%).

Third, the four founders, via their holding company JPN Fixations, created with a group of business angels an explicit pact agreement that took effect on the first day of the IPO. This group of business angels, on the first day of the IPO, held 19.0 percent of cash flow rights and 15.4 percent of voting rights. The pact agreement forbade, for a period of five years, any sale or transfer of shares by contracting shareholders that would result in crossing below the 50 percent threshold of voting rights controlled by the signatories of the agreement. Signatories of the pact decided also to act in concert with each other in respect of major strategic and governance-related decisions. On the first day of the IPO, the pact members controlled 64.7 percent of voting rights in Rigiflex International.

Thus, through the implementation of three layers of defensive mechanisms (double voting rights, two-tier pyramid control structure and pact agreements) the four founders of Rigiflex International could noticeably leverage their control over and above their equity stake. In particular, they finally controlled 64.7 percent of voting rights in the company while owning only a 31 percent cash-flow stake. More essentially, the simple example of Rigiflex International shows how the effects of dual-class shares, pyramid control structures and pact agreements can be additive. That is, the combination of several types of defensive mechanisms significantly increases the wedge between cash flow rights and voting rights. As a result, shareholders who are strongly motivated to reduce loss of control risks at IPO are likely to line up several defensive mechanisms at the same time. We now provide a theoretical framework to explain why founder-CEO shareholders are more likely than any other types of pre-IPO controlling shareholders to combine several defensive mechanisms similar to the ones used by the Rigiflex International founders.

Founder-CEO Inclination to Use Defensive Mechanisms at IPO

A large body of research suggests that founder-CEOs are more apprehensive about post-IPO shifts of control than other types of CEOs. By virtue of their status as founders, founder-CEOs have stronger feelings of psychological ownership and duties of protection, care and nurturing towards their firm (Arthurs et al., 2007; Ikävalko et al., 2010; Pierce et al., 2001). For the same reason, they are more strongly identified with and emotionally attached to their firms relative to other types of CEOs (Anderson et al., 2009; Arthurs and Busenitz, 2003; Gao and Jain, 2011; He, 2008; Souder et al., 2012; Wasserman, 2006, 2008). As a result, they are more inclined to exclude other stakeholders from controlling the firm (Arthurs et al., 2007; Gao and Jain, 2011; Gimeno et al., 1997; Wasserman, 2006).

Indeed, although both founder-CEOs and non-founder-CEOs may feel a sense of psychological ownership towards the firm, this perception is likely to be deeper for founder-CEOs. Psychological ownership is defined as 'the feeling of possessiveness and of being psychologically tied to an object. One's possessions are felt as extensions of the self' (Pierce et al., 2001, p. 299). Three characteristics, much more salient for founder-CEOs than non-founder CEOs, reinforce this state of mind: (1) control of the company; (2) familiarity with the company; and (3) self-investment in the company (Pierce et al., 2001).

Founder-CEOs are probable to exercise greater control over the company compared to non-founder-CEOs because they commonly unite four sources of power: ownership, structural, expertise and prestige (Buyl et al., 2011; Finkelstein, 1992). Indeed, founder-CEOs generally own larger ownership stakes in their companies than non-founder-CEOs (Fahlenbrach, 2009; Gao and Jain, 2011; He, 2008; Nelson, 2003). Stronger economic ties to the company provide founder-CEOs with rights and legitimacy to imprint their own vision, mission, values and goals upon the company. This will ultimately grant them more control over the company (Davis et al., 1997; Le Breton-Miller and Miller, 2009). Further, founder-CEOs are more likely to retain structural power as they typically implement founder-centric governance structures and pick friendly directors on supervisory boards, which in turn provide them with greater decision-making power and control-related benefits (Gao and Jain, 2012; Nelson, 2003; Souder et al., 2012). Additionally, founder-CEOs are by definition the longest-tenured employees in their companies (Le Breton-Miller et al., 2011; Souder et al., 2012; Wasserman, 2006). Longer tenure allows founder-CEOs to gather specific knowledge and expertise about the company's history, culture and underlying political structure (Fahlenbrach, 2009; Souder et al., 2012). As a consequence, founder-CEOs have more occasions to develop credibility, to centralize decision-making processes, to control information flow and, finally, to impose their power in the company (He, 2008). Lastly, status as founder-CEO confers prestige, reputation and charismatic roles. This eases the exercise of influence and power (Adams et al., 2005; Buyl et al., 2011; Le Breton-Miller et al., 2011).

In terms of familiarity with the company, research shows founder-CEOs to enjoy more occasions to intimately know the company than a non-founder CEO. Indeed, the prime way to develop familiarity with an organization is to create it (Wasserman, 2006). The long time spent since creation allows founder-CEOs to amass explicit and tacit knowledge of internal and external stakeholders linked to the company, and hence accrue familiarity with the company (He, 2008; Pierce et al., 2001). Founder-CEOs' longer tenure also implies that they have dedicated more personal investment of time, skills, wealth, human capital and energy in the process of creating and developing the company than any other externally hired CEO (Fischer and Pollock, 2004; Gimeno et al., 1997; Le Breton-Miller et al., 2011; Pierce et al., 2001; Wasserman, 2008). All in all, these arguments point to the conclusion that founder-CEOs are likely to experience stronger psychological ownership feelings than other types of CEOs, because of their greater control of, familiarity with and self-investment in their companies.

The state of psychological ownership triggers several behavioral effects including stronger identification, attachment and commitment as well as a deeper sense of responsibility to invest more time and energy than any other stakeholder (Fahlenbrach, 2009; He, 2008; Hoang and Gimeno, 2010; Ikävalko et al., 2010; Pierce et al., 2001; Souder et al., 2012). For instance, Gimeno et al. (1997) found that founder-CEOs ensured the survival of their ventures, despite enduring below-average performance, because of their strong attachment and feeling of responsibility towards their firm.

Moreover, several studies have shown that founder-CEOs' stronger feelings of psychological ownership lead to a tendency to exclude others from controlling the firm (Arthurs and Busenitz, 2003; Ikävalko et al., 2010; Pierce et al., 2001). For example, research indicates that founder-CEOs' strong psychological ownership increased their overconfidence and self-efficacy compared to non-founder-CEOs (Busenitz and Barney, 1997; Chen et al., 1998; Forbes, 2005), making them believe that they are the only competent and legitimate managers to successfully run the firm (Wasserman, 2008). Similarly, Nelson (2003) suggests that founder-CEOs' socio-emotional attachment and desire to keep control over their company cause them to consider venture capital backing or IPOs as last-resort solutions, which if implemented need to be accompanied by efficient defensive mechanisms. Such resistance to delegation of authority and dilution of ownership significantly limits founder-CEO-led companies' expansionary initiatives (Souder et al., 2012). In addition, founder-CEOs' intrinsic motivation and strong economic ties enable them to aim at longer investment horizons relative to non-founder-CEOs. This makes conservation of control in the long term a primary issue for founder-CEOs (Certo et al., 2001; Gao and Jain, 2011; Gao and Jain, 2012; He, 2008; Nelson, 2003).

Greater feelings of psychological ownership towards the company come at an economic cost for founder-CEOs. For example, Wasserman (2006) found that founder-CEOs' higher levels of psychic income make them willing to voluntarily accept lower cash compensation than non-founder-CEOs. Likewise, He (2008) suggests that founder-CEOs demand lower pecuniary compensation for their efforts in the company and do not need pay-for-performance incentives, because intrinsic satisfaction compensates for the need for extrinsic rewards.

Gómez-Mejía et al. (2007) report similar behaviors in the context of family companies. Indeed, their study indicates that families prioritize control over the company even if this implies increased risk of poor pecuniary benefits. Gómez-Mejía et al. (2007) examined the behavior over 54 years of 1237 family-owned olive mills in Southern Spain that were facing two options. The first option is to join a co-operative. This leads to loss of family control but at the same time reduces economic risk. The second option is not to join a co-operative. This preserves the family control over the mill but increases the economic risk. Gómez-Mejía et al.'s (2007) empirical findings indicate that families consistently choose the second option because they cognitively frame the loss of control situation as the 'worst-case scenario'. Keeping family control over olive mills preserves socio-emotional wealth, and hence constitutes a key family goal (Gómez-Mejía et al., 2007). Families are more willing to bear threats to their financial well-being, believing that this threat can be managed, than to endure costs of loss of socio-emotional well-being (Gómez-Mejía et al., 2007).

Moved to the context of this study, findings highlighting the dominance of socio-emotional considerations in family companies may suggest that founder-CEOs are more likely to frame the loss of control at IPO as a worst-case scenario compared to non-founder-CEOs. Therefore, they should be more inclined than non-founder-CEOs to amass several defensive mechanisms at IPO to maximize the gap between cash-flow rights and voting rights. This is despite the risk of larger economic penalties, such as a larger underpricing at IPO.

There also exists an extrinsic characteristic which explains differences in behaviors with respect to company control preferences. Indeed, founder-CEOs typically have much higher company-specific human capital relative to non-founder-CEOs (Certo et al., 2001; Gao and Jain, 2011; He, 2008; Nelson, 2003). As a result, it is harder for founder-CEOs to find corresponding alternative executive positions in other companies compared to professional managers, who enjoy more general human capital and longer experience in the external labor market (Gao and Jain, 2012; He, 2008). This increases founder-CEOs' employment risk aversion, and hence resistance to any change of control scenarios (Gao and Jain, 2012). Furthermore, organizational life cycle theory proposes that founder-CEOs' employment risk aversion is particularly acute post-IPO because founder-CEOs generally lack skills, abilities and resources required to face new competitive, financial, regulatory and managerial challenges typically faced by CEOs of publicly traded companies (Certo et al., 2001; Gedajlovic et al., 2004; He, 2008; Souder et al., 2012; Wasserman, 2008). Accordingly, the outlook of turning over executive responsibility to a professional manager, better able to deal with new post-IPO challenges, is likely to prompt founder-CEOs to anticipate such an unwanted consequence by setting up several defensive mechanisms blocking leadership transitions.

Thus, entrepreneurship research suggests that founder-CEOs' spirit of psychological ownership, identification, attachment and commitment towards the company are stronger than those of other types of CEOs (Gómez-Mejía et al., 2007; Wasserman, 2006). Such emotional ties tend to disappear as company ownership and management transition into subsequent generations of the founder's family and professional managers hired externally (Gómez-Mejía et al., 2007; Mishra and McConaughy, 1999; Schulze et al., 2001; Wasserman, 2006). Consequently, founder-CEOs are more inclined than non-founder-CEOs to pool several defensive mechanisms in parallel to oppose any possible loss of control of their company at IPO.

EMPIRICAL EVIDENCE FROM THE FRENCH IPO MARKETS

We empirically investigated the propensity to implement defensive mechanisms using the whole population of IPOs undertaken from January 1992 to December 2010 on the French capital markets. We started to collect data from 1992 because IPO prospectuses are reliably available from Bloomberg and Thomson ONE databases only after the year 1991. The French capital market exemplifies a particularly interesting empirical context because defensive mechanisms such as dual-class shares, pyramid control structures and pact agreements are used widely, in contrast to some other countries where such devices are legally prohibited.

In total, the population of all French IPOs undertaken over the 1992–2010 period included 467 IPOs after excluding IPOs which: (1) were not completed on regulated markets; (2) involved transfers from different capital markets; (3) involved non-French companies undertaking IPOs on French stock markets; and (4) resulted from stock listings following mergers, acquisitions and spin-offs of publicly listed companies. Of these 467 IPOs, 287 IPOs involved founder-CEOs (61.5 percent) and 180 IPOs (38.5 percent) were led by non-founder-CEOs. Primary data sources used in this research are SDC New Issues, Datastream, Bloomberg and Thomson ONE databases supplemented by IPO prospectuses and reference documents filed with the French Financial Markets Authority (AMF).

Table 12.2 shows the distribution of IPOs by industry for the observation period. The distribution of the number of IPOs over time puts in evidence the influence of cycles of bubble periods and subsequent recessions on IPO activity. Although IPOs are undertaken in all sectors of the economy, they are not evenly distributed. A large number of IPOs were performed in industrial, technology and consumer goods sectors; very few IPOs were done in highly regulated sectors such as oil and gas, utilities and basic materials.

Table 12.3 describes the major features of IPO companies, broken down by founder-CEO-led companies and non-founder-CEO-led companies. Companies involving founder-CEOs are considerably smaller and younger than other companies. However, smallness and newness do not translate into differences in performance (that is, return on equity ratio) or leverage (that is, debt to assets ratio).

In terms of ownership and voting rights structures, five findings should be highlighted. First, founder-CEOs retain significantly more voting rights at IPO than non-founder-CEOs. Second, venture capital and private equity voting rights are lower in companies involving founder-CEOs than in other companies. Third, public equity released at the IPO is smaller in founder-CEO led companies than in other companies. Fourth, the proportion of family controlled companies is considerably higher in founder-CEO managed companies than in other companies. Two conditions were used to identify family controlled companies: (1) family members must, either individually or as a group, retain the largest shareholding or voting rights; and (2) at least two members of the family must exercise an executive or a director position (Gomez-Mejía et al., 2003). Companies satisfying both conditions are considered as family-controlled companies. Fifth, companies managed by founder-CEOs are associated with less prestigious underwriters than other companies. We use two variables to measure underwriters' prestige (Bruton et al., 2010; Certo, 2003). First, we used the logarithm of average market capitalization of IPOs performed by the underwriter over a three-year period prior to IPO date. Second, we used the logarithm of average number of IPOs completed by the underwriter over a three-year period prior to IPO date.

In terms of CEO characteristics, there are four important differences. First, founder-CEOs are younger than non-founder-CEOs. Second, they possess less human capital and social capital than non-founder-CEOs. We measure CEOs' human capital using a dummy variable taking a value of

Table 12.2   Distribution of IPOs by industry over the 1992–2010 period (full sample)

Year	1992	1993	1994	1995	1996	1997	1998	1999	2000	2001	2002	2003	2004	2005	2006	2007	2008	2009	2010	Total
Oil and gas	0	0	1	0	0	0	0	0	0	0	0	0	0	1	0	0	0	0	0	2
Basic materials	0	0	1	1	1	1	3	0	1	0	0	0	0	0	0	1	0	0	0	9
Industrials	2	2	13	5	7	15	24	6	7	4	1	0	4	4	4	2	0	1	0	101
Consumer goods	0	2	6	1	12	11	19	8	7	1	3	0	2	1	1	0	0	0	0	74
Health care	0	0	2	0	4	5	11	2	1	1	1	0	1	2	4	1	0	4	4	39
Consumer services	0	2	4	4	9	8	19	12	11	4	1	0	1	5	1	4	0	0	0	85
Telecommunications	0	0	0	0	0	1	3	1	0	1	0	0	0	0	1	1	0	0	0	8
Utilities	0	0	1	0	0	0	0	0	1	0	0	0	0	2	1	0	0	0	0	5
Financials	0	0	4	0	1	2	2	2	4	2	0	0	1	3	10	2	2	0	0	35
Technology	0	0	0	2	9	11	20	24	36	3	1	0	1	0	2	0	0	0	0	109
Total	2	6	32	13	43	54	101	55	68	15	7	0	10	18	24	11	2	1	4	467

Table 12.3   Summary statistics: full sample, founder-CEO firms and non-founder-CEO firms

Variables	Full sample (N = 467)		Founder-CEO firms (N = 287)		Non founder-CEO firms (N = 180)	
	Mean	SD	Mean	SD	Mean	SD
Number of mechanisms	1.23	0.83	1.42***	0.76	0.94***	0.85
Dual class shares (dummy)	0.73	0.44	0.83***	0.38	0.58***	0.49
Pyramid control structures (dummy)	0.33	0.47	0.39***	0.49	0.24***	0.43
Pact agreements (dummy)	0.17	0.37	0.20*	0.40	0.12*	0.32
Total sales†	3.52	1.8	2.99***	1.32	4.36***	2.13
Firm age†	2.26	0.96	2.06***	0.83	2.59***	1.06
VC/Private equity voting rights	16.4	22.89	11.26***	16.42	24.58***	28.7
CEO voting rights	40.96	33.24	51.21***	28.21	24.62***	34.18
Public equity released	23.63	11.17	22.78*	9.73	24.97*	13.06
Family controlled firm (dummy)	0.46	0.50	0.55***	0.50	0.31***	0.46
CEO age	48.42	9.31	47.25***	9.35	50.3***	8.97
CEO human capital (dummy)	0.28	0.45	0.22***	0.41	0.38***	0.49
CEO social capital	1.12	0.48	1.06**	0.38	1.21**	0.6
CEO duality (dummy)	0.77	0.42	0.87***	0.34	0.61***	0.49
Return on equity†	8.22	0.41	8.20	0.52	8.24	0.01
Total debt to assets ratio	27.32	110.42	27.37	139.35	27.24	26.76
CEO lockup (period length)	5.99	10.78	8.06***	11.9	2.68***	7.64
CEO lockup (shareholding)	30.64	42.68	40.16***	44.4	15.44***	34.86
Underwriter prestige (IPOs size)†	3.65	2.11	3.38*	1.77	4.08*	2.5
Underwriter prestige (nb. of IPOs)†	0.93	0.7	0.98*	0.71	0.85*	0.67
Founder-CEO status	0.61	0.49				

Note: A statistically significant difference in mean or proportion between founder-CEO and non-founder-CEO firms at the .1 %, 1 % and 5% significance levels are indicated by ***, ** and *, respectively based on two-sample tests of proportions for dummy variables and two-sample t tests for other variables.

1 if they graduated from a prestigious institution, as classified by Maclean et al. (2006), and 0 otherwise. To proxy CEOs' social capital, we counted the number of directorship mandates they held in companies belonging to the SBF250 index (Belliveau et al., 1996; Tian et al., 2011). This index includes the 250 largest companies in terms of market capitalization listed on the Paris stock exchange. Third, founder-CEOs are more likely to combine executive and chairman positions than non-founder-CEOs. Fourth, founder-CEOs bear significantly stronger lock-ups in terms of both period length and shareholding than non-founder-CEOs.

In the population of all 467 French IPOs undertaken over the 1992–2010 period, the most popular defensive mechanism is undeniably dual-class shares (73 percent), followed by pyramid control structures (33 percent) and voting pact agreements (17 percent). In total, 80 percent of CEO-shareholders took advantage of at least one defensive mechanism at IPO. More specifically, 43 percent of them used one mechanism, 32 percent combined two mechanisms and 5 percent used all three mechanisms. Accordingly, 37 percent of CEO-shareholders have cumulated more than one defensive mechanism, which may imply that dual-class shares, pyramid control structures and voting pact agreements protection effects are additive rather than substitutable (Almeida and Wolfenzon, 2006).

Are companies with founder-CEOs more likely to use defensive mechanisms than companies led by non-founder-CEOs at IPO? On average, companies led by founder-CEOs implemented a larger number of defensive mechanisms than companies run by non-founder-CEOs. More specifically, companies led by founder-CEOs implemented on average 1.42 defensive mechanisms. Non-founder-CEO companies introduced only 0.94 mechanism. This difference is statistically significant at $p < 0.01$. Examination of the distribution of each type of defensive mechanism across the two groups revealed the same trend. Indeed, 83 percent of companies led by founder-CEOs implemented dual-class shares at IPO whereas only 58 percent of companies led by non founder-CEOs put in place dual-class shares at IPO. This difference is statistically significant at $p < 0.01$. Similarly, 39 percent of founder-CEOs used pyramid structures to control the company at IPO. This percentage falls to 24 percent for non-founder-CEOs. Again, the difference between founder-CEOs and non-founder-CEOs in their propensity to implement pyramid control structures is statistically significant at $p < 0.01$. Likewise, 20 percent of founder-CEOs were involved in shareholder pact agreements at IPO whereas only 12 percent of non-founder-CEOs participated in pact agreements. This difference is statistically significant at $p < 0.05$.

Taken together, these results indicate that at IPO, founder-CEOs are more likely than non-founder-CEOs to use dual-class shares, pyramid control structures and pacts. As a result, founder-CEOs tend to use several defensive mechanisms concurrently while non-founder-CEOs adopt only a few mechanisms. Given that the gap between ownership and control created by a combination of several mechanisms in parallel is significantly stronger than the gap obtained by one isolated mechanism, our findings provide convergent indication for the predominance of founder-CEOs' defensive postures relative to non-founder-CEOs at IPO.

DISCUSSION

This chapter hopefully increases our understanding of the implementation of defensive mechanisms by both founder-CEOs and non-founder-CEOs. First, drawing upon a longitudinal database covering the whole population of French IPOs undertaken between 1992 and 2010, this study demonstrates that only 20 percent of CEO shareholders did not put in place defensive mechanisms at IPO. Moreover, almost one-third of CEO shareholders implemented several mechanisms in parallel. This result confirms the additive effects of dual-class shares, pyramid control structures and voting pact agreements in shielding CEO shareholders from undesired change of control (Almeida and Wolfenzon, 2006).

Second, the empirical analysis described in this study provides an answer to the question of whether founder-CEOs are more prone to use dual-class shares, pyramid structures and pact agreements than non-founder-CEOs at IPO. More specifically, the number of defensive mechanisms used by founder-CEOs is significantly larger than the number of mechanisms implemented by non-founder-CEOs. The combination of several mechanisms increases the gap between cash-flow rights and voting rights and provides successive defensive lines that may be useful if one particular mechanism fails (for example, if a shareholder refuses to renew a pact agreement).

Third, the theoretical framework developed in this study provides a logic explaining why founder-CEOs are more likely than non-founder-CEOs to use defensive mechanisms at IPO. In particular, the more forceful defensive posture adopted by founder-CEOs is likely to be the consequence of both intrinsic and extrinsic distinct attributes. For example, founder-CEOs' stronger attachment, identification, commitment and feelings of psychological ownership towards their company make them more inclined to resist control change and to consider that they are the only legitimate, capable and suitable managers of the company. Moreover, because founder-CEOs' employment risk aversion is greater than that of non-founder-CEOs, who possess more general human capital and longer experience in the external labor market, they are more likely to resist leadership transitions by implementing several defensive mechanisms. For these reasons, founder-CEOs are more likely than non-founder-CEOs to apply defensive mechanisms at IPO.

This study has several limitations, which offer opportunities for future research. For instance, we examine the relationships between founder status and defensive mechanisms in a specific context. The French context is an appropriate setting for this study because defensive mechanisms are legally allowed and popular. However, future research should investigate whether the results presented here hold in other institutional contexts. Perhaps more importantly, future research should examine the size of financial costs and penalties endured by founder-CEOs, in the short and long terms, as a result of defensive mechanisms implementation.

In sum, this study demonstrates how intrinsic and extrinsic differences between founder- and non-founder-CEOs influence corporate governance decisions in the specific context of IPOs. By doing so, it contributes to streams of research in entrepreneurship and corporate governance which suggest that founder-CEOs cognitively frame the loss of control situation as the worst-case scenario and that protecting socio-emotional wealth constitutes a key goal in and of itself.

REFERENCES

Adams, R.B., Almeida, H. and Ferreira, D. (2005), 'Powerful CEOs and their impact on corporate performance', *Review of Financial Studies*, **18** (4), 1403–1432.

Almeida, H.V. and Wolfenzon, D. (2006), 'A theory of pyramidal ownership and family business groups', *Journal of Finance*, **61** (6), 2637–2680.

Anderson, R., Duru, A. and Reeb, D. (2009), 'Founders, heirs, and corporate opacity in the United States', *Journal of Financial Economics*, **92** (2), 205–222.

Arthurs, J.D. and Busenitz, L.W. (2003), 'The boundaries and limitations of agency theory and stewardship theory in the venture capitalist/entrepreneur relationship', *Entrepreneurship Theory and Practice*, **28** (2), 145–162.

Arthurs, J.D., Hoskisson, R.E., Busenitz, L.W. and Johnson, R.A. (2008), 'Managerial agents watching other agents: Multiple agency conflicts regarding underpricing in IPO firms', *Academy of Management Journal*, **51** (2), 277–294.

Arthurs, J.D., Townsend, D.M., Busenitz, L.W., Liu, K. and Hoskisson, R.E. (2007), 'Founders, governance and firm valuation: Does the market perceive psychological ownership?', *Frontiers of Entrepreneurship Research*, **27** (12), Article 1.

Bebchuk, L.A., Kraakman, R. and Triantis, G. (2000), 'Stock pyramids, cross-ownership, and dual class equity: The mechanisms and agency costs of separating control from cash-flow rights', in *Concentrated Corporate Ownership*, Chicago, IL: University of Chicago Press, pp. 295–318.

Belliveau, M.A., O'Reilly III, C.A. and Wade, J.B. (1996), 'Social capital at the top: Effects of social similarity and status on CEO compensation', *Academy of Management Journal*, **39** (6), 1568–1593.

Bennedsen, M. and Wolfenzon, D. (2000), 'The balance of power in closely held corporations', *Journal of Financial Economics*, **58** (1–2), 113–139.

Bhaumik, S.K. and Gregoriou, A. (2010), 'Family ownership, tunnelling and earnings management: A review of the literature', *Journal of Economic Surveys*, **24** (4), 705–730.

Brau, J.C. and Fawcett, S.E. (2006), 'Initial public offerings: An analysis of theory and practice', *Journal of Finance*, **61** (1), 399–436.

Bruton, G.D., Chahine, S. and Filatotchev, I. (2009), 'Founders, private equity investors, and underpricing in entrepreneurial IPOs', *Entrepreneurship Theory and Practice*, **33** (4), 909–928.

Bruton, G., Filatotchev, I., Chahine, S. and Wright, M. (2010), 'Governance, ownership structure, and performance of IPO firms: The impact of different types of private equity investors and institutional environments', *Strategic Management Journal*, **31** (5), 491–509.

Busenitz, L.W. and Barney, J.B. (1997), 'Differences between entrepreneurs and managers in large organizations: Biases and heuristics in strategic decision-making', *Journal of Business Venturing*, **12** (1), 9–30.

Buyl, T., Boone, C., Hendriks, W. and Matthyssens, P. (2011), 'Top management team functional diversity and firm performance: The moderating role of CEO characteristics', *Journal of Management Studies*, **48** (1), 151–177.

Certo, S.T. (2003), 'Influencing initial public offering investors with prestige: Signaling with board structures', *Academy of Management Review*, **28** (3), 432–446.

Certo, S.T., Covin, J.G., Daily, C.M. and Dalton, D.R. (2001), 'Wealth and the effects of founder management among IPO-stage new ventures', *Strategic Management Journal*, **22** (6–7), 641–658.

Chen, C.C., Greene, P.G. and Crick, A. (1998), 'Does entrepreneurial self-efficacy distinguish entrepreneurs from managers?', *Journal of Business Venturing*, **13** (4), 295–316.

Claessens, S., Djankov, S., Fan, J.P. and Lang, L.H. (2002), 'Disentangling the incentive and entrenchment effects of large shareholdings', *Journal of Finance*, **57** (6), 2741–2771.

Cronqvist, H. and Nilsson, M. (2003), 'Agency costs of controlling minority shareholders', *Journal of Financial and Quantitative Analysis*, **38** (4), 695–719.

Daily, C.M., Certo, S.T. and Dalton, D.R. (2005), 'Investment bankers and IPO pricing: does prospectus information matter?', *Journal of Business Venturing*, **20** (1), 93–111.

Daily, C.M., Certo, S.T., Dalton, D.R. and Roengpitya, R. (2003), 'IPO underpricing: A meta-analysis and research synthesis', *Entrepreneurship Theory and Practice*, **27** (3), 271–295.

Dalziel, T., White, R.E. and Arthurs, J.D. (2011), 'Principal costs in initial public offerings', *Journal of Management Studies*, **48** (6), 1346–1364.

Davidoff, S.M. (2013), 'Thorny side effects in silicon valley tactic to keep control', *New York Times*, 3 September.

Davis, J.H., Schoorman, F.D. and Donaldson, L. (1997), 'Toward a stewardship theory of management', *Academy of Management Review*, **22** (1), 20–47.

Faccio, M. and Lang, L.H. (2002), 'The ultimate ownership of Western European corporations', *Journal of Financial Economics*, **65** (3), 365–395.

Fahlenbrach, R. (2009), 'Founder-CEOs, investment decisions, and stock market performance', *Journal of Financial and Quantitative Analysis*, **44** (2), 439–466.

Fattoum, A. and Delmar, F. (2011), 'The impact of separated voting and cash-flow rights on French IPO valuation: A principal agent perspective', *Frontiers of Entrepreneurship Research*, **31** (11), 351–363.

Fattoum, A. and Delmar, F. (2013), 'Kings today, rich tomorrow: How do steward founder-CEOs succeed IPOs?', *Academy of Management Proceedings* (Best Papers), **2013** (1), 16898.

Finkelstein, S. (1992), 'Power in top management teams: Dimensions, measurement, and validation', *Academy of Management Journal*, **35** (3), 505–538.

Fischer, H.M. and Pollock, T.G. (2004), 'Effects of social capital and power on surviving transformational change: The case of initial public offerings', *Academy of Management Journal*, **47** (4), 463–481.

Forbes, D.P. (2005), 'Are some entrepreneurs more overconfident than others?', *Journal of Business Venturing*, **20** (5), 623–640.

Gao, N. and Jain, B.A. (2011), 'Founder CEO management and the long-run investment performance of IPO firms', *Journal of Banking and Finance*, **35** (7), 1669–1682.

Gao, N. and Jain, B.A. (2012), 'Founder management and the market for corporate control for IPO firms: The moderating effect of the power structure of the firm', *Journal of Business Venturing*, **27** (1), 112–126.

Gedajlovic, E., Lubatkin, M.H. and Schulze, W.S. (2004), 'Crossing the threshold from founder management to professional management: A governance perspective', *Journal of Management Studies*, **41** (5), 899–912.

Gianfrate, G. (2007), 'What do shareholders coalitions really want? Evidence from Italian voting trusts', *Corporate Governance: An International Review*, **15** (2), 122–132.

Gimeno, J., Folta, T.B., Cooper, A.C. and Woo, C.Y. (1997), 'Survival of the fittest? Entrepreneurial human capital and the persistence of underperforming firms', *Administrative Science Quarterly*, **42** (4), 750–783.

Gómez-Mejía, L.R., Haynes, K.T., Núñez-Nickel, M., Jacobson, K.J.L. and Moyano-Fuentes, J. (2007), 'Socioemotional wealth and business risks in family-controlled firms: Evidence from Spanish olive oil mills', *Administrative Science Quarterly*, **52** (1), 106–137.

Gómez-Mejía, L.R., Larraza-Kintana, M. and Makri, M. (2003), 'The determinants of executive compensation in family controlled public corporations', *Academy of Management Journal*, **46** (2), 226–237.

Gompers, P.A., Ishii, J. and Metrick, A. (2010), 'Extreme governance: An analysis of dual-class firms in the United States', *Review of Financial Studies*, **23** (3), 1051–1088.

He, L. (2008), 'Do founders matter? A study of executive compensation, governance structure and firm performance', *Journal of Business Venturing*, **23** (3), 257–279.

Hoang, H. and Gimeno, J. (2010), 'Becoming a founder: How founder role identity affects entrepreneurial transitions and persistence in founding', *Journal of Business Venturing*, **25** (1), 41–53.

Ikävalko, M., Pihkala, T. and Kraus, S. (2010), 'The role of owner-managers' psychological ownership in SME strategic behavior', *Journal of Small Business and Entrepreneurship*, **23** (3), 461–479.

ISS, Shearman & Sterling, and ECGI (2007), 'Report on the proportionality principle in the EU', http://ec.europa.eu/internal_market/company/shareholders/indexb_en.htm and http://www.ecgi.org/osov/documents/final_report_en.pdf.

Johnson, S. (2000), 'Tunneling', *American Economic Review*, **90** (2), 22–27.

La Porta, R., Lopez-de-Silanes, F. and Shleifer, A. (1999), 'Corporate ownership around the world', *Journal of Finance*, **54** (2), 471–517.

La Porta, R., Lopez-de-Silanes, F., Shleifer, A. and Vishny, R.W. (1998), 'Law and finance', *Journal of Political Economy*, **106** (6), 1113–1155.

Le Breton-Miller, I. and Miller, D. (2009), 'Agency vs. stewardship in public family firms: A social embeddedness reconciliation', *Entrepreneurship Theory and Practice*, **33** (6), 1169–1191.

Le Breton-Miller, I.L., Miller, D. and Lester, R.H. (2011), 'Stewardship or agency? A social embeddedness reconciliation of conduct and performance in public family businesses', *Organization Science*, **22** (3), 704–721.

Lowry, M. and Schwert, G.W. (2002), 'IPO market cycles: Bubbles or sequential learning?', *Journal of Finance*, **57** (3), 1171–1200.

Maclean, M., Harvey, C. and Press, J. (2006), *Business Elites and Corporate Governance in France and in the UK*, Basingstoke: Palgrave Macmillan.

Mishra, C.S. and McConaughy, D.L. (1999), 'Founding family control and capital structure: The risk of loss of control and the aversion to debt', *Entrepreneurship: Theory and Practice*, **23** (4), 53–64.

Modigliani, F. and Miller, M.H. (1963), 'Corporate income taxes and the cost of capital: A correction', *American Economic Review*, **53** (3), 433–443.

Morck, R. and Yeung, B. (2003), 'Agency problems in large family business groups', *Entrepreneurship Theory and Practice*, **27** (4), 367–382.

Nelson, T. (2003), 'The persistence of founder influence: Management, ownership, and performance effects at initial public offering', *Strategic Management Journal*, **24** (8), 707–724.

Nenova, T. (2003), 'The value of corporate voting rights and control: A cross-country analysis', *Journal of Financial Economics*, **68** (3), 325–351.

Nenova, T. (2007), 'How to dominate a firm with valuable control? Dual class firms around the world: Regulation, security-voting structure, and ownership patterns', SSRN Scholarly Paper No. ID 1017603, Rochester, NY: Social Science Research Network.

OECD (2004), 'Corporate governance principle', available at: http:www.oecd.org (accessed 4 October 2013).

Pierce, J.L., Kostova, T. and Dirks, K.T. (2001), 'Toward a theory of psychological ownership in organizations', *Academy of Management Review*, **26** (2), 298.

Roosenboom, P. and Schramade, W. (2006), 'The price of power: Valuing the controlling position of owner–managers in French IPO firms', *Journal of Corporate Finance*, **12** (2), 270–295.

Schulze, W.S., Lubatkin, M.H., Dino, R.N. and Buchholtz, A.K. (2001), 'Agency relationships in family firms: Theory and evidence', *Organization Science*, **12** (2), 99–116.

Smart, S.B. and Zutter, C.J. (2003), 'Control as a motivation for underpricing: A comparison of dual and single-class IPOs', *Journal of Financial Economics*, **69** (1), 85–110.

Smith, A., Davies, P.J. and Foley, S. (2013) 'Exchanges divided by dual-class shares', *Financial Times*, 3 October.

Souder, D., Simsek, Z. and Johnson, S.G. (2012), 'The differing effects of agent and founder CEOs on the firm's market expansion', *Strategic Management Journal*, **33** (1), 23–41.

Tian, J., Haleblian, J. and Rajagopalan, N. (2011), 'The effects of board human and social capital on investor reactions to new CEO selection', *Strategic Management Journal*, **32** (7), 731–747.

Villalonga, B. and Amit, R. (2006), 'How do family ownership, control and management affect firm value?', *Journal of Financial Economics*, **80** (2), 385–417.

Villalonga, B. and Amit, R. (2009), 'How are US family firms controlled?', *Review of Financial Studies*, **22** (8), 3047–3091.

Volpin, P.F. (2002), 'Governance with poor investor protection: Evidence from top executive turnover in Italy', *Journal of Financial Economics*, **64** (1), 61–90.

Wasserman, N. (2006), 'Stewards, agents, and the founder discount: Executive compensation in new ventures', *Academy of Management Journal*, **49** (5), 960–976.

Wasserman, N. (2008), 'The founder's dilemma', *Harvard Business Review*, **86** (2), 102–109.

World Bank's (2013), 'Doing Business 2013', available at http://www.doingbusiness.org (accessed 4 October 2014).

Zingales, L. (1994), 'The value of the voting right: A study of the Milan stock exchange experience', *Review of Financial Studies*, **7** (1), 5–148.

13. Corporate governance and accounting in small growing firms: a comparison of financial reporting and cost of debt across Gazelles and Non-Gazelles
Marita Blomkvist and Mari Paananen

INTRODUCTION

Small and growing privately held firms cause a lot of public debate due to their importance as contributors to job creation, regional development and economic growth. Specifically, there is a particular focus on high-growth firms, often referred to as Gazelles, as these are known to be outstanding job creators (Birch, 1979; Davidsson et al., 1994; Acs et al., 2004; Jermakowicz and Epstein, 2010; Li et al., 2011; Henrekson and Johansson, 2010). For example, the European Commission (EC) lists the support for small high-growth firms as an important political objective in its European Strategy Report (EC, 2010), and in business media successful fast-growing firms (e.g. 'Gazelles', 'Inc-500 companies') are identified and praised for their success.

Prior research suggests that Gazelles, on average, are younger and smaller than other firms (Davidsson and Henrekson, 2002; Bishop et al., 2009). However, despite the fact that they are small, they still generate a significant proportion of the total creation of new jobs in society. This is particularly manifested in times of recession, when Gazelles are more likely to continue to grow while other firms decline. While prevalent across most industries, it seems that Gazelles are over-represented in service industries (Henrekson and Johansson, 2010). Furthermore, prior research shows that Gazelles are more innovative than other firms, especially in countries with highly developed technological sectors (Hölzl, 2009). A key challenge for Gazelles is to secure access to financial resources to support their high-growth trajectory. However, raising capital by borrowing often results in complex contractual relationships between owner-managers and creditors (Armstrong et al., 2010). Managers have firm-specific information that may create or exacerbate a wide range of agency conflicts. For example, there is a risk that managers attempt to increase their personal wealth at the expense of other shareholders and/or creditors (Jensen and Meckling,

1976). The potential conflicting interests among contracting parties generate a demand for monitoring and contracting mechanisms that help mitigate such various agency conflicts. The corporate governance system of a firm is viewed as an essential mechanism by which the shareholders make sure that the board of directors oversees that the actions and choices of managers are aligned with the interests of shareholders and creditors. As Gazelles both are typically younger and smaller than the average small firm (Davidsson and Henrekson, 2002; Bishop et al., 2009) it is plausible to assume that the corporate accounting information environment is less developed in these firms. An important function of the corporate governance system in small privately held firms is to ensure the quality of financial reporting information. The financial reporting information provides relevant and reliable information that aids the monitoring and control of management. Also, financial reporting information reduces information asymmetry between existing and future creditors. Increased transparency and higher-quality financial reporting improves the corporate governance system, therefore enhancing the efficiency of contractual arrangements between the firm and external parties.

Privately held firms are often managed by a single owner or have owners who play a direct role in the management of the company (Chen et al., 2011). Owners and other stakeholders, such as lenders, may instead access inside information from the private companies with which they interact (Ball and Shivakumar, 2005), and may rely on other sources of information than published financial reporting, such as information about the character and reliability of the firm's owner (Berger and Udell, 2002). Financial reporting among privately held firms may instead to a greater extent reflect other objectives such as tax reporting, dividend policy or insurance requirements (Ball and Shivakumar, 2005; Burgstahler et al., 2006).

In spite of the recently considerable attention to small and growing firms in the literature (Landström, 2010) scholars interested in corporate governance and accounting have only recently started to explore financial reporting information issues among different types of small privately held firms. This lack of research is partly due to limited data available on private firms since in many constituencies they are not required to prepare and/or file statutory financial statements. In this chapter, we contribute to this stream of research by examining the quality of financial reporting information among different types of privately held small firms. Dividing the sample into Gazelles and Non-Gazelles, we posit that Gazelles have a greater incentive to attract external funding to finance their growth, and therefore also have a greater incentive to produce high-quality financial reporting compared to Non-Gazelles.

Although prior research concurs on the general conception of Gazelles as fast-growing firms, there is no commonly accepted definition of Gazelles (e.g., Gabrielsson et al., 2014). Recent research, however, tends to measure growth in terms of sales or turnover of assets. Thus, for the purpose of this study, we define Gazelles as small privately held firms with more than ten employees and that double their sales over a period of three consecutive years. Furthermore, we define high-quality financial reporting as the strength of the association between current accruals and past, present and future cash flow (Dechow and Dichev, 2002). We predict that Gazelles exhibit a higher quality of financial reporting manifested by showing more persistent accruals and being less prone to engage in earnings management (Dechow and Dichev, 2002; Givoly et al., 2010). In addition, we also examine differences in the degree of exhibited conservatism across Gazelles and Non-Gazelles.[1]

In Sweden,[2] all limited liability companies must prepare and file annual financial statements. We use these data to contribute to the literature and further explore financial reporting quality across Gazelles and Non-Gazelles. Controlling for endogeneity using Heckman's two-step selection model (Heckman, 1979), we find no significant difference in accrual persistence across the two groups and only weak evidence that Gazelles are less conservative. However, these results should be interpreted with caution, since we use growth measured as a doubling of the sales over a consecutive three-year period to identify Gazelles, and therefore this measure is intrinsically related to changes in accruals. We try to control for this by using Heckman's two-step procedure; however, the specification used may not fully take care of this problem. We also investigate tendencies to manage earnings by exploiting the link between financial reporting and tax regulations in Sweden. We test the association between the accumulated appropriations[3] and the change in earnings before interest and tax (EBIT). A high proportion of accumulated appropriations are interpreted as an indication of that a profitable company has exhausted or is close to exhausting legal opportunities to avoid taxation and would therefore be more prone to manipulate earnings. That is, a significant negative association between accumulated appropriations and change in EBIT may suggest that a firm is manipulating EBIT downwards. Finally, we test the difference in cost of debt across Gazelles and Non-Gazelles and find that creditors are able to assess the credit risk regardless of the financial reporting quality, which result in lower cost of debt for Gazelles. Although we do not argue that financial reporting is of no consequence, the test of cost of debt levels suggests that, on average, other corporate governance factors such as a qualified audit opinion drives interest rates upwards and the use of a Big Four auditor reduces interest rate levels. Further, we find that a larger number of board members result in lower cost-of-debt levels. We interpret this as creditors identifying a higher level of corporate governance, assuming that a larger number of board members is a sign of external parties in addition to the owner-manager on the board of directors. In addition, we also find that the cost of debt decreases for both Gazelles and Non-Gazelles during times of recession.

The remainder of the chapter is organized as follows. The next section provides a literature review and the hypothesis development. The following section then outlines the research design. The chapter then describes the sample selection process, before offering the empirical results. The final section summarizes our main conclusions.

LITERATURE REVIEW AND HYPOTHESIS DEVELOPMENT

The literature review covers two main areas of research. The first subsection reviews research on financial reporting quality. The second subsection covers research on cost of debt capital.

Research on Financial Reporting Quality

Financial reporting plays a key function in the corporate governance system of an enterprise as it contributes to reducing information asymmetry between contracting parties. Prior research on privately held firms tends to focus on comparing financial reporting quality in private firms to publicly traded firms, as opposed to comparing across types of private firms. Using a large sample of United States (US) firms Hope et al. (2013) compare financial reporting quality across private and publicly traded firms and find that privately held firms exhibit lower financial reporting quality, a finding consistent with the notion that publicly traded firms respond to a greater demand for high-quality financial statement information from external stakeholders.

These results concur with the findings of Ball and Shivakumar (2005). Using a United Kingdom (UK) sample of privately held firms, they show that these firms' financial reporting is also of lower quality, which they also interpret as a result of different market demands across privately held and publicly traded companies. Also, Burgstahler et al. (2006) report similar results in a study using the level of earnings management as a measure of accounting quality. They document that privately held European Union (EU) firms exhibit higher levels of earnings management compared to public EU firms. However, Givoly et al. (2010) find contrary results and conclude that privately held firms in the US exhibit higher financial reporting quality compared to publicly traded firms, although the difference in results may be explained by the fact that Givoly et al.'s (2010) sample of privately held firms are privately held firms with public debt, suggesting that the stakeholders of public debt may have a similar, if not greater, demand of high-quality financial reporting.

In this chapter, we examine the role of financial reporting among different groups of privately held small firms. Such firms are often owner-managed (Chen et al., 2011) and where capital providers, including providers of both equity and debt, typically have insider access to corporate information (Van Tendeloo and Vanstraelen, 2008; Chen et al., 2011). The main users of financial reporting in privately held small firms are owners, creditors, employees, suppliers and the government. Prior research suggests that tax incentives affect the quality of financial reporting negatively, and more so among private companies as their financial reporting is less widely distributed and therefore to a greater extent influenced by factors such as taxation and dividends (Ball and Shivakumar, 2005). Furthermore, this is exacerbated in an environment with a strong book-tax conformity level, such as in Sweden (Atwood et al., 2010). Despite the above arguments that financial reporting in private companies is assumed to be of a lower quality compared to publicly traded firms, the weaker information disclosure environment compared to publicly traded companies might make financial reporting disclosures very important because of the lack of competing information sources (Chen et al., 2011).

Recent research on variation within privately held firms show that high accounting quality increases with the demand of equity investors, lenders and suppliers (Hope et al., 2013). They also reveal that accounting quality in private firms is associated with the ability to predict future cash flow and with the quality of investment decisions. Using a sample of privately held firms in Belgium, Beuselinck et al. (2009) show that firms with private equity (PE) involvement have higher-quality financial statements than comparable private companies without PE involvement. This is explained as a natural outcome of PE investors' monitoring that often takes place in the board of directors. Furthermore, the proportion of equity stake held has an effect on a firm's financial reporting quality. The reporting quality is lower in firms where private equity investors have high ownership stakes than firms in which private equity investors have low equity stakes, suggesting that PE investors with high-equity stakes have greater access to inside information (Beuselinck and Manigart, 2007). Finally, prior research also indicates that private equity governance has a positive effect on accounting information production by compelling management to implement management control systems and employ accountants to maintain an overview of the company (Davila and Foster, 2005).

In sum, prior research is inconclusive as to whether privately held firms have an incentive to produce higher-quality financial reporting in general. However, prior research suggests that firms with prominent external stakeholders such as shareholders or creditors face a greater demand for high-quality financial reporting. We therefore predict that Gazelle firms that need to attract external funding to finance growth have a corporate governance function with greater incentive to produce high-quality financial reporting, as follows:

H1: Gazelle firms produce higher-quality financial reports compared to Non-Gazelle firms.

Research on Cost of Debt

Prior research on publicly traded firms suggests that financial reporting aids investment efficiency by reducing adverse selection, liquidity risk and information risk (Diamond and Verrecchia, 1991; Leuz and Verrecchia, 2000; Easley and O'Hara, 2004; Francis et al., 2005; Lambert et al., 2007; Chen et al., 2011). Diamond and Verrecchia (1991) develop a model showing that in most cases, increased disclosure results in reduced information asymmetry by providing information about a firm's potential future cash flows, which in turn improves market liquidity and decreases the cost of capital for those firms (Diamond and Verrecchia, 1991). This model has since been tested in several studies, such as Lambert et al. (2007) which demonstrates that the quality of accounting information influences cost of capital directly and indirectly, and Francis et al.'s (2005) study that documents the equity market pricing of accrual quality. However, most prior research examines financial reporting quality among publicly traded companies as opposed to private companies and it could be argued that this reasoning may not apply for privately held firms where lenders may rely on other sources of information than financial information data, such as information about the character and reliability of the firm's owner (Berger and Udell, 2002). Nevertheless, there is reason to believe that financial reporting of private companies is useful for debt financing as well. Small firms are more dependent on bank finance and other financial institutions for external funding compared to large firms which have access to public capital markets (Berger and Udell, 2002). Chen et al. (2011) investigate financial reporting quality among private firms from emerging markets and find that financial reporting quality increases if firms are bank financed and decreases when incentives to minimize taxation exist. Further, Paananen et al. (2016) create an index which captures choices of accounting standards, auditor quality and board size that reflect improvements in the information environment, and investigate the causes and consequences of improvements in the information environment for a sample of Swedish small and mid-sized firms. They find that increases in short-term financing trigger improvements in the information environment: the most common actions are to switch to a Big Four auditor or a chartered accountant and to add independent board members. These improvements result in a switch to more long-term debt and a reduction of the cost of debt.

To conclude, it seems fair to argue that small privately held firms to a large extent are bank financed and have incentives to minimize taxes, although we argue that Gazelles need external funding to a greater degree compared to Non-Gazelles to finance their rapid growth, and therefore have an incentive to produce higher-quality financial reporting in order to raise debt capital, and the higher quality of Gazelles' financial reporting helps creditors to assess the risk, resulting in a lower cost of debt. Based on the above we predict the following:

H2: Privately held Gazelle firms experience a lower cost of debt compared to Non-Gazelle firms.

RESEARCH DESIGN

We examine the quality of financial reporting information among different types of privately held small firms. Given our interest in entrepreneurial settings characterized by high growth, we investigate whether Gazelles are more prone to maintain a higher quality of financial reporting compared to Non-Gazelles, and whether this is reflected in their cost of debt. The first part of our research design develops a determinant model to establish that our proxy for capturing Gazelles is in agreement with characteristics suggested by prior research on Gazelles. We then use this model to carry out the Heckman two-step procedure controlling for endogeneity in all subsequent tests. We use three measures to capture the quality of financial reporting. These measures are two accrual-based measures: accruals persistence relative to cash flows and the degree of conservatism; and a measure of prevalence of earnings management measured as the association between reported change in EBIT and prior year's accumulated closing balance of tax appropriations, that is, whether firms manipulate earnings when the room to manoeuvre using legal tax appropriations is exhausted or close to being exhausted. Finally, to capture differences across Gazelles and Non-Gazelles' cost of debt we use a model regressing interest rate expenses as a measure of cost of debt on an indicator for Gazelles, and a number of control variables identified by prior research.

Determinants Test of the Construct Used to Define Gazelles

We define Gazelles as small privately held firms that double their growth in three years and have more than ten employees. In order to validate whether our definition of Gazelles is comparable to prior research on Gazelles, we estimate a binary logit model using previously identified characteristics. Our first characteristics are age (*AGE*) and size (*SIZE*), since prior research suggests that Gazelles are small and relatively young firms (Birch, 1979; Birch and Medoff, 1994; Davidsson et al., 2002; Henrekson and Johansson, 2010). Moreover, prior research also shows that Gazelles are more innovative than Non-Gazelles, especially firms from countries known for their highly developed technological sector (Hölzl, 2009). We therefore include a variable for level of investment in terms of research and development (R&D) capitalization (*R&DCAP*). We also include a variable capturing region (*REGION*), since some research finds that most Gazelles are located in larger metropolitan areas (Davidsson et al., 1994; Davidsson, 1995). Finally, in order to capture differences in the use of financial services provided by accounting firms, we also include two variables capturing the relative amounts spent on auditing (*AUDITFEE*) and other services (*SERVFEE*). Based on the above we specify the following model:

$$Gazelle \ (0, 1)_i = \beta_0 + \beta_1 SIZE_{i,t} + \beta_2 AGE_{i,t} + \beta_3 R\&D \ CAP_{i,t} + \beta_4 REGION_{i,t} + \beta_5 AUDITFEE_{i,t} + \beta_6 SERVFEE_{i,t} + \varepsilon_{i,t} \qquad (13.1)$$

Models to Test Financial Reporting Quality across Gazelles and Non-Gazelles

To investigate the difference in quality of financial reporting across Gazelle and Non-Gazelle firms, we use three models. The extant literature tends to use either market-related or accounting-related measures to proxy for accounting quality (Dechow and Dichev, 2002; Schipper and Vincent, 2003; Barth et al., 2008). We examine privately owned companies and therefore we look at accounting-related measures only. However, as a second step we also examine the logical consequence of financial reporting quality, which is the level of cost of debt.

Our first measure of financial reporting quality is accrual persistence relative to cash flows and we capture this using the following model (Givoly et al., 2010):

$$OI_{i,t+1} = \beta_0 + \beta_1 CF_{i,t} + \beta_2 ACCR_{i,t} + \beta_3 GAZELLE_i + \beta_4 GAZELLE_i * CF_{i,t}$$
$$+ \beta_5 GAZELLE_i * ACCR_{i,t} + \beta_k CONTROLS_{i,t} + \varepsilon_{i,t} \qquad (13.2)$$

$$CONTROLS_{i,t} = \{+SIZE_{i,t} + LEV_{i,t} + GROWTH_{i,t}\}$$

where *OI* is operating income after depreciation, *CF* is operating cash flow component of earnings measured as the cash flow part of the total operating income defined as *OI* minus *ACCR*. *ACCR*, in turn, is proxied using the change in net operating assets (*NOA*) between year *t*–1 and *t*. *NOA* comprise all short-term operating assets such as inventories and long-lived assets used for the operation of the business minus operating liabilities. All continuous variables are tested using the natural log. We assess the model by comparing the incremental difference in persistence of earnings and cash flows across Gazelles and Non-Gazelles represented by β_4 and β_5. We also control for size (*SIZE*) measured as the natural log of total assets, leverage (*LEV*) measured as shareholders' equity to total assets, and growth (*GROWTH*) measured as the change in sales compared to prior year since prior research suggests that these factors affect reported earnings (Van Tendeloo and Vanstraelen, 2008; Givoly et al., 2010; Chen et al., 2011).

For our second test of financial reporting quality we use conservatism. Following prior research we assume that a more timely recognition of losses compared to gains produces a systematic asymmetric undervaluation of net assets (Givoly et al., 2007; Watts, 2003; Givoly et al., 2010). The question whether conservatism reflects high-quality accounting is controversial: some argue that conservatism creates hidden reserves which is used for earnings management, while others argue that conservatism is beneficial for evaluating stewardship (Penman and Zhang, 2002; O'Connell, 2007; Givoly et al., 2010). Given the different views of the appropriateness of this test, we use it in conjunction with other tests such as the above test of accrual persistence relative to cash flows and an earnings management test. Following prior research, we measure conservatism as the speed at which earnings reflect bad news compared to good news (Basu, 1997; Ball and Shivakumar, 2005). We assess this speed by comparing β_3 across Gazelles and Non-Gazelles from the following regression:

$$\Delta EBIT_{i,t} = \beta_0 + \beta_1 D\Delta EBIT_{i,t-1} + \beta_2 \Delta EBIT_{i,t-1} + \beta_3 GAZELLE_i +$$
$$\beta_4 D\Delta EBIT_{i,t-1} * \Delta EBIT_{i,t-1} + \beta_5 GAZELLE_i * D\Delta EBIT_{i,t-1} + \beta_6 GAZELLE_i$$
$$* \Delta EBIT_{i,t-1} + \beta_7 GAZELLE_i * D\Delta EBIT_{i,t-1} * \Delta EBIT_{i,t-1} + \varepsilon_{i,t-1} \qquad (13.3)$$

where $\Delta EBIT$ is the change in EBIT between year t and $t-1$ and $D\Delta EBIT$ is a dummy variable equal to 1e if $\Delta EBIT$ is negative and 0 otherwise. We assume that reporting of gains is deferred until cash flows are realized and therefore gains are the persistent positive component of income in that it will not reverse while losses are recognized more timely decreasing income, which results in subsequent reversals (Givoly et al., 2010). We therefore predict that $\beta_2 = 0$ and $\beta_2 + \beta_4 < 0$. In addition, we analyse the difference between Gazelles and Non-Gazelles by comparing β_4 and β_7, if $\beta_7 < \beta_4$, then Gazelles are recognising losses in a more timely fashion than Non-Gazelles.

Finally, our third measure to assess differences in financial reporting quality across Gazelles and Non-Gazelles is a proxy capturing the tendency to manipulate earnings. We posit that Gazelles are less prone to engage in manipulation of earnings compared to Non-Gazelles, since they need to raise external capital to finance their high growth and they thereby need to provide external stakeholders with information to obtain that funding (Hope et al., 2011). Prior research uses a measure capturing the tendency of reporting a small positive income (Barth et al., 2008; Givoly et al., 2010). For the purposes of this study, however, we exploit the regulatory link between accounting and taxation in Sweden and analyse negative changes in EBIT when the room to manoeuvre using allowed tax appropriations is exhausted or close to exhaustion. Under Swedish generally accepted accounting principles (GAAP), all changes made to tax appropriations must be reported on the face of the income statement, and accumulated appropriations are shown on the face of the balance sheet.[4] We design a test regressing change in EBIT on Gazelles and the level of accumulated tax appropriations at the end of the previous year. The rationale is that a company with high levels of appropriations would be more prone to manage earnings to avoid taxation. We specify the following model:

$$\Delta EBIT_{i,t} = \beta_0 + \beta_1 GAZELLE_i + \beta_2 APPR_{i,t-1} + \beta_3 GAZELLE * APPR_{i,t-1} + \beta_4 QRATIO_{i,t} + \beta_5 \Delta SALES_{i,t} + \beta_6 SIZE_{i,t} + \beta_7 LEV_{i,t} + \varepsilon_{i,t} \qquad (13.4)$$

We interpret a negative association between $APPR$ from the previous year end and the change in $EBIT$ as a sign of earnings management to avoid taxes controlling for other reasons for a decrease in income. We predict a positive coefficient for the variable $GAZELLE$ as we expect these firms to be more profitable. In addition, we also predict that the coefficient for the interaction of $GAZELLE$ and $APPR$ to be positive, indicating that Gazelles are less likely to engage in earnings management. We control for $QRATIO$ as the short-term liquidity would affect the likelihood that firms engage in earnings management. Similarly, we also control for change in sales since this directly affects the change in *EBIT*, and also for size (*SIZE*) and leverage (*LEV*).

Model to Compare Cost of Debt across Gazelles and Non-Gazelles

We posit that a higher quality of financial reporting of Gazelles results in a reduced cost of debt. We assess this assertion using a model where the dependent variable is the percentage cost of debt (*INTRATE*) and the test variable is an indicator variable reflecting whether a firm is a Gazelle or not. We predict that the coefficient for the variable *GAZELLE* is negative and statistically significant.

We also include variables controlling for other factors affecting creditors' interest rate decisions. Prior research show that firms with greater financial reporting creditability (that is, annual financial statements reviewed by an auditor) experience significantly fewer perceived problems in gaining access to external finance (Hope et al., 2011). Minnis (2011) uses a large proprietary database of privately held US firms for which the financial statements audits are not mandated. He finds that accruals from audited financial statements are better predictors of future cash flow and therefore more informative and influence lenders' decisions. Moreover, Lisowsky and Minnis (2014) examine the financial statement production of privately held US firms and show that younger, high-growth firms with intangible assets and losses are more likely to engage an auditor when attracting external capital, both debt and equity. Firms raising new capital without an audit are typically mature, profitable firms with tangible assets. Dedman et al. (2014) show that companies in the UK are more likely to purchase audits after the mandate is relaxed in 2004 if they have greater agency costs, are riskier, wish to raise capital, purchase non-audit service from their auditor, and exhibit greater demand for audit assurance in the mandatory regime.

Moreover, variation in the characteristics of the auditors such as auditor size, qualification and opinion may affect the quality of verification and the cost of debt. Karjalainen (2011) studies a sample of privately held firms in Finland and he shows that audit quality, captured as Big Four audits and number of auditors, affects firms' ability to access capital. Further, he finds that Big Four audits, and audits conducted by more than one responsible auditor, are associated with a decrease in cost of capital. However, there are also studies that imply that Big Four audits do not contribute to the pricing of debt in private firms (Chaney et al., 2004; Fortin and Pittman, 2007). In several Scandinavian countries a privately held firm can choose between two different types of qualified auditors: a chartered accountant or an approved public accountant. Therefore, we control for Big Four (*BIG4*) and chartered accountant (*CHARTERED*) audits, since a perceived high-quality audit would decrease the creditor's risk to lend capital. Further, we control for whether the firms received a qualified audit opinion (*AUDIT_OP*), since that would increase the creditors' risk. In addition, we also control for board size (*BOARD*) since prior research suggests that independent board members increase the level of corporate governance (Armstrong et al., 2010).

Prior research emphasizes the role of independent board members for effective corporate governance (Armstrong et al., 2010). Jaggi et al. (2009) find that board independence is important for financial reporting quality as it is associated with less opportunistic earnings management behaviour. We presume that if the number of board members is greater, external parties in addition to the owner-manager are likely to be on the board of directors.

We also control for the proportion of utilized overdraft at the end of the previous year (*OVERDRAFT*) and leverage (*LEV*) to control for the level of borrowing affecting interest rates. Finally, we also control for size (*SIZE*) and the ongoing recession (*RECESSION*). Recession is a variable equal to 1 from 2008 onwards and 0 otherwise. The model is specified as below:

$$INTRATE_{i,t} = \beta_0 + \beta_1 GAZELLE_i + \beta_2 BIG4_{i,t} + \beta_3 CHARTERED_{i,t} + \beta_4 AUDIT\_OP_{i,t} + \beta_5 BOARD_{i,t} + \beta_6 OVERDRAFT_{i,t-1} + \beta_7 SIZE_{i,t} + \beta_8 LEV_{i,t} + \beta_9 RECESSION + \varepsilon_{i,t} \quad (13.5)$$

SAMPLE SELECTION PROCESS

All limited liability companies domiciled in Sweden are regulated under the Companies Act (CA).[5] This Act stipulates that these firms provide an audited annual report.[6] These reports are prepared under the Bookkeeping Act[7] and the Annual Accounts Act[8] which provide a framework of generally accepted accounting principles. Swedish enterprises have to register with the Swedish Companies Registration Office (Bolagsverket) and supply this government body with annual reports.[9] Retriever Sverige AB (Retriever) supplies the information from these annual reports to subscribers in a downloadable format. We extracted Swedish small company data from 2002 to 2011, using 2002 as the base year to calculate the growth rate of sales in order to identify Gazelle firms. That is, we used data from 2002 to 2011 to categorize small firms into Gazelles and Non-Gazelles, defining Gazelles as firms that double their sales in three years during any

Table 13.1   Sample selection process

	Firms	Firm-year observations
All Swedish SMEs* not part of a group (2002–11)	29058	135888
Less 2002 to 2004 observations used to identify Gazelles and lagged variables (2004)	−2495	−18970
Less observations 2011 observations used for lead variables	−7016	−26027
Missing data	−13829	−46020
Total	5718	44871
From which a random sample for the years 2005 to 2010 is extracted	2000	12000
Missing data	−213	−5289
	1787	6711
Of which:		
Gazelles	590	2171
Non-Gazelles	1197	4540

Note: * For the purposes of our study, we define small and medium-sized enterprises (SMEs) as companies with ten or more employees and revenues more than €2 and less than €50 million.

three years during 2002 and 2011. We then excluded 2002 to 2004 as these data were used to identify Gazelles and to create lagged variables, and we also excluded 2011 since this part of the data was used to create lead variables. This yields a total dataset of 5718 firms and 44871 firm-year observations, after excluding firm-year observations with missing data. We drew a random sample of 2000 firms 12000 firm-year observations from this dataset. We manually collected data related to type of auditor, audit fees, audit opinions and number of board members. The final sample used for our analysis of financial reporting quality levels and cost of debt capital comprises 1787 firms (6711 firm-year observations), of which 590 firms (2171 firm-year observations) are Gazelles and 1197 firms (4540 firm-year observations) are Non-Gazelles. Finally, regional information was extracted from databases provided by Statistics of Sweden.[10] Table 13.1 shows the sample selection process for data used for our analysis.

Table 13.2 shows that the industry distribution across Gazelles and Non-Gazelles is fairly similar, with most firms operating in the retail, construction, manufacturing and transport sectors. The only material difference across the two groups of firms is that the number of firms in the consulting sector is somewhat larger among Gazelles (9 per cent) compared to Non-Gazelles (4 per cent).

Table 13.2   Industry distribution across Gazelles and Non-Gazelles

Industry	Gazelles			Non-Gazelles		
	Firms	Firm-year observations	%	Firms	Firm-year observations	%
Retail	102	384	18	286	1055	23
Construction	117	392	18	184	697	15
Manufacturing	97	379	17	228	905	20
Transport	56	194	9	115	440	10
Consulting	51	183	9	47	159	4
Hotel and restaurants	22	80	4	53	183	4
Financial services	19	66	3	45	170	4
Real estate	16	64	3	49	183	4
Care	16	60	3	41	179	4
Education	18	58	2	24	102	2
Information technology	15	49	2	12	52	1
Other	61	262	12	113	415	9
Total	590	2171	100	1197	4540	100

RESULTS

Our analysis comprises four sections. We start with an analysis and discussion on descriptive statistics followed by the analysis of our test of determinants of Gazelles versus Non-Gazelles that we use as the selection model in a two-step Heckman model to control for endogeneity. We then analyse and discuss our test of accounting quality levels across Gazelles and Non-Gazelles. We end our analysis by discussing our results related to differences in cost of debt across Gazelles and Non-Gazelles.

Descriptive Statistics

Table 13.3, Panel A provides descriptive statistics for the variables used to control for endogeneity related to our measure of Gazelles. As expected, we find that Gazelles are larger and younger than Non-Gazelles; however, the difference is not statistically significant. We also find that Gazelles report capitalized R&D to a significantly greater extent compared to Non-Gazelles (p-value < 0.01). We interpret this difference as Gazelles being more prone to engage in innovative projects which most likely are a part of a strategy for future growth. It should also be noted that when Gazelles are capitalizing R&D they are actually using an accounting treatment not allowed (or to a lesser extent allowed) under SFASC/IFRS at that point

Table 13.3   *Descriptive statistics across firm type*

Panel A: Descriptive statistics of variables used for determinants test by firm type

Variable	Firm type	N	Mean	Median	Standard deviation
SIZE	Gazelle	2171	8.583	9.038	1.980
SIZE	Non-Gazelle	4540	8.565	8.996	2.001
Difference			0.018	0.042	
AGE	Gazelle	2171	19.719	17.000	11.852
AGE	Non-Gazelle	4540	25.852	22.000	14.358
Difference			−6.133***	−5.000***	
R&DCAP	Gazelle	2171	0.000	0.000	0.003
R&DCAP	Non-Gazelle	4540	0.000	0.000	0.002
Difference			0.000***	0.000**	
REGION	Gazelle	2171	0.429	0.000	0.495
REGION	Non-Gazelle	4540	0.383	0.000	0.486
Difference			−0.046	0.000	
AUDITFEE	Gazelle	2171	0.004	0.002	0.004
AUDITFEE	Non-Gazelle	4540	0.004	0.002	0.004
Difference			0.000	0.000***	
SERVFEE	Gazelle	2171	0.002	0.001	0.005
SERVFEE	Non-Gazelle	4540	0.003	0.001	0.005
Difference			−0.001***	−0.000***	

Panel B: Descriptive statistics of variables used for tests of accounting quality by firm type

Variable	Firm type	N	Mean	Median	Standard deviation
OI	Gazelle	2171	0.423	0.107	1.079
OI	Non-Gazelle	4540	0.256	0.094	0.720
Difference			0.167***	0.013***	
CF	Gazelle	2171	0.101	0.175	1.586
CF	Non-Gazelle	4540	0.186	0.138	0.888
Difference			−0.085***	0.037***	
ACCR	Gazelle	2171	0.396	0.053	1.839
ACCR	Non-Gazelle	4540	0.133	0.038	0965
Difference			0.263***	0.015**	
ΔEBIT	Gazelle	2171	−0.014	0.003	0.176
ΔEBIT	Non-Gazelle	4540	−0.004	0.002	0.105
Difference			−0.010***	0.001**	
APPR	Gazelle	2171	0.079	0.049	0.091
APPR	Non-Gazelle	4540	0.090	0.061	0.100
Difference			−0.011***	−0.012***	

Table 13.3   (continued)

Panel C: Descriptive statistics of variable used for test of cost of debt by firm type

Variable	Firm type	N	Mean	Median	Standard deviation
INTRATE	Gazelle	2171	2.045	1.580	2.062
INTRATE	Non-Gazelle	4540	2.185	1.790	2.169
Difference			−0.140**	−0.210**	

Panel D: Descriptive statistics of control variables by firm type

Variable	Firm Type	N	Mean	Median	Standard deviation
BIG4	Gazelle	2171	0.457	0.000	0.498
BIG4	Non-Gazelle	4540	0.437	0.000	0.496
Difference			−0.020	0.000	
CHARTERED	Gazelle	2171	0.670	1.000	0.470
CHARTERED	Non-Gazelle	4540	0.649	1.000	0.477
Difference			0.021*	0.000*	
AUDIT_OP	Gazelle	2171	0.070	0.000	0.255
AUDIT_OP	Non-Gazelle	4540	0.056	0.000	0.230
Difference			0.014**	0.000*	
BOARD	Gazelle	2171	2.390	2.000	1.611
BOARD	Non-Gazelle	4540	2.449	2.000	1.789
Difference			0.059	0.000	
LEV	Gazelle	2171	0.283	0.251	0.211
LEV	Non-Gazelle	4540	0.303	0.277	0.201
Difference			−0.020***	0.026***	
QRATIO	Gazelle	2171	1.292	1.124	0.866
QRATIO	Non-Gazelle	4540	1.304	1.094	0.893
Difference			−0.012	0.030	
ΔSALES	Gazelle	2171	−0.028	0.079	0.718
ΔSALES	Non-Gazelle	4540	−0.007	0.040	0.325
Difference			0.021	0.039***	
OVERDRAFT	Gazelle	1265	0.292	0.000	0.469
OVERDRAFT	Non-Gazelle	2885	0.248	0.000	0.371
Difference			0.044***	0.000***	

Panel E: Descriptive statistics of cost of debt by firm type and pre-recession and recession

	Pre-recession (year 2005 to 2007)			Recession (year 2008 to 2010)				
	Mean	Median	Std dev.		Mean	Median	Std dev.	Difference	Difference
Gazelles N = 1135	1.893	1.540	1.845	Gazelles N = 1037	2.212	1.605	2.268	−0.319***	−0.065**

Table 13.3   (continued)

Panel E: Descriptive statistics of cost of debt by firm type and pre-recession and recession

Pre-recession (year 2005 to 2007)			Recession (year 2008 to 2010)				
Mean	Median	Std dev.		Mean	Median	Std dev.	Difference Difference
Non-Gazelles	2.020	1.770	1.876	Non-Gazelles	2.375	1.830	2.453	−0.355*** −0.060***
N = 2445				N = 2095			
Difference	−0.013* −0.230**				−0.163* −0.225		

Notes:
*, **, *** = Significant at the 0.10, 0.05 and 0.01 levels, respectively.
All continuous variables are winsorized on the 1% level.
SIZE is the natural log of total assets.
AGE is the number of years between the firm registration date and year *t*.
R&DCAP is the total R&D balance reported in the balance sheet in year *t* scaled by total assets.
REGION is a dummy variable taking equal to 1 if the firm is operating in the two major Swedish metropolitan regions (Stockholm and Göteborg).
AUDITFEE is the total audit fee scaled by total assets for year *t*.
SERVFEE is the total fee for other accounting services scaled by total assets for year *t*.
OI_{t+1} is the operating income measured as earnings before interest and tax (EBIT) scaled by net operating assets (NOA) at time *t*.
CF_t is cash flow from operation measured as EBIT in year *t* scaled by NOA in year *t* − 1, minus *ACCR*.
$ACCR_t$ is the change in NOA from year *t* − 1 to *t*, deflated by NOA at *t*−1.
NOA is the net operating assets calculated as total current assets less current liabilities.
$\Delta EBIT_{t-1}$ is the change in EBIT from year *t* − 1 to year *t* scaled by sales.
$D\Delta EBIT_{t-1}$ is a dummy variable equal to one if $\Delta EBIT_{t-1} < 0$ and zero otherwise.
APPR is accumulated appropriations balance scaled by total assets.
INTRATE is the interest expense charged divided by the average total long-term liabilities.
BIG4 is a dummy variable equal to 1 if the firm uses a Big Four auditor firm.
CHARTERED_ACC is a dummy variable if the firm uses a qualified chartered accountant.
AUDIT_OP is a dummy variable equal to 1 if the company received a qualified audit opinion.
BOARD is the number of board members.
LEV is total liabilities divided by total assets.
QRATIO is the quick ratio defined as current assets minus inventory divided by current liabilities.
$\Delta SALES$ is the percentage change in sales between year *t* and *t*−1.
OVERDRAFT is the utilized proportion of the company overdraft.

in time, which might be an indication that Gazelles hypothetically would be even less likely to opt for a full adoption of SFASC/IFRS compared to Non-Gazelles. We do not find any differences in prevalence of Gazelles and Non-Gazelles across different regions. Finally, we find that Gazelles tend to pay less audit and service fees compared to Non-Gazelles, which we interpret as these companies being more likely to prefer to keep this expertise within the company. Overall, we interpret the results of this univariate analysis as an indication that our proxy for Gazelles is comparable to findings of prior research.

Turning to descriptive statistics related to our tests of accounting quality shown in Table 13.3, Panel B, we find that the operating income (*OI*) scaled by net operating assets is significantly higher for the Gazelles (p-value < 0.01). We also find that the accrual component of earnings (*ACCR*) is significantly larger among Gazelles compared to Non-Gazelles (p-values < 0.01). We also find that the change in EBIT is greater among Gazelles but the difference is very small. This result might be explained by the high growth among Gazelles. However, we find that the average operating cash flows (*CF*) of Non-Gazelles is significantly larger compared to Gazelles (p-value < 0.01), while the median operating cash flows is higher among Gazelles. We acknowledge that this is due to a skewed distribution, and the means of all of the above variables used to test accounting quality should be interpreted with caution.[11] The measure used to capture the incentive to resort to earnings management, accumulated appropriations (*APPR*) is significantly smaller among Gazelles. This might be explained by the difference in age across the two groups: it takes five years to maximize the appropriations allowed, and Gazelles are significantly younger than Non-Gazelles. Panel C, Table 13.3 shows descriptive statistics for the dependent variable of our test of cost of debt implications (*INTRATE*) across Gazelles and Non-Gazelles. The result of a univariate comparison supports our prediction that Gazelles are experiencing a lower cost of debt (p-value < 0.05).

Finally, Table 13.3, Panel D provides descriptive statistics for the control variables used in various models to test earnings management and cost of debt. We find no significant difference in opting to use a Big Four auditor (*BIG4*) or a chartered accountant (*CHARTERED*) across the two groups; around 45 per cent of all small firms chose a Big Four auditor and about 65 per cent chose a chartered accountant. We find some significant differences in frequency of qualified audit reports (*QUALIFIED*), where Gazelles are more likely to receive a qualified audit report. We find that the number of board members (*BOARD*) is smaller compared to Non-Gazelles, though the difference is not significant. Gazelles are also significantly less leveraged (*LEV*), considering that Gazelles are utilizing their overdraft (*OVERDRAFT*) to a greater extent and have a lower quick ratio (*Q-RATIO*); we interpret this as Non-Gazelles relying on other funding sources, such as loans, while Gazelles rely heavily on current capital and their overdraft to fund their expansion. Finally, we find that Gazelles' sales increases (*ΔSALES*) are significantly higher.

The final part of Table 13.3, Panel E, compares the cost of debt before and after the start of the recession. The analysis reveals that Gazelles are experiencing a lower level of cost of debt (*INTRATE*) compared to Non-Gazelles both before and after the recession, and both groups have experienced a slight increase since the start of the recession. The question is whether this difference is driven by an increase in reliance on interest-bearing debt or an increase in interest rates.

Table 13.4, Panel A describes the pairwise correlations between the variables used in the two-step Heckman procedure to control for endogeneity. We find that the pairwise correlations confirm the univariate comparisons across means and medians and Gazelles seem to be significantly younger (*AGE*), invest more in R&D (*R&DCAP*), and use less service from accounting firms (*SERVFEE*). In addition, they are also more likely to locate in a metro area (*METRO*). Further, Panels B and C of Table 13.4 show that Gazelles are more profitable (*OI*), have a lower cash flow level (*CF*), higher level of accruals (*ACCR*), but are less leveraged (*LEV*). We interpret this as Gazelles using current liquid assets to a greater extent to fund their growth compared to Non-Gazelles. This reliance on non-interest-bearing capital could partially explain the lower interest rate among Gazelles. We also see that the recession has reduced profitability and size (*SIZE*), and increased leverage across the board, which stands to reason. We also find that the reduction in EBIT (*ΔEBIT*) is significantly larger among Gazelles, especially during the recession.

Turning to Panel D, as in the means and medians comparisons above, we see that Gazelles exhibit significantly lower levels of accumulated appropriations (*APPR*). We also find that accumulated appropriations are positively related to current liquidity (*Q-RATIO*) which makes sense since high profitability increases cash flow levels and a greater used of allowed tax appropriations. Finally, Panel E, Table 13.4 reveals the pairwise correlations of the variables used for the test of cost of debt. Overall, interest rates (*INTRATE*) among Gazelles are lower and interest rates are significantly increased by the recession (as mentioned above, this may be caused by a greater use of interest-bearing capital), qualified audit opinions (*AUDIT_OP*), the more of the overdraft a firms utilize (*OVERDRAFT*), and the larger the company is (*SIZE*). The interest rates (*INTRATE*) decrease with the members on the board of directors (*BOARD*) and leverage (*LEV*). We also find that Gazelles utilize the overdraft (*OVERDRAFT*) to a significantly higher extent and are less leveraged (*LEV*), supporting the notion that they tend to utilize current liquid assets and their overdraft to finance their growth. Moreover, we see that Gazelles are slightly more likely to use a chartered accountant (*CHARTERED*) compared to Non-Gazelles, and are slightly more likely

Table 13.4   Pairwise correlations

Panel A: Variables used to control for endogeneity

	GAZELLE	RECESSION	SIZE	AGE	R&DCAP	REGION	AUDITFEE	SERVFEE
GAZELLE	1.00							
RECESSION	0.015	1.00						
SIZE	0.00	−0.45***	1.00					
AGE	−0.21***	−0.06***	0.12***	1.00				
R&DCAP	0.04***	0.00	0.01	−0.04***	1.00			
REGION	0.04***	−0.00	−0.02	−0.07***	0.01	1.00		
AUDITFEE	−0.00	0.00	−0.27***	−0.14***	0.03**	0.14***	1.00	
SERVFEE	−0.03***	−0.01	−0.14***	−0.02	−0.00	−0.08***	0.35***	1.00

Panel B: Variables used to test persistence of accruals

	GAZELLE	RECESSION	OI	CF	ACCR	SIZE	LEV
GAZELLE	1.00						
RECESSION	0.01	1.00					
OI	0.09***	−0.10***	1.00				
CF	−0.03***	−0.01	0.10***	1.00			
ACCR	0.09***	0.00	−0.00	−0.60***	1.00		
SIZE	0.00	−0.45***	−0.10***	−0.01	0.02	1.00	
LEV	−0.05***	0.05***	−0.05***	−0.08	0.13***	0.08***	1.00

Panel C: Variables used to test conservatism

	GAZELLE	RECESSION	ΔEBIT
GAZELLE	1.00		
RECESSION	0.01	1.00	
ΔEBIT	-0.04***	-0.09***	1.00

Panel D: Variables used to test earnings management

	GAZELLE	RECESSION	APPR	Q-RATIO	ΔSALES	SIZE	LEV
GAZELLE	1.00						
RECESSION	0.02	1.00					
APPR	-0.05***	-0.00	1.00				
QRATIO	-0.01	0.03**	0.15***	1.00			
ΔSALES	-0.02	-0.08***	0.02	-0.02*	1.00		
SIZE	0.00	-0.45***	-0.03**	0.02*	0.13***	1.00	
LEV	-0.05***	0.05***	0.01	0.64***	0.00	0.08***	1.00

Panel E: Variables used to test cost of debt

	INTRATE	GAZELLE	RECESSION	BIG4	CHARTERED	AUDIT_OP	BOARD	OVER DRAFT	SIZE	LEV
INTRATE	1.00									
GAZELLE	-0.03**	1.00								
RECESSION	0.08***	0.01	1.00							
BIG4	-0.01	0.02	-0.01	1.00						
CHARTERED	0.01	0.02*	0.02*	-0.01	1.00					
AUDIT_CP	0.12***	0.03**	0.03***	0.03***	-0.06***	1.00				
BOARD	-0.03**	-0.02	0.00	0.00	0.11***	-0.11***	1.00			
OVERDRAFT	0.26***	0.05***	0.05***	-0.02	0.02	0.11***	0.01	1.00		
SIZE	0.12***	0.12***	0.00	-0.45***	0.08***	-0.08***	0.19***	0.05***	1.00	
LEV	-0.20***	-0.20***	-0.05***	0.05***	0.014	-0.20***	0.07***	-0.25***	0.08***	1.00

353

to end up with qualified auditor opinions (*AUDIT_OP*). Finally, we also find that the recession has significantly increased the number of qualified audit opinions, decreased firm size, and increased leverage across the board.

Variables Used to Control for Endogeneity

As shown in Table 13.5, our logit results of the test of determinants for Gazelles suggested by prior research generally concur with the findings of the above univariate analysis. We find that Gazelles are larger (p-value < 0.05) and younger than their Non-Gazelle counterparts (p-values < 0.01). However, no other variable in the model is significant. Despite the fact that we do not find any evidence of more investments in R&D, a higher concentration in metro areas or a greater use of accounting firms consultation, we are reasonably confident that our proxy to capture Gazelles allows cross-study comparisons, and we use this model to control for

Table 13.5   Results test of the proxy used for identifying gazelles

$Gazelle\ (0,\ 1)_i = \beta_0 + \beta_1 SIZE_{i,t} + \beta_2 AGE_{i,t} + \beta_3 R\&DCAP_{i,t} + \beta_4 REGION_{i,t} + \beta_5 AUDITFEE_{i,t} + \beta_6 SERVFEE_{i,t} + \varepsilon_{i,t}$

Variable	Coefficient	Robust std error	p-value
Intercept	0.291	0.126	0.021
SIZE	0.018	0.009	0.048
AGE	−0.007	0.001	0.000
R&DCAP	4.715	4.103	0.251
REGION	0.027	0.024	0.259
AUDITFEE	−0.663	2.949	0.822
SERVFEE	−1.902	2.117	0.369
YEAR	Yes		
INDUSTRY	Yes		
Pseudo R^2	0.065		
N	6711		

Note:
SIZE is the natural log of total assets.
AGE is the number of years between the firm registration date and year *t*.
R&DCAP is the total R&D balance reported in the balance sheet in year *t* scaled by total assets.
REGION is a dummy variable taking equal to 1 if the firm is operating in the two major Swedish metropolitan regions (Stockholm and Göteborg).
AUDITFEE is the total audit fee scaled by total assets for year *t*.
SERVFEE is the total fee for other accounting services scaled by total assets for year *t*.

endogeneity in the Heckman two-stage procedure for all other tests presented below.

Tests of Financial Reporting Quality across Gazelles and Non-Gazelles

We first test financial reporting quality, measured as the persistence of the accrual components of earnings across Gazelles and Non-Gazelles. We test the persistence of accruals by comparing the coefficients of the accrual ($ACCR$) and the cash flow (CF) components of earnings. If the accrual component is more persistent compared to the cash flows component, then it is the significantly larger of the two.

Table 13.6 shows that the coefficient for the cash flow component for Non-Gazelles is larger than the accrual component of earnings, suggesting that the accrual component of earnings is less important for predicting future earnings. Turning to the interaction variables capturing the incremental difference related to Gazelles, contrary to prediction we find similar results. This suggests that the accrual component is not a better indicator of future earnings for either type of firm; however, none of these interaction variables are significant. As shown in Table 13.6, these results are qualitatively similar whether including or not including the various control variables and regardless of controlling for endogeneity, although the control for endogeneity ($LAMBDA$) should be included in the regression since it is significant. Based on the test of differences across coefficients, we conclude that the test of accrual persistence does not support hypothesis 1. Finally, the inverse Mills variable ($LAMBDA$) is significant, suggesting the presence of endogeneity.

As a second test of financial reporting properties we test the degree of conservatism. As discussed above, we test whether or not earnings increases are more persistent than earnings decreases. The results concur with prior research as earnings increases are more persistent than earnings decreases for both groups, and we conclude that financial reporting is overall conservative. As shown in Table 13.7, when controlling for endogeneity we find that $\beta_3 + \beta_6$ is significant and negative (p-value 0.045). However, the interaction variable coefficient representing persistence of earnings declines over earnings decreases for Non-Gazelles (β_3) is not significant. We find that Gazelles exhibit an interaction variable coefficient representing persistence of earnings declines over earnings decreases (β_6), which is positive and significant suggesting that Gazelles' financial reporting is less conservative than that of Non-Gazelles. However, considering the small coefficient (0.0003) in conjunction with the insignificant coefficient for the measure of persistence of earnings declines over earnings decreases for Non-Gazelles (β_3), we conclude that we do not find any

Table 13.6   *Results of tests of persistence of accruals across Gazelles and Non-Gazelles*

$OI_{i,t+1} = \beta_0 + \beta_1 CF_{i,t} + \beta_2 ACCR_{i,t} + \beta_3 GAZELLE_i + \beta_4 GAZELLE_i * CF_{i,t} + \beta_5 GAZELLE_i * ACCR_{i,t} + \beta_k CONTROLS_{i,t} + \varepsilon_{i,t}$

Panel A: Persistence of accruals across Gazelles and Non-Gazelles for the period 2005–10

Variable	Estimation without controlling for endogeneity		Primary variables		Primary and control variables	
	Coefficient	p-value	Coefficient	p-value	Coefficient	p-value
Intercept	−0.213	0.707	−1.226	0.051	0.347	0.631
CF	0.302	0.000	0.304	0.000	0.276	0.000
ACCR	0.271	0.000	0.267	0.000	0.243	0.000
GAZELLE	−0.108	0.520	−0.043	0.797	−0.033	0.894
*GAZELLE * CF*	−0.069	0.385	−0.070	0.375	−0.071	0.354
*GAZELLE * ACCR*	−0.064	0.292	−0.061	0.302	−0.052	0.380
LAMBDA			0.533	0.000	0.366	0.012
CONTROL VARIABLES:						
SIZE					−0.148	0.000
LEV					−0.113	0.786
GROWTH					0.251	0.163
INDUSTRY	Yes		Yes		Yes	
YEAR	Yes		Yes		Yes	
R²	0.244		0.303		0.316	
N	1236		1236		1236	

Statistical tests:		p-value		p-value		p-value
F-test:	$\beta_1 = \beta_2$	0.572	$\beta_1 = \beta_2$	0.481	$\beta_1 = \beta_2$	0.521
F-test:	$\beta_4 = \beta_5$	0.963	$\beta_4 = \beta_5$	0.938	$\beta_4 = \beta_5$	0.862
F-test:	$\beta_1 + \beta_4 = \beta_2 + \beta_5$	0.800	$\beta_1 + \beta_4 = \beta_2 + \beta_5$	0.761	$\beta_1 + \beta_4 = \beta_2 + \beta_5$	0.874

Notes:
$OI_{i,t+1}$ is the natural log of operating income measured as earnings before interest and tax (EBIT) scaled by net operating assets (NOA) at time t.
CF_i is the natural log of cash flow from operation measured as EBIT in year t scaled by NOA in year $t–1$, minus $ACCR$.
$ACCR_i$ is the natural log of the change in NOA from year $t–1$ to t, deflated by NOA at $t–1$.
$GAZELLE$ is a dummy variable equal to 1 if the firm is classified as a Gazelle and 0 otherwise.

Table 13.6 (continued)

NOA is the net operating assets calculated as total equity plus financial liabilities less financial assets.
LAMBDA to control for potential endogeneity related to the variable used to proxy for the decision to apply a fast-growing strategy (becoming a Gazelle), we follow Heckman (1979) and estimate a probit model including the variables age, size, R&D investments, choices related to quality of the audit captured by a dummy for chartered accountant and Big Four, the choice to locate in one of the two metro areas in Sweden, and the audit fee and fees related to other services supplied by the auditors etc. as predictors used to compute an inverse Mills ratio, this ratio is labelled lambda and is included in the above regressions as a control variable. The regression is estimated using 1236 firm-year observation sample generated in the Heckman two-step estimation.
SIZE is the natural log of total assets.
LEV is total liabilities divided by total assets.
GROWTH is a percentage difference in net sales between *t* and *t*–1.

support for hypothesis 1. Finally, the inverse Mills variable (*LAMBDA*) is significant suggesting the presence of endogeneity.

Our third and final test of financial reporting quality is based on tests of the prevalence of earnings management (Barth et al., 2008; Givoly et al., 2010), as shown in Table 13.8. We posit that Gazelles are less prone to engage in manipulation of earnings compared to Non-Gazelles since they need to raise external capital to finance their rapid growth and they therefore need to provide external stakeholders with useful information to raise funding (Hope et al., 2013). For the purposes of this study, we decided not to use the reporting of a small positive income commonly used in prior research because of the link between accounting and taxation in Sweden (Barth et al., 2008; Givoly et al., 2010). Instead, we exploit this regulatory link between accounting and taxation in Sweden and analyse negative changes in EBIT when the room to manoeuvre using allowed tax appropriations is exhausted or close to exhaustion. Under Swedish GAAP, all changes to tax appropriations made must be reported on the face of the income statement and the balance sheet.[12] We test the association between the change in EBIT and the level of accumulated tax appropriations at the end of the previous year and compared Gazelles to Non-Gazelles. The rationale is that profitable companies would maximize the allowed appropriation opportunities and once these are exhausted, a company would have an incentive to manipulate EBIT and this would result in a decrease in EBIT. As noted above, we predict that Gazelles are less likely to resort to downward manipulation of EBIT compared to Non-Gazelles. We find that there is an overall negative change of EBIT for all firms which are most likely explained by the ongoing recession. However, only the negative

Table 13.7   *Results of tests of conservatism of accruals across Gazelles and Non-Gazelles*

$\Delta EBIT_{i,t} = \beta_0 + \beta_1 D\Delta EBIT_{i,t-1} + \beta_2 \Delta EBIT_{i,t-1} + \beta_3 GAZELLE_i + \beta_4 D\Delta EBIT_{i,t-1} * \Delta EBIT_{i,t-1} + \beta_5 GAZELLE_i * D\Delta EBIT_{i,t-1} + \beta_6 GAZELLE_i * \Delta EBIT_{i,t-1} + \beta_7 GAZELLE_i * D\Delta EBIT_{i,t-1} * \Delta EBIT_{i,t-1} + \varepsilon_{i,t-1}$

Variable	No control for endogeneity			Controlling for endogeneity		
	Coefficient	St. dev.	p-value	Coefficient	St. dev.	p-value
Intercept	0.084	0.059	0.015	0.091	0.060	0.127
$D\Delta EBIT_{t-1}$	0.029	0.009	0.002	0.030	0.009	0.001
$\Delta EBIT_{t-1}$	−0.000	0.000	0.001	−0.000	0.000	0.000
$D\Delta EBIT_{t-1} * \Delta EBIT_{t-1}$	−0.193	0.227	0.394	−0.189	0.227	0.404
$GAZELLE$	0.011	0.012	0.340	0.011	0.012	0.321
$GAZELLE * D\Delta EBIT_{t-1}$	−0.009	0.020	0.662	−0.010	0.020	0.612
$GAZELLE * \Delta EBIT_{t-1}$	−0.000	0.000	0.108	−0.000	0.000	0.109
$GAZELLE * D\Delta EBIT_{t-1} * \Delta EBIT_{t-1}$	0.000	0.000	0.005	0.000	0.000	0.008
$SIZE$	0.017	0.004	0.000	0.016	0.004	0.000
LEV	0.024	0.016	0.149	0.022	0.017	0.175
$LAMBDA$				−3.248	1.990	0.046
$INDUSTRY$	Yes			Yes		
$YEAR$	Yes			Yes		
$\beta_4 + \beta_7 = 0$			0.037			0.045
R^2	0.115			0.117		
N	4211			4211		

Notes:
$\Delta EBIT_{i,t-1}$ is the change in EBIT from year t–1 to year t scaled by sales.
$D\Delta EBIT_{i,t-1}$ is a dummy variable equal to 1 if $\Delta EBIT_{i,t-1} < 0$ and 0 otherwise.
$GAZELLE$ is a dummy variable equal to 1 if the firm is classified as a Gazelle and 0 otherwise.
$LAMBDA$ to control for potential endogeneity related to the variable used to proxy for the decision to apply a fast-growing strategy (becoming a Gazelle), for further description please refer to Table 13.6. The regression is estimated using 4211 firm-year observation sample generated in the Heckman two-step estimation.
$SIZE$ is the natural log of total assets.
LEV is total liabilities divided by total assets.

Table 13.8   Results of tests of earnings management across Gazelles and Non-Gazelles

$$\Delta EBIT_{i,t} = \beta_0 + \beta_1 GAZELLE_i + \beta_2 APPR_{i,t-1} + \beta_3 GAZELLE_i * APPR_{i,t} + \beta_4 QRATIO_{i,t} + \beta_5 \Delta SALES_{i,t} + \beta_6 SIZE_{i,t} + \beta_7 LEV_{i,t} + \varepsilon_{i,t}$$

Variable	No control for endogeneity			Controlling for endogeneity		
	Coefficient	St. dev.	p-value	Coefficient	St. dev.	p-value
Intercept	−0.066	0.029	0.023	−0.008	0.354	0.819
GAZELLE	−0.044	0.039	0.256	−0.044	0.039	0.255
APPR	−0.011	0.005	0.037	−0.011	0.005	0.037
GAZELLE * APPR	0.006	0.006	0.282	0.006	0.006	0.290
QRATIO	−0.000	0.003	0.877	−0.000	0.003	0.888
ΔSALES	0.106	0.030	0.001	0.105	0.030	0.000
SIZE	0.007	0.003	0.032	0.007	0.003	0.034
LEV	0.038	0.013	0.003	0.041	0.013	0.001
LAMBDA				−0.036	0.020	0.065
INDUSTRY	Yes			Yes		
YEAR	Yes			Yes		
$\beta_2 < \beta_3$			0.059[a]			0.058[a]
R^2	0.180			0.182		
N	2689			2689		

Notes:
[a] One-tailed test
$\Delta EBIT_{t-1}$ is the change in EBIT from year t–1 to year t scaled by sales.
GAZELLE is a dummy variable equal to 1 if the firm is classified as a Gazelle and 0 otherwise.
APPR is the natural log of accumulated appropriations balance at t–1.
QRATIO is the quick ratio defined as current assets minus inventory divided by current liabilities.
$\Delta SALES$ is the percentage change in sales between year t and t–1.
SIZE is the natural log of total assets.
LEV is total liabilities divided by total assets.
LAMBDA to control for potential endogeneity related to the variable used to proxy for the decision to apply a fast-growing strategy (becoming a Gazelle), for further description please refer to Table 13.6. The regression is estimated using 2689 firm-year observation sample generated in the Heckman two-step estimation.

trend among Non-Gazelles, represented by the intercept, is statistically significant (p-value 0.023).

Further, we find that there is a significant negative association between appropriations and Non-Gazelles (p-value 0.037 regardless of whether we control for endogeneity). We also find that the interaction variable representing the association between change in EBIT and appropriations among Gazelles is positive, however neither the dummy variable representing Gazelles nor the interaction variable is statistically significant. We test the difference between the changes in EBIT related to appropriations across Gazelles and Non-Gazelles and find that Gazelles seems to be significantly less likely to manipulate earnings downwards when the possibility to use allowed appropriations is getting close to be exhausted. However, since none of the coefficients related to Gazelles are significant we cannot say that this supports hypothesis 1. Finally, as in previous tests, the inverse Mills variable (*LAMBDA*) is significant suggesting the presence of endogeneity.

Tests of Cost of Debt across Gazelles and Non-Gazelles

Our final test investigates the capital cost implications of the quality of financial reporting. As discussed above, we predict that small high-growth firms have an incentive to produce high-quality financial reporting to raise capital to fund their growth. Better-quality financial reporting helps creditors to assess the risk and thereby provide a lower cost of capital. We test the cost of credit measured as the interest expense for the year scaled by the average liabilities.

As shown in Table 13.9, we find that Gazelles are experiencing a 0.26 per cent lower interest level, which supports our prediction in hypothesis 2 (p-value = 0.01). Furthermore, we also find that small firms opting for a Big Four accounting firm would decrease their interest expense by about 0.2 per cent. We find this interesting, considering that our univariate test suggests that Gazelles are slightly more committed to the quality of the audit, which is demonstrated by their tendency to opt for qualified chartered accountants to a greater extent than Non-Gazelles. However, it appears that this is not recognized by creditors, who do not differentiate between the choice of a qualified chartered accountant or one who is not.

As can be expected, we find that a qualified audit opinion increases the interest rate of borrowed capital by almost 0.9 per cent. We interpret this as creditors identifying a higher level of corporate governance, assuming that a larger of number of board members is a sign of external parties in addition to the owner-manager on the board of directors. We also control for the proportion of utilized overdraft at the end of the previous year (*OVERDRAFT*) to make sure that we capture cost of debt as opposed to a shift from using current liquid assets to utilizing the overdraft. We find that a higher level of utilization of the overdraft increases cost of debt with almost 0.9 per cent.

We also find that leverage (*LEV*) is significantly and negatively asso-

Table 13.9 Results of tests of cost of debt across Gazelles and Non-Gazelles

$INTRATE_{i,t} = \beta_0 + \beta_1 GAZELLE_i + \beta_2 BIG4_{i,t} + \beta_3 CHARTERED_{i,t} + \beta_4 AUDIT\_OP_{i,t} + \beta_5 BOARD_{i,t} + \beta_6 OVERDRAFT_{i,t-1} + \beta_7 SIZE_{i,t} + \beta_8 LEV_{i,t} + \beta_9 RECESSION + \varepsilon_{i,t}$

Variable	No control for endogeneity			Controlling for endogeneity		
	Coefficient	St. dev.	p-value	Coefficient	St. dev.	p-value
INTRATE	−0.426	0.652	0.513	−0.431	0.738	0.559
GAZELLE	−0.260	0.098	0.008	−0.260	0.101	0.010
BIG4	−0.233	0.099	0.019	−0.233	0.100	0.019
CHARTERED	0.022	0.101	0.828	0.022	0.101	0.828
AUDIT-OP	0.845	0.182	0.000	0.845	0.182	0.000
BOARD	−0.097	0.033	0.003	−0.097	0.032	0.003
OVERDRAFT	0.898	0.187	0.000	0.898	0.188	0.000
SIZE	0.286	0.049	0.000	0.286	0.050	0.000
LEV	−1.839	0.327	0.000	−1.840	0.334	0.000
RECESSION	−1.183	0.096	0.058	−0.183	0.097	0.059
LAMBDA				0.003	0.192	0.988
INDUSTRY	Yes			Yes		
YEAR	Yes			Yes		
R^2	0.169			0.169		
N	2790			2790		

Notes:
INTRATE is the interest expense charged divided by the average total long-term liabilities shown as a percentage.
GAZELLE is a dummy variable equal to 1 if the firm is classified as a Gazelle and 0 otherwise.
BIG4 is a dummy variable equal to 1 if the firm uses a Big Four auditor firm.
CHARTERED is a dummy variable equal to 1 if the firm is audited by a qualified Chartered Accountant and 0 otherwise.
AUDIT_OP is a dummy variable equal to 1 if the company received a qualified audit opinion and 0 otherwise.
BOARD is the number of board members.
OVERDRAFT is the utilized proportion of the company overdraft at $t-1$.
SIZE is the natural log of total assets at $t-1$.
LEV is total liabilities divided by total assets at $t-1$.
RECESSION is a dummy variable equal to one for the period 2008 to 2010 and zero otherwise.

ciated with interest rates, and size (*SIZE*) is significantly and positively associated to interest rate levels. The positive association related to size might be explained by a very strong negative correlation between size and recession shown in the pairwise analysis, and the same analysis shows that leverage is strongly and negatively correlated to the level of use of the overdraft. We also find that interest rate levels have decreased since the start of the recession. Contrary to previous tests, the inverse Mills variable (*LAMBDA*) is insignificant, suggesting there is no presence of endogeneity. We conclude that although we cannot put forward a strong argument that Gazelles are producing high-quality financial reporting, we find that the interest levels are significantly lower for this group of firms and therefore creditors have been able to adequately assess the risk and rewards, which supports hypothesis 2.

CONCLUSIONS

Financial reporting plays an important function in the corporate governance system of small privately held firms. In this chapter we have examined differences in the quality of financial reporting across Gazelles and Non-Gazelles. We find no significant difference in accrual persistence across the two groups and only weak evidence that Gazelles are less conservative. However, these results should be interpreted with caution, since we use growth measured as a doubling of the sales over a consecutive three-year period to identify Gazelles, and therefore this measure is closely related to changes in accruals. We try to control for this by using Heckman's two-step procedure; however, it may be that the specification used does not control for this problem. Furthermore, our test of prevalence of earnings management shows no significant difference across Gazelles and Non-Gazelles. Finally, we also test the difference in cost of debt across Gazelles and Non-Gazelles and find that creditors seem to be able to assess the credit risk regardless of financial reporting quality, and this results in lower cost of debt for Gazelles.

The findings in this chapter contribute to the growing stream of research of corporate governance and accounting in entrepreneurial settings by showing that the quality of financial accounting among different groups of private firms is of less importance among small firms, and that these firms manage to provide creditors with information to assess the credit risk regardless. However, we do not argue that financial reporting is of no value. On the contrary, financial reporting is relevant from a corporate governance perspective. The result shows that corporate governance mechanisms that influence financial reporting quality have an indirect impact on the cost of debt of private small firms. The test of cost of debt levels shows that, on average, a qualified audit opinion drives interest rates upwards, and the use of a Big Four firm reduces interest rate levels. Also, we interpret the results as creditors identifying a higher level of corporate governance, assuming that a larger number of board members is a sign of external parties in addition to the owner-manager on the board of directors. The interest rates decrease with the members on the board of directors. Instead, we interpret our results as indicating that small firms are using the financial reporting in conjunction with other information, 'soft' data gathered by the loan officers over time (Berger and Udell, 2002), not included in the financial report to inform creditors about the risk of their business. Our results build on prior research and show that if book-tax conformity is prevalent, financial reporting usefulness decreases, but our study also indicates that firms use other means than financial reporting to disclose information to creditors when the book-tax link exists, and that creditors are indeed able to evaluate the firms (Chen et al., 2011).

As discussed above, this chapter shows some indication that financial reporting quality reduces the cost of debt, and that firms with a greater incentive to increase financial reporting quality benefit from doing so in terms of reduced cost of debt. Future research could further these findings by investigating which corporate governance measures are most effective and which source of financing that these firms gain access to. Moreover, in the light of the recent financial crisis, how has this changed corporate governance processes and finance sourcing among different types of private firms.

The results should be interpreted with caution, because we use growth measures based on sales growth to identify Gazelles, and this measure is intrinsically related to changes in accruals. We try to control for this by using Heckman's two-step procedure; however, the specification used may not fully take care of this problem.

NOTES

1. We do not predict a direction for the degree of conservatism due to it could be questioned whether conservatism reflects high quality accounting, some argue that conservatism creates hidden reserves which is used for earnings management while others argue that conservatism is beneficial for evaluating stewardship (Penman and Zhang 2002; O'Connell 2007; Givoly, Hayn and Katz 2010).
2. All limited companies domiciled in Sweden are regulated under the Companies Act (Aktiebolagslagen (ABL) Svensk författningssamling, SFS 1975:1385). This act stipulates these firms to provide an audited annual report.
3. Appropriations are deductions allowed under Swedish tax legislation under the condition that they are reported in the balance sheet and all changes are reported on the face of the income statement (Kommunalskattelagen (SFS 1928:370)).
4. Kommunalskattelagen (SFS 1928:370).
5. Aktiebolagslagen (ABL) (SFS 1975:1385).
6. During the period (2002–2011) all firms in the sample were required to have a financial audit regardless of firm size.

7. Bokföringslagen (SOU 1996:157).
8. Årsredovisningslagen (SFS 1995: 1554).
9. http://www.bolagsverket.se/.
10. The Swedish government's official statistics provider.
11. We control for outliers by winsorizing the data on the 1 per cent level. We also rerun all tests and estimations removing outliers greater than two standard deviations with qualitatively similar results.
12. Kommunalskattelagen (SFS 1928:370).

REFERENCES

Acs, Z.J., Arenius, P., Hay, M. and Minniti, M. (2004), *Global Entrepreneurship Monitor 2004 Executive Report*, Wellesley, MA, USA and London, UK: Babson College and London Business School.

Alle, K.D. and Lombardi Youn, T. (2009), 'The demand for financial statements in an unregulated environment: An examination of the production and use of financial statements by privately held small businesses', *Accounting Review*, **84** (1), 27–51.

Armstrong, C.S., Guay, W.R. and Weber, J.P. (2010), 'The role of information and financial reporting in corporate governance and debt contracting', *Journal of Accounting and Economics*, **50**, 179–234.

Atwood, T.J., Drake, M.S. and Myers, L.A. (2010), 'Book-tax conformity, earnings persistence and the association between earnings and future cash flows', *Journal of Accounting and Economics*, **50**, 111–125.

Ball, R. and Shivakumar, L. (2005), 'Earnings quality in UK private firms: Comparative loss recognition timeliness', *Journal of Accounting and Economics*, **39** (1), 83–128.

Barth, M.E., Landsman, W. and Lang, M.H. (2008), 'International accounting standards and accounting quality', *Journal of Accounting Research*, **46** (3), 467–498.

Basu, S. (1997), 'The conservatism principle and the asymmetric timeliness of earnings', *Journal of Accounting and Economics*, **24**, 3–37.

Berger, A.N. and Udell, G.F. (2002), 'Small business credit availability and relationship lending: The importance of bank organizational structure', *Economic Journal*, **112** (February), 32–53.

Beuselinck, C., Deloof, M. and Manigart, S. (2009), 'Private equity involvement and earnings quality', *Journal of Business Finance and Accounting*, **36** (5), 587–615.

Beuselinck, C. and Manigart, S. (2007), 'Financial reporting quality in private equity backed companies: The impact of ownership concentration', *Small Business Economics*, **29**, 261–274.

Birch, D.L. (1979), *The Job Generation Process*, Cambridge, MA: MIT Program on Neighbourhood and Regional Change.

Birch, D.L. and Medoff, J. (1994), 'Gazelles', in Solomon, L.C. and Levenson, A.R. (eds), *Labor Markets, Employment Policy and Job Creation*, Boulder, CO: Westview, pp. 159–167.

Bishop, K., Mason, G. and Robinson, C. (2009), 'Firm growth and its effects on economic and social outcomes: Literature and statistical review', Report to the National Endowment for Science, Technology and the Arts, NIESR, London.

Burgstahler, D., Hail, L. and Leuz, C. (2006), 'The importance of reporting incentives: Earnings management in European private and public firms', SSRN Working Paper.

Chaney, P.K., Jeter, D.C. and Shivakumar, L. (2004), 'Self-selection of auditors and auditor pricing in private firms', *Accounting Review*, **79** (1), 51–72.

Chen, F., Hope, O.K., Li, Q. and Wang, X. (2011), 'Financial reporting quality and investment efficiency of private firms in emerging markets', *Accounting Review*, **86** (4), 1255–1288.

Davidsson, P. (1995), 'Culture, structure and regional levels of entrepreneurship', *Entrepreneurship and Regional Development*, **7** (1), 41–61.

Davidsson, P. and Henrekson, M. (2002), 'Determinants of the prevalence of start-ups and high-growth firms', *Small Business Economics*, **19** (2), 81–104.

Davidsson, P., Kirchhoff, B., Abdulnasser, H.J. and Gustavsson, H. (2002), 'Empirical analysis of business growth factors using Swedish data', *Journal of Small Business Management*, **40** (4), 332–349.

Davidsson, P., Lindmark, L. and Olofsson, C. (1994), *Dynamiken i svenskt näringsliv*, Lund: Studentlitteratur.

Davila, A. and Foster, G. (2005), 'Management accounting systems adoption decisions: Evidence and performance implications from early-stage/startup companies', *Accounting Review*, **80** (4), 1039–1068.

DeAngelo, L.E. (1981), 'Auditor size and audit quality', *Journal of Accounting and Economics*, **3** (3), 183–199.

Dechow, P.M. and Dichev, I. (2002), 'The quality of accruals and earnings: The role of accrual estimation errors', *Accounting Review*, **77** (Supplement), 35–59.

Dedman, E., Kausar, A. and Lennox, C. (2014), 'The demand for audit in private firms: Recent large-sample evidence from the UK', *European Accounting Review*, **23** (1), 1–23.

Diamond, D.W. and Verrecchia, R.E. (1991), 'Disclosure, liquidity, and the cost of capital', *Journal of Finance*, **46** (4), 1325–1359.

Easley, D. and O'Hara, M. (2004), 'Information and the cost of capital', *Journal of Finance*, **59** (4), 1553–1583.

EC (2003), 'Definition of micro, small and medium sized enterprises in Europe' (2003/361/EC), 6 May.

Fortin, S. and Pittman, J.A. (2007), 'The role of auditor choice in debt pricing in private firms', *Contemporary Accounting Research*, **24** (3), 859–896.

Francis, J., LaFond, R.Z., Olsson, P. and Schipper, K. (2005), 'The market pricing of accruals quality', *Journal of Accounting and Economics*, **39**, 295–327.

Gabrielsson, J., Lindholm Dahlstrand, Å. and Politis, D. (2014), 'Sustainable high-growth entrepreneurship: A study of rapidly growing firms in the Scania region', *International Journal of Entrepreneurship and Innovation*, **15** (1), 29–40.

Givoly, D., Hayn, C. and Katz, S.P. (2010), 'Does public ownership of equity improve earnings quality?', *Accounting Review*, **85** (1), 195–225.

Givoly, D., Hayn, C. and Natarajan, A. (2007), 'Measuring reporting conservatism', *Accounting Review*, **82**, 65–106.

He, X., Wong, T.J. and Young, D. (2012), 'Challenges for implementation of fair value accounting in emerging markets: Evidence from China', *Contemporary Accounting Research*, **29** (2), 538–562.

Heckman, J.J. (1979), 'Sample selection bias as a specification error', *Econometrica*, **47**, 153–161.

Henrekson, M. and Johansson, D. (2010), 'Gazelles as job creators: A survey and interpretation of the evidence', *Small Business Economics*, **35** (2), 227–244.

Hölzl, W. (2009), 'Is the R&D behaviour of fast-growing SMEs different? Evidence from CIS data for 16 countries', *Small Business Economics*, **33** (1), 59–75.

Hope, O.-K., Thomas, W.B. and Vyas, D. (2011), 'Financial credibility, ownership, and financing constraints in private firms', *Journal of International Business Studies*, **42** (7), 935–957.

Hope, O.-K., Thomas, W.B. and Vyas, D. (2013), 'Financial reporting quality in US private firms', *Accounting Review*, **88** (5), 1715–1742.

Jaggi, B., Leung, D. and Gul, F. (2009), 'Family control, board independence and earnings management: Evidence based on Hong Kong firms', *Journal of Accounting Public Policy*, **28** (4), 281–300.

Jensen, M.C. and Meckling, W.H. (1976), 'Theory of the firm: Managerial behaviour, agency costs and ownership structure', *Journal of Financial Economics*, **3** (4), 305–360.

Jermakowicz, E.K. and Epstein, B.J. (2010), 'IFRS for SMEs – an option for US private entities?', *Review of Business*, **30**, 72–79.

Karjalainen, J. (2011), 'Audit quality and cost of debt capital for private firms: Evidence from Finland', *International Journal of Auditing*, **15**, 88–108.

Lambert, R., Leuz, C. and Verrecchia, R.E. (2007), 'Accounting information, disclosure, and the cost of capital', *Journal of Accounting Research*, **45** (2), 385–420.

Landström, H. (2010), *Pioneers in Entrepreneurship and Small Business Research*, New York: Springer.

Leuz, C. and Verrecchia, R.E. (2000), 'The economic consequences of increased disclosure', *Journal of Accounting Research*, **38**, 91–124.

Li, X., Roca, P.S. and Papaoikonomou, E. (2011), 'SMEs' responses to the financial and economic crisis and policy implications: An analysis of agricultural and furniture sectors in Catalonia, Spain', *Policy Studies*, **32**, 397–412.

Lisowsky, P. and Minnis, M. (2014), 'Financial reporting choices of US private firms: Large-sample analysis of GAAP and audit use', Working Paper.

Minnis, M. (2011), 'The value of financial statement verification in debt financing: Evidence from private US firms', *Journal of Accounting Research*, **47** (2), 457–506.

Niskanen, M., Karjalainen, J. and Niskanen, J. (2011), 'Demand for audit quality in private firms: Evidence on ownership effects', *International Journal of Auditing*, **15**, 43–65.

O'Connell, V. (2007), 'Reflections on stewardship reporting', *Accounting Horizons*, **21** (2), 215–227.

Paananen, M., Renders, A. and Blomkvist, M. (2016), 'Causes and consequences of improvements in the information environment for Swedish small and mid-sized firms', *Accounting in Europe*, **13** (1), 21–42.

Penman, S.H. and Zhang, X.J. (2002), 'Accounting conservatism, the quality of earnings, and stock returns', *Accounting Review*, **77** (2), 237–264.

Schipper, K. and Vincent, L. (2003), 'Earnings quality', *Accounting Horizons*, **17**, 97–110.

Svensk författningssamling (1975), SFS 1975:1385, Aktiebolagslag (ABL).

Van Tendeloo, B. and Vanstraelen, A. (2008), 'Earnings management and audit quality in Europe: Evidence from the private client segment market', *European Accounting Review*, **17** (3), 447–469.

Watts, R. (2003), 'Conservatism in accounting, Part I: Explanations and implications', *Accounting Horizons*, **17**, 207–221.

Watts, R.L. and Zimmerman, J.L. (1983), 'Agency problems, auditing, and the theory of the firm: Some evidence', *Journal of Law and Economics*, **26** (3), 613–633.

PART V

CORPORATE GOVERNANCE AND CORPORATE ENTREPRENEURSHIP

14. Corporate governance and corporate entrepreneurship in different organizational forms
Elin Smith and Sven-Olof Collin

INTRODUCTION

In today's society, products and services are offered in a number of different organizational forms: leisure activities are offered by not-for-profit associations or privately held firms, waste disposal services by local government corporations or administrations, manufactured products and services by listed corporations or state-owned corporations. Independent of organizational form and type of products and services offered, the long-term survival and success of the organization should benefit from a governance system that supports the exploration of novel opportunities that are in line with the purpose of the organization. As such, an intertwinement between a governance system of an organization and the exploration of novel opportunities for the advancement of the organization is suggested. Aspects of governance can be found in the literature of corporate governance (e.g., Shleifer and Vishny, 1997) and tend to have a disciplining emphasis. Aspects of the exploration of novel opportunities can be found in the literature of entrepreneurship (Covin and Lumpkin, 2011; Zahra et al., 2000) and tend to have an enabling emphasis.

The starting point for an intertwinement between governance and entrepreneurship is that organizations are present to serve the interests of the holders of property rights (sometimes diffusedly termed owners, members or, in agency theory, principals) and as such, entrepreneurship should be in accordance with and aligned to these interests. Corporate governance mechanisms serve as a way to align the interests of property rights holders, for example, as in agency theory, to align the interests of the principals and the agents (Schleifer and Vischny, 1997). Therefore, corporate governance mechanisms appear to be a relevant starting point for considering the influence on entrepreneurship at the organizational level, hereafter termed corporate entrepreneurship. Such an intertwinement is moreover in line with researchers' identification of interesting and insufficiently explored topics (e.g., Caruana et al., 2002; Corbett et al., 2013; Lacetera, 2001; Phan et al., 2009).

The point of departure for the intertwinement is corporate governance, conceptualized as corporate governance mechanisms, where each and every mechanism, separate and as a set, is considered to be influential on corporate entrepreneurship. One example is the governance mechanism of the joint stock company board of directors, which is to represent the interests of the principal, whether it is the shareholders in a United States (US) system, or shareholders and employees in a German system. The role of the board is that of providing service, setting strategy, monitoring, and being an arena for conflict resolution (Collin, 2008). As such, the board is a mechanism that sets the rules and the direction through which the manager's attention can be directed towards effective use of resources, such as the identification of capabilities that can be used for proactive behaviour.

The present conceptual linkages between governance and entrepreneurship tend to treat the influence on entrepreneurship from a general point of view. For example, Covin and Slevin (1991) consider external variables, strategic variables and internal variables as influential on entrepreneurial posture. Lumpkin and Dess (1996, 2001) contribute a comprehensive theoretical connection between a set of environmental and organizational factors and their relation to an entrepreneurial orientation which later is empirically evaluated. Kearney et al. (2008) focus on the public sector and present the main antecedents and relation to corporate entrepreneurship. Although some governance issues are included in these frames, for example strategy and the top management team, they lack a coherent model of how the corporate governance mechanisms can be used to influence entrepreneurship at the organizational level.

Moreover, what is neglected in present studies on governance and entrepreneurship is the range of different organizational forms. The present studies tend to take the organizational form of the corporation as a default, neglecting the full range of different organizational forms that are used for organizing economic activity. To avoid this shortcoming, we propose that a theory of corporate governance and corporate entrepreneurship starts with acknowledging the distribution of property rights and liabilities among participants of different organizational forms. In this way, a theory of governance and entrepreneurship would be applicable to different empirical manifestations of the firm, not merely the commonly studied corporation.

In this chapter, we present results from a research project aiming at exploring the intertwinement between a disciplining side and an enabling side of the firm, where 'the firm' refers to any empirical manifestation of organizations. The research project's point of departure was the assumption that corporate governance and corporate entrepreneurship and the theories of these fields are as applicable, for example, to democratic associations as they are to capitalistic joint stock companies. The empirical objects of the studies belong to two industries. One is the equestrian industry, specifically Swedish riding schools that offer riding activities primarily for youth. The industry has developed from an authoritarian military school to a sport for the people. The other empirical object is the waste management and water and sewerage industries, which are a part of the technical supply system under municipal responsibility. We chose these industries because the research project demanded studies of economic activity that was performed in different organizational forms. The riding industry includes a variety of organizational forms, mainly not-for-profit associations and sole proprietorships. The waste management and water and sewerage industries historically have been organized as local government corporations and local government administrations. The rest of this chapter reports the main findings and experiences of the various studies that have come out of this research project.

First, we present the theoretical frame including: (1) the conception of property rights, which distinguishes rights and liabilities among important input owners and enables their applicability to different organizational forms; (2) corporate governance, which represents the disciplining side of the firm; (3) the field of entrepreneurship, which represents the enabling side of the firm; and (4) a synthesis of these fields, which presents the research model that has served as the foundation for the research. We follow with a presentation of the empirical setting and the findings, separated into conceptual and empirical issues; and a final discussion of the opportunities and limitations

THEORETICAL FRAME

Property Rights

With the aim of including different organizational forms in the intertwinement of governance and entrepreneurship, the studies in this research project have applied a property rights approach. This approach is inspired by Alchian and Demsetz (1972) and Furobotn and Pejovich (1972), who suggest that property rights specify the norms of people's behaviour and influence their behaviour, as both principals and agents. Considering the firm, the factors of production are all owned or controlled by someone (Alchian and Demsetz, 1973), and someone will experience the benefits and costs of each particular factor. For example, the prominent holder in a privately held firm is the proprietor, and the proprietor has a direct influence on some corporate governance mechanisms such as the strategy and structure of the firm. In the corporation, the board of directors can be the central party and exercise influence on the corporate governance mechanisms. The manager is also an important holder in the corporation through having all or part of the right to observe input behaviour and to alter membership of the team.[1] In the local government administration, the influence of the politicians has been described as dominating the influence of the manager. The distribution of rights and liabilities in various organizational forms is suggested to influence the incentives and actions of actors, which by extension characterize the corporate governance mechanisms and how they are used to explore novel opportunities.

Corporate Governance

Corporate governance is a research field including a range of different theories and viewpoints (Aguilera and Jackson, 2010), but it can be defined as the processes and structures used to control organized economic activities in an organization. Theories underlying its development are primarily agency theory (Jensen and Ruback, 1983) and transaction cost theory (Williamson, 1996), and it all started when the debate about the joint stock company arose at the beginning of the eighteenth century. Corporate governance deals primarily with the issue of separation between ownership and control, where shareholders making financial investments want to secure profit on invested capital (Berle and Means, 1932). Corporate governance pays attention to how organizations, especially top managers, are disciplined in order to satisfy the principals of the organization (Jensen and Meckling, 1976). One way to conceptualize corporate governance is to consider it through mechanisms (Schleifer and Vishny, 1997; Thomsen, 2008); these in turn exist among the organization's input factors, within the organization and its transformation process and at the output markets (Elsayed, 2011). See Figure 14.1 for an overview.

Mechanisms among the organization's input factors are the market for capital, be it debt or equity, and the external market for managerial labour. The market for external managerial labour includes the supply and demand of managers. One important aspect concerns the signals from the external labour market, for example reputation. With an increasing number of business schools, trainee programmes and management training, the supply of suitable managers has increased. However, in relation to different organizational forms, it might be that capitalistic corporations have a larger supply of individuals to choose from, compared to local government administrations, one reason being the better reputation achieved by being appointed to a corporation. The capital market consists of equity and debt capital, where equity is supplied by shareholders and debt is

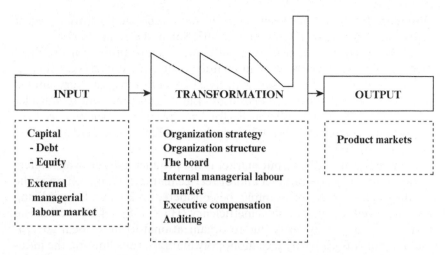

Figure 14.1   The set of corporate governance mechanisms

supplied by banks, suppliers and market debt. An internal quasi-capital market exists, however, where the cash flow of the firm is distributed, typically existing in large and diversified corporations (Stein, 1997).

Mechanisms within the organization are its strategy and structure, the board of directors, the internal managerial labour market, executive compensation and auditing. Strategy focuses on the formal and informal direction of operations, whereas structure focuses on how to implement the strategy. Studies have examined, for example, the coherence between an organization's strategy and its structure (Fligstein, 1985; Grinyer et al., 1980; Hamilton and Shergill, 1992), but attention has also been given to strategy as an important governing mechanism of public entities (Collin and Tagesson, 2010). In the field of corporate governance, the board of directors, especially of capitalistic corporations, is a well-researched mechanism (e.g., Pugliese et al., 2009), primarily because an important role of the corporate board is to represent the owners' interests and to monitor managerial activities, provide service, set the strategy and/or contribute resources in the sense of directors' experiences and backgrounds, and to create value (Golden and Zajac, 2001; Huse, 2007; Judge and Zeithaml, 1992; Zahra and Pearce, 1989). Researchers have turned their attention, not only to the corporate board, but also to boards of not-for-profit associations (Miller, 2002; Miller-Millesen, 2003; Olson, 2000). The internal managerial labour market concerns the internal side of the managerial labour market and actions taken by the organization in order to socialize suitable individuals to management positions. Compensation is another mechanism used to influence managerial behaviour (Gomez-Mejia and

Wiseman, 1997) and has been given substantial public scrutiny in recent years (Adut et al., 2003; Cyert et al., 2002; Sun and Cahan, 2009).

In the interest of considering different organizational forms, these mechanisms are likely to vary in characteristics; thus, local government administration, in comparison with listed corporations, has very limited possibilities for financial compensation. But it is also relevant to consider other ways of providing rewards, for example fringe benefits. A final important mechanism is the audit, which is differently regulated according to organizational form.

A mechanism at the output market is the product market, which refers to the competition on product and/or service markets. Competition in the product market can, for example, be considered as a way of disciplining because it reduces individuals' inefficiency (Hart, 1983). This mechanism is likely to vary in intensity due to organizational form as local government organizations partly face monopoly markets, thus limiting the influence of this mechanism, whereas the mechanism can be more prominent, for example, in internationally operating corporations (Collin et al., 2013). These would be the governing mechanisms aimed at facilitating the governance of different organizational forms. To this disciplining view of the firm, we next add a more enabling view: that of entrepreneurship.

Corporate Entrepreneurship

Entrepreneurship can be exercised by individuals, organizations or states (e.g., Schumpeter, 1934) and has been stressed as being of importance for societal development (Covin and Slevin, 1991; Miller, 1983; Pinchot, 1985; Zahra, 1991, 1993) as well as organizational success (Corbett et al., 2013; Heavey and Simsek, 2013; Hornsby et al., 2013; Zampetakis and Moustakis, 2007), which has led to the establishment of a field of study focusing on entrepreneurship where the organization is the unit of analysis.

Corporate entrepreneurship is described by many different terms, for example, entrepreneurial posture (Covin and Slevin, 1991), innovative strategy making (Miller and Friesen, 1983), corporate entrepreneurship (Corbett et al., 2013; Guth and Ginsberg, 1990; Stevenson and Jarillo, 1990; Stopford and Baden-Fuller, 1994; Zahra, 1991, 1993, 1996), intrapreneurship (Antoncic and Hisrich, 2003) and entrepreneurial orientation (Knight, 1987; Lumpkin and Dess, 1996). The studies reported in this chapter have predominantly used the term 'corporate entrepreneurship' to include the dimensions of strategic opportunism and risk taking, in line with the ideas of strategic renewal found in earlier as well as recent studies (Corbett et al., 2013; Guth and Ginsberg, 1990). Strategic opportunism refers to the organization's capacity to perceive new opportunities and to

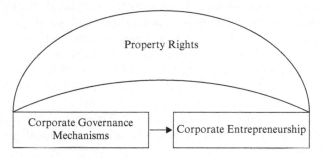

Figure 14.2   The research model

develop new strategies, be they new products or markets, and to redirect its resources without being bound by the present strategy (Collin and Smith, 2007). It has also been described as a capacity to discover new demands and to act upon these demands, for example through combining the firm's resources in a new way. Risk taking is considered a common characteristic of entrepreneurship (Antoncic and Hisrich, 2003). Its essence is the commitment of different types of resources to a venture; the entrepreneurial risk taking is high when it implies a threat for the survival of the firm. Focusing on public entities, a more proper term appears to be 'public entrepreneurship', where the exploration of novel opportunities is considered through acts of innovation, risk taking and proactiveness, inspired by previous studies in this area (e.g., Caruana ct al., 2002). Regardless of the term used, corporate entrepreneurship can be considered on a continuum, ranging from highly conservative to highly entrepreneurial organizations (Miller and Friesen, 1982).

Corporate Governance and Corporate Entrepreneurship

The suggested research model (see Figure 14.2) refers to an intertwinement between corporate governance mechanisms and corporate entrepreneurship, and the model takes different organizational forms into account (Collin and Smith, 2007; Smith, 2012b). The advantage of such a model is that the influence of each and every governance mechanism and its specific characteristics is given full and separate attention.

FINDINGS

The empirical base for data collection regarding corporate governance mechanisms' influence on corporate entrepreneurship is twofold. One part is devoted to the Swedish equestrian industry, specifically Swedish riding schools where the core activity is to teach riding with priority on learning to take care of horses. Riding schools can be differently organized and data have been collected from privately held firms, not-for-profit associations, corporations and constellations of organizational forms, such as public–private partnerships. The other part of the database is the Swedish waste management and water and sewerage industries, which represent activities that are municipal responsibilities. These services are commonly organized in local government administrations and local government corporations.

The main reason for choosing these diverse industries is based on the theoretical frame and its focus on property rights, which is a way of considering economic activity organized in different ways, that is, in different organizational forms. This focus has implications on the choice of industry, where one important criterion has been to identify and study industries with a diverse set of organizational forms. The two chosen industries meet this criterion. The method of data collection was through interviews and questionnaires, with some variability in the approach, depending on the study at hand. One paper, for example, takes an overall approach to governance and entrepreneurship (Collin and Smith, 2007) and uses interviews for collecting data, whereas another focuses on board composition and influence on corporate entrepreneurship (Smith, 2007), using questionnaires. The next section of this chapter presents the most interesting findings to be drawn from our various studies on corporate governance and corporate entrepreneurship in different organizational forms.

Conceptual and Methodological Issues

How to observe entrepreneurship at the organizational level
Entrepreneurship at the organizational level can be observed in different ways, as evidenced in the papers reported here. Initially the term 'corporate entrepreneurship' (e.g., Smith, 2007) including the dimensions of strategic opportunism and risk taking was used. The measures of strategic opportunism and risk taking were inspired by previous researchers (e.g., Lumpkin and Dess, 1996; Zahra, 1991), and then developed to fit the riding school industry. One conclusion from these studies is that corporate entrepreneurship is two-dimensional, that is, risk and strategic opportunism captured different phenomena and moreover were influenced by different corporate governance mechanisms. Thus, in a study on board composition and its influence on corporate entrepreneurship, the separation turned out to be essential for detecting influence relating to a high proportion of female directors and strategic opportunism (Smith, 2007).

Hence, taking actions of strategic opportunism implied low risk for the survival of the organization. Evidently the riding schools did not associate taking actions of strategic opportunism with high risk. One speculation about this finding could be the nature of not-for-profit associations, where members make no financial investments and might not identify the danger of starting new activities that represent high strategic opportunism. Another speculation could be that the municipality has an interest in the continuance of activities; sometimes the municipality owns the land where the riding school is located, hence it is the municipality that assumes the risk. The negative correlation could indicate that the municipality assumes the downside risk while the organization assumes the upside risk. Investing in new activities, such as those of high strategic opportunism, will increase the probability of survival, that is, low risk. If it turns out to be bad for the organization – that is, high risk – there will be some probability of the municipality entering into the organization and saving it. Thus, our findings indicated that the property rights distribution, where financial downside and upside risk were separated, had effects on incentives of entrepreneurial actions.

A speculative reasoning could be advanced here, that the extensive use of options, which are financial instruments with only an upside risk, are instruments well suited to large bureaucratic organizations in strong need of corporate entrepreneurial actions. That could be one explanation for the extensive use of options during the 1990s in the large US corporations (Fich and Shivadasani, 2005).

Our conclusion is that corporate entrepreneurship could be considered as a multidimensional concept, but the dimensionality at this stage of theory development is more an empirical than a theoretical case. Possibly, our findings indicate that dimensions of corporate entrepreneurship vary with the distribution of property rights, where especially risk distribution influences the number of dimensions.

The multiple functions of corporate governance mechanisms
Corporate governance is mostly conceptualized as governance mechanisms (Shleifer and Vishny, 1997). The metaphor of governance as separate mechanisms with governance as their function is a conceptual simplification. The mechanisms are elements of organizational structures and processes with governance as one of several functions. Since these elements have other functions, the governance function could vary in its intensity in a specific situation, with the effect that the expected correlation between the element and an expected governance outcome, such as level of corporate entrepreneurship, can be hard to observe.

One example is the organization's equity. It has been identified as a governance mechanism (Jensen, 1993) where increasing leverage puts pressure on managers to produce cash flow to pay the interest to the constantly aware debt holders, thus putting a strong disciplining pressure on managers. The 'pecking order' theory of corporate finance (Myers and Majluf, 1984), claiming that corporations prefer financing through internal cash flow, then debt and, last in line, equity, has been interpreted as signifying managerial interest of discretion. However, research and development (R&D)-intensive firms (Hall, 2002) and family firms (Lopez-Gracia and Sánchez-Andújar, 2007) tend to have low financial leverage. In both cases, the low leverage can be interpreted as a means of infusing risk propensity into the organization and giving management discretion. Since the financial risk is low, the business risk can be higher, thus promoting and supporting entrepreneurial actions, for the managers in the entrepreneurial firms and for the family in the family firm. Low leverage could also be a signal of trust towards suppliers, since low leverage will reduce the suppliers' business risk. Additionally, the pecking order could also indicate how much information the corporation needs to disclose: not to the owners, but to the competitors. In intensely competitive industries, it could be the case that 'less is more', that internal financing implies less risk of distributing sensitive information to competitors. It could therefore be expected that entrepreneurial firms use equity to stimulate entrepreneurial action, to avoid distributing sensitive information and to send a signal of trust to important stakeholders. Equity is presumably of insignificant importance as a governance restraining mechanism in entrepreneurial firms, implying that these firms have to use other mechanisms to discipline management.

Another example is the board of directors. According to the legislation in most countries, a corporation has to have a board, and its legal responsibility is monitoring (Thomsen, 2008). Research in corporations has also found that the board, besides monitoring, contributes service, such as advice and network connections (Hillman and Dalziel, 2003; Huse, 2007). In order to be able to fulfil these functions, researchers and consultants have claimed the need for directors of boards – so-called independent directors – not to have strong connections to the management and the dominant owners. Absence of independent directors has been interpreted to represent deviation from 'good governance' (Oxelheim and Randøy, 2005). However, boards can be a distinctive decision organ of the corporation (Judge and Zeithaml, 1992), thus shouldering the responsibility of management, including the entrepreneurial function. Boards can also be arenas where the principals of the corporation meet and negotiate the goals of the corporation, that is, fulfil a conflict resolution function, not between the principal and the agent, but between the principals (Collin, 2008). These functions, when stressed through composition, could very well imply a strong presence of managers and of owners. In the ideology of 'good governance' (Ponomareva and Ahlberg, 2016), boards composed to fulfil the functions of decision-making and conflict resolution would be deemed inefficient. But in the case of decision-making, they could be composed to stress entrepreneurial action, while monitoring is performed through other mechanisms.

The top management of the firm could be externally or internally recruited. External recruitment could be interpreted as representing a strong governance function, where collusion within the organization is reduced through the threat of dismissal of the management team. However, it could be the case that external recruitment is used when the organization is in need of strategic change, as it requires new ideas and new viewpoints which might be harder to get from a person inside the organization. Internal recruitment, creating high levels of tenure (e.g.,Watson et al., 1998; Watson et al., 1993), exploiting the strength of an internal culture with strong and fast communicative links, could be an efficient recruitment strategy when in need of strong action capacity which could be stimulated by knowing the organization, that is, efficiently implementing a strategy (Collin and Smith, 2007). Thus, one could expect that external recruitment is used when the window of entrepreneurship is open, that is, when corporate entrepreneurship will be emphasized; and internal recruitment is used when the window is closed, in order to exploit the entrepreneurial achievements.

Finally, observing the ownership function, a separation of shareholder rights into control rights and profit rights can be interpreted as an arrangement of minority exploitation, thus representing weak governance. This policy, however, could also be claimed to be a division of labour among owners, where exit-oriented owners assume the financial risk and voice-oriented owners – that is, those with entrepreneurial capacity and ambitions – achieve a credible contract of power, securing their opportunity to influence the corporation through voice. An entrepreneurial owner, or a corporation in need of an entrepreneurial owner, can arrange an ownership structure with a division of control and profit rights. While this arrangement is deemed as indicating a departure from the ideology of 'good governance' it could, according to our interpretation, indicate a need to make it possible for less wealthy entrepreneurs to be engaged through the ownership function. The conclusion is that structures and processes that traditionally are considered to be governance mechanisms need to be understood in their entirety since they could be activated to promote other interests of the principal and the agent, for example entrepreneurial actions or creating trust in the business environment.

Governance strategy: a praxis concept

Scientists tend to assume *ceteris paribus* and scientists in corporate governance tend to consider principals such as shareholders as weak and subject
to the strong opportunistic manager, the agent. The principal is assumed
to be restricted to a rather passive monitoring capacity, which is a function
of the concentration of the ownership. In reality, in many corporations the
principals have not abdicated from power: for example, in most European
corporations, where the owner has a higher level of presence; in family
firms, where the owner is distinctively present; and in voluntary organizations, where members are strongly involved in the organization. These
principals influence the corporation, and they cannot indolently rely on
ceteris paribus actions, dealing with one mechanism at a time, but must try
to simultaneously influence all available mechanisms.

The *ceteris paribus* tendency has been counteracted recently in corporate governance research. One attempt is to use the conception of bundles
of governance mechanisms, first mentioned by Rediker and Seth (1995),
but recently developed by García-Castro et al. (2013). Bundles of mechanisms are based on the von Bertalanffy (1968) systems idea of equifinality,
claiming that different set-ups can create the same result. This approach
includes studies using the idea of substitution, that one mechanism can be
substituted for another, having different influence but producing the same
effect; and the idea of complementarity, that one mechanism has stronger
influence if complemented by other mechanisms (e.g., Azim, 2012; Poppo
and Zenger, 2002; Ward et al., 2009; Wirtz, 2011).

Related to the idea of bundles of mechanisms is the notion that governance mechanisms are not present and available in a similar fashion, and
therefore cannot perform the same function and produce the same effect
on all corporations. This has been stressed in comparative corporate governance (Lubatkin et al., 2007), suggesting that every country has its own
opportunity set of corporate governance mechanisms.

Combining the ambition to avoid the *ceteris paribus* limitation and to
conceptually empower the principal, making the conception more realistic, the concept of governance strategy has been created (Collin, 2007). It
suggests that the principal influences the individual governance mechanisms and the mix of the mechanisms, with the intention of disciplining
and enhancing the entrepreneurial capacity of the managers to make it
possible for management to satisfy the will of the principal through the
organization's operations. The corporate governance mechanisms and the
mix of the mechanisms are believed to be influenced by four forces:

1.   The principal, which to different degrees has interest and capacity to
     engage in creating a governance strategy.

2. Exogenous forces, for example national regulation and culture defining the actual property rights of the principal and the agent, thereby defining the opportunity set of governance mechanisms.
3. The agent, for example when the agent influences the mechanisms in order to create credible commitment towards the principal, or when agents act to exploit the client effect (Dyl et al., 2002).
4. Functional diversity of the mechanism, which is the need to design the mechanism in order to fulfil functions other than governance.

These governance mechanisms influence entrepreneurial propensity and strategy implementation – that is, the actual management of the organization – which produce the performance of the organization. The performance is efficient to the degree that it satisfies the interest of the principal, thus closing the governance circle.

This conception puts the principal – for example, the ownership of the corporation or the membership of the association – into the driving seat of the organization, together with the agent, and it lets the mechanisms and especially the mix of mechanisms vary depending on different forces, where one important force is the principal's interest and capacity to create a governance strategy.

The conception has been used to describe and understand the governance of business groups and riding school associations (Collin, 2007), municipal governance of riding schools (Collin and Smith, 2008), municipal corporations (Collin and Tagesson, 2010), international corporations (Collin et al., 2013) and executive compensation in listed corporations (Collin et al., 2014). These organizations exist in very diverse institutional milieus, and are diverse in their property rights set-up and their market conditions. This has made it possible to derive empirically based propositions that are not limited to a specific institutional milieu or specific organizational conditions.

It is proposed that 'tough environments create tough beasts'; that is, organizations situated in environments that strongly influence the corporation will have principals that create a governance strategy that is strong and will utilize more intensively the available mechanisms in order to govern the corporation. The 'beast proposition' (Collin, 2007, p. 232) arose when comparing governance strategies applied in a business group and in a riding school association. The business group consisted of corporations engaged in international markets, with strong competition on almost all factor markets, whereas the riding school experienced rather limited competition. The principal of the business group utilized all governance mechanisms, and in a distinct manner, while the riding school principal utilized only some of the available mechanisms.

Another proposition is the 'orchestra proposition', implying that a principal has a limited supply of mechanisms available, which then have to be used with the force needed. The riding school could not use all mechanisms, because some of them were not available and some were available, but could only be used in a limited fashion due partly to resource scarcity and partly to organizational norms. One of the remaining mechanisms was the board, which was therefore used with strength and intensity. This observation was supported in a study of municipal corporations (Collin and Tagesson, 2010) where one actual available mechanism, executive compensation, was not utilized, mainly because of a tradition in the municipal sector not to consider compensation as an instrument of governance, or even management. A similar observation was made in a case study of municipal governance strategies towards riding schools that received support from the municipality (Collin and Smith, 2008). Riding schools experiencing hard environmental conditions were supported and even promoted to be highly entrepreneurial, while riding schools experiencing good resource conditions were not supported, or were even hampered in their entrepreneurial actions. The principals used the instruments they needed and that were available, whereas availability was influenced by norms, traditions, knowledge and governance capacity. Fewer instruments induced the principal to use the existing instruments more intensely.

Entrepreneurial action is influenced by the governance strategy, where the level and orientation is partly determined by the principal and the principal's interest and capacity. This conception makes it possible to consider the variety of the mechanisms, their multi-functionality and their conditioned presence, where their effect is conditioned in interaction with the other mechanisms.

Empirical Issues

Methodological and conceptual difficulties notwithstanding, empirical studies have been performed and some findings have been observed which contribute to our understanding of the interconnection between corporate governance and entrepreneurship at the organizational level. The following four subsections present empirical findings on the variety of entrepreneurship in different organizations and on the governance mechanisms influencing corporate entrepreneurship.

Systems of compensation and entrepreneurship at the organizational level
How managers are rewarded is assumed to influence how they will act. There are numerous forms of rewards: material (for example, wage) and immaterial (for example, status); actual (for example, hierarchical

position) and prospective (for example, career opportunities). Studies in corporate governance tend to focus on material rewards and their division between actual and prospective.

Prospective material rewards, such as bonus and options, appear to be the most frequently observed rewards in capitalistic corporations when the intention is to stimulate entrepreneurial action (Manne, 2011; Sushil and Momaya, 2011). Capitalistic corporations, having publicly traded equity securities such as shares, can use both bonus and options, and the distribution between bonus and options can be assumed to depend on the time horizon of the action and the possibility of informing the stock market about the entrepreneurial action. But it has been hard to find the performance effects of prospective rewards, such as inspiring high levels of entrepreneurship (Lerner et al., 2009). The observation that prospective material rewards are frequent could be explained by tradition, or that entrepreneurial firms typically cannot offer high material rewards today, but could have a promising future. Yet it is claimed, more or less dogmatically, that prospective (contingent) rewards are important in high-performance organizations (Pfeffer and Veiga, 1999).

Immaterial rewards, such as status, power, personal development and absence of monitoring are less observed as reward instruments. In institutional milieus that are not characterized by capitalistic values, such as voluntary organizations, it could be assumed that immaterial rewards are more frequent. One reason could be material resources scarcity, as in poorly funded riding schools. Another reason could be the difficulty of directing behaviour towards goal attainment that cannot be quantified and is therefore not possible to correlate with an economic value. A third reason could be that the institutional milieu cultivates other values than material ones and therefore cannot support actions through material rewards. What is important to note, however, is that immaterial rewards also have an element of prospect. Opportunities of promotion to more exciting tasks could be as strong a motivator as the actual salary.

Voluntary organizations need entrepreneurial action as much as capitalistic organizations, even if they do not have material resources to support their needs. Then immaterial rewards enter into the picture. In one case (Collin and Smith, 2007) we observed a manager's entrepreneurial action that appeared to be more than the organization needed or wanted. But the board, which is the preferred and available governance mechanism, did not intervene, even if certain actions created tensions in the organization and were clearly not positive for the organization. Our interpretation was that the board was lax in directing and monitoring, but strong in governance when it was needed. The board gave the manager large degrees of freedom, which partly benefited the organization, but also motivated the manager. Through these actions the manager became visible on the labour market and later gained a much more prestigious position in another organization. In this case, it can be claimed that the board used an immaterial actual and prospective reward to motivate the manager to entrepreneurial actions. Having a large freedom of action was the actual reward, and the prospective reward was the possibility to become visible on the labour market, with the probability of a more prestigious employment. Thus, we suggest an entrepreneur reward proposition: entrepreneurial freedom is a reward of entrepreneurial action (cf. Rule and Irwin, 1988).

Our conclusion is that prospective rewards could influence behaviour and support entrepreneurial propensity. The character of the reward varies, however, among organizations, probably due to their institutional milieus, where capitalistic organizations use more material rewards and the not-for-profit sector uses more immaterial rewards. The governance challenge of entrepreneurial firms would rather be to handle the entrepreneur reward proposition, to govern through freedom of action in order to achieve entrepreneurial actions and their outcomes.

The board and corporate entrepreneurship

One well-researched corporate governance mechanism is the board of directors (Dalton et al., 1998; Hillman and Dalziel, 2003; Huse, 2000, 2007; Pugliese et al., 2009). The board's connections to entrepreneurship have been the focus of numerous previous studies (e.g. Gabrielsson, 2003, 2007; Hung and Mondejar, 2005; Taylor, 2003).

We found in our studies that the board appeared to be an important stimulator for entrepreneurship. In a comparative case study (Collin and Smith, 2007) we analysed two riding schools. The riding schools were organized in two different forms. One was as a not-for-profit association. The other school had recently outsourced the riding activities to a privately held firm, thus having one part consisting of a not-for-profit association comprising members and membership activities, and one private part comprising the riding activities and horses. In the first case it was a dramatic crisis that brought about a change in board composition and induced the board to assume action. In the second outsourcing case, the board had the desire and active capacity to carry through the rather dramatic reorganization of outsourcing. In both cases the board opened up and created the possibilities for entrepreneurship.

Another study (Smith, 2007) was conducted on a topic that lately has attracted increased researchers' interest: how to compose the board of directors in order to gain positive performance effects (Elsayed, 2011). In particular, the gender composition of boards has over the years become a growing area of study (Burgess and Fallon, 2003; Burke, 2000; de Cabo et al., 2012; Huse and Solberg, 2006; Nielsen and Huse, 2010). Despite intense debates regarding gender equality and gender quotas on boards (Adams and Ferreira, 2009; Rose, 2007), boards of listed firms are dominated by male directors (Burke, 2003; McCormick Hyland and Marcellino, 2002; Singh and Vinnicombe, 2004), and even though advantages due to gender have been found, the relation between gender composition and output measures is not evident (Carter et al., 2010). With this background, a study was conducted on gender composition of the board of directors in not-for-profit riding schools and its influence on corporate entrepreneurship, where it was defined and observed through risk taking and strategic opportunism (Smith, 2007). The study indicates that the overall gender composition of not-for-profit boards in the Swedish riding school industry has no correlation with the measures of corporate entrepreneurship. These were the findings when considering the board at large. However, in order to understand women's contribution to boards, it has been suggested that the presence of women in certain key positions on the board should be given closer attention (Dalton et al., 1998; Ellstrand et al., 1999). Even though women are appointed to boards, it could be that they are excluded from specific powerful positions, thereby implying limited possibilities to influence output measures. Thus, in order to understand the influence of different directors, it is important to observe the power structure of the board. In this study it was found that in observing the gender composition of the power structure, with respect to the positions of chairperson, secretary and treasurer, a positive correlation was found: the more female directors in these positions, the higher the levels of strategic opportunism.

It can thus be concluded that the board is an important stimulator for entrepreneurship in the riding industry. One speculation about these results could be linked with another study including riding schools (Collin, 2008), which emphasizes a fourth board function, that of conflict resolution, adding to the three traditional ones of monitoring, resource provision and decision-making (Daily et al., 2003; Carpenter and Westphal, 2001; Forbes and Milliken, 1999; Hillman and Dalziel, 2003; Judge and Zeithaml, 1992). A reason for its apparent presence could be the specific characteristics of riding schools, namely that their roots in people's movements and their accessibility for children and youth (Svenska Ridsportförbundet, 2006). As members populate the board, different coalitions can be formed with the aim of realizing different interests (Collin, 2008). What our studies indicate is that when the board is oriented towards stimulating entrepreneurship, the conflict resolution function appears to be less prominent. On the contrary, board stimulation regarding entrepreneurship appears to be more linked with the function of resource provision (that is, board composition) and with the function of

shaping and taking formal decisions about strategy (for example, the decision to reorganize). This would indicate that when the board of a riding
school has a stimulating influence on entrepreneurship, functions other
than conflict resolution, such as decision-making and resource provision,
become predominant. A proposition could therefore be suggested: corporate entrepreneurship is positively correlated with a board's emphasis on
resource provision and decision-making, and negatively correlated with an
emphasis on monitoring and conflict resolution.

A similar conclusion was arrived at in studies of local government
organizations in the waste management and water and sewerage industries
(Smith, 2012a, 2014). The board of a local government corporation is large
and mainly composed of politicians. Because of its diverse political composition, discussions assume more of a political than a business-oriented
nature. It is not, however, board composition that influences entrepreneurship; instead it appears to be the size of the board. The board's large
size implies that the meetings are framed as formal discussions, which
do not allow much room for innovative exchange. To circumvent this
problem, a smaller group with specific board members was created. This
smaller group was found to be active in the search for new business activities and found to stimulate entrepreneurship (Smith, 2014).

Our conclusion is that, in line with previous research (e.g., Baysinger et
al., 1991; Brunninge and Nordqvist, 2004; Gabrielsson, 2003, 2007; Hung
and Mondejar, 2005; Huse, 2007; Taylor, 2003; Zahra, 1996; Zahra et al.,
2000), the board appears to be an important actor in the governance of
organizations. We found that its functional emphasis and composition,
especially the existence of a sub-group within the board, could influence
entrepreneurship.

Entrepreneurship at the organizational level as a propensity
Entrepreneurship on both the individual and organizational levels has
been conceptualized in the literature through aspects such as innovation,
risk taking, proactiveness and strategic renewal (Antoncic and Hisrich,
2003; Covin and Slevin, 1991; Lumpkin and Dess, 1996). Organizations
displaying these characteristics have been claimed to be entrepreneurial,
that is, to have an entrepreneurial posture (Covin and Slevin, 1991; Zahra,
1991). This presents a rather static view of entrepreneurship as existing or
not existing. Entrepreneurship at the organizational level could, however,
be studied from a more dynamic view, suggesting it to be a propensity or
a latent capacity, which it is possible to set free and to restrict through the
influence of corporate governance mechanisms (Collin and Smith, 2007).

Entrepreneurial propensity could be characterized as a window of entrepreneurship, which it is possible to open and close through the influence

of the corporate governance mechanisms. In a study by Collin and Smith (2007) that focused on a not-for-profit association and a privately held firm in the riding school industry it was found that the opening of the window was initiated by the board of directors. The closing of entrepreneurship in the private riding school was influenced by the product market, and in the not-for-profit riding school it was influenced by the managerial labour market.

The opening and closing of the window of entrepreneurship have been identified in other studies (Smith, 2007, 2012a, 2014). From these studies it can be concluded that different mechanisms are active in opening and closing the window. In line with previous research, the power of the board (Brunninge and Nordqvist, 2004; Baysinger et al., 1991; Gabrielsson, 2003, 2007; Hung and Mondejar, 2005; Taylor, 2003; Zahra, 1996; Zahra et al., 2000) appears to be conducive in the opening of the window of entrepreneurship (Collin and Smith, 2007; Smith, 2014). Yet the external environment, strategy and organizational culture are found to open the window (Smith, 2012a, 2014), while strategy and organizational culture are found to close it (Smith, 2012a).

The opening of the window of entrepreneurship has also been found in different constellations of organizational forms. In a study of governance and entrepreneurship in public–private partnerships (Collin and Smith, 2008) it was found that a municipality with an adaptive governance strategy is conducive to opening a window of entrepreneurship in a private organization that was dependent on the municipality. Our conclusion is that corporate entrepreneurship can be considered a latent capacity, a propensity, which it is possible to influence through governance mechanisms, either through a stimulating influence depicted by opening the window of entrepreneurship, or through a restraining influence depicted by closing that window.

Entrepreneurship in different organizational forms

We claim that corporate entrepreneurship is present in different organizational forms (Collin and Smith, 2007; Smith, 2007). In particular, studies on public entrepreneurship tend to argue that there are low levels of public entrepreneurship within the sector, yet our studies (Smith, 2012a, 2014) identify entrepreneurial actions in all organizational forms and find that corporate entrepreneurship can be positively and negatively influenced in these different organizational forms.

One influential mechanism is the board, and a stronger influence has been found in the not-for-profit associations compared to organizations at the local government level. One explanation of this finding is that it might be due to sector belongingness and thereby also organizational form. The organizational forms at the local government level – that is, local government corporations and local government administrations – are politically initiated organizations directed by politicians. The board members are politicians and the board function could be that of representing a political agenda, that is, focusing on conflict resolution and monitoring operations. This could be contrasted with the not-for-profit boards of the riding schools, which are most likely populated by members very close to the activities, such as those taking riding lessons themselves or arranging instruction for their children, which would make it easier for them to identify and act on novel opportunities.

Another mechanism influencing corporate entrepreneurship is the labour market pool. One difference between the organizational forms is the character of this mechanism. The not-for-profit association faces a limited managerial market and has problems finding suitable candidates, which restrains the possibility for entrepreneurship (Collin and Smith, 2007). The local government administration has candidates to choose among; however, the strongest labour market in this set of organizations appears to be present for the local government corporation. This organizational form has a rather good supply of well-educated, experienced individuals to choose from, implying the possibility of finding suitable candidates and the opportunity to stimulate entrepreneurship if that is the goal. An explanation for these differences could be the differences in reputation, that is, a better reputation from working in a corporation compared to employment in a not-for-profit association; but differences in resources and rewards are also most likely present where a local government corporation has a better opportunity to offer higher salaries than a not-for-profit association.

The need to take account of organizational form in any investigation has gained support in the literature. The discussion on the issue of separation between owners and managers is founded in the corporation, where shareholders invest capital and expect some return on invested capital, and where the monitoring of the manager is delegated to the board of directors. A similar attenuation of rights is found in the not-for-profit association, yet with the exception that the members do not make any financial investments and do not have the right to the residual. This can be contrasted with the single proprietorship where the property rights are vested in one person, that is, the single proprietorship who is the liable entity. This implies, for example, that failure of the organization would affect the single proprietor personally. The distribution of rights implies that members of a not-for-profit association have less incentive for strong monitoring of the activities, compared to a single proprietor. The single proprietor's desire for governance has been observed through studying the structure of the organization (Smith, 2009). Single proprietorships have been found to have a centralized organizational structure, thus retaining direct control over activities, whereas the structure in not-for-profit associations has a more decentralized character, with a less strong monitoring orientation (Smith, 2009).

CONCLUSIONS

Our findings start with the notion that organizations differ, and one means of conceptualizing this difference is through describing them as a collection of different property rights and liabilities. These organizational characteristics define the principal and the agent; they influence the opportunity set of governance mechanisms and the specific formation of each mechanism. In interplay between the principal and the agent, mechanisms are formed and influence the organization, and thereby its developmental character and capacity; that is, they influence corporate entrepreneurship.

We found that corporate entrepreneurship can vary and that it can therefore be viewed as a propensity. It can be triggered by different governance mechanisms and their specific formations. For example, the specific formation and composition of the board of directors have been shown to influence level of corporate entrepreneurship. The compensation system can promote entrepreneurial action through rewarding with freedom. Due to tradition in specific organizational forms, certain mechanisms are not available for use, with the implication that others are used with more strength in governing corporate entrepreneurship. We found indications of principals using the available governance mechanisms to influence corporate entrepreneurship, and termed this action 'governance strategy'.

These findings contribute to an understanding of how organizations function and how governance mechanisms are influenced in order to direct, that is, to promote or to limit corporate entrepreneurship. But we have also reported theoretical voids and limitations that restrain the development of a theory of corporate governance and corporate entrepreneurship. We have pointed to the multiple functions of governance mechanisms, which limit our capacity to understand to what extent they influence and to what extent they have been used as governance mechanisms. We have indicated the opportunity to operationalize corporate entrepreneurship in a variety of ways, which may create not only diversity, but also confusion.

As scientists in a modern society, and situated as we are in a modern university, we would like to create theories that are more general than specific (Popper, 2002), and we notice that there is a political interest in creating knowledge that could be used in the advancement of society. We cannot claim that, at our present stage of knowledge, that we have a general theory of corporate governance and corporate entrepreneurship. The knowledge tends to be limited to specific organizational forms and even to specific geographical areas (Lubatkin et al., 2007). Following in Popper's (2002) steps, we would strive towards theories that cover more phenomena and that are as simple as possible.

We suggest in this chapter, firstly, that a commonality of all organizations is the presence of property rights, with principals and agents and their rights and liabilities. Secondly, stressing both corporate governance and entrepreneurship, we suggest that organizations have structures and processes restraining and empowering actors of the organisation. And thirdly, as a consequence, neither the agent nor the principal is assumed to be active or passive, but their actions are embedded in the property rights and liability setup.

The drawback of this view is that the current trend in demand for social engineering – that our knowledge should be of use to manipulate organizations for the advancement of society – cannot be fulfilled. As researchers of corporate entrepreneurship and corporate governance, it is tempting to continue striving towards the goal of reaching conclusions based in praxis. We all want organizations to function well and to develop towards prosperous futures. Society at large, especially those with political tasks, has a strong interest in finding the keys to development.

Our review of property rights and the findings from the studies reported here, however, is rather pessimistic concerning the ambition to finding the key to development. We can nevertheless claim that corporate entrepreneurship has been promoted through different mechanisms in different organizations, while experiencing different conditions. Certain mechanisms are available in some situations and can trigger corporate entrepreneurship. The principals, if they are interested and have the necessary capacity, can create a governance strategy and, in cooperation with the agent, promote development of the organization.

NOTE

1. 'Team' refers to the ideas in team production theory emphasizing that people working together in a firm are more productive than the market (Alchian and Demsetz, 1972). Together with a property rights view, it implies that the firm is considered as including a team of different actors with different rights and liabilities. For example, in the single proprietorship, the proprietor, also given the title 'owner', has the most rights, that is, the right: (a) to be a residual claimant; (b) to observe input behaviour; (c) to be the central

party common to all contracts with inputs; (d) to alter the membership of the team; and (e) to transfer the rights (Alchian and Demsetz, 1972).

REFERENCES

Adams, R.B. and Ferreira, D. (2009), 'Women in the boardroom and their impact on governance and performance', *Journal of Financial Economics*, **94**, 291–309.

Adut, D., Cready, W.H. and Lopez, T.J. (2003), 'Restructuring charges and CEO cash compensation: A re-examination', *Accounting Review*, **78** (1), 169–93.

Aguilera, R.V. and Jackson, G. (2010), 'Comparative and international corporate governance', *Academy of Management Annals*, **4** (1), 485–556.

Alchian, A.A. and Demsetz, H. (1972), 'Production, information costs and economic organisation', *American Economic Review*, **62** (5), 777–95.

Alchian, A.A. and Demsetz, H. (1973), 'The property right paradigm', *Journal of Economic History*, **33** (1), 16–27.

Antoncic, B. and Hisrich, R.D. (2003), 'Clarifying the intrapreneurship concept', *Journal of Small Business and Enterprise Development*, **10** (1), 7–23.

Azim, M.I. (2012), 'Corporate governance mechanisms and their impact on company performance: A structural equation model analysis', *Australian Journal of Management*, **37** (3), 481–505.

Baysinger, B.D., Kosnik, R.D. and Turk, T.A. (1991), 'Effects of board and ownership structure on corporate R&D strategy', *Academy of Management Journal*, **34** (1), 205–15.

Berle, A.A. and Means, G.C. (1932), *The Modern Corporation and Private Property*, New York: Macmillan.

Brunninge, O. and Nordqvist, M. (2004), 'Ownership structure, board composition and entrepreneurship: Evidence from family firms and venture-capital-backed firms', *International Journal of Entrepreneurial Behaviour and Research*, **10** (1–2), 85–105.

Burgess, Z. and Fallon, B. (2003), 'A longitudinal study of women directors in Australia', *Women in Management Review*, **18** (7), 359–68.

Burke, R.J. (2000), 'Company size, board size and numbers of women corporate directors', in Burke, R.J. and Mattis, M.C. (eds), *Women in Management: International Challenges and Opportunities*, Dordrecht: Kluwer Academic, pp. 157–67.

Burke, R.J. (2003), 'Women on corporate boards of directors: The timing is right', *Women in Management Review*, **18** (7), 346–48.

Carpenter, M.A. and Westphal, J.D. (2001), 'The strategic context of external network ties: Examining the impact of director appointments on board involvement in strategic decision making', *Academy of Management Journal*, **44** (1), 639–60.

Caruana, A., Ewing, M. and Ramaseshan, B. (2002), 'Effects of some environmental challenges and centralization on the entrepreneurial orientation and performance of public sector entities', *Service Industries Journal*, **22** (2), 43–58.

Carter, D.A., D'Souza, F., Simkins, B. and Simpson, W.G. (2010), 'The gender and ethnic diversity of US boards and board committees and firm financial performance', *Corporate Governance – An International Review*, **18** (5), 396–414.

Collin, S-O. (2007), 'Governance strategy: A property right approach turning governance into action', *Journal of Management and Governance*, **11**, 215–37.

Collin, S-O. (2008), 'The board's functional emphasis: A contingency approach', *Corporate Ownership and Control*, **6** (2), 73–88.

Collin, S-O., Gustafsson, L., Petersson, E. and Smith, E. (2014), 'Options are a CEO's best friend: Executive compensation and ownership in Swedish listed corporations', *IUP Journal of Corporate Governance*, **8** (3), 40–71.

Collin, S-O. and Smith, E. (2007), 'Window of entrepreneurship: Explaining the influence of corporate governance mechanisms on corporate entrepreneurship in two riding schools', *International Journal of Entrepreneurship and Small Business*, **4** (2), 122–37.

Collin, S-O. and Smith, E. (2008), 'Democracy and private property: Governance of a three party public–private partnership', *Public Organization Review*, **8**, 53–68.

Collin, S-O., Smith, E., Umans, T., Broberg, P. and Tagesson, T. (2013), 'Mechanisms of corporate governance going international: Testing its performance effects in the Swedish economy 2004', *Baltic Journal of Management*, **8** (1), 79–101.

Collin, S-O. and Tagesson, T. (2010), 'Governance strategies in local government: A study of the governance of municipal corporations in a Swedish municipality', *International Journal of Public Policy*, **5** (4), 373–89.

Corbett, A., Covin, J., O'Connor, G. and Tucci, C. (2013), 'Corporate entrepreneurship: State-of-the-art research and a future research agenda', *Journal of Product Innovation Management*, **30** (5), 812–20.

Covin, J.G. and Lumpkin, G.T. (2011), 'Entrepreneurial orientation theory and research: Reflections on a needed construct', *Entrepreneurship Theory and Practice*, **35** (5), 855–72.

Covin, J.G. and Slevin, D.P. (1991), 'A conceptual model of entrepreneurship as firm behaviour', *Entrepreneurship Theory and Practice*, **16** (1), 7–25.

Cyert, R.M., Kang, S-H. and Kumar, P. (2002), 'Corporate governance, takeovers, and top-management compensation: Theory and evidence', *Management Science*, **48** (4), 453–69.

Daily, C.M., Dalton, D.R. and Cannella Jr, A.A. (2003), 'Corporate governance: Decades of dialogue and data', *Academy of Management Review*, **28** (3), 371–82.

Dalton, D.R., Daily, C.M., Ellstrand, A.E. and Johnson, J.L. (1998), 'Meta-analytical reviews of board composition, leadership structure, and financial performance', *Strategic Management Journal*, **19** (3), 269–90.

De Cabo, R.M., Gimeno, R. and Nieto, M.J. (2012), 'Gender diversity on European banks' boards of directors', *Journal of Business Ethics*, **109** (2), 145–62.

Dyl, E.A., Elliott, W.B. and Handley, J.C. (2002), 'Do share prices matter?', *Accounting and Finance*, **42** (3), 225–37.

Ellstrand, A.E., Daily, C.M., Johnson, J.L. and Dalton, D.R. (1999), 'Governance by committee: The influence of board of directors' committee composition on corporate performance', *Journal of Business Strategies*, **16** (1), 67–88.

Elsayed, K. (2011), 'Board size and corporate performance: The missing role of board leadership structure', *Journal of Management and Governance*, **15** (3), 415–46.

Fich, E.M. and Shivdasani, A. (2005), 'The impact of stock-option compensation for outside directors on firm value', *Journal of Business*, **78** (6), 2229–54.

Fligstein, N. (1985), 'The spread of the multidivisional form among large firms, 1919–1979', *American Sociological Review*, **50** (3), 377–91.

Forbes, D.P. and Milliken, F.J. (1999), 'Cognition and corporate governance: Understanding boards of directors as strategic decision-making groups', *Academy of Management Review*, **24** (3), 489–505.

Furobotn, E.G. and Pejovich, S. (1972), 'Property rights and economic theory: A survey of recent literature', *Journal of Economic Literature*, **10** (4), 1137–62.

Gabrielsson, J. (2003), *Boards and Governance in SMEs: An Inquiry into Boards' Contribution to Firm Performance*, Halmstad: Lund University, SIRE.

Gabrielsson, J. (2007), 'Boards of directors and entrepreneurial posture in medium-size companies: Putting the board demography approach to a test', *International Small Business Journal*, **25** (5), 511–37.

García-Castro, R., Aguilera, R.V. and Ariño, M.A. (2013), 'Bundles of firm corporate governance practices: A fuzzy set analysis', *Corporate Governance: An International Review*, **21** (4), 390–407.

Golden, B.R. and Zajac, E.J. (2001), 'When will boards influence strategy? Inclination x power = strategic change', *Strategic Management Journal*, **22** (12), 1087–1111.

Gomez-Meija, L. and Wiseman, R. (1997), 'Reframing executive compensation: An assessment and outlook', *Journal of Management*, **23** (3), 291–374.

Grinyer, P.H., Yasai-Ardekani, M. and Al-Bazzaz, S. (1980), 'Strategy, structure, the environment, and financial performance in 48 United Kingdom companies', *Academy of Management Journal*, **23** (2), 193–220.

Guth, W.D. and Ginsberg, A. (1990), 'Guest editors' introduction: Corporate entrepreneurship', *Strategic Management Journal*, **11** (4), 5–15.

Hall, B.H. (2002), 'The financing of research and development', *Oxford Review of Economic Policy*, **18** (1), 35–51.

Hamilton, R.T. and Shergill, G.S. (1992), 'The relationship between strategy–structure fit and financial performance in New Zealand: Evidence of generality and validity with enhanced controls', *Journal of Management Studies*, **29** (1), 95–114.

Hart, O.D. (1983), 'The market mechanism as an incentive scheme', *Bell Journal of Economics*, **14** (2), 366–82.

Heavey, C. and Simsek, Z. (2013), 'Top management composition effects on corporate entrepreneurship: The moderating role of perceived technological uncertainty', *Journal of Product Innovation Management*, **30** (5), 837–55.

Hillman, A.J. and Dalziel, T. (2003), 'Boards of directors and firm performance: Integrating agency and resource dependency perspectives', *Academy of Management Review*, **28**, 383–96.

Hornsby, J.S., Kuratko, D.F., Holt, D.T. and Wales, W.J. (2013), 'Assessing a measurement of organizational preparedness for corporate entrepreneurship', *Journal of Product Innovation Management*, **30** (5), 937–55.

Hung, H. and Mondejar, R. (2005), 'Corporate directors and entrepreneurial orientation: An empirical study', *Journal of Entrepreneurship*, **14** (2), 114–29.

Huse, M. (2000), 'Boards of directors in SMEs: A review and research agenda', *Entrepreneurship and Regional Development*, **12** (4), 271–90.

Huse, M. (2007), *Boards, Governance and Value Creation*, Cambridge: Cambridge University Press.

Huse, M. and Solberg, A.G. (2006), 'Gender-related boardroom dynamics: How Scandinavian women make and can make contributions on corporate boards', *Women in Management Review*, **21** (2), 113–30.

Jensen, M.C. (1993), 'The modern industrial revolution, exit and the failure of internal control systems', *Journal of Finance*, **48** (3), 831–80.

Jensen, M. and Meckling, W. (1976), 'Theory of the firm: Managerial behaviour, agency costs and ownership structure', *Journal of Financial Economics*, **3** (4), 305–60.

Jensen, M. and Ruback, R.S. (1983), 'The market for corporate control: The scientific evidence', *Journal of Financial Economics*, **11**, 5–50.

Judge Jr, W.Q. and Zeithaml, C.P. (1992), 'Institutional and strategic choice perspectives on board involvement in the strategic decision process', *Academy of Management Journal*, **35**, 766–94.

Kearney, C., Hisrich, R. and Roche, F. (2008), 'A conceptual model of public sector corporate entrepreneurship', *International Entrepreneurship and Management Journal*, **4** (3), 295–313.

Knight, G.A. (1987), 'Cross-cultural reliability and validity of a scale to measure firm entrepreneurial orientation', *Journal of Business Venturing*, **12** (3), 213–25.

Lacetera, N. (2001), 'Corporate governance and the governance of innovation: The case of pharmaceutical industry', *Journal of Management and Governance*, **5** (1), 29–59.

Lerner, M., Azulay, I. and Tishler, A. (2009), 'The role of compensation methods in corporate entrepreneurship', *International Studies of Management and Organization*, **39** (3), 53–81.

Lopez-Gracia, J. and Sánchez-Andújar, S. (2007), 'Financial structure of the family business: Evidence from a group of small Spanish firms', *Family Business Review*, **20** (4), 269–87.

Lubatkin, M., Lane, P.J., Collin, S-O. and Very, P. (2007), 'An embeddedness framing of governance and opportunism: Towards a cross-nationally accommodating theory of agency', *Journal of Organizational Behavior*, **28** (1), 43–58.

Lumpkin, G.T. and Dess, G.G. (1996), 'Clarifying the entrepreneurial orientation construct and linking it to performance', *Academy of Management Review*, **21** (1), 135–72.

Lumpkin, G.T. and Dess, G.G. (2001), 'Linking two dimensions of entrepreneurial orientation to firm performance: The moderating role of environment and industry life cycle', *Journal of Business Venturing*, **16** (5), 429–51.

Manne, H.G. (2011), 'Entrepreneurship, compensation, and the corporation', *Quarterly Journal of Austrian Economics*, **14** (1), 3–24.

McCormick Hyland, M. and Marcellino, P.A. (2002), 'Examining gender on corporate boards: a regional study', *Corporate Governance*, **2** (4), 24–31.

Miller, D. (1983), 'The correlates of entrepreneurship in three types of firms', *Management Science*, **29** (7), 770–91.

Miller, D. and Friesen, P.H. (1982), 'Innovation in conservative and entrepreneurial firm: Two models of strategic momentum', *Strategic Management Journal*, **3** (1), 1–25.

Miller, D. and Friesen, P.H. (1983), 'Strategy-making and environment', *Strategic Management Journal*, **4** (3), 221–35.

Miller, J.L. (2002), 'The board as a monitor of organizational activity: The applicability agency theory to nonprofit boards', *Nonprofit Management and Leadership*, **12** (4), 429–50.

Miller-Millesen, J.L. (2003), 'Understanding the behaviour of nonprofit boards of directors: A theory-based approach', *Nonprofit and Voluntary Sector Quarterly*, **32** (4), 521–47.

Myers, S.C. and Majluf, N. (1984), 'Corporate financing and investment decisions when firms have information that investors do not have', *Journal of Financial Economics*, **13** (2), 187–221.

Nielsen, S. and Huse, M. (2010), 'The contribution of women on boards of directors: Going beyond the surface', *Corporate Governance – An International Review*, **18** (2), 136–48.

Olson, D.E. (2000), 'Agency theory in the not-for-profit sectors: Its role at independent colleges', *Nonprofit and Voluntary Sector Quarterly*, **29** (2), 280–96.

Oxelheim, L. and Randøy, T. (2005), 'The Anglo-American financial influence on CEO compensation in non-Anglo-American firms', *Journal of International Business Studies*, **36**, 470–83.

Pfeffer, J. and Veiga, J.F. (1999), 'Putting people first for organizational success', *Engineering Management Review*, **27** (3), 50.

Phan, P.H., Wright, M., Ucbasaran, D. and Tan, W. (2009), 'Corporate entrepreneurship: Current research and future directions', *Journal of Business Venturing*, **24** (3), 197–205.

Pinchot, G. (1985), *Intrapreneuring: Why You Don't Have to Leave the Organisation to Become an Entrepreneur*, New York: Harper & Row.

Ponomareva, Y. and Ahlberg, J. (2016), 'Bad governance of family firms: The adoption of good governance on the boards of directors in family firms', *Ephemera: Theory and Politics in Organization*, **16** (1), 53–77.

Popper, K.R. (2002), *Conjectures and Refutations*, London: Routledge.

Poppo, L. and Zenger, T. (2002), 'Do formal contracts and relational governance function as substitutes or complements?', *Strategic Management Journal*, **23** (8), 707–25.

Pugliese, A., Bezemer, P-J., Zattoni, A., Huse, M., van den Bosch, F. and Volberda, H.W. (2009), 'Boards of directors' contribution to strategy: A literature review and research agenda', *Corporate Governance: An International Review*, **17** (3), 292–306.

Rediker, K.J. and Seth, A. (1995), 'Boards of directors and substitution effects of alternative governance mechanisms', *Strategic Management Journal*, **16**, 85–99.

Rose, C. (2007), 'Does female board representation influence firm performance? The Danish evidence', *Corporate Governance: An International Review*, **15**, 404–13.

Rule, E.G. and Irwin, D.W. (1988), 'Fostering intrapreneurship: The new competitive edge', *Journal of Business Strategy*, **9** (3), 44–47.

Schumpeter, J.A. (1934), *The Theory of Economic Development: An Inquiry into Profits, Capital, Credit, Interest, and the Business Cycle*, Cambridge, MA: Harvard University Press.

Shleifer, A. and Vishny, R.W. (1997), 'A survey of corporate governance', *Journal of Finance*, **52** (2), 737–83.

Singh, V. and Vinnicombe, S. (2004), 'Why so few women directors in top UK boardrooms? Evidence and theoretical explanations', *Corporate Governance*, **12** (4), 479–88.

Smith, E. (2007), 'Gender influence on firm-level entrepreneurship through the power structure of boards', *Women in Management Review*, **22** (3), 168–86.

Smith, E. (2009), 'The sport of governance: A study comparing private and non-profit Swedish riding schools', *European Sport Management Quarterly*, **9** (2), 163–86.

Smith, E. (2012a), 'Explaining public entrepreneurship in local government organisations', *State and Local Government Review*, **44** (3), 171–84.

Smith, E. (2012b), 'Corporate governance and entrepreneurship at the organisational level in a frame of property right', Doctoral dissertation, Lund University, Media Tryck.

Smith, E. (2014), 'Entrepreneurship at the local government level: Stimulating and restraining forces in the Swedish waste management sector', *Public Management Review*, **16** (5), 708–32.

Stein, J.C. (1997), 'Internal capital markets and the competition for corporate resources', *Journal of Finance*, **52**, 111–33.

Stevenson, H.H. and Jarillo, J.C. (1990), 'A paradigm of entrepreneurship: Entrepreneurial management', *Strategic Management Journal*, **11** (5), 17–27.

Stopford, J. and Baden-Fuller, C. (1994), 'Creating corporate entrepreneurship', *Strategic Management Journal*, **15** (7), 521–36.

Sun, J. and Cahan, S. (2009), 'The effect of compensation committee quality on the association between CEO cash compensation and accounting performance', *Corporate Governance: An International Review*, **17** (2), 193–207.

Sushil, B.R.B. and Momaya, K. (2011), 'Drivers and enablers of corporate entrepreneurship: Case of a software giant from India', *Journal of Management Development*, **30** (2),187–205.

Svenska Ridsportförbundet (2006), *Driva ridskola – Policy och rekommendationer för ridskoleverksamhet* (Managing a riding school: Policy and recommendations for the riding school industry).

Taylor, B. (2003), 'Board leadership: Balancing entrepreneurship and strategy with accountability and control', *Corporate Governance: The International Journal of Effective Board Performance*, **3** (2), 3–5.

Thomsen, S. (2008), *An Introduction to Corporate Governance: Mechanisms and Systems*, Copenhagen: DJØF Publishing.

Von Bertalanffy, L. (1968), *General System Theory: Foundations, Development, Applications*, New York: George Braziller.

Ward, A.J., Brown, J.A. and Rodriguez, D. (2009), 'Governance bundles, firm performance, and the substitutability and complementarity of governance mechanisms', *Corporate Governance: An International Review*, **17** (5), 646–60.

Watson, W.E., Johnson, L., Kumar, K. and Critelli, J. (1998), 'Process gain and process loss: Comparing interpersonal processes and performance of culturally diverse and non-diverse teams across time', *International Journal of Intercultural Relations*, **22** (4), 409–30.

Watson, W.E., Kumar, K. and Michaelsen, L.K. (1993), 'Cultural diversity's impact on interaction process and performance: Comparing homogeneous and diverse task groups', *Academy of Management Journal*, **36**, 590–602.

Williamson, O.E. (1996), *The Mechanisms of Governance*, New York: Oxford University Press.

Wirtz, P. (2011), 'The cognitive dimension of corporate governance in fast growing entrepreneurial firms', *European Management Journal*, **29**, 431–47.

Zahra, S.A. (1991), 'Predictors and financial outcomes of corporate entrepreneurship: An exploratory study', *Journal of Business Venturing*, **6** (4), 259–85.

Zahra, S.A. (1993), 'Environment, corporate entrepreneurship, and financial performance: A taxonomic approach', *Journal of Business Venturing*, **8** (4), 319–40.

Zahra, S.A. (1996), 'Governance, ownership, and corporate entrepreneurship: The moderating impact of industry technological opportunities', *Academy of Management Journal*, **39** (6), 1713–35.

Zahra, S.A., Neubaum, D.O. and Huse, M. (2000), 'Entrepreneurship in medium-size companies: Exploring the effects of ownership and governance systems', *Journal of Management*, **26** (5), 947–77.

Zahra, S.A. and Pearce II, J.A. (1989), 'Boards of directors and corporate financial performance: A review and integrative model', *Journal of Management*, **15** (2), 291–334.
Zampetakis, L.A. and Moustakis, V. (2007), 'Fostering corporate entrepreneurship through
internal marketing implications for change in the public sector', *European Journal of
Innovation Management*, **10** (4), 413–33.

15. Corporate entrepreneurship in a large company: skunk works or guided evolution?

Seppo Laukkanen, Martin Lindell and Anssi Vanjoki

INTRODUCTION

Scholarly studies suggest that the governance system of an enterprise may have a major impact on its conditions for corporate entrepreneurship (Guth and Ginsberg, 1990; Taylor, 2001; Huse, 2007). Prior studies of how corporate governance influences corporate entrepreneurship have primarily employed statistical methods to examine how governance mechanisms and corporate entrepreneurship efforts correlate (e.g., Zahra, 1996; Zahra et al., 2000; Brunninge and Nordqvist, 2004; Gabrielsson, 2007). While this stream of research has contributed valuable insights into the governance–entrepreneurship relationship in corporate settings, there is a lack of recent studies that address corporate entrepreneurship as an organization-wide process operating at multiple levels and involving multiple strategic actors (e.g., Newey and Zahra, 2009). As a result, we know relatively little about how corporate governance interacts with cultural, strategic and administrative processes that foster successful corporate entrepreneurship over longer periods of time. Therefore, in this chapter we discuss corporate governance and entrepreneurial development processes. We specifically analyse three entrepreneurially driven strategic projects of a major company. The aim is to develop understanding on how corporate governance and leadership can advance entrepreneurship in a large corporation.

The concept of corporate governance has been elaborated from several perspectives. Most of these perspectives concern the relationship between owners, boards and top management (Davis and Useem, 2002; Monks and Minow, 2011). Huse (2007) divides the definition of corporate governance into four categories: a shareholder definition, stakeholder definition, managerial definition and firm definition. In this chapter, we use the firm definition, which focuses on value creation. According to this definition, the purpose of corporate governance bodies is to facilitate cooperation;

in addition, these bodies resolve conflicts between stakeholders and they monitor control (Huse, 2007, p. 22f). A board's role is to ensure that managers and the organization focus on long-term value creation and corporate entrepreneurship. Entrepreneurial activities usually have a long-term perspective.

Our view of corporate entrepreneurship is in accordance with Ireland et al.'s (2009, p. 21) definition: corporate entrepreneurship is a vision-directed, organization-wide reliance on entrepreneurial behaviour that purposefully and continuously rejuvenates the organization and shapes the scope of its opportunities through the recognition and exploitation of entrepreneurial opportunities. Dess et al. (2003) identify four categories of corporate entrepreneurship: (1) sustained regeneration; (2) organizational rejuvenation; (3) strategic renewal; and (4) domain redefinition. This chapter examines categories 1 and 4. In category 1, sustained generation, firms develop cultures, processes and structures to support and encourage a continuous stream of new product introductions in their current markets as well as enter into new markets with existing products. In category 4, the firm proactively seeks to create a new product market position in markets that competitors have not recognized or have underserved.

This chapter begins with a brief literature review of the concepts of intrapreneurship and corporate entrepreneurship, and simultaneously clarifies our view on these concepts. The review summarizes the influence of top management on the organizational context of corporate entrepreneurship. The empirical material consists of three entrepreneurial cases in the company, Nokia. The projects are analysed and compared. The chapter concludes with a multilevel discussion on corporate entrepreneurship that brings to the fore the mechanisms through which corporate governance and leadership support or inhibit entrepreneurship.

INTRAPRENEURSHIP AND CORPORATE ENTREPRENEURSHIP: SKUNK WORKS AND GUIDED EVOLUTION

The early characterizations of intrapreneurship in large companies emphasize the bottom-up aspects of the entrepreneurial process. The entrepreneurial projects were seen as self-driven 'skunk works' (Ahmed and Shepherd, 2010). The driving force was viewed to be an autonomous entrepreneur at an operational level in the organization. The projects were considered to be lower-level employee initiatives involving something new; projects were innovations created unasked by subordinates and, occasionally, against the desires of senior leadership (Vesper, 1984, p. 295).

Intrapreneurship was entrepreneurship that just happened to occur in a large corporate context. The management or strategy articulations had little to do with inspiring or driving intrapreneurship. The inspiration arose from the intrapreneur's own aspirations.

In the above characterizations of intrapreneurship, the company's top management played a minimal role in initiating and guiding the projects. The primary role of top management was a retrospective rationalization of emergent entrepreneurial initiatives, a rather passive role for top management. Bower (1970) and Burgelman (1983) both argue for a bottom-up process. However, in Burgelman's model, champions at operational and middle management levels are central catalysts of renewal. They orchestrate the process through which individuals inside organizations pursue opportunities independently of the resources they currently control (Stevenson and Jarillo, 1990).

To augment this operational view of entrepreneurship in large organizations, the concept of corporate entrepreneurship was introduced. In the corporate entrepreneurship conceptualization, top management's role is more active (Sharma and Chrisman, 1999). Quinn (1978) previously introduced the concept of logical incrementalism, in which the strategic topics are generated in a series of 'strategic subsystems' and are governed by broad goals. Later, both Noder and Bower (1996) and Burgelman (1991) argued for more active senior management roles. Based on the analysis of several businesses, Noda and Bower claim that top managers exercise critical influence over the strategic initiatives of lower-level managers by establishing the context in which these managers make decisions and take actions. This insight is echoed by Burgelman's proposition (1991, p. 256): 'Firms that are relative successful over long periods of time, say ten years or more, will be characterized by maintaining top driven strategic intent while simultaneously maintain bottom-up driven internal experimentation and selection processes'. Burgelman reasons that firms have both variance-increasing and variance-reducing mechanisms. The actual realized strategy evolves as an outcome of induced and self-driven activities (Ahmed and Shepherd, 2010).

The strategic intent works as a variance-reducing mechanism. It loosely articulates the long-term goals that reflect the preferred future position of the firm (Hamel and Prahalad, 1989). The strategic intent sets direction and inspires analysis, interpretation and decisions at lower levels in the organization. Yet, the intent gives necessary latitude for entrepreneurial initiatives, the key source and driver of organizational learning.

Learning works its way through organizational fabric, as Dutta and Crossan (2005) discuss in their 4I organizational learning framework. According to these researchers, the learning begins when individual(s) develop an intuition regarding business opportunities on the basis of their prior experience and their recognition of patterns as external events unfold. In the next phase the individual interpretation gains strength as a group shares it and develops a shared understanding of a feasible business opportunity. Dialogue and joint actions are important for the development of shared understanding, that is, integrating. The final phase is that the shared understanding gets institutionalized at an organizational level in the form of systems, structures, procedures and strategy; this entails some sort of formalization of the outcome of corporate entrepreneurship.

In advancing corporate entrepreneurship, Gupta et al. (2004) have summed the tasks of top management: (1) framing the challenge, which includes simultaneously setting ambitious goals and setting limits of what can be achieved; (2) absorbing the uncertainty, which is creating vision and unburdening responsibility for being wrong regarding the future; (3) path-clearing, which is negotiating within inside and outside environments; (4) building commitment and enabling the energy to accomplish the set of goals; and (5) setting limits to override self-imposed, limiting ideas of the team members. Gupta et al.'s view of the management's tasks inherently indicates that management through levels of organization has an active role in fostering corporate entrepreneurship.

The top level is heavily involved in strategy formulation and competitive advantage reformulation (Amo, 2006). Top management's proactiveness, which refers to initiative and risk taking, is stressed; bold and competitively aggressive actions by senior management are emphasized as well (Antoncic and Hisrich, 2001).

EVERYBODY IS AN INNOVATOR: FIRM IS BOTH FOUNDATION AND TEST BED FOR ENTREPRENEURIALLY DRIVEN INNOVATIONS

However, common strategic intent and governance is not sufficient. Nahapiet and Ghoshal (1998) note the importance of corporate culture in fostering the productive interplay of strategy and emergent actions. They even claim that internal corporate culture is more important for a long-term competitive advantage than a single competitive advantage at any given point in time.

Lovas and Ghoshal (2000) have further developed the evolutionary perspective of an organization. In their conceptualization, all employees generate ideas. The initial screening of ideas is made in the social structure of a company; the people working on initially selected strategic initiatives perform another screening. Ultimately, the ideas are verified by their success in the actual business. The members of the top management group have five main responsibilities: (1) to develop and articulate strategic goals that define the strategic intent of the organization; (2) to sponsor strategic initiatives; (3) to allocate financial capital to strategic initiatives; (4) to recruit people to the organization; and (5) to take responsibility for the development of the social capital and knowledge in the organization.

Along the lines of evolutionary perspective the entrepreneur intuits and takes the initiative. In order to obtain support and resources from the surrounding organization, the entrepreneur needs to convince the organization of the merits of the case. For this to happen, the entrepreneur's interpretation and judgement of the situation needs to be sufficiently shared and internalized by the decision-makers. The governance and leadership principles of the company define the arenas and set the tone for instances in which the merging of entrepreneur's subjective views and the company's common strategic agenda occurs.

The role of the company's administrative system is to facilitate the replication of a natural selection environment inside the firm, thus enabling and guiding the strategy process without traditional, hierarchical mechanisms of command and control. The purpose of the administrative systems is not solely to control the retention of predefined strategies (Lovas and Ghoshal, 2000): the intention is also to ensure that variation, selection and retention of strategic initiatives and human and social capital are informed by the local knowledge of people within the firm.

In this conceptualization, the role of top management is: (1) to create a set of administrative systems that would replicate the processes of natural selection within the organization; and (2) to guide those processes by defining the strategic intent and the units of selection in the evolutionary process (Lovas and Ghoshal, 2000). The dynamic capabilities that underlie a firm's competitive advantage are grounded in people and their relationships, that is, in the firm's human and social capital. Lovas and Ghosal's hypothesis is that firms that are able to choose strategic initiatives, which effectively leverage their existing human and social capital, will perform better in the long run than those that are not able to attain this synergy.

DOES THE LEADERSHIP AND GOVERNANCE MATTER?

Thus far, the short literature review describes corporate entrepreneurship fundamentally as a bottom-up process. The individual entrepreneurs and the team members involved in the projects are the initiators and developers of the process. They also are the driving force for substantial new ventures in a large company and, perhaps, are the most critical resource for a large company's long-term survival. However, the entrepreneurial core process is in symbiosis with entrepreneurial leadership and governance: the leadership, governance and ultimately the board has several roles in the creation and fostering of corporate entrepreneurship.

The board's role is to determine and decide the long-term orientation of the company and the strategic intent. Ultimately, it is the board that decides, or at least confirms, the strategy and structure of the company. The board also decides the most strategic investments of a company.

In a large company, individual board members are not involved in the day-to-day activities of corporate entrepreneurship. However, they can contribute with advice, networking and lobbying (Huse, 2007). In particular, board members are expected to have the greatest input in decisions with high complexity and uncertainty within a turbulent environment. Rindova (1999) suggests that when board members participate in scanning, the decision-making group will collect more diverse information on a broader range of issues related to the decision-making situation than will an internal top management group. The decisions and decision alternatives will be more thoroughly analysed and discussed with the board's involvement. The expectation is that board members contribute significantly to complex strategic decisions, such as the assessment of ambiguous entrepreneurial opportunities. Studies also show that board members' involvement in strategy development has a positive impact on internal innovation, while financial control has a negative impact (Huse, 2007).

Top management has a substantial role in developing the company's culture; it shapes the organizational context in which action occurs. Despite the fact that most of the decisions and development activities can be delegated to lower levels in the organization, top management has a role in motivating and facilitating distributed and self-generated initiatives (Ghoshal and Bartlett, 1994, p. 105). The senior management also determines the internal governance structure of the company, which in turn defines the instances of operational decision-making in terms of participants and mandates.

Identification with the organization provides direction for the development activities. Shared ambitions and objectives lead to a context in which employees are ready to do even more than expected. Expectations, obligations and disciplines, in terms of repeatable processes, are stated as success factors for self-driven work. Different types of support from top management, such as encouragement, trust and resources, are important for development work. Ultimately, organizational learning results from a combination of distributed initiatives and organizational contexts as supporting factors.

The fundamental question at the end of this theory discussion is whether corporate entrepreneurship can be seen as a guided evolutionary process. If yes, what are the driving forces, governance mechanisms and leadership activities that support such a process? Can we identify concrete governance and leadership recommendations that companies could use for advancing entrepreneurship in their organizations?

EMPIRICAL DATA

This discussion is based on three Nokia innovation cases. The entrepreneurial processes of the cases were thoroughly examined from the entrepreneurs' viewpoints in Laukkanen's doctoral dissertation (Laukkanen, 2012). In augmenting the cases, we build on the notion that the interplay between senior management and entrepreneurs – that is, the leadership – is reciprocal. Both strategy articulations and activities evolve through continuous iteration of strategic intent and actions (Laukkanen, 2012). The formal governance and organizational structure defines the arenas in which this interplay takes place. The normative governance principles, such as opportunity orientation versus control orientation and trust, set the tone for the interplay. The objective is to develop a narrative view of corporate entrepreneurship as a reciprocal interplay between top management and entrepreneurial actions. We leveraged the rich empirical data and analysis from purposely selected innovation projects that occurred at Nokia from 2006 to 2008.

The empirical data were gathered from intrapreneurs who initiated and executed three selected innovation projects. In addition, the empirical data contain the insights collected from middle managers and executives that led and supported the corporate entrepreneurs' work in these projects. In addition, a book by chief executive officer (CEO) and chairman of the board, Jorma Ollila (Ollila and Saukkomaa, 2013), has been used; this book describes Nokia's development since the mid-1980s.

To dive into the governance aspects of corporate entrepreneurship, the empirical analysis is augmented by the reflections of the senior executive who was in charge of the business unit, in which the innovation projects occurred; reflections by senior executives that otherwise played a critical role in executing the cases are also included. Senior executive participation in the governance bodies at all organizational levels of the subject company opens a unique view into how the governance structure and corporate culture influenced entrepreneurship. This also creates an opportunity to understand more regarding the dialogue of senior management and corporate entrepreneurs during the innovation process. The case description begins with a short description of the board and, particularly, the management style of CEO Jorma Ollila, a key Nokia manager for more than two decades.

THE NOKIA GROUP

Jorma Ollila was nominated as CEO of Nokia in 1992; his tenure continued until 2006. He held a double role for a long time, also serving as chairman of the board from 1999 to 2012.

Board

In the corporate governance guidelines for Nokia, the basic responsibility of the board members is to act in good faith and to exercise due care in their business judgement on an informed basis; in other words, board members must act in what they reasonably and honestly believe to be in the interests of the company and its shareholders. In discharging that obligation, the directors must avail themselves of all relevant information reasonably accessible to them.

In Nokia, strategy creation belongs to top management; top management presents it to the board. Following a dialogue with the board, the board makes decisions regarding the agreed-upon strategy. The board is not where strategy or an important organizational structure change is planned. The board is international: approximately 50 per cent of the board members reside outside Finland. The minimum number of board members is seven, and the maximum is 12. The board members convened 13 times during 2006; however, the number of meetings varies widely from year to year. In 2013, when divesting the mobile phone business, the number of board meetings was very high, at 34. Nokia has an active board with many informal contacts also occurring between board meetings.

Creative organizational culture and a favourable context
When Jorma Ollila became CEO, Nokia already had 25000 employees. To manage such a huge number of employees required common values. The values governing Nokia's business, which the CEO stressed, were previously established in the 1990s. These were: (1) customer orientation, which included the development of value-added products and services for the customer; (2) respecting the individual, meaning that all employees' needs were to be met openly and honestly; (3) achievement, meaning that all employees supported the achievement of company goals and were promised rewards; and (4) continuous learning, meaning learning on the job,

in negotiations, in customer relations and in processes. This constituted value-based management in Nokia. The company's values were summarized in the slogan 'The Nokia Way'.

CEO Jorma Ollila claims that he is not particularly creative himself, but that he endeavoured to develop the organization in a creative direction and provide possibilities for creative people and their occasionally very risky projects. For the CEO, managers and foremen must be seen as mentors who draw from employees' competences. Trust is vital; everything is built around trust in people and trust in their work. Within the company an entrepreneurial spirit existed, and mistakes were allowed. Common culture and common values were the driving forces for growth; this meant loyalty and trust toward the best in the company, an ability to listen and avoidance of politicking in the organization.

Strategy

Since the early 1990s Nokia's primary expansion strategy was organic growth in growing markets, not acquisitions. At the beginning of his tenure, Jorma Ollila defined the future of Nokia using four concepts to increase the company's profitability: (1) focus, entailing a concentration on core competencies (mobile phones, telecommunication and cable); (2) globalization; (3) telecommunication; and (4) high-value-added products.

The strategic annual discussion at Nokia began with a joint meeting of 200–400 top managers. In these meetings, all important future demands were discussed. According to Ollila, strategic thinking is very much a daily undertaking; it involves business plans, including goals, directions, and means of reaching these goals. However, the company must be adaptive; it must be possible to correct business plans and directions impacted upon by a turbulent environment.

The structure for strategy development is the strategic discussions; at Nokia, a strategic panel met with top management every month. This was a useful discussion forum. Ollila relied significantly on the top management group and 400 key managers; he had direct contact with all of these individuals.

Administrative and management processes

From the very beginning, Jorma Ollila wanted to freely recruit key managers without any board involvement. The organization needed to be flat and decentralized, system-efficient, with a working style based on teamwork. The core processes were strategic planning, economic control and human resource management based on the values defined above.

Four top management levels could be observed: (1) CEO; (2) five core managers (named 'the dream team' in the media); (3) top management executive group; and (4) 200–400 key managers. The five core executives had a very important role. Ideas and the future of Nokia were the frequent topic of informal discussions in this group; minutes were not recorded. 'Silent trust' was built between the members of the dream team, meaning that core executives could make rapid decisions and take risks without going through formal processes or agreement rituals. The CEO also discussed topics individually with the members of the dream team and other top managers. He saw himself as best in a one-to-one discussion. The characteristic of day-to-day work was frequent communication and openness.

During the 1990s the organization evolved through multiple stages. A common denominator of organization models was a strong entrepreneurial drive in the business units. At the time of examined cases the company was organized into three business group units: Multimedia, Enterprise Solutions and Mobile Phones. The Multimedia and Enterprise Solutions business groups were set to explore new opportunities in mobile internet and enterprise services. Mobile Phones was set to aggressively exploit the company's leading position in an established market of conventional mobile phones.

Sponsoring, resources and support

According to the CEO, the most important company resource was its employees; he saw himself as responsible for them. He attempted to know all the 300–400 top managers well and, simultaneously, he attempted to maintain satisfactory contact with all levels of the organization. Promising young people were quickly promoted in the organization. Nokia valued education and knowledge and supported continuous learning. For many decades, improvising had long been a part of the Nokia culture. All flowers had been allowed to grow. If the idea had growth potential, Nokia had been willing to invest in the project. The aforementioned has provided an overarching context for the entrepreneurial activities in Nokia.

Organizational setting for examined entrepreneurial business projects

At the time of the development of the products and services examined in this chapter, Nokia was the mobile phone industry's undisputed leader, with a 40 per cent global market share. The company built its industry leadership during the previous 15 years by proactively exploring opportunities within the rapidly growing mobile phone market. The company was viewed as the mobile phone industry's innovation powerhouse. Nokia had a strong opportunity-oriented entrepreneurial legacy.

In 2007, Nokia's industry leadership built on the mastery of a wide array of products for different markets around the world. The markets had well-established trade customers such as operators and distributors, with which Nokia had strong commercial ties. The Multimedia Business Group was in charge of advanced multimedia-oriented smart phones targeting consumer markets. In addition to the smart phones, the business group had the responsibility of developing mobile internet services for consumers.

Innovation cases examined in this study were all introduced to the markets in 2007 and 2008. The development time varied from a year and a half to five years. As a consequence of differences in development time, the organizational context of the cases varies slightly.

As noted by Anssi Vanjoki, the executive vice-president in charge of the business, one must take a longer view to understand the organizational context in which these three cases occurred. The cultural heritage of the Multimedia Business Group can be traced back to the mid-1990s and the development of the first wireless data product, Nokia Communicator. The development of the first Nokia Communicator was driven by a few technology nerds with strong strategic foresight into the convergence of information technology (IT) and telecom technologies. The CEO, Jorma Ollila, Nokia's executive board, and the president of Nokia Mobile Phones, Pekka Ala-Pietilä, were sufficiently open-minded and future-oriented to allow the skunk works team to act in a decidedly autonomous way.

The autonomy and resources the team was given enabled it to choose technologies that differed from the mainstream. The team was also given responsibility to develop its own strategy; it had latitude to bend standard development processes when necessary to achieve its strategic objectives. The Wireless Data Unit developed a highly entrepreneurial culture characterized by extremely high ambitions, progressive opportunity orientation, uncompromising work ethics, high trust, risk tolerance and non-hierarchical structure.

At the end of the 1990s this cultural hegemony was nurtured in the Digital Convergence Unit (DCU), which was a continuation of the Wireless Data Unit. The DCU was a somewhat larger organizational entity tasked to address a broader opportunity space stemming from the convergence of telecom, IT and internet technologies. The DCU had the mission of bringing together digital imaging, music, games, internet media and mobile communications. The innovators and managers were working together to scope opportunities and conceptualize new products and services. In addition, product development was more collegial in this unit than in the mainstream business. Due to the technical complexity of new concepts the efficiency, in terms of man-years per new product, was compromised. The unit developed the first smart phones with digital cameras and true internet browsing capability. In parallel with the development of these radically innovative products, the managers and innovators developed a specific strategy for each new product category. The DCU's top management was actively participating in the development of those strategies; through this practice of participation and engagement the emerging strategies migrated and integrated effectively into Nokia's overall strategy.

All examined cases belonged to the Multimedia Business Group's strategic scope. The N 95 was executed entirely by the Multimedia Business Group. The development activities leading to the Comes-With-Music proposition were originally initiated in the Digital Convergence group, but the development occurred primarily in the Multimedia Business Group. The Sports Tracker activities were initiated at the Nokia Research Centre, which also implemented the pre-commercial service proposition.

THE CASES

The N 95 departed from the business group's established strategy. The mission and strategic intent of the business unit drove the innovation. However, the N 95's development activity substantially changed the product strategy framework used for positioning and specifying products. In addition to an innovative product, the activity created a fundamentally new way of positioning advanced Multimedia products; it created a new strategy framework. Existing product development processes drove the development activity for the N 95. The developers had the capacity to modify the processes as the development task required. However, in essence, the innovation was rooted in the operational and strategic tradition of the business group and Nokia.

The Comes-With-Music and Sports Tracker cases both represented new businesses, which were only loosely connected to Nokia's business tradition. Comes-With-Music was driven by the business unit's strategy, whereas self-driven entrepreneurial researchers at the Nokia Research Centre initiated the development of Sports Tracker. Neither Comes-With-Music nor Sports Tracker relied on Nokia's traditional business processes.

N 95 Case

The Nokia N 95 was a high-performance multimedia phone, which changed the perception of what mobile devices are capable of. The product introduced new path-breaking capabilities, such as true internet browsing and Global Positioning System (GPS) navigation, to the market. Moreover, in terms of imaging and multimedia functionality, the N 95 represented the state of the art in the industry. The N 95 was viewed as the most innovative product of the industry; it also became a great commercial success.

The key phases of development

The mission of the Multimedia Business Group, which was the rapid take-off of consumer internet services and accumulated experience regarding the usage patterns of multimedia mobile phones, drove the initial goal setting for the N 95. An entrepreneurial and powerful portfolio management team took the initiative in defining the product. The team members had versatile professional backgrounds and were well connected, both to operations and to management.

The product conceptualization work was preceded by a systematic exploration of innovative technologies in accordance with the business's overall strategic direction. The goal was to create maximum consumer value with sophisticated multimedia functionalities. With Nokia's decade-long mobile multimedia research and development, the team had a broad portfolio of technologies, inventions and insights to build on. Clear strategic intent, a broad mandate and the efficacy of the portfolio planning team fostered the development of a holistic understanding regarding the opportunity. With its strengths, the team was in a position to identify the building blocks for the product and draft initial conceptualizations for product development. The creation of a radical concept required a holistic view of the market as well as a comprehensive understanding regarding implementation options. Moreover, with its experience and influence, the team was able to drive the necessary changes to the product strategy and sales practices. Those changes legitimized the innovative proposition and enabled its implementation.

Through this early conceptualization work the product strategy framework of the Multimedia Business Group was fundamentally changed from narrowly focused products to multipurpose devices with maximum market value. Without the change in the product category strategy, the N 95 concept could not have been legitimized. The drastic change in the product category strategy triggered a flood of combinatory innovations.

The development of the N 95 concept benefited from the entrepreneurial leadership of the Multimedia product business. The leadership challenged the established tight pricing assumptions, which provided leeway for a more aggressive deployment of value-adding technologies. The changes in the positioning framework and pricing assumptions provided latitude for integrating new, innovative functionalities into the product. The leadership was also persistent and urged exploring all avenues in creating an innovative product concept. This persistence led to the discovery of a novel double slide concept; this concept made the product distinctive and resolved usability challenges stemming from the N 95's wide array of functionalities. In fact, the 'revolutionary' concept was found in the 'rubbish bin' of old concept experiments.

During the conceptualization work, the actual product development evolved into a large-scale product programme, which was executed according to established product development practices. Following well-defined and disciplined processes was essential to managing the vastly complex development of an ambitious product. Product development benefited from the high priority given the product by the business group and Nokia's senior management. Additionally, the sense of ownership among the doers was a critical success factor for the development of the complex product; this was established through participation in the conceptualization work. Moreover, the complex and interdependent product development activity could not have been accomplished without the experienced core team, which was well connected to parties that were contributing to the N 95 product implementation.

The senior vice-president of the product business and the senior vice-president of product development championed the product development work and acted as an escalation route for securing resources and deliverables from other parts of the organization. This work required substantial amounts of their time.

Obtaining the necessary internet services to accompany the product required changes to the business's critical sales and marketing processes. The business development that created specific internet services for the N 95 required an early introduction of a secret product to trusted business partners. The change in the business-critical sales and marketing process was enabled by the shared strategic interest between the Multimedia Business Group and the N 95 programme, to establish the capability to launch holistic propositions containing both hardware and service elements. In addition, the fact that many key stakeholders in the sales organization had participated in the conceptualization work of the N 95 was instrumental in obtaining the required decisions from the sales management team, as well as from the Multimedia Business Group's management team.

In parallel with the decision-making, the actual business development was conducted through an organic set-up consisting of key stakeholders from the sales organization and product business. The working model relied heavily on the internal business networks of the key actors, as well as on the commitment of the people who had participated in the conceptualization of the N 95. The service business development activity of the N 95 created a new product launch process for Nokia, which was documented; this process spread as the practice to launch sophisticated products that required complementary internet services. A critical success factor in developing internet services for the N 95 was the selection of a single lead market; a strict focus on the lead market enabled comprehensive integration and synchronization of global and local service elements.

Following the launch in the lead market, the country-specific launches were adaptively replicated from country to country. The replication of the experiences from the lead market to the follower markets occurred through both headquarters and at the operational level, from market to market. This process was an adaptive and organic replication process, which entailed replication of the core concept and local adaptation, as well as continuous learning from the local adaptations. The sense of ownership established during the product definition phase was a major supporting factor in this dispersed learning and execution phase. The senior vice-presidents of the product business, service business and Multimedia sales divisions all supported the dispersed activity; in addition, the key director-level stakeholders supported the activity with their own efforts. The trio of senior vice-presidents had the capacity to secure resources and align the high-level target settings of their respective organizations. The hands-on support of the middle managers drove the effectiveness of the dispersed business development activity in Nokia's country organizations. The middle managers were also crucial in obtaining the support of key business partners for the complex product launch.

Critical success factors
The decisive factor making the N 95 the most innovative product in the industry was the way it was conceptualized. The product's conceptualization was done as part of a holistic portfolio planning process; the work was tightly linked to the overall strategy discourse of the Multimedia Business Group. The aim was to create maximum value to consumers and business partners. Ultimately, the N 95's conceptualization reframed the principles by which the products were positioned and defined; this change 'authorized' the new combinations of technologies and capabilities, which led to novel value-adding inventions.

The N 95 conceptualization activity elevated the portfolio planning process of the Multimedia Business Group to a core process that had a major influence on the business group's strategy. The process engaged key stakeholders from sales, product planning, product development and technology development. The collaborative entrepreneurial effort in conceptualizing the N 95 spurred entrepreneurship and commitment among the participants. The committed entrepreneurship of participants in the conceptualization work of the N 95 was a crucial resource for executing and bringing to market the revolutionary product and associated services.

The elevation of the portfolio planning process was enabled by the pro-active and opportunity-oriented mind-set of the entire senior leadership of the business group. The vice-president of portfolio planning managed the actual process; he engaged key stakeholders from sales, marketing, product development and service development in the process. The diverse participants brought a broad set of inputs and cognitive frames to the conceptualization work. Without the broad locus of influence, the participants in the process would have been unable to envision the value of the innovative proposition in such a broad context. The executive vice-president of the business group and the senior vice-president of the product business supported the work by assigning it a high priority and by supporting the risk taking. These senior managers were also engaged in the conceptualization to extend the internalization of the merits of the concept; they also developed a personal commitment to the product development.

The fact that the participants in the planning process developed a strong sense of ownership for the innovation was instrumental in the development work's later stages. The dispersed action necessary in implementing such a holistic innovation was easier to execute as the key stakeholders in different parts of the organization were driving and supporting the work.

In addition to the fact that the team members were influential, well connected and knowledgeable, the process was effectively tied to the actual ongoing business, because it covered products in active sales, products under development, and products in the process of being defined. Operating over multiple time horizons created a ripe environment for organizational learning; it enabled a second and even a third organizational learning loop. The product planning community developed a highly entrepreneurial mind-set. The opportunity-oriented strategy and leadership of the Multimedia Business Group formed the context in which such entrepreneurial mind-sets could emerge. Ultimately, the entrepreneurship mind-set spread to the product and business development groups, as well as to the sales group.

Outcome
The commercial launch of the N 95 was strong, impactful and rapidly replicable across markets. The innovative product had worked itself to the core of the new product strategy and the internal organization supported the sales and marketing of the product. In addition, the business partners adopted the product and its associated strategy. In fact, the N 95 product became a strategic product for most customers. It reversed the rapid price erosion of the industry for a while.

Consequently, the N 95 became a commercial success, which substantially strengthened Nokia's position in accordance to the company's intended strategy. With its success, the N 95 changed the actual strategy of the company markedly by converting the product category approach of the Multimedia Business Group from categories defined by narrow functionalities, such as Imaging and Music to broad all-in-one propositions.

Sports Tracker Case

At the time of its introduction, Sports Tracker was a revolutionary internet service innovation that enabled people to link their self-created multimedia content, such as pictures, to a location on a map. In practice, Sports Tracker users could tag a digital map with the user's personal training data or other self-created content, such as photographs or videos. The application opportunities were very versatile; it won the Best Mobile Service award in 2007.

Sports Tracker was launched solely as a pre-commercial service. It received an outstanding reception from its users. The enthusiastic user community viewed Sports Tracker as the best service ever introduced by Nokia. However, Nokia never commercialized the service because, as a stand-alone service, it was in strategic conflict with the location services of the recently acquired Navteq. In addition, the attempts to integrate the key functionalities of Sports Tracker with other internet services failed.

The key phases of development

Three self-driven researchers had diverse business backgrounds and a great interest in sports; they created the original idea regarding attaching training data to a location on a digital map. The idea of tagging maps with self-created content had utility value in a variety of application areas, such as sports, imaging and games.

In the first instance, the inventors focused on creating a value-adding feature to a rugged sports phone. The first innovation attempt was terminated due to a change in Nokia's overall product strategy; the sports-oriented phones category was terminated. Following the change in the product strategy, the inventors shifted their focus to another application area, the 'wellness diary'. The plan was to create a spin-off venture that provided a wellness diary service to Nokia smart phone users. Nokia Ventures hosted the activity. As the corporate venturing activity of Nokia was scaled down, the inventors were forced to seek a new home for the activity; therefore, the inventors also revisited the application area, returning to the original application area, that is, to sports. They started working on a holistic sports tracking service proposition they termed 'Sports Tracker'.

The Sports Tracker development activity was executed at the Nokia

Research Centre. The work was only loosely connected to the business strategy work of Nokia and the Multimedia Business Group. In addition, on the operational level the connections to commercial services development were minimal. The Sports Tracker service proposition development team consisted of entrepreneurially oriented technology experts who developed relationships with the operational service business of their own accord. Nokia Research Centre's senior management were not in a position to mentor or champion business-related matters; they lacked both a mandate and competence in such matters. The Sports Tracker team's relationships to the businesses became sporadic. The interests of the innovators and the interests of the operational service business were in conflict. The innovators were keen to develop a vertical business with its own strong identity, whereas the operational services unit was seeking an add-on 'contextual' feature for a wide array of services.

In addition, the operative processes were different in the operational service business and research unit. As the development team members had strong faith in and commitment to their invention, they eventually proceeded alone. The Sports Tracker was introduced to the market through an experimental setting in the Nokia Research Centre; it attracted an enthusiastic user community and generated a great deal of excitement both internally and in the market.

The top executives at Nokia were aware of the Sports Tracker proposition, its merits and its users' excitement. The stance was supportive; the innovation was viewed to be well in accordance with the overarching strategic direction of the company. In fact, the executive vice-president of the Multimedia Business Group insisted on a prompt implementation of the proposition in the operational service business. To support the implementation, he assigned the most capable and respected executives to determine how to commercialize the Sports Tracker proposition. However, the issues of the prioritization of critical resources in the operational service business, lack of ownership among middle management and stakeholders, personal conflicts between operations personnel, and harsh technical realities prevented the commercial deployment of the Sports Tracker innovation; it was never commercialized.

Eventually, some novel ideas from the innovation migrated to the plans for other company service propositions. The novelty value of the Sports Tracker proposition shrank with time. Finally, the team worked out a plan to spin off Sports Tracker and its experimental implementation from Nokia; Sports Tracking Technologies Ltd was established.

Comes-With-Music Case

The Comes-With-Music proposition was a revolutionary service and business model innovation that introduced an alternative pricing scheme to consumers and a new sales channel to the music industry. In concrete terms, it enabled users of Nokia smart phones to purchase rights to a practically unlimited music library. It added value to the smart phones.

For the record companies, Comes-With-Music opened a new service category, which expanded their music market to mobile phone users. To succeed in the market, it was crucial to bundle the introduction of the service with the launch of a compelling and distinctive product, Nokia 5800. The bundling with a distinctive product connected Comes-With-Music to a massive launch campaign and Nokia's global sales presence. The bundled approach made the Comes-With-Music irresistible to the record labels. The music industry perceived Comes-With-Music as an opportunity to, with minimal effort, sell and distribute their digital music to the audiences that would have otherwise been apt to copy illegal music.

The key phases of development
The Comes-With-Music proposition arose as an outcome of an explorative search for opportunities to add value within the convergence of digital music and mobile telephony. The original target setting for the explorative search was to see how Nokia could add value to its mobile phones with digital music. Initially, a small team of young entrepreneurial business developers were given the task of exploring the opportunity. The work was led by the vision and inspiration of the executive vice-president in charge of the Digital Convergence Unit and by the vice-president of business development.

Reflecting technical progress, Nokia's capabilities, and the leeway provided by the operator customers, several innovations were introduced during the exploration journey. The early market experiences gained with FM radios, music players and dedicated music devices added to the overall music competences of Nokia. These early steps also improved Nokia's capability and credibility to interact with the music industry.

Eventually, in 2005 Nokia initiated a systematic search for substantial strategic opportunities with music services. The search entailed a number of elaborative discussions with opinion leaders and experts in the music and internet services industry. The goal was to search for disruption and value creation opportunities that would leverage Nokia's strongholds in mobile technologies, its global reach, leading market share and marketing capabilities.

The idea of the Comes-With-Music proposition arose out of these discussions with the music industry. The concept was simply to create a fixed price bundle that would allow its buyers to download an unlimited quantity of music from the associated record labels. The timing of the idea's invention cleverly coincided with the acquisition of a relatively small digital music service company, Loudeye. The acquisition of Loudeye was critical because it added to Nokia's music service competences and resources. Those competences and resources were critical in the later stages of development. The acquisition of Loudeye can be viewed as an entrepreneurial act by the executive vice-president of the Multimedia Business Group. Through this risky acquisition he supported the creation of a sufficient competence base for building a presence in the new field.

To achieve maximum impact, the introduction of the Comes-With-Music service proposition was attached to the launch of a phone which was specifically designed for the youth market. Once the guiding principles of the service proposition were fixed, a massive contract negotiation process began. The executive vice-president of the Multimedia Business Group and the senior-vice president of services development were the key actors negotiating the agreements with the first record labels; these senior executives put much personal effort into obtaining signatures for the first deals. The strong commitment and involvement partially stemmed from the fact that these very same executives had originally initiated the search for digital music-related business opportunities; these executives were committed to the overall agenda and to the personnel involved.

As the probability of success for the Comes-With-Music service increased, Nokia made a corporate-level decision to bundle the service that had been created by the Multimedia Business Group, with a youth-oriented product that was being developed by the Mobile Phones business group. The cross-business group decision was justified by the fact that the Nokia 5800 was the most strategic product in Nokia's portfolio in 2008. It was the first mass-market touch-screen phone. In addition, this targeted the right consumer segment, that is, youth. The plan was to create a bundled value proposition and a massive youth focused marketing campaign to launch it.

The bundling decision was made at a fairly late stage of the product development. Nokia 5800 had previously been conceptualized; its core functionality was defined to be navigation. The change from a navigation focus to a music focus was dramatic and could not have happened without corporate-level involvement. The fundamental change in the product functionality of Nokia 5800 and the change in Nokia's organizational structure from a business group structure to an 'integrated structure' in which mobile devices – that is, the whole range of mobile phones – were developed in the Devices unit occurred simultaneously. Following the changes, Mobile services were developed in the Services unit and the sales and marketing was integrated into the Markets unit. In this structure the development work of the Nokia 5800–Comes-With-Music-bundle was divided into three interdependent streams: (1) the development of the service proposition; (2) the development of the product proposition; and (3) the market development activities.

Based on the experiences of earlier service launches, the market-making activity was organized as a dispersed yet globally concerted effort. This new working model was created by the self-driven initiative of a small team in charge of global marketing. The working model facilitated entrepreneurial ownership in the markets as well as in product and service development. This entrepreneurial ownership was particularly apparent in the lead market, in which the activity's owner improvised the knitting together of a complex service ecosystem.

The creation of the local service ecosystem was interdependent with the global service creation and product development activities; locally, this was strongly connected to marketing and retail activities. The area sales organization's senior management provided support, both with resources and with facilitation of the creation of new working practices; these practices were created, in particular, to work with the retailers and with local record labels. The experiences from the lead market were replicated through both a concerted global effort and from country to country; this interconnected way of working enabled improvisation and entrepreneurship on multiple fronts. Moreover, it facilitated rapid replication of experiences. In this dispersed working style, the loosely networked Go-To-Market routine, in association with common strategy and leadership, and the key executives' attention and encouragement, inspired and motivated personnel.

Outcome

The innovation became clearly distinctive in the target markets. This was in accordance with Nokia's intended strategy and had a major influence on the realized strategy in the short term. The Nokia 5800 became very popular and was the most profitable product in Nokia's line-up in 2009. The Comes-With-Music service proposition received massive visibility in the market and was ultimately bundled with a large portion of Nokia products in 2009 and 2010. The service was launched in 33 markets, which included nearly all prominent mobile internet services markets.

Comes-With-Music was likely the most visible service proposition in Nokia's portfolio of digital services in 2009. Despite the forceful distribution and marketing of the Comes-With-Music proposition, the active use of the service was modest; a few hundred thousand consumers were actively using the service at the end of 2010. In 2011, as part of an overall review of Nokia's strategy for internet services, the Comes-With-Music service was terminated.

At the end of 2007 Multimedia was discontinued as a unit, divided up and integrated into the functional organization across Nokia. This structural change very quickly began to slow down innovation and hamper the entrepreneurial management approach; most decisions became committee debates resulting in compromises and uncertainty. In particular, service propositions began to be guided by strict financial performance targets rather than by their value added to Nokia's overall business. Even the clearly driven initiatives were diluted into a broad portfolio of products and activities. Rather than having focused programmes with influence over the resources, the development programmes were designed functionally, with laborious hand-over processes. This increased need for coordination by the senior executives. Entrepreneurially oriented employees felt empty. Gradually, many entrepreneurial employees left the organization, which further amplified the migration of the corporate culture towards a mainstream business mentality. As the executive vice-president of the Multimedia Business Group summarized:

> entrepreneurial culture is hard to create and takes a long time. Functional organizations and traditional control mechanisms are prime enemies of entrepreneurial culture. Even in the case where the culture is strong, the control-oriented leadership on the top and traditional functional management mechanisms can fast destruct entrepreneurship. The result is mediocrity, average performance and slowed down renewal.

CROSS-CASE ANALYSIS: WHAT DOES IT TAKE TO CREATE A RADICAL INNOVATION IN A LARGE COMPANY?

The Nokia cases were all executed in project teams through an entrepreneurial process. The process quite clearly divides into: (1) opportunity recognition; (2) concept development; (3) entrepreneur's judgement and commitment; (4) development; and (5) diffusion. The contextual realities in the phases, as well as the factors leading to success, varied markedly case by case. Table 15.1 summarizes critical success factors for each phase of the projects.

The cases that were successfully launched to the market were both inspired by the overarching strategic intents of Nokia and its multimedia business. The focus was on creating value to the consumers with new

Table 15.1 *Supporting factors and inhibiting factors (italics) in each phase of the case projects as well as the critical success factors for each phase of entrepreneurial process*

	Opportunity recognition	Concept development	Judgement and commitment	Development	Diffusion
N 95	Opportunity-oriented and ambitious culture Focus on value creation Mission of Business Group Inspiration and drive from the leadership Lots of exploration in Multimedia domain Versatile team	Versatile and capable team Attitude of risk taking Pragmatic hands-on attitude of leadership	Mission Culture for proactive risk taking Commitment to value creation Trust and drive from leadership Versatile and influential team, hands-on experience Iterative process	Professional middle management Broad commitment and support created during conceptualization Acceptance of additional cost Ability to act through governance system-developed strategy and processes	Broad commitment fostered dispersed action Capable team matched product with market Business development and commitment of sales Progressive risk taking in ramping up business
Sports Tracker	Inspiration and intuition of entrepreneurs	Opportunity orientation Skills, competences and interests of inventors	Strong intuition Alignment with Nokia's strategy *Support from the management of Research Centre*	Ability to hack and create an experiment *Alienated from the business Was not able to implement a commercial environment Identity conflict: vertical vs. horizontal*	*No support from the business units Detached from the doers of business unit Technical disalignment*

Table 15.1 (continued)

	Opportunity recognition	Concept development	Judgement and commitment	Development	Diffusion
Comes-with-music	Strategic mission: value creation Search over long period of time Interplay between entrepreneurs and leadership Engagement with external experts	Insights from external experts 'Think big' attitude Networks of champions Support from the champions	Leadership's sponsorship and sharing of risk	Ability to mobilize internal action, resources and acquisitions through champions	Leadership's support Peer support Ability to mobilize internal action Dispersed entrepreneurship *The ownership was diluted through organizational change*
Critical success factors across the cases	Culture Mission Focus on value creation Extensive exploration Diversity Connection to relevant parties	Versatile team Broad set of skills Latitude Iterative and networked working practices	Culture Inspiring mission Support in risk taking Accept compromises vis-à-vis the old paradigm Courage	Right skills and resources Support from contributors Adaptive processes or network approach Ability to overcome obstacles	Extensive business network Broad support from the organization

multimedia capabilities. In the N 95 case, the exploration of new ideas occurred primarily within the company's boundaries. The ideas were developed in close dialogue with business management and the markets; the elaboration and concept development occurred through practical processes that involved prominent actors from technical, design, sales and business management. The success of exploration and conceptualization can be attributed to the following: (1) inspiring, consumer value-focused mission of the business unit; (2) sufficient amount of ongoing exploration and technical solutions in relevant domains; (3) opportunity-oriented culture; (4) latitude given to the work; (5) appropriate diversity of participants; and (6) creative skills and practices of the key actors. For Comes-With-Music, the exploration occurred in close dialogue with music industry experts; the concept was crafted in the dialogue with the music industry. Both cases were appropriately connected to the ongoing business, to operations and to senior management. The N 95 case – that is, the case closest to the operational tradition – remained connected with the ongoing business through a robust and iterative product planning process, whereas the connection between Comes-With-Music and the ongoing business built on networking on the operative level as well as networking through the product's champion.

The positive judgement of the innovators and senior management of Nokia's multimedia business demonstrated created a strong commitment among innovators and managers. The positive outcome in both cases resulted from the business unit's proactive and risk-tolerant culture, as well as from the commitment to add value to the consumers. The fact that senior leadership was involved in making positive assessments in these cases provided the innovators with the confidence to propose propositions with rather high risk levels. At the same time, this strengthened the senior management's commitment and support to the projects.

For both successfully launched products, that is, N 95 and Comes-With-Music, the innovators were in a position to shape the strategy and process of the company during product conceptualization and development. This ability to shape the strategy and rework processes was a critical factor to the success of the cases; they simply could not have been implemented without the changes in the strategy and certain critical business processes. Senior management's commitment and support was crucial in making necessary changes to the strategy and processes.

For the N 95, this influence over Nokia's strategy and processes was continuous; it occurred through established working practices and can be characterized as the collective influence of the innovators. The process through which the strategy and innovation influenced one another was iterative in character; several iterative rounds of conceptualization and strategizing were required to achieve a fit between strategy and innovation.

For Comes-With-Music, the rudimentary strategy was created in joint exploration with a music industry expert. The specific conceptualization of the proposition was done internally; refinement occurred as part of the business development activity. The proposition and strategy were verified through market experiments, which led to a confirmation and firming of the strategy.

The fact that Sports Tracker was not connected to the operative business during its development became an impediment during the commercialization phase; it was disconnected from the outset and grew alien to the organization during its development. The technology choices, operative working practices and even the team culture were far apart from the realities of the operative business. In addition, the positioning of Sports Tracker was in gross conflict with Nokia's service business. Commercialization of Sports Tracker within Nokia's organizational and operational setting had become practically impossible.

Entrepreneurs Live and Shape the Strategy, Structure and Culture of Company

The direction of corporate entrepreneurs is influenced by loose strategy articulations, such as strategic scope, vision, intent and mission. However, the initiative towards the case is of the entrepreneur's own making. As the entrepreneur proceeds with the case they develop more specific articulations and framings that often get integrated into the strategy of the company. Table 15.2 summarizes governance and leadership mechanisms through which this interplay of entrepreneurship and strategy takes place in each phase of the entrepreneurial process.

Viable Leadership and Governance Principles

Opportunity recognition
In the first phases of the entrepreneurial process, the search for ideas and technical solutions occurs through networks. A strategically important theme or mission drives the work. Both successful projects – that is, N 95 and Comes-With-Music – highlight the importance of a proactive and opportunity-oriented culture that emphasizes the creation of new value. In accordance with the cases examined herein, the search for radical innovations in ongoing business occurs primarily within the company, whereas the search for new business opportunities relies heavily on external inputs. To develop an opportunity-oriented culture and a sufficient repository of ideas and solutions is a gradual process; it takes several years and requires continuous investment in competence building.

Table 15.2   *Characteristics of the entrepreneurial process mapped with the*
desired attributes of corporate culture, leadership and strategy

	Opportunity recognition	Concept development	Judgement and commitment	Development and diffusion
Entrepreneurial process	Network-oriented Requires continuous investment	Iterative Intensive	Across multiple organizational levels	Tight vs. Loose vs. Networked Reflects proximity to the 'old' business
Culture and mind-set	Opportunity-oriented Proactive with focus on value creation	Proactive Creative Multi-disciplinary	Committed to the mission High trust Risk tolerant	Committed to the mission Strong work ethic Persistent
Leadership and governance	Inspiring External networks Exploration	Participating Appreciates diversity Ambidextrous	Participating Risk sharing Non-political	Clear Vertical/aligned with task Exploitation
Strategy	Theme and mission Market-oriented	Strong intent and adaptive in specifics	Strong mission Case specific metrics	Strong mission Prepared to carry the cost and risk

Concept development

Creating a radical and implementable concept requires an iterative and elaborative process across multiple levels of abstraction. Often, a radical concept challenges or adds to the existing strategy and cannot be legitimized without considering strategy. Senior management's involvement facilitates this reciprocal interplay between the concept and strategy. The conceptualization work benefits from a diversity of participants and the involvement of key stakeholders. Key stakeholders' participation encourages operative people to be more forward-leaning and holistic in addressing the business opportunity.

Judgement

Stakeholder involvement in the conceptualization improves their understanding of the project; this was central to building the ability to assess each project. The projects were still very ambiguous at decision time, regarding deployment of significant resources. Stakeholders' earlier involvement enables them to internalize the opportunity and the concept. Internalization over a longer period of time enables decision-making in an ambiguous situation. Still, the decisions regarding radically innovative projects rely heavily on professional and personal trust between senior leaders and innovators. The alignment between the proposition, strategic intent and business value of the projects appears to be the key decision-making criterion in assessing the projects.

Development and diffusion
The key success factor influencing the later resource-intensive stages of innovation appears to be management's overall involvement in the conceptualization and decision-making. Early involvement builds profound commitment to the case. The examined cases bring to the fore that it is essential to obtain support from the management level that actually controls the resources and that can influence stakeholders in a large organizational sphere. For instance, commercialization requires dispersed business development activities, which cannot be executed without the support from the very top of the organization.

The cases examined herein note that the core research and development (R&D) activity follows the company's disciplined process, whereas dispersed business development activities are improvisational in character; the dispersed business development activities execute the mission that was created and shared in the conceptualization phase. The persistence of development work is achieved best by sharing a common goal and collective mind-set; a strong work ethic and organizational mission are crucial for dispersed execution.

DISCUSSION: THE GOVERNANCE AND MANAGEMENT ACTIONS FOSTER CORPORATE ENTREPRENEURSHIP

The goal of this chapter is to elaborate and articulate the interplay of corporate governance and corporate entrepreneurship in a large corporation. Earlier quantitative researchers, for example Brunninge and Nordqvist (2004), Gabrielsson (2007) and Zahra et al. (2000), have identified corporate governance background factors that appear to have an impact on corporate entrepreneurship. However, they do not create much insight regarding the mechanisms through which corporate governance influences corporate entrepreneurship. Therefore, in this chapter we have studied corporate entrepreneurship as a multilevel organizational phenomenon that is influenced by the organizational context. Our special focus has been leadership and governance principles of the company, because they set the context in which the entrepreneurial initiatives take place. Figure 15.1 is our summary of the key leadership and governance mechanisms that have an effect on entrepreneurship in a large company.

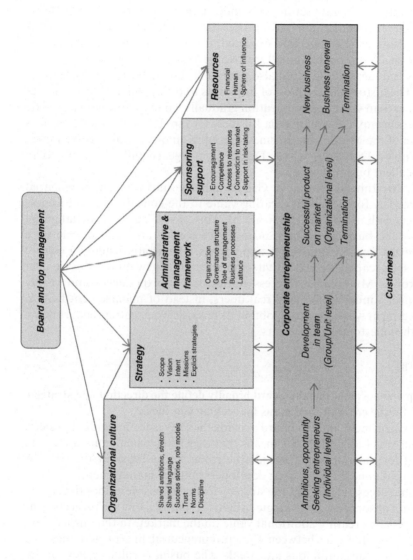

Figure 15.1   The mechanisms for board and top management to govern and support corporate entrepreneurship in a large company

Culture

1. Senior management is the creator of the organizational culture

The culture of the organization in which action takes place is at the heart of renewal in a corporate setting. To understand the organizational context in which profoundly innovative propositions such as the N 95 or Comes-With-Music were started and executed, it is necessary to understand the evolution of the enabling culture. Nokia had a heritage of supporting efforts and ideas; these could also potentially create businesses outside its core. The historical evolution of initiatives to utilize wireless technologies for other than voice communication gradually led to establishing a specific business group, the Multimedia Business Group. From 1994 until the formation of the Multimedia Business Group a unique culture evolved from the Wireless Data entity to the Digital Convergence unit and finally to an independent business group.

The Multimedia Business Group actively nurtured entrepreneurial culture. The focus was on creating value to the consumers and business partners with innovative propositions. This was reflected to the language used in the business group. Successes were celebrated and people were recognized for new innovative approaches. The group fostered a culture and a social capacity for creativity and attempting new things; this element was key in Multimedia. Success stories, shared experiences and visibly recognising innovators made real doers, instead of management heroes. Management was assumed to obtain its rewards when entrepreneurs delivered the milestone-based results.

Strategy

2. Top management and the board broadly define the direction and strategic intent for the company and areas for seeking new ideas

Top management and the board provide the canvas for individual projects (Belousova et al., 2010); this means that they show where innovations are crucial for the company, provide the resources and delimit the risks. A dialogue is conducted between developers and top management.

In the successful projects the strategy formulations were adaptive, emergent and absorbed new strategic insights resulting from the projects. The focus was on creating additional value on the market. In the unsuccessful project, the dialogue between the entrepreneurial line of activities and strategy was discontinuous and weak. The business value of new inventions was not clear.

Administrative and Management Framework

3. Top management and, ultimately, the board set the governance structure that determines the instances in which the merging of entrepreneurial activities and strategy occurs

Corporate entrepreneurship benefits from the governance structure that brings together a viable range of functional disciplines from the units that are central for the development and deployment of innovative propositions. In the existing business, the entrepreneurial innovator is in a position to build sufficient momentum to advance his case in the management forums. In creating an entirely new business, advocacy by senior executives appears to be necessary to obtain the decisions required from variety of management forums. In the Multimedia Business Group, leadership and management practices were developed to allow rapid multidisciplinary decision-making throughout the organizational layers. Specific management responsibilities for key programmes were assigned and strong empowerment for programme managers was endorsed. The programmes operated in a multidisciplinary setting with a high degree of functional diversity and reach. Decision-making was distributed and top management involvement was contributory, rather than controlling. Business target selection was done in careful milestone planning sessions, not in a budgetary fashion.

Another important aspect of governance is what the governance bodies and leaders are tasked to do. The focus on creating market value fosters entrepreneurship, whereas a cost-focused business bureaucratic approach kills entrepreneurial initiatives.

4. Management provides the freedom and subordinates functions to entrepreneurial actors

Entrepreneurial autonomy is supported with the governance structure that subordinates the knowhow of functional disciplines to entrepreneurially driven activities. The successful project groups could act autonomously, yet responsibly. For instance, in the Nokia Multimedia Business Group, resource fluidity was achieved primarily by making programme managers the key resource holders. The responsibility of functional line organizations focused on ensuring the competence levels of individuals and their functional disciplines; the functional disciplines were clearly subordinated to entrepreneurial programmes. Resource and schedule conflicts were quickly resolved by the top management in multidisciplinary decision forums. Critical resources were rapidly transferred from programme to programme to ensure that competence would grow and spread in the fastest possible manner.

In addition, the Multimedia Business Group had its own sales and marketing arm, which had much freedom in defining positions and prices, as well as in selecting distribution channels, creating marketing messages and advertising. Creative advertising and a creative marketing approach were equally important in making new products and services stand out as innovative. Marketing was as innovative as the products and services themselves. However, the pricing decisions were all determined centrally by the executive vice-president and backed by strong market knowledge and programme involvement.

Sponsoring and Support

5. The management sponsors the new ventures: the importance of case-specificity and connection to actual business
For a leader in a corporate entrepreneurial setting, being involved and genuinely interested are key qualities. Progress reporting should be very frequent, not intermittent, and preferably based on jointly agreed milestones, rather than on a finance and control calendar. The focus should be on the activity's value rather than on business bureaucratic metrics. These management principles do not mean that criteria would be loose, but focus is more on creation of value and thus the criteria are more case-specific. This requires more dialogue than a conventional command-and-control approach.

Sponsors help entrepreneurs obtain access to resources for developing the ventures. Furthermore, they legitimatize and support the project and provide advice and guidance for project development. All the Nokia cases we examined had support from senior management; the successful innovation cases were supported by management of the actual business units. The case for which initial support was solely obtained from the research unit's management did not succeed with commercialization; it was alienated from the mainstream business and faced difficulties in obtaining support on the operational level. The cases that were examined provide evidence regarding the importance of active sponsorship by the operative business.

6. Management supports risk taking
The executive vice-president noted that the most important leadership qualities in an entrepreneurial entity are tolerance for failure and sponsorship of risk taking. The leadership that contributes, rather than controls, is instrumental in fostering entrepreneurship in an organization. Entrepreneurs require freedom, responsibility and a sense of ownership. However, risk is ultimately shared by entrepreneurs and leaders. In an entrepreneurial business entity, such as the Multimedia Business Group at

Nokia, it is important for managing risk that the leaders are curious and proactive in exploring new things; seeking renewal must be continuous.

7. Management connects to customers and markets

Being closely connected to market and effective go-to-market mechanisms are vital business enablers in an entrepreneurial business unit. Market introduction of products and services with innovative features and functionalities requires specific competences. In particular, pricing, positioning and business development capacities are essential for the successful conceptualization and market launch of products. The lack of contacts with the operative business and market led to the failure of Sports Tracker.

Resources

8. Senior management assigns personnel and networks, team composition

To succeed with radical innovation the project group must have influence over a large organizational sphere. This calls for substantial direct resource allocation at risk. The key entrepreneurs of the project team must also have capacity to influence people in the surrounding organization. In the examined cases this took place through networks. Furthermore, the project team must have appropriate diversity of competences and must include creative employees. Moreover, the entrepreneurs must be persistent, yet socially sensitive in execution.

CORPORATE ENTREPRENEURSHIP: A GUIDED EVOLUTION STRONGLY INFLUENCED BY THE LEADERSHIP AND GOVERNANCE

To get back to our original question as to whether corporate entrepreneurship can be seen as a guided evolutionary process. If the answer is yes, what are the driving forces, governance principles and leadership activities that support such a process?

Through analysis of the Nokia cases, the answer to the question is a clear yes. All projects were initiated by entrepreneurs, who were driven by the strategy of the company. The entrepreneurial culture and overarching vision of Nokia had a lot to do with the initiation and development of the cases. Two of three cases were closely connected to the missions of the business unit they came from. The leaders of the unit were continuously inspiring and supporting, and at times challenging, the successful cases. In fact their involvement and positive judgement of the cases made leaders co-entrepreneurs in the cases. The examined cases strongly support our definition of corporate entrepreneurship as vision-directed, organization-wide reliance on entrepreneurial behaviour that purposefully and continuously rejuvenates the organization and shapes the scope of its opportunities through the recognition and exploitation of entrepreneurial opportunities.

The most important selection mechanisms through the whole development and commercialization process were the strategic intent, company culture, administrative setting and leadership that fostered entrepreneurship. In Nokia's case all those factors reflected the core values (the Nokia way) of the company. The values were defined by the CEO and the 'dream team' in the early 1990s. Nokia was truly a value-driven company.

Administratively, the development work was conducted in project teams. The recruitment of project team members was very important; the team required a broad competence and power base to push the project forward in the organization. Team members with well-developed networks were chosen. The driving force behind the main development efforts was the developers and project managers. To perform well, they needed to have clear project ownership. The projects were evaluated based on their future value, not on detailed financial analyses of the present. The management and governance of the projects was lean; the management style was supportive, yet stretching. Ambitious, market-oriented, encouraging and risk tolerant climate supported entrepreneurs.

To succeed and make an impact a project must integrate with the broader organization. In particular the N 95 and Comes-With-Music projects were also in interaction with top management throughout the project. In reality the projects did not move from one level to another as in Burgelman's (1983) model. Several levels of organization had already been involved in the initial concept development. This observation supports the 4I organizational learning model of Dutta and Crossan (2005).

As the product development went on, the product strategy evolved, which in turn had implications for the unit's business strategy. The study highlights *strategy development, business development and product development as parallel processes*. They all have an evolutionary character and adapt to each other over time. This evolution reflects technical development, market situation and project team decisions. It is clearly an iterative learning process. Newey and Zahra (2009) have made a similar observation of operative and dynamic capabilities of a company.

As pointed out in the theory discussion the purpose of the administrative systems is not solely to control the retention of predefined strategies (Lovas and Ghoshal, 2000). The aim is to ensure that variation, selection and retention of strategic initiatives and human and social capital are informed by the local knowledge of people within the firm. That was the case in the Nokia Group in the years 2005–07. Dess et al. (2003) discuss this and refer to 'clan control'. In clan control employees' commitment is driven by identification to organization and corporate culture; furthermore, instead of seeking the right answer, clans reduce uncertainty by creating a communality that reduces opportunism due to a similarity in norms, beliefs and priorities between members (Dess et al., 2003). The role of the leadership is to stretch and challenge the clan to exceed its inherent norms and to go beyond the obvious. This was the case in the successful Nokia N 95 and Comes-With-Music projects.

The study identified eight distinct areas where senior management and ultimately the board have a substantial role in leading corporate entrepreneurship. The role of corporate governance is to organize coordination and engagement of local knowledge in the collective processes of search and discovery (Huse, 2007). The board of directors appoints the CEO and often confirms the selection of other key leaders. Board decisions on these matters set the tone of the leadership of the company. In addition, governance has a role of directing the attention of the organization through compositions of the governance bodies, as well as by influencing the vocabulary and cognitive frameworks used in governing the company. Strict focus on facts and present financials hampers entrepreneurship, whereas proactive market and value-oriented discussions foster entrepreneurial behaviour.

One additional factor can be observed in the Nokia Group. A CEO's leadership style and direct communication with a very wide range of top managers (200–400 top managers) is rather unusual; this created an informal and business-oriented leadership style. The style built trust and amplified weak signals in decision-making. This pattern of informal communication spread in the organization. The communication was intensive and called in subjective 'local views' from the subject matter specialists. This type of intensive communication across organizational levels resonates well with corporate entrepreneurship and organizational learning. This factor is not often stressed in the corporate entrepreneurship or corporate governance literature. The role of informal leadership style in fostering entrepreneurship deserves more research attention in the future.

In summary, corporate governance and corporate entrepreneurship interact through multiple touch-points: they synergize with one another through organizational culture, strategy, administrative frameworks and sponsoring of entrepreneurial activities, as well as through critical decisions on resources. A synergy leads into productive corporate entrepreneurship and rich organizational learning, the ultimate sources of strategic renewal of a company. The leadership and ultimately the board of directors set the scene, and at best challenge and stretch entrepreneurs to go beyond their inherently ambitious norms. Entrepreneurship of a large company is guided evolution across the layers of organization. The process is driven by dispersed entrepreneurial behaviour that is strongly influenced by concrete leadership and governance actions.

REFERENCES

Ahmed, P. and Shepherd, C.D. (eds) (2010), *Innovation Management. Context, Strategies, Systems and Processes*, Harlow, UK: Pearson Education.

Amo, B.W. (2006), 'The influence from corporate entrepreneurship and intrapreneurship on white-collar workers' employee innovation behavior', *International Journal of Innovation and Learning*, 3 (3), 284–298.

Antoncic, B. and Hisrich, R.D. (2001), 'Intrapreneurship: Construct refinement and cross-cultural validation', *Journal of Business Venturing*, 16, 495–527.

Belousova, O., Gailly, B. and Basso, O. (2010), 'A conceptual model of corporate entrepreneurial behavior', Working Paper 06/2010, Louvain School of Management, Belgium.

Bower, J.L. (ed.) (1970), *Managing the Resource Allocation Process*, Homewood, IL: Richard D. Irwin.

Brunninge, O. and Nordqvist, M. (2004), 'Ownership structure, board composition and entrepreneurship: Evidence from family firms and venture-capital backed firms', *International Journal of Entrepreneurial Behavior and Research*, 10 (1–2), 85–105.

Burgelman, R.A. (1983), 'A process model of internal corporate venturing in the diversified major firm', *Administrative Science Quarterly*, 28 (2), 223–244.

Burgelman, R.A. (1991), 'Intraorganizational ecology of strategy making and organizational adaption: Theory and field research', *Organization Science*, 2 (3), 239–262.

Davis, G.F. and Useem, M. (2002), 'Top management, company and corporate control: Top management, company directors and corporate control', *Handbook of Strategy and Management*, pp. 232–258.

Dess, G.G., Ireland, R.D., Zahra, S.A., Floyd, S.W., Janney, J.J. and Lane, P.J. (2003), 'Emerging issues in corporate entrepreneurship', *Journal of Management*, 29 (3) 351–378.

Dutta, D.K. and Crossan, M.M. (2005), 'The nature of entrepreneurial opportunities: Understanding the process using the 4I organizational learning framework', *Entrepreneurship Theory and Practice*, 29 (4), 425–449.

Gabrielsson, J. (2007), 'Boards of directors and entrepreneurial posture in medium-size companies: Putting the board demography approach to a test', *International Small Business Journal*, 25 (5), 511–537.

Ghoshal, S. and Bartlett, C.A. (1994), 'Liking organizational context and managerial action: The dimensions of quality of management', *Strategic Management Journal*, 15, 91–112.

Gupta, V., MacMillan, I.C. and Surie, G. (2004), 'Entrepreneurial leadership: Developing and measuring a cross-cultural construct', *Journal of Business Venturing*, 19 (2), 241–260.

Guth, W. and Ginsberg, A. (1990), 'Guest editor's introduction: Corporate entrepreneurship', *Strategic Management Journal*, 11, 5–15.

Hamel, G. and Prahalad, C.K. (1989), 'Strategic intent', *Harvard Business Review*, 67 (3), 63–76.

Huse, M. (ed) (2007), *Boards, Governance and Value Creation*, Cambridge: Cambridge University Press.

Ireland, R.D., Covin, J.G. and Kuratko, D.F. (2009), 'Conceptualizing corporate entrepreneurship strategy', *Entrepreneurship Theory and Practice*, 33 (1), 19–46.

Laukkanen, S. (2012), *Making Sense of Ambidexterity: A Process View of the Renewing Effects of Innovation Activities in a Multinational Enterprise*, No. 243, Helsinki: Hanken School of Economics, Economics and Society.

Lovas, B. and Ghoshal, S. (2000), 'Strategy as guided evolution', *Strategic Management Journal*, **21** (9), 875–896.
Monks, R.A.G. and Minow, N. (eds) (2011), *Corporate Governance*, New York: John Wiley & Sons.
Newey, L.R. and Zahra, S.A. (2009), 'The evolving firm: How dynamic and operating capabilities interact to estable entrepreneurship', *British Journal of Management*, **20** (s1), 81–100.
Noda, T. and Bower, J.L. (1996), 'Strategy making as iterated processes of resource allocation', *Strategic Management Journal*, **17** (s1), 159–192.
Ollila, J. and Saukkomaa, H. (eds) (2013), *Mahdoton menestys. Kasvun paikkana Nokia*, Helsinki: Otava.
Quinn, J.B. (1978), 'Strategic change: Logical incrementalism', *Sloan Management Review*, **20** (1), 7–21.
Rindova, V.P. (1999), 'What corporate boards have to do with strategy: A cognitive perspective', *Journal of Management Studies*, **36** (December), 953–975.
Sharma, P. and Chrisman, J.J. (1999), 'Toward a reconciliation of the definitional issues in the field of corporate entrepreneurship', *Entrepreneurship Theory and Practice*, **23** (3), 11–27.
Stevenson, H.H. and Jarillo, J.C. (1990), 'A paradigm of entrepreneurship: Entrepreneurial management', *Strategic Management Journal*, **11**, 17–27.
Taylor, B. (2001), 'From corporate governance to corporate entrepreneurship, *Journal of Change Management*, **2** (2), 128–147.
Vesper, K.H. (1984), 'Three faces of corporate entrepreneurship: A pilot study', in Hornaday, J.H., Tarpley Jr, F., Timmons, J.A. and Vesper, K.H. (eds), *Frontiers of Entrepreneurship Research*, Wallesley, MA: Babson College, pp. 294–326.
Zahra, S.A. (1996), 'Governance, ownership and corporate entrepreneurship: The moderating effect of industry technological opportunities', *Academy of Management Journal*, **39** (6), 1713–1735.
Zahra, S.A., Neubaum, D.O. and Huse, M. (2000), 'Entrepreneurship in medium-size companies: Exploring the effects of ownership and governance systems', *Journal of Management*, **26** (5), 947–976.

Index